Texte und Studien zum Antiken Judentum

herausgegeben von
Martin Hengel und Peter Schäfer

7

The Jews in Hellenistic and Roman Egypt

The Struggle for Equal Rights

by

Aryeh Kasher

J. C. B. Mohr (Paul Siebeck) Tübingen 1985

Revised and translated from the Hebrew original: יהודי מצרים ההלניסטית והרומית‎
במאבקם על זכויותיהם‎ (= Publications of the Diaspora Research Institute and the Haim
Rosenberg School of Jewish Studies, edited by Shlomo Simonsohn, Book 23). Tel Aviv
University 1978.

CIP-Kurztitelaufnahme der Deutschen Bibliothek

Kasher, Aryeh:
The Jews in Hellenistic and Roman Egypt:
the struggle for equal rights / Aryeh Kasher. –
Tübingen: Mohr, 1985.
   (Texte und Studien zum antiken Judentum; 7)
   ISBN 3-16-144829-4

NE: GT

First Hebrew edition 1978
Revised English edition 1985

© J. C. B. Mohr (Paul Siebeck) Tübingen 1985.
Alle Rechte vorbehalten. / All rights reserved.
Printed in Germany.
Säurefreies Papier von Scheufelen, Lenningen. Typeset: Sam Boyd Enterprise, Singapore.
Offsetdruck: Gulde-Druck GmbH, Tübingen. Einband: Heinr. Koch, Tübingen.

In memory of my parents
Maniya and Joseph Kasher

Preface

The Jewish Diaspora has been part and parcel of Jewish history since its earliest days. The desire of the Jews to maintain their national and religious identity, when scattered among the nations, finds its actual expression in self organization, which has served to a rampart against external influence. The dispersion of the people in modern times has become one of its unique characteristics. Things were different in classical period, and especially in the Hellenistic period, following the conquests of Alexander the Great, when dispersion and segregational organization were by no means an exceptional phenomenon, as revealed by a close examination of the history of other nations. Colonists — Hellenic and others — dotted the Mediterranean and Euxine basins with hundreds and thousands of colonies. Eastward migration in the Hellenistic period has turned into common sight, and attempts were made by the authorities to encourage it. Groups of immigrants were on the whole shown an attitude of utmost consideration, and they were enabled to maintain their ancestral traditions, and to organize themselves in their own religious, social, and political frameworks.

From the beginning of the Ptolemaic period Egypt was the destination of a great variety of immigrant groups, among which Jews were not absent. Their basic right to "live by the Law of their Fathers" was liable to generate many legal difficulties. Had every ethnic group been granted the permission to maintain its laws and usages entirely intact, we should have heard of a tremendous legal disorder in Egypt as well as in countries in a similar position. As it would be unreasonable to assume that people could keep all litigation within their own group, it seems plausible that the basic right to keep old traditions was limited in certain areas.

The question of the legal status of Egyptian Jews deserves treatment in a wider context which is not restricted to Jews only, and which comprises the question of the legal status of other groups. It is generally agreed that one of the most important criteria for the civic stratification of Egyptian population is ethnic origin. It will be pointed in the sequel that many Jews mentioned in official documents have various other (non Jewish) *ethnica* beside their names. Research has shown that these were *pseudo-ethnica* and that they had a functional significance. It is therefore important to find out to what extent was their civic stratification modified by this functional classicification.

It is a well known fact that modern scholarship has focused its interest on the problem of the civic status of Alexandrian Jews. The main question was whether the Jews of this *polis* were or were not its citizens. The relative abundance of sources about this particular area seems to have stimulated the absorption in this question still further, since it has been widely assumed that Alexandria could be treated as model for Jewish civic rights in other parts of the Hellenistic and Roman Diaspora. No scholar has so far challenged the assumption that the struggle of the Jews for their rights was in fact the struggle for citizenship in the *polis*. The main evidence for this was adduced from the writings of Josephus, and to a lesser degree from those of Philo. The fact that Jews styled themselves citizens (πολῖται) and Alexandrians (Ἀλεξανδρεῖς) has been reckoned the ultimate proof, and there has been almost no one who has sought a different meaning behind these terms. Josephus' terminology with regard to this subject, viz. ἰσπολιτεία, ἰσονομία, ἰσοτιμία, ἰσομοιρία, ἰσοτελεία, has strengthened this impression, but almost no attempt has been made to get to the bottom of this legal terminology. Scholars have varied in their conclusions according to their evaluation of Josephus as source: those who believed his veracity regarded the Jews as citizens in the *polis*, whereas those who suspected him of apologetic falsehood denied the Jews any claims to such a status. The discovery in 1924 of *P. Lond. 1912*, containing Claudius' Letter to the Alexandrians, strengthened the position of the latter and deepened their mistrust of Josephus' truthfulness. The document appeared to them as plainly contradictory to an edict quoted under Claudius' name by Josephus (*Antiquitates,* XIX 280 ff.).

Leading the ranks of these sceptics was the German philological school, whose prominent representatives Wilrich, Wilcken, Schubart and Laquer, attacked with eager enthusiasm other papyrological finds in order to expose Josephus' lack of credibility, and were not always innocent of antisemitic motivation. Their profound learning and their world-wide reputation added weight to their view. Their fundamental conclusions have so far not been contested.

Among modern Jewish scholars their most faithful follower has been A. Tcherikover, though he has managed to purify their theories of stains of antisemitism. On the basis of their conclusions he erected the edifice of his own investigations, revealing like them profound scholarship equipped with a sound and enticing logic. Adopting the method of historical analogy he projected the Jewish struggle for "emancipation" in the 18th and 19th Centuries backwards to the Hellenistic and Roman period. The Jews emerged as a national minority struggling for equal civic rights, the Alexandrians keeping their own ranks close, to prevent Jewish infiltration. For him this was the real essence of the "Jewish question".

The fault of this method is evident. The term "war of emancipation" was coined in a strange and remote historical reality from which it would be dangerous to conclude about classical antiquity. Furthermore, it will be shown later on, that no source provides an explicit piece of evidence that the Jews aspired to citizenship in the *polis*.

The political and the municipal organization in the period under discussion was strongly linked with the municipal cult. Religious apostasy was therefore involved in obtaining full citizenship, and it is doubtful whether Jews were willing to surmount this obstacle. Their struggle for equal political rights does not necessarily have to be interpreted as one for citizenship in the *polis*, and it is unfortunate that no other possibility has been examined.

The purpose of the present study is to suggest a new interpretation of the whole problem, and to try to demonstrate that the equality which the Jews strove to obtain is to be conceived as an equality between two separate political bodies, the Jewish community (πολίτευμα) and the Greek *polis*. In other words, the Jews fought for the right of self organization within the *polis*, on an equal footing with the Greeks, without this right being dependent on the *polis*, but on the central government. The Greeks in truth attempted to prevent this from happening, and to bring the authority of the *polis* to bear on all its inhabitants.

The discussion will be chronologically limited to the period up to the Jewish insurrection under Trajan (115-117 A.D.). This period is characterized by continuity of orderly and organized communal life, interrupted only by temporary shortlived episodes such as the riots under Caligula and Claudius (38-41 A.D.) and at the times of the great insurrection in Judaea (66-71 A.D.). Another reason for the particular interest of this period stems from the fact that it witnessed no far reaching demographic changes. Nor was there any significant change in the status of the Jews and in the system of their basic rights. Yet, in spite of this chronological limitation, earlier and later sources will have to be consulted for the sake of comparison and clarification.

Bibliographical Note

Several works of reference will be referred to by the author's name only (e.g. Fraser, Vol. 1 etc.), other works by key words related to the title (e.g. Bell, *Jews and Christians*). Articles will be mostly referred to by the common abbreviated titles of periodicals, yearbooks, Jubilee Volumes etc.

Acknowledgements

The original version of this book was in the form of a doctoral dissertation submitted to the Senate of Tel-Aviv University in 1972, and was prepared under the direction of Prof. J. Efron and Prof. S. Applebaum. Recent discoveries and research have been incorporated into this version.

I wish to express my gratitude to those who assisted me in my work:

Prof. J. Efron who was the first to inspire me to undertake this research in the spirit of the thesis here offered, even before 1968 when I was accepted as a doctoral candidate. His remarkable loyalty and devotion, and especially his scholarly care and his erudition guided and encouraged me throughout.

Prof. S. Applebaum who offered much learned advices concerning epigraphy and the classical world was helpful especially in drawing comparisons with the Jewish communities of ancient Cyrene. In 1972, while surpervising my research, he wrote two articles on related subjects (published in *The Jewish People in the First Century*, edited by S. Safrai and M. Stern), and allowed me to read his work before it went to press.

Prof. B. Bar-Kochva, Prof. A. Oppenheimer and Prof. Z. Rubin, who kindly helped me with their advice and thoughtful criticism.

Mr. M. Borek who helped me to read some articles written in Russian, and Dr. H. Ben-Amram who contributed to the editorial work.

Special thanks are due to the Memorial Foundation for Jewish Culture, which supported me during my work on this project.

Many thanks are also due to Tel-Aviv University's Prof. S. Simon-sohn (Chairman of the Diaspora Research Institute) and to Prof. M. Gil (Chairman of the School of Jewish Studies) whose help made the publication of this book possible.

I am particularly indebted to Miss Na'omi Hendelman for her contribution in translating the Hebrew version of this book into English. I take this opportunity of acknowledging my sincere thanks to the Melton Center for Jewish Studies (Ohio State University) for the assistance in the preparation of the English translation.

I was greatly honored by the bestowal on me of the Prof. S.W. Baron Prize by the School of Jewish Studies of Tel-Aviv University for this book.

Finally, I want to express my profound gratitude to my wife Tamar whose patient encouragement and efforts to free me from daily cares made the writing of this book both possible and enjoyable.

Tel-Aviv.

Contents

Contents

Abbreviations

1. Inscriptions, Papyri, Ostraca

BGU = *Ägyptische Urkunden aus den königlichen Museen zu Berlin – Griechische Urkunden*, I-VIII (1895-1933).

CIG = *A. Boeckh et al. (eds.), Corpus Inscriptionum Graecarum*, Berlin 1828-1877.

CIJ = J.B. Frey (ed.), *Corpus Inscriptionum Judaicarum*, I-II (1936, 1952).

CPJ = V.A. Tcherikover. A. Fuks. M. Stern (eds.), *Corpus Papyrorum Judaicarum*, I-III (1957-1964).

FGrH = F. Jacoby (ed.), *Fragmente der griechischen Historiker*, Berlin-Leiden 1923-.

IG = *Inscriptiones Graeca*, Ausgabe der Preussischen Akademie der Wissenschaften zu Berlin, 1873-.

IGLS = L. Jalabert, R. Mouterde, C. Mondesert, J.P. Ray-Coquais (eds.), *Inscriptions Grecques et Latines de la Syrie*, 1929-.

IGRR = R. Cagnat (ed.), *Inscriptiones Graeca ad Res Romanas Pertinentes*, 1911-1927.

MAMA = W. Calder et al. (eds.), *Monumenta Asia Minoris Antiqua*, 1928-1962.

M. Chr. = L. Mitteis, U. Wilcken., *Grundzüge und Chrestomatie der Papyruskunde*, II: 2, Berlin-Leipzig 1912.

O. Bodl. = J.G. Tait (ed.), *Greek Ostraca in the Bodlian Library at Oxford and Various other Collections*, 1930.

OE = *Fouilles franco-polonaises*, Rapport I, *Tell Edfou*, 1937 (pp. 141f.); 1938 (pp. 137f.).

OGIS = W. Dittenberger (ed.), *Orientis Graeci Inscriptiones Selecta*, Lipsia 1903-1905.

O. Mich. = L. Amundsen (ed.), *Greek ostraca in the University of Michigan Collection*, Ann Arbor 1935.

O. Strassb. = P. Viereck (ed.), *Griechische und griechisch-demotische Ostraka der Universität- und Landesbibliothek zu Strassburg in Elsass*, Berlin 1923.

O. Theb. = J.G. Milne (ed.), *Theban Ostraca*, London-Oxford 1913.

PCZ = C.C. Edgar (ed.), *Catalogue général des antiquités égyptiennes du Musée du Caire; Zenon Papyri*, Cairo 1925-1931.

P. Col. Zen. = W.L. Westermann et al. (eds.), *Zenon Papyri, Business Papers of the Third Century B.C. dealing with Palestine and Egypt*, I-II, New York 1934, 1940.

P. Cornell = W.L. Westermann, C.J. Kraemer, *Greek Papyri in the Library of Cornell University*, New York 1926.

P. Eleph. = O. Rubensohn (ed.), *Elephantine Papyri*, Berlin 1907.

P. Ent. = O. Guéraud (ed.), *ENTEYΞEIΣ: Requêtes et plaintes adressées au roi d'Égypte au III*^{e} *siècle avant J-C.*, Cairo 1950.

P. Fay. = B.P. Grenfell, A.S. Hunt, D.G. Hogarth (eds.) *Fayûm Towns and their Papyri*, London 1900.

P. Flor. = D. Comparetti, G. Vitelli (eds.), *Papiri greco-egizii*, Milan 1906-1915 (1962).

P. Freib. = W. Aly, M. Gelzer, J. Partsch, U. Wilcken (eds.), *Mitteilungen aus der Freiburger Papyrussumlung*, Heidelberg 1927.

P. Giss. = O. Eger, E. Kornemann, P.M. Meyer (eds.) *Griechische Papyri im Museum des oberhessischen Geschichtsvereins zu Giessen*, Leipzig-Berlin 1910-1912.

P. Gurob = J.G. Smyly (ed.), *Greek Papyri from Gurob*, Dublin 1921.

P. Hal. = *Dikaimata: Auszüge aus Alexandrinischen Gesetzen und Verordnungen in einem*

Papyrus des philologischen Seminars der Universität Halle mit einem Anhang weiterer Papyri derselben Sammlung, herausgergeben von der Graeca Haelnsis, Berlin 1913.

P. Hamb. = P.M. Meyer (ed.), *Griechische Papyrusurkunden der Hamburger Staats- und Universitätsbibliothek*, Leipzig-Berlin 1911-1024.

P. Hibeh = B.P. Grenfell, A.S. Hunt et al. (eds.), *The Hibeh Papyri*, I-II, London.

P. Lille = P. Jouguet (ed.), *Papyrus grecs* (Institut Papyrologique de l'Université de Lille), 1907-1928.

P. Lips. = L. Mitteis (ed.), *Griechische Urkunden der Papyrussalmlung zu Leipzig*, 1906.

P. Lond. = F.G. Kenyon, H.I. Bell (eds.), *Greek Papyri in the British Museum*, London 1893-1917.

P. Magd. = *P. Lille*, Vol. ii (Papyri from Magdola) 1912.

P. Merton = H.I. Bell et al. (eds.), *The Greek Papyri in the Collection of Wilfred Merton*, I, London 1948; II. Dublin 1959.

P. Mich. = C.C. Edgar, A.E.R. Boak, J.G. Winter et al (eds.), *Papyri in the University of Michigan Collection*, I-VIII, Ann Arbor 1931-1951.

P. Mich. Zen. = C.C. Edgar (ed.), *Zenon Papyri in the Universiy of Michigan Collection*, Ann Arbor 1931.

P. Oxy. = B.P. Grenfell, A.S. Hunt et al. (eds.), *The Oxyrhynchus Papyri*, London 1898-.

P. Par. = A.J. Letronne, W. Brunet de Presle (eds.), *Notices et textes des papyrus grecs du Musée du Louvre et de la bibliothèque impériale*, Paris 1865.

P. Petr. = J.P. Mahaffy, J.G. Smyly (eds.), *The Flinders Petrie Papyri*, I-III, Dublin 1891-1905.

P. Reinach = P. Collart (ed.), *Les Papyrus Théodore Reinach*, Cairo 1940.

P. Ryl. = A.S. Hunt, J. de M. Johnson,V. Martin, C.H. Roberts, E.G.Turner (eds.), *Catalogue of the Greek and Latin Papyri in the John Rylands Library*, Manchester 1911-.

PSI = G. Vitelli, M. Norsa et al. (eds.), *Publicazioni della Società Italiana per la ricerca dei Papiri greci e latini in Egitto*, Firenze 1912-.

P. Strassb. = F. Preisigke (ed.) *Griechische Papyrus der Kaiserlichen Universitäts-und Landesbibliothek zu Strassburg*, Leipzig 1912, 1920.

P. Tebt. = A.S. Hunt, J.G. Smyly et al. (eds.), *The Tebtunis Papyri*, London 1902-1938.

P. Tor. = A. Peyron (ed.), 'Papyri graeci R. Musei Aegyptii Taurinensis', *Mem. R. Accad. Torino*, XXXI (1826), pp. 9-188; XXXIII (1827), pp. 1-80.

SB = F. Preisigke, F. Bilabel, E. Kiessling (eds.), *Sammelbuch griechischer Urkunden aus Ägypten*, Göttingen 1915-.

SEG = *Supplementum Epigraphicum Graecum*, Leiden 1923-.

SP = A.S. Hunt, C.C. Edgar (eds.), *Select Papyri* (Loeb Classical Library), London 1932-1934.

Syll. = W. Dittenberger (ed.), *Sylloge Inscriptionum Graecarum*, Leipzig 1915-1924.

TAM = E. Kalinka (ed.), *Tituli Asiae Minoris*, II, fasc. I, II, Vienna 1920, 1930.

UPZ = U. Wilcken, (ed.), *Urkunden der Ptolemäerzeit*, I-II, Berlin-Leipzig 1922-1927, 1957.

W. Chr. = L. Mitteis, U. Wilcken (eds.), *Grundzüge und Chrestomatie der Papyruskunde*, I: 2, Leipzig-Berlin 1912.

WO = U. Wilcken (ed.), *Griechische Ostraka aus Aegypten und Nubien*, I-II, Leipzig-Berlin 1899.

2. Periodicals and Series

Aegyptus = *Aegyptus: Rivista italiana di egittologia e di papirologia*
AIP = *Annuaire de l'institut de philologie et d'histoire Orientales et Slaves*
AJA = *American Journal of Archaeology*
AJAH = *American Journal of Ancient History*
AJPh = *American Journal of Philology*

AJTh = American Journal of Theology
ASAE = Annales du Service des Antiquités de l'Egypte
Archiv = Archiv jür Papyrusforschung
BA = The Biblical Archaeologist
BASOR = Bulletin of the American Schools of Oriental Research
BCH = Bulletin de correspondance hellénique
BIFAO = Bulletin de l'Institut français d'Archéologie orientale
BSAA = Bulletin de la Société archéologique d'Alexandrie
BSAC = Bulletin de la société d'archéologie copte
CAH = Cambridge Ancient History
Chr. d'Ég. = Chronique d'Égypte
Class. Philol = Classical Philology
DLKIW = Deutsche Literaturzeitung jür Kritik der internationalen Wissenschaft
HTR = Harvard Theological Review
HUCA = Hebrew Union College Annual
IEJ = Israel Exploration Journal
JBL = Journal of Biblical Literature
JEA = Journal of Egyptian Archaeology
JHS = Journal of Hellenic Studies
JJP = Journal of Juristic Papyrology
JJS = Journal of Jewish Studies
JNES = Journal of Near Eastern Studies
JPOS = Journal of the Palestine Oriental Society
JQR = Jewish Quarterly Review
JRS = Journal of Roman Studies
JSS = Jewish Social Studies
JTS = Journal of Theological Studies
MGWJ = Monatsschrift für Geschichte und Wissenschaft des Judentums
NTS = New Testament Studies
OTS = Old Testament Studies
PAAJR = Proceedings of the American Academy for Jewish Research
PEF = Palestine Exploration Fund
PEQ = Palestine Exploration Quarterly
QAL = Quaderni del archeologia della Libia
RB = Revue Biblique
REA = Revue des études anciennes
REG = Revue des études grecques
REJ = Revue des études juives
REV. Arch. = Revue archéologique
Rev. d. Philol. = Revue de Philologie
RHR = Revue de l'histoire de religions
Riv. d. Fil = Rivista di filologia classica
TAPA = Transactions of the American Philological Association
VDI = Vestnik Drevnej Istorii
YCS = Yale Classical Studies
Yediot = Bulletin of the Israel Exploration Society (Hebrew)
ZNW = Zeitschrift für die neutestamentliche Wissenschaft

3. Encyclopedies and Dictionaries
The Jewish Encyclopedia, I-XII (1901-5).

Encyclopaedia Judaica, I-X (A-L), (1928-1934).
RE(PW) = *Real-Encyclopädie der classischen Altertumswissenschaft* (Pauly A., and Wissowa G. Kroll W. eds), 1894-.
Encyclopaedia Talmudica: Enziklopediah Talmudit (1948-Hebrew).
Encyclopaedia Biblica: Enziklopediah Mikraït (1954-1982 Hebrew).
Encyclopaedia Judaica, I-XVI (1971).
Liddell H.G., Scott R., *A Greek-English Lexicon*,[9] Oxford 1973.

4. Works of reference (by author's name only)

Appelbaum S., *Jews and Greeks in Ancient Cyrene*, Leiden 1980
Bar-Kochva B., *The Seleucid Army, Organization and Tactics in the Great Campaigns*, Cambridge 1976.
Bevan E.R., *History of Egypt under the Ptolemaic Dynasty*, London 1927.
Bouché-Leclerq A., *Histoire des Lagides*, I-IV, Paris 1903-1907.
Box G.H., *Philonis Alexandrini Legatio ad Gaium (edited with an introduction, translation and commentary)*, Leiden 1961.
Cowley A.E., *Aramaic Papyri of the Fifth Century B.C.*, Oxford 1923.
Fraser P.M., *Ptolemaic Alexandria*, I-III, Oxford 1972.
Fuchs L., *Die Juden Ägyptens in ptolemäischer und römischer Zeit*, Wien 1924.
Heichelheim F., 'Die auswärtige Bevölkerung im Ptolemäerreich', *Klio*, Beiheft 18, 1925.
Johnson A.C., *Roman Egypt to the Reign of Diocletian*, in T. Frank's *Economic Survey of Ancient Rome*, II, Baltimore 1956.
Jouguet P., *La vie municipale dans l'Égypte Romaine*, Paris 1911.
Juster J., *Les Juifs dans l'empire Romain — Leur condition juridique, économique et sociale*, I-II, Paris 1914.
Launey M., *Recherches sur les armées hellénistiques*, I-II, Paris 1949-1950.
Leon H.J., *The Jews of Ancient Rome*, Philadelphia 1960.
Lesquier J., *Les institutions militaires de l'Égypte sous les Lagides*, Paris 1911.
Musurillo H.A., *The Acts of the Pagan Martyrs — Acta Alexandrinorum, edited with commentary*, Oxford 1954.
Preaux C., *L'économie royale des Lagides*, Bruxelles 1947.
Rostovtzeff M.I., *Social and Economic History of the Hellenistic World* (= *SEHHW*), I-III, Oxford 1941.
—— *Social and Economic History of the Roman World* (= *SEHRW*), I-II, Oxford 1957.
Ruppel W., 'Politeuma-Bedeutungsgeschichte eines staatsrechtlichen Terminus', *Philologus*, LXXXII, N.F. XXXVI (1927), pp. 268-312, 433-454.
Schürer E., *Geschichte des jüdischen Volkes im Zeitalter Jesu Christi*,[4] Leipzig 1901-1909.
—— (eds. E. Vermes & F. Millar), *The History of the Jewish People in the Age of Jesus Christ*, I-II, Edinburgh 1973, 1979.
Smallwood, E.M., *Philonis Alexandrini Legatio ad Gaium (Edited with an Introduction, Translation and Commentary)*, Leiden 1961.
Tarn W.W., Griffith G.H., *Hellenistic Civilization*,[9] London 1952.
Taubenschlag R., *The Law of Greco-Roman Egypt in the Light of the Papyri 332 B.C.-640A.D.*, I-II, New York 1944, 2° Ed. Warszawa 1955.
Uebel F., *Die Kleruchen Ägyptens unter den ersten sechs Ptlemäern*, Abhand. d. Deutschen Akad. d. Wiss. z. Berlin, 1968.
Wallace S.L., *Taxation in Egypt from Augustus to Diocletian*, Princeton 1938.
Wilcken U., Mitteis L., *Grundzüge und Chrestomatie der Papyruskunde*, I-II, Berlin-Leipzig 1912.

Introduction

Milestones in the political history of the Jews in Egypt

Jews began settling in Egypt long before its conquest by Alexander the Great. The first foundations of that settlement were laid already at the time of the XXVI Saite Dynasty which dislodged the Assyrian yoke and at the end of the seventh century B.C.E. sought to reinstate Egyptian hegemony in Palestine and Syria. During the Babylonian period Egyptian involvement in Palestine increased, and concomitantly the land of the Nile became a target for Jewish immigration whether for political or purely economic reasons. The chief waves of immigration were undoubtedly connected with the national tragedy represented by the destruction of the First Temple. Despite the tragedy, however, all the exiles to Egypt of that time were not inveitably helpless war refugees, for many of them were absorbed into the Egyptian military forces. One of the outstanding examples was the immigration of Johanan son of Kareah and "the captains of the forces", who proceeded to Egypt after the murder of Gedaliah son of Ahikam, and were settled in Migdol and Tahpanhes (in Lower Egypt), in Noph (Memphis in Middle Egypt) and in "the land of Pathros" (i.e., the southern country or Upper Egypt)[1]. During the reign of Zedekiah, the last king of Judah, for instance, Jewish soldiers served in the army of Psammetichus II (594-589 B.C.E.), as reported in the *Letter of Aristeas* (§13) and indirectly confirmed in Herodotus (II 161) and in epigraphy[2]. The Aramaic papyri from Elephantine too confirm that the beginnings of extensive Jewish settlement on Egyptian soil occurred during the Saitic dynasty, although the exact circumstances of the establishment of the military colony at Elephantine are unclear. That well-known colony, whose residents were offi-

---

1 *Jer.*, 44:1; and see *Encyclopaedia Biblica*, vol 4, p. 635f.; vol. 5, pp. 212-216; vol. 6, p. 642.

2 For details see Porten, *Archives from Elephantine*, p. 8f.

cially known as (*Ḥaylā Yehudeia*) (= Jewish garrison) and defended
Egypt's southern border, reached its apogee under the Persians from
525 B.C.E. until about 399 B.C.E.[3]

The *Letter of Aristeas* implies a further wave of Jewish immigration that started after the Persian conquest (*loc. cit.*) in the wake of
which evidently quite a number of Jews joined the local garrisons
(like that of Elephantine). Later, at the end of the Persian period,
many Jerusalemites were forcibly transported to Egypt (*ibid.*, 35)
but the scantiness and vagueness of the information available does
not allow for any accurate historical conclusions[4].

The information we have on the immigration of Jews from Palestine to Egypt in the Hellenistic period attributes the initial impetus
to Alexander the Great[5]. Most scholars tend to ascribe apolgetic
tendencies to the reports in their view the reports were aimed at
ascribing the privileges accorded the Jews of Alexandria to Alexander
the Great himself. Although such a claim is not totally refutable, the
reports do appear to be qiuite credible[6].

Better founded information on the immigration of Jews from
Palestine to Egypt relates to the period of the Diadochs, Alexander's
successors, between 323 and 301 B.C.E.[7] As Josephus, who preserved that information, clearly noted its sources, it has generally
been regarded as reliable. One of Josephus' statements (*C. Apionem*,
I 186-189) based on Hecataeus of Abdera (a contemporary of
Alexander the Great and Ptolemy I) tells of the willing immigration
of a considerable group of Jews led by the priest Hezekias, who
moved to Egypt following the battle of Gaza (312 B.C.E.) in which

---

3 *Ibid.*, p. 19f.

4 I believe this hint in the *Letter of Aristeas* refers to the secret events which occurred in
the reign of Artaxerxes III Ochus (359/8-338/7 B.C.E.) which fit in with the troubles
hinted at in the writings of the Apostolic Fathers (see Schürer, vol. 3, pp. 7-8 and n. 11)
and *C. Apionem*, II 191, 194. See also Klausner, *History of the Second Temple* vol. 2,
p. 13f.; Grinz, *The Book of Judith*, p. 18f.; Barag, *BASOR*, 133 (1966), pp. 6-12; E. Stern,
The Material Culture of the Land of the Bible in the Persian Period, p. 250ff.

5 See *Bellum*, II 487; *C. Apionem*, II 35, 42.

6 For extensive treatment see Kasher, *Beth Mikra*, 20 (1975), pp. 187-208; see also chap.
IV, *C*. On the credibility of Josephus in this case, see lately: D. Golan, "Josephus, Alexander's visit to Jerusalem, and modern historiography", in: *Josephus Flavius, Historirian of
Eretz-Israel in the Hellenistic-Roman Period* (ed. U. Rappaport), Jerusalem 1982, pp.
29-55 (Hebrew).

7 For the general background of these wars, see Tcherikover, *Hellenistic Civilization and
the Jews*, pp. 50-59; Will, *Histoire politique*, vol. 1, pp. 39-70.

Ptolemy I and Demetrius Poliorcetes confronted each other[8]. In that connection Josephus based himself on another excerpt from Hecataeus, and noted that the war of the Diadochs actually led to Jewish immigration in various directions — to the Phoenician cities in the north and Egypt in the south (*ibid.*, 194). The two testimonies perhaps indicate a rift in the Jewish community between adherents of Antigonus Monophthalmus and his son Demetrius Poliorcetes on the one hand, and on the other the adherents of Ptolemy, so that the opposite directions of immigration suggest a polarity in political positions. When the Ptolemaic kingdom was officially established in 306 B.C.E., extensive opportunities to settle in Egypt became available to Jews, for the rulers encouraged immigration from foreign countries for the purpose of defending their throne again t the native population, and they set up numerous military colonies throughout the kingdom[9]. Most of the Palestinian Jews were evidently more inclined toward Antigonus Monophthalmus, who besides being a more gifted commander, manifested a more liberal attitude to his subjects. If not for that preference, Ptolemy I would not have had to conquer Jerusalem by a trick on the Sabbath. Testimony on that episode is provided by Josephus (*ibid.*, 205-211; *Antiquitates*, XII 5-6) citing the Greek writer Agatharchides of Cnidus of the second century B.C.E., apparently relating to 302 B.C.E.[10] The *Letter of Aristeas* (§§12-14) adds a few details, noting that Ptolemy I transported 100,000 Jewish captives to his country, drafted the 30,000 men into his army, and assigned them to garrison duty in fortresses, selling the rest (women, children and the elderly) into slavery. According to this source (§§14-27, 37) they were latter redeemed by Ptolemy II Philadelphus. Today there is no doubt of the historic truth of those reports, although the number of captives must be taken with a grain of salt and viewed as simple literary exaggeration[11]. Presumably the immigration of Jews from Palestine to Egypt in Ptolemy I's time, whether forced or free, was not a single instance but a continuous

---

8 See a full analysis of this report on p. 41 below.

9 See full coverage in the studies of Lesquier, Launey, Bouché-Leclerq and Bevan.

10 See Tcherikover, *Hellenistic Civilization and the Jews*, pp. 55-58; M. Stern, *Greek and Latin Authors*, I, pp. 104-109. On the problem of war on the Sabbath mentioned in the same report, see Bar Kochva, *The Wars of the Hasmonaeans*, p. 331f.

11 See Wilcken, *Archiv*, 12 (1936), p. 221f.; Wilhelm, *Archiv*, 14 (1941), p. 30f.; Hadas, *Aristeas to Philocrates*, pp. 28-32, 104; Westerman, *AJPh*, 59 (1938), pp. 1ff., esp. 19-38; M. Gutmann, *Dinaburg Aniversary Book*, pp. 76-79.

process associated with his wars in Coele-Syria and lasting about a generation (320-301 B.C.E.). It should be noted in this connection that tombstones found in the vicinity of Alexandria and dated to the start of the Hellenistic period confirm the settlement of Jews in Egypt at that time (*CIJ*, II 1424-1431).

Under Ptolemy II Philadelphus (284-246 B.C.E.) the development of Jewish community life, particularly in Alexandria, was greatly advanced. Epigraphic and papyrological findings indicate that from that time on there was a steady increase in the number of Jews absorbed in the army, in administrative services, and in sentry and police duty (specified below). Like other ethnic groups, the Jews of Egypt too enjoyed, as much as circumstances permitted, the great privilege of maintaining community life within the framework of military and administrative service. In Ptolemaic terms, a community of that kind was called a *politeuma*, that is, a national (or religious) group enjoying certain political privileges, first and foremost the maintenance of an independent judicial system and community establishment, on the basis of the right to preserve ancestral customs[12]. We shall see below that the Jewish community in Alexandria was organized according to that pattern, and content ourselves here just with mentioning the well-known document from the *Letter of Aristeas* (§§ 308-310).

In the reign of Ptolemy II Philadelphus, Alexandria was already one of the most important centers of Hellenistic culture, and the royal court was the seat of philosophers and scholars, writers and poets. They all took an active part in the political life of Egypt and contributed a great deal to the formation of its laws and political regime in the spirit of their philsophical aspirations and thought[13]. The close acquaintance they had with the Jewish religion and Jewish people evoked considerable admiration and deep intellectual interest on their part. According to the *Letter of Aristeas*, the initiative to translate the Pentateuch into Greek came from the court. The idea was proposed by the director of the royal library, Demetrius of Phaleron, who quickly gained the vigorous support of the king himself. In his enthusiasm, Ptolemy II Philadelphus despatched an official delegation to the High Priest Eleazar in Jerusalem, to ask for help in the

---

12 For details see below p. 30 and n.5.
13 Fraser, vol. 1, p. 305f.

planned translation. The latter responded by sending to Egypt seventy-two sages who knew both the Torah and the Greek language. It took seventy-two days to complete the translation (generally known as the Septuagint, that is, "the translation of the seventy") whereupon it was read aloud to the amazement of the audience, in the presence of the Jewish *politeuma* with its elders and leaders. After the reading, the translation was officially approved at the ceremony, and it was decided to consecrate the text in perpetuity (*Letter of Aristeas*, 308-311). In the end the translation was read to the king himself, who expressed his appreciation for the pearls of wisdom in it, and recognized its sanctity.

Despite the tinge of legend coloring the story, it is hard to doubt the fact that intellectual circles at the Ptolemaic court found the values of Judaism of great interest, which led to the production of the Septuagint[14]. Yet some scholars believe that a translation was needed by the Jews, whose involvement in Hellenistic culture had led to their abandonment of the Hebrew language[15] (a view apparently based on a retroprojection from Moses Mendelssohn's translation of the Pentateuch into German to fill the needs of the "enlightened" Jews of Germany). At any rate, there is nothing in the sources to support or confirm such a hypothesis. Nor does it seem likely that the Jews became so quickly and deeply rooted in Greek culture so that within a single generation the Alexandria community already needed the Torah in Greek to meet its religious needs. Furthermore, it is hard to imagine that captivity and slavery, which were the lot of many Jews till Ptolemy II Philadelphus freed them, could create the proper conditions for cultural assimilation. The close ties with Judaea during the century of Ptolemaic rule there (301-200 B.C.E.), the geographic proximity and the immigration that proceeded throughout the Syrian Wars would all likewise counter the above view[16]. It is more reasonable to suppose that the Ptolemies' loss of Palestine and the severance of the ties between Egyptian Jews and their brothers in Jerusalem produced new historical conditions that made the Jews of Egypt more open to the external influence of Hellenistic culture,

---

14 See J. Gutman, *The Beginnings of Jewish Hellenistic Literature*, vol. 1, pp. 115f.; 189-192.
15 The first to express this view was Zechariah Frankel, *Vorstudien zu der Septuaginta*, p. 5f.; see also Tcherikover, *op.cit.*, pp. 348ff.; Fraser, vol. 1, p. 687f. For a different opinion see Hengel, *Judaism and Hellenism*, p. 101f., 162f.
16 Cf. J. Gutman, *op.cit.*, p. 119f.

while there was no convenient, regular possibility of "recharging the batteries" of Jewish values. Consequently it is more likely that the initiative for translating the Pentateuch into Greek did indeed come from the intellectual circles of the Ptolemaic court, and did not derive from internal Jewish needs. It should be noted that talmudic sources too suggest Greek initiative for the translation[17]. It is hard to determine exactly when the text of the translation was sanctified by the Jewish community of Alexandria, but this does not appear to have been done before the middle of the second century B.C.E. One way or the other, the translation was one of the most important spiritual creations for Hellenistic Jewry, particularly since it provided inspiration for a whole series of Greek-speaking Jewish writers and philosophers in succeeding generations.

The Ptolemaic court's enlightened interest in Jews and Judaism, as well as the monumental Pentateuch translation projects, fostered the growth of anti-Jewish works already in the time of Ptolemy II Philadelphus. It developed in Hellenized circles of the Egyptian priestly aristocracy, whose first spokesman was Manetho. Just as the Septuagint provided inspiration to Jewish philosophers in subsequent generations, so the anti-Jewish libels of Manetho supplied a literary base for many-storied structures of anti-Jewish literature[18].

Little literary information has survived on the Jews of Egypt in the reign of Ptolemy III Euergetes I (246-221 B.C.E.), except for a rather muffled echo in the story of the Tobaid Joseph reported by Josephus[19]. It is told that Joseph son of Tobias wished to marry his daughter to one of the prominent members of the Alexandria Jewish community (*Antiquitates*, XII 187), indicating the prosperity of that community already then, and perhaps also its independent organization headed by an aristocratic leadership. Joseph's endeavor to hide his sin of fornication, which he himself said was contrary to the prohibition against a Jew approaching a Gentile woman, is readily explainable in the literary context against the background of strict

---

17 *T.J. Megillah*, I 10 (71d); *Mekhilta* for *Ex.* 12:40; *Masekheth Soferim*, 1:7; *Aboth de-Rabbi Nathan*, version B, 37:1; cf. above n.14.

18 Kasher, *Studies in the History of the Jewish People and the Land of Israel*, vol. 3 (1975), pp. 69-84.

19 See M. Stern, *Tarbiz*, 32 (1963), pp. 35-47, for an exhaustic historical analysis of this story.

compliance with precepts on the part of the Alexandria Jews at the time.

The reign of Ptolemy IV Philopator (221-205 B.C.E.) was marked by religious fanaticism and the persecution of Egyptian Jews in general and Alexandrian Jews in particular. A detailed literary survey of that period is preserved in *III Maccabees*, which has been a matter of dispute in modern scholarly literature. Although several scholars have treated the story as entirely fictional, and sought to find its historical core in later periods, they do not seem to have been able to shake its foundations[20].

There is no surviving literary information on Egyptian Jewry under Ptolemy V Epiphanes (205-180 B.C.E.) either. However, one of the fateful events of the life of that community occurred in his reign — the detachment from Palestine following the Seleucid victory in the Fifth Syrian War (202-200 B.C.E.) The effects of that event on the life of the Jews of Egypt were discernible during the reign of Ptolemy VI Philometor (180-145 B.C.E.) and thereafter. The deterioration of relations between the Jewish community of Palestine and the Seleucid authorities from the time of Seleucus IV (187-175 B.C.E.) on turned the Jews into an important factor in Ptolemaic policy, since they could contribute a great deal to the ejection of the Seleucid from the region. The development of a pro-Ptolemaic orientation in Jerusalem, as can be seen from the Onias III episode[21], is thus not surprising. His removal as High Priest in 175 B.C.E. by pro-Seleucid Hellenizers, and his foul murder shortly thereafter, did not lessen opposition to the Antioch authorities, quite the contrary. When Onias IV, the legitimate successor to the High Priesthood, realized that the authorities had turned the high office into a toy for sale to the highest bidder, and had abolished his family's claim to it by appointing Menelaus and after him Alcimus, he lost all hope and left for Egypt.

In Egypt Onias IV found a loyal ally in Ptolemy VI Philometor, and through him was able to entertain hopes of one day returning to Jerusalem. For the Ptolemies had not reconciled themselves to the loss of Palestine. In 172 B.C.E. they undertook a new initiative that

---

20 See chapter VI, section b, below for details.
21 M. Stern, *Zion*, 25 (1960), p. 5f.

involved them heavily in the Sixth Syrian War (170-168 B.C.E.)[22]. It is reasonable to suppose that under such circumstances, Ptolemy VI considered Onias IV an ally, and perhaps even more than that, a political instrument likely to be extremely helpful in reinstating Egypt's political influence in Palestine. It is against this background that one should judge Josephus' testimony on the establishment of the military colony of Land of Onias, that stretched along the eastern tributaries of the Delta, and at whose center, in the town of Leontopolis, was erected the sanctuary known as the Temple of Onias[23].

The strategic importance of the Land of Onias for the defense of Egypt was very great, for Egypt could not be conquered except by invasion from that direction. From the geo-strategic point of view, Egypt was like an island surrounded by impassible natural obstacles. To the north was the Mediterranean, to the south the mountains of Ethiopia, to the west the Libyan desert and the Sahara, to the east the Red Sea and the Indian Ocean. The conquest of Egypt, including Alexandria, was thus contingent upon the seizure of the region along the eastern arm of the Delta to its head. To cross the Delta breadthwise (directly to Alexandria) was completely senseless because of the intervening aquatic obstacles and areas that could be flooded and blocked. The fact that the Jews were assigned to the defense of that sensitive area for about a hundred years certainly indicates the authorities' view of both their political reliability and their military qualifications[24].

However aggrandized Josephus' report of the appointment of Onias IV and his friend Dositheus as commanders of the Ptolemaic army (*C. Apionem*, II 49) is considered, their military importance and high rank cannot be ignored, and Josephus may not have exaggerated at all in regard to the role they played in the history of Egypt in the short reign of Cleopatra II in 145 B.C.E. It is reasonable to suppose that their unreserved loyalty to her and their readiness to defend her throne against her foes — Ptolemy VIII (Euergetes II) and the Alexandrian *polis* — placed them in the higher echelons of the military command, and increased their political importance to the highest degree (*ibid.*, 50f.). It is inconceivable that Onias IV could

---

22 Will, *Histoire politique*, p. 257f.
23 See pp. 119ff. below.
24 See Stern, *Greek and Roman Authors*, vol. I, p. 404f.

have defended Cleopatra's throne with only a small military force[25],
if he did not have the help of the Alexandria Jews. The location of
the Jewish quarter known as "Delta" in the rear of the royal palace
in Cape Lochias[26] may support the conclusion that Onias was helped
by Jews within the city, and that was probably the reason they were
persecuted by Ptolemy VIII Physcon (Euergetes II) in 145 B.C.E.[27]
Although Josephus' description of this episode, including the miracle
that happened to the Jews (*C. Apionem*, II 53-55) is a weak diluted
paraphrase of what *III Maccabees* relates about the religious persecutions by Ptolemy IV Philopator, that description has been accorded
more credibility as a historical source. In fact, however, the two
episodes should be distinguished, and should not necessarily be considered as referring to a single event[28].

It is reasonable to suppose that the marriage of Ptolemy VIII
(Euergetes II) to Cleopatra II solved the problem of Jewish political
loyalty, at least for a while. But the rift in the royal family did not
heal, and in 131 B.C.E. a new conflict emerged which escalated into
a protracted civil war (to 124 B.C.E.) and ended with another recon-
ciliation[29]. Presumably the Jews remained loyal to Cleopatra, and
consequently it is not at all clear whether the miracle reported by
Josephus took place in 145 B.C.E. as Tcherikover proposed[30], or in
124 B.C.E. In any case the fact that Ptolemy VIII came to terms
with the Jews and resumed normal relations with them is shown by
inscriptions dedicated to him in various synagogues[31].

Onias IV's move to Egypt was part of a great wave of immigration
in the wake of the stormy events in Palestine after the persecutions
of Antiochus IV Epiphanes and the revolt of the Hasmonaeans, and

---

25 The source states the Onias went up to Alexandria at the head of a small army (στρατὸν
ὀλίγον). Some scholars have corrected the text and added οὐκ (= not) before the word
ὀλίγον, which complicates matters unacceptably; cf. J. Cohen, *Judaica et Aegyptiaca*,
p. 33.

26 *Bellum*, II 495; *C. Apionem*, II 33-37; and see Fraser, vol. 1, p. 35; vol. 2, p. 109 and
n.270.

27 For detailed surveys of the general background, see Bevan, p. 306f.; Otto & Bengston,
Zur Geschichte des Niederganges des Ptolemäerreiches, p. 23f.

28 See pp. 211ff. below (ch. 6, B.).

29 Fraser, vol. 1, p. 121f.

30 Tcherikover, *Hellenistic Civilization and the Jews*, p.283; Bickermann, *PAAJR*, 20
(1957), p. 130f.

31 *CIJ*, II 1441-2, 1449.

its effect extended as far as Cyrene. A considerable portion of the
immigrants were no doubt ordinary war refugees, seeking to better
their situation in the traditional land of opportunity, Egypt. Others
were certainly political exiles who wanted a haven until anger dis-
sipated. Among the latter were also Hellenizers looking for refuge
abroad from the ire of the Hasmonaean rebels (*I Maccabees*, XV
15-24).

When the Hasmonaeans defeated the Seleucids, the bonds between
the Jews of Egypt and their brothers in Zion became closer. Jewish
volunteers from Egypt and Cyrene may even have taken an active
part in the Hasmonaean revolt[32]. At any rate, the religious and
national identification of the Jews of Egypt with the goals of the
Hasmonaean rebels was expressed in the Hanukkah Letter (*II Maccabees*, I 1f.)[33]. The spiritual and religious affinity with Jerusalem was
interestingly revealed by Josephus in reporting on penertrating discussions the Alexandrian Jews held with the Samaritans regarding the
holiness of the temples in Jerusalem and Mount Gerizim (*Antiquitates*,
XIII 74-79), reportedly in the presence of Ptolemy VI Philometor.
The discussion may well have exceeded the limits of a verbal religious
disagreement, and become a serious violent conflict that required
high level mediation. Although absolute truth cannot be inferred
from the sources, the testimony does show how close the Jerusalem
temple was to the hearts of the Jews of Alexandria, and how zealous
they were in defending its sanctity. The spiritual ties between the
Alexandria Jews and Jerusalem are indicated also in the translation
into Greek of the book of Ben-Sira (Sirach) after 118 B.C.E., by the
author's grandson, who even proceeded to Egypt (132 B.C.E.) for
this purpose[34]. One of the foremost representatives of the Jewish
intelligentsia in Alexandria in those days was the philosopher Aristobulus, a member of the high priestly family who served in the court
of Ptolemy VI Philometor as "the teacher of King Ptolemy" (*II
Maccabees*, I 10) and who was the recipient of the famous Hanukkah
Letter. His "Exegesis to the Law of Moses" of which vestiges have
survived in the works of the Church Fathers, was dedicated to

---

32 Appelbaum, *Jews and Greeks in Ancient Cyrene*, pp.139-140; Bar Kochva, *Beth. Mikra*,
   45 (1974), p. 432f.
33 See Bickermann, *ZNW*, 32 (1933), p. 233f.
34 Segal, *The Complete Book of Ben-Sira*, Foreword, p. i; see also Tcherikover, *op.cit.*,
   p. 142ff.; Hengel, *Judaism and Hellenism*, vol. 1, p. 131f.

Ptolemy VI, and flaunted the influence of the Jewish Torah on the greatest Greek philosophers[35].

In the reign of Cleopatra III Selene (116-101 B.C.E.)[36] the relationship between the Jews and the royal family reached an apogee, with the appointment of Helkias and Hananiah, the sons of Onias IV, as high officers in her army (*Antiquitates*, XIII, 284-287). In her first regnal year, she was compelled to share her throne with her son Ptolemy IX Lathyrus by the pressure of the Alexandrian *polis*. In practice, her control of the capital was conditional on the loyalty of the Jews to her rule and her strong alliance with them. The accession in 114/113 B.C.E. of Ptolemy X (Alexander I) further complicated matters and a civil war was inevitable. From 108/107 B.C.E. on, Ptolemy IX Lathyrus, who left for Cyprus, conducted a campaign against his mother and brother with actual Seleucid help. The military endeavor focused first on Palestine (103/102 B.C.E.) where Ptolemy IX Lathyrus sought to establish a bridgehead for the conquest of Egypt. That fact and his political ties with the Seleucids led to a political alliance and military cooperation between King Janaeus and Cleopatra III. Soon after, Ḥelkias was killed in one of the battles waged on Palestinian soil, while Ḥananiah continued to serve his queen and even foiled the plot of some of her advisors to nullify the alliance with Jannaeus and conquer his country (*ibid.*, 348-355)[37]. Presumably the defeat Cleopatra inflicted on Ptolemy Lathyrus further reinforced the status of the Jews in her kingdom, and the political inconsistency of the Alexandrian *polis* evidently made a considerable contribution to this. It is therefore no wonder that as the alliance between the Jews and the queen was strengthened, her rivals' hatred grew, and threatened to erupt into anti-Jewish violence at the first opportunity.

The coregency of Cleopatra III and Ptolemy X (Alexander I) came to an end in 101 B.C.E., when the mother-queen was murdered by her son following a dispute between them. It is not clear how that affected the fate and status of the Jews, for the information avail-

---

35 About him see J. Gutman, *op.cit.*, pp. 186-220, 276-286; Walter, *Der Thoraausleger Aristobulos*. See also pp. 59-60 below.
36 On her reign, see Otto & Bengston, *Zur Geschichte des Niederganges des Ptolemäerreiches*, pp. 145-193.
37 See Stern, *Tarbiẓ*, 33 (1964), p. 326f.

able on the reign of Ptolemy X is extremely scanty. In 89 B.C.E. he
was forced to leave Alexandria under obscure circumstances, when
his army and the citizens of the capital turned their backs on him[38].
He was replaced by Ptolemy IX Lathyrus who gained the political
support of Alexandria due to the great popularity of his wife,
Berenice III. Presumably the persecution of the Jews in 88 B.C.E. of
which we have only a muffled echo was perpetrated on the initiative
of Ptolemy IX Lathyrus and was a consequence of his protracted
struggle against his mother and brother. There may however have
been other reasons, perhaps connected with the persecutions of the
Jews of Antioch and Cyrene which took place just at that time[39].

The wars of succession for the Ptolemaic throne waxed rather than
waned. With the death of Ptolemy IX Lathyrus in 80 B.C.E., Egypt
became totally subject to Roman influence, and Sulla's intervention
led to the crowning successively of Ptolemy XI (Alexander II) and
Ptolemy XII Auletes. The citizens of Alexandria were entirely
opposed to Roman intervention, which influenced the succession
noted. The slaying of Berenice III at the instigation of Ptolemy XI
led to an outbreak of anti-Roman and vengeful feelings in Alexandria,
which expressed themselves in the murder of the king. The Alexandrians considered Ptolemy XII Auletes too a Roman puppet, and
opposed him in every possible way, until in 58 B.C.E. riots protesting
his reign forced him to leave the city[40]. It is reasonable to suppose
that the Jews were involved in the riots one way or another, willingly
or not. It is simply unlikely that the citizens of Alexandria would
have allowed them to remain indifferent or neutral[41], besides which
there is every reason to assume that they themselves would have
sought to safeguard their interests through an alliance with the most
stable element in the distintegrating kingdom. Their support of
Ptolemy XII Auletes is clearly indicated by the fact that in 55 B.C.E.
Jewish soldiers opened the gates of Pelusium for him after he returned
from exile with the assistance of the Roman commander Gabinius

---

38 See Fraser, vol. 1, p. 123.
39 It is not clear, e.g., to what extent these persecutions were connected with Sulla's
   campaigns in the east. See Tcherikover, *CPJ*, 1 (1957), p. 25; Willrich, *Hermes*, 39
   (1904), pp. 244f.; Appelbaum, *Jews and Greeks in ancient Cyrene*, pp. 201f.
40 On the entire affair, see Fraser, vol. 1, p. 124f.
41 Schubart, in commenting on some papyri dating from 58 B.C.E. (*BGU*, 1762-1764),
   thought they hinted at anti-Jewish agitation.

(*Bellum*, I 175; *Antiquitates*, XIV 98-99).

In the winter of 48/47 B.C.E. Jews faced a similar situation when they helped Julius Caesar in the Alexandrian war he was unwillingly drawn into. In his review of the entire affair, Josephus (*Bellum*, I 187-194; *Antiquitates*, XIV 127f.) lauded the aid provided by the Jews of "the Land of Onias" to the auxiliary troops headed by Mithradates of Pergamon, who surrounded the Delta on the way to Alexandria in order to extricate Julius Caesar. At the outset the Jews stopped Mithradates' army (*Antiquitates*, XIV 131) but after a short persuasion by the High Priest Hyrcanus II and Antipater the Idumaean (Herod's father), they took their places clearly in the camp of Caesar's supporters. Does this imply that the Jews of Egypt supported Cleopatra VII against her brother Ptolemy XIII? It is known that she discriminated against the Jews of Alexandria in the distribution of grain during a famine in Egypt at a later date (*C. Apionem*, II 60). However, the real dilemma facing the Jews at the time was whether to support the political arrangements of Rome, in this case those made by Julius Caesar. In adopting a favorable stand[42], they placed themselves on Cleopatra's side whether they intended to do so or not. Her unfairness to the Alexandrian Jews in the distribution of grain at a later date does not necessarily indicate uneasy relations between her and the Jews in 48-47 B.C.E., for there could be a thousand reasons for the subsequent deterioration in relations. The fact that in 48 B.C.E. the Jews were no longer charged with guarding Pelusium[43] demands an explanation. Since in 48 B.C.E. that responsibility was borne by forces under the command of Achillas who were loyal to Ptolmey XIII, and their goal was to prevent the possible return of Cleopatra VII from her Syrian exile[44], the fact that they opened the way to Pelusium for Gabinius made them thenceforth unsuitable for the task, or at least suspect in the eyes of Ptolemy XIII. The support given him by the Alexandrians only reinforces the conclusion that the Jews found themselves — whether against their

---

42 The surrender to Rome was effected in accordance with the Ptolemaic political tradition several generations old; perhaps that is the secret of the success Hyrcanus II and Antipater had in convincing the Jews of the Land of Onias (*Antiquitates*, XIV 131).

43 Its geo-strategic value as the key to the gates of Egypt was clearly demonstrated in Julius Caesar's time, as can be seen in *Bell. Alex.*, 26.

44 Caesar, *Bell. Civ.*, III 103; *Bell. Alex.*, 26; Cassius Dio, XLII 36, 2; Strabo, XVII 1, 11; Florus, II 13, 52.

will or at their own initiative — on the other side of the fence. It should be noted in this connection that in their assemblies the Alexandrians expressed the fear that Julius Caesar's arrival in their city was just another step in the process, begun in Gabinius' time, of turning Egypt into a Roman province (*Bell. Alex.*, 3).

When Caesar landed at the port of Alexandria on 2 October 48 B.C.E., he had only a few thousand troops, which diminished his self-confidence even before he left his ship[45] . According to the available information, matters quickly escalated from angry demonstrations by the urban rabble to violent assemblies that deteriorated into street skirmishes. In the end Caesar was in straits that he considered an emergency and described as a *tumultus* in the full sense of the world[46] . As required in an emergency, he called on all possible resources for help, took rapid defensive measures, and spared no effort to gain time through diplomatic negotiations pending the arrival of help[47] . The enemy forces were extremely numerous, and Achillas' troops summoned from Pelusium alone accounted for twenty thousand soldiers. Despite the professional inferiority of the Ptolemaic soldier compared to the battle-tried warriors under Caesar's command, it must be borne in mind that the core of the Ptolemaic army that confronted Caesar consisted of former Roman soldiers who had served with Pompey, and been brought to Egypt in 55 B.C.E. by Gabinius and settled there. In addition, Caesar was faced with the multitude of citizens of the Alexandrian *polis*, the wealthier members of which even enlisted their slaves in order to swell the ranks and attain decisive numerical superiority over Caesar. However much we exaggerate the genius and wiliness of Caesar, it is hard to believe he could hold out for six months (the war ended only on 27 March 47 B.C.E.) without considerable help from an internal element in Alexandria. In only one instance, and that incidentally, is there notice that in part of the city held by Caesar there was a large mass

---

45 For details see Rice-Holmes, *The Roman Republic*, vol. 3, p. 180f.
46 See e.g. *Bell. Civ.*, III 106, 4; Lucan, IX 1007-1010; Cassius Dio, XLII 7, 2-3; 34, 2; 35, 2; Appian, *Bell. Civ.*, II 90. On the term *tumultus* as indicating an emergency of the highest degree see Sachers, *RE (PW)*, vol. 7, A2, s.v., p. 1344f.; Mommsen, *Strafrecht*, p. 660f.; Kromayer & Veith, *Heerwesen*, pp. 285, 305; Daremberg & Saglio, *Dictionnaire*, vol. 5, p. 532. Cf. also Applebaum, *Jews and Greeks in Ancient Cyrene*, pp. 308-310.
47 *Bell. Civ.*, III 107, 1f.; *Bell. Alex.*, 1, 1f.; Cassius Dio, XLII 35, 1f.; Lucan, X 14-19; Frontinus, *Strat.*, I 1, 5; Appian, *Bell. Civ.*, II 89.

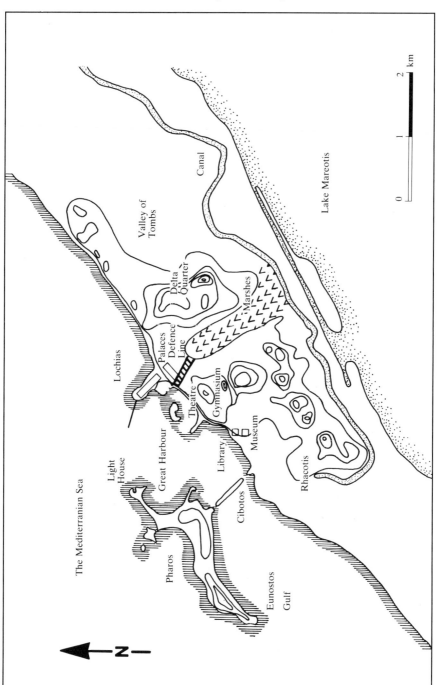

Alexandria in the „Alexandrian War" of Julius Caesar

of urban residents which he did not evacuate from their homes, "for they proved openly their loyalty to us" (*Bell. Alex.*, 7.3). Evidently that large mass not only demonstrated passive loyalty, but actually helped the Roman commander in various ways. Aside from actual combat, Caesar had to devote considerable effort to digging ditches, building fortifications, and drilling wells for drinking water, since the city's water channels had deliberately been filled with salt water. These tasks demanded quite a lot of manpower, and it is doubtful whether Caesar could have supplied it without local help.

It seems to me that the residents who helped the Roman imperator should be identified with the members of the Jewish community[48]. The topographical descriptions in the sources on the "Alexandrian War" indicate that Julius Caesar established himself in the neighborhood of the royal palaces at the base of Cape Lochias on the edge of the Jewish quarter, the Delta, to the east, while his enemies held most of the western sectors of the city[49]. In those days the division of the city between east and west was very definite, as a swampy extension of Lake Mareotis separated them. The division was especially distinct in the fall when the Nile overflowed and flooded extensive areas. Caesar arrived in Alexandria just at that time (2 October) and not unexpectedly understood how to exploit the swampy terrain for the improvement of his defensive system by digging a deep ditch that connected the seacoast with the swamp. That can only reinforce the conclusion that his strategic conception was based on a total separation between the two sections of the city, and on his absolute trust of the population living in the eastern section. Why then is no Jewish help specifically mentioned in the authoritative work on that war, *Bellum Alexandrinum*? The answer may lie in the literary objective of the author, Hirtius, which was to glorify Caesar whether by concealing facts likely to diminish his achievements, or by focusing the laudatory spotlights on Caesar's own deeds and ingenuity. It is also possible that Hirtius, who did not himself take part in the war, received incomplete information from Caesar[50], and may have interpreted his commander's descriptions in slightly distorted form, thus

---

48. Further details in Kasher, *Newsletter, World Union of Jewish Studies*, 14-15 (1979), pp. 15-23.
49 *Bell. Civ.*, III 112, 4-8; *Bell. Alex.*, 1, 4-6; Rice-Holmes, *The Roman Republic*, p. 489f.; Fraser, vol. 2, p. 80, n.184.
50 See the introduction to Book 8 of *The Gallic Wars*.

failing to distinguish between the Jews and the citizens of the *polis*, and treating them all as "Alexandrians". If the author got such an impression, it may have derived also from the fact that the Jews customarily represented themselves as "Alexandrians" in line with their struggle for equal rights with the citizens of the *polis*.

The direct positive evidence in *Bellum Alexandrinum* of help the Jews of Alexandria extended to Julius Caesar appears in the privileges accorded them after his victory[51]. Some have cast doubt on the authenticity of Josephus in this matter, claiming that the name of Julius Caesar was mistakenly substituted for that of Augustus. The main justification for this claim contends that Julius Caesar was not the official ruler of Egypt, and as it had not yet become a Roman province, he was not empowered to grant the Alexandria Jews any privileges at all[52]. However, it can be argued that it is more likely that the privileges of the Alexandria Jews were established within the framework of the political arrangements Julius Caesar imposed on Egypt. It should be recalled that for several generations, the Ptolemaic kingdom had been under Roman influence and protection, and no political matter worthy of the name was dealt with in the absence of Roman intervention. Furthermore, the rights granted the Alexandria Jews parallel those extended by Julius Caesar himself (or at his behest) to the Jews of Ionia and Asia Minor. The latter are cited at length by Josephus in the same connection (*Antiquities*, XIV 213f.) and their authenticity is unquestioned. As to the argument on the absence of any official authority to grant privileges, we may ask whether the privileges Caesar granted John Hyrcanus II derived from a legal and political situation whereby Judaea was considered a Roman province. It is logical to conclude that no benefits are granted without underlying practical justification, and thus Julius Caesar compensated the Jews of Alexandria for substantial help they gave him. On the basis of the same principle, the High Priest John Hyrcanus II and Antipater the Idumaean acquired many privileges (*Bellum*, I 193ff.; *Antiquitates*, XIV 137 ff.) and although Hirtius, the author of *Bellum Alexandrinum*, did not make the slightest

---

51 *Antiquitates*, XIV 188-189; *C. Apionem*, II 37; and cf. *ibid.*, 61.
52 Tcherikover, *CPJ*, vol. 1, Prol., p. 123; Th. Reinach, *REJ*, 79 (1924), p. 123; Tcherikover, *Hellenistic Civilization and the Jews*, p. 324, 514 (n.81); Smallwood, *The Jews Under Roman Rule*, p. 233.

reference to them, there is no doubt of Josephus' reliability on this matter[53].

The bill of rights that Julius Caesar granted the Jews of Alexandria in effect established the political and legal foundations for Jewish rights throughout the Roman empire in subsequent generations. On the basis of those rights, for instance, Jewish communities were not counted as forbidden *collegia* (*Antiquitates*, XIV 215f.; Philo, *In Flaccum* 4; *Legatio ad Gaium* 316) and their right to religious and judicial autonomy was recognized (*Antiquitates*, XIV 213-216, 227, 235, 241-246, 256-264). One of the celebrated privileges concerned Jews with Roman citizenship who were exempt from military service in the Roman legions (*ibid.*, 223-240)[54]. A perusal of the wording of these rights might easily lead to the impression that the Jews within the Roman empire were treated like a "nation"[55]. But there are restrictions to this generalization[56], for it applied only to Jews whose right to organize into a legal political body known as *politeuma* was recognized.

The transformation of Egypt into a Roman province in 30 B.C.E. was a turning point in its history, and this of course had important implications for the life of the Jews there as well. According to Philo, Augustus confirmed their right to maintain an autonomous community based on ancestral laws, and that right accorded with his policy regarding their coreligionists in the empire[57]. Eventually Emperor Claudius confirmed it in an edict, noting that Augustus had actually continued to maintain Jewish rights as in the past, because he wanted all his subjects to live in accordance with their own customs and not be coerced into abandoning their ancestral religion (*Antiquitates*, XIX 282f.). Further confirmation appears in the papyrus containing Claudius' letter to the Alexandrians (*P. Lond.*

---

53 Schürer, vol. 1 (ed. Vermes), p. 271 f.; see also Gilboa, *Studies in the History of the Jewish People* etc., vol. 1, (1970), pp. 71-77. Note in this connection the general statement of Hirtius (*Bell. Alex.*, 65) that when he was in Syria, Caesar liberally rewarded everyone who helped him in the Alexandrian war, both private individuals and public bodies.

54 Smallwood, *The Jews Under Roman Rule*, p. 133f.

55 *natio, gens* or γένος, ἔθνος, that was the view of Radin, *The Jews Among the Greeks and Romans*, p. 267f.; Mitteis, *Richsrecht*, pp. 34, 94, 1890; Cf. Wilcken-Mitteis, *Grundzüge*, vol. 1, p. 56f., Colorni, *Leggi ebraici*, p. 13f.

56 Cf. Juster, vol. 2, p. 19f., Applebaum, "The Legal Status, etc." p. 455f.

57 *In Flaccum*, 50; *Legatio*, 152-158, 240, 294-297, 311-318.

1912, lines 82-88). Thus Augustus made no changes in the legal and political status of the Jews, which they undoubtedly found satisfactory. The only change was the community establishment, which was adapted to the standards of the Augustan principate, but that did not constitute any real change in the content and scope of the Jewish rights[58].

It is customarily believed that the poll-tax (*laographia*) levied on all Egyptian subjects (*dediticii*) applied to the Alexandria Jews as well, as the only exemptions were Roman citizens and the citizens of the Alexandrian *polis*[59] . In fact, however, we have no information clearly and definitely indicating that it was levied on all the Jews of the city. We shall see that there were quite a few Jews who were *laographia*-paying subjects, but there is good reason to think that the members of the Jewish *politeuma* in Alexandria enjoyed *isoteleia* (tax equality) with the citizens of the *polis*, a privilege apparently extended to anyone entitled to be called an "Alexandrian"[60]. The only deterioration that took place in Jewish life after the Roman conquest was connected with the dissolution of the Ptolemaic army, including the military settlements. However, the Greek population in Egypt was similarly affected. The offspring of the military settlers were not deprived of their lands in the first generations after the conquest, but later (in the first century and particularly in the reigns of the Flavian emperors) deep cracks appeared in that regard. On the other hand, the economic opportunities open to the Jews under Roman rule were much greater than they had known in the past[61].

On the history of the Egyptian Jews under Tiberius (14-37 C.E.) we have no information beyond the obscure episode concerning their being discriminated against in the distribution of grain during the visit of Germanicus in 19 C.E.[62] That same year the Jews of Rome were persecuted on the initiative of L. Aelius Sejanus, head of the Praetorian Guard and Tiberius' right hand man, and their situation improved only in 31 C.E. when he was executed[63]. Philo reported these persecutions in a separate essay, apparently entitled "Against

---

58 *In Flaccum*, 74; *Antiquitates*, XIX 283, and see p. 253f. below (cap. VII, b).
59 In Tcherikover, *Jews in Egypt*, pp. 77ff.
60 Cf. *Antiquitates*, XVI 161; and see p. 288 below.
61 See Tcherikover, *CPJ*, vol. 1, Prol., p. 48f.
62 See pp. 341ff. below.
63 See detailed information in Leon, *The Jews of Ancient Rome*, pp. 16-20.

Sejanus" which may have been joined with his other two historical works, *In Flaccum* and *Legatio ad Gaium*, to form a complete literary trilogy.

In 32 C.E. Aulus Avilius Flaccus was appointed prefect (=governor) of Egypt, and at the end of his incumbency (in 38 C.E.) the severest persecutions ever encountered by the Jews of Alexandria began. The stormy events were reported in detail in Philo's two works, *In Flaccum* and *Legatio ad Gaium*[64]. Briefly, toward the end of his term Flaccus quarreled with two of the leaders of the Alexandrian *polis*, Isidorus and Lampo, who acted as gymnasiarchs, in connection with corruption and bribery. Isidorus was even tried and exiled after being found guilty by Flaccus' court. When Gaius Caligula became emperor (in 37 C.E.) Flaccus began to be concerned about his own fate, partly because of his close friendship for Tiberius whom Caligula hated, and partly becausse of his considerable involvement in Tiberius' intrigues against Caligula's mother. The execution in Rome early in the summer of 38 C.E. of his personal friends — Gemellus (Tiberius' grandson) and Macro (head of the Praetorian Guard) — added to his insecurity and brought him to the brink of despair. Under such circumstances he fell into the net of the Alexandrian leaders, first and foremost Isidorus. It appears that the latter had a hand in the overthrow of Macro, and since Caligula liked him, he was not afraid to return to Alexandria. The political price Flaccus was required to pay in return for a promise that he would be safe from Caligula's vengeance was turning the Jews of Alexandria over to the *polis*. It was a bargain for him, because in any case he had little fondness for the Jews, as shown by the fact that he did not transmit to Rome their congratulations and best wishes on the accession of Caligula. In August 38 C.E. on the occasion of the unexpected visit of King Agrippa I (the grandson of Herod and Miriam the Hasmonaean) on his way to actualize the kingdom he was given by Caligula in northern Palestine (the estate of his uncle Philip), the signal for violence was given. Although Agrippa wished to conceal the visit, it became known and engendered great excitement in town. The Jews were very enthusiastic and hoped through Agrippa to repair the damage

---

64 For a more extensive treatment see M. Stein, *Philo of Alexandria — Historical Writings* (Hebrew), p. 7f.; Box, Introduction, p. xxxviiif.; Smallwood, Introduction, p. 14f.; Smallwood, *The Jews Under Roman Rule*, p. 235f.

Flaccus had done them by not forwarding their greetings to Caligula, especially since they construed Agrippa's arrival as constituting a block against possible future intrigues. The Alexandrians, on the other hand, became most envious at the sight of the Jewish king, and expressed their disrespect in a mocking comedy in which a madman played the role of Agrippa. Flaccus' failure to respond only encouraged the people to continue baiting the Jews. Evidently they had no fear that the friendship between Agrippa and Caligula would interfere, for they planned to harass the Jews in a manner that would pander to the latter's deification craze. At first they desecrated synagogues by setting up statues in honor of the new god, Caligula; thereafter, when the Jews took steps to defend their holy places, the urban mob had an excuse for real violence.

For his part Flaccus prepared the legal grounds for a war against the Jews. He invalidated Jewish rights (both communal and individual) and issued an order turning the members of the Jewish community over to the *polis* and proclaiming them aliens and foreigners, or enemies whose lives and property were expendable[65]. When the signal was given the mob attacked the Jews, robbing and murdering them. Most of the harm befell those who lived in mixed neighborhoods, but even the purely Jewish areas were by no means safe. Many Jews were evicted from their homes and crammed into a quarter that was too small to contain them, and the terrible overcrowding, hunger and epidemics common in such circumstances completed the work the riots had started. In addition to daily killings, the Alexandrian mob lost no opportunity to torment its victims in plays of horrible torture presented in the municipal theater. Flaccus did not lift a finger to restore order and security in the city. He even accused the Jews of armed subversion, conducted searches for arms in their homes and arrested many of them. He did not recoil from taking part in the basest intrigues. Thus he summoned the heads of the Jewish *gerousia* (= council of elders) ostensibly to discuss the restoration of peace, and in fact turned them over to their enemies, in order to humiliate them in a public whipping ceremony customary for ordinary Egyptian native criminals.

Ultimately Flaccus proved to have been mistaken in hoping to

---

65 For a detailed discussion of the legal and political import of the decree see pp. 240ff. below.

escape the emperor's vengeance through his alliance with the Alexandrian leaders. The uprisings in the city, and probably also the condemnatory report of King Agrippa, who had meanwhile arrived in Palestine, focused Caligula's attention on Flaccus, and the emperor acted to settle accounts. At the end of 38 C.E., a new prefect (Vitrasius Polio) was assigned to Egypt, and Flaccus was despatched to Rome in chains, sentenced to exile on the island of Andros (in the Aegean Sea, south of Euboia) and eventually executed at the emperor's order.

Due to the fragmentary nature of Philo's survey, the events of 39 C.E. are unclear, but presumably order was restored by the new prefect. During that time the Jews seem to have licked their wounds and begun to rehabilitate themselves, and may even have accumulated arms in order to fight back should the hostile activities recommence. At the same time they initiated a judicial struggle aimed at eliminating any doubt about their legal and political rights as an organized community and as individuals. The new prefect allowed the two rival groups to send representaitves to Rome to submit their case to the emperor. The two delegations, one headed by Philo and the other by Apion, reached Rome in the winter of 39/40 C.E.[66], but were unable to appear before the emperor, as he then set out on a campaign against the Germans. No progress in settling the dispute was made thereafter either, for between his return to Rome on 31 August 40 and his assassination on 24 January 41, Caligula consistently avoided dealing with the affairs of the Jews. In his brief meetings with the rival delegations, the last and most important of which took place in January 41, he did not refrain from insulting and baiting the Jews, and gave them no opportunity to present their arguments. As a matter of fact, Philo had no illusions as to Caligula's hostility, for with Agrippa's panic-stricken arrival in Rome (in September 40, approximately) the terrible decree that threatened to place the emperor's statue in the Temple at Jerusalem became known[67]. In Philo's opinion that decree turned the struggle of the Alexandrian Jews for their rights into a secondary and marginal

---

66 Smallwood, pp. 47-50; Smallwood, *The Jews Under Roman Rule*, p. 242f.
67 For a chronological reconstruction of the whole episode see Smallwood, pp. 31-36, and Smallwood *Latomus*, 16 (1957): 13-17. Cf. Balsdon, *JRS*, 24 (1934); 19-24; idem, *The Emperor Gaius*, pp. 135-140.

matter, as the decree struck at the very existence of the Jewish religion. Under those circumstances he could only put his trust in Divine Providence and wish for the tyrant's death. His wish was granted on 24 January 41, and thereafter a drastic change took place in the situation of the Jews and the clarification of their affairs.

When the news of Caligula's death and Claudius' coronation reached Alexandria in mid-February, the Jews regained courage, armed themselves, and attacked the Alexandrians to avenge their past suffering (*Antiquitates*, XIX 278). Upon learning of the resumption of hostilities in Alexandria, Claudius despatched a rescript to his prefect there insturcting him to use the Roman troops to restore order. At the same time he applied himself to a thoroughgoing clarification of all the legal and political problems affecting the rights of the Jews in Alexandria, and in about mid-April, under the influence of his childhood friend, King Agrippa, issued two imperial edicts (*ibid.*, 280-285, 287-291) conforming to the spirit of the charters granted by Julius Caesar and Augustus. On 30 April and 1 May 41, a trial took place before the imperial council at which the Alexandrian leaders Isidorus and Lampo made serious accusations against King Agrippa. The verdict completely exonerated him and sentenced Isidorus and Lampo to death. The Alexandrians were deeply disappointed, and it is hardly surprising that they expressed their bitterness, tension and frustration in renewed acts of hostility late in September and early in October of 41[68].

Alexandrian attempts to force a change in imperial policy led to an additional judicial confrontation before Claudius, after new rival delegations were sent to Rome. This time the Jews were not united, but appeared in two delegations, differing in their opinions and stances. The more moderate represented the interests of the aristocratic circles and adhered to the policy adopted by Philo which was content with a return of the *status quo*. The other was more extreme and fanatic, representing the opposition and popular groups who were not satisfied with past achievements, and intended to submit new demands to Claudius[69]. The emperor was perplexed, and also weary of dealing so much with Jewish matters within the short

---

68 See Kasher, *Zion*, 39 (1974), pp. 1-7; idem. *Semitica*, 26 (1976), pp. 99-108; see also pp. 272ff. below.
69 See Tcherikover, *CPJ*, vol. 2, p. 50f.; and see pp. 321-323 below.

time since his accession. He was also taken aback by the Alexandrians'
eagerness to accord him divine veneration, especially since it was
designed to pave the way for a change in his Jewish policy as formulated in his two edicts. Above all, however, he was angered at the
resumption of disorders, which were completely contrary to his
policy of *Pax Romana* which was his watchword. He therefore
irately ended the matter and sent a detailed *Letter to the Alexandrians*
(*P. Lond.*, 1912) in which he stressed his adherence to the policy of
Augustus, without favoring either side. At the same time, threatening
dire consequences, he warned them both to refrain from hostile
action and make peaceful co-existence possible in practice[70].

The Jewish-Alexandrian conflict was not resumed till the reign
of 'Nero (54-68 C.E.). In 66 the Alexandrian *polis* discussed de-
spatching a delegation to Rome for the purpose of persuading the
emperor to cancel the Jews' rights in their city (*Bellum*, II 490). The
timing provides grounds for believing that the *polis* was encouraged
by the results of the similar conflict in Caesarea Maritima which was
concluded that same year. After a protracted legal consideration,
Nero had decided to cancel the "equal rights" of the Jews in Caesarea
and recognized the exclusive sovereignty of the Greek *polis* over all
residents of the city[71]. The Alexandrians may well have realized that
the conflict in Caesarea was the signal for the outbreak of the Great
Revolt in Judaea. For them it was convenient from the political
propaganda point of view, because it might present all Jews as
enemies of the Romans. The attempts of the Alexandrian Jews to
sabotage the public discussions regarding the despatch to Rome by
the citizens of the *polis* of a delegation was the spark that reignited
the fire of conflict. When three Jews were seized and dragged off to
the municipal amphitheater to be burned at stake, the furious Jewish
crowd planned to set fire to all the spectators of that event. The
Roman prefect, Tiberius Julius Alexander, did not hesitate to oppose
them with the two Roman legions permanently stationed in the city
and 2,000 soldiers from Libya who happened to be there. Although
the Jews stubbornly opposed the Roman troops and inflicted con-

---

70 For a detailed analysis of the letter see Bell, *Jews and Christians*, p. 23f.; Tcherikover,
   CPJ, vol. 2, p. 153; Tcherikover, *Jews in Egypt*, p. 139f.; and see pp. 310ff. below (chap.
   IX, *A*).

71 This matter is dealt with further in pp. 289f.

siderable casualties, they could not overcome the Roman superiority in arms, organization and experience, expecially since the Alexandrian mob took an active part in the riots. According to Josephus, some 50,000 people[71a] were cruelly slaughtered at the time, among them women, children and eldsters. The Alexandrian hooligans on the other hand escaped all punishment despite even their multilation of corpses (*Bellum* II 494-498).

While the Jewish-Alexandrian confrontation in 66 was the outcome of the domestic relations, in 70-73 the background was different. Immediately after the destruction of the Temple in Jerusalem in 70, the citizens of Alexandria as well as Antioch sought in vain to impel Vespasian and Titus to officially repeal the rights of the Jews in their cities, exploiting the personal involvement of those two Roman leaders in the Great Revolt[72]. The seeds of insurrection and violence now blossomed on Jewish ground. Thousands of refugees of the *Sicarii* emigrated at the time from Judaea to Egypt and found among their coreligionists there rather extensive groups ripe to absorb their rebellious notions. The fact that they did not hesitate to assassinate a number of prominent Jews who stood in their way and prevented them from inciting in Alexandria community to insurgence shows that the social circles they operated in were composed mainly of ordinary folk. The resolute response of the heads of the Jewish *gerousia*, a decision to pursue the *Sicarii* in order to turn them over to the Romans, testifies to the division of the community (signs of which were evident earlier as well) between two polar political positions: a) moderation and the aspiration to peaceful coexistence with the Graeco-Roman world, favored by the ruling aristocratic leadership circles; b) rebellious extremism inspired by the Zealot philosophy, favored by the oppositional groups in the population. There was evidently an identical development in Cyrene, judging by the events that took place there from 70 C.E. on[73]. It

---

71a cf. *Bellum*, VII 369 which states "more than sixty-thousand". It appears that the larger number refers to the total Jewish victims in Egypt (not merely in Alexandria) who died at the time, including the Jews of the Land of Onias whose temple was closed in 73 C.E. On the revolutionary agitation in the Egyptian *chora*, see Cf. chap. VII, n.44 below.

72 *Antiquitates*, XII 120-124; *Bellum*, VII 100-110. There were acts of violence against Jews in Antioch as well at that time; see *Bellum*, VII 41-62. For more details see Smallwood, *The Jews Under Roman Rule*, p. 356f.

73 A fuller treatment is to be found in Applebaum, *Jews and Greeks in Ancient Cyrene*, p. 218f.

appears that the rebellion fomented in Egypt and Cyrene by the *Sicarii* was not confined to the large cities, but spread to the rural regions of the *chora* (χώρα; the "country" outside the limits of the *polis*) even the remoter ones[74]. Probably the agrarian policy of the Roman emperors in the first century, which led to the gradual decline in small-scale farming in Egypt and Cyrene[75], affected the Jews as well and prepared them psychologically for rebellious aggression. Their close religious and national ties with Jerusalem likewise deepened their hatred of Rome. But under the conditions then obtaining, the strongest influence was exerted by the direct live contact with the *Sicarii* refugees who generated great admiration for their bravery and devotion to their cuase (cf. *Bellum*, VII 407-419). Despite internal dissension, the fact that that the refugees captured in the *chora* (*ibid.*, 416) need not be construed as the result of a purely Jewish initiative. It cannot be denied that the *chora* communities may likewise have had moderate leaders influenced by the Jewish leadership in Alexandria, but the fact that the prefect Lupus found it necessary to destroy the temple of Onias (*ibid.*, 420f.) is suggestive[75a]. The aggressive messianic activity of the false prophet who made his way to Judaea from his native Egypt during the term of the procurator Felix (A.D. 52-60?)[76] perhaps indicates that he did not sprout on barren soil. Moreover, the scope and dimensions of the Jewish uprising during Trajan's reign (115-117) show the extent to which the Jewish communities in the Egyptian *chora* were fertile ground for the seeds of revolt.

The Jewish rebellion of Trajan's time is the last milestone in this introductory survey. Its background, course and outcome have however been thoroughly reconstructed by other scholars[77], and just

---

74 *Bellum*, VII 416 mentions the Egyptian *chora* in general, particularly the union of Theban districts (Upper Egypt) which spreads southward to the Elephantine region. In connection with Cyrene, cf. *Bellum*, VII 437-438, 441.

75 On this policy and its results, see p. 99f. below and Applebaum, *op.cit.*, p. 201f.

75a The "ammunition dump" of *ballista* stones there might indicate to that event, see Applebaum, *Tarbiẓ*, 28 (1959), p. 422, n.10; but cf. Petrie, *Hyksos* etc., p. 26.

76 *Bellum*, II 261-263; *Antiquitates*, XX 169-172; *Acts*, 21:38.

77 See e.g. Alon, *History of the Jews in Eretz Israel*, p. 202f.; Tcherikover, *Jews in Egypt*, p. 160f.; Fuks, *Aegyptus*, 33 (1953), pp. 131-158; idem, *JRS*, 51 (1961), pp. 98-104; Tcherikover & Fuks, *CPJ*, vol. 1, Prol., pp. 85-93; vol. 2, pp. 228-260; Applebaum, *op. cit.*, p. 201f. Kasher, *Zion*, 41 (1976), pp. 127-138, and recently, Smallwood, *The Jews Under Roman Rule*, p. 389f.

a few remarks are in order. There is no doubt that the roots of the events that fanned the flame of revolt lie in the traditional struggles and conflicts between Jews and Greeks in the large cities of the Hellenistic-Roman Diaspora, and especially in Alexandria and Cyrene. As the social-political strength of the Jewish people waned following the destruction of the Second Temple, Jew-haters increased their attempts to assail the rights and legal status of the Jews. Although the Roman rulers did not support these efforts and did not permit the Jews to become subjects deprived of all rights, in practice their policy was systematically eroded. The first manifestation was the "Jewish tax" which applied to Jews everywhere even if they were Roman citizens[78]. Then the situation deteriorated to the extent that actual persecutions were conducted under the aegis of Emperor Domitian[79]. Venemous anti-Jewish literary propaganda, renewed judicial confrontations between Jews and Alexandrians, and recurrent hostilities and violent clashes as early as the start of Trajan's reign certainly contributed to escalating the storm that erupted in 115 C.E. The socio-economic ills of the *chora* Jews who had been dispossessed of their land by the Roman agrarian policy further completes the picture of the local reasons for the revolt. Among the external factors the most influential was the Zealot spirit brought to Egypt from Palestine by the rebel refugees (Zealots and *Sicarii*) and by the prisoners of war sold into slavery. All these created a convenient climate for messianic ferment and eschatological expectations.

In 114 C.E. Trajan set out to fight the Parthians in order to stop their constant menace to the eastern Roman provinces. The size of the armies engaged in the battle, the extensive preparations in the Roman empire, and the fact that the Romans were not yet able to defeat the Parthians aroused the Jews to great excitement, involving a yearning for the realization of messianic expectations. A popular literary expression of the mood appears in the talmudic traditions concerning the tannaitic personages of the first half of the second century, Rabbi Jose ben-Kisma and Rabbi Simeon bar-Yohai[80]. As a matter of fact, the hope of restoring Jewish national life with Parthian help was quite ancient, having appeared during the struggle of Antigonus the Hasmonaean against Herod in 40-37 B.C.E.

---

78 Smallwood, *The Jews Under Roman Rule*, p. 371f. 79 *Ibid.*, p. 376f.
80 *T.B. Sanhedrin*, 98a-b; *Ekhah Rabbati*, I 13 (Buber ed. 39a); *Shir ha-Shirim Rabbah*, VIII 10.

Petronius, the Roman legate for Syria, took note of the threat from the Euphrates following Caligula's decree (Philo, *Legatio ad Gaium*, 216-217). Agrippa II in his celebrated oration at the start of the Great Revolt also indicated the existence of national and political expectations for help from Parthia[81]. As a result of the transfer of large numbers of troops to the front line facing the Parthians in 115 C.E., there was a considerable reduction in the number of troops stationed in the provinces adjacent to Palestine. That of course provided a convenient opportunity and reason for starting the revolt, and explains its success as well.

The outcome of the rebellion was fateful for the Jews of Egypt, as the Talmud shows in its depictions of the terrible cost in lives[82]. The papyrological reports indicate that the Jews were slaughtered in most of the rural areas and provincial towns of the *chora*. The community in Alexandria, although not completely annihilated, never regained its former glory, and its experience evidently paralleled that of its great synagogue. The injuries to the community were not confined to loss of life and physical destruction, but included the loss of its well-known legal autonomy[83], and the decline of its unique spiritual life which had long aspired to a symbiotic relationship between Judaism and Hellenism. The intensity of the hatred and cruelty, the extreme fanatic aggressiveness, the fierceness of the fighting, and the vast dimensions of the destruction on the part of all who were involved in the rebellion — the Jews, the Greeks, the native Egyptians and the Roman troops — left their mark on subsequent generations. Thereafter it was no longer possible to bridge the gap between the pagan world and that of the Jews, and thus the history of Egyptian Jewry, which seemed to be approaching a synthesis between the cultures of Jerusalem and Athens, came to a dead end. The Byzantine period witnessed some renascence of Jewish life in various communities, but their development was restricted and sometimes completely stopped by the Church. It would therefore be no exaggeration to say that in 117 C.E. one of the most glorious chapters in the history of the Jewish people in the Diaspora came to an end.

---

81 *Bellum*, II 388-389; cf. *ibid.*, I 5, and cf. also with Titus's oration, *Bellum*, VI 343.

82 *T.J. Sukkah*, V 55b; *T.B. Gittin*, 57a; *Seder Eliahu Rabbah* (ed. M. Friedmann)[2], ch. 29 (30), p. 151.

83 *Tosefta Pe'ah*, IV 6, Zuckermandel, p. 23; *Tosefta Ketuboth*, III 1, Zuckermandel p. 263.

Chapter I

The Civic Stratification of the Jews
in Ptolemaic Egypt

A. Civic Stratification according to Ptolemaic Law[1]

It is generally thought that the Ptolemaic government of Egypt was the direct heir of the Pharaonic[2], but it would be a mistake to believe that the accession of the Ptolemies amounted merely to a change of dynasty. Their conquest in fact marked a turning point in the history of the land of the Nile, and its impact was discernible in various domains. An examination of the legal system and its effect on civic stratification is important for the understanding of the legal principles that determined the status of the Jews. Egypt was then the home of many different ethnic groups; it is thus reasonable to suppose that the legal system there provided answers to the complex of problems that situation produced, and that the legislator did not consider each ethnic group separately.

Scholarly literature contains a sharp debate on the legal principles that prevailed in the Classical world, including Egypt, in regard to civic stratification. As papyrological finds supplied additional clues to the legal system in Egypt, the debate became more acrimonious. One of the central questions was the nature of the principle that guided the Ptolemaic lawmaker in determining the laws and judicial system for the non-Egyptian population. Many jurists agreed that the *Personalitätsprinzip* operated in regard to the native-born, who accordingly were subject to the "law of the land" (ὁ τῆς χώρας νόμος) and a separate judicial system which defined their civic status precisely. The most authoritative definition of the *Personalitätsprinzip* states that according to it the laws of the state applied only to the

---

1 In general, see Rostovtzeff, *SEHHW*, pp. 316f., 1057f., 1394-1395; Taubenschlag, p. 1f.; and this contains a detailed bibliography.
2 See, e.g., Wilcken and Mitteis, p. 2f.; Ehrenberg, *Der griechische und der hellenistische Staat*, p. 73f.

citizens of the state and not to foreigners who lived there[3]. Bickermann strongly objected to the notion of the particular application
of that principle, since he interpreted it differently. He invested it
with territorial significance, meaning that people were tried according
to the laws of their native land[4]. That interpretation naturally did
not affect the native-born, but made a difference in regard to immigrants. If that interpretation is accepted without reservations, it
would mean denying the existence of the "personality principle", for
the Ptolemaic legislator was unlikely to recognize the existence of
many varied legal systems fitting the many colors of the ethnic
mosaic of his country. Such recognition would have produced
juridical confusion, arising from real-life situations, since people of
any particular ethnic origin could not be expected to confine their
disputes to their own group. It should be kept in mind that the non-
Egyptian population was for the most part organized into independent political units, civil or military, mainly of the *polis* or
politeuma type[5]. Legally and politically the members of these
units were considered citizens ($\pi o \lambda \hat{\iota} \tau a \iota$)[6], and as such enjoyed some
juridical independence that amounted to the right "to live according
to ancestral laws"[7]. The question is whether that juridical indepen-

---

3 Taubenschlag, p. 2f., where there are extensive bibliographical details. For the definition,
  see Tcherikover, *Jews in Egypt*, p. 95; and the reference is to permanent residents in the
  country, not to temporary ones.
4 Bickermann, *Archiv*, 8 (1929), p. 225f.
5 The accepted definitions of the term *politeuma*: (1) "Ein organisierter Zusammenschluss
  von Männern gleich politischen Rechtes ausserhalt ihrer eigentlich $\iota \delta \iota a$" (Preisigke,
  Fachwörterbuch, s.v.); (2) "Die nicht stadtmässigen politischen Organisationen" (*P. Hal.*,
  p. 38); (3) "$\pi o \lambda \iota \tau e \upsilon \mu a \tau a$ liberae sunt civitates, sive Graecorum, sive aliarum gentium, in
  territorio cuiusdam urbis cum aliis incolis collocatae" (Engers, *Mnemosyne*, 54 (1926),
  p. 161); (4) "ein mit bestimmten politischen Vorrechten ausgestattete Gemeinde auf
  ethnischer Grundlage" (Ruppel, p. 306); and cf. Tcherikover's definition — "a community founded on an ethnic base and enjoying certain political rights" *CPJ*, I, (Prolegomena), p. 6; see also Fuchs, p. 89; Launey, II, p. 1064f.; H. St. Jones, *JRS*, 16 (1926),
  p. 27. See finally Smallwood's excellent definition: "A *politeuma* was a recognized,
  formally constituted corporation of aliens enjoying the right of domicile in a foreign
  city and forming a separate, semi-autonomous civic body, a city within a city; it had its
  own constitution and administered its internal affairs as an ethnic unit through officials
  distinct from and independent of the host city." — Smallwood, *The Jews under Roman
  Rule*, p. 225.
6 The matter is clearly indicated by inscription *OGIS*, 592. Cf. Ruppel, pp. 288, 310f.;
  Taubenschlag, p. 584; Smallwood, p. 8f.
7 On common versions of this right see Polybius, II, 70.4; XVIII, 44.2; 46.5; *OGIS*, 222;
  Syll., 390, 572; and see also Bickermann, *REJ*, 100 (1935), pp. 27f.; and also Tcherikover,
  Jews in Egypt, p. 99; *CPJ*, I (Prolegomena), p. 7.

dence derived from the territorial principle as Bickermann would have it, or from specific legislation. Scholarship has opted for the second alternative, but despite unanimity in regard to the application of imperial law[8], it has not been able to ignore the fact that the latter was itself also based on legal principles embodied in the heritage of the immigrants' countries of origin[9]. In Bickermann's view, however, the Ptolemaic kings (especially Ptolemy VIII Physcon, Euergetes II) strove in their legislation for "juridical nivelation" as he put it, so that the various ethnic groups would become one group of "Hellenes" from the legal viewpoint[10]. He did not claim that the old legal systems the immigrants had brought along consequently disappeared, but that the priorities set gave first place to imperial legislation. He found most important evidence of this in *P. Gurob.* 2, lines 41-51[11], which explicitly notes the following order of preference: a) the ordinacnes and regulations of King Ptolemy[12]; b) the civic laws (πολιτικοὶ νόμοι)[13]; c) the discretion and reasoning

---

8 See full details in Taubenschlag, *Actes du Ve congrès intern. de papyrologie*, (1938), p. 471f.

9 The point did not escape Tcherikover, either (*Jews in Egypt*, p. 95); see also Bickermann, *Archiv*, 8 (1929), pp. 226, 228.

10 Bickermann, *ibid.*, pp. 220-221, especially p. 230f.

11 Lines 41-51. This document is in the Tcherikover papyrus collection (*CPJ*, I, 19) and will be discussed separately below.

12 Bickermann, for some reason, did not mention the royal "laws", and a distinction should be made between them and royal "edicts". On this see Schubart, *Klio*, 10 (1910), pp. 44-45; and also Taubenschlag, pp. 8-10, n.7.

13 The exact legal meaning of "civic laws" has not been agreed upon. At first Wilcken and Bickermann thought that this meant only the laws of Alexandria itself (Wilcken, *UPZ*, II, p. 82f.; Bickermann, *Archiv*, 8 (1929), p. 228). However, Taubenschlag correctly noted that a distinction must be made between πολιτικὸς νόμος (in the singular) and πολιτικοὶ νόμοι (in the plural). The singular refers to Alexandrian law, while the plural includes the laws of other cities in Egypt and outside it, and also the regulations of various ethnic bodies like the *politeumata* (see Taubenschlag, p. 8f. and n.28). Zucker (*Beiträge*, p. 52f.) thought likewise, and even emphasized the inclusion of the *politeumata* regulations. Schubart (*Klio*, 10 (1910), p. 66, n.1) and Segré (*Aegyptus*, 8 (1927), p. 299) expressed similar opinions, although they were more tentative. In Zucker's opinion, it is not inconceivable that Jewish law was also included in this category, but in general his opinion has been rejected. At present the accepted scholarly view is that of Schubart, that the "civic laws" in fact constituted the Greek law that applied in Egypt (Schubart, *op.cit.*, pp. 41-47). Taubenschlag carefully avoided definite conclusions, and only stated that Greek law in Egypt was based on a combination of various "civic laws'", but that royal legislation held pride of place, even though the influences of "laws" and "decisions" from all over the Greek world can be distinguished in it (see his book, pp. 8-14; and see also n.8 above. Cf. also Restovtzeff, *SEHHW*, pp. 1066-1070, 1592.

of the judges. Thus the "terrotirial principle" was taken into account by the Ptolemaic legislator, but was by no means predominant. Tcherikover sharply attacked Bickermann's notion of leveling (*Nivelierung*), arguing primarily that such a thesis disregards the fact that there were ethnic organizations in Ptolemaic Egypt that preserved their national-cultural characteristics and enjoyed a degree of legal autonomy, especially since these groups refused to abandon their uniqueness, and their refusal to do so was respected by the regime[14]. This fact by no means contradicts Bickermann's view. Actually the independent existence of ethnic frameworks accords nicely with the "territorial principle", which in his opinion determined the imperial condification only partially. In accordance with that principle or, more precisely, with the right "to live according to ancestral laws" that derived from it, the various ethnic groups were granted their legal autonomy. As noted, the principle was not applied exclusively, but did influence the Ptolemaic legislator who sought to compromise with reality. From this point of view, those enjoying independent jurisdiction in Ptolemaic Egypt can be compared with the *metoikoi*, the permanent residents without citizens' rights in Athens[15]. It must logically be concluded that their autonomy was extremely limited, for otherwise it would have been impossible to avoid judicial confusion, which indeed imperial legislation sought to prevent. Most probably the autonomy was restricted to the narrow areas where the ethnic groups differed, such as religion, matrimony, and national customs. It might be argued that so long as the right "to live according to ancestral laws" was maintained, the differences between the various ethnic groups persisted, thus supposedly justifying Tcherikover's criticism regarding juridical leveling. However, Bickermann's evidence on the existence of the process cannot be ignored. At most the actual outcome might be questioned, and it might be claimed that Bickermann exaggerated a bit, as will be shown below. The notion of juridical leveling raises an additional difficulty: Did the connection of "Barbarians" (= non-Greeks) with such organizations and with "civic laws" make them legally "Hellenes"? Unfortunately no decisive unequivolcal answer is as yet available. In any case, a distinction needs to be made between two aspects of the question: a) the

---

14 Tcherikover, *Jews in Egypt*, p. 96, n.5, and see other evidence there.
15 Bickermann, *Archiv*, 8 (1929), p. 226, n.1; p. 228.

connection with the Greek organizations; b) the connection with independent, non-Greek organizations.

The first aspect has been dealt with extensively, and it appears that non-Greeks (Persians, Jews, and even autochthonic Egyptians) who joined legal-political frameworks of clearly Hellenic character thereby changed their ethnic adherence and enjoyed complete naturalization, especially on the military plane. Lesquier devoted considerable attention to this matter and reached some illuminating conclusions. He proved, for instance, that from the second century B.C.E. on, several *politeumata* became pseudo-ethnic, making possible the alteration of national designations, for military purposes[16]. Moreover, he showed that the military *politeumata* became successful juridical instruments for the ethnic naturalization of the soldiers, to the point that natives were accepted into the regular army[17]. These facts are enough to support Bickermann's conclusion regarding the goal of juridical leveling in the Ptolemaic state. Tcherikover himself admitted that the use of the term "Hellenes" made its way into official language but contended that this incidental phenomenon should not be accorded the value of a principle[18]. Regrettably he ended with a generalization lacking verified proof. However, in military matters at least, the official term "Hellenes serving in the army"[19] speaks for itself, especially in view of Lesquier's thesis[20].

---

16 Lesquier, p. 142f.; see especially p. 150, cf. also Bickermann, *ibid*, p. 230.

17 Lesquier, p. 150f., also p. 126.

18 Tcherikover, *Jews in Egypt*, p. 97, n.5. It is interesting that in *The Jews in the Greek and Roman World*, p. 236, Tcherikover noted that in the Adler Papyri one man (Horos son of Nehotas — an Egyptian name) at the end of the Ptolemaic era, was called a "Persian of the Epigone", a term which in demotic is translated as "a Greek born in Egypt" (on the meaning of the terms "Epigone" and "Persian of the Epigone" see below, n.22); which shows that for the natives all foreigners were "Hellenes" (i.e. Greeks). What is interesting is that Tcherikover quotes Bickermann's interpretation for this double term, as though he did not realize that in so doing he was bolstering up the latter's proof for legal leveling (Bickermann, *Archiv*, 8 (1929), p. 220f.).

19 στρατευόμενοι Ἕλλενης (*P. Tebt.*, I, 5, lines 168-9).

20 See nn.16-17 above. Cf. also *P. Freiburg*, III, 36/7; *P. Ent.*, 15 where the names of the Thessalian hipparchy is the title "The hipparchy of the Thessalians and the other Hellenes". See also Kornemann — *Aegyptus*, 13 (1933), pp. 644-650 — who believed that the term "Hellenes" had a definite official meaning and was meant to indicate non-Egyptians who included a jumble of alien peoples. He also presented a wealth of examples for the version of "Macedonians and other Hellenes". Cf. also the opinion of Peremans (*Chr. d'Égypte*, 11 (1936), pp. 517-521) who argued, among other things: "Nous proposons d'appeler 'Hellènes' ceux, parmi les étrangers, qui se distinguent par leur situation social et leur richesse."

Among the documents Bickermann did not take into account are
P. Tebt. 427 (of the second century B.C.E.) which mentions "Hellenic
farmers" from the Arsinoë district, at least some of whom were not
of Greek origin[21] ; *P. Strassb.*, 21, in which a person of non-Greek
descent is called in Demotic *Wnjn ms n kme* (= a Greek of the
Epigone)[22]. It is surprising that Bickermann failed to consider the
testimony of Polybius (quoted by Strabo, XVII, 1, 12) that the
Alexandrians were "a mixed people" and yet "Hellenes" in origin
and well-versed in Hellenic customs. The trend toward leveling is
indicated also by the fact that the "civic laws" were clearly the outcome of deliberate condification designed to set a common judicial
norm for all the "Hellenes" in Egypt. Even Tcherikover did not
disregard the logical conclusion that the process was likely to erase
the ethnic differences that existed in the variegated population of the
foreign-born[23], and noted the pseudo-ethnicity of some *politeumata*
in the Ptolemaic army[24]. The third Cyrenean edict of Augustus quite
clearly shows that the term "Hellenes" was used to classify inhabitants of various races and different political groups in one unit, for
purely official purposes (imposing military liturgies) and to distinguish
them from the "Romans". Atkinson rightly assumed that the distinction was part of the Ptolemaic heritage, as can be concluded as well
in regard to a well-known group of military settlers ("the 6475
Hellenes") mentioned in several documents in Arsinoe of the first
and second centuries C.E. which likewise derived from the same
tradition[25]. The same is true of the "Macedonian" Jews of Alexandria, mentioned in two documents of the Augustan period (*CPJ*, II
142-143) as well as by Josephus (*C. Apionem,* II 35-36).

As to the second aspect, we have no clear authoritative answer.
Circumstances point to the existence of non-Greek ethnic groups
organized in independent political frameworks, following a com-

---

21 See Bell, *Aegyptus*, 12 (1932), p. 546.
22 See Heichelheim, p. 14, who believed he was a "Persian". Cf. Uebel, p. 347, No. 1445(f.)
   and n.5; Bickermann, *Archiv*, 8 (1929), p. 221. The term "of the Epigone" has usually
   been interpreted as referring to the descendants of soldiers (a sort of military reserve),
   but in recent years this has been questioned, e.g. Oates, *YCS*, 18 (1963), pp. 5-129,
   and see also Fraser, vol. I, p. 50. Since the problem has not yet been solved definitively,
   I will adhere to the accepted interpretation.
23 Tcherikover, *Jews in Egypt*, p. 95.
24 *Ibid.*, pp. 37-38; 97.
25 Atkinson, *Ancient Society and Institutions*, p. 25f.; SEG, IX, 19, 8.

pletely Greek pattern[26]. Such organization deserves to be interpreted as political "Hellenization" inspired and permitted by the central government or, more accurately, as legal and political assimilation to Hellenic models and standards[27]. Thus in regard to the second aspect as well there is support for Bickermann's view regarding the juridical leveling that the Ptolemaic rulers of Egypt strove to achieve. Let us not, however, adopt his extreme position that this legislative process eventually produced a monolithic group of "Hellenes" which was homogeneous as regards its rights. The aim of the legislator was, as noted above, to avoid the juridical and administrative complications inherent in the multiplicity of ethnic designations by creating an inclusive legal infrastructure common to all the foreign-born, the "civic laws" (πολιτικοὶ νόμοι). Differences between the various ethnic groups may well have emerged in the rights they had beyond that base, and on that score there is no comparison between the rights of *polis* citizens and *politeuma* members. There may also have been differences between one *politeuma* and another, perhaps between those that were "Hellenic" and the "Barbaric" ones. It therefore appears that the general Hellenistic law in Ptolemaic Egypt applying to the foreign-born was actually a legal infrastructure (of the "Hellenic" pattern) for additional civic stratification, and that the criteria for it were both political and ethnic; that is, membership in a political or ethnic unit, or both together, determined to a great extent the civic status of the foreign-born population in Egypt. The political criterion certainly derived from the tradition of the

---

26 E.g., the Idumaean *politeuma* — *OGIS*, 737 (on this see Ruppel, p. 307f.; Rappaport, *Rev. de Philol.*, 43 (1969), pp. 73-82); a *politeuma* of unknown origin which existed in Cos — *OGIS*, 192; the *politeuma* of the Caunians in Sidon — *OGIS*, 592; and also the *politeumata* in Alexandria, such as the Phrygian — *OGIS*, 658; the Lycian — *SB*, 6025 (= *SEG*, VIII, 359; *IGRR*, I, 1078) and the Boeotian — *SB*, 6664 (= *SEG*, II, 871) and also the Cilician in Arsinoë — *SB*, 1270. On the separate organization of "Persians of the Epigone" as a pseudo-ethnic *politeuma*, see F. Zucker, *RE(PW)*, XIX, 1, pp. 911-913. The same applies to other forms of organization such as κατοικία (a military settlement), ἔθνος (a "people" or "national community"), σύνοδος (an association), etc. Similar organizations also of non-Greek origin are known outside of Egypt also, such as in Sidon (*OGIS*, 592) and the famous Jewish *politeuma* of Berenice (*SEG*, XV, 913; *IGRR*. I, 1024; *CIG*, 5361-5362) and there are other examples.

27 It should be intimated, as early as this, that even Josephus's statements about the "iso-politeia" of the Jews in reference to the "Hellenes" should not be interpreted as political and legal emancipation, but as juridical and political assimilation in accordance with Hellenic standards and models, in the spirit noted above.

Classical world, and as it embodied nothing new need not be re-
examined. The ethnic criterion was however definitely the creation
of the Hellenistic period, and as such merits attention.

Research has shown that every individual in Ptolemaic Egypt was
required to note in official documents, aside from his name, his
ethnic group (that is, his homeland, in Greek πατρίς), in the absence
of which it was impossible to determine his civic status in relation to
the state authorities and institutions. A broad spectrum of ethnic
designations is discernible in the early generations of the Ptolemaic
kingdom, but the absence of documentary evidence makes it difficult
to provide satisfactory answers to some of the problems arising from
that situation. What is clear and accepted by all scholars is that the
ethnic designations were registered in official documents by government order[28] and, as noted, for the purpose of civic stratification.
Even a cursory examination of the various documents indicates a
decided difference between two types of ethnic designations, general
and individual. The general ones derived from general national names
such as Macedonians, Thracians, Thessalians, Persians and the like.
The individual ones bore names derived from Greek cities, such as
Athenians, Corinthians, Cyreneans, etc. Furthermore, the latter
appeared mainly early in the Ptolemaic period and disappeared in
the course of time. While the names related primarily to the citizens
of Greek *poleis* or their offspring, to indicate descent, they at the
same time indicated the civic status in Egypt of those bearing them.
However, as the Ptolemaic monarchy did not need only the Classical
qualification (such as citizenship in a *polis*) to determine civic
stratification, and employed also ethnic qualifications[29], there was
no real difference between an "Athenian" and a "Macedonian".
The regime considered both terms equally indicative and adequate
for civic stratification.

Research has shown that the general ethnic designations had a
functional significance as well, mainly in connection with military
service. In other words they could often be viewed as technical terms
in military langauge, describing the nature of various units, including
the type of warfare they engaged in, the weapons they used, and so

---

28 One of the more detailed documents on this matter from the end of the 3rd century
   B.C.E. was published in 1954; *P. Hamburg*, II, 168.
29 Lesquier discussed this problem at length, particularly in his writings on military service;
   see n.16, 17 above.

on[30]. Thus the term "Macedonians" was applied to heavily armed infantry in the units trained in the combat methods of the Macedonian phalanx, while "Cretans" referred to units of archers. The same was the case with "Thracians", "Thessalians", "Libyans", "Persians", and others, terms which also referred to specific functions in the military context[31]. Most probably at the start of the Ptolemaic period the ethnic identity of the soldiers corresponded to the ethnic designation of their units. But the documents show that in the course of time, particularly after the second century B.C.E., the general ethnic designations became pseudo-ethnic, and the ones whose names came from Greek cities disappeared entirely. Thus actual ethnicity was sacrificed to functionality. Nevertheless even then the designations of ethnicity continued to fill a juridical role for the purpose of civic stratification. As such they facilitated and simplified the legal process of naturalizing the soldiers in accordance with the needs of the regime[32]. And yet the influence of tradition was strong enough to leave clear traces of ethnic, religious and social organization in the army[33].

The question of primary concern is of course how the Jews fitted into that picture. There were three distinct population sectors in the land of the Nile — foreigners who were settled in the *chora* and employed in government service such as the army and civilian administration; citizens of the Greek *poleis*; the autochthonic Egyp-

---

30 See, e.g., Lesquier, pp. 88f., 296f.; Launey, I, pp. 321, 330, 360f.

31 Tcherikover rejected the possibility that the private ethnic designations taken from the names of cities had a similar significance, since he found it difficult to imagine that such a heterogeneous army could be maintained in fact (*Jews in Egypt*, p. 37). However, his approach is based on mdoern military thinking. It seems to me that the heterogeneity of the Ptolemaic army (like the Seleucid) is demonstrated in the descriptions of the great battles in ancient literature, such as the battle of Raphiah. It appears that this situation was characteristic particularly at the beginning of the Hellenistic period, when recruitment from abroad was still growing. At any rate, it should be kept in mind that at least the mercenary troops could very well have been very heterogeneous in composition. On the other hand, there is no need to exaggerate the difficulties, for in the last analysis, they were all Greeks, and even if the units differed in their combat methods, could easily be combined. It is possible that the numbered hipparchies (in the Ptolemaic army) were a product of such an action, and therefore they did not have a definite ethno-functional character.

32 See Lesquier, p. 142f.

33 For example, the association (κοινά) from Cyrpus, whose ethnic mixture is quite impressive: Achaeans, Cilicians, Cretans, Greeks and Thracians; see details in San Nicolò, *Aeg. Vereinswesen*, I, pp. 198-199; Lesquier, pp. 124, 143f.

tian population — and it is necessary to ascertain first the legal status of the Jews in relation to the first and third sectors[34].

The study below of the Jews in government services provide information on the functional factor in their civic status, further illuminated by an investigation of the Jews in the Ptolemaic army in general, with emphasis on their organization into independent frameworks and their absorption in various units.

B. Jews in the Ptolemaic Military Service within Independent Organizations

During the Persian period Egyptian Jews already served in the army in separate independent units, as shown in the Elephantine papyri. Various aspects of their organization shed light on Ptolemaic practices based on the heritage of that earlier time:

a) The Jewish inhabitants of Elephantine were organized in a distinct framework, militarily and ethnically, which was called the Jewish garrison (*Ḥaylā Yehudaia*)[35], but was under Persian command.

b) The Jews formed a separate community, that is, they lived in a settlement or residential quarter of their own[36].

c) The whole military settlement in Elephantine, including the Jews, was charged with the defense of Egypt's southern border and preservation of order and security in the region; and may have been assigned special missions as well[37].

d) A distinction must be made between "Jew" and "Aramaean" although the latter was applied to Jews as well[38]. Probably the second term referred generally to members of a large Aramaic-speaking unit, Jews among them, while the first designated members

---

34 The main question, of whether the Jews integrated with the citizens of the *poleis*, particularly in Alexandria, is discussed in detail in ensuing chapters.

35 See Cowley, Nos. 21, 22. It should be noted that the two fortresses of Elephantine and Syene included soldiers of quite varied ethnic origins, as can be seen, e.g., in Papyrus No. 24.

36 On this subject see E.G. Kraeling, *BMAP*, p. 18; Aime-Giron thought that the word *Ḥayla* is likely to be understood as "colony" or "quarter", and that the Greek term στρατόπεδον (camp) is an equivalent, judging by the mention of "the Tyrian camp" in Memphis in Herodotus, II, 112; and see Aime Giron, *Textes*, p. 59. On the military settlement, see also Korngreen, *Jewish Military Colonies* (Hebrew), 1947; and the most important study, Porten, *Archives from Elephantine*, 1968.

37 See E.G. Kraeling, *ibid.* pp. 41-42.

38 Cowley, Nos. 5, 6, 12; and cf. also Poten, *ibid.*, pp. 17f., 33f.

of a specific unit, in this case the Jewish garrison.

e) The Jewish military settlement also contained people who were not in the army. Both they and the soldiers normally engaged in farming, trade, moneylending, etc. This fact alone shows that the way of life typical of military settlements of the Hellenistic period had its roots in earlier practices.

f) The Jews of Elephantine had their own religious leadership headed by a supreme board and a priesthood[39]. These conducted the religious life of the ocmmunity, the worship in its temple, and also served as its official representatives to the authorities[40].

g) The Jews of Elephantine had their own court[41], whose jurisdiction is however hard to determine. In matrimonial matters at least there are signs of Jewish law and terminology, along with a strong non-Jewish influence[42].

As noted above, the Ptolemies inherited the political arrangements of their predecessors and in the early period no doubt avoided far-reaching revolutionary changes. It is no wonder then that the character of military settlement, that of the Jews as well, did not change. Some scholars have tried to minimize the military value of the Jews and claimed that only later, after proving themselves in the Hasmonaean revolt, did they gain the appreciation which opened the way for their service in the Hellenistic armies[43]. The testimony of Hecataeus of Abdera quoted by Diodorus Siculus is enough to refute that assessment[44]. No one now doubts the information given in the *Letter of Aristeas* (§13) and supported by Josephus (*C. Apionem*, II 44; *Antiquitates*, XII 8) on the settlement of Jewish captives in Egyptian forts by Ptolemy I[45]. Epigraphical and papyrological find-

---

39 Cowley, No. 30, lines 1, 4, 22. The overall name for the leadership may have been בעלי יב

40 Cowley, Nos. 27, 30, 31.

41 Cowley, Nos. 1, 7, 8, 13, 15, 16, 18, 28, and more. See also E.G. Kraeling, *ibid.*, pp. 5-9; Yaron, *The Law of the Elephantine Documents*, 1961.

42 I cannot go into the depths of this complex problem, particularly since it is not relevant to the subject of inquiry.

43 Even Tcherikover was influenced by this idea to some extent: see *Hellenistic Civilization and the Jews*, p. 278 and also pp. 317-318, n. 10; *Jews in Egypt*, p. 39.

44 Diodorus Siculus, XL, 3: "... in matters of war the legislator (Moses) evinced much anxiety for the future, and forced the young men to develop courage and power to withstand any misfortune."

45 See, e.g., Tcherikover, *Jews in Egypt*, p. 33 and n.7; *CPJ*, I (Prolegomena), p. 12. See below for an analysis of the reports.

ings too definitely prove that Jews served in the Ptolemaic army from the third century B.C.E. on.

The main questions are how the Jews fitted into the Egyptian army: were they assimilated into various units or were they organized in separate units of their own? Tcherikover concluded in several places quite decisively that a purely Jewish unit is not mentioned anywhere in the documents and was probably not a reality till the time of Onias IV[46]. Influenced as he was by the thesis that diminished the military capability of the Jews, he came to the conclusion that the change in the Ptolemiac attitude to Jewish troops took place around 150 B.C.E. as a result of the Hasmonaean victories. It was only then, he believed, that Jewish army units commanded by Jews were set up. There does not however seem to be any basis for that conclusion, and in fact there are traces in both literary testimony and epigraphical and papyrological findings of separate Jewish units even before the time of Onias IV.

The testimony of Hecataeus of Abdera quoted by Josephus (C. Apionem, I 186-205) on the immigration to Egypt of a group of Jews led by the priest Ḥezekiah (in the reign of Ptolemy I) was at first deemed suspect by scholars but has now been accepted as authentic[47]. The settlement of Ḥezekiah and his followers should

---

46 *Hellenistic Civilization and the Jews*, p. 335; cf. also *Jews in Egypt*, pp. 38-40. *CPJ*, I, pp. 13-14.

47 See, e.g., a negative evaluation: Schürer, vol. 3, p. 603f.; Bousset-Gressman, *Religion des Judentums*, p. 26; ed. Meyer, *Ursprung*, II, pp. 24, 28; Willrich, *Judaica*, p. 86f., and see other bibliographical details in Schürer, (*op.cit.*). Tcherikover at first also tended to this evaluation (*Jews and Greeks*, 1931, pp. 278-279 and also *Jews in Egypt*, p. 94 n.9), but later retracted: see *Hellenistic Civilization and the Jews*, pp. 56, 425-427, nn.46, 49, mainly because of the influence of Hans Levy's article (*Studies in Jewish Hellenism*, p. 44f.; cf. *ZNTW*, 31 (1932), p.117f.) Numismatic finds from Beit Zur and Tel Gamma reveal that חזקיה (or יחזקין) was one of the last Jewish satraps at the end of the Persian era see Rahmani, *IEJ*, 21 (1971), pp. 158-160; Naveh, *BASOR*, 203 (1971), pp. 27-32. In regard to the description of Ḥezkiah as "high priest", which was one of the main reasons for rejecting the report, it can be said, in the spirit of Levy's words (*ibid'*, p.49) that possibly Hecataeus exaggerated because of his tendency to rely on priestly traditions, and beeause of the idealization apparent in the entire report. In fact, Büchler's claims about the frequency of this title in Josephus and in the New Testament, in regard to priests belonging to the high priestly family, even though they did not actually fill this high office, may also justify the application of the title to Ḥezkiah. See Büchler, *Tobiaden*, p. 33. Cf. Thackeray, *Josephus — The Life*, p. 283; and see also Smallwood, *JTS*, 13 (1962), p. 16. The dispute over the authenticity of Josephus' report (citing Hecataeus) has continued up until recently, and on this see Schaller, *ZNW*, 54 (1963), pp. 15-31; Gager, *ZNW*, 60 (1969), pp. 130-139.

be considered a military settlement (*katoikia*) judging by the use of the term κατοίκησις in that testimony (*ibid.* 189); and its rights seem to have been defined in a "written *politeia*" (πολιτεία γεγραμμένη; *ibid.*). Presumably those rights included the terms of the contract covering the military service of Ḥezekiah's people[48], as was customary in such circumstances since the legitimate basis for service of military settlers was in effect contractual. If so, that *politeia* certainly defined the the right of Ḥezekiah's group to be organized as a *politeuma* or, to be more exact, as a *katoikia* organized and institutionalized "according to ancestral laws". To Tcherikover's credit it must be said that he made some suggestions in that line, even believing that a kind of "charter" or settlement permit was the "written law" (πολιτεία γεγραμμένη) of the new community which outlined its political organization[49].

It is important to note that the position of a priest as the chief leader of a military settlement indicates a unit organized on a definitely religious basis, as in the case also of Onias IV at Leontopolis. Interestingly enough, Dorion, the leader of the Idumaean *politeuma* in Memphis, was both priest and commander of his community-unit[50]; and it appears that that was not the only such instance among non-Jews[51]. Evidently the practice was inherited from the Persian period, judging by Josephus' testimony on Daniel who "built at Ecbatana in Media a fortress (βάρις) ... and the person to whose care it is entrusted is a Jewish priest" (*Antiquitates*, X 264-5)[52]; or judging by information on the leadership by priests in the military settlement at Elephantine. At any rate, the dual role cannot

---

48 Hans Levy interpreted the entire report, including the terms mentioned above, in a completely different way. In his opinion, it describes a public occasion for the reading of the Torah, as is usual on holidays and Sabbath (*Studies in Jewish Hellenism*, pp. 50-51). His suggestion should, I believe, be rejected, mainly becuase it is based on rather labored linguistic corrections.

49 *Jews in Egypt*, p. 98, n.9; *Hellenistic Civilization and the Jews*, pp. 57, 299-301, 506 (nn.11-120; *CPJ*, I (Prolegomena), p. 7 (and n.18).

50 See *OGIS*, 737, lines 5-6; and also Ruppel's excellent explanation, pp. 306-307. The person concerned here is a priest for the Apollo-Cos rite, in Launey's opinion (II, p. 1075); and see also Rappaport, *Rev. de Philol.*, 13 (1969), 80f.

51 E.g., *OGIS*, 658, 871; the ethnic "associations" in Cyprus were also headed by priests (see Lesquier, p. 145).

52 Applebaum ("The Organization etc.", p. 471f.) provides more information on this subject, and deals with the significance of the offices of שר הבירה and איש הבירה found in our sources, in the spirit of what is written here.

be considered the invention of Ptolemy VI Philometor. The *Letter of Aristeas* (§ 310) too refers to priests as part of the leadership of the Jewish *politeuma* in Alexandria, whose primarily military character is discussed below. It is only reasonable to suppose that the right to keep ancestral laws while serving in the army was exercized among other ways by enlisting soldiers in units of the same religion and ethnic origin. Such consolidated units served in Ptolemaic Cyprus, for instance. Evidently that is the way to interpret Alexander the Great's call to the Jews to serve in the army, and as Josephus reports (*Antiquitates*, XI 339), "when he said to the people that if any wished to join his army while still adhering to the cusoms of their country, he was ready to take them". A similar case is the testimony on the establishment in Phrygia in the reign of Antiochus III of a Jewish *katoikia* whose people were promised that they would be allowed to keep their special laws (*Antiquitates*, XII 147-153). On the basis of the term ὑπηρέτης which in Josephus (*Antiquitates*, IV 214) and *Lucas* (IV:20) refers to a *hazzan*, Abraham Schalit inferred that there were religious officials among the commanders of the Jewish military settlement. Possible, but not likely[53]. Schalit himself admitted that they were religious officials of lower rank, and it is strange that only they are mentioned in the letter, and not higher ranking ones. It is rather the military use of the term that should be stressed, as it appears in various Hellenistic sources[54]; in that case the tesimony refers to people working in military administration.

The *Letter of Aristeas* too indicates independent Jewish organization in military service under the early Ptolemies. Paragraph 13 says Ptolemy I settled Jews from among the captives he brought

---

53 See Schalit's translation of *Antiquitates*, XII 152, and also *JQR*, 50 (1959/60), p. 312f. In contrast, Ralph Marcus translated the words τάς χρείας ὑπηρετοῦσι as "those engaged in public service", even relating this phrase to *Antiquitates*, XIII 67, where he translated a similar expression, παῖς σαῖς ἐξυπηρετεῖν χρείας, as "to serve your (i.e. Philometer's) interests". On the other hand, Schalit remained faithful to his system and translated it "לעבוד (את האלוהים) למענך" (= to serve God for you). It should be noted that as against this the title ὁ ἐπί τῶν χρείων was applied in the *Letter of Aristeas* (§§ 37, 110, 172) to government officials.

54 See, e.g., Polybius, VI 24, 5, and cf. its use in papyri such as *P. Reinach*, 14, lines 15, 20, 30-31; *P. Ent.*, 62, lines 2-3; *P. Petr.*, III 112(a), line 25; 112(d), line 5; *W. Chr.*, 336, line 25. It must be pointed out that this term appears in the *Letter of Aristeas*, (§§ 26, 111) with the same meaning. In Athens ὑπηρέτης was considered the arms bearer of a heavy foot soldier (hoplite) and perhaps for this reason the term was usually applied to service and auxiliary personnel (see Liddell and Scott, s.v.). On the military significance of the term discussed see also Lesquier, p. 99f., especially p. 101.

from Palestine in the forts (φρούρια) of his country[55]. Further on, verse 36 notes that Ptolemy attached many of the Jews to the units of his army (τὸ στρατιωτικὸν σύνταγμα)[56] and repeats that he entrusted them with guarding the forts. Their connection with the regular army is discernible also in the fact that they were listed among "the mercenaries" (μισθοφόροι). Josephus added an important piece of information, testimony on the dispatch of some of the Jews to Cyrene and other Libyan cities, and their settlement during the reign of Ptolemy I, in accordance with his policy of ensuring a political and military foothold there[57]. There is no doubt that the term κατοικῆσον in that context relates to military settlement[58]. The use of the word σύνταγμα is most illuminating. It was common in epigraphical and papyrological sources in Egypt itself and generally meant a tactical and administrative infantry unit[59]; it could however also designate a military unit organized as a socio-religious and political body. Applebaum noted that Strabo applied the very term to Jewish communities in Cyrene and Egypt[60]. In his view it indicates the community organization of the Jews[61]. Indeed the independent organizational framework of those bodies is very clearly reflected in that testimony which states that they "observe the national Jewish laws" (*Antiquitates*, XIV 116).

Ptolemy II Philadelphus' order releasing the Jewish captives brought to Egypt during his father's reign (The *Letter of Aristeas*, 22-25)[62] led many of them to undertake military service (*ibid.*, 37). They undoubtedly joined up in groups, and may well have organized

---

55 The authenticity of the report stands the test of criticism in the light of another report (*P. Petr.*, II 29(b) = *W. Chr.*, 334) about the transfer of "captives from Asia" to Egypt and their settlement as soldiers on the "king's land". Cf. also Diodorus Siculus, XIX 85, 4. And see Fraser, vol. 1, p. 57.

56 Cf. the parallel in Josephus, *Antiquitates*, XII 45.

57 Josephus, *Antiquitates*, II 44. On the history of Jewish military settlement in Cyrene, see Applebaum, *Jews and Greeks in Ancient Cyrene*, p. 130f.

58 Applebaum, *ibid.*, p. 134. Cf. a similar usage in the *Letter of Aristeas*, 35 (κατῳκίσθαι) and also in *C. Apionem*, I 189 (see p. 41 above).

59 See Lesquier, pp. 95-96; and cf. Bar-Kochva, p. 208, n.9. Josephus, in *Antiquitates*, XIII 326, also employed this meaning.

60 Strabo, in Jos., *Antiquitates*, XIV 116, and this is said about Jewish immigrants of the second wave of the middle of the 2nd century B.C.E.

61 Applebaum, *ibid.*, pp. 139, 192.

62 About the authenticity of the order, see Westermann, *AJPh*, 59 (1938), 1-30; Rostovtzeff, *SEHHW*, pp. 340-346 Préaux, pp. 313-315; Fraser, vol. 2, p. 974, n.126.

into completely Jewish units. On this matter we have mainly papyrological evidence.

It should be noted at the outset that the term "Jew" ('Ιουδαῖος) which is quite common in the papyri should be considered an ordinary general ethnic designation, which like others defined a person's origin and thus his classification with the foreign-born. It should be recalled that in the early Ptolemaic period the general ethnic classification reflected the independent association in their own communities (*politeumata*) of persons of the various peoples. Although in the course of time some of them lost their real ethnic significance, not all the foreigners were inclined to abandon their ancestral customs and national laws, particularly since the authorities were extremely considerate, allowing them to continue their community organization in and out of the army[63]. Why then should the Jews be deemed an exception who were not organized in independent military units until the second century B.C.E.?

The sources themselves provide testimony on Jewish independent detachments in the military framework. An important document from Arsinoe (Crocodilopolis) of 226 B.C.E. (*CPJ*, I 19) refers to soldiers bearing the ethnic designation "Jew". Taking into account the existence of a Jewish community in the place, as several documents indicate, it can definitely be posited that the Jewish military settlers had an organizational framework of their own[64].

In the Fayûm region, the names of settlements such as "the Syrians' Village", "Magdola" and "Samareia" suggest the original, primary ethnicity[65]. It is not unlikely that other settlements too were purely Jewish, as was the case in later periods[66]. At any rate it is reasonable to suppose that just as Samaritans were allowed to settle in a village of their own, so were Jews. Be that as it may, there is evidence of Jews organized in an independent military unit. The matter is illuminated by document *CPJ*, I 22 of 201 B.C.E. which

---

63 Tcherikover, *Jews in Egypt*, pp. 96-97, cf. *CPJ*, I (Prolegmena), pp. 6-7.
64 See a detailed discussion of this subject below c.1 and in chap. 3 (*passim*).
65 See Tcherikover, *ibid*. pp. 18-19, cf. *CPJ*, I (Prolegomena), p. 9. A precipitous identification of these settlements as Jewish should be avoided, for widespread "Syrian" settlement in Egypt is known. Even the name "Magdola" may be misleading, and this is shown by document *P. Ent.*, 13, which attests to the existence of a shrine to the goddesses Berenice-Aphrodite in that place to serve a particular military settlement.
66 The reference is to "the village of the Jews" and "Babylon" (see pp. 121-122 below).

actually comes from Samareia. The document is a special agreement of renunciation (παραχώρησις) of a Jewish soldier named "Theodotos son of Kasandros a Paeonian"[67], who ceded a quarter (σταθμός)[68] out of his Father's legacy to four Egyptian "King's peasants". The mention of the names of six witnesses, described as "Jews", indicates a considerable concentration of Jews and a unit organization to suit. On the other hand, the additional designation of "Paeonian" shows that Theodotos belonged functionally to a non-Jewish unit, and the name was undoubtedly pseudo-ethnic so far as he was concerned. The fact that his six "Jewish" witnesses were readily available might mean there was close daily contact between the two units which may have been under a single command and stationed near each other. A careful reading reveals that Theodotos' unit membership is defined in further details which also indicate his specific job. It appears that he served as a *taktomisthos*[69], and belonged to "Phyleus' troop" composed of the "Paeonian" and "Jewish" sub-units. The document shows that when it was written he lived in Samareia[70], but as his father's property was in nearby Kerkesephis, he probably came from there. His reason for moving is not clarified, but it was probably because of increased authority and duties (in addition to those in his permanent unit, which he continued to belong to). In other words, as a "Paeonian" he came from Kerkesephis where his sub-unit was settled; but as a *taktomisthos* of "Phyleus' troop" he worked for the higher command of the mother-unit centered at Samareia, and consequently moved there[71]. Document *CPJ*, I 28[72] of 155 B.C.E.

It appears that the list should also include the place called Σάδη (שדה =field) which was within the boundaries of the village of Bacchias in the northern Fayûm (*P. Ryl*, 154, 66 C.E.). Its affinity to military settlement in the Ptolemaic era is proven clearly by its definition as "*katoikic* land". The same is true of the "village of the Syrians" near Oxyrhynchus (*P. Oxy.*, 1424-1425, 1448, 2124, 316 C.E.), which was simply named after its founder. All the documents dealing with these villages, by the way, were not included in the *Corpus Papyrorum Judaicarum*.

67 Tcherikover's reasons for calling him a Jew are most convincing, see *CPJ*, I 22 (p. 161).

68 This term has a clearly military significance, and see Lesquier, pp. 210f., 224, and 235f.

69 An administrative and financial position in the framework of military service; usually paymaster. See Lesquier, p. 99f.

70 Cf. also Uebel, p. 189 and n.1.

71 See also chap. III (Samareia) below. It is interesting that Tcherikover, in the introduction to document *CPJ*, I 28, also from Samareia, noted that the residents like their counterparts from Psenyris (*CPJ*, I 31), were divided into separate national groups.

72 The document is a list made by "the village scribe" of flock-owners from among the soldiers stationed in Samareia.

contains a concentration of more than twenty Jewish names, indicating that there was a Jewish unit in Samareia and its surroundings. It is even possible to distinguish between soldiers and officers, and there is no doubt of the Jewish identity of the latter[73]. It is probable that in Alexandrou-Nesos too there was a Jewish sub-unit (and perhaps also a Jewish command) connected with the mother-unit in Samareia.

The voluntary segregation of Jewish military settlers as early as the third century B.C.E. is seen also in *CPJ*, I 33. This document from the village of Psenyris in the Fayûm tells of the division of the local settlement into two separate and officially distinct sections: "Hellenes" and "Jews". Why should those "Jews" not be viewed as constituting a military sub-unit organized independently? It should be noted that a similar distinction, between "Macedonians" and "Jews", occurs in another Fayûm document (*CPJ*, I 30) of mid-second century B.C.E.[74]

The papyrological findings also prove that even before Onias IV there were high-ranking Jewish officers who operated both in integrated units and in Jewish ones. As *CPJ*, I 28 has shown, Jews were part of the officers' complement at Samareia. Evidently one of the first high-ranking Jewish officers was Tobias, commander of a cleruchy (= military settlement) in Transjordania whose men came from a variety of ethnic backgrounds[75].

An important inscription found at the Fayûm (*CIJ*, II 1531) refers to Ela'azar son of Nicolaus, the *hegemon* (ἡγεμών). Frey's notion that the title applied to a community or synagogue function[76] must be rejected as the term generally designated a high officer in the Ptolemaic army next in rank to the *strategos*. Sometimes the reference was to the commander of some military post such as a φρούαρχος, or of a tactical unit of infantry or the like[77]. Although the ethnic

---

73 The list of officers (owners of plots of 80 and 30 *aruorai; aroura* – a measure of area of about half an acre) was distinguished from and separated from the list of soldiers (see lines 4-5). The same is true of Frag. 2 of this document, in which wives of officers were also listed separately, not together with the wives of regular soldiers (see lines 31-32).
74 Should they not be considered a sub-unit of "Macedonian Jews"? Cf. Fraser, vol. 2, p. 138, n.134.
75 See, e.g., *PCZ*, 59003, 59075, 59076.
76 See the remarks of Lewis, *CPJ*, III 1531, p. 163.
77 See details in Lesquier, p. 83f. and Bar-Kochva, p. 93 and n.26.

composition of his unit cannot be definitely determined, the fact that the officer was Jewish provides a basis for thinking that most of his men were his coreligionists. The fact that he operated in the Fayûm strengthens that impression, for it is well known as a region of Jewish military settlement[78].

Another instance of high Jewish command figures in *P. Tebt.*, 818 (= *CPJ*, I 24) of 174 B.C.E. from Trikomia in the Fayûm. Line 26 of that document notes that two Jewish cavalrymen from the First Hipparchy, owners of 80 *aròurai* (one *aroura* is of 1,975 square meters) were among those who received their estates through Dositheos (τῶν διὰ Δωσιθέου). The man's theophoric name and the fact he settled two Jewish cavalrymen on the land support Launey's contention that he too was Jewish, the more so since all those involved in the agreement recorded in the document were Jews[79]. His being part of the command at Trikomia is clearly shown by the fact that his name is a kind of eponymous appellation that fits the usual formula τῶν διὰ τοῦ δεῖνος[80]. The number of Jewish names (nine) in a single document suggest a distinct Jewish unit in the place including cavalry (who were the military aristocracy). It is important to note that besides Dositheos, the document refers to another Jewish official who was a τακτόμισθος, as in the case in Samaraeia. The presence of two Jews in the local command complement further supports the conclusion that there was at least a Jewish sub-unit in Trikomia. The same village at the end of the third century B.C. had a high-ranking police officer named Simon (Σίμων, probably *Simeon* in Hebrew) reported in *P. Ent*, 82 (= *P. Magd.*, 33)[81], and it is quite possible that he commanded an entire police unit composed of

---

78 Cf. *CPJ*, I 27, line 7, and also Launey, I p. 545; Fraser, vol. 2, p. 443, n.775.

79 See Launey, p. 546, 1233; and also Willrich, *RE(PW)*, vol. 2, p. 1605. Both of these scholars suggested that this Dositheus should be identified with the person mentioned in Jos., *C. Apionem*, II 49, but that appears doubtful, if only because of the early date — 174 B.C.E.

80 That is, "those who (were settled) by someone" (= τῶν διὰ τοῦ δεῖνος); see details in Uebel, (*Eponybezeichnungen*) as per index. On the meaning of the formula and the office-holder, see Lesquier, p. 196f.

81 The document is not included in the *Corpus Papyrorum Judaicarum*, perhaps because there was some doubt about his Jewishness; and see also Tcherikover's correct conclusions in regard to the identification of the name Simon (Σίμων) as Jewish, in his book, *Jews in Egypt*, pp. 10, 181-182. Cf. *CPJ*, I (Prolegomena), pp. 29-30. Indeed, since many Jews were found in the ranks of the police, (see below, pp. 55ff.), it is reasonable to assume that he was a Jew.

fellow Jews. In the middle of the third century B.C.E. another village
in the Fayûm, called Phebichis, had an ethnically mixed cavalry unit
known by the name of its commander Zoilos (*CPJ*, I 18). It included
Jews as well, one of whom was an officer with the low rank of
δεκανικός. As the rank was low and of secondary importance[82],
it is reasonable to suppose that the local unit of "Zoilos' troop"
included a Jewish sub-unit under Jewish command.

   Closer to the time of Onias IV a Jew named Iasibis ('Ιασῖβις) was
the "epistates of a hipparchy", (ἐπιστάτης ἱππαρχίας) in Diospolis-
Magna (*CPJ*, I 27, col II 1.7; col. III 1.8). We do not know what
exact authority connected with that function, for documents point
variously to judicial and police work, and even to economic management of holy places, and the like[83]. While the document does not
indicate that the man was connected with a Jewish unit, it is certainly
possible and even logical.

   Adding up the facts noted above, we must conclude that they are
enough to cast doubt on Tcherikover's assumption that before the
time of Onias IV Jews did not organize into independent units under
Jewish command.

C. The Legal Status of Jews in Military and Government Service

1. Army

Document *CPJ*, I 18 of 260/259 B.C.E. is an agreement to settle
claims between two people, at least one of whom was a Jew in military service belonging to the cavalry unit of "Zoilos' troop" in the
Fayûm village of Phebichis[84]. The document shows that the unit was
ethnically mixed, for five different ethnic designations are listed, and
in fact the list can be added to from other documents[85]. "Zoilos'
troop" thus seems to have consisted of military settlers gathered from
various units who received land holdings (κλῆροι) under Zoilos' com-

---

82 Lesquier, pp. 91-92.
83 Lesquier, p. 193. On his judicial-disciplinary functions, see also Taubenschlag, pp. 486,
   537, 540.
84 Uebel thought that Jew was not a soldier, contrary to most scholars (p. 276, n.4; but cf.
   Bilabel, *Aegyptus*, 5 (1924), p. 161f.; Bouché-Leclerq, 4, p. 240; Tcherikover, *CPJ*, I
   28 (p. 148f.)). I do not believe he is correct, if only because of the man's witnesses,
   who were evidently all Jewish soldiers.
85 Uebel, p. 275f., Nos. 1151-1157.

mand. Most probably the parties involved in the contract signed it in the presence of witnesses close to them. According to the juridical logic then applied in Ptolemaic Egypt, it would be reasonable to assume that the witnesses had the same status as the principals, and as these were cavalrymen, they too belonged to the military aristocracy. There may well have been Jews among them, even though we cannot verify this through their names or ethnic designations. At any rate, the one definite Jew was a cavalryman in the Ptolemaic army[86], with all the privileges and status deriving from the function, such as the size of his estate and his connection with the "civic laws".

Document *CPJ*, I 19 from Arsinoë-Crocodilopolis (dating from 225 B.C.E.) containing an official record of the trial of two "Jewish" litigants (a man and woman) provides further information on the legal status of Jewish soldiers. It is particularly important because of its juridical nature. The court, all agree, was Greek, but there is a scholarly difference of opinion on its exact nature[87], which will not be dealt with here. However, there is a close resemblance between the terminology it used and that current in certain types of courts in Alexandria. As in Alexandria, the court in Arsinoe-Crocodilopolis was called a Court of Ten ($\delta\iota\kappa\alpha\sigma\tau\acute\eta\rho\iota\upsilon\nu$)[88], and thus involved $\delta\iota\kappa\alpha\sigma\tau\alpha\acute\iota$, that is, judges who were appointed and sworn in for the exclusive purpose of a particular trial. Moreover, as in Alexandria, one of the judges functioned as the president ($\pi\rho\acute\delta\epsilon\delta\rho\sigma\varsigma$) and matters of court procedure were entrusted to a special official known as the Clerk of the Court ($\epsilon\grave\iota\sigma\alpha\gamma\omega\gamma\epsilon\acute\upsilon\varsigma$). The close resemblance might lead to the mistaken notion that the Alexandrian court (which sat in the *chora*) is meant, and that it dealt with citizens of Alexandria[89]. However, the ethnic designations of the litigants leave no doubt that in the case of Arsinoë-Crocodilopolis, the people were members of the local *katoikia*. The important thing is that the resemblance shows that the pair involved in the case had a civic status like that of Alexandrian citizens, that is, they too were considered $\pi\upsilon\lambda\tilde\iota\tau\alpha\iota$[90]. The illuminating fact, extremely significant for our investigation, is that the court was

---

86 It is reasonable to suppose that among his witnesses there was at least one Jew.

87 See Taubenschlag, p. 484, and also Tcherikover, *Jews in Egypt*, p. 109.

88 See Taubenschlag, p. 484.

89 The legal procedures are also similar; and see Taubenschlag, pp. 508, 519, on this.

90 However, it must not be assumed that they had equal status *in all matters*, for the Alexandrian *polis* was more important.

not one that judged the native Egyptian population (λαοκρίται) nor one of the special kind that handled civil suits involving Greeks and natives[91]. That means that the two parties to the dispute, designated as "Jews", had the status of *politai*. However, if they were not citizens of Alexandria, what legal and political framework did they belong to? Both of them were members of the *katoikia* in Arsinoe-Crocodilopolis. It was an ethnically mixed military settlement[92], but we know of a synagogue there at that very time (the reign of Ptolemy III), which shows that the Jews were already organized in an independent framework officially recognized by the authorities, which was probably a *politeuma*[93], and the members of such a body naturally had the status of *politai*[94]. To sum up, the document proves definitely that the legal procedures and the structure and composition of the court were of the "Hellenic" pattern, familiar and usual in Alexandria itself. Even the legal bases — "royal regulations" (τὰ διαγράμματα) and "civic laws" (οἱ πολιτικοὶ νόμοι) in *CPJ*, I 19, lines 43-44 — for the woman's claims support this conclusion. Thus it can be argued that the litigants were considered *politai* in relation to the state authorities, and if that status did not derive from Alexandrian citizenship, it derived from membership in the Jewish *politeuma* in Arsinoe. As the establishment of that body was the result of government policy on military service, it can be seen that the functional factor was extremely influential in the civic stratification of the Jews. In other words, their independent organization and legal status was determined in large measure by their military service in general and their specific function in particular.

Another question is raised by the document under discussion. One of the litigants, the Jewess Herakleia, appeared at the trial with her guardian, that is her κυρίος, described as "an Athenian of the *Epigone*" (line 38). Generally the "guardian" was one of the woman's

---

91 Courts like those called κοινοδίκιον are mentioned in *P. Ent.*, 11, line 7; 44, line 9; 65; line 19; 70, line 19.

92 This is shown by the document itself, in which three other ethnic designations besides the "Jews" are mentioned (lines 5, 30, 34). On the basis of other documents from the same place, another two ethnic designations can be added, and see Uebel, p. 168, Nos. 123-124.

93 Full details of this are given in the chapter on Jewish communities in Egypt (below, p. 128f.).

94 On the affinity of the terms *politai* and *politeuma* see above p. 30 and nn.5-6.

closest relatives — a husband, father, son, brother, uncle and the like[95] — as confirmed by all the documents referring to Jewish women[96]. We must therefore conclude that there were ties of kinship between the woman and her guardian, although this document, unlike others, does not state it. How can this be explained? It appears that a distinction must be made between contracts and litigation. In the first case by law the trustee or guardian had to have equal civic status and the same ethnic designation as the woman, and it was understandably only natural that relatives most easily met those conditions. In cases of litigation, however, the laws allowed the appointment, either in a will or by the authorities, of a guardian who was not actually a member of the family[97], although there was a tendency in these cases too to appoint relatives[98]. Probably then, there was some relationship, albeit indirect, between the "Jewess" Herakleia and her "Athenian" guardian, based on some matrimonial connection. The fact that both were described as residents of the same *katoikia* may explain the background of that connection[99]. Whatever the nature of the ties, obviously the man's willingness to serve as "guardian" and his appointment as such by the authorities show that the civic status of the "Jews" in that *katoikia* was not inferior to that of the Greeks, at least in the judgement of the competent authorities. It appears that the connection between guardianship described above and the status of the litigants as *politai* is demonstrated by the functional stratification common to all the parties involved.

Document *CPJ*, I 23 of 182 B.C.E., likewise from Arsinoe-Crocodilopolis, is a contract regarding a mortgage loan between two "Jews of the Epigone". As in the preceding document, a "royal regulation"

---

95 See Taubenschlag, p. 170f. and n.7.
96 See *CPJ*, I 26; II 144, 146, 148, 149; III 453, 455; Tcherikover, *Jews in Egypt*, p. 110 and n.42; *CPJ*, I (Prolegomena), pp. 34-35.
97 Taubenschlag, *ibid.*, and also p. 173.
98 Thus, e.g., in *P. Ent.* 22, of 218 B.C.E., a "Persian" woman requested the appointment of a "guardian" (for purposes of litigation, because her husband and sons were deceased) from a different ethnic group (Thracian). However, it appears that this man was her husband's brother-in-law (married to his sister).
99 In fact, Tcherikover's explanation (*CPJ*, I p. 156, explication of line 38) about friendship between families is satisfactory. But if the possibility of matrimonial ties is considered, this attests to the fact that an "Athenian" did not fear any damage to his offspring's status because of marriage to a "Jewess".

was the applicable legal basis[100]. The amount of the loan (two talents and 3,000 copper drachmas) and the value of the security show the wealth and lofty status of the signatories. As such agreements were made before the local *agoranomos*, and both signatories were "Jews", the inference is that the relationship of Jewish military settlers to the authorities followed the usual "Hellenic" pattern, as indicated in the previous document[101].

Document *CPJ*, I 22 from Samareia, dating from 201 B.C.E., provides additional data clarifying the functional element in the civic stratification of the Jews. It is an official renunciation contract made by Theodotos son of Kassandros "the Paeonian" in favor of four "king's peasants" in respect of a quarter ($\sigma\tau\alpha\vartheta\mu\acute{o}\varsigma$) in Kerkesephis (near Samareia) which had belonged to his father. The contract was made in Samareia in the presence of six local witnesses, all "Jews". Theodotos was undoubtedly Jewish despite the ethnic designation "Paeonian". As noted above, that designation was inherited from his father, and because he served in a "Paeonian" military sub-unit. The mother-unit was a typical eponymous one (that is, the soldiers were described by the commander's name) known as "Phyleus' troop". The fact that the "Jewish" and "Paeonian" sub-units were subordinate to the former explains why Theodotos' witnesses were "Jews"[102]. At any rate, what is important here is that the Paeonian witnesses were "Jews", in an official document. That means that their status was not inferior to that of the principal insofar as the state authorities were concerned.

There are a number of documents listing military settlers of Greek and Jewish descent with no distinction being made between them. One such (*CPJ*, I 29) from mid-second century B.C.E., recorded the desert land cultivated by a group of military settlers in the Fayûm region. Of the seventeen names listed, six are clearly Jewish and the rest Greek. In the absence of data for determining the national identity of those eleven, they must be considered non-Jewish. If so, the list attests an ethnically mixed unit. The listing of the names together, with no distinction or separation, indicates that Jews and Greeks were equal in the eyes of the local administration. This is the practice

---

100 See Tcherikover's explanation of line 20 (*CPJ*, I p. 164).
101 Cf. additional documents as well: *CPJ*, I 24-26.
102 See p. 45 above.

in another document as well, of the same period, and likewise from the Fayûm, in which the names of "Jews" and "Macedonians" are mixed together (*CPJ*, I 30). There too the reason for order in which the names appear is not manifest nor is the purpose of the listing. Be that as it may, the document demonstrates that those who composed it did not rank the "Jews" lower than their "Macedonian" counterparts[103].

Another list dating from the mid-second century B.C.E. (*P. Tebt.*, 79b), likewise from the Fayum[104], contains more than twenty-five names, including a number of Jewish ones, without however the ethnic designation "Jewish". Unfortunately Tcherikover did not copy the entire document, extracting only the lines clearly relating to Jews[105], so that no proper conclusions could be drawn. An examination of the document in its entirety shows that the listing begins with proprietors of large estates (about 80 to 100 *arourai*) designated as "Macedonian", "Sidonian" and "Persian"[106]. Judging by the size of their properties, they were probably cavalrymen, and perhaps even part of the local command[107]. Prominent among them is Seuthes son of Dositheos, who owned 61¾ *arourai*. In comparison with the others, the size of his estate indicates he was among the wealthiest and highest-ranking settlers, since eight settlers had allotments of 40 *arourai*, and eight other had plots of between 20⅜ and 51¼ *arourai*. The size of these suggests that their owners were infantry *katoikoi* attached to a cavalry unit, particularly since one of their officers described as a *hegemon* (ἡγεμών) had a 40-*aroura* estate (line 25). Tcherikover assumed that the Thracian name of the Jew referred to above could indicate he belonged to the Thracian hipparchy[108]. The size of his property, however, does not place him

---

103 See n.74 above.
104 The exact location is unknown, but it can be understood from the document that it lay opposite the village of Psenyris in the Polemon meris of the Arsinoite nome.
105 It is possible that other Jews are hidden there, in addition to those who can be positively identified, the lines dealing with whom Tcherikover cited in *CPJ*, I 31.
106 See *P. Tebt.*, 79(b), lines 7, 11, 57, 60.
107 Infantry soldiers usually had a holding of thirty *arourai* and cavalry of seventy or more. From the present standpoint, it is important to note that there was no significant difference in the size of the holdings of the three. It appears that the command in this military colony was given to a man who was among the "first friends", and he had 124 3/16 *arourai* (*ibid.*, line 44).
108 See *CPJ*, I p. 177, commentary on line 63.

in the cavalry, and it is more reasonable to suppose that he was an
infantry *katoikos* attached to a cavalry unit because of some particular development and for a circumstantial military purpose.
In fact, the document records four definitely Jewish names in a
military unit called τῶν εἰς τὴν Θηβαίδα ἀπὸ τῶν 'Δ[109]. The
meaning of that designation is clarified by three other documents
where it is given in full: τῶν ἀναξευξάντων εἰς τὴν Θηβαίδα ἀπὸ
τῶν 'Δ ἀνδρῶν[110], that is, "the four thousand who set forth on the
expedition against Thebes". The unit was probably recruited in the
reign of Ptolemy V Epiphanes upon the eruption of the great Theban
revolt, which was suppressed in 187/6 B.C.E.[111] As the document
dates from mid-second century, presumably the men mentioned
were the descendants of the original recruits (perhaps the second
generation)[112]. They had subsequently remained in their original
unit, apparently in accordance with the government policy of pre-
serving peace in the region. The relevant point here is that the
estates of the four Jews in the unit (49³⁄₁₆, 32⅝, 49³⁄₁₆, and 50
arourai) were not smaller than those of the others (20⅜, 51⁵⁄₁₆,
49³⁄₁₆, and 51¼ *arourai*). Judging by the size of Seuthes son of
Dositheos' estate, he may have been the leader of the Jewish soldiers
who joined the unit, or at least been a man of importance from the
viewpoint of his military function. As estate size generally reflected
the status of the soldiers[113], it can definitely be posited that all five
of the Jewish soldiers were in the middle rank, if not higher, in their
military settlement.

Another document, *P. Gurob.*, 26, also from the Fayûm, dating
from 217 B.C.E.(?), mentions fifteen military settlers with allotments
of from 60 to 100 *arourai*, five of them Jews according to their
names[114]. There is no doubt that they were counted as part of the

109 *Ibid.*, col., II line 69 (as to the names of the Jews, see *CPJ*, I 31).
110 Both documents are from Kerkeosiris: *P. Tebt.*, 62, lines 43-45; *P. Tebt.*, 63, lines 42-
43; while the third is from Berenice Tesmophoris (*P. Tebt.*, 998, line 3). It should be
noted that the two settlements mentioned here lie in the very same area, the Polemon
meris of the Arsinoite nome.
111 Cf. Lesquier, p. 163; Uebel, p. 165, n.1.
112 The documents from Kerkeosiris, on the other hand, are from the end of the second cen-
ury B.C.E. (119 and 116 B.C.E.) and it is therefore reasonable to assume that the soldiers
mentioned in them were at least the third generation since the establishment of the unit.
113 See Lesquier, p. 173f.
114 Only a passage dealing directly with the Jews was included by Tcherikover in the Corpus,

military aristocracy of the Ptolemaic kingdom, and had obtained that status because of their military functions.

2. Police

It would be logical to assume that as for the army, for the police too the Ptolemies avoided engaging ordinary Egyptians[115], as the latter were suspected of disloyalty and an inclination to revolt, and policing is by nature authoritarian and representative and not suitable for people of such low status. However, the dearth of Greek manpower intervened, and as early as the third century B.C.E. Egyptians of the warrior class (μάχιμοι) carried out police duties[116], and of course were more privileged than others. The situation changed in the second century, chiefly as a result of the cleruch system that was developed and refined[117]. The police force was affected, so that it can be considered to have become part of the regular army. The majority of the regular police (φιλακῖται) were still recruited from among the Egyptians[118], but quite a number were foreign-born. These were mainly from neighboring peoples who were accustomed to desert life and were thus suited for guard duty in regions bordering on the desert. It is not by chance that we find many Arab policemen in various documents, and Tcherikover rightly pointed out that in the third century B.C.E. "Arab" was a synonym for "policeman"[119]. Probably the same policy accounted for the recruitment to the police force in Memphis of a group of Idumaeans as a unit of μαχαιροφόροι

---

namely *CPJ*, I 32. It is interesting that Frag. b mentions another Jew who, judging by his description, ὧν οὐκ εὑρίσκομεν ἐν τῶι κληρουχικῶι, is not inevitably a soldier. But on the other hand, cf. Uebel, p. 253, n.4.

115 Not in vain did Tcherikover mention one document (*PCZ*, 59610) in which there is a specific reservation about assigning guard duty to Egyptian natives, see *Jews in Egpt*, p. 44 and n.31; *CPJ*, I (Prolegomena), p. 17 and n.47.

116 Lesquier, p. 260. Later they even joined the army as a result of the reforms of Ptolemy IV Philopator after the battle of Raphiah.

117 The term κληροῦχος indicated a military settler from among the natives, while κάτοικος indicated a military settler from among Macedonians and Hellenes; see Oertel, *RE(PW)*, XI, pp. 17-18.

118 See Lesquier, pp. 260-264; Oertel, *Die Liturgie*, p. 59; Bouché-Leclerq, vol. 4, pp. 52-62; *P. Tebt.*, I, App. I pp. 550-551; Uebel, p. 377. The bibliography on this subject is fairly large. For examples of the service of Egyptians in the police, see, e.g., *P. Tebt.*, I 112, lines 81, 86; *P. Hibeh*, I 41, line 18; *P. Lille*, I 25, lines 45, 64; *P. Tebt*, I 116, line 57; I 120, line 128. And additional examples are plentiful.

119 *Jews in Egypt*, p. 44; *CPJ*, I (Prolegomena), p. 17, n.47.

(bearers of short, curved pointed swords) and its organization as a
politeuma[120]. It is quite likely that the authorities also considered
the Jews suitable for such duty, and that organized groups of Jews
joined the police force like their Idumaean compatriots. The status
of policemen in general as cleruchs (=military settlers of the lower
class of natives) certainly reflected their civic stratification. In comparison with regular army personnel, they were considered to be the
lowliest. Foot soldiers received allotments of thirty *arourai* and
cavalry of seventy to eighty, while the ordinary policeman was
allotted only ten[121]. Special duty policemen such as the χερσέφιπποι
(the police patrol which guarded the desert border and the cultivated
land), the ἐρημοφύλακες (desert patrol) or the ἔφοδοι (the guard for
the tax collectors) were sometimes given as much land as ordinary
soldiers, twenty-five to thirty *arourai.* The status of police officers,
especially the high-ranking ones, was closer to, if not identical with,
that of army of officers. At any rate, the impression gleaned from
the documents is that the highest-ranking positions were not filled
by Egyptians, at least not till toward the end of the Ptolemaic
period[122]. All in all, the status of policemen was much higher than
that of other Egyptians but inferior to that of regular army personnel.

　　As to the Jews, there are in all just three pieces of direct papyrological or epigraphical evidence on Jewish policemen: *OGIS,*
96 (= *CIJ*, II 1443), *CPJ*, I 25 and *P. Ent.*, 82. The first, from the
second century B.C.E., is a dedication of a synagogue by Ptolemy
son of Epikides, "the chief of the policemen" (ὁ ἐπιστάτης τῶν
φυλακιτῶν) in conjunction with "the Jews in Athribis", in honor of
the royal family. The man ranked very high among the officers of
the police, and we know that he was in command of all the policemen of the district (*nomos*)[123]. Subordinate to him were all police
commanders with the rank of ἀρχιφυλακίτης, those in charge of
toparchies or forts who led sub-units, and the village police. In other
words, he was responsible to the *strategos* for all police work in the

120　See *OGIS*, 737, and also Launey, pp. 1072-1077; Ruppel, pp. 306-309; Fraser, vol. 1,
　　　pp. 280-281.
121　Lesquier, p. 177f.; Bevan, p. 143.
122　Lesquier, pp. 190; 262-263; Bevan, p. 163.
123　Lesquier, p. 261; Bevan, p. 143.

nome, and second to him in rank[124]. Presumably the "Jews in Athribis" were cleruchs in the police force as was usual in second-century B.C.E. Egypt, like their Idumaean counterparts in Memphis. In regard to their land holdings, except for their officers they were certainly inferior to regular army soldiers.

The second document (*CPJ*, I 25), likewise dating from the second century B.C.E., records a Jewish policeman as a witness to a loan contract between two soldiers of the regular army. It shows that from the juridical point of view that policeman was deemed to be of suitable status to serve as a witness in an official transaction of regular soldiers. The fact that the other witnesses, like the parties to the contract, were soldiers proves that he was in good company.

The third document (*P. Ent.*, 82 = *P. Magd.*, 33) which was not included in the *Corpus Papyrorum Judaicarum*, is the earliest, dating from 220 B.C.E. It is a legal petition of a woman from the village of Trikomia (in the Fayûm) in which she requests the local *strategos* to instruct Simon the ἐπιστάτης and the superintendent (ἀρχιφυλακίης) to investigate the terrible deed of the person in charge of the local women's bathhouse who deliberately poured boiling water on her and caused serious burns. The presence of Jewish military settlers, members of the military aristocracy (i.e. the cavalry) in Trikomia at the start of the second century B.C.E. (*CPJ*, I 24) supports the impression that the police *epistates* there was a Jew, and that the Greek name was derived from the Hebrew *Simeon*[125].

Among the less explicit testimony is an inscription from the synagogue of Nitriai (*CIJ*, II 1442) which will be dealt with below. In regard to literary evidence, Tcherikover was of the opinion that the defective testimony of Josephus (*C. Apionem*, II 64) on the "river guard" (*fluminis custodia*) does not relate to the garrisons that defended Egypt's eastern portals, but it is more reasonable to assume that Josephus was thinking of police who was charged with maintaining order along the Nile, for that is how the Nile guard (ποταμοφυλακία) is referred to in the ostraca[126]. That conclusion seems most reason-

---

124 Some think he also had judicial functions, see Jouguet, p. 53; Taubenschlag, pp. 486, 491.
125 See p. 47 and n.81 above.
126 Tcherikover, *Jews in Egypt*, p. 43. In Tcherikover's opinion, then, this report cannot be based on *Bellum*, I 175, which relates that Jews were entrusted with guarding the border fortresses in the Pelusium area, and therefore served as a military garrison and not as police. Cf. also *CPJ*, I (Prolegomena), p. 53 and n.14.

able and should perhaps be applied as well to the Jewish police unit
from Athribis, which may have formed part of the extensive network
of the Nile guard.

3. Administration

In contrast to the army, the Ptolemaic administrative system was
more open to autochthonic Egyptians. At the time of Alexander the
Great's conquest, they were even admitted to the higher echelons of
civil administration. Arrian tells us (III 5) that Alexander appointed
two of them nomarchs (district heads). They directed the administration in Memphis and Pelusium, working together with the Macedonian commanders. Some scholars have considered that situation as
indicative of Alexander's goal of administrative decentralization, and
of his aspirations for the integration of the conquerors and the conquered. Be that as it may, it is a fact that native Egyptians already
occupied high positions in the civil administration in his time.

The situation was totally different in the reigns of his successors,
the first Ptolemies. The centralism that characterized their regimes
was indicated by the elimination of the post of *nomarch*, and the
concentration of both civil and military authority in the hands of the
strategos alone, so that the parallelity or division of authority was no
longer possible[127]. Thus the bureaucracy of Ptolemy II Philadelphus
was primarily Greek, except in the lowest ranks that were open to
Egyptians, such as "village scribe"[128], of which there were thousands
in the villages of Egypt. However, the "Hellenization" of the administration did not last very long. Even in the reign of Ptolemy IV
Philopator, Egyptians of the Hellenized aristocratic class could serve
in high positions, and at the end of the second century B.C.E. in the
most eminent[129].

As to the Jews, they were to be found in the administration in the
earliest times. The author of the *Letter of Aristeas* states that among
the courtiers of Ptolemy II Philadelphus were the most loyal and
gifted Jews who were taken captive by his father Ptolemy I and freed

---

127 It is true that in the Fayûm the office of nomarch remained, but this was exceptional
    (see Bevan, p. 142), and it is interesting that of the seven holders of this office, five were
    Greeks and two Egyptians.
128 See Bevan, p. 143; *A.H.M. Jones, The Greek City*, p. 18f; idem., *CERP*, p. 308.
129 See, e.g., *OGIS*, 132, and also *P. Tor.*, 5-7. *P. Lond.*, II p. 13 even has a mention of an
    epistrategos of Egyptian origin, from Thebes.

by him[130]. They may have ranked as "the king's friends", but in any case they were definitely attached to the court, as is evident from the *Letter* and from Josephus' paraphrase. Tramontano even proved that the phrasing in the *Letter of Aristeas* accords with that in other sources[131], so that there is no doubt of its reliability. It may very well be that they were "the men powerful at court" (τῶν περὶ τὴν αὐλὴν δυνατῶν) mentioned as being cultivated by Hyrcanus son of Joseph son of Tobias (*Antiquitates*, XII 215)[132]. The *Letter of Aristeas* may even have mentioned the name of one of them (*ibid.*, 182ff.), Dorotheus, who was charged with providing food and other necessities for the seventy-two elders translating the Pentateuch. The fact that he was a Jew is evident from his theophoric name and his familiarity with Jewish customs. That is particularly clear in Josephus who notes that "Dorotheus being put in charge of these matters because of his exactness in the details of living" (*Antiquitates*, XII 94-97). It would not be wrong to say that in describing the Ptolemaic court the author of the *Letter* demonstrated the greatest familiarity with its protocol, manners and practices. This suggests that he had access to the court and was himself one of the courtiers. The impression is strenghened by his precise information on the titles at the court and the arrangements[133]. During the reigns of Ptolmey II and Ptolemy III very good relations were developed with the Jews of Palestine as well. It is is not by chance that Tobias was the commander of a military settlement in Transjordania, and he most likely had civilian administrative authority in the area under his command. In the reign of Ptolemy III, Joseph son of Tobias was appointed chief tax collector for Palestine (*Antiquitates*, XII 175-179). And, as noted above, he was not the only Jew to be given a lofty post by the king,

---

130 *Letter of Aristeas,* 37, and cf. Jos., *Antiquitates,* XII, 47.

131 Tramontano, *La Lettera di Aristea, ad loc.*

132 And it is reasonable to hypothesize the "one of the Jews of high rank" (τινί τῶν ἐπ' ἀξιώματος Ἰουδαίων) to whom the niece of Joseph son of Tobias was to be betrothed (*Antiquitates,* XII 187) was one of this group, to be more exact, a descendant of those who attained their status at the time of Ptolemy II Philadelphos.

133 He was well acquainted with the following officials: "the president of the king's library" (*ibid.,* 9); "the chief of bodyguards" (*ibid.,* 40 and cf. also 12); "the paymasters of the forces and the royal bankers" (*ibid.,* 26); "those who had custody of the officers" *ibid.,* 33); "judges", "legal officers for every district and their assistants" ((*ibid.,* 110-111); "the lord high steward" (*ibid.,* 182; cf. Andrews, *ap.* Charles, *The Apocrypha and Pseudepigrapha,* vol. ii, p. 111).

since his niece was to be married to "one of the high ranking Jews" in Alexandria (*ibid.*, 187). In the same king's reign the Jewish convert, Dositheos son of Drimylos, began his great career which continued on to that of Ptolemy IV Philopator[134]. No information is available on when or why he converted, whether his conversion occurred before he was appointed royal "memorandum writer" (ὑπομνηματογράφος) or perhaps on being appointed eponymous priest of Alexander and the deified Ptolemies. Be that as it may, his Jewish origin does not seem to have been an obstacle to advancement; at most it could have interfered with the last post.

For the second century B.C.E. more plentiful information is available on Jewish functionaries in the Ptolemaic administration. One of the prominent ones was the person to whom Herod the *dioiketes*, (i.e. the "manager", the chief assistant of the king in matters of finance and economics) addressed a letter in 164 B.C.E. (*CPJ*, I 132 = *UPZ*, 110). It was Wilcken who first proposed identifying the addressee as Onias and defining him as the *strategos* of Heliopolites (= the nome of Heliopolis)[135]. It was Tcherikover's view that the courteous tone of the letter and the greetings of the royal family it begins with indicate that Onias was not an ordinary *strategos* but a familiar of the court who had personal ties with the king and *dioiketes*[136]. Taking into account the fact that the king mentioned in the letter was Ptolemy VI Philometor who was fond of Jews, the addressee is probably identifiable as Onias IV, the *strategos* of Heliopolites who founded the military colony known as the "Land of Onias" and established the temple called the "House of Onias"[137]. Tcherikover too considered that possibility. At first he rejected it mainly on the basis of *Antiquitates*, XII 387, which reports that Onias IV emigrated to Egypt after the assassination of Menelaus and the appointment of Alcimos as High Priest, that is, after 162 B.C.E. He therefore believed that the reference could not be to the Onias of the papyrus but must be another member of the same family in which Onias was a common name[138]. Subsequently,

---

134 *III Macc.*, I 2-3; and see the papyrological information about him and their analysis: Fuks, *CPJ*, I 127, pp. 230-236; idem., *JJP*, 7/8 (1953/4), pp. 205-209.

135 Wilcken read it as Ὀνί[αι]; even so he refrained from identifying him with Onias III or IV.

136 Tcherikover, *Jews in Egypt*, p. 45, and cf. also his commentary to *CPJ*, I 132.

137 See his title as *strategos* – *C. Apionem*, II 49.

138 Tcherikover, *Jews in Egypt*, p. 45; and cf. *UPZ*, 110 (pp. 487-488).

however, he concluded that they were the same person, chiefly because of the identity in name, period, position as *strategos* in the same neighborhood, and close relations with the court. As he put it, "Such coincidences are far too unlikely to be credible"[139]. Tcherikover then reasoned that Onias may well have moved to Egypt immediately after the assassination of his father Onias III (in 170 B.C.E.), rightly claiming that Josephus is unreliable on the chronology of the affair. The truth is however that the shadow of a question mark falls on all these assumptions: Was Wilcken's reading really correct? For only one letter in the name — V — is legible, and some scholars read it as [Θέω]νι[140].

Along with Onias, Josephus mentions Dositheos who served as *strategos* under Philometor and his wife Cleopatra (*C. Apionem*, II 49-50). We do not know who he was, though some scholars have been inclined to identify him with the Dositheos mentioned in *P. Tebt.*, 818 (= *CPJ*, I 24) of 174 B.C.E.

Reference to another Jewish *strategos* appears on the Ḥelkias, Stone (*CIJ*, II 1450) but the state of preservation of the inscription makes it impossible to determine whether it is Ḥelkias, the celebrated commander of Cleopatra III who is meant (*Antiquitates*, XIII 284-287, 348, 351)[141] or his son, as the name is in the genitive, Χελκίου[142].

The testimony of Josephus (*C. Apionem*, II 40; *Antiquitates*, XIII 285) implies that two Jews held the position of *strategos* in the reign of Ptolemy VI Philometor and Cleopatra III. They may have been in charge of two different districts (νόμοι). If so, the "Land of Onias" included more than one district. It is not known how long after Cleopatra III Jews continued to hold the position of *strategos* in their districts. Probably their great influence at court was at a peak during that queen's reign and gradually declined under her successors.

II Maccabees (I 10) mentions the name of Aristobulus, "the teacher of King Ptolemy", as the recipient of one of the "Ḥanukka letters" sent from Jerusalem. The identity of the. man is a matter of

---

139 See his commentary on *CPJ*, I 132; *Hell. Civil.*, pp. 276-7, 497-8 (n.26).
140 E.g., Letronne, *P. Par.*, 63, I-VII.
141 Tcherikover, *Jews in Egypt*, p. 463, and cf. also *CPJ*, I p. 17, n.45.
142 Th. Reinach in *REJ*, 40 (1900), pp. 50-54, for example, read it as [Onias (?) son of] Ḥelkiah": that is, the third generation after Onias IV, the founder of the colony. Cf. also Fuchs, p. 16; Schürer, vol. 3, p. 132.

great dispute, but the general view tends to identify him with the famous Jewish philosopher and historian whose writings have been preserved in fragmented form by the Apostolic Fathers[143]. Clemens Alexandrinus (*Strom.*, I 150, 1-3) explicitly asserted that he belonged to the reign of Ptolemy VI Philometor, and a similar assertion was made by Eusebius (*Preparatio Evangelica*, VIII 9, 38), and both referred to *II Maccabees*, I 10[144]. Two other proposals are of interest. One puts Aristobulus later, to the time of Ptolemy IX Soter, called Lathyrus, who reigned in 116-107 and 88-80 B.C.E.[145]; the other pushes him back to the reign of Ptolemy II Philadelphus[146]. Both these proposals must however be rejected mainly because the chronological determinations of Clemens Alexandrinus, Eusebius and Hieronymus are too numerous and specific to be denied, and because Eusebius explicitly says that Aristobulus dedicated his exegesis of the Pentateuch to Ptolemy VI Philometor, and even turned to him at times to clarify problems that arose from his biblical interpretations (*ibid.*, VIII 10, 1; 7; XIII 12, 2). That perhaps explains the *II Maccabees* epithet, and Aristobulus can be considered a teacher of philosophy[147] at the court of Ptolemy VI. It may be not only Aristobulus' philosophical stature but also his high priestly genealogy (*ibid.*) that goes a long way to account for his status at court, for that was one of the reasons for the political and social advancement of Onias IV in the very same period.

This is the sum total of the information available on high-ranking Jews in the service of the Ptolemies. There is quite a good deal of data however on Jews serving in the lower ranks of the administrative hierarchy. most of them were tax-farmers, tax-collectors, granary officials and bankers, in other words, part of the financial administration[148]. Such posts were generally allotted to the wealthier mem-

---

143 See, e.g., Guttman, *The Beginnings of Jewish-Hellenistic Literature*, pp. 187f., 280f.

144 See a full collection of the patristic reports in Schürer, vol. 3, p. 512f., and also in Walter, *Der Thoraausleger*, p. 9.

145 See, e.g., Stahlin, *Gesch. der griesch. Literatur*, vol. II, 1, p. 606; Praechter, *Die Philosophie des Altertums*, p. 571.

146 See Walter, *Der Thorauausleger*, p. 13f. and especially p. 19f.

147 The term "teacher" (διδάσκαλος) should not be interpreted in its Jewish sense as a "teacher of the Torah", but rather in its Greek sense; and see Walter's comment on the subject (*ibid.*, p. 36, n.3). Most of the commentaries on II *Macc.* considered this title to denote an advisor or a teacher of philosophy as noted above.

148 See details in Tcherikover, *Jews in Egypt*, pp. 46-50, and also in *CPJ*, I p. 194f. (Section V).

bers of the local population. This was true in particular in regard to the tax-farmers, whose property was the guarantee for the annual rental due. Their legal status is not verifiable, but it is reasonable to suppose that the officials in the metropolitan administrative centers were mainly Greek, while those in the villages were well-to-do Egyptian natives who were deemed loyal collaborators. Representative of these was the Jew Simon son of Jazaros, a tax-farmer from Thebes, who was illiterate and needed the help of someone else in writing receipts[149].

Document *BGU*, 1730 from Herakleopolis, containing a royal *prostagma* of Ptolemy XII and Cleopatra VII (dating from 50/49 B.C.E.) mentions a Jewish scribe (γραμματεύς) named Onias who worked with a "district scribe" (τοπογραμματεύς) named Horos[150]. The title of the latter indicates that he served in one of the toparchies of the Herakleopolitan nome. As the name of the higher-ranking official of the two is Egyptian (Horos) it may be deduced that he was counted as a native, as was the Jewish colleague subordinate to him.

D. "King's Peasants", Tenants and Simple Craftsmen among the Jews

The vast majority of the Egyptian population that was settled in the villages of the *chora* belonged to the autochthonic class, the *laoi*. They were generally lease-holders who cultivated the land of the military settlers, paying an annual rental. The lease-holders of royal lands, known as "king's peasants," paid their rent to government officials at the regional banks or granaries, while those of the military settlers remitted the rent directly to the proprietors of the land they leased. Their inferior legal status as natives was defined in specific legislation which established a separate set of laws and a separate judicial system. Details of their obligations and restrictions have been satisfactorily dealt with in modern scholarship[151]. The tenant farmers were the most numerous among the natives, but the class included also simple workers and craftsmen such as shepherds, fishermen, potters, weavers, tanners, and dyers, as well as unskilled day laborers.

---

149 See *CPJ*, I 107. See also additional documents about him, *ibid.*, Nos. 61, 62, 63, 90.
150 In the Corpus Tcherikover quoted only the final lines (*CPJ*, I 137).
151 See Taubenschlag, pp. 2f., 295f., which also provides very extensive bibliographical details.

As to the Jews in that class, many questions remain unanswered. What proportion of the Jewish population was in that class? What determined their status? Were they descendants of Jews who had settled in Egypt before the Hellenistic conquest, or of those captives from Judaea brought to Egypt at the time of the first Syrian Wars? The last two questions may be answered affirmatively, though only partially.

An examination of the traces of Jews of the native class shows that a considerable concentration of them lived in the Fayûm and were "king's peasants". Zenon's papyrus archives have documents, all from the third century B.C.E., on a number of Jews who worked on the estate of Apollonius the *dioiketes* at Philadelphia as tenants, shepherds, watchmen, servants and even slaves. Among the tenants, for instance, was "Antigones the Jew" who leased (probably from Apollonius) a vineyard (*CPJ*, I 8), but it is not clear whether he was in fact a native. Another case was that of "Pasis the Jew" (*CPJ*, I 9a-b) who leased a piece of land described as ἡ διὰ τῶν λαῶν that is, land leased to native peasants or cultivated by them[152]. Pasis was subordinate to Zenon (Apollonius' official) and subject to his orders, which indicates that it was he who leased the land to Pasis. The testimony on the latter shows that besides being a tenant farmer, he was also a shepherd and, by the terms of his contract with his master, undertook to supply a quantity of wool for mattresses.

Another document (*CPJ*, I 13) is a memorandum of a claim submitted by two peasants, Ismaelos and Alexander, enjoining Zenon to fulfill the contractual condition and let them have the loan agreed upon. It notes that as Zenon did not meet his obligations their land dried up for lack of water and produced no crop. The financial straits of the two and the small size of their leased plots[153] testify to their sad situation as poor tenant farmers.

Document *CPJ*, I 14 mentions two Jewish vine-dressers, Samoelis and Alexander, who leased a 60-*aroura* vineyard from Zenon and Sostratos. They inform the local police officer that 30,000 reed canes (probably to be used for trellising the vines) were stolen from the leased vineyard. Thus presumably the contract covered the

---

152 See the introduction to the document *PCZ*, 59292 (ed. Edgar).
153 One was of 3½ *arourai*, and while the size of the other is unknown, it is reasonable to assume that it was no different.

reed canes as well as the land[154]. The two men figure also in Zenon's letter to his partner Sostratos (*CPJ*, I 15) consulting the latter about the intention of the Jewish tenants to abandon the vineyard. They wished to do so because of the difficulties neighbors put in their way by not allowing them to pass through their holdings. The vineyard was of sixty *arourai*, and as thirty was the normal size of the property of an ordinary military settler, it was enough to provide a decent living for the two. Thus the tenant farmers in this case were quite well-to-do. The document mentions the quite considerable sum of 630 drachmas (line 39) which may well have been the annual rent[155]. The wealth of the two, who were probably partners, is suggested by the fact that Zenon reported his fear that he and Sostratos were going to lose them as tenants. Papyrological evidence indicates that vineyard work was mainly in Greek hands[156], which means that it was more respectable and profitable than other agricultural work. That finding reinforces the impression that the two were ordinary tenant farmers so far as the law was concerned, but not the lowliest among them. In fact the annoyances perpetrated by the neighbors may perhaps be attributed to envy. Zenon wrote to his partner upon receipt of a letter from the tenants and assumed that Sostratos had received a similar one. The tenants' letters no doubt reported the neighbors' doings to the landlords, and indicated that failure to find a solution to the problem[157] would be an infringement of the tenancy contract. Zenon seems to have sent a reply that amounted to a legal warning, but its contents are unverifiable because the document is in bad condition (line 41ff.). All the available information points to the fact that the two Jews were not miserable hard-pressed tenant farmers, but quite well established people who could act rather freely and apply pressure against their masters, the owners of the vineyard.

Aside from information on tenant farmers, the Zenon papryi provide some on Jews of the same class engaged in other work.

---

154 Cf. *CPJ*, I 15 on this matter.
155 Edgar, the editor of the document (*PCZ*, 59367, Col. II) thought so, and even determined the rate of 10 drachmas as the usual rent for one *arura* (according to *PCZ*, 59269). It appears, then, that the sum of 630 is correct, since the size of the holding was about sixty *arourai*.
156 For details of viniculture in Ptolemaic Egypt, see Rostovtzeff, *Large Estate*, p. 93f.; Schnebel, *Die Landwirtschaft*, p. 239f.
157 *CPJ*, I 15, lines 31-40; it seems that the theft of reeds, which is mentioned in *CPJ*, I 14 is part of the neighbors' campaign of harassment.

Document *CPJ*, I 12 is a letter from a Jew named Somoelis who was a watchman in Apollonius' estate. He complains to Zenon about the treatment an official accorded him and his son. The letter indicates that besides being a watchman, the man worked at sowing wheat and buying barley. According to him, guarding the granary at Philadelphia paid very little, only 1½ *artabai* of wheat provided by the local farmers, and as this was not enough to support his family, he had to take on other work. In short, his economic situation was very bad, and he felt he was greatly exploited.

Another document (*CPJ*, I 10) is a detailed report, apparently submitted by a mason, of the number of bricks brought from the village of Tanis to Apollonius' estate at Philadelphia in the course of a week, from the 5th to the 11th of Epeiph (the year is not known). The seventh of that month was a Saturday according to the Jewish calendar, and no work is listed for that day, but the word $Σάββατα$[158] appears in place of the daily tally of bricks (line 6). The question is why no work was done on Saturday. The document mentions two men (probably donkey-drivers) who transported the bricks, but their names provide no basis for identifying them as Jews[159]. Tcherikover rightly speculated that the work was unlikely to be stopped because of a single donkey driver or laborer, who could easily be replaced. He was therefore of the opinion that the writer of the report (a mason, or the construction foreman on the estate) was the Jew. It seems more likely that the work stoppage was connected with a number of drivers, and perhaps also a number of masons. Some support for this assumption appears on the verso of the document where the name $Σαββατ(αῖος)$ in rather blurred form appears as another person making a report on the receipt of bricks, whom Edgar thought to be a driver[160]. Quite possibly then all the people mentioned in the document were Jews, and the construction work on the estate of Apollonius was carried out by Jewish bricklayers and Jewish porters. It is not clear whether they were day laborers or forced labor[161], but obviously the work would not have stopped on

---

158 The source has it as $Σάββατα$. As Tcherikover pointed out, the pluralization of the word "Sabbath" is not unusual, but fairly frequent in the Septuagint; see *CPJ*, I p. 137.

159 One was called Phileas and the other Demetrios.

160 See Tcherikover's explanations of the verse (*CPJ*, I p. 137). As to Edgar's opinion, see *PCZ*, 59762.

161 Such as that mentioned in *CPJ*, I 12.

Saturday if they had not been Jews.

The Zenon papyri mention a number of clearly Semitic names whose national identity cannot be determined but which may have belonged to Jews. Three documents refer to a man by the name of Βανναῖος which certainly derived from the Aramaic or Hebrew *Bannai, Benaiah, Benaiahu*[162]. The documents were written in the 28th regnal year of Ptolemy II Philadelphus, during a journey of Apollonius' in the *chora*, and all of them refer to that man as the servant of Apollonius, the minister of finance[165]. A man named *Natinas* is mentioned in a memorandum from Asklepiades (an official of Apollonius) to Zenon (*PCZ*, 59406) as having handed over a certain number of sheep, rams and lambs, so that he was probably a shepherd in the employ of Apollonius. Another man, *Zabdaios*, is referred to in one of the documents (*PCZ*, 59701) as an unskilled laborer. If all these were indeed Jews, a possibility that cannot be totally rejected, then they were Jews of an inferior socio-economic status who were undoubtedly classed with the "natives"[164].

If Edgar's view is accepted, an additional Jew is identifiable in the Zenon papyri. He is the man referred to in one of the complaint-petitions (*CPZ*, 59618) as "a Jew" ('Ιουδ[αῖος]). It is interesting to note that among the names of Jews at the estate of Apollonius (or Zenon) is 'Ιωάνα, a house slave[165]. As the document also mentions slaves that Nicanor (Apollonius' agent) dispatched from Syria, Tcherikover's assumption that she was one of them is reasonable, for Syria was a term then inclusive of Palestine. It is quite possible that document *PCZ*, 59710 (= *CPJ*, I 11) also mentions a person who came to Egypt in similar circumstances, one Χανουναῖος who was in charge of the dogs on Apollonius' estate. In Tcherikover's view the name is the Greek transcription of *Cana'an* or *Ḥananiah*[166], in which case the man was a Jew. His job indicates that he was a house slave or low ranking servant.

---

162 See *CPJ*, I p. 132, n.1.
163 *PCZ*, 59087, 59674, 59676. His employment as a servant is especially evident in the last document.
164 Cf. with Tcherikover's commentary – *CPJ*, I 16 (p. 146).
165 *SB*, 6769 = *P. Cornell*, 1. Tcherikover, in the Corpus, copied only 159-168 (see *CPJ*, I 7).
166 See the commentaries on *CPJ*, I 11, line 41. Cf. also with the village in the Fayûm called Χανααναῖν which name may also have been derived from כנען – *P. Petr.*, III, 43(2).

Those are the data on Jews provided by the Zenon papyri. In order to round out the picture for the Fayûm, some other documents are of interest. Document *P. Lille*, I 5[167], an order of 259/8 B.C.E. on the distribution of seed among farmers, includes a list of recipients of allotments, among them a number of "king's peasants". Some of them sound distinctly Jewish, e.g. Ptolemaios son of Ananias (᾽Ανανίας, line 14), Simeon (Σίμων, lines 4 and 39), Jonathan or Jonah (᾽Ιωνᾶτος, line 18), Theophilos (line 6) and Theodoros (lines 19, 25, 62)[168]. It is interesting to note that one of the recipients was of Syrian descent (line 14) which explains to a considerable degree the presence of Jews. The location of the document in the Fayûm supports the conclusion that they were settled on the "king's land" as tenant farmers[169].

A clear illustration of the situation of a Jewish "king's peasant" appears in document *CPJ*, I 43 of the second century B.C.E. It is a petition requesting the head of the district financial administration. (known by the title of ἐπιμελητής) to deal with the injury done to the petitioner by the village scribe. It appears that the farmer leased a 3-*aroura* tract of arid land and invested a lot of work and money in it. His rental had been four *artabai* of wheat per *aroura* (an *artaba* was a measure of volume equal to about thirty liters) and the scribe suddenly demanded a rental based on 5⅔ *artabai* per *aroura*. The case seems to reflect the sad fate of this farmer and others like him. As it is hard to imagine that three *arourai* (1½ acres) of arid land were his only source of livelihood, he must have worked other land as well. The description of the 3-*aroura* tract suggests that it was wasteland on the edge of the desert, which the Jewish farmer was evidently obliged to cultivate under orders, in accordance with the prevailing policy of conquering the desert and preparing additional land for agriculture. It thus appears that after the farmer invested hard labor in the parched soil and succeeded in improving it, the government representative (the village scribe) came and set a new rate that was applicable to productive land. The farmer felt he was defrauded as he had not even managed to reap the fruits of his toil,

---

167 Tcherikover copied only a few lines from the document; see *CPJ*, I 35.

168 The last two names are typical theophoric ones. See Tcherikover, *Jews in Egypt*, p. 11; *CPJ*, I (Introduction), p. xix.

169 The place is called Ghorân today. See details in Rostowzew, *Kolonatus*, p. 52.

and considered the new assessment to be arbitrary extortion and blatant exploitation.

A few meager pieces of information on Jewish "king's peasants" are provided in two lists of payers of tax (in kind) to the public granaries in the Fayûm, early in the first century B.C.E. (*CPJ*, I 44; 45). Another document (*CPJ*, I 42), of mid-second century B.C.E., lists five or six Jews paying what seems to be land taxes. The same is true of another document from the Arsinoite nome in the Fayûm (*CPJ*, I 47) but it is not clear whether the Jews were "king's peasants" or military settlers.

Document *CPJ*, I 126 from Arsinoe-Crocodilopolis in the Fayûm (238/7 B.C.E.), the testament of a man named Philo son of Hera-kleides, mentions a Jew as being a "debt slave". It states that "Apollonius, a resident alien, also known by the Syrian name of Jonathas, is a debtor in bond "according to a sentence recorded in the public archives" (lines 14-16)[170]. As the writer of the testament had the ethnic designation of "Cyrenean" (lines 6-7) and was a per-manent resident of the Fayûm, and as his witnesses were all "of the *Epigone*" (lines 21, 23, 25), he was obviously a military settler. Of special interest are the Jew's legal status and connection with the testament writer. Tcherikover's treatment of this text and his conclu-sion on this matter were correctly based on Westermann's investi-gation of the celebrated Rainer Papyrus, and he decided that this was an instance of a free man enslaved for debt, as was the case in the Rainer papyrus of "enslaved persons who are free"[171]. On the basis of the research of Westermann and others, Tcherikover established that Apollonius-Jonathas was "a free man" legally speaking, and that his enslavement was temporary pending the repayment of his debt. The two documents have several points in common. Both were written in the reign of Ptolemy II Philadelphus, and both mention "debt slavery". It is especially noteworthy that the Rainer papyrus too dealt with the enslavement of "free" natives from Syria and

---

170 The translation here is based on Tcherikover's textual reconstruction.
171 See Westermann, *AJPH*, 59 (1938), pp. 1-30. The papyrus was first published by Liebesny (*Aegyptus*, 14 (1936), p. 275f.; cf. *SB*, 8008), and it was in disagreement with his con-clusions that Westermann wrote his article. Tcherikover's reconstruction was done mainly by comparison with the terminology used in the Reiner papyrus in regard to "debt slaves" (line 23). *P. Col. Inv.*, 480, from 197 B.C.E., especially lines 23-24 can be added.

Phoenicia. The royal decree (*prostagma*) quoted in the document sought to limit the practice and even stated explicitly that nobody would be permitted on any pretext to buy or accept as security free men from among the natives, except the ones sold by the officer in charge of the revenue of Syria and Phoenicia when carrying out the sequestration of a person enslaved on the basis of the lease regulations[172]. The fact that document *CPJ*, I 126 notes explicitly that the "debt slavery" of Apollonius Jonathas was "in accordance with a sentence recorded in the public archives" (line 14) shows that the requirements of the royal decree cited in the Rainer papyrus were taken into account. That Apollonius Jonathas came from Palestine can be inferred from two points: the clarification "called the Syrian Jonathas" appended to his name, and his classification as a "resident alien" ($\pi\alpha\rho\epsilon\pi\acute{\iota}\delta\eta\mu\sigma\nu$, line 15)[178]. It is quite likely then that Apollonius-Jonathas had previously been "a free native" ($\lambda\alpha\iota\kappa\grave{o}\nu\ \dot{\epsilon}\lambda\epsilon\acute{\nu}\vartheta\epsilon\rho\sigma\nu$) like those mentioned in the Rainer papyrus, and had been taken into slavery by Philo son of Herakleides the Cyrenean because of debt, during the latter's military service in Palestine. The enslavement is easily understood against the background of the relations between a military settler and his tenants. At any rate it is agreed that it was at cases such as these that the *prostagma* of Ptolemy II Philadelphus (cited in the Rainer Papyrus) was directed. The fact that the testament of Philo son of Herakleides was executed at Crocodilopolis in the Fayûm was probably due to the transfer of his army unit to there[174]. It was only natural for him to take along to Egypt his slaves[175] including his Jewish "debt slave". In his will he bequeathed his slaves, along with his other property, to his wife and daughters, and probably the Jewish "debt slave" would continue to serve them until his debt was repaid.

Three other documents from the Fayûm are interesting. *CPJ*, I 38 is a complaint of a wool dealer from Crocodilopolis against a Jewish

---

172 See *SB*, 8008, recto, lines 12f.
173 Bickermann (*Archiv*, 8 (1929), p. 232) already recognized the origin of those called by this title outside of Egypt. Taubenschlag even distinguished clearly between "alien permanent residents" ($\xi\acute{\epsilon}\nu\sigma\iota\ \kappa\alpha\tau\sigma\iota\kappa\sigma\tilde{\upsilon}\nu\tau\epsilon\varsigma$) and "alient temporary residents" ($\pi\alpha\rho\epsilon\pi\iota\delta$-$\eta\mu\sigma\tilde{\upsilon}\nu\tau\epsilon\varsigma$), and supported the distinction in a number of examples, most of them from the period under consideration; see also his book, p. 590.
174 In the Fayûm there was a large concentration of Cyrenian military settlers.
175 These are mentioned in the document in lines 13-14.

shepherd named Seos from the village of Alabanthis, in 218 B.C.E., because the latter did not deliver the wool the dealer had bought and paid a deposit on before the shearing. The Egyptian name of the Jew and his occupation indicate his low status and civic stratification as a "native". The second document (*CPJ*, I 46), from the second or first century B.C.E., is an agreement between two Jewish potters from the "Syrian Village" and three Egyptian potters regarding the use of a workshop in the village of Neiloupolis owned by another Jew. The contract stipulates that they will pay the tax (φόρος) together, each according to his percentage in the partnership (lines 11-12) and most likely a government tax is meant. The occupation of the Jews, their partnership with Egyptian natives who were illiterate (lines 19-20), their being obliged to pay a government tax, the Egyptian name of one of them (line 1) and the fact that the Jewish owner of the workshop lived in an Egyptian village all point to their status as ordinary natives. The third document from mid-second century B.C.E. (*CPJ*, I 133) mentions a Jew who was one of the hired workers in an unnamed village in the Fayûm. Although his occupation was not specified, the fact that he was a day laborer suggests the status of native.

As to Upper Egypt, the ostraca from Diospolis-Magna (Thebes) might appear to provide information on the lower class Jews there, but in fact the available data are quite unclear. The ostraca served as receipts for payments to the granaries, and thus list farmers, but it is impossible to determine definitely which of them were "king's peasants" and which military settlers. It might be thought that a small payment would indicate a tenant on a small plot of land. In fact, however, some people had holdings that were scattered, and made various and separate payments accordingly[176], so that the farmer's economic situation cannot be deduced from the size of the payments. Still, an examination of receipts issued by the royal granaries during that period (edited by Wilcken and Tait) shows that the majority recorded small amounts no greater than ten *artabai*[177].

---

176 A good example is Hellen son of Dositheos, who paid $7^2/_3$ *artabai* for his holding in Thebes (*CPJ*, I 82), but at the same time paid $46^1/_3$ *artabai* for another holding in the Koptic nome (*ibid.*, 83). Another example is the case of Simon son of Horaios, who paid two sums in one year, 90 and 5¼ *artabai* (*CPJ*, I 91-92).

177 Wilcken's collection includes only six ostraca recording who paid more than 50 *artabai* (*WO*, 702, 710, 1253, 1254, 1341, 1342), and Tait's only another four (*O. Bodl.*, 147,

The same is true of the Jewish ostraca from Thebes where only four record amounts larger than fifty *artabai*[178]. Thus, despite the reservations noted above, it can be said that most of the small payments were made by small farmers settled as tenants on "king's land". Some of the receipts are for no more than five *artabai*. As that was the annual rate per *aroura*, evidently those small amounts were payments from the crops of especially tiny plots; some however represented partial payments, as in a number of other documents as well[179]. In short, it is reasonable to suppose that the farmers concerned had little land. The receipts for "chaff levy" were also relatively small, thus providing additional evidence of their penury[180]. Further support is deducible from the fact that one of the local Jews, who paid the royal granary 7½ *artabai* of wheat, was also a weaver (*CPJ*, I 95), an indication that his leased land alone must have provided only a very meager livelihood. His situation was strikingly different from that of another craftsman, the tax-farmer Simon son of Iazros, quite a wealthy man who paid 90 *artabai* on his property (*CPJ*, I 90). Another document (*CPJ*, I 94) mentions a Jew and his partners as paying 2½ *artabai* in all to the public granary. It is difficult to decide whether the term "partners" (οἱ μέτοχοι) refers to a group of farmers who leased a tract of land together, or tax farmers who also leased some land in partnership[181].

Not all the Theban farmers raised grain crops. Some had vineyards or orchards, as indicated by receipts for "wine tax" (*CPJ*, I 48-49), for *apomoira*, a tax levied on vineyard and orchard owners (*CPJ*, I 64, 70, 71, 72), and for "tax on the fruit trees" and "tax on the date trees" (*CPJ*, I 110-111). Generally the owners and even the lessees of orchards were in much better condition than ordinary peasants (wheat growers)[182], and this is evident from the Jewish ostraca of Thebes. A man who leased a date grove and paid a tax of two thousand drachmas for it (*CPJ*, I 110) was certainly a man of means. Another Jew, Apollonius son of Dositheos, an orchard owner

---

150, 159, 169).
178 *CPJ*, I 82, 83, 84, 90, 91.
179 See, e.g., documents *CPJ*, I 75, 78, 84, 96.
180 For details, see *CPJ*, I 97-103.
181 See details in Tcherikover, *CPJ*, I p. 195 and n.2; and also in his *Jews in Egypt*, p. 47 and n.40.
182 See Tcherikover, *ibid.*, pp. 59-60.

mentioned in *CPJ*, I 111, was undoubtedly wealthy. While the amount of tax he paid is not known (the ostracon is defective), he was a tax-farmer (for the *apomoira* — *CPJ*, I 70-72), and it was the Ptolemaic practice to assign tax farming to well-to-do men whose property constituted security for the payments.

Cattle and sheep raisers may also have enjoyed relative ease. Two ostraca from mid-second century B.C.E. mention Jews as paying "pasture tax" (*CPJ*, I 50, 108). Although it is not clear whether they were flock owners or tax-farmers[183], it is evident that there were Jews in Thebes who owned flocks (*CPJ*, I 104, 106). The "pasture tax" was paid for grazing flocks (of sheep or cattle) on royal land[184]. The tax payers were generally simple shepherds, sometimes flock owners forced to use royal land because no other pasture was available. One of the latter had 137 head of sheep and cattle (*CPJ*, I 106) and another 62 head (*CPJ*, I 104) so that they seem to have been quite prosperous. It is not clear, however, whether their only source of livelihood was their flocks. They may have engaged in another activity, and earned their living mainly from tilling the soil as military settlers. An example appears in *P. Tebt*, 882 (= *CPJ*, I 28) from Samareia in the Fayûm, which mentions Jewish military settlers who also had flocks.

The Theban ostraca also mention other artisans, among them a weaver (*CPJ*, I 95), dyers (*CPJ*, I 65), shoemakers (*CPJ*, I 66-68) and fishermen (*CPJ*, I 61-63, 107). The weaver was certainly not wealthy, as he engaged in both agriculture and weaving. As to the others, their economic situation cannot be verified, for the ostraca mentioning them record only the total sum delivered by the tax-farmers, and not the amount for each individual. By the nature of their work, however, they were simple people earning meager living by the sweat of their

---

183 The second possibility seems more likely, if we judge by the sum mentioned in one ostracon — 3,740 drachmas (*CPJ*, I 108), and by the fact that the second ostracon records two poeple who paid it jointly (*CPJ*, I 50); see Tcherikover's introductory remarks about "pasture-tax" (*CPJ*, I p. 196).

184 See Wilcken, *Grienchisch. Ostraka*, p. 191f. On the other hand, there were those who thought the tax was levied on all flock-owners (Rostovtzeff, *SEHHW*, p. 295), but it appears that this was not the case, for the tax levied on the owners according to the size of their herds is called τέλος προβάτων. About this distinction see Avogadro, *Aegyptus*, 14 (1934), p. 293f.; Wallace, *JEA*, 25 (1939), p. 60ff.; Wallace, *Taxation*, p. 37; Tcherikover, *Jews in Egypt*, p. 62.

brow. It seems proper therefore to place them on the lower rungs of
the social ladder, and that position was probably reflected in their
civic stratification[185] .

---

185 For supplementary details see Tcherikover's excellent survey, *CPJ*, I (Section V), p. 194f.

Chapter II

The Status of the Jews in the Roman Civic
Stratification

Scholars are in agreement that the Romans in Egypt adopted the Ptolemaic legal system without making any drastic changes, at least in the early period of the principate. Naturally juridical modifications were made in accordance with the political developments, so that royal legislation became imperial, and the king's regulation were replaced by those of the prefects. The basic distinction between the Egyptian legal systems and those applying to "Hellenes", however, remained in force.

It might be expected that the Romans, known for their pragmatic approach, would intensify the process of juridical leveling of the Ptolemaic period and recognize a single bloc of "Hellenes" that was homogeneous from the point of view of rights. In practice, however, although the term had a certain legal significance, a distinction was made among the several groupings it included. The Romans abandoned the ethnic and functional criteria for civic stratification, and introduced a simple, rigid administrative criterion. Their system stipulated that the civic status of inhabitants of Egypt was determined exclusively on the basis of the registration of place of residence and membership in local associations[1]. Like the Ptolemies, the Romans differentiated citizens of the *poleis* (Alexandria, Ptolemais, Naucratis and later also Antinoopolis) so that they were the highest stratum from the viewpoint of their legal status, albeit still inferior to Roman citizens. They were designated in official documents as *politai* or *astoi* and through their tribes (φυλαί) or demes (δῆμοι)[2]. Permanent residents of those cities who were not citizens (of the *poleis*) had the right of *origo*, which gave them certain privileges compared with

---

1 See Bickermann, *Archiv*, 9 (1930), pp. 24ff., esp. 36-41.
2 For more detailed information about the rights of this class, see Taubenschlag, pp. 582-609.

temporary residents and Egyptian natives. But the important thing is
that all the non-citizens were designated without exception in official
documents as οἱ ἀπὸ... (= those from...); thus it was their place of
residence or membership in local political associations that determined their status. From the Roman legal standpoint, all of them
were considered at least theoretically *peregrini dediticii* (= foreign
subjects) who must pay the *laographia* (poll-tax), indicating they
were deemed Egyptian natives[3]. Still, the Romans recognized a need
to make things easier for certain sectors of that population, in particular for those considered "Hellenes" because of their descent,
education, or political organization. They were not exempt, but
paid a reduced tax. In practice they were a middle class, between the
citizens of the Greek *poleis* and the rural native population. In this
manner the term "Hellenes" acquired recognized legal meaning[4] that
covered three distinct groups: a) descendants of military settlers
(κάτοικοι); b) "those of the gymnasium" (οἱ ἀπὸ γυμνασίου); c)
residents of the *metropoleis* (οἱ ἀπὸ μετροπόλεως). A special test
called the ἐπίκρισις determined whether the inhabitants belonged
to one of those sectors, and those who passed the test were called
ἐπικεκριμένοι[5]. Their "Hellenism" was thus not decided on an ethnic
basis[6], but through a legal and political criterion. In her study of
Augustus' third Cyrenean edict, Atkinson showed that the term
"Hellenes" was applied to inhabitants of all races who belonged to
certain groups composed of persons with various privileges[7]. The
Romans took the three groups of "Hellenes" into account for two
main reasons: a) Most had enjoyed similar privileges under the
Ptolemies, and the Romans endeavored to keep to the old arrangements as much as possible and b) they provided the manpower for
the Roman administration throughout the *chora*. This was true in
particular of gymnasium graduates who were the elite of the *metro-*

---

3 Taubenschlag, p. 588; and cf. with Bickermann also, *ibid.*, 40-42.

4 Thus, e.g., the 6475 "Hellenes" from the Arsinoite nome of the Fayûm, and also the
  "Hellenes" in the Delta and in Thebes (*OGIS*, 709), and see details in Bickermann, *ibid.*,
  42ff.

5 See Bickermann, *ibid.*, 30f.; Wilcken-Mitteis, *Gründzüge der Papyruskunde*, pp. 216ff.;
  Wallace, *Taxation*, p. 109; Taubenschlag, p. 640; *CPJ*, I pp. 59-61.

6 The Romans knew very well that the descendants of the Greeks in the Eastern provinces
  did not preserve their racial purity, not even in the Greek *poleis*. Sometimes this fact was
  even a subject of scorn and derision, as can be seen, e.g., in Livy, XXXVIII 17, 3.

7 Atkinson, *Ancient Society*, pp. 21-26. Cf. also Tcherikover, *Jews in Egypt*, p. 135.

poleis and filled all the municipal positions. Gymnasium education may be said to have become an important criterion for civic stratification in the Roman period. It was very strictly supervised, to the point of leaving no room for the type of individual initiative that was possible in the Ptolemaic period[8].

A. The Jews as Roman Citizens

There were three ways of acquiring Roman citizenship: military service, manumission, and imperial award. Theoretically, only Roman citizens could serve in the Roman legions, but in practice, due to the manpower shortage, *peregrini* (= foreigners) too, selected from among the *epikekrimenoi*, could serve, and thereby become Roman citizens[9]. Prima facie, Jews too could serve in the legions, for many were Roman citizens. However, their absence is a definite fact, particularly in comparison with their considerable presence in the Hellenistic armies. The exemption from military service granted to Jews (who were Roman citizens) from Asia Minor during the Civil Wars (49-43 B.C.E.) was explained on religious grounds[10], and it is illuminating that one of the men who granted the exemption — Lucius Lentulus Crus — had been despatched by the Senate to recruit two legions in Asia[11]. Tacitus testified that in the deliberations of the Roman Senate (during the reign of the emperor Tiberius) on proscription of the Egyptian and Jewish rites, it was decided that four thousand of them, of the freedmen class (*libertini*) would be mobilized and sent to Sardinia to destroy the bandits, in the hope that they would perish in the oppressive climate. Josephus adds an important point, that many who refused to serve in the army because they wished to abide by their ancestral law were exiled from Rome[12]. In regard to Tiberius Julius Alexander, a nephew of Philo's who had a brilliant career in the Roman army[13], Josephus stressed that his

---

8 Taubenschlag, p. 639; see additional details in Tcherikover, *ibid.*, pp. 131-136.
9 Segré, *Atti della Pont. Accad. Rom. di Archeol,* 17 (1940-41), p. 167ff.; Taubenschlag, p. 621.
10 *Antiquitates*, XIV 225-232, 234, 236-240; cf. also XVI 28.
11 Caesar, *Bell. Civ.*, III 4.
12 See Tacitus, *Annales*, II 85; and cf. also Suetonius, *Tiberius*, 36; Jos., *Antiquitates*, XVIII 84. It is interesting that according to Suetonius, some of those deported tended toward beliefs like theirs; but it is not clear if he meant those inclining towards Judaism.
13 For full details about him, see Burr, *Tiberius Julius Alexander.*

religion differed from his father's, and that he "did not stand by the
practice of his people" (*Antiquitates*, XX 100). It is no wonder that
as the highest ranking officer at Titus' headquarters he participated
in the siege of Jerusalem, and he may even have been responsible for
burning the Temple down. Two of his descendants who bore the
same name followed in his foot-steps in military careers, and went
further than he had in regard to religion[14]. Evidently service in the
Roman legions was a serious constraint for Jews, and probably led
to conversion[(x)]. It was otherwise in the Hellenistic armies where
ethnic and religious groups (including Jews) were allowed to maintain
their own units, and were not required to conform to an official
religion. The life of the Roman legion, on the contrary, included
obligatory religious elements such as the *auspicia*, *signa* and *auguria*,
ceremonials, sacrifices, oaths, and the imperial cult[15]. Consequently,
it is not likely that for Jews service in the Roman army was a common
means of obtaining Roman citizenship. From the standpoint of religious obligations and the risk of conversion, service in the legion
differed from that in the auxiliary forces (*auxilia*) and indeed there is
considerable evidence that Jews served in the latter throughout
the empire[16].

Traces of Jewish soldiers in the Roman army in Egypt are discernible only in a single ostracon, of 116 C.E., found in the Jewish
quarter of Apollinopolis Magna (*CPJ*, II 229). It is a receipt for the
payment of the "Jewish tax" by the slave of a centurion (commander
of a *centuria*, a 100-man unit) named Άνινιος. Even a cursory
inspection shows that the centurion was Jewish, for his name is a
Greek transcription of the Hebrew Ḥanina (or Ḥanani or Ḥananiah)[17],
especially since the same name appears on another ostracon dated

---

14 See details in Schürer, vil. 1, p. 568, n.9.

(*) In the time of Hadrian's persecutions there is mentioned " אסטרטיום אחד משומד ",
     see *Bereshith Rabbah*, 82,9 (Albeck ed., p. 985); see also Alon, *History of the Jews*,
     vol. 2, p. 59; and cf. also Appolebaum, "Jewish Diaspora etc.", p. 56.

15 See Applebaum, *Roman Frontier Studies*, pp. 181-184.

16 In fact, most of the material gathered by Juster on Jewish military service for Rome
     deals with auxiliary troops (see Juster, vol. 2, p. 269f.). Tcherikover criticized his conclu-
     sions harshly and correctly (see *Jews in Egypt*, p. 43; cf. *CPJ*, I (Prolegomena), p. 52 and
     n.12.

17 The possibility that the slave was a Jew is unacceptable, not only because of his Egyptian
     name (in contrast to the Jewish name of the *centurio*), but also for other reasons. See
     Tcherikover, *CPJ*, II Section IX, 3 (p. 114).

107 C.E.[18]. In view of the general Roman practice, the fact that a Roman centurion was Jewish must evoke surprise. Even more amazing is the fact that a Jewish centurion was retained in 116 C.E., that is, during the Jewish revolt in Trajan's reign. But a careful examination of the chronology reveals that the revolt in Egypt spread to the Edfu region only after the date on the ostracon (18 May 116) though very shortly after it. In fact that date is the latest known for the regular collection of the "Jewish tax" in Edfu, after which there is an archaeological hiatus regarding Jews until 151 C.E.[18]. Probably the Jewish centurion was demobilized when the revolt spread to his area. Even so, the centurion's clearly Jewish name itself represents a difficulty, because it may indicate that he did not deny his Jewish identity, which does not fit in with Roman military service (as a centurion at that). The only explanation is that the man was a centurion in an auxiliary unit rather than in a legion.

Another document (*CPJ*, II 405) from the Jewish quarter of Edfu mentions a Jew named Jesous son of Papios as a δεκανός (commander of ten). He might have served as a low-ranking officer (*decurio*) in one of the Roman auxiliary units, for he was not a Roman citizen, and other documents referring to him indicate that he paid the *laographia*[20]. The fact that he was not a Roman citizen is evident as well from his name and the Egyptian and Jewish names of the others mentioned along with him. All in all it is more reasonable to suppose that he was a police officer, as Jews were in other places in Egypt (e.g. *P. Tebt.*, 27; *P. Oxy.*, 387).

No information on Jewish soldiers among regular Roman troops in Egypt is available for later periods either. On the other hand, one document (*CPJ*, III 463) from the end of the second century, a list of soldiers in an auxiliary unit, contains information on Jews, in the opinion of its publisher[21]. The document is in a bad state of preservation, and the only traces of Jews are the letters *Ebra* which may be reconstructed as *Ebra[eos]*, and the name Abdior which sounds

---

18 *CPJ*, II 212; it is even possible that it was the same man. Both ostraca were receipts for the payment of the "Jewish tax" by slaves bearing Egyptian names, and both were found in the Jewish quarter Delta. The time difference (nine years) does not obviate such a possibility.

19 See below, p. 151f.; see also Tcherikover, *Jews in Egypt*, p. 171f.; Applebaum, *Jews and Greeks in Ancient Cyrene*, pp. 265ff.

20 *CPJ*, II 298, 304, 311, 321.

21 See *P. Mich.*, VII 448.

Semitic. The interpretation may be correct; in any case, the unit in question is an auxiliary unit and not a regular Roman legion.

Another document, *P. Oxy.*, 735, of 205 C.E. has likewise been cited as attesting to Jews serving in Roman legions[22]. The conclusion is dubious, however, since it has been shown that although they sound Semitic, most of the names are not Jewish[23].

A number of documents from Karanis in the Fayûm (from early second century) relate to a legion officer called Julius Apollonaris[24] whose grandmother was named Sambathion. Tcherikover showed that doubt must be cast on the Jewishness of many persons bearing that name who lived in Roman Egypt, and that their involvement with people bearing Egyptian and Greek names was especially common in the villages of Karanis and Theadelphia in the second century C.E.[25] The members of Julius Apollonaris' family had a mixture of Roman, Greek and Egyptian names; thus it was most probably a Hellenized Egyptian family that gained Roman citizenship through past military service. The nature of the family is indicated also by their references to Egyptian deities, so that Tcherikover's view that they were not Jewish can be unhesitatingly accepted.

Summing up the evidence on Jews in the regular Roman army, it can be asserted that there is not a single document attesting that Jews in the Roman legion remained Jewish. If some Jew became a Roman citizen through such military service, he undoubtedly converted and abandoned Judaism, so that this case is irrelevent.

The second way of acquiring Roman citizenship was through manumission, and that method was more common not only in Egypt but in all the provinces of the Roman empire. The earliest reference to this process in Egypt (from 13 B.C.E.) concerns an imperial freedman ($\kappa\alpha\iota\sigma\alpha\rho\sigma\varsigma$)[26], but no other information is available on the

---

22 See, e.g., Juster, vol. 2, p. 274, n.3; Fuchs, pp. 42, 50f.

23 Tcherikover, in his commentary on the same document (*CPJ*, III 465), correctly supported the conclusion that the names originated in Palmyra.

24 *P. Mich.*, VII 465-466, 486-487 (and see *CPJ*, III 486 a-b). His rank was *Principalis* and *liberarius legionis*. He was very well integrated in the Roman army, as is apparent from his letters to his family, which are written in typical military language.

25 See a detailed discussion on the subject of "Sambathions" in his book, *Jews in Egypt*, p. 194f., especially pp. 196-197; and also *CPJ*, III p. 43f. The large number of women's names can be understood in view of the fact that Karanis was the site of a cult to the goddess named Sambatis.

26 If Schubart's reconstruction is correct ($\kappa\alpha\iota\sigma\alpha[\rho\sigma\varsigma]$ – *BGU*, 1129), cf. also *M. Chr.*, 254;

man, not even his full Roman name. He was called Tryphon son of Simon, and he purchased from a very wealthy Alexandrian citizen a tract of $49^{11}/_{16}$ *arourai* of *"Katoikic* land" in the Busirite nome of Lower Egypt. It is not clear whether he acquired the land for himself or acted as agent for his Roman master, and some knowledge on this point would have clarified his situation. At any rate, his title, καίσαρος, should not lead to the conclusion that he belonged to the urban Alexandrian tribe of that name, which is first mentioned in Nero's time[27], especially since the citizenship of Jews in the Alexandrian *polis* is inconceivable (see below).

The other information on Jewish *libertini* comes from ostraca found in the Jewish quarter of Apollinopolis Magna (Edfu). For instance, in Vespasian's time, there is reference to a whole Jewish family whose head was a Roman citizen named Antonius Rufus[28] Tcherikover logically deduced that he was a freedman who was called by the name of his master, of the Antonian clan (*gens Antonia*)[29]. A number of questions arise. Was he born a slave or captured? If he was a captive, where and when was he taken? And when was he freed? These questions are practically unanswerable, mainly because there is no direct information on him. References to him appear in ostraca that were receipts for various taxes paid by his sons. The earliest is from 70 C.E. (*CPJ*, II 239) and cites his son Nikon. The latter was then quite an old man, because there is an ostracon of the same year referring to his grandson Tryphas[30]. Thus we know only that the father of the family was a *libertinus* at around the middle of the first century A.D. However, astonishing, Antonius Rufus' sons and grandsons were not Roman citizens, for they paid the *laographia*[31]. How can this be explained, since under the republic and the first emperors the title of *libertinus* was generally applied also to descendants, who were exempt from the poll-tax (*tributum capitis*)[32]? The explanation is that not all freedmen gained

---

CPJ, II 145.
27 See details on the subject in Schubart, *Archiv*, 5 (1909), p. 94, n.3. On the legal status of freedmen so designated in the reign of Augustus, see *ibid.*, pp. 116-118.
28 For details on the family see *CPJ*, II Index, s.v., and also the geneological chart in *CPJ*, II p. 117.
29 See *ibid.*, p. 116.
30 See *CPJ*, II 238, and see also No. 237, from 69 C.E.
31 *Ibid.*, 239, 243, 246, 248, 249, 253, etc.
32 Cf. Suetonius, *Claudius*, 24; and see details in Duff, *Freedmen*, pp. 51f., 71.

Roman citizenship. It was Augustus who sought to bloc the proliferation of freedmen by initiating various technical restrictions. The
Lex Aelia Sentia of 4 C.E., for instance, established a new status for
libertini suspected of committing crimes or disturbing public order
(such as during the last civil wars) so that when freed they were legally
known as *dediticii* (= subjects). This policy of Augustus' had already
been evident in an earlier law, *Lex Iunia* (of 17 B.C.E.) which awarded
freedmen the status of Latin citizens (*Latini Iuniani*) who were only
potentially Roman citizens. Legally they were freed before being
found worthy of bearing the full responsibility of Roman citizens-
ship or their emancipation was unofficial (*manumissio minus iusta*)
being unaccompanied by the formal ceremonies required to be legally
complete. In short, they were *libertini*, no longer enslaved, but their
Roman citizenship was conditional. The *Lex Aelia Sentia* further
restricted the right to Latin citizenship to people past thirty. The
provision was designed to limit the number of freedmen among a
former slave's offspring, on the theory that he was likely to be less
prolific when older. Another provision stipulated that the unofficial
libertini could not request Roman citizenship for any child at all.
All these applied up to 75 C.E.[33] As for Antonius Rufus, he can
reasonably be assumed to have been an unofficial freedman with
intermediate status. In other words, he did not automatically acquire
Roman citizenship when he was freed, and even if he did gain it some
time or other, it did not apply to his sons. Satisfactory as this
explanation is, the date of the first ostracon — 70 C.E. — suggests
another alternative. It is possible that the family was enslaved following the Zealotic ferment that beset the Jews of Egypt from 66 C.E.
on (*Bellum* VII 499ff.) and freed a short time later. Or perhaps the
father was taken to Egypt as a rebel from Judaea long before, and
freed prior to 66 C.E.

Another Rufus, Achillas Rufus[34], was probably connected with
the same clan (*gens*) and family. That was initially Tcherikover's
view[35], but in discussing *CPJ*, II 378 he changed his mind and was
inclined to assign him to the Caecilii. His reason was that Achillas

---

33 Fuller details of these problems and of the laws dealing with the "libertini" are provided
   in Duff, *Freedman*, pp. 72-82, 210f. (App. I).
34 *OE*, 168-195; and see *CPJ*, II Index 2, s.v.
35 *Jews in Egypt*, p. 157.

Rufus paid the wine-tax for a Rufus, "Sara's freedman", whom Tcherikover believed to be a member of the Rufii family, and since three other documents[36] refer to another Sara who had a freedman named Caecilias, he attached all of them to the same clan. The geneology is however speculative. Tcherikover himself realized that the Saras had to be differentiated, for one is mentioned as of 162 C.E. (*CPJ*, II 378) and the other in 75 and 80 C.E. (*CPJ*, II 171, 179, 180), and undoubtedly she cannot be the same woman. If the likelihood that they were both converts to Judaism is accepted, their identical names are easily explained, as the name Sara was common in such cases[37]. In this connection it should be recalled that at the end of the republican period, one of the Caecilii, nameed Quintus Caecilius Niger, who was the *quaestor* of Veres, governor of Sicily, was suspected of adhering to the Jewish faith[38]. The dictionary of Suidas also contains an interesting item regarding a member of that clan, a rhetor named Caecilius, likewise from Sicily in the reign of Augustus, who was "a Jew in his faith" (τὴν δε δόξαν Ἰουδαῖος). Schürer had difficulty in deciding the source of his Judaism, as there are two possibilities: either he was the son of a Jewish *libertinus*, or he converted[39]. One way or the other, he was definitely a Jew and a member of the Caecilii. In view of these data and those from Apollinopolis Magna regarding the Caecilian convert Sara and her freedman, evidently conversion to Judaism or the manumission of Jewish slaves was not uncommon in that clan, which should thus be added to the list of clans sympathizing with Jews that Stern wrote of[40] Furthermore, "Sara's freedman" was called Ἀκυντᾶς Κακιλλίας[41], which is no doubt a somewhat distorted transliteration of the Roman name, Quintus Caecilius. Is that name only accidentally identical with that of Veres' *quaestor*, who was suspected of being Jewish? Although there is a lapse of time, names often recurred in families in succeeding generations. Since the first ostracon mentioning

---

36 *CPJ*, II 171, 179, 180.
37 Cf. *CIJ*, I 523; and see also Leon, *The Jews of Ancient Rome*, p. 254.
38 Plutarch, *Cicero*, 7, 5; and scholars have commented that Plutarch was wrong in supposing him to have been a freedman. See Th. Reinach, *REJ*, 26 (1893), p. 36f.; Schürer, vol. 3, p. 632; Leon, *ibid.*, pp. 15-16.
39 See Schürer, vol. 3, pp. 629-633 and especially p. 630.
40 Stern, *Zion*, 29 (1964), p. 155f.
41 *CPJ*, II 171, 180.

Akyntas Kaekilias has been dated 75 C.E., the man was probably captured between 66 and 73 C.E. (if not earlier) and freed shortly after the latter date. He may possibly have been brought to Egypt as a war captive, or taken as a slave in Egypt itself in the course of the disturbances in the wake of the revolt in Judaea. Finally it should be noted that his Roman citizenship did not exempt him from paying the "Jewish tax"[42].

Three other Jews with Roman names are Marcus Annis, mentioned in an ostracon of 78 C.E. (*CPJ*, II 268), Marcus Verrius, mentioned in an ostracon of 71 C.E. (*CPJ*, II 241) and Verrius, grandson of Tedisos (perhaps a relative of Marcus Verrius), mentioned in an ostracon of 93/4 C.E. (*CPJ*, II 293). All three appear to have had Roman citizenship, acquired through manumission, like *Akyntas Kaekilias*.

Two Jews with Roman names, a man and woman, appear in a document of 85 C.E. from Oxyrhynchus (*CPJ*, II 423 = *P. Oxy.*, 335). The man Paulus sold one sixth of a house in the Jewish quarter to Nicea Silvanus, daughter of Psoubius. These names are not based on clan names, but are *praenomina*, which were widely adopted in the Roman period. Consequently, it is by no means certain that their bearers in this case were in fact Roman citizens[43]. The law in Roman Egypt did not, it is true, permit the free choice of names, and any name change required a special license and administrative supervision. But how misleading Roman names could be as to civic status is shown by the fact that the sons of Antionius Rufus of Edfu, who were called Niger, paid the *laographia*. If there were nevertheless two Jews mentioned in *CPJ*, II 423 as Roman citizens, they must have acquired the status through manumission.

Another ostracon from the Jewish quarter of Apollinopolis Magna is a double receipt for the payment of the *laographia* and other taxes by Senpeamys son of Achillas Rufus, and for the payment of some unspecified taxes by a person whose father was Licinius (*CPJ*, II 398). The name shows the latter was a Roman citizen belonging to one of the prominent Roman clans. It is not certain that he paid the poll-tax, but seems likely in view of the first part of the ostracon.

---

42 For another example of this type see *CPJ*, II 199, from 103 C.E.

43 The same is true of the name of Sambathion, daughter of Sabinius, who is mentioned in a document from 73 C.E. in Arsinoë in the Fayûm (*CPJ*, II 421).

If so, his father Licinius acquired Roman citizenship as the Rufus described above did, that is, as a freedman, without the right of bequeathing that status to his offspring. The date of the ostracon, 159 C.E., suggests he may have been born in slavery, and that his father was taken into slavery when the Jewish revolt in Egypt was suppressed in Trajan's reign. It is equally possible, however, that he himself was brought to Egypt as a slave after the Bar-Kokhba revolt.

Finally there is Pollia Maria, a young woman from Thebes (*CPJ*, III 462a-h) who lived in the middle of the second century C.E. Her Roman name may seem a bit strange, as though based on two clan names (*nomina gentilicia*), Pollius and Marius. The name Maria, however, may be a definitely Jewish name, but romanized[44]. This possibility is supported by two Jewish ostraca from Apollinopolis Magna (*CPJ*, II 223, 227) of 114-116 C.E mentioning two women by that name, although their patronymics are no clue to their Roman citizenship. The case is otherwise with Pollia Maria, who was clearly a Roman citizen of the Pollius clan. The adjective "young" attached to her name may mean that her mother bore the same name, indicating that the younger woman acquired her citizenship by inheritance. There is no way of knowing whether the woman's family were originally Jewish, or converts. The second alternative is not likely because in that case the conversion would have taken place at about the time of the Jewish revolt (115-117 C.E.) and it is hard to believe that Judaism then attracted Roman citizens. On the other hand, the timing is right for the first alternative; that is, she was a member of a Jewish family taken into slavery when the revolt in Trajan's reign was suppressed, and was later freed by her Roman master.

The third way to acquire Roman citizenship was by imperial grant, but the number of Jews in Egypt during the principate who bore the names of an imperial clan is extremely small. We know in all of two Jews from Alexandria, one called Iulianus (*CIJ*, II 1439) and the other Iulianus Isaac (*CIJ*, II 1446), but it is not known whether they were actually connected with the Julii[45]. There is also a reference in a first or second century ostracon from Edfu (Apollino-

---

44 See Stern's explanations in the introduction to the above-mentioned documents (in n.2).

45 We know that one of the descendants of Tiberius Julius Alexander was also called Julianus (see n.56 below). It is not impossible, therefore, that there was some sort of connection between people of such names and Tiberius Julius Alexander.

polis Magna) of one Arthenatas son of Julius (*CPJ*, II 408b) whose
Roman citizenship may have been inherited from a father who was
granted it by one of the émperors in gratitude for some service; he
may however have been a freedman of one of the Julian families[46].

Better examples of Roman citizenship acquired by imperial grant
are found in the family of Tiberius Julius Alexander. Information on
them comes from quite numerous sources and has been dealt with in
the literature, but there is no agreement on who granted them citizenship. Some scholars contended that it was Julius Caesar or Augustus, on the basis of the founders name — Gaius Julius Alexander —
but the majority believed it was Tiberius, which impelled the father
to name his first-born Tiberius Julius Alexander[47]. The father was a
landowner in Euhemeria of the Fayûm[48], a successful banker, and
supervisor of the finances of Antonia, the mother of the emperor
Claudius[49]. His commercial and social connections in Italy provided
access even to the political arena. Consequently it is not at all surprising that he was awarded Roman citizenship by direct imperial
grant. According to Josephus he was also involved in the high Roman
officialdom in Egypt as Ἀλαβάρχης or, as scholars prefer, Ἀραβάρχης,
that is, the inspector-in-chief of the customs duties collected on the
eastern (i.e. Arab) borders of Egypt[50].

His son had a most impressive military career in the empire. His
first known appointment was as *epistrategos* of the Thebaid in Upper
Egypt in 42 C.E., and it does not appear to be coincidental that his
brother Marcus Julius Alexander conducted profitable business in the
reign at the time (*CPJ*, II 419). After that he was procurator of Judaea
in 46-48. He seems not to have neglected the economic interests of
his family while absent from Egypt, for during his incumbency
Queen Helene of Adiabene purchased grain in Egypt to alleviate the
famine in Judaea. In 63 he took part in the campaign against the

---

46 Thus, e.g., the noted Jewish rich man, Gaius Julius Alexander (whose way of acquiring
    citizenship will be discussed later) and a land agent named Gaius Julius Amarantus, who
    apparently attained Roman citizenship as a freedman, and so also bore the name of his
    paster (except for the *cognomen*, of course), as was customary in such cases. About this
    man, see *CPJ*, II 420a.
47 About him see *CPJ*, II 420, where bibliographical details are given.
48 See Fuks, *CPJ*, II 419-420.
49 *Antiquitates*, XIX 276.
50 *Antiquitates*, XVIII 159, 259; XIX 276; XX 100. See Schürer, vol. 3, p. 132f. (N.9);
    CPJ, I p. 49, n.4.

Parthians as commander of the troops sent from Egypt to reinforce
Corbulo (Tacitus, *Annales*, XV 20). In 66 Nero appointed him
praefectus Aegypti and he was in charge of containing the Jewish
uprising that erupted in Alexandria at the time of the Great Revolt
in Judaea. He left his mark on Egyptain life through an important
edict issued in 68 designed to remedy a number of administrative
deficiencies such as official corruption, inequitable taxation, ineffi-
cient tax collection, calumny, oppression, etc.[51] On 1 July 69,
Tiberius Julius Alexander announced his recognition of Vespasian
as emperor, and the day became the coronation day (*dies imperii*) of
the new ruler[52]. At the end of 69 or beginning of 70, he was transferred to Titus' headquarters in Judaea, to suppress the Great
Revolt[53]. According to Josephus (*Bellum*, VI 237) he was appointed
"the prefect of all the forces", and this is confirmed by an inscription from Arados[54]; in other words, he was Titus' highest ranking
officer, second only to him. He reached the pinnacle of his career in
70, with his appointment as *praefectus praetorio* (commander
of the imperial bodyguard) in Rome[55]. His children seem to have
followed in his footsteps and had impressive military and political
careers. One of them — Julius Alexander — served as *legatus* when
Emperor Trajan was fighting the Parthians; in 117 he was consul, and
in 118-119 a member of the collegium of Roman priests[56]. Another
son, also named Tiberius Julius Alexander, was commander of the
first Cohort Flavia, and *agoranomos* (= market supervisor) of the B
quarter of Alexandria during the reign of Antoninus Pius[57].

---

51 See *P. Hibeh*, II 135; Burr, *Tiberius Julius Alexander*, p. 100.

52 Tacitus, *History*, II 74; see Burr, *ibid.*, pp. 60f., 103, n.37. See also *CPJ*, II 418a.

53 One of the epigraphic finds shows that even when he was Prefect in Egypt he helped
    put down the rebellion in Judaea by lending Agrippas II one of his cohorts; see Avi-
    Yonah, *IEJ*, 16 (1966), pp. 258-264.

54 *OGIS*, 586 = *CIG*, III 4536(f).

55 See *P. Hibeh*, 215 = *CPJ*, II 418(b). Turner, who published the papyrus (see also Turner,
    JRS, 44 (1954), p. 61f.) suggested two possibilities: a) he filled this post when he was
    Titus' chief of staff, and this is indicated by his title in Josephus and in the Arados'
    inscription, or b) he was appointed later, and his title in the papyrus refers to the post of
    commander of the Pretorian guard in Rome itself (*P. Hibeh*, 215, line 7).

56 See Schürer, (ed. Vermes & Millar), vol. 1, p. 458 n.9. His full name was Ti(berius)
    Julius Alexander Julianus.

57 See *OGIS*, 705, and also Hirschfeld, *Verwaltungsbeamten*[3], p. 235. From this they
    deduced that the B quarter was the second Jewish quarter of those mentioned by Philo
    (*In Flaccum*, 55), one of which was called by Josephus, but this seems very doubtful.

The family of Julius Alexander thus produced rotten fruit in the
persons of these apostate careerists. The departure from Judaism of
the first of these (Tiberius Julius Alexander) evoked a vigorous response in the family, as attested to by the considerable intellectual
effort applied by his celebrated uncle, Philo[58]. History has however
ironically decreed that the son of one of the most generous contributors to the Temple in Jerusalem (*Bellum*, V 201-205), and perhaps
a member of a priestly family[59], should be one of the men primarily
responsible for its destruction. As to Philo himself, there is no evidence that he was a Roman citizen, although in view of his family
and his own lofty status, he probably was.

All in all, there is a paucity of data on Jews holding Roman citizenship in Alexandria. Presumably there were many such Jews in
that city, as there were in other cities of the empire, in Asia Minor,
for instance. Because of local climatic conditions, however, papyrus
documents have not survived and a reliable picture cannot be drawn.

B. Jews as Descendants of Military Settlers

As noted above, the offspring of military settlers belonged to the
intermediate class, the "Hellenes", but had two great advantages
compared with others of their status: a) They enjoyed a greater
reduction in the *laographia* they paid, and were sometimes even
exempt; b) In practice, their holdings were viewed as private land[60].

Quite clear information on such Jews has come down from the
reign of Augustus. The earliest document, (*CPJ*, II 142-143) from
13-14 C.E., refers to two brothers described as "Macedonians", who
owned land in the Alexandrian *chora* near the "Syrian village"
(*ibid.*, 142, lines 3-11). Josephus too mentions such Jews in Alexandria: "Down to the present time their local tribe bore the name of
Macedonians" (*C. Apionem*, II 36). Leaving aside the question of
their rights in Alexandria, it can be stated that they were descendants of the most prestigious *katoikoi*, and apparently for that reason
remained in possession of land in the *chora* of Alexandria. It appears

---

58 It was for this purpose that he wrote his essay *De Providentia*. See, e.g., Wolfson, *Philo*,
    I p. 53.
59 See Schürer, vol. 3, p. 636.
60 See, e.g., Oehler, *RE(PW)*, XI 1, p. 201; *British Museum Papyri*, 260, p. 124f.

that during the Ptolemaic period there was some military connection between the Jewish "Macedonian" unit in Alexandria and the neighboring "Syrian village". While there is no definite proof that the village was inhabited by descendants of military settlers, a hint that was the case is suggested by the fact that one of the "Macedonian" Jews had land bordering on the village land, and had real estate actually within it as well (*CPJ*, II 142, lines 18-19). The property included homes and other buildings and had previously belonged to a woman named Aristion daughter of Ariston (*ibid.*)[61]. The woman's possession of such property is explainable on the assumption that she acquired it by inheritance from her father who was a military settler and a man of status in the village at the end of the Ptolemaic period. Furthermore, the woman seems to have been a Jewess and a sister-in-law to a Jew named Theodoros, for his wife was called Dionysia daughter of Ariston (*ibid.*, 141, lines 2, 20). Probably Aristion died childless and her sister Dionysia and brother-in-law Theodoros therefore inherited her property.

Another document (*BGU*, 1129 = *CPJ*, II 145) of 13 B.C.E., an συγχώρησις (= agreement) on the sale of a property, provides information on the presence in the Bousirite district of Lower Egypt of descendants of Jewish *katoikoi*. The description of the borders of that property, which belonged to a wealthy Alexandrian citizen, mentions two other properties, one "the land of Ḥelkias" (Χελκίου γῆ, *ibid.*, line 16) and the other "the land of Heron and Ḥelkias" ("Ηρωνος καὶ Χελκίου γη, *ibid.*, lines 16-17). Schubart, who published the papyrus first, believed that "the land of Ḥelkias" previously belonged to Cleopatra III's famous commander. Fuks, however, suggested that since two properties naming Helkias are mentioned, it is more logical to assume the ownership at the time by a man of that name of both properties, one in partnership with Heron. At most, the name was given to the man because the Jews of the place were fond of the famous commander. At any rate, the document leaves no doubt that it was "*katoikic* land" (*ibid.*, line 11). Evidently the purchaser, Tryphon son of Simon, wished to buy land in a Jewish neighborhood,

---

61 The woman's name is unclear (line 18) as follows: 'Αριστίου τῆς 'Αριστίωνος. To me it appears that this is not the inevitable reconstruction of the name, and that it is possible to delete the ι after the τ so that it reads 'Αριστωνος ; on the conclusion arising from this, see below.

so that there must have been a considerable concentration in the place of descendants of Jewish military settlers[62].

For the period after Augustus' reign, information relating to Jews of that category is sparser. The 66 C.E. document, *P. Ryl.*, 154 (which is not included in the *Corpus Papyrorum Judaicarum*) mentions a tract of land near the village of Bacchias in the northern Fayûm, defined as "*katoikic* land" (κλῆρον κατοικικὸν), that was called Σάδη (= field, in Hebrew). Such a name most likely derived from the military settlement in the Ptolemaic period. Although the names mentioned in the document are not Jewish, their bearers may well have been. At any rate, if the owners of a *katoikic* property called *Sadeh* were not Jewish, they acquired the property from Jews who had a military past.

A document from Oxyrhynchus (*P. Oxy.*, 270) of 94 C.E. may likewise refer to descendants of Jewish military settlers. It mentions "*katoikic* land" connected with the adjacent "Syrian village", which suggests a possible Jewish origin (cf. below, Chap. III, pp. 144-146). Other documents from Oxyrhynchus (*CPJ*, II 445, 448) contain hints at confiscation of Jewish land and property there after the great Jewish uprising in Trajan's time, and the original Jewish ownership could be explained on the basis of the military past of their ancestors.

Document *CPJ*, III 453 of 132 C.E. from the Hermoupolite district mentions two farmers from the village of Magdola-Mire who wished to lease a tract of "*katoikic* land". It was owned by two women only one of whom, Tryphania daughter of Nearchos, is named. For the signing of the contract she was represented by her son, "Hermaios also called Phibion son of Onias" (*ibid.*, lines 20-21). All those involved in the transaction may well have been of Jewish descent, because the joint ownership suggests that the two women were related and inherited the land together; thus Stern seem to have been justified in his interpretation that the women were descendants of Jewish military settlers. The name "Onias" lends further support to this supposition, particularly in this location to which a tradition of Jewish military settlement is attached.

---

62 Mainly because the Roman authorities had no interest in maintaining local garrison troops according to the Ptolemaic system. We even know that a definite policy was implemented to eliminate the γῆ κληρουχική and rent or sell it to small farmers or influential Roman landlords. See Rostowzew, *Kolonatus*, pp. 112-114.

A number of documents mentions Jews described as "Persians of the *Epigone*". The problem of this term, though dealt with at length, has not been solved to general satisfaction, nor shall any attempt be made to do so here. However, it appears that at the start of the Ptolemaic period the "Persians" were organized into a hipparchy (= cavalry unit) which already then was pseudo-ethnic in nature. The trend toward pseudo-ethnicity in military units gained greater impetus from the middle of the second century B.C. on when the Ptolemies permitted many autochthonic Egyptians in the ranks of the "Persians"[63]. This lifting of restrictions undoubtedly diminished the military value of the unit and led to limitation in its military assignments in general[64], and of course in the legal status of its members. The scholarly community has more or less accepted the view that by the time of the later Ptolemies, the term "Persians of the *Epigone*" had a special legal significance, unrelated to military service. The people so defined were subject to the "extradition clause" (ἀγώγιμος) designed to prevent them from seeking asylum in temples if sued in connection with business transactions. The Romans inherited that legal fiction from the Ptolemies and the term was applied to people not permitted to avoid legal responsibility in commercial affairs; in practice it appears to have designated debtors in particular. It has been shown that at least those figuring in documents of the Roman period were almost all people of little means, among them freedmen who had to lease land or houses and apply for small loans in money or grain. Because of their particular legal status as debtors (that is, "Persians of the *Epigone*") they were subject to effective supervision by the other party to the transaction[65]. It is thus impossible to determine whether Jews bearing such a designation in the Roman period were in fact the descendants of the original "Persians" of the early Ptolemaic period.

Of the five documents dealing with such Jews — *CPJ*, II 146, 149, 411, 417 and *CPJ*, III 518a — four concern simple impecunious men

---

63 See F. Zucker, *RE(PW)*, XXXVII, p. 910f.; Heichelheim, pp. 78, 100f., 127f.

64 It appears that their military duties were gradually reduced, so that they turned to ordinary civilian pursuits such as commerce, craft, and administration.

65 See, e.g., Tcherikover, *CPJ*, I (Prolegomena), p. 59, n.10; *Jews in Egypt*, p. 41. See also the comprehensive study which Tcherikover did not know, Oates, *YCS*, 17 (1963), pp. 5-129; and see also Fraser, vol. 1, pp. 58-59.

involved in simple, limited transactions, who apparently belonged
to the class of the Egyptian natives. Only one — CPJ, II 417 of 59
C.E. — mentions three members of a family, described as "Jews,
Persians of the *Epigone*" who were quite well-to-do and a party to
quite a large transaction involving land. A father and his two sons
from the "Village of the Syrians" in the Heliopolite nome, they
borrowed from a Roman cavalryman serving in the military camp
at Babylon the considerable sum of 600 silver drachmas given in
imperial Ptolemaic coins. The borrower undertook to repay the debt
in genuine silver coins that were legal tender, assigned suitable security from their property, and were also responsible for each other.
One of the provisions even stipulated that in case of arrears, they
would lose their security deposits and still be required to repay the
debt and pay interest and a fine of 120 drachmas. The amount of
the loan, the property guarantee and the terms of the contract show
that the borrowers were certainly not indigent, for they could not
have taken such a great risk if they were incapable of handling it.
They presumably had a good deal of property, probably real estate.
Their provenance from the "Village of the Syrians" in the Heliopolite nome which in Ptolemaic times had been part of "the land of
Onias" and the name Ḥelkias which was common in the family as a
papinomic[66] reinforce the impression of their descent from military
settlers. This cannot be deduced here from the term "Persians of
the *Epigone*" which defined the legal status of debtors.

Another important document from the Fayûm is *CPJ*, III 459[67],
of 149 C.E., which is a report by the *sitologoi* (= tax collector) of
the village of Berinikis Aigialou on revenue from land tax paid in
grain. Among those listed is "Didymus, also called Ptolemaios, son
of Didymus", who paid the "tax on the *katoikoi*" through his wife
(lines 297-298). His status as a descendant of a military settler is
noteworthy in contrast to that of other Jews from the village who
paid the δημοσίων as tenants cultivating crown land (lines 371-372).
This evidence suggests that after the Jewish uprising in Trajan's time
it was possible for Jews in certain places to regain their rights, perhaps

---

66 That is, the custom of naming the grandson after the grandfather, see lines 4-5 in the
document.
67 Only a few lines from the long document (*BGU*, 1893) were included in the *CPJ* since
they were the only ones clearly referring to Jews.

thanks to the conciliatory policies of Hadrian and Antioninus Pius. A similar juxtaposition of *demosion*-payers and *katoikic* tax-payers appears in connection with residents of the village of Theadelphia in the Fayûm in the 170s (*CPJ*, III 489f,g,h).

There seems to be some traces of descendants of Jewish military settlers as late as the fourth century in the Oxyrhynchus area, judging by a number of document relating to the "Village of Dositheos" (*P. Oxy.*, 1224, 1225, 1448, 2124)[68]. The theophoric name may have come down from the Ptolemaic period when the village was named after its Jewish founder who headed a group of military settlers. At any rate the distinction one of the documents makes between land tax on private land the *demosion* (*P. Oxy.*, 2124, lines 10, 16) suggests that the owners of the private land were the descendants of military settlers or at least purchased "*katoikic* land". The fact that one of the people mentioned in the document — Jacob son of Horion, a well-to-do man who was one of the local tax-farmers (lines 4, 20) — was Jewish reinforces that impression.

In general, the paucity of documents on descendants of Jewish military settlers has three possible explanations: a) the Roman tendency early in the principate to abolish so far as possible the Ptolemaic military customs; b) numerous changes in land ownership leading to the disappearance of traces of those descendants; c) the inability of many Jews, because of intermarriage with fellow Jews from other classes, to prove *katoikic* descent through the *epikrisis* test.

C. Jews Resident in the Metropoleis

The attempt to trace Jews among the citizens of Egyptian *metropoleis* during the principate period is frustrating because no document has as yet come to light demonstrating the participation of Jews in the community organizations of the metropolitan cities. That does not mean Jews did not reside in them; on the contrary, papyrological, epigraphical and archaeological finds indicate that they did, from the early Ptolemaic period on. However, those finds show that Jews were organized in their own associations, separate from but parallel to the Greek urban associations. It should be noted that in the Roman

---

68 All these documents were not included in the *CPJ*.

period, the *metropolitai* were subjected from time to time to strict
and accurate investigation, and supervision of the cities was the
responsibility of the district *strategoi*. It does not seem likely, therefore, that it was easy to infiltrate into their ranks without being
caught and punished. The exclusivity of the members of this group
too was a natural obstacle to the infiltration of undesirable and
foreign elements. The question of the independent organization of
the Jews is dealt with below[69]; the question of interest here is the
legal status of members of the Jewish communities in the metropolitan cities.

As noted above (p. 75 f.) the Roman authorities viewed the permanent dwelling place of the inhabitants and nautre of their political associations as the criteria of civic stratification. It is therefore
important to ascertain to what extent the Jews' own associations in
the *metropoleis* were recognized as bodies entitling their members
to tax reductions, which were after all the chief indicators of the
legal status of the inhabitants of Egypt in general. An examination of
the *laographia* payments made by the Jews of Apollinopolis Magna
reveals a most interesting situation.

Tcherikover was inclined to believe that Jews did not differ from
their Egyptian neighbors in that respect, and paid the rate usual in
Upper Egypt, sixteen drachmas[70]. An inspection of the sums recorded
on the ostraca indicates that there were a considerable number of
Jews who did pay that amount. Nikon son of Antonius Rufus, for
instance, paid the full sum six times (*CPJ*, II 239, 246, 253, 257,
263, 226), so that the single ostracon recording just half that amount
(*ibid.*, 271) must be regarded as a receipt for a partial payment. The
same must be said in respect of his brother Theodotos son of
Antonius Rufus, who paid the full sum three times (*ibid.*, 263,
264, 274), and another time made two payments of eight drachmas
each for the same year only ten days apart (*ibid.*, 269, 270). Their
nephew, Niger son of Ptollis, also paid the full amount (*ibid.*, 257).
Another Jew, Thedetos son of Alexion, made payments of twelve
and four drachmas on different days of the same month, and these
are recorded on the same ostracon (*ibid.*, 258). Consequently other

---

69 See below, chap. III.
70 Tcherikover, *Jews in Egypt*, pp. 80-82; cf. *CPJ*, II p. 111f.

payments he made, of eight or four drachmas[71] must also be regarded as partial. As another Jew, Melchion son of Pesouris by name, paid sixteen drachmas in 101 C.E. (*ibid.*, 310) and in 109 (*ibid.*, 358), the payments of four, eight and twelve drachmas he made in the intervening years (*ibid.*, 317, 323, 324, 338, 351) may reasonably be viewed as partial. His father too, Pesouris son of Jason Philo, in 108 made three separate payments — of eight, four and four drachmas (*ibid.*, 348-350) — totalling sixteen. There are additional instances of payments of sixteen drachmas by several Jews, recorded together on ostraca (*ibid.*, 295, 337, 339, 401) and also installments recorded on two or more ostraca. Thus for example Jacobos son of Thaumasios paid 4 + 12 drachmas recorded on different dates on one ostracon (*ibid.*, 325). The ostracon of Panibekis son of Senpeamys son of Achillas Rufus showing eight drachmas (*ibid.*, 380) was doubtless a receipt for a partial payment since in another year he paid sixteen at one time (*ibid.*, 401). His brother Senpeamys was unlikely to have differed from him, so that the ostraca relating to him (e.g., *ibid.*, 381) represented half the annual tax. That is further supported by the fact that the same man paid poll-tax and other taxes in two installments (in 159, Antoninus Pius' twenty-third regnal year), one of twelve drachmas and the other of an unspecified amount (*ibid.*, 397, 398) which however was probably four. He made similar payments in 163/4, Marcus Aurelius' third regnal year (*ibid.*, 385). The same is true of his brother Senpetestheus, for whom the ostraca list sums smaller than sixteen drachmas (*ibid.*, 384, 393-396, 399) which were also evidently only partial payments.

The examples noted might lead to the conclusion that the official tax rate applying to all the Jews in Apollinopolis Magna (in the Jewish quarter) was sixteen drachmas. A number of scholars thought that the sum was the regular rate for Upper Egypt, and Tcherikover accepted their view. It has not, however, been proven definitely that sixteen drachmas was the maximum payment[72]. A comparison of

---

71 *Ibid.*, 230, 285, 308, 316, 336. It is odd that a man of the same name was mentioned in both 56 C.E. (*ibid.*, No. 230) and 106 C.E. (*ibid.*, No. 336). It does not appear likely that the same man is meant, since even if he were only 14 years old in 56 C.E. he would have been 64 in 106 C.E. and so in any case exempt from the laographia. Therefore, either the references are to two individuals, or the first ostracon was wrongly dated.

72 Wilcken, *Ostraka*, p. 233; Wallace, p. 128; and see n.70 above. Wallace (*ibid.*) points out that there is no evidence that the cities of Upper Egypt recognized a class of holders of tax exemptions.

that rate with those customary in other districts of Egypt shows that
it fits the one applying to *metropolitai*. In Arsinoë in the Fayûm, for
instance, members of that class paid twenty drachmas compared
with the forty to forty-four that the natives paid[73], while in Oxyrhynchus the *metropolitai* paid twelve[74]. It would be unreasonable
for people of that class in Arsinoe, who enjoyed a partial exemption,
to pay twenty while ordinary natives from Apollinopolis Magna paid
only sixteen. Furthermore, in other towns of Upper Egypt (and even
in the Apollinopolis Magna region) receipts have survived showing
larger *laographia* payments of even twenty, twenty-four and thirty
drachmas[75]. Why then should the sixteen-drachma amount not be
viewed as a special assessment for people entitled to a partial exemption? Furthermore, it is hard to accept the notion that descendants
of Roman citizens, even if they did not inherit the citizenship of the
founder of their family, were counted with the lowliest populations
of Egypt[76]. It is likewise hard to imagine that the Jew, Jesus son of
Papios, listed as a *laographia* payer[77], was deemed on a par with the
lowly natives, for he was a *dekanos*, a junior police officer (p. 79
above) and as such was certainly eligible for at least a partial exemption.

The small number of farmers among the local Jews[78] somewhat
reinforces the estimate above, since that occupation was the province mainly of autochthonic Egyptians. Of the Jewish farmers, one
was the proprietor of an estate and, as it was included in the metropolitan lands (*CPJ*, II 241, 294), he could not possibly have been
classified as a native. At first glance it might seem he could be one
of the *metropolitai*, but his residence in the Jewish quarter shows
that organizationally he belonged to the Jewish community. He may

---

73 Wallace, p. 121f.
74 See, e.g., *P. Oxy.*, II 258; III 478; IV 714; VII 1028. At the end of the second century
   C.E. there were mentioned "*metropolitai* who pay eight drachmas"; see Taubenschlag,
   p. 613.
75 Tcherikover knew this; see *Jews in Egypt*, p. 82; and see Wallace, p. 130f.
76 On these, see above, p. 81f.
77 See *CPJ*, II 298 (from 96 C.E.) — payment of 8 drachmas; No. 304 (99 C.E.) — the
   same; No. 311 (101 C.E.) — 6 drachmas and 4 obols; No. 321 (104 C.E.) — 4 drachmas;
   and it appears that all these were installment payments, and that the annual total was 16
   drachmas in these cases also.
78 Fewer than fifteen ostraca (out of 250) mention taxes connected with agriculture, and
   they refer to just a few farmers, who can be counted on the fingers of one hand.

be compared with those Alexandrian Jews who owned land in the *chora* of Alexandria and at the same time clearly belonged to the Jewish *politeuma* in the city[79]. The comparison certainly entails further explanation of the way the local community was organized. The presence of Jewish vine-dressers among the few landowners (*ibid.*, 378, 392) may well support the conclusion that they were not on the same level as the low native class, as from the Ptolemaic period on vineyard owners belonged to a higher socio-economic class (pp. 72-73 above). Another landowner, Tryphas son of Nikon, who paid various land taxes appears not to have been a small farmer either. As he himself lived in the Jewish quarter of Apollinopolis Magna while his land was in the village of Thmouos (*ibid.*, 237, 238, 247), it may be assumed that it was worked by tenants. The evidence of Jewish ship owners in the first or second century (*ibid.*, 404) and the proprietor of a land-transport business (*ibid.*, 282, 362) provides further information on the occupational cross-section of the local Jews. Philo placed the Jewish "ship owners" of Alexandria in the highest economic stratum, of the city (*In Flaccum*, 57), and those in Apollinopolis Magna must have had a similar status. In that remote place probably the owners of land-transport businesses were classed with them. All these facts together suggest that the Jews of Apollinopolis Magna had a relatively high social position which makes it difficult to class them with the lowly natives.

On the hypothesis that a reduced poll-tax applied, the sixteen-drachma payments made by so many Jews there may be viewed as evidence of their inclusion in a higher class that was equivalent to that of the *metropolitai*. While the Jews in Apollinopolis Magna were not members of the Greek community organization, they enjoyed ἰσοτελεία (= tax equality) with the *metropolitai*. Most probably this derived from their own community organization that paralleled the Greek one and was officially recognized by the Roman authorities[80]. All the same, there may have been Jews in Apollinopolis Magna who did not enjoy the same privilege, but due to insufficient data that possibility cannot be explored.

---

79 See *CPJ*, II 142, lines 9-10; 143, lines 7-8.
80 This matter will be dealt with in detail in chap. III.

D. "Those of the gymnasium"

There is no question that Bickermann was right in stating that the people classified as "those of the gymnasium" were a restricted, exclusive group in the cities of Egypt, including the *metropoleis*, who because of their high status fulfilled important functions in the administration and economy[81]. In the Egyptian *Poleis* of the Roman period they were considered the most eminent citizens, that is, the ones registered in tribes and demes.

Any attempt to find Jews in this class throughout the *metropoleis* is doomed to failure, as not a single piece of supporting evidence is available, for the entire Roman period, from the conquest of Egypt to the fourth century. Two documents of 304 and 306 C.E. (*CPJ*, III 474a-b) mention a man named Johannes who was evidently a gymnasiarch in the Fayûm village of Karanis. In Stern's view despite his Jewish name it is not clear whether he was a Jew or only of Jewish descent[82]. Indeed in that period the name was more likely to be borne by a Christian. If however he was Jewish, he might have headed a Jewish gymnasium, perhaps like the one in Hypaipa in Lydia at the end of the second or beginning of the third century, in connection with which "the young Jews" are noted[83].

Despite ostensibly contradictory testimony in a number of important documents — Hellenos son of Tryphon's petition regarding the *laographia* (*BGU*, 1140); the *Boulé* papyrus (*PSI*, 1160); *Claudius' letter to the Alexandrians* (*P. Lond.*, 1912); the *Acts of the Alexandrian Martyrs* — which are discussed in the chapters on Alexandrian Jewry, the conclusion that there are no signs of Jews among "those of the gymnasium" in Roman Egypt is firm and unshaken.

E. Jews as Natives (λαοί)

As we have seen, in the Roman period all inhabitants who were not Roman citizens or citizens of the Greek *poleis* were considered Egyptian natives from the purely legal viewpoint, but in practice administrative distinctions were made between various sectors of

---

81 Bickermann, *Archiv*, 9 (1930), pp. 37-40; cf. Jouguet, p. 80f.; A.H.M. Jones, *CERP*, p. 318. See also pp. 76-77 above and n.8.

82 See *CPJ*, III p. 37 (commentary on line 3).

83 See Schürer, vol. 3, p. 91; S. Reinach, *REJ*, 10 (1885), p. 74; and perhaps it was also the same as regards the list of Jewish ephebes from Jasos (in Asia Minor) — see L. Robert, *REJ*, 101 (1937), p. 73f.; idem., *Hellenica*, 3 (1943), p. 100.

"Egyptians" in particular as regards taxation. It is therefore necessary to avoid automatically classifying all Jewish *laographia* payers in one category, and to carefully examine and verify all the rates. Only evidence showing the maximum poll-tax payment will permit the determination of a lower class status.

Document *CPJ*, II 421 from Arsinoe (72/3 C.E.) explicitly mentions Jews included in the list of maximum *laographia* payers, an indication that they were counted as inferior natives. The ostraca from Apollinopolis Magna, on the other hand, do not supply grounds for the same conclusion, for the sixteen-drachma rate suggests that it was not the highest, and that the Jews there were equal to the *metropolitai*. Despite such difficulties the Jews of the lower class can be rather successfully traced using social and occupational criteria. In other words, Jews are to be found in the social and occupational strata typical of this class.

The vast majority of the lowest native class were tenant farmers, the descendants of the "king's peasants" of the Ptolemaic period, and the agrarian policies of the Roman emperors in the first and second centuries worsened their condition. Augustus found Egypt in a low political and economic situation. On the one hand there were rich Alexandrians, an inflated administration of Greek officialdom, thousands of merchants spread throughout the country, a powerful rural aristocracy (descendants of the *katoikoi*) and rich temples and a privileged and extremely influential priesthood. On the other, the extensive native population which included myriads of tenant farmers and simple artisans was subject to the constant oppression of tax collectors, tax farmers and government officials. The evils of a complicated bureaucracy, corruption and inefficiency likewise made their contributions to the crisis.

Augustus energetically embarked upon the rehabilitation of Egypt's economy and administrative arrangements. First he freed a considerable part of the population from economic bondage to the temples, and reintroduced taxation on temple land and revenue. While the responsibility of the officials to the central authorities was increasingly stressed, no fundamental changes were made in the administration, and Augustus concentrated on improving the economy of the country. Retaining the Ptolemaic tax system and financial and economic organization, he turned his attention primarily to agrarian reform. He was the first to give people of means and initiative a free hand to purchase neglected land, in order to increase the productivity of Egypt as an imperial province. Subsequent emperors too continued that policy and encouraged the acquisition of land, chiefly lands of former cleruchs which had been abandoned for various reasons and confiscated by the authorities. The policy led to the proliferation of large estates (οὐσίαι), for the owners paid a minimum price — twenty drachmas per *aroura*. They also enjoyed great tax reductions, sometimes even total exemptions (ἀτέλεια, κουφοτέλεια). Their lands were considered nominally "purchased land" (γῆ ἐωνημένη) and a kind of "private land". Generally the owners of these estates were familiars of the emperors, such as members of their families, prominent Romans, influential courtiers, freedmen the emperors were fond of, and also rich Alexandrians.

Obviously, small farmers could not compete, and more and more land became concentrated in the hands of the emperors' friends. The results of that agrarian policy were soon evident. Farming improved in efficiency, more land was cultivated, but the imperial revenue did not increase. As Egypt was an imperial province, its land was subject to exploitation through land taxes (*agri tributarii*) and the unrestricted growth of private land holdings eventually had an adverse effect on the emperor's treasury. It is no wonder that at the end of the first century attempts were made to decelerate this growth, as indicated for example by a provision in the edict issued by the prefect Tiberius Julius Alexander. The emperors dared not put an end to the "private estates" altogether, but began to control their untrammeled expansion. Awareness and fear of diminished income led the Flavian emperors to adopt an aggressive policy of augmented pressure on the tax collecting administration on the one hand, and of a calculated confiscation of estates on the other. They sought to reestablish small local farmers linked to the land which would ensure orderly tax payment and collection, including the levying of liturgies and various types of forced labor. The confiscation of estates was continued in the second century as well, and there is no doubt that it revived the system of crown tenants and small local farming. The new policy somewhat stemmed the abandonment of land by small farmers, but did not reduce the pressure and shameful exploitation they were subjected to by the tax administration. The encouragement of small local farming also resulted in the expansion of the metropolitan cities. It was easier for the farmers to manage their affairs from there, as their land was generally scattered throughout the nomes. Residence in the *metropolis* enabled them to supervise its cultivation more efficiently, and also engage in some craft or commerce. Most of these landowners were Greeks or Hellenized Egyptians, and only a few were Roman citizens. The various agrarian policies and the different developments which ensued had an unsettling effect on the Egyptian economy but made no change in the basic condition of the rural population. The vast majority remained permanent tenants, on crown land, public land or private land. In certain respects their situation was even aggravated, for the land taxes and tenancy fees were continually raised, and in the second century the tenants were permanently attached to their villages as serfs.

In the vicissitudes of Egyptian agriculture[84], traces of Jewish tenants (δημόσιοι γεωργοι) can be found in various villages of the *chora*, especially in the agricultural region of the Fayûm. A papyrus from Philadelphia (*CPJ*, II 416) of 25 C.E., which is a list of συντάξιμον payers, gives the names of several Jews. The term was originally Ptolemaic, and in Roman times in the Fayûm villages denoted the poll-tax combined with other levies. The rate there was as high as forty-four drachmas, probably applicable to the lowest native class[85]. The Jews listed were certainly tenants settled on crown or public land, like most tenants in that neighborhood. A Jew of that class figures in a notice (*ibid.*, 427, of 101 C.E.) sent to the "royal scribe" (βασιλικός γραμματεύς) of the Arsinoite nome, reporting the death of a son, in order to bring the *laographia*-payer list up to date. The members of that rural family were thus small farmers or crown tenants, legally classed as "subject to the poll tax" (λαογραφόμενοι). Another Fayûm papyrus of 110 C.E. (*ibid.*, 431) mentions a Jew who was required to provide "forced agricultural labor" (γεωργία) by the authorities (line 17). In this matter the Romans retained the Ptolemaic policies[86]. The early editors of the papyrus, along with other scholars, believed that the term indicated a status of tenancy on public land[87]. Tcherikover concurred, adding interesting points

---

84 On the survey above, see Rostowzew, *Kolonatus*, p. 85f.; Rostovtzeff, *SEHHW*, p. 285f.; idem., *Journal of Economic and Business hist.*, 1 (1928/9), p. 337f.; Milne, *JRS*, 17 (1927), p. 1f.; Martin, *La fiscalité romaine en Égypt*; see also Wilcken-Mitteis, p. 237f. The literature on this subject is fairly extensive.

85 Cf. Johnson, p. 533; Wallace, p. 121f.

86 See Taubenschlag, p. 618.

87 See *P. Fay*, 123, and also Rostowzew, *Kolonatus*, p. 55f.; Johnson, p. 107.

showing that the person concerned was a small, poor farmer forced
to lease public land[88]. As such he had to pay the full *laographia*. A
document from Oxyrhynchus (*P. Oxy.*, XIV 1747) of the end of the
third century also mentions two Jews required to provide labor by
the authorities. That document contains a list of villages and estate-
owners each of which was obligated to supply one person for public
work. The inclusion in the list of the names of two Jewish farmers
(lines 40, 52) thus clearly shows their low status.

Document *CPJ*, III 455 of 137 C.E. from the Fayûm village of
Theadelphia mentions a Jewish widow's complaint, through her
guardian son, about the theft of six *artabai* of wheat from the small
threshing floor she inherited from her husband which was located
in the "public lands" in her vicinity. The small size of the theft and
the reference to public land suggest that hers was a family of simple,
poverty-stricken tenants. In the same category were also other people
of her village described in *CPJ*, III 489a-f as having paid the *laographia*
and other taxes. Another document from the Fayûm (*CPJ*, III 459,
col. xi) of 149 C.E., which is a report by the *sitologoi* of the village
of Berenikis-Aigialou on revenues from land tax, mentions tenants on
public land (line 372) among them members of the Jewish "people"
(or "neighborhood"; line 373)[89]. The same document also lists
payers of the "*katoikoi* tax" (col. ix, line 298) so that the contrast
between them and those who paid the *demosion* is well defined. The
same contrast is evident also in a list of taxpayers from the Fayûm
village of Theadelphia (*CPJ*, III 489f-h). Another document (*CPJ*,
III 471) of the third century from the village of Sebennytos has a
Jew among the twenty Egyptian tenants listed as *demosion* payers,
so that he was obviously a member of their class.

One Jew from the Fayûm village of Karanis paid the "Jewish tax"
in 145/6 (or 167/8) C.E. as recorded in document *CPJ*, III 460,
which is an annual report on the collection of various taxes including
the *laographia*. The nature of the taxes suggests that most of the
villagers were tenant farmers and craftsmen, and probably the Jew

---

88 *CPJ*, II 431, line 17 (pp. 219-220); Tcherikover, *Jews in Egypt*, pp. 60-61.
89 The garbled text — ὁ αὐ(τὸς) ᾽Ιουδαϊκ[...] — does not permit definitive reconstruction.
    To me λαύρα seems more acceptable, mainly because of the comparison with the
    existence of Jewish quarters in Hermopolis (*CPJ*, III 468, line 10) and Oxyrhynchus
    (*ibid.*, 454, line 9).

was as well. (The presence of a single Jew among non-Jews is explainable against the background of the uprising in Trajan's time).
Registers of 171-174 C.E. from the same village list fourteen people
named Sambathion, mostly women (*ibid.*, 492) among *laographia*
payers, but there are not enough grounds for identifying them as
Jewish[90]. Two third-century ostraca from that village (*O. Mich.*,
332, 595) contain Jewish names, and as they list chiefly Egyptian
farmers who paid various taxes, it may be inferred with considerable
assurance that the Jews among them were of the same class. An early
fourth century ostracon, likewise from Karanis, notes the name of a
Jew as having paid "on behalf of the villagers" ($ὑπὲρ$ $κωμητῶν$) a
certain amount of chaff to the government granary[91]. He may have
been a "chaff tax" collector or a farmer representing a group of
peasants from his village[92], but in either case his status cannot have
been higher than that of his colleagues. The date of the ostracon also
shows the continuity of Jewish residence in Karanis whose population consisted for the most part of small farmers or simple tenants.

A second-century list of Roman landowners from the village of
Soknopaiou-Nesos near Karanis (*CPJ*, III 464) contains information
on the size of their holdings in nearby villages, and the names of the
tenants who cultivated them. Two of the latter are undoubtedly
Jewish, judging by their names[93]. The other bear Egyptian names[94],
and here again the juxtaposition suggests that the Jews had the
equivalent legal status.

Tenants sometimes leased land from other tenants rather than
directly from the owners. Such was the case with Hatres son of
Sambathion who in 157 C.E. together with a partner bearing a
definitely Egyptian name wished to sign a tenancy contract regarding
a tract of six *arourai* in a Fayûm village (*CPJ*, III 491). The lessors
were tenants as well (line 6) and they therefore stipulated that the
lease was conditional on the payment of the *demosion* (line 9f.). The
actual owners of the land are not named, but they were probably of

---

90 See Tcherikover , *Jews in Egypt*, p. 194f.; and also *CPJ*, I p. 43f.
91 In Stern's opinion (*CPJ*, III 480) the chaff was required for heating the public baths or
   for military use.
92 Tcherikover suggested both possibilities in *Jews in Egypt*, p. 59.
93 One was called Simon (line 4) and the other "Heras known as Ezekiel" (lines 23-24).
   There may have been another Jew among them, if that can be concluded from the name
   Diodorus (line 20).

the government service class, for their land was described as cleruchic land (line 5).

The tenants of private estates seem to have been in a better situation than those of imperial land. Their lords protected them, for instance, from forced labor required by the authorities. In that connection there is an interesting document of 110 C.E. from the Fayûm (*CPJ*, II 431) referring to a Jew named Teophilos. Evidently assigned to forced agricultural labor which he wished to avoid, he appealed to a rich Roman estate owner to take him under his protection as a tenant in his service[95]. It is not clear whether he had previously been a crown tenant or a hired farm laborer, but in any case there was no difference from the legal standpoint. That Jew's interest in the patronage of an estate owner shows the plight of the crown tenants and the relative security (from government oppression) of other tenants.

As to other agricultural workers, the shepherds definitely belonged to the native class, and differed not at all from hired farm laborers in their legal status. Only two documents testify to Jewish shepherds in the Roman period, one of 27/8 C.E. from the Oxyrhynchite nome (*P. Oxy.*, 353) and the other from early in the first century from the Fayûm (*CPJ.*, III 482)[96]. It should be noted that the three Apollinopolis Magna Jews who paid "sheep tax" in the first and second centuries were flock owners rather than simple shepherds[97]. This is shown by the fact that the tax was a property tax based on the number of heads, in contrast to the "pasture tax" paid by shepherds or flock owners for the right to graze their sheep on state land[98]. Moreover one of them was a Roman citizen[99], and another the son of a *libertinus* (without Roman citizenship)[100]. As the amount of the tax paid indicates the flocks were too small to provide a livelihood, they probably served to fill household needs, and are an example of typical

---

94 It is interesting that one of the leaseholders bears a definitely Roman name, Sabinus son of Julius (*ibid.*, line 16). Apparently he was the son of a freedman, franchised by *manumissio minus iusta*, and did not pass on his Roman citizenship to his son.

95 See Tcherikover's excellent explanation of line 17f. (*CPJ*, II pp. 219-220).

96 See Tcherikover, *Jews in Egypt*, p. 62 (Nos. 9-10).

97 See *CPJ*, II 268, 284, 377, 383, 391; the ostraca concern only three people.

98 See chap. I above, p. 73f. and n.184 (where a bibliography on the subject is given); and also Tcherikover, *Jews in Egypt*, p. 62, n.74.

99 See *CPJ*, II 268.

100 *Ibid.*, 377, 388, 391.

supplimentary farming. Evidently those Jews sometimes collaborated to hire a single shepherd for their combined flocks, as indicated in *CPJ*, II 412 relating to such flock owners in the Oxyrhynchus district in 8/9 C.E. Thus flock owners must be distinguished from simple shepherds, and only the latter placed in the native class.

It is difficult to find Jews of this native class engaging in non-agricultural pursuits, due to the paucity of papyrological and archaeological evidence. The Jewish wet nurse of Alexandria mentioned in *CPJ*, II 146 of 13 B.C.E. seems to have been one such (the epithets "Persian" applied to her and "Persian of the *Epigone*" to her husband do not necessarily indicate a military past, for the terms had a legal meaning connected with contractual obligations[101]. Another was perhaps a second wet nurse, also of Alexandria, mentioned in *CPJ*, II 147 of 14 C.E.

---

101 See above, p. 91f.

Chapter III

Jewish Communities in the Egyptian Chora and their Organization

Little basic data is unfortunately as yet available on the community organization of Jewish settlements throughout the Egyptian *chora*. It is therefore necessary to be content with meager information and to conduct comparative studies of other ethnic groups in Egypt and of Jewish communities in other countries of the Hellenistic-Roman Diaspora. The subject is of vital importance in illuminiating the nature and scope of the rights accorded to the Jews. Tcherikover wisely proposed a reliable indicator of organized Jewish communities that could be discerned in epigraphical and papyrological documents: Since the synagogue occupied a crucial place in the social, organizational, religious and cultural life of Jews everywhere, the existence of of a synagogue presupposes a well-ordered community organization[1]. A number of points derive from that hypothesis:

a) Since unauthorized building of a synagogue is hardly credible (in particular in a country like Egypt) the legal basis for its construction and operation must have been the right "to live according to ancestral laws".

b) Synagogues were built only in places where a considerable Jewish population had need of their services, that is, in the heart of. the Jewish settlement area.

c) A synagogue was presumably public property owned by all the Jewish inhabitants of the place.

d) The construction and maintenance of a synagogue involved considerable funds which could be provided only by a community of at least several dozen families.

e) The existence of a synagogue generally implies a regular religious leadership, and perhaps also a court, archives, community foundations for various purposes, a ritual bath, and so on.

---

1 See *CPJ*, I (Prolegomena), p. 7f.

f) As the existence of most of the synagogues was revealed by dedicatory inscriptions within them or on their gates, evidently the Jewish community involved was empowered to make decisions of an official nature and implement them, an indication that the decisions derived from a legal right and a body having a legal status.

g) The wording of the inscriptions and also of papyri relating to the Jewish communities of Egypt which established the synagogues follows the accepted official forms. Thus phrases like "the Jews from such-and-such a place" (οἱ ἀπὸ ... Ἰουδαῖοι) or "the Jews in such-and-such a place" (οἱ ἐν... Ἰουδαῖοι) testify to Jewish organization separate from the Gentile community organization in the place by whose name the Jewish community was designated[2].

It thus seems evident that Jewish congregation that had a synagogue was organized as a community and was a legal entity recognized and defined by law. Epigraphical and papyrological evidence on some communities supplies definite grounds for positing organized Jewish community life there.

A. Lower Egypt

Schedia

The place now known as Kafr ed-Dawar was originally located about 20 kilometers east of Alexandria on the main canal that lead to the capital through the Canopic Branch of the Nile (*Strabo*, XVI 1, 16). Σχεδία means "ferry", "raft" or "float", from which it can be inferred that the place of that name must have been a harbour through which cargo passed on the way to Alexandria. This is suggested by the writings of *Strabo* (XVI 1, 16).

At the beginning of the twentieth century there was discovered in Schedia one of the oldest Jewish inscriptions extant, carved on a marble slab, and containing a dedication to King Ptolemy III Euergetes I (246-221 B.C.E.) and his family[3]. It reads as follows: ὑπὲρ

---

2 In the cities of Egypt, including the metropoleis, these terms (οἱ ἐν κτλ., οἱ ἐκ κτλ., οἱ ἀπό κτλ.) described permanent residents with the right of *origo* who were not members of the urban communal organizations. See, e.g., Jouguet, p. 55f. However, papyrological and epigraphical research has shown that formulas of this kind also indicated membership in an independent local organization (see Bickermann, *Archiv*, 8 (1929); 234-235; Ruppel, p. 448, n.289.

3 *CIJ*, II 1440 (= *CPJ*, III 1440).

βασιλέως Πτολεμαίου καὶ βασιλίσσης Βερενίκης ἀδελφῆς καὶ γυναικὸς καὶ τῶν τέκνων τὴν προσευχὴν οἱ Ἰουδαῖοι. Th. Reinach, taking into consideration the close proximity in which Schedia lay to the capital, concludes that the local Jewish community constituted a "daughter" community of the Alexandrian one[4]. The suggestion seems a reasonable one, particularly since it gives credence to Josephus' testimony regarding the antiquity of the "mother" community (*Bellum*, II 487; *C. Apionem*, II 35, 37, 42). The extent to which Alexander the Great settled Jewish soldiers in Alexandria may be controversial (see Chap. IV, C below), but what is certain is the fact that Jews were buried in the suburb of the capital (now Al-Ibramiyeh) at the beginning of the third century B.C.E. This means that they were settled there during the reigns of Ptolemy I and Ptolemy II too[4a].

Obviously these conscripts must have been called up either by Ptolemy I, or by his son. It seems fairly certain that they were in some way connected with the policing of the Nile (ποταμοφυλακία). I agree with Tcherikover (*CPJ*, I p. 53, n.14) that the *fluminis custodia* of the Roman period, referred to by Josephus in *C. Apionem*, II 64, is to be identified with the ποταμοφυλακία mentioned in certain of the ostraca[4b]. It has to be noted that Josephus made it very clear that Jews had indeed served in this capacity in the Ptolemaic period[4c]. As recorded in *III Maccabees* (iv 11), Schedia was the last stage in the Journy made by the Jews condemned to death by Ptolemy IV Philopator. The place was chosen for its suitability in exposing the former to the public gaze so that those entering the city of Alexandria, and those leaving for the country (i.e. χώρα), could have a good view of them. It was also a position from which "they could neither make contact with the army nor obtain protection from the walls". Since police service in Ptolemaic Egypt was frequently connected with the regular army see pp. 55-58 above , the citation may serve to reinforce the assumption that Jewish settlers in Schedia were somehow connected with the policing of the Nile[5].

---

4 See Th. Reinach, *REJ*, 45 (1902), pp. 161-164.
4a Cf. *CIJ*, II 1424-1426; *Letter of Aristeas*, 12ff., 36ff.; *Antiquitates*, XII 8; 45-47; *C. Apionem*, II 44.
4b *Ostr. Theb.*, 36, 93; *WO.* 507; *Ostr. Ashm.*, 41; cf. Wilcken, *Griechische Ostraka*, pp. 282ff.; Mitteis & Wilcken, vol. 1, pp. 392, 396.
4c Juster, vol. 2, p. 257.
5 Strabo, *loc.cit.*; Agatarchides, *Geog. Gr. Min.*, I p. 122; for further details, see Wallace, pp. 258, 262, 268; Fraser, vol. 1, pp. 144, 149.

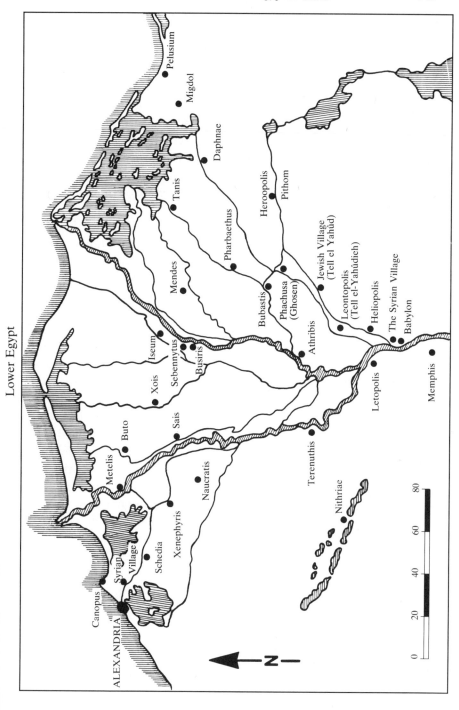

The existence of an organised local community is indicated in the last word of the inscription, οἱ Ἰουδαῖοι (*CIJ*, II 1440, line 8). Its full designation appears to have been οἱ ἐν Σχεδία Ἰουδαῖοι or οἱ ἀπὸ Σχεδίας Ἰουδαῖοι. Designations of this kind are used for permanent residents of Ptolemaic cities (*poleis* and *metropoleis*) who enjoyed the privilege of *origo* and were called κατοικοῦντες or μέτοικοι. The same designation is used in the case of self-organised communities as well as in that of provincial towns or rural districts (see n. 2 above). We do not know exactly to what extent corporate bodies of this type were accorded full legal representation[5a]. However, when classed with the Ptolemaic system of associations, they seem to fall into place as legal organisations.

It is quite obvious that the Jewish dedication from Schedia was official, from which it can be concluded that the community had full public recognition. In other words, consequent on their being organised as a legal body, the Jews had royal sanction for erecting a synagogue, owing and administering public property, as well as for issuing public decrees, i.e. Ψηφίσματα. It would seem that the Synagogue was under royal protection as regards violation, a fact to be inferred from another inscription, probably dating from the same period, where the granting of asylum (ἀσυλία) to a synagogue somewhere in Lower Egypt[6] is recorded. It seems that the Jewish community of Schedia must in any case have been endowed with official leadership, for there is no other way of explaining the fact that it held the right to pass resolutions, as is proved in the dedication, as well as the right to implement them. Clearly, privileges conferred on them by Ptolemy III must have earned the gratitude of the Jews, a fact that emerges from the dedication, as well as from that of a similar inscription from Arsinoë-Crocodilopolis containing a dedication to the same monarch[7]. It has been noted at this point that Josephus likewise cited the good relations that were obtained between the same ruler and the Jews of Judaea (*C. Apionem*, II 48; *Antiquitates*, XII 167-179; 185). His testimony serves to reinforce the positive character of the situation described hitherto.

5a Jouguet, pp. 55ff.; Bickermann, *Archiv*, 8 (1929), p. 234ff.; Ruppel, p. 448, n.289; Taubenschlag, vol. 1 (1944 ed.), p. 43ff. (especially p. 47).

6 *CIJ*, II 1449; cf. also *CIJ*, II 1433. For further details see note 10 below.

7 Vogliano, *Riv. di Filologia*, 57 (1939), p. 247ff.; cf., *CPJ*, III 1532A.

Xenephyris

The place is southeast of Damanhur, near the northwest edge of the delta, not far from Alexandria. In that neighborhood, specifically at the ruins of Kom el-Akhdar, and inscription was found on the "gate house" (πυλών) of the synagogue which contains a dedication to the family of Ptolemy VIII (Euergetes II) Physcon (143-116 B.C.E.)[8]. Presumably that dedication was made only for the erection of the "gate house", which means that the synagogue itself was built earlier. The Jewish construction terminology suggests that such a structure was generally placed at the entrance to a courtyard around the main building, as a kind of sentry post[9]. Thus the synagogue at Xenephyris was situated on a lot that was walled or fenced, so that the gate house made it possible to observe whoever came in. It is reasonable to assume that the yard was called "the holy square", as was the case in other synagogues in and out of Egypt[10].

The Xenephyris inscription provides important information on the leadership of the congregation, as it states that the dedication was made "in the days of the incumbency of the *prostatai* (προστάντων) Theodorus and Achilion" (lines 7-8). Reinach logically inferred that the participial form of *prostatai* (προστάντες) denoted functionaries heading an organized body and representing it[11], but he does not seem to have considered other data relating to that office. First of all, account should be taken of the general terminology in the Hellenistic world regarding *prostates*[12]; for it must be assumed that the independent body of the Xenephyris Jews was organized in accordance with the usual practice in the Ptolemaic

8 For details see Th. Reinach, *REJ*, 65 (1902), pp. 135-137; Juster, vol. 1, p. 348f.; *CIJ*, II 1441.
9 M. *Ma'asroth*, III 6; *Erubin*, VIII 4; *Sotah*, VIII 3.
10 Cf. *CIJ*, II 1433 from Alexandria, and Philo, *In Flaccum*, 48; *Legatio*, 137. The right of asylum (ἀσυλία) granted to one of the synagogues in Upper Egypt (*CIJ*, II 1449) confirms the existence of a "holy square" around it. In regard to communities outside Egypt, cf., e.g., the inscriptions from Phocaea (*CIJ*, II 738). The same is true of the synagogues in Miletus, Priene, Stobi and that of Dura Europos (see Sukenik, *Ancient Synagogues*, pp. 40, 42, 49, 79, 83) and in Thyateira in Lydia (*CIJ*, II 756). Cf. also synagogues in Palestine such as Capernaum, Chorazin and Na'aran (Sukenik, *ibid.*, pp. 8, 22, 28). On the right of asylum in Egypt see the exgensive survey in Rostovtzeff, *SEHHW*, p. 899f. F.V. Woess, *Dass Asylwesen Ägyptens in der Ptolemäerzeit*, München 1923.
11 Th. Reinach, *REJ*, 65 (1902), p. 137; the wording of this inscription should be compared with that of another inscription from Alexandria (*CIJ*, II 1447).
12 See Liddell & Scott, s.v.; see esp. Schaefer, *RE(PW)*, Suppl. 9, pp. 1287-1304.

kingdom, and did not differ in that respect from that of other similar
ethnic or religious groups. According to the terminology employed
there in regard to the heads of various associations, they were evidently *prostatai* who were leaders representing religious organizations[13]. Sometimes they were identified as managers of estates or
other property, or as heads of various unions[14], and sometimes they
filled managerial jobs in military units[15]. The mention of the names
of the Jewish *prostatai* of Xenephyris should be viewed accordingly.
There is no doubt that they were entrusted by the community with
certain leadership functions, but exactly what they were is not clear.
They may have been managers of the local synagogue, or they may
have acted in the much more important capacity of representatives
of the community before the authorities. In that connection the use
of the participial form ("in the days of the incumbency of the *prostatai*", etc.) may indeed indicate representational functions as
Reinach believed, especially since the indication of the date is
eponymous; which resembles what was also found in another inscription from Alexandria (*CIJ*, II 1447).

It is important to note that during the Hellenistic period the term
was used in Palestine too, probably in accordance with government
practice. First, as Hecataeus of Abdera said, "the heading of the
people" or "the leadership of the people" — προστασία τοῦ ἔθνους)
was always entrusted to a person considered to be the priest with the
greatest wisdom and virtues[16]. That testimony suggests that aside
from their religious function, the *prostatai* also headed the political

---

13 Otto, *Priester*, vol. 1, p. 362; vol. 2, p. 75; Index, s.v. προστάτης; Poland, *Vereinwesen*,
    p. 363ff.; San Nicolo, *Aegyptisches Vereinswesen*, vol. 2, p. 58ff.; Oertel, *Die Liturgie*,
    p. 133ff.; Preisigke, *Wörterbuch*, vol. 3, p. 1503; id., Suppl. 1, p. 436; Schaefer, *ibid.*,
    p. 1303.
14 Bouché-Leclercq, vol. 3, p. 191; Fraser, vol. 2, p. 322, n.439. Note also documents
    BGU, 1134-1136 mentioning Tryphon son of Ptolemais as *prostates* of a loan company
    in Alexandria (at the end of the first century B.C.E.) who may have been a Jew accord-
    ing to *BGU*, 1134. On that document see also Fuks (*CPJ*, II 149, p. 24) and Tcheri-
    kover, *Jews in the Greek and Roman World*, p. 314, n.52.
15 See Preisigke, *Wörterbuch*, vol. 3, p. 218; Lesquier, pp. 146, 192ff. Lesquier suggested
    the possibility that in another case the protates could be identified as the leaders of the
    Cretan *politeuma* in Arsinoë (*P. Tebt.*, I 32, lines 8-9, of 145 B.C.E.). In any case it is
    clear that *prostates* headed one of the military *politeumata* of Alexandria. See Fraser,
    vol. 2, pp. 476 (n.121), 977 (n.148).
16 In Diodorus Siculus, XL 3, 5; see Gutman, *The Beginnings of Jewish — Hellenistic
    Literature*, vol. 1, p. 275.

leadership. Josephus indicates the same about Onias II, who fulfilled two parallel tasks — the High Priesthood and the "leadership of the nation"[17]. It was Joseph son of Tobias who dislodged Onias from the latter position and took it over, thus causing the separation of the two functions[18]. The same passage indicates that "the *prostates* of the people" was also responsible for the payment of the "tax for the people" (*Antiquitates*, XII 158f., 161f.). Without going into the problems connected with that tax, here irrelevant, it can be concluded that the description applies to a function involving political and representational leadership, which is very explicitly shown by the fact of Joseph son of Tobias' mission to the Ptolemaic court "for the sake of the nation" (*ibid.*, 163; and cf. *ibid.*, 167).

It should be noted that in Jewish literature of the Hellenistic period too, prostates has the same meaning. For instance in the apocryphal Ezra (1:8) Sheshbazzar is described as "*prostates* of Judaea" (in contrast to "prince of Judaea" in the scriptural Ezra [1:8] and "*archon* of Judaea" in the Septuagint), further indicating the political and representational nature of the job.

Other sources have *prostatai* fulfilling managerial-economic functions. *II Maccabees* (II 4ff.) for example, mentions Simeon, a leading Hellenizer, as "administrator of the Temple" (προστάτης τοῦ ἱεροῦ) who undermined the leadership of High Priest Onias III and clashed with him in regard to the *agoranomia* (management of the market) in Jerusalem. He was apparently supervisor of the household of the Temple, and sought to extend his authority beyond it. The nature of his post is confirmed by the Septuagint use of the term *prostates*[19]; and there is no doubt that this accorded with Hellenistic practice[20].

There were *prostatai* also in other communities of Lower Egypt

---

17 *Antiquitates*, XII 161; XX 238. Note that *Jesus Sirach* (45:24) describes the priest Phinees as filling two posts, apparently in accordance with the terminology current in the author's time.

18 The same situation seems to have prevailed later as well, in Gabinius' time and the reigns of Herod and Archelaus (*Bellum*, I 69; *Antiquitates*, XX 251). That Josephus construed *prostates* to have a political connotation is clear also from his reporting Judas Maccabeus as having inherited from his father the "management of affairs" (προστασία τῶν πραγμάτων), that is, the leadership of the revolt (*Antiquitates*, XII 285).

19 See *I Chron.*, 27:31; 29:6; *II Chron.*, 8:10; 24:11.

20 See Oertel, *Die Liturgie*, p. 137ff.; cf. esp. *ibid.*, p. 138 and n.4, regarding the use of the term "governor of the Temple" in *II Maccabees*.

in the Hellenistic period (*CIJ*, II 1447). An Aramaic papyrus from
Oxyrhynchus of about 400 C.E. (*JEA*, II p. 212) mentions *prostatin*.
Two inscriptions from the Jewish community of Rome from the first
(or second) century C.E. refer to the post: one was found in the
Via Appia catacomb (*CIJ*, I 100) and the other in the Monte Verde
catacomb (*ibid.*, 365). Johannes Chrysostomos too noted the presence of such officials in Antioch in the fourth century C.E. (*Chrys.
Adv. Jud. Orat.*, V 3) and a sixth century inscription from Venosa
in Italy (*CIL*, 6200) likewise mentions a *prostates*. Some scholars
have sought to identify the office with the political and representational leadership of the communities (as political organizations)
and even equate it with that of the gerousiarch[21]; others tried to
equate it with the "patronus" especially in view of the practice in
Rome[22]. A clear decision is difficult, because there is support for
both views in antiquity. The terms *prostasia* and *prostates* themselves have very general meanings, and their actual content can
only be stipulated in relation to specific cases. In evaluating the
function it is necessary too to take into account the time and the local
traditions.

Thus the functions of the *prostatai* in Xenephyris cannot be
definitely ascertained, but the fact that they figure in a congrega-
tional dedication indicates that they were legal personages recognized
by the authority, and that they had prominent positions in the
community which was an organized body that had legal status.

Nitriai

Nitriai is located in the north-east of the Great Libyan Desert,
in the so-called Wadi Natrun, not far from the south-western limits
of the delta. The only evidence of a local Jewish community of the
Ptolemaic period is found in an honorary inscription dedicated to
Ptolemy VIII Physcon (Euergetes II) and his family (*CIJ*, II 1442).

The inscription informs us concerning appurtenances (τὰ συγκύροντα)
attached to the synagogue. Unfortunately, no details that can explain
the exact meaning of this term, exist. The term does, however,

---

21 See, e.g., Juster, vol. 1, p. 443; Kruass, *Syn. Alt.*, p. 145; C.H. Kraeling, *JBL*, 51 (1932),
    p. 132. Cf. also Tcherikover, *Jews in Egypt*, p. 101.
22 See, e.g. Schürer, vol. 3, p. 89 and n.52; idem, *Gemeindeverfassung*, p. 131; Frey, *CIJ*,
    Introd. I, pp. xcivf.; Leon, p. 191f.

appear again in a contemporary synagogue at Alexandria, which, since it was surrounded by a sacred precinct ($\iota\epsilon\rho\grave{o}\varsigma\ \pi\epsilon\rho\acute{\iota}\beta o\lambda o\varsigma$)[23] may be taken as a case corresponding to that of Nitriai. In other cases $\tau\grave{a}\ \sigma v\gamma\kappa\acute{v}\rho ov\tau a$ seem to consist of structures such as the *exedra* of Athribis[23a], the $\pi v\lambda\tilde{\omega}v$ of Xenephyris[23b], a ritual bath and public water supply[23c], and possibly a communal archive[23d], a lodging house[23e], and accommodation for the study of the Torah. We cannot be certain that all of these were connected with the synagogue at Nitriai. In all events, the synagogue was not the only building which served the local Jews. This very fact indicates that the community was sufficiently well-organised and big enough to provide its members with communal services. In addition, the routine administration of such considerable holdings as allegedly existed in Nitriai, implies the existence of a capable local leadership.

Two questions now arise: what were the Jewish settlers in Nitriai like? And what reason had they for living in such a remote spot bordering on the desert? The answer to both lies in the geographical nature of the area in which Nitriai was located. Wadi Natrun consists of a stretch of marshland, about seventy kilometers long and five kilometers wide. Its bottom is twenty-three meters below sea level, and it contains several shallow salines, of high salinity, with various minerals such as sodium carbonate, sodium bicarbonate, sodium chloride and some sulphates. It is no wonder that since antiquity this area has been one of the richest sources of salts in Egypt. The whole region is called by Strabo $v\acute{o}\mu o\varsigma\ N\iota\tau\rho\iota\acute{\omega}\tau\eta\varsigma$[24] and its saltworks and natron pits were without doubt state monopolies, at least in the

---

23 *CIJ*, II 1433 and see n.10 above.

23a *CIJ*, II 1444 (discussed below).

23b *CIJ*, II 1441. As a matter of fact, the very existence of a *pylon* indicates that the synagogue was within an enclosure. The so-called "gatehouse" (*Beth ha-Sha'ar*) was usaully erected at the entrance of an enclosure, being designed for sentry. See, for example, *M. Ma'asseroth*, iii 6; *M. Erubin*, viii 4; *M. Sota*, viii 3.

23c The like of which is supposed to have been in Arsinoë-Crocodilopolis, cf. *CPJ*, II 432.

23d The kind of which is mentioned in *CPJ*, II 143 as regards the Jewish community of Alexandria. This institution existed also in other communities outside Egypt, see for example, *CIJ*, II 775 from Hierapolis in Phrygia.

23e Like that mentioned in *CIJ*, II 1404 $\tau\grave{o}v\ \xi\epsilon v\tilde{\omega}va$ from a synagogue located in the Ophel (Jerusalem). Cf. C.H. Kraeling, *The Excavations at Dura Europos* (1956) Final report, vol. 7, p. 328; Meisler, *Yediot*, 9 (1942), pp. 15-16; Ben-Zvi, *JPOS*, 12 (1933), pp. 94-96.

24 Strabo, XVII 1, 23; cf. Pliny, *Historia Naturalis*, XXXI, 111. Even the Arab name *Wadi Natrun* still preserves the original name and its sound.

Ptolemaic period[25]. Perhaps this fact can shed some light on the occupation of the Jewish settlers there in the middle of the second century B.C.E. They would have hardly been salt miners; for workers of this kind were for the most part condemned criminals or slaves[26]. On the contrary, they must have been present in the area as members of a security force, either of a police unit or a military detachment, and their job must have been present to deal with rebellions as they arose. Perhaps they were even part of the general defence system of the western border of the Delta. Jews, along with other Semitic groups in Egypt, were welcomed into the Ptolemaic desert-police, it seems; for, accustomed as they were to nomadic life, they were best able to keep raiding nomads in check[27]. The high percentage of Arabs in the desert police illustrates this phenomenon[27a], as do the Idumaeans in Memphis and Hermopolis Magna[28].

Athribis

This town is located near Benha at the southern tip of the delta, on the Damietta Branch of the Nile, about forty-five kilometers directly north of Cairo. The Jewish inscriptions containing references to the local synagogue were found there (*CIJ*, II 1443-1445). The exact date of these inscriptions is uncertain though there is a tendency to link them with Ptolemy V Epiphanes, Ptolemy VI Philometor, Ptolemy VIII Physcon (Euergetes II), and even with Ptolemy IX Lathyrus, each of whom had a queen called Cleopatra. But in view of the fact that Ptolemy VI Philometor was known for his friendship towards the Jews, it seems right to assume that they date from his reign[29]. Mainly for linguistic reasons, I have to disagree with Lewis' contention that the second inscription is later than the first (*CPJ*, III 1444, p. 143) In my view, the word τήνδε (line 5) connects the second with the first inscription being logically and syntactically continuous with it. It is only thus that its use here can be explained. Apparently, it was recorded so as to make a distinction between the

25 Wilcken, *Grünzuge*, p. 252; idem, *Ostraka*, vol. 1, p. 264; Tarn, p. 192.
26 Rostovtzeff, *SEHHW*, pp. 309, 1219-1220.
27 Tcherikover, *Jews in Egypt*, p. 44.
27a Tcherikover, *loc.cit.*; idem. *CPJ*, vol. 1 (prolegomena), p. 17, n.47.
28 *OGIS*, 737; *SB.*, 681, 4206, 8066, cf. n.40c below.
29 S. Reinach, *REJ*, 17 (1888), pp. 235-238; Schürer, vol. 2, p. 500; vol. 3, pp. 43, 93; *OGIS*, 96, 101; *CPJ*, III 1443-1445.

donors and their contributions, these having been mentioned separately in the inscriptions. This alone is a good enough reason for assuming that one date is implied.

The dedication of the synagogue to the "Most High God" (in *CIJ*, II 1443) is not to be related to the cult of ϑεὸς ὕψιστος which gained a wide footing in the Roman Empire only at a later date[30]. Since this epithet recurs in the Septuagint and in Jewish-Hellenistic literature[31] with great frequency, there is some justification in concluding that it was employed as a name for God by the Jews of Egypt too. It is, in fact, in no way surprising that yet another synagogue of the period found in Alexandria was also dedicated to ϑεὸς ὕψιστος. (*CIJ*, II 1443).

Some scholars have, however, unfortunately failed to grasp the meaning of the ἐξέδρα. Goodenough, to take one example, has interpreted it as the "Seat of Moses", meaning the seat of honour in a Jewish synagogue[32]. In point of fact, this object, examples of which were discovered in the synagogue of Dura Europos, Chorazin and Hammath (Tiberias)[33], became known as "Moses' Cathedra" only at a much later date[34]. Clearly, what is meant by ἐξέδρα is a hall or arcade at the front of important public buildings such as the gymnasia[35]. This type of structure is frequent in ancient Jewish construction terminology, and is found in the *Mishnah* and *Tosefta*[36].

It seems obvious that the Jewish community in Athribis functioned as a legal body enjoying the same privileges as its "sister"

---

30 On this cult see Schürer, *Sitzungsberichte der Berliner Akademie* (1897), pp. 220-225; Robert & Skeat & Nock, *HTR*, 29 (1936), p. 36; Cumont, *Les religions orientales* etc., pp. 59ff.

31 See, for example, *Gen.* 14:18-20, 22; *Psalms*, 7:18, 17:14, 49:14, 77:35; *II Macc.*, 3:31; *III Macc.*, 7:9 and many places in Philo's writings as well. Cf. Wolfson, *passim*; Tcherikover, *Jews in Egypt*, p. 102.

32 Googenough, *Jewish Symbols*, vol. 2, p. 85; Lewis in *CPJ*, III p. 143.

33 Cf. *Matthew*, 23:22; *Pesikta De-Rab Kahana* (ed. Mandelbaum), p. 11.

34 Krauss, *Synagogale Altertümer*, p. 386; Sukenik, *op.cit.*, pp. 57-61; Googenough, *op.cit.*, vol. 3, figs. 554, 568.

35 See: Liddell & Scott, *Greek-English Lexicon*, s.v. Certain scholars had in mind the *pronaos* which was mentioned in a Jewish inscription from Mantinea (*REJ*, 34 (1897), pp. 148-9). See further the details discussed by Krauss, *op.cit.*, p. 350; S. Reinach, *REJ*, 17 (1888), p. 238; Frey in *CIJ*, II 1440; Fraser, vol. 2, p. 443, n.773.

36 *M. Ma'asseroth*, iii 6; *M. Erubin*, viii, 4; *M. Sotah*, viii 3; *M. Oholoth*, vi 2; *T. Erubin*, viii 4 (ed. Zuckermandel, p. 147). For further details see: Krauss, *Griechische und lateinische Lehnwörter*, vol. 2, pp. 44ff.; idem, *Talmudische Archaeologie*, vol. 1, p. 52; idem, *Synagogale Altertümer*, p. 349.

community in Schedia. Furthermore, the inscriptions found in
Athribis prove that the Jewish community was entitled to administer
public funds as well as to solicit gifts from private donors for public
use. The importance of this fact lies in the light it sheds on the controversial question of whether bodies of this kind had the right to
own property, or not, in Ptolemaic Egypt[37]. The aspect of the
Athribis inscription which is of particular interest here is that which
concerns the character of the local Jews. The title carried by Ptolemy
son of Epikides, one of the donors mentioned in *CIJ*, II 1443, ὁ
ἐπιστάτης τῶν φυλακιτῶν, a leader of φυλακῖται surely, not of
φύλακες, who with his subordinates was no doubt engaged by the
authorities as a policeman and not as a private watchman[37a], has
great relevance to this problem. Even though his Jewish origins are
doubted by some scholars[38], their arguments have to be rejected on
the grounds of their being based on a popular prejudice which has
minimised the military significance of the Jews. Any further cause
for doubts is cleared up by Tcherikover who asks rhetorically, "Why
should a non-Jew associate himself with the Jewish community in
the dedication of a synagogue?"[38a]. It is true that the aforementioned individual carved out a fine career for himself as a superintendent of police, but this has no bearing at all on the religious
restrictions under discussion.

Officers of this rank were usually in command of all the policemen in a certain nome[39] being only second to the *strategos* himself
in police matters, and possibly in juridicial ones too[39a]. Since Athribis
was a *metropolis* (of the Athribic nome), it would seem certain that
an official of such high standing would be resident there, which, in
turn, would imply the existence of a Jewish unit under his command
for, as a rule, officers of this kind commanded units belonging to
their own ethnic group[39b]. This assumption gains support from the

---

37 On this question, see Taubenschlag, pp. 650-651.
37a Tcherikover, *CPJ*, I (Prolegomena), p. 17 and n.47.
38 S. Reinach, *loc. cit.*; *OGIS*, 96; and cf. Schürer, vol. 3, p. 132.
38a Tcherikover, *op.cit.*, n.46.
39 Lesquier, p. 262; Bevan, p. 143.
39a Lesquier, p. 193, Bouché-Leclercq, vol. 3, pp. 139-140; vol. 4, pp. 225-231; Jouguet, p. 53.
39b Cf. *CPJ*, I 24 which refers to two Jewish cleruchs settled by a Jewish officer called Dositheos. We may also take into account the example of Tobias, the head of a military

fact that the synagogue bears the joint dedication of the officer and the community. It appears then, that the nucleus of the local Jewish community consisted of a police unit under the command of this officer, which probably belonged to the ποταμοφυλκία too.

There does not appear to have been any difference between the regular army and the Ptolemaic police of the second century B.C.E.[40] The Jews of Athribis can, therefore, be regarded as κληρουχοι in the service of the police. The location of the "Land of Onias", the well-known Jewish military settlement, in the vicinity strengthened this impression. There is, too, a papyrus (*P. Oxy.*, 500 = *CPJ*, II 448) dated 130 C.E. which proves that the Jews were landowners in the Athribic nome. There is no doubt that their lands, confiscated after the great revolt of 115-117 C.E., came down to them through an ancient Ptolemaic inheritance. These lands, called δημοσία in the papyrus (lines 13, 16)[40a], probably were once classified as γῆ ἐν ἀφέσει or more correctly, γῆ κληρουχική.

The third inscription from Athribis is the last link in the chain of proofs offered here. It hints at the military character of the local Jewish settlement in explicit terms with: οἱ ἐκ τῆς...[στρα]τιωτικῆς...

The conclusion that can be drawn from this set of facts is that the communal organisation of Jewish cleruch-policemen in Athribis follows that of the κοινόν or πολίτευμα model, corresponding to other ethnic units within the Ptolemaic army[40b]. The inscription on the Idumaean *politeuma* of policemen in Memphis[40c] gives further support to this conclusion.

Leontopolis

Scholars seeking to identify Leontopolis encountered two main difficutlies: a) Josephus located it both in the Heliopolite nome

cleruchy in Trans-Jordan, and of course that of Onias IV and his sons, the heads of several Jewish military settlements in the so-called "Land of Onias". Cf. also to the *politeuma* of the Idumaeans in Memphis (n.40c below and n.28 above).

40 Lesquier, pp.260-264; Bouché-Leclercq, vol. 4, pp. 52-62; Grenfell & Hunt, *P. Tebt.*, I App. I, pp. 550-551; Uebel, p. 37 *et al. multa.*

40a Or *ager publicus* in Latin. This term referred to the land, which was confiscated from the Jews, as a result of the crushing of their revolt in 115-117 C.E.

40b See, for example, Lesquier, pp. 142-155; Launey, vol. 2, p. 106ff; Ruppel, p. 299ff.

40c *OGIS*, 737, Ruppel, pp. 306ff.; Launey, pp. 1072-1077; Rapaport, *Rev de Phil.*, 40 (1969), pp. 73-82; Fraser, vol. 1, pp. 280-281; cf. n.28 above.

(*Antiquitates*, XIII 65, 70; *Bellum*, VII 426) and at the fort of
Bubastis (*Antiquitates*, XIII 66, 70). b) There are two places known
as Tel el-Yehoudieh, one of them six miles southeast of present day
Belbis (at a spot called Gheyata) not far from ancient Bubastis which
lay in the middle of another nome (north of that of Heliopolis)[41],
and the other two miles south of presentday Shibin al-Kantir within
the Heliopolite nome. Naville managed to overcome the difficulties
and argued persuasively that the second site was the Leontopolis
of Onias[42]. His view is supported by the fact that Josephus actually
said the place was near the temple, rather than the town, of Bubastis
(*Antiquitates*, XIII 66, 70), and since a number of places in Egypt
(especially in this region) were connected with the cult of Bast, it
is quite possible that there was a temple to that goddess in Leontopolis as well. That is actually proven by an archaeological find, the
statue of Horus holding the sanctuary of that goddess, as Petrie
already showed[43]. Following Naville's suggestion, the city of Onias
has been identified with the "camp of the Jews" (*castra Judaeorum*)
mentioned in an early Byzantian source (*Notitia Dignitatum Orientis*)
which was located in the *Augustamnica* district east of the delta.
Among the convincing evidence of this identification are archaeological finds from Tel el-Yehoudieh indicating that it was definitely a
military site[44].

On the other hand Duncan appears justified in objecting to Naville's
identification of Tel al-Yehoudieh with another place called *Scenae
Veteranorum*, likewise known from Byzantian times, because it
would not accord with the distance cited in *Itinerarium Antonini*. In
his view the second place should be identified with nearby El-Manir

---

41 About which Herodotus attested (II 137). See Strabo, XVII 1, 19 (802c); Pliny, V 9, 49;
    Ptolmaeus, IV 5, 51.

42 Naville, *The Mound*, p. 19f.

43 The same scholar gave additional reasons for identifying the place, and relied to a great
    extent on Josephus, devoting, e.g., a special discussion to the distances indicated in his
    writings, and apparently solving the matter satisfactorily. He considered an important
    archeological find – large piles of burnt animal bones discovered outside of the city, on
    the north side – to be the collection of bones of the sacrifices from the temple of Onias.
    In his opinion the Hellenistic shards from the second century B.C.E., the style of the
    city's buildings and forts, and especially the remains of the temple validate Josephus's
    report. For full details see Petrie, *Hyksos*, pp. 19-27; Schürer, vol. 3, pp. 42-43, 145,
    n.34.

44 See Naville, *ibid.*, Petrie, *ibid.*; support for this appears also in the reports of Josephus,
    which described the temple of Onias as a fortress (*Antiquitates*, XIII 66).

which has no connection with Jews. Apparently an Arab garrison was stationed there, and furthermore there is not a sign of a Jew in the local graveyard (of enormous size) from the first century (to the fourth). As to northern Tel el-Yehoudieh which borders on Belbis, Duncan argued convincingly that it should be identified with the "village of the Jews" (*Vicus Judaeorum*) mentioned in *Itinerarium Antonini*, 42[46]

Concurring in Naville's identification of Leontopolis, Juster was of the opinion that *Castra Judaeorum* was what Josephus called τὸ Ἰουδαίων στρατόπεδον (*Antiquitates*, XIV 133), the place where Mithradates and Antipater fought the Egyptians when they set out to extricate Julius Caesar from his military difficulties in Alexandria[47]. Schürer on the other hand cautiously avoided that identification, believing that the battle site was west of the delta. At first glance that could be the inference from Josephus' statement on encircling the delta[48], but the wording is somewhat misleading, and cannot be construed to mean that Mithradates' troops had already crossed the river. They undoubtedly meant to proceed southwards to the head of the delta and there cross the Nile westwards. Such a course would be tactically correct, because it obviates the need to move troops through the cleft terrain of the delta, and from that southern point Alexnadria can be approached directly along the west branch of the Nile without any intervening aquatic obstacles. Crossing the Nile at the vertex of the delta was preferable also because that region was inhabited by Jewish communities willing to collaborate. Most likely the Egyptian foe gathered at Memphis understood Mithradates' movements very well and wished to hinder them. Consequently it is reasonable to locate the battle in the vicinity of Heliopolis, east of the Nile[49]. The description of the course of the

---

45 For full details on this problem see Duncan (in Petrie, *Hyksos*, p. 55); and cf. Petrie's own words on the problem of distances (*ibid.*, p. 66f.).

46 Cf. also Schürer, vol. 3, pp. 43, 146. He also distinguished between the two places that were called Tel el-Yehoudieh.

47 Juster, vol. 1, p. 205, n.5; and cf. also *Bellum*, I 191. Because of the similarity of the names, Tcherikover also tended to this view, see *Hellenistic Civilization etc.*, p. 279; *Jews in Egypt*, p. 23.

48 *Bellum*, I 191; *Antiquitates*, XIII 133. Cf. Rice-Holmes, 3, p. 496f.; Sijpesteijn, *Latomus*, 24 (1965), pp. 123-124, n.8.

49 Cf. the description of the operation by Hirtius, *Bell. Alex.*, 26-31; and see also Andrieu, *César*, Intr. p. XLIIIf.; Sijpesteijn, *ibid.*, p. 122f.

battle seems to support this choice. Josephus testifies that the
right wing under the command of Mithradates was pushed back,
while Antipater's right wing rushed forward (after its victory) along
the river bank to help (*Antiquitates*, XIV 134). If the battle did
take place because of an attempt to cross the river, its course is more
easily understood if both the opposing armies are assumed to have
been east of the Nile. Thus Schürer's view must be rejected. Yet
this does not confirm Juster's proposal, for Leontopolis (according
to Naville's identification) lay far from the vertex of the delta. The
site of τὸ Ἰουδαίων στρατόπεδον must therefore be located around
Heliopolis itself, apparently a bit south of it. The similarity of this
name to *Castra Judaeorum* should not lead to the conclusion that a
single place is meant. It appears that there was an additional place
near Heliopolis — Babylon — that likewise had a similar name,
and in the first century was a "camp" (παρεμβολή) for the Roman
army[50], evidently built on the foundations of a Ptolemaic camp. It is
that place that should be identified with Josephus' τὸ Ἰουδαίων
στρατόπεδον, for its location east of the Nile exactly at the vertex
of the delta accords with military logic in regard to crossing the river.
The name "Babylon" of course implies an Eastern or Semitic origin[51]
and it does not seem incorrect to identify its ancient settlers with the
people of the "land of Onias". As the place is in the Heliopolite
nome, it may reasonably be assumed to have been a forward outpost
on the southern border. Its propinquity to the nome of Memphis
explains the town's participation in the blocking of the forces of
Mithradates and Antipater, and its attempt to prevent the crossing of
the river and the subsequent rescue of Julius Caesar.

The site of Leontopolis having been determined, findings having
some direct bearing on the community organization there can be
examined. These are provided in the main by excavations directed by
Naville which uncovered a Jewish cemetery about two kilometers
away from the town, bordering the desert. It is about a kilometer
and a half long and several hundred meters wide. All the graves are

---

50 See de Villard, *Aegyptus* 5 (1925), p. 174f. The place is mentioned as a military "camp"
in *CPJ*, II 417 (= *P. Hamb.*, 2) from 59 C.E., and was in the vicinity of the "Syrian village" of the Heliopolis district. The residents of the village were certainly descendants of
the people from the land of Onias, as the editor of the document thought.
51 Tcherikover, *Jews in Egypt*, p. 23 and n.34.

below ground level, some in what can be identified as family catacombs (see Plate in p. 124).

The catacombs from the Roman period were more symmetrical
and precisely planned. Four stone steps led down to a low stone door
that turned on a hinge and was locked. It opened into a central hall
from the sides of which long narrow crypts the size of a human body
were hewn out of the rock. Some still contained parts of bodies, with
no trace of embalmment or decoration, and a clump of earth at the
head. Naville noted that the design and interior arrangements of the
tombs indicate a sytle brought from outside Egypt, in which the
influence of Phoenicia and Palestine are clearly recognizable. The
absence of embalmment and decoration as well as the clump of earth
at the head he rightly considered characteristic of Jews[52]. These
signs are important because they serve to identify as Jewish many
tombs whose inscriptions have not survived. In fact to this day
the Egyptians call the place the "tomb of the Jews", confirming that
it was that in ancient times. The epigraphical finds come to more
than eighty tombstone inscriptions mostly from the first century,
with only a few earlier ones[53].

In regard to the local Jewish community, the size of the cemetery
and the valuable nature of the findings indicate first of all that it was
a large community, quite well established economically. That it was
institutionalized in its organization is evident, for the allocation of
plots for family tombs presupposes effective organization. Naville
found various qualities of rock in different sections of the cemetery, so that there were "good" sections and "bad" ones, which
might have led to difficulties in assigning them. The community may
have had a burial society (*Ḥebrah Kadisha*) which solved such problems, as another Fayûm community had[54].

One of the inscriptions, known as the "Ḥelkias stone"[55] (*CIJ*, II

---

52 Naville, *The Mound*, pp. 13-15.
53 The earliest of them (*CIJ*, II 1490) is from 117 B.C.E.
54 Its nature is unknown. In any case, one of the papyri dealing with it (*CPJ*, I 138) mentions the burial society which met in the local synagogue, and see Stern's commentary
   (*ibid.*).
55 The reference may be to the famous strategos, Ḥelkias, one of Cleopatra III's commanders, or perhaps to his son. See Lewis's comments on this inscription (*CPJ*, III 1450),
   and also Tcherikover's opinion — *CPJ*, I p. 17, n.45. Reconstruction of the inscription
   (Th. Reinach, *REJ*, 40 (1900), pp. 50-54) was apparently done on the basis of the Jewish inscription from Berenice in Cyrene (*CIG*, 5361 = *REG*, LXII p. 283) but it is ex-

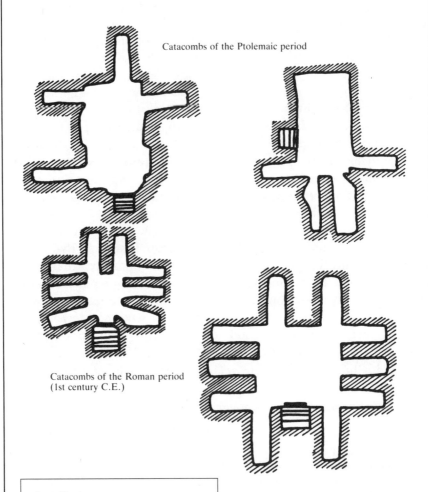

Examples of Jewish catacombs from Leontopolis

Catacombs of the Ptolemaic period

Catacombs of the Roman period
(1st century C.E.)

According to:
Ed. Naville, F. L. Griffith,
*The Mound of the Jewish catacombs from
Leontopolis*
Pl. XVI

1450), though badly preserved provides considerable information on the community organization. The inscription has the form of a reverential "decision" by the "public (πλῆϑος) in the sacred district" (line 3) showing that the Jewish community in Leontopolis was an organized body empowered to make decisions (ψηφίσματα). The use of the word πλῆϑος is most illuminating, and as it accords with the wording of the *Letter of Aristeas* (§ 310) in regard to the Jewish *politeuma* in Alexandria as well as the members of the Idumaean police *politeuma* in Memphis[56], leads to the conclusion that the Jewish community in Leontopolis was also organized into a *politeuma*.

This is confirmed by an important inscription (*CPJ*, III 1530A = *SB* 5765) on the tombstone of a prominent man named Abramos, described as the "head (πολιτάρχης of two places" (line 7). Etymologically the title may be a combination of *archon* (= ruler) and *polis* (= city), and in a number of cities of the Hellenistic-Roman world it was conferred on the most important local magistrates[57]. Luckily there is mention of an official with that title in an Egyptian city, Oxyrhynchus (*P. Oxy.*, IV 745) in the first century, and Jouguet proved that he was actually a "city governor" subordinate to the *strategos* of the nome[58]. The presence of a Jewish *politarches* (or *politarchon*) in Leontopolis suggests that its administration was all Jewish. This is not surprising for in the Hellenistic period the *strategoi* of the whole nome were Jews[59], and besides, the city was the religious center for the Jews of the entire region. Although it might be argued

---

tremely doubtful; see also Fuchs, p. 16; Willrich, *Archiv*, 1 (1901), p. 48f.; Strack, *Archiv*, 2 (1903), p. 554; Cohen, *Judaica et Aegyptiaca*, p. 58; Stern, *Greek and Latin Authors*, p. 270.

56 *OGIS*, 737, line 6. Cf. the use of the term πλῆϑος in the inscription from Syrian Apamea, *CIJ*, II 804, and see on this matter Schwabe (*Kedem*, 1 (1941), pp. 85-93), who discussed similar usages in the New Testament.

57 This was so, e.g., in Thessaloniki — *Acta apostolorum*, XVII: 6, 8 and also *CIG*, II 1967; or in the city of Letae — *Syll.* 700 (1, 48). And see also Perdrizet, *BCH*, 18 (1894), p. 420; idem., *op.cit.*, 21 (1897), pp. 161-162; and also Holleaux, *REG*, 10 (1897), p. 451. All these citations are from the Roman period. Tarn (p. 67) believed that the appearance of the *politarches* was a result of administrative reform of the Roman authorities, and was designed to give them more efficient control of the cities. M. Stern, *The Diaspora in the Hellenistic-Roman World*, pp. 175, 336 (n.84).

58 Jouguet, p. 66.

59 A matter which has epigraphical and papyrological confirmation. See, e.g., *CPJ*, I 132; *CPJ*, III 1450, and, of course, Josephus — *C. Apionem*, II 49-50; *Antiquitates*, XIII 284-287.

that the inscription dates from the Roman period when the Jewish
military settlement in the place was already disbanded and the
strategoi were no longer Jewish, there is no evidence that the Romans
had implemented the same policy of dissolution in regard to administration and non-military political and organizational matters. In
other words, despite the demilitarization of the "land of Onias"
during the Roman period, it is reasonable to assume that it remained
demographically Jewish, and therefore its capital, Leontopolis,
could well have had a Jewish "city governor" (πολιτάρχης).

Robert was the first scholar to make an important deduction
regarding the local community organization, the *politeuma*, for the
title of *politarches*. In his view it was based on a federative union of
two groups, one in Leontopolis itself, and the other in one of the
other place in the vicinity, which is why Abramos was described as
"*politarches* of two places"[60]. Organizationally speaking, two aspects
are discernible. On the one hand there appears to have been a type of
landsmannschaft association in each place (δισσοί τόποι) and on the
other a community roof organization suggested by Abramos' double
function (διμερῆ δαπάνην). The first has an analog in Arsinoe where
there was a *landsmannschaft*-type association of Jews from Thebes
(Diospolis Magna) which had its own synagogue and *archontes*[61].
In the city of Rome too there were thirteen separate congregations
organized around separate synagogues each with its own magistracy.
The same applied to an Antioch congregation which established an
organization of its own in Apamea on the Orontes[62], and to similar
congregations in Palestine[63]. However, there are no other definite
instances of a federative union involving a community roof organization[64].

A careful examination of the inscription on the Abramos tombstone reveals additional clues suggesting that his community was
organized as a *politeuma*, for he is described as wearing "the wreath

---

60 See Robert, *Hellenica*, 1 (1940), pp. 18-24.
61 *CPJ*, II 432, lines 56-57 (from 113 C.E.), and this will be discussed at greater length
    below.
62 *CIJ*, II 804; and see Schwabe, *Levy Memorial Volume*, p. 216f.
63 E.g., in Jerusalem – see *Acts*, 6:9; or in Caesarea Maritima, – *CIJ*, II 772; and cf. Schwabe,
    Yediot, IX (1942), pp. 21-30. See also *J.T. Sanhedrin*, x 28a; *J.T. Shebiith*, ix 39a.
64 For a survey of research on this problem, especially as regards the Jews of the city of
    Rome, see Leon, *The Jews of Rome*, p. 168f.

of magistracy for the whole people (ἀρχῇ πανδήμῳ ἐθνικῇ; lines 5-6). The use of the term *ethnos* is most instructive, for it not only fits the ethnic criterion for the formation of a *politeuma*, but was also the term applied to the Jewish community of Alexandria[65]. The *ethnarches* in Alexandria may even be the equivalent of *politarches* (or *politarchon*) in Leontopolis, so that the two communities seem to have been organized in the same way, each as a *politeuma*.

Information culled from other Leontopolitan documents provide support for this hypothesis. A first century inscription designates the members of the community as πολῖται[66] and others describe them as ἄστεοι as distinct from "foreigners" (ξένοι)[67]. It is reasonable to suppose that those epithets referred not to any of the three Greek *poleis* in Egypt, but to "citizenship" in Leontopolis. And since the town was not a *polis*, the inevitable conclusion is that they point to membership in the Jewish *politeuma* of which Abramos was *politarches*. The same indication is given by another tombstone, calling to the passerby to mourn the man who left the σεμνότα[τον -?-]and his city (καὶ πόλιν)[68]. While the reconstruction of the missing word is by no means certain, it could very well be *politeuma* (σεμνότα[τον πολίτευμα])[69].

The Leontopolitan Jews conception of their town as their "homeland" is shown in a young woman's tombstone inscription, in the form of a poetic dialogue (*CIJ*, II 1530). To a question on her "homeland (πατρίς) and birth-place" (line 2) the proud answer is "the famous land of Onias reared me" (line 4), and there is no doubt that the reference is to Leontopolis (where she was buried). Such an attitude is not at all unusual or astonishing, for the Jews of Alexandria

---

65 E.g., in Strabo, who is quoted by Josephus in *Antiquitates*, XIV 117; and also in the Claudian Edict — *Antiquitates*, XIX 284, 285. Cf. also Philo's usage: *Legatio*, 133, 137, 161, 178; *In Flaccum*, 117, 124 (this is only a small sample of his frequent use of the term). Other communities in the Roman diaspora were also called by the name, such as Smyrna — *CIJ*, II 741. Cf. also L. Robert, *Hellenica*, 1 (1940), p. 20.

66 *CIJ*, II 1489, line 6.

67 See particularly *CIJ*, II 1531, line 1; cf. also *ibid.*, 1490, line 1; 1508, lines 2, 10; 1509, line 9. The identity of the terms ἀστοί and πολῖται does not seem to be deducible from this (see chap. V, b below) since the term ἀστοί here has a purely rhetorical significance.

68 *CIJ*, II 1490, lines 5-6.

69 See bibliographical details on the possibility of such a reconstruction in *CPJ*, III 1490 (p. 153). If it is accepted, the complete translation of line 5 of the inscription would be: "Weep for the man who has left the most dignified *politeuma* and his city".

Chapter III

Jewish tomb stones from Leontopolis

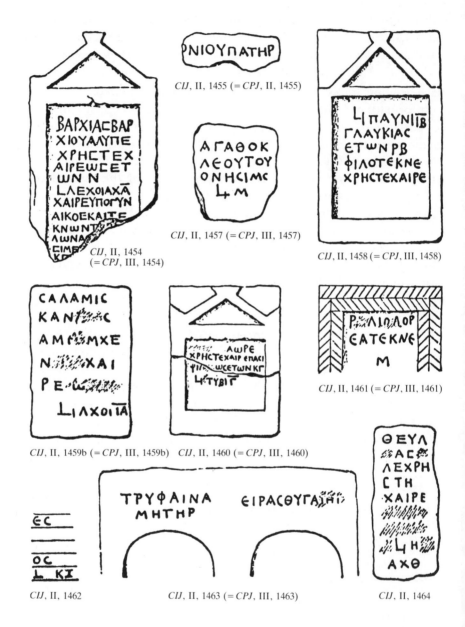

CIJ, II, 1455 (= CPJ, II, 1455)

CIJ, II, 1457 (= CPJ, III, 1457)

CIJ, II, 1454
(= CPJ, III, 1454)

CIJ, II, 1458 (= CPJ, III, 1458)

CIJ, II, 1461 (= CPJ, III, 1461)

CIJ, II, 1459b (= CPJ, III, 1459b)   CIJ, II, 1460 (= CPJ, III, 1460)

CIJ, II, 1462   CIJ, II, 1463 (= CPJ, III, 1463)   CIJ, II, 1464

Jewish tomb stones from Leontopolis

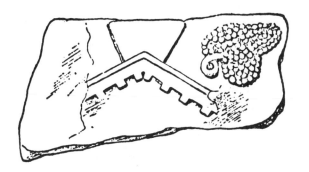

MEKAINYN ... ΠѠϹΕΙΤΑΟΓΕΝ
ΝΗϹΑϹΓΑΡΜ ... ΠΕΝΘΕΙΤΗΚΟ
ΜΕΝΟϹΨΥΧΗ ΥΝΓΕΝΕΙΗΔΕΦΙ
ΛΟΙϹΕΙΔΕΘΕΛ ϹΓΝѠΝΑΙΔΥΝΑ
ϹΑΙΠΟϹΕΗΠΙ ΙϹΗΔΕΧΑΡΙϹΚΑΙ
ΠѠϹΠΑΝΤΕϹ ΔΥΡΜΟϹΕΧΕΙΔΕΥ
ΡΙΘΙΚΙΕΡѠΤΗϹ ΝϹΟΜΟΗΔΟΝ
ΥΙΟΝΑѠΡΑΤΟϹ ΠΟΤΑΠΟϹ

CIJ, II, 1451 (= *CPJ*, III, 1451)

MIKKOϹΝΕΘΑΝΕѠϹ
ΠΑϹΙΦΙΛΕΧΡΗϹΤΕΑѠΡΕ
ΧΑΙΡΕѠϹΕΤѠΝΛΕ
ЦΘΦΑѠΦΙΙΑ

CIJ, II, 1452 (= *CPJ*, III, 1452)

ΕΛΕΔΖΑΡΕ
ΑѠΡΕΧΡΗϹΤΕ
ΠΑϹΙΦΙΛΕ
ѠϹΕΚΜϹ

CIJ, II, 1453 (= *CPJ*, III, 1453)

referred to their city in the same terms[70]. Thus the political ties that the Leontopolitan Jews had to their city were based on their own organization, and like the Alexandrian Jews they were *politai* of the local Jewish *politeuma*. Confirmation of this is provided by Strabo (quoted by Josephus in *Antiquitates*, XIII 287): "And only the Jews of the district named for Onias remained faithful to her [Cleopatra III] because their fellow-citizens (τοὺς πολίτας) Ḥelkias and Ananias, were held in special favour by the queen"[71]. It is Strabo too who employed the term *politeia* in regard to the Jewish community of Alexandria (*Antiquitates*, XIV 117).

Some information is available also on the establishment and practices of the Leontopolis Jewish community. One of the steles (*CIJ*, II 1529) marks the tomb of a Jew who lived outside the town, but there is no evidence of others in the same situation. The deceased came from the village of Teberkythis whose location is unknown, but was probably a small nearby place. Its Jewish inhabitants may have brought their dead to Leontopolis for burial, or even been formally connected with the town. On the other hand, the burial of a "stranger" in Leontopolis may suggest a movement of Jews, in particular from neighboring communities, to that place, which might be the explanation for Abramos' double post as *"politarches of two places"*. The demilitarization policy of a Romans which led to the disbanding of the Jewish military settlements in the region may well have resulted in a move to Leontopolis and the subsequent formation of *Landsmannschaft* within the larger community.

Another stele, *CIJ*, II 1514, of 27 B.C.E. mentions a woman named Marion described as ἱέρισα, that is, "of priestly descent". An early researcher, Edgar, had trouble with the meaning, and hesitantly suggested it might be her patronymic[72]. Lietzmann contended it signified her descent[73], and Frey even found a similar designation on

---

70 See, e.g., Philo, *In Flaccum*, 46. A detailed discussion of this problem is to be found below, p. 238. Compare to πατρίς mentioned in an inscription from Acmonia (*CIJ*, II 771) and one from Tiberias (Schwabe, *Levy Memorial Volume*, p. 226, No. 15). See also Ramsay, *The Cities*, pp. 622-651; and see pp. 236-238 below.

71 Although the translation could be "their conationals" or even "their brothers", the fact that Strabo used this term when he could have used others (more literary and simpler) may indicate that this was actually the official term applied to the members of the Jewish community of Leontopolis.

72 Edgar, *ASAE*, 22 (1923), p. 13.

73 Lietzmann, *ZNW*, 22 (1923), p. 234, n.25.

Leontopolis – The city and Onias' temple

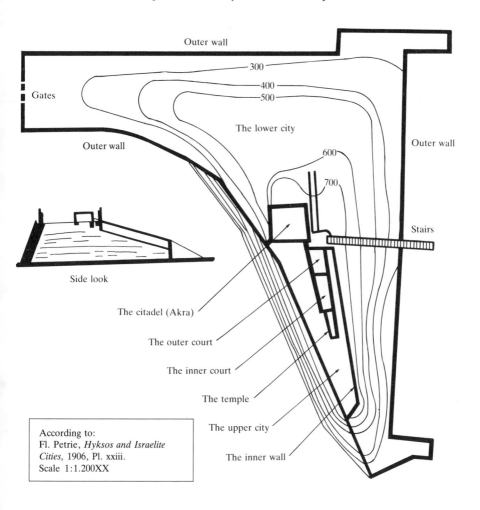

Outer wall

300

400

500

Gates

Outer wall

The lower city

Outer wall

600

700

Side look

Stairs

The citadel (Akra)

The outer court

The inner court

The temple

The upper city

According to:
Fl. Petrie, *Hyksos and Israelite
Cities,* 1906, Pl. xxiii.
Scale 1:1.200XX

The inner wall

a tombstone in Rome[74]. The designation of preistly descent is interesting and important, all the more so in view of Josephus' testimony that generalogical records of priestly families were preserved in Jewish community archives in every locality (*C. Apionem*, I 31-36; *Vita*, 6). Surely such records were preserved in Leontopolis as well, especially since it was the site of the temple of Onias which was operated by priests of the High Priestly family. As there is no mention on the tombstone of that lineage, Marion must have belonged to a less prestigious family of lay priests. In any case, the inscription helps confirm Josephus' assertion regarding community archives where the family trees of the priestly families were kept. Josephus also reported the presence in Leontopolis of religious functionaries (*Antiquitates*, XIII 63, 73) and Tcherikover noted that the temple of Onias was supposed to serve the military settlement, obviously not only in Leontopolis but in all of the "land of Onias"[75]. It is quite possible then that the genealogical records of the priestly families settled throughout the whole region were likewise kept in Leontopolis.

A number of chronological problems arise in connection with the establishment of the temple of Onias and of the military settlement in Leontopolis, since Josephus has two versions of Onias' departure for Egypt and the erection of the temple, one in *Bellum* and the other in *Antiquitates*, each logical and solid so that it is difficult to harmonize them. Aside from Josephus' erroneous identification (in *Bellum*) of Onias as III rather than IV[76], his chronology is systematic. First of all, that version does not separate Onias' move to Egypt from the construction of the temple. Secondly, as all the testimony connects the events with the defilement of the Jerusalem temple in the region of Antiochus IV Epiphanes (ca. 168/7 B.C.E.)[77], that may even be construed as the main and greatest motivation for the erec-

---

74 See *CIJ*, I 315. It appears that there are other parallels, e.g. in inscriptions from Beth She'arim, see Schwabe-Lifshitz, *Beth She'arim*, vol. 2, Nos. 66, 68. About the emphasis on priestly descent in the cities of the Roman Diaspora, see also p. 162 below and n.190.

75 Tcherikover, *Jews in Egypt*, p. 222.

76 Murray's choice of Onias III (*JTS*, 18 [1967], p. 362f.) must be totally rejected.

77 *Bellum*, I 33; *Bellum*, VII 422-425. According to *Bellum*, VII 436, the time that elapsed from the founding of the temple until its closing was 343 years. If this number is deemed a mistake, or a simple scribal error, and changed to 243, which many scholars believed to be correct, we can count back from 73 C.E. (the date of its closure) and arrive at 170 B.C.E., which fits the date stated almost exactly.

tion of the temple of Onias[78]. The *Bellum* version mentions (disparagingly) two other motivations. One was that Onias vied with the Jews at Jerusalem "against whom he harboured resentment for his exile", and the other suggesting that he had pretensions to personally implementing Isaiah's prophecy[79]. Josephus did not however identify the Jerusalemites that Onias wished to compete with, and as there are a variety of possibilities it seems preferable to refrain from speculating, and to adhere to the one explicit reason, the desecration of the Temple in Jerusalem by Antiochus IV Epiphanes.

In *Antiquitates* Josephus gave entirely different dates both for Onias' emigration and for the construction of his temple in Egypt. In XII 387 he connected the emigration with the appointment of Alcimus to the High Priesthood in Jerusalem, that is, in about 162 B.C.E., even stressing that the assignment of that high post to a member of a different priestly family was what led Onias to leave for Egypt[80]. In that passage Josephus hinted at the establishment of Onias' temple, but deferred the report on it so as to include it in a later chronological framework. That deferment alone suggests that the *Antiquitates* version attributed the building of the temple to a later period. In addition, however, the description is connected with Alexander Balas' accession to the Seleucid throne. Furthermore, the treatment is broken off in XIII 62 and resumed only in XIII 80. Between these two paragraphs are two matters connected with the Jews of Egypt, one relating to the temple of Onias (XIII 62-73) and the other to a dispute between Samaritans and Jews in Alexandria about the sanctity of the temples in Jerusalem and Gerizim (XIII 74-79)[81]. This insertion suggests that according to *Antiquitates* Onias' temple was erected after the rout of Demetrius I in his war with Alexander Balas. Consequently Onias' letter to the Ptolemaic kings regarding the help he gave them in the war in Syria and Phoenicia refers to the conflict between Demetrius I and Alexander Balas

---

78 See particularly *Bellum*, VII 422-425.
79 *Bellum*, VII 431-432 (*Isaiah*, 19:19 — "on that day there will be an altar for the Lord within the Land of Egypt").
80 Cf. *Antiquitates*, XX 235-236. There is no doubt that Josephus was in error here, since in fact the appointment of Menelaus was what caused Onias' family to be deprived of the high priesthood, but Josephus thought Menelaus was a relative.
81 Josephus gave no reason for relating the two episodes in one context. The reason seems to be their nearness in time (the period of Ptolemy Philometor) and their connection with Egypt. The relation is apparently only associational.

who was an ally of the Ptolemies[82]. All in all, the *Antiquitates* version intimates that Onias arrived in Egypt some considerable time before his temple was built[83].

It is important to note that in contrast to his version in *Bellum*, Josephus in *Antiquitates* did not once connect the construction of Onias with the defilement of the Temple in Jerusalem. He proffered a totally different reason, definitely stressing that Onias acted out of his desire "to acquire for himself eternal fame and glory" (XIII 63) and realize the prophecy of Isaiah[84]. This scriptural support made its way as well into talmudic legend[85], and Josephus evidently took it from a common popular tradition. It is reasonable to suppose that the reference to the prophecy served as halakhic support for the legality of the temple of Onias[86], and if so there was sense to it only after the Temple at Jerusalem was in regular operation, that is, at least after 164 B.C.E. Josephus was obviously consistent as well in the *Antiquitates* version where he postponed the events connected with Onias IV, while in *Bellum* they were set earlier. Moreover, in *Antiquitates* (XII 237) he clearly states that when Onias III was dismissed from the High Priesthood by Jason (175 B.C.E.), Onias IV was still an infant (νήπιος). In XII 387 he further notes that when Alcimus became High Priest (162 B.C.E.) Onias IV was a child (παῖς). It thus appears that Onias IV was a young man when he erected his temple, close to the time of Demetrius' defeat by Alexander Balas (XIII, 62ff.), that is, some time after 150 B.C.E.

---

82 Tcherikover at first identified the war under consideration with the civil war which occurred between Ptolemy VI Philometor and Ptolemy VIII Eurgetes II, see: *Jews and Greeks*, 1931, pp. 286-287. Later, (after the papyrological discovery of *UPZ*, 110), he avoided any definite identification and proposed other possibilities, such as a rebellion of natives in Egypt, or Philometor's last war against Alexander Balas, but he did not eliminate his first suggestion, either (*Hellenistic Civilization and the Jews*, p. 278f.; 499 (n.30).

83 And Tcherikover thought so, see *CPJ*, I (Prolegomena), p. 45; and also Stern, *Zion*, 25 (1960), p. 16 and n.99.

84 *Ibid.*, p. 64, 68, 71. *Bellum*, VII 432 also gives this reason, but as an unimportant one compared with the reason connected with the desecration of the Temple (*ibid.*, 425).

85 *T.J. Yoma*, VI 43c etc.; *T.B. Menaḥoth*, 109b etc.

86 It should be noted in this context that Rabbi Judah Bar Ilai considered the Temple of Onias an acceptable altar according to this tradition, and this was also the attitude of the *Mishnah* (*Menaḥoth*, XIII:10) although it considered its priests "who have a blemish". Perhaps in the latter matter there is an indirect hint of a competitive motif which is found in Josephus regarding the establishment of the Temple of Onias (*Bellum*, VII 431).

The question is which of the two Josephus versions is correct. Tcherikover was inclined to credit the *Antiquitates* version which is more detailed, especially since Josephus made corrections in it as regards the identity of Onias. He therefore preferred to postpone the date for the erection of the temple and set it around the time of Ptolemy VI Philometor's death (145 B.C.E.). In his view the temple was supposed to serve the Jewish military settlement at Leontopolis, and it can therefore be assumed that the settlement was founded before the temple was built[87]. On the basis of *UPZ*, 110 (= *CPJ*, I 132) Tcherikover suggested that Onias made his way to Egypt earlier, in about 170 B.C.E., because that papyrus was written in 164 B.C.E. and because he was inclined to identify the addressee as Onias IV. However, as noted above, that identification is based on an uncertain reading by Wilcken, and also contradicts the chronological data of *Antiquitates*. Consequently in the absence of a definite conclusion, the problem remains unsolved. Even if Wilcken's reading is accepted, it is by no means self-evident that the Onias of the papyrus is Onias IV[88] But if that identification is adopted, it would be necessary to conclude that Onias IV was already *strategos* in 164 B.C.E. Such a conclusion contradicts the *Antiquitates* version, making it necessary to accept that of *Bellum*, so that this complicated problem does not lend itself to a clear solution.

B. Middle Egypt

The most important district of Middle Egypt was the Fayûm, a large settlement area since the time of Ptolemy II Philadelphus[89]. Since most of the population was new there at the time, testimony on the presence of Jews there is of great interest. The papyrological and epigraphical evidence shows that Jews settled there from the third century B.C.E. on, distributed in about thirty different localities[90]. Some of them were characterized by organized communities, as the documents show.

---

87 See full details in *Hellenistic Civilization*, etc., p. 275f.
88 See chap. I, pp. 60f. above.
89 See Rostovtzeff, *SEHHW*, p. 360f.
90 See, e.g., Tcherikover, *Jews in Egypt*, p. 24f. Among the Jews there were quite a few military colonists, and on this see Launey, pp. 541-550.

Middle and Upper Egypt

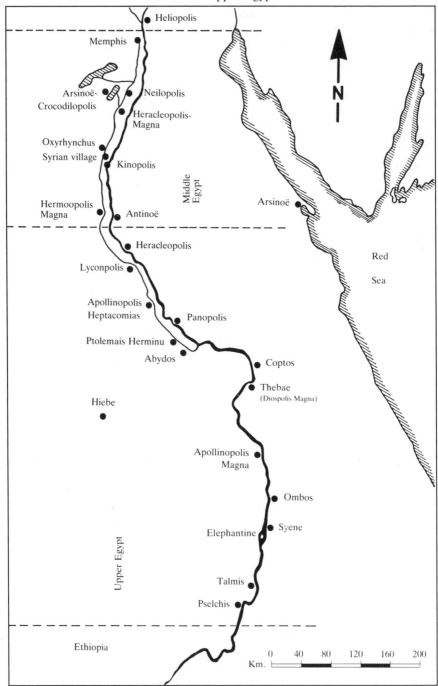

Heliopolis

Memphis

Arsinoë-
Crocodilopolis

Neilopolis

Heracleopolis-
Magna

Oxyrhynchus
Syrian village

Kinopolis

Middle
Egypt

Arsinoë

Hermoopolis
Magna

Antinoë

Heracleopolis

Red

Sea

Lyconpolis

Apollinopolis
Heptacomias

Panopolis

Ptolemais Herminu

Abydos

Coptos

Thebae
(Diospolis Magna)

Hiebe

Apollinopolis
Magna

Ombos

Elephantine

Syene

Upper Egypt

Talmis

Pselchis

Ethiopia

N

0   40   80   120   160   200
Km.

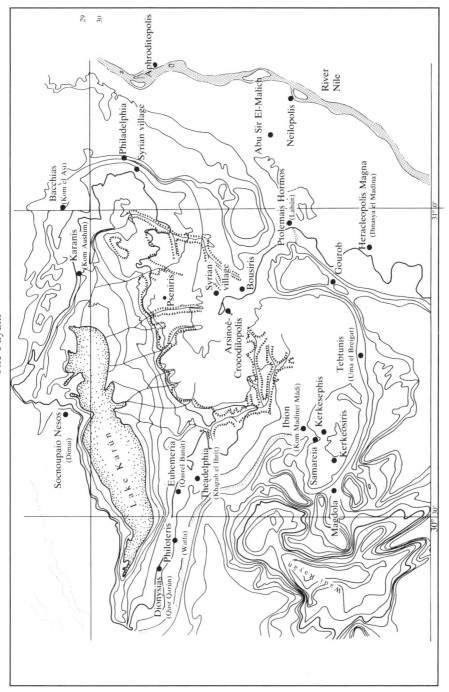

The Fayûm

Arsinoe Crocodilopolis

The *metropolis* of the Fayûm district, Arsinoe, already had an
organized Jewish community in the early days of the Ptolemaic
settlement program, as definitely proven by a dedicatory inscription
in honour of Ptolemy III Euergetes I and his family from a local synagogue (*CPJ*, III 1532A = *SB*, 8939). Papyrological evidence too
points to the antiquity of the Jewish community in that city[91]. *P.
Tebt.*, 86 (= *CPJ*, I 134) may refer to the same synagogue, but as a
place of the size certainly had several, the reference may be to
another[92]. The papyrological testimony is included in a land survey
of the city from the end of the second century B.C.E. which indicates
that the synagogue was built on a tract of land in the northwestern
part of the city[93], in an area listed in the Ptolemaic registry as
"sacred land" (ἱερὰ γῆ). The area was parceled out into various
holdings, some of which were leased and some of which were turned
over to private owners (apparently as "private land" — γῆ ἰδιωτική).
Thus, for example, two tracts bordering that of the synagogue were
defined as a "consecrated garden" (ἱερὰ παράδεισος), one of them
"private land" of some unnamed woman, and the other leased to
someone else (lines 14, 19-20). It is not clear what the status of the
synagogue land was, whether it was leased to the community or
turned over to it as "private land". In either case, the inescapable
conclusion is that the community was a recognized legal entity. The
fact that the synagogue land was marked "sacred land" is itself
illuminating, as the first editor of the papyrus notes[94]. The synagogue was certainly recognized as a holy place by the authorities
along with other sacred sites allotted suitable land and designated as
sacred. This is not surprising, for there are other examples from other
synagogues in Egypt[95]. It is not clear whether the adjacent "consecrated garden" that was leased (line 20) belonged to the com-

---

91 See, e.g., *CPJ*, I 126, from 238/7 B.C.E.; *CPJ*, I 19, from 226 B.C.E.
92 See *CPJ*, I pp. 247-248; and see also below, regarding *CPJ*, II 432.
93 See lines 16-17, 21-22, 29, 31. See also Tcherikover's commentary in *CPJ*, I p. 249.
94 Except that they did not really grasp the full significance (*P. Tebt.*, 86).
95 E.g., the inscription in one of the synagogues in Alexandria, which mentions "a holy
   square" (*CIJ*, II 1433); cf. Philo, *In Flaccum*, 48. An inscription from a synagogue in
   Upper Egypt (*OGIS*, 129 = *CIJ*, II 1449) mentions the granting of ἀσυλία at the order of
   the king. The sacredness of areas around Jewish synagogues is attested to in Asia Minor
   also, see *Antiquitates*, XVI 163-164, 168; *ibid.*, XIV 261, and others; cf. n.10 above.

munity or not. If it did, then the community had a small income from it, for the land survey notes that flowers and vegetables were grown on it. Although the names of the lessees are definitely Gentile, they may well have been Jews, for as a synagogue is after all designed to serve a considerable community, it was most likely situated in a Jewish residential area. Moreover, since the synagogue was given legal protection as a holy place, it is logical to suppose that it was surrounded by tracts of land assigned to Jews[96].

The location of the synagogue at the northwestern limits of the town suggests the existence of a Jewish residential neighborhood at the perimeter, a convenient place for maintaining a regular Jewish way of life with a minimum of interference. The neighborhood may have been within the Syrian quarter (Ἄμψοδον Συριακῆς) mentioned in fifteen documents from the second to the fourth century C.E.[97], or the entire quarter may in fact have been Jewish[98]. In any case, at the time Arsinoe contained neighborhoods designated by particular ethnic groups such as Bithynians, Macedonians, Thracians, Cilicians, etc[99]. That feature was a heritage from the Ptolemies and may be a muffled echo of the organization of *politeumata* based on military settlement in the place. That the Jewish community was similarly organized seems obvious.

The document in question (*CPJ*, I 134) indicates that the official representative of the community to the authorities was a man named Pertollos (line 18). He probably held a public office with administrative-representative duties, such as that of a *prostates*[100]; or perhaps he was a *frontistes*, which was likewise a familiar post in the com-

---

96 Their Egyptian names cannot be cited as proof that they were not Jewish. The Jews of Egypt did not hesitate to adopt the most pagan names, see Tcherikover, *Jews in Egypt*, p. 191. cf. *T.B., Gittin*, 11b. Thus the names mentioned in the document — Demetrios, Hermione, Apollonides, Sarapion, Petesouchos and Marres — may have been Jewish, especially since most of them are mentioned in several other documents (cf. *CPJ*, III, Appendix II, s.v.). Of these names, only Petesouchos has no parallel, but since the name of the man who represented the synagogue before the authorities, Pertollos, also has no equivalent, and there can be no doubt that *he* was Jewish, we must not hasten to reject the possibility of Petesouchos being a Jew.

97 Vaggi, *Aegyptus*, 17 (1937), p. 33.

98 So thought Heichelheim (p. 71).

99 See Wessely, *Die Stadt Arsinoë*, p. 21f.; Jouguet, pp. 287-288; see also *P. Ryl.*, 103, lines 4, 9-10, 20. Cf. as regards the existence of a "Hellenic quarter" *BGU*, 18, line 30.

100 See chap. III, Xenephyris.

munities of the Diaspora, involving matters like the supervision and management of the community's common property[101]. He may however have been one of the local *archontes*, who are mentioned in another document (*CPJ*, II 432, see below) as representing the community in regard to public water consumption. While the data are insufficient to allow for an unequivocal conclusion, the last alternative seems the most likely. In any case, Pertollos was presumbly a respected, wealthy man, with enough property of his own to guarantee the community property for the authorities.

Important information on the community is provided by document *CPJ*, II 432 of 113 C.E., which is an official report of income and expenditure in connection with the municipal water supply, submitted by the four competent officials to the city auditor. Among the debtors are two Jewish institutions, one called the "synagogue of the Thebans" (Προσευχὴ Θηβαίων; line 57) and the other just "synagogue" (or "prayer house" — εὐχεῖον —; line 60). The distinction made suggests that the local Jews at the time were organized into two *landsmannschaft*-type bodies, one of people from Thebes (Diospolis Magna)[102] and the other probably of local people. How the leadership and the connections between the two operated is intimated by line 57 (ἀρχόντων Ἰ[ου]δαίων προσευχῆς Θηβαίων). It was translated by the editor, Fuks, as "from the *archontes* of the synagogue of the Theban Jews"[103] which implies that the Thebans had their own leadership, and in that case it is surprising that no *archontes* are mentioned in connection with the local synagogue (line 60). The genitive case of the phrase suggests a slightly different meaning, however: "From the Jewish *archontes* for the synagogue of the Thebans... and similarly for the prayer house", etc.[104] Only in this way is the failure to mention *archontes* in connection with the local synagogue explicable. In brief, the men were *archontes* for both synagogues, each of which was billed separately for water. Evidently then the Jewish community of Arsinoë was a federative organization

---

101 See *CIJ*, I pp. xcif.; Baron, *The Jewish Community*, p. 102. Cf. also Schwabe, *Tarbitz*, 12 (1941), p. 231.
102 The circumstances under which they reached Arsinoe are unknown, but see n.180 below.
103 Cf. Tcherikover's identical translation, *Jews in Egypt*, p. 100.
104 Cf. line 30 — "for the bath of Severianus"; line 36 — "for the street fountain"; line 40 — "for the Macedonian fountain", etc. (cf. also lines 44, 51).

of *landsmannschaft*-type groups, with a roof leadership. The document seems to indicate as well that the municipality and government considered the Jewish community a separate collective which paid its water bills in an organized manner through its authorized representatives, the *archontes*. The document lists a great many consumers of water and sets water rates, but never once refers to any officials in connection with the payments, except for the Jewish *archontes*. The reason is simple: All the other consumers were affiliated with the metropolitan communal organization. Thus the fact that the bill was submitted to and paid by the Jewish *archontes* emphasizes the special nature of the Jewish community and its separate organization.

The information on the Arsinoë community may be summed up as follows:

a) The existence of synagogues in the city indicates organized community life.

b) The constitutional basis for the construction and operation of the synagogues was undoubtedly the right to "live according to ancestral laws" granted by the central government.

c) The placement of a local synagogue on "sacred land" shows its protected status recognized by government and law.

d) The Jewish community was located in its own residential area making regular community life possible.

e) As an organized body recognized by law, the community had the right of ψήφισμα (= public decision).

f) The community had its own leaders, separate from those of the *metropolis*, who had representational functions in connection with public services.

g) The Jewish community had communal property which it maintained and managed on its own.

These facts lead to a single important conclusion: The Jewish community in Arsinoe-Crocodilopolis was considered a recognized, political and legal body, which seems to have been organized as a *politeuma*.

As to the legal status of individual members of the community, document *CPJ*, I 19 of 226 B.C.E. shows that the community included Jews with the status of *politai*. In a case involving two Jews (a man and woman), all the procedures, constitutional bases, and the court itself, followed the Greek norms. That is especially clear from the descriptions of the grounds for the judges' decision, which included the "civic laws" (πολιτικοὶ νόμοι). It should be kept in mind that the document was written in the court itself, so that the descriptions and terms faithfully reflect the actual juridical situation. As the official designation for the two litigants are "Jewess" and "Jew of the *Epigone*", and the "civic laws" were the basis for their case, it is obvious that there was a legal connection between their being "Jewish" and those laws. Their Jewishness, or to be more exact, their membership in the Jewish *politeuma* of Arsinoë, established their legal status as *politai*. Probably that status was connected with military settlement[105].

CPJ, I 19 also contributed to conclusions regarding juridical leveling in the Ptolemaic kingdom[106]. At any rate the organization of Jews into their own *politeuma* can be interpreted as Hellenization at least on the political plane, for it followed the Hellenistic pattern. Tcherikover rightly stressed that "presumably besides maintaining national customs such as traditional holidays, religious ceremonies and the like, in all legal matters members of the *politeuma* acted in accordance with the general Hellenistic law that applied in the country and used to have recourse to the ordinary court of the government"[107]. The Jewish *politeuma* was no exception, and in one of his most brilliant chapters Tcherikover showed that in most aspects of their legal existence the principle prevailing was the famous rabbinic one of "the law of the state is the law (and must be obeyed)"[108]. This is evident from the type of promissory notes Jews wrote, the courts they used, the way Jewish women were legally represented, the interest-bearing loans made between Jews, legal petitions, etc. It is thus not by chance that members of the Jewish *politeuma* of Arsinoe relied on the "civic laws" and the Hellenic court.

However, not all the Jews of the town had the same status. Document *CPJ*, II 421 (of 73 C.E.) proves that at the time of the Flavian

---

105 The title of the defendant may indicate his military role. The wording "a Jew of the Epigone" may be an indication that the Jewish military settlers in the place were already the second generation; this is especially instructive because of the date of the document, 226 B.C.E. On other military settlers in Arsinoë in the Ptolemaic period and also in the Fayûm as a whole, see Launey, pp. 541-550.

106 See pp. 31ff. above, especially p. 35.

107 Tcherikover, *Jews in Egypt*, p. 97.

108 *Ibid.*, chap. 4 — "Jewish Law and Hellenistic Law" (pp. 95-115), especially p. 105f; cf. *CPJ*, I pp. 32ff. Most of his conclusions on this subject can be depended on, and will be discussed here only where they are especially relevant.

emperors, there were quite a few Jews in Arsinoe with the status of "natives". The document includes a list of payers of the "Jewish tax" ('Ιουδαίων τέλεσμα) complied by one of the town *amphodarches* (an official in charge of a city quarter). To make up the list he utilized two sources — a list of *laographia* payers (lines 180, 203) and a list of *epikrisis* (lines 139, 163, 174, 184). The first provided the names of five men, and the second of six women and four minors. Since the *laographia* in Egypt applied only to men (aged 14 to 60-62), it is reasonable to assume that all fifteen were considered "natives". However, hasty conclusions must be avoided for the document was written in 73 C.E. and it is possible that the destruction of the Temple in Jerusalem and the suppression of the incipient Jewish rebellion in Egypt (including the closing of the temple of Onias) adversely affected the legal status of certain groups of Jews in the Egyptian *chora* so that they were marked as subjugated by having to pay the full *laographia* as well as the "Jewish tax". Be that as it may, the document can prove neither that all the Jews of Arsinoe were lowly "natives" nor the contrary. Ironically, in fact, the "Jewish tax" can be viewed as official recognition of the continued existence of the Jewish religion, and of the community organization involved[109]. There is no doubt that the tax was discriminatory, as it applied to all Jews from 3 to 62[110], and there was no connection between its payment and the legal status of those paying it.

At first glance, *CPJ*, II 432 (the water bill report) might lead to the conclusion that the Arsinoe Jews were of lower status than other residents, for the synagogue paid more than other consumers. However, Fuks rightly rejected the notion that consumers were billed according to their status. The document does not allow for such an interpretation[111], for the criterion for setting the amounts is clearly quantitative, and it was due to the Jewish purification rules that the synagogues used more water than any of the other institutions

---

109 I am grateful to Prof. S. Applebaum for calling my attention to this. In this context it is worthwhile citing Davis's instructive remarks about the *Fiscus Iudaicus*: "But this did not mean that the existence of the Jewish nation was no longer recognized: the religious privileges that the Jews originally enjoyed were maintained; farther, the creation of the *Fiscus Judaicus* on the same line as the *Fiscus Asiaticus* and the *Fiscus Alexandrinus* implied the recognition of the Jews as a separate entity." (Davis, *Race Relations*, p. 156).

110 See *CPJ*, II p. 114; Tcherikover, *Jews in Egypt*, p. 91.

111 See his commentary on document *CPJ*, II p. 221.

listed[112]. It was no accident that Jews tried to locate their synagogues close to water sources[113], or made proper arrangements near the synagogues[114]. In the Ptolemaic period one of the Arsinoe synagogues was built near the municipal water channel[115], and in Roman times synagogues arranged to have a regular supply of water from permanent installations. In Fuks' view these installations probably provided also for the domestic consumption of the local Jews (which supports the hypothesis that the synagogue was in the midst of a Jewish residential area). One way or another, it was the quantity of water used rather than the status of the users that determined the amount paid.

The Syrian Villages

The best known of the Syrian villages which lay between Philadelphia and Arsinoe, south of the Heraclidean district[116], is mentioned in more than twenty papyri, from 245 B.C.E. to the eighth century C.E.[117] It should not be confused with another, likewise near

---

112 Actually, Schürer already suggested this, vol. 2, p. 519, n.63; vol. 3, p. 48; and see also Alon, *Studies*, etc., vol. 1, pp. 148-176. It is quite likely that in building their synagogues near places of water, Jews in the Diaspora wanted to avoid "the uncleanness of Gentile land" (cf. Sukenik, *Ancient Synagogues*, p. 50). Yet this could eventually derive from an interpretation to some biblical phrases such as *Numeri*, 24:6; *Ezechiel*, 1:3; *Daniel*, 8:2; 10:4; *Psalmi*, 24:1-2; 130:1; *Ecclesiastes*, 1:7; *Nehemiah*, 8:1. See: *Mechilta d'Rabbi Ismael* (eds. H.S. Horovitz, I.A. Rabin), 1930, p. 3; *J.T. Kila'im*, IX 32c; *J.T. Ketubboth*, XII 35b; *B.T. Berakhoth*, 15b-16a; cf. Krauss, *Syn. Alt.*, pp. 282, 288.

113 See, e.g., *Antiquitates*, XIV 259; *Acta Apostolorum*, XVI:13, and see details on this in Schürer, vol. 2, p. 519, n.63; vol. 2 (eds. Vermes & Millar), p. 441, n.65. The archaeological findings prove also that the synagogues of Delos, Aegina and Miletos were located near the sea (Sukenik, *ibid.*).

114 E.g., in the excavations in Sardis a special building with installations for water was found near the synagogue (*BASOR*, 187 [1967], pp. 10, 18, 62). An inscription from Philadelphia in Lydia mentions a donation of "a water basin" (Lifshitz, *Donateurs*, No. 28) "to the holy synagogue of the Hebrews". A similar gift was made in Side in Pamphilia (*ibid.*, No. 37). Also, the Theodotus inscription from Jerusalem attested to the presence of water installations (a ritual bath) in the synagogue built to house guests from abroad (see, e.g., Schwabe, *Sefer Yerushalayim*, vol. 1 (1956), pp. 362-365). On the water arrangements in synagogues, see L. Robert, *Rev. de Philol.*, 32 (1958), pp. 45-48.

115 See *CPJ*, I 134, lines 17, 23, 30.

116 Wessely, *Denkschr.*, p. 19; Rostovtzeff, *A Large Estate in Egypt*, p. 87.

117 See full and exact details in Vaggi, *Aegyptus*, 17 (1937), p. 31. In Rostovtzeff's view (*SEHHW*, p. 1366, n.28) the "Syrian village" was founded by captives of war who were exiled to Egypt in the reign of Ptolemy II Philadelphus, or in the time of Ptolemy III (Eurgetes I).

Arsinoe close to the districts of Themistes and Polemon, for that one was founded later, the earliest reference to it dating from the third century C.E.[118] As noted above, the town of Arsinoe had a "Syrian quarter" mentioned in about fifteen documents, but that quarter's existence is attested only from the second to the fourth century C.E.[119] There may have been some connection between one or both of the Syrian villages and the urban Syrian quarter, but the data available do not permit a definite conclusion on this.

The names "Village of the Syrians" and "Syrian quarter" suggest some form of ethnic organization. As "Syrians" was a common ethnic designation in the Ptolemaic military terminology[120], it can be assumed to have come down as such to the Roman period, while losing all real military significance. It is unfortunately impossible to say definitely that the "Village of the Syrians" in question was Jewish. As Tcherikover correctly noted, the term "Syria" covered Palestine as well, and therefore for Egyptians "Syrians" applied to all immigrants from that area, Jews and non-Jews[121]. As the Fayûm was a region of considerable Jewish military settlement in the Ptolemaic period, this "Village of the Syrians" may have been part of it. The possibility is supported by the mention of another "Village of Syrians" (near the Alexandrian *chora*) where Jewish "Macedonians" (= Jewish military settlers in the Ptolemaic period) owned real estate and on which their estates bordered (*CPJ*, II 142). Unfortunately there is no direct documentary backing for such an assumption, except the fact that there were Jews living there (*CPJ*, I 46). It is also possible that in the Arsinoe area the term "Syrians" was applied particularly to Jews, judging by document *CPJ*, I 126 which mentions the Jew Apollonius "also known by the Syrian name Jonathas" (lines 15-16).

Still another "Village of Syrians" figures in a document of 94 C.E. from Oxyrhynchus (*P. Oxy.*, 270). The fields of that village were classified as "*katoikic* land", indicating that their owners were descendants of military settlers. While the precise ethnic origin of the

---

118 *Ibid.*, 31-32.

119 *Ibid.*, 33.

120 Heichelheim, p. 63f.

121 Tcherikover, *Jews in Egypt*, pp. 17-18, and nn.14-15. In this context, note the Fayûm village of Χαναανaὶν — mentioned in a document from 245 B.C.E., *P. Petr.*, III 43 (2), line 30 — whose name possibly derived from "Canaan" or "Canaanites".

inhabitants cannot be inferred from the document, they may well
have included Jews, in view of the considerable number of the latter
in the Oxyrhynchus region (see below).

Alexandrou-Nesos

Papyrus *CPJ*, I 129 from Alexandrou-Nesos, though badly preserved, provides important information on the local Jewish community and its organization. It is a petition (ἔντευξις) of an unnamed
woman dating from 218 B.C.E., complaining that a local Jew called
Dorotheos stole her cloak, and demanding justice. She states that
when she shouted for help, Dorotheos fled to the local synagogue
with his loot. Thanks to the intervention of another man — a respected man named Lezelmis who owned 100 *arourai* of land — the
stolen cloak was deposited with Nikomachos, the *nakoros* (the Doric
form of νεωκόρος) of the synagogue (see the explanation of the post
below), pending the verdict. In view of these developments the
woman petitioned the king to instruct the local *strategos* in writing
to write to the *epistates* of Samareia to order Dorotheos and Nikomachos to turn the cloak over to him (i.e. to the *epistates*) and after
the truth of her statement has been ascertained to have the cloak
returned to her or its cost paid to her.

The question arises as to why Dorotheos fled to the synagogue
with the loot. Tcherikover proffered three alternatives: a) He may
have sought refuge and the protection of friends from the woman
who called for help (assuming she and her friends were not Jews).
b) He may have sought safety in the synagogue which like all holy
places had the right to provide asylum. c) The plaintiff too may have
been Jewish and Dorotheos may have meant to clarify the matter
with her before the Jewish authorities sitting in the synagogue[122].
The third alternative is impossible in this case, however, because the
Jewish courts were not authorized to deal with criminal cases. Of the
two remaining alternatives, the fact that the cloak was kept in the
synagogue until the matter could be settled makes the second more
likely.

What can be learned from the case about the nature of the Jews in
the place and their settlement? The key to the solution is the figure

---

122 See *CPJ*, I p. 240. Except that Tcherikover, considering them all reasonable, did not
   choose among the possibilities he mentioned.

of Lezelmis. Tcherikover rightly noted that his intervention should be considered mediation by a rich, influential inhabitant of the village. His Thracian name is no proof that he was not Jewish[123]; as a matter of fact his appearance in the synagogue and his success in depositing the cloak there imply that he was. His intervention may also indicate that he was in a position of authority in regard to the plaintiff and both Dorotheos and Nikomachos, evidently because of his military rank. The fact that he was a military settler is very clear from the document, and the size of his estate (100 *arourai*) places him among the commanding officers. In brief, all the people involved seem to me to have been Jews; they may even have had some military connection with the Jewish military settlers in nearby Samareia[124], for the complaint was sent there and was to be dealt with there. The possibility that there was a Jewish sub-unit in Alexandrou-Nesos is supported also by the presence there of Jewish military settlers who owned vineyards, as shown by two other documents from the third century B.C.E. which Tcherikover did not include in the *Corpus Papyrorum Judaicarum*[125]. In any case it cannot be denied that there were a considerable number of Jewish settlers in the place, organized into a community which maintained a synagogue employing a *nakoros* (or *neokoros*), a title which in the Greek world meant "sacristan" or "custodian of a temple"[126]. Called *ḥazan*[127] (or may be *shamash*) in Hebrew, he was in charge of the services, and of the maintenance and supervision of the synagogue property[128].

Thus, no conclusions can be drawn as to the independence or affiliation of the Alexandrou-Nesos Jewish community with that of nearby Samareia. What is evident is that the Jews of Alexandrou-

---

123 We know that in nearby Samareia there was a Jewish solider named Theodotus son of Kassandros who was called "the Paeonian" (*CPJ*, I 22). In his commentary on this document Tcherikover justifiably decided that he belonged to the Thracian hipparchy, which would explain the name Kassandros (see *CPJ*, I p. 161). Could not the same apply to Lezelmis?

124 See above, pp. 44-46.

125 The reference is to *P. Petr.*, II 29a (see lines 13, 16), and also *P. Petr.*, II 43a (line 24); and see details in Uebel, p. 123, n.358.

126 Liddell and Scott, s.v.; Oertel, *Die Liturgie*, pp. 338f., 371f.

127 Krauss, *Syn. Alt.*, p. 128; *CPJ*, I p. 241.

128 Josephus (*Bellum*, I 153) and Philo (*De Specialibus Legibus*, I 156; *De Praemis et Poenis*, 74) used this term in reference to the functionaries in Jerusalem, who were charged with the maintenance and safeguarding of the Temple; Philo even indicated specifically their affinity to the Levites.

Nesos had a community organization, the nucleus of which must have been a military settlement.

Samareia

Samareia was in the Arsinoite nome of the Fayûm. A papyrus of 201 B.C.E. (*CPJ*, I 22) mentions seven Jews who were military settlers in that village. One of them owned *statmos*[129] in the nearby village of Kerkesephis inherited from his father (lines 9, 23-24). Thus Jews were settled there at least a generation earlier, circa 225 B.C.E., and perhaps even earlier[130].

The name of the place probably refers to the original settlers, apparently from Samaria in Palestine. They may have been the off-spring of Sanbalat's soldiers who settled in Egypt in Alexander's time (*Antiquitates*, XI 345) or of the Samaritans brought there with their Jewish compatriots by Ptolemy I (*Antiquitates*, XII 7). Ptolemy II Philadelphus may have sent them there in carrying out his military settlement program in the Fayûm. Some document record peoples designated as Σαμαρίτης and Σαμαρεῖτα[131], which Zucker believed should be understood to refer to *origo*, so that the people came from the village of Samareia[132]. Launey and Übel on the other hand contended that the reference was to military settlers[133]. The two views seem to complement each other, and it seems likely that the terms designate military settlers from that particular place. There is no possibility of deciding whether the people so designated were Jews or Samaritans in origin, nor is any information available on the fate of the original Samaritan settlement. Probably in the course of a generation or two it lost its particularity, and its members inter-married with the Jews (who were settled near or with them), so that by the end of the third century B.C.E. there was no trace of its existence aside from the place name[134]. The explanation may be the

---

129 On the military significance of this term see chap. 1, n.68.
130 That is, at the time of the implementation of Ptolemy II Philadelphus's settlement project in the Fayûm.
131 See, e.g., *P. Tebt.*, 62, lines 2-3.
132 F. Zucker, *Aegyptus*, 13 (1933), pp. 217-218. He believed this form was characteristic of the third century B.D.E. and presented some examples from the Zenon papyri referring to various villages where titles of a similar nature were noted.
133 Launey, p. 554; Uebel, p. 198, n.1.
134 Contrary to Schürer, who decided, on the basis of the words τῶν περὶ Σαμαρείαν

merger of the two villages, Samareia and Kerkesephis[135], and that explains also why one of the Jewish military settlers from Samareia owned houses in Kerkesephis (*CPJ*, I 22, lines 9, 23-24), and his move to Samareia may be a clue to the date of the merger. Information on the prosperity of the military settlement in Samareia in the middle of the second century B.C.E. (the reign of Ptolemy VI Philometor) is provided by document *CPJ*, I 28, which indicates also that the military command was Jewish[136]. Information on the local community arrangements is unavailable, but it was most probably organized in the usual way.

Magdola

The name Magdola is definitely of Semitic origin, and in biblical times a similar name, Migdal, was given to one of the settlements near Pelusium[137]. The meaning and its application in Pharaonic Egypt indicate it was used in connection with forts and watchtowers, and the same holds true for Ptolemaic Egypt[138]. The adoption of the name as a term in the official Greek lexicon is most interesting: The guards of such towers in Egyptian villages (even in considerably later periods) were called *magdolophilakes* and the tax levied on the villages for their maintenance was called *magdolophilakeia*[139].

At the end of the third century B.C.E., Magdola in the Fayûm was the seat of the local *strategos*. It was therefore the address for petitions submitted by people in the area, among them Jews[140]. Unfortunately the Jewish petitions cannot throw much light on the local community, for three of the five emanate from other places[141]. One of them refers to "the civil law of the Jews" in Tcherikover's reading

---

that a group of people (whose names are mentioned in a papyrus from the second century B.C.E.) were Samaritans, see Schürer, vol. 3, pp. 45-46. These words do not necessarily refer to Samaria in Palestine. On the contrary, it is more reasonable to connect them with the Egyptian village under consideration.

135 According to document *BGU*, 94 (from 289 B.C.E.) the two places are one and the same; and cf. also *P. Tebt.*, II p. 383f. regarding their proximity.

136 See pp. 45-46 above.

137 *Ex.*, 14:2; *Num.*, 38:7; *Jer.*, 44:1, 46:14; *Ezek.*, 29:10, 30:6.

138 See *Entzyklopedia Mikra'it*, vol. 4, p. 636; Tcherikover, *Jews in Egypt*, p. 19.

139 Tcherikover, *ibid.*, nn.20, 23; see also *CPJ*, III 489 (a-b).

140 See *CPJ*, I 37, 38, 127b, 128, 129.

141 *CPJ*, I 37 − from Herakleia; *CPJ*, I 38 − from Arsinoë (Crocodilopolis); *CPJ*, I 129 − from Alexandrou-Nesos.

of the damaged text[142]. In his view the term has the same meaning as the πολιτικοὶ νόμοι of the Greeks, and thus defines the body of laws of the Jewish *politeuma*[143]. It is not clear, however, whether that *politeuma* was in Magdola or one of the surrounding settlements. It may have been a federative organization of several (small) military settlements of Jews in the region. In any case, it is important to note that the petition dealt with marital laws (a conflict between husband and wife), indicating the legal area in which the Jewish *politeuma* operated[144].

Oxyrhynchus

A considerable number of papyri pertaining to Jews have survived from Oxyrhynchus, most of which relate to private matters of the Roman and Byzantine periods. The existence of an organized Jewish community there is first attested in *P. Oxy.*, II, 335 (= *CPJ*, II 423). This badly preserved document (dated 85 C.E.) contains a declaration submitted by a certain Theon son of Sarapion to the local *agoranomos* in order to register legally the sale of one-sixth of a house "in the Jewish Quarter" (ἐπ' ἀμφόδου Ἰουδαϊκοῦ). It appears that the house had passed through the hands of two Jewish owners at least, who are referred to officially in the documents as "those among the Jews of the city of Oxyrhynchus" (τῶν ἀπ' Ὀξυρύγχων πόλεως Ἰουδαίων). Such a formal reference was made in accordance with the legal terminology used in Roman Egypt. In other words, since affiliation to the local Jewish community was legally defined, the implication is that the organized body of Jewish residents in Oxy-

---

142 *CPJ*, I, 128, ll. 2-3: [κατὰ τὸν νόμον π]ολιτικὸν τῶν ['Ιου]δαίων. See Tcherikover's reasons for this reconstruction and cf. his proposals for another reconstruction of another lacuna in line 3: [νόμου Ἰουδ]αικοῦ or [νόμου πολι]τικοῦ. The document, which is in very poor condition, allows for many possible reconstructions, but as regards lines 2-3, there is a good deal of agreement among scholars. See also n.143 below.

143 See *CPJ*, I p. 238. Tcherikover did not ignore the possibility of a different reconstruction, such as [πρὸς τὸ ἀρχεῖον π]ολιτικὸν τῶν ['Ιουδ]αίων. Perhaps this reconstruction is preferable, especially in view of the existence of such archives in other communities in the Hellenistic-Roman Diaspora, such as *CPJ*, II 143 — Alexandria; *CIJ*, II 775-779 — Hierapolis in Phrygia; *CIJ*, II 741 — Smyrna; and see L. Robert, *BCH*, 67 (1947), p. 105. This possibility does not contradict the first, on the contrary, the Alexandrian example supports it.

144 On this subject there is again an insturctive parallel to *CPJ*, II 143 for its subject is the deposit of a will in the Jewish archives in Alexandria, a subject which touches upon the laws of matrimony also.

rhynchus had won political recognition from the Roman authorities.

The concentration of Jews in a quarter bearing their name was by no means unique in Egyptian urban life. Wilcken's idea that the Jewish Quarter should be reckoned as a *Ghetto* is wholly unacceptable[145]. Wilcken was influenced by a much later historical phenomenon; it is improper and incongruous to draw any conclusion concerning this earlier period from modern times. Furthermore, ethnic or national quarters occurred frequently in Egyptian cities, as elsewhere; such practices were not confined to Jews alone[146]. With a common centre in their own residential quarter, the Jews could manage their communal and religious life more easily; and the same may be said of other ethnic or religious groups. There are references to Jews living outside the Jewish Quarter; they were nevertheless active in Jewish circles. This is indicated in an official announcement (*P. Oxy.*, 100 = *CPJ*, III 454) issued in 133 C.E., which mentions some Jewish property located "in the Cretan Quarter and in the Jewish <street>" (ἐπ' ἀμφόδον Κρητικοῦ καὶ Ἰουδαϊκῆς <λαύρας>)[147]. Opinions vary on the exact meaning of ἄμφοδον and λαύρα[148], but no one can deny the fact that both terms referred to residential areas which were accepted as such by the local administration. If one follows P. Jouguet's logical views about these terms, the implication is of a "Jewish street" (or rather "lane" or "close") being situated in the "Cretan Quarter". Quite similar picture is presented with regard to Hermopolis, too, where a "Jewish street" was located within one of the city quarters[149]; in keeping with Philo's writing, the same may be said of Alexandria itself[150].

The prosperity of the Jewish community in Oxyrhynchus was adversely affected by the well-known uprising during the reign of Emperor Trajan (115-117 C.E.). Tcherikover rightly maintained that

---

145 Wilcken, *Antisemitismus*, p. 8; Mac Lennan, *Oxyrhynchus*, p. 14; Wessely, *Studien z. Palaeographie u. Papyruskunde*, 13 (1913), pp. 8-10. Against this view, see: Tcherikover, *CPJ*, I (Prolegomena), p. 5.

146 Rink, *Strassen*, pp. 25-6; Wessely, *Das Stadt Arsinoë*, p. 21ff.; Jouguet, p. 283ff.; cf. cary, *A History of the Greek world*, pp. 268, 274.

147 The completion of the word λαύρας was made by Rink (p. 17); cf. *CPJ*, III 454 (p. 12). For other possibilities, such as ὁδός or ῥύμη, see: Th. Reinach, *REJ*, 37 (1898), p. 221.

148 See, for example, Wilcken, *Griechische Ostraka*, p. 712; Jouguet, pp. 283-5; Grenfell & Hunt, *The Oxyrhynchus Papyri* vol. 1, p. 190, n.1.

149 *CPJ*, III 468 (lines 9-10); 485 (lines 4, 7, 26).

150 *In Flaccum*, 55; cf. Box, *ad. loc.*

P. Oxy., 100 (= *CPJ*, III 454) includes a direct reference to one instance of confiscation of Jewish property after that revolt[151]. The strength of the community and its traces in city life of Oxyrhynchus can be gathered indirectly from surviving pieces of papyrological evidence. A relevant document, of 117 C.E., appears to have been promulgated by the local *agoranomos*. It is a contract compelling the city's bakers to supply bread in quantitites proportionate to their official grain allocation in order to prevent hoarding, and at fixed rather than speculative prices[152]. This may suggest that the economic situation in Oxyrhynchus at the time was extremely adverse. Another document echoes the damage inflicted upon the city by Jewish rebels; marks of destruction remained for at least a generation[152a]. It was no mere formality that the victory over the Jews was celebrated annually by the local population even so late as 199/200 C.E. (*CPJ*, II 450). To strengthen the impression of the misery of Oxyrhynchus and of its deep hatred of the Jews, we may note that an important chapter of the so called 'Pagan Martyrs' literature, including a direct reference to the Jewish uprising, was found there. The heavy fighting in the city area provides evidence of the martial qualities of the Jews in those days. One may wonder how they could have acquainted themselves in the art of warfare when because of religious reasons they were exempt from military service in Roman legions[152b]. In fact, Jews could serve in auxillary forces, a practice for which there is evidence in several instances from Egypt and from Oxyrhynchus itself[152c]. In addition, traces in the city's vicinity of descendants of Jewish military settlers from the Ptolemaic period substantiate this view[153]. It is probable that these descendants still cherished, if only

---

151 See: Tcherikover, *CPJ*, III 454 (p. 11); cf. also *CPJ*, II 445.

152 *P. Oxy.*, 1454.

152a See *P. Oxy.*, 707 (recto) (= *CPJ*, II 447).

152b Cf. Josephus, *Antiquitates*, XIV 225-232, 234, 236-240; XV 28; XVIII 84; Applebaum, *Roman Frontier Studies*, 1967, pp. 181-184.

152c *CPJ*, II 229, 405; III 463, 465, 468 a-b.

153 The existence of a Jewish quarter along with other ethnical quarters, from the first century on, might be better understood through consideration of the heritage of the Ptolemaic military settlements. References to Oxyrhynchus are "The Quarter of the Lycian Camp" (*P. Oxy.*, 478, 513) and "The Cretan Quarter", alluding to the frequency of Cretans in Hellenistic armies; see Launey, passim; Bar-Kochva, *The Seleucid Army*, passim. In *P. Oxy.*, 270 (dated 94 C.E.) there is a reference to "*katoikic* land" in the neighbouring Syrian Village. The name of this village might also denote a Jewish origin,

for self-defence, the soldierly traditions of their ancestors.

It is difficult to suggest an exact date for the reconstitution of the Jewish community of Oxyrhynchus[154]. It can be deduced from *CPJ*, II 473 that it was well established again by the end of the third century. This document deals with the liberation from slavery of a Jewish woman and her two sons in 291 C.E. "by the Jewish community" (παρὰ τῆς συναγωγῆς τῶν Ἰουδαίων), an event neither extraordinary nor unfamiliar in Jewish life in the Diaspora[155]. The formal involvement of the community in such a case implies clearly enough that it represented a legal personality while serving as a juridical party to an official transaction. The fact that the Jewish community paid the ransom implies that it possessed public funds and authority to use them, a right reserved exclusively for legal bodies. As such, the community was represented by two deputies who had been empowered to negotiate terms with the slave owners. Their appointment and the allocation of the ransom money imply that these acts were preceded by appropriate communal decisions. Both deputies must have been important figures in the Jewish congregation of Oxyrhynchus. Otherwise, they would not have been chosen to carry out such a task. One of them, Aurelius Dioscorus, was a local Jew, and apparently one of the community's leaders. His precise position is obscure, and it is difficult to decide whether he was the *archisynagogos* (according to Tcherikover's interpretation)[156], or rather a *prostates*[157]. The second deputy, aurelius Justus,

since all people originating from either Syria or Palestine were referred to in Egypt as "Syrians" (cf. *CPJ*, I, Prolegomena, p. 5). However, other documents of the fourth century mention another village in the vicinity of Oxyrhynchus which bore the name of Dositheos; at least one of its prominent residents was a Jew (*P. Oxy.*, 2124; cf. also nos. 1424-5). These papyri suggest that a Roman detachment was stationed there, a fact which might allude to the military character of the place, possibly derived from a Ptolemaic heritage. As "Dositheos" was a typical Jewish name, the impression is that the village could have been named after a certain Jewish commander who had settled there with a unit of co-religionist soldiers.

154 See: Stern, *CPJ*, III 452b.
155 Cf. *CIJ*, I 683 (Panticapaeum in the Crimea); *CIJ*, I 690 (Gorgippia in the Crimea); *CIJ*, I 709-711 (Delphi in Greece). The manumission of captives sold into slavery has been an obligation of Jews ever since that time; see, for example, *Mishna Gittin*, iv 9; *J.T. Gittin*, 45d-46a; *B.T. Gittin*, 46a; *B.T. Kidushin*, 14b, 21a; cf. Krauss, *Talmudische Archaeologie*, vol. 2, pp. 98, 497 (n.674).
156 *CPJ*, III 473 (p. 35). On the functions of the *archisynagogos*, see Krauss, *Synagogale Altertümer, passim.*
157 On this office see pp. 156-157 below.

was a Palestinian Jew, bearing the title of *"Bouleutes* of Ono in
Syria-Palestina and *Pater-Synagogos"*. Both his origin and title are
puzzling; how could a Palestinian Jew represent the Jewish community of Oxyrhynchus while being at the same time a *Bouleutes*
of Ono? The answer to this lies in the last component of his title:
Pater-Synagogos. Such an appellation was quite common in Jewish
communities, and was born by persons of high dignity[158]. It was
conferred on a man either because of his economic and social position or because of his outstanding personality and achievements in
public life.

A *"Bouleutes* of Ono in Syria-Palestina., *Aurelius Justus,* could
ipso facto simultaneously be raised to the exalted position of a
Pater-Synagogos in Oxyrhynchus. This seems the only likely explanation since honorary membership of the Jewish community of
Oxyrhynchus alone could enable him to serve as its deputy.

Why was a *"Bouleutes* of Palestinian Ono" involved in the redemp-
tion of three Jewish slaves in Egypt? It is conceivable that the slaves
had some connection with Ono, or even relation to Aurelius Justus
himself. The woman is described here as a born slave (οἰκογενὴς
δουλή) manumitted at the age of forty; the inference being that her
parents had been sold into slavery prior to her birth. Taking into
account the date of the document (291 C.E.), one may conclude that
their enslavement might have occurred before 251 C.E. Here it
should be recalled that following the Severan Emperors crisis and
anarchy prevailed in Palestine after 235 C.E. The exact circumstances in which the parents were enslaved and deported to such a
remote place as Oxyrhynchus are unknown, but it is reasonable to
think that they might have lost their freedom because of some political involvement. As commercial connections between Oxyrhynchus
and Palestinian cities of Ascalon and Gaza are known to have
existed[158a], Aurelius Justus might have received information about
the enslaved family through some travelling merchants. Thus, having
succeeded in tracing the family, he might have felt obliged to purchase its freedom. That the transaction of liberating the slaves was
carried out by the agency of the Jewish community of Oxyrhynchus,
and not privately by Aurelius Justus himself, may indicate the exis-

---

158 Schürer, vol. 3, pp. 88-89; Juster, vol. 1, pp. 448-9; Leon, pp. 186-188.
158a Cf.P. Oxy., 924.

tence of difficulties which required such intermediation as the community alone was able to supply. The excessively high ransom-price of fourteen silver talents provides an oblique hint of those difficulties[159].

The document under discussion (*CPJ*, III 473) sheds some light upon the civic status of the Jews in Oxyrhynchus as well. In it at least two people were designated to the class of *Aurelii*; there are similar references to Jews in other documents[160]. They may have been entitled to that appellation by virtue of the famous *Constitutio Antoniniana* (issued in 213 C.E.)[161], which bestowed Roman rights upon the inhabitants of the whole Roman Empire. As the juridical implications of the *Constitutio Antoniniana* have not yet fully resolved, it is difficult to draw any decisive conclusions as to the legal status of all the Jewish inhabitants of the Roman Empire. Opinions vary on the interpretation of this edict as cited in *P. Giss.*, 40[161a]. Whatever the degree of Roman citizenship granted to people in the provinces, it is obvious that a considerable section of the imperial population was not awarded this status. This may be deduced from the exclusion of the *dediticii* in that edict, and from the many papyri indicating that, even after 213 C.E., there were still people liable to *laographia*[162]. Like the other *metropoleis* in Egypt, Oxyrhynchus became a *civitas*[163]; and *ipso facto* its citizens enjoyed the privileges of Roman citizenship. In this context the question remains whether or not all the local Jewish inhabitants had been granted this status. Tcherikover suggested that the small number of Aurelian Jews mentioned in Oxyrhynchus' papyri might indicate a very strict limitation on the granting of Roman citizenship to Jews; nevertheless, he rightly insisted that sufficient documents do not exist to allow any conclusive judgement[164]. There is no reason to think that the Jewish right of self-organization was affected by the *Constitutio Antininiana* in any way. On the contrary, according to *P. Giss.*,

---

159 For prices of slaves at the time, see Johnson, pp. 279ff.
160 Cf. *CPJ*, III 474a, 477, 503, 508, 513.
161 Millar, *JEA*, 48 (1962), pp. 124ff.; Rubin, *Latomus*, 34 (1975), pp. 430-436.
161a Bickermann, Das *Edict des Kaisers Caracalla*. For further bibliography, see Taubenschlag, pp. 40ff., 589ff.
162 Taubenschlag, pp. 593-4 and n.45.
163 See *P. Oxy.*, 1114 (237 C.E.); *SB*, 1016 (249 C.E.).
164 Tcherikover, *The Jews in Egypt*, p. 159.

40, all those civic groups in the Roman Empire which had been organized as self-contained political bodies (viz. πολιτεύματα) were permitted to remain such[165]; it is unreasonable to think that the Jewish communities alone would have been deprived of this privilege. Indeed, *CPJ*, III 473, in itself proves that the communal organization of Jews of Oxyrhynchus remained unaltered. In some fragmentary later (fifth century) Hebrew papyri, the community is still mentioned, but referred to by the Hebrew name *Knesseth* (synagogue) *Benei ha-Knesseth* or "the holy congregation"[166]. The term *Knesseth* (or συναγωγή in Greek) fully corresponds the official terminology used at the time in the Roman world[167] and is equivalent to πολίτευμα of previous days. A similar terminological modification occurred in the Jewish community of Berenice (in Cyrenaica) in the first century[168].

The aforementioned Hebrew papyri from Oxyrhynchus inform us of local communal institutions: the *Roshei ha-Knesseth* (the heads of the synagogue), *Ziknei ha-Knesseth* (the elders of the synagogue) and *Prostatin* (προστάται in Greek, namely the superintendents or simply the leaders). The first are to be identified with the repeatedly mentioned in Jewish epigraphy ἀρχισυνάγωγοι, who appear to have functioned as the spiritual leaders and the highest religious authorities in each community[168a]. The "elders" are also noted, though less frequently, in Jewish communities of the Greco-Roman world, where they constituted the communal council (γερουσία)[168b]. In several communities, there was a definite distinction between ordinary members of the council and the executive committee (the archons)[168c]. But as the latter are not mentioned in Oxyrhynchus, it is difficult to draw any conclusion about the structure of the council there. It seems, however, that the aforementioned *prostatin* were connected

165 See the reconstructed text in *M. Chr.*, 372.
166 Cowley, *JEA*, 2 (1915), pp. 209-213.
167 Krauss, *Syn. Alt.*, pp. 13-15; Schürer, *op.cit.*, p. 504ff.
168 *CIG*, 5361-2; *REG*, 52 (1969), pp. 283, 290; *SEG*, XVII 823; cf. Applebaum, *Jews and Greeks in Ancient Cyrene*, p. 162.
168a Schürer, vol. 2, pp. 509-512; vol. 3, pp. 88ff.; idem (eds. Vermes & Millar), vol. 2, pp. 433-436; Krauss, *op.cit.*, p. 114ff; Leon, pp. 172-3, 194, 246.
168b Schürer, vol. 3, pp. 72, 76, 89ff.; Leon, pp. 150-151, 181; Tcherikover, *CPJ*, I (Prolegomena), p. 9 and n.24.
168c Schürer, vol. 3, p. 84ff.; Juster, vol. 1, p. 443ff.; Baron, *The Jewish Community*, p. 95ff.; Frey, *CIJ*, I, p. lxxxii ff.; Leon, p. 173ff.; Applebaum, "The Organization of the Jewish Community", p. 493ff.

somehow to the executive body of the community council. In the common terminology of the Greco-Roman world, the title προστάτης seems to have referred to either the presiding officer, chief leader of various councils and committees (religious, social, professional and political), or to the *patronus* or legal representative of a certain body to the central authorities[169]. Both interpretations are in accordance with our knowledge of that office in Jewish communal life[169a]; and it appears that quite a variety of local traditions exerted influence upon Jews in the matter of communal life. For this reason the representative of the Jewish community in Oxyrhynchus, who is mentioned in *P. Oxy.*, 1205 (= *CPJ*, III 473), has been described as a *prostates* rather as *archisynagogos*. Whatever conclusion one may reach, it is quite obvious that the *prostatai* in Oxyrhynchus were identified collectively as the leadership of a well-organized community. The use of Hebrew in local papyri may suggest that Palestinian Jewry exerted a great influence on Egyptian Jews at the time, and this impression is supported by Talmudic traditions[169b]. In spite of this nationalistic revival, the use of Greek terms such as *prostatai* remained a feature of Jewish communal life in Oxyrhynchus.

We may state in conclusion that Jews in Roman-Byzantine Oxyrhynchus were well organized as a self-contained body (i.e. a community), dwelt together in their own quarter and enjoyed the privilege of living by their ancestral laws. There is evidence to indicate that their community controlled its own funds and property, and was empowered with self-administration. It clearly follows that, as a distinct ethnic and religious unit, the Jewish community of Oxyrhynchus constituted a legal body fully recognised by the central authorities.

Hermoupolis Magna

The date when Jews first settled in Hermoupolis has not been established. The earliest document referring to Jews are unfortun-

---

169 See Liddell & Scott, s.v.; Schaefer, *PW(RE)*, Suppl., IX (1962), cols. 1287-1304; Otto, *Priesten und Temple im hellen. Aegypten*, vol. 1, p. 362; vol. 2, p. 75; San Nicolo, *Aegyptische Vereinswesen*, vol. 2, p. 132ff.; Preisigke, vol. 3, p. 436; cf. Applebaum, *op.cit.*, pp. 496-7.

169a Schürer, *Die Gemeindeverfassung*, p. 31; Juster, vol. 1, p. 443; Krauss, *op.cit.*, p. 145; C.H. Kraeling, *JBL*, 51 (1932), p. 137; Frey, *op.cit.*, p. xciv ff.; Leon, pp. 191-192; Applebaum, *Loc.cit.*

169b Tcherikover, *CPJ*, I, Prolegomena, p. 106ff.

ately quite late and connected with the great uprising during the reign of Trajan (115-117 C.E.). Jewish settlement in the vicinity may have begun in the Ptolemaic period and been military in character, judging by the proximity of Hermoupolis to four villages called Magdola, suggesting "Syrian" settlement like that in the Ptolemaic Fayûm. The impression is strengthened by the fact that Hermoupolis was an important military center in the Ptolemaic period which absorbed also a group of Idumaean military settlers[170]. In any case there is mention in 132 C.E. of a Jew in one of these villages — Magdola Mire — acting a guardian (= legal master) for his mother in connection with a contract on leasing her estate which was classified as *"katoikic* land". The name of the man — "Hermaios known also as Phibion son of Onias" (*CPJ*, III 453, lines 20-21) — likewise supports this impression, especially since his place of residence is connected with a tradition of Jewish military settlement.

During the Jewish uprising (115-117 C.E.) Hermoupolis and its nome were hard hit, as a long series of papyri show[171]. The fact that the area underwent so much suffering indicates that there were many Jews in the town and its environs and that they were quite strong. Furthermore, an uprising of that kind could not succeed without efficient organization and obedience to a firm leadership, and these could only be the product of a local community establishment. No direct information is available on the independent community organization of the Hermoupolis Jews, but indirect evidence is provided by a bill of sale for real estate from the end of the second century C.E. (*CPJ*, III 468)[172]. It shows that the term "Jewish street" (line 10) was in current usage by the local people, indicating that in the past Jews had lived in a neighborhood of their own. That fact is enough to permit the assumption of organized community life, no different from the practice in other cities of Egypt.

C. Upper Egypt

Thebes — Diospolis Magna

The earliest testimony on Jews in Thebes during the Ptolemaic

---

170 See Fraser, vol. 1, pp. 234, 280-281; vol. 2, pp. 438-439, nn.750-752.

171 *CPJ*, II 436-444; 446.

172 The purchaser and seller were both Graeco-Egyptians, but the property in question was Jewish property which had been confiscated around the time of the suppression of the Jewish uprising in 115-117 C.E.; see also Tcherikover's commentary, *CPJ*, III p. 29.

period appears on two fragments of Aramaic papyri containing commercial reports which mention among others Jews with Greek names. Cowley dated them to ca. 300 B.C.E. on the basis of the logical assumption that Aramaic did not survive much beyond the time of Alexander the Great[173]. The circumstances under which the Jews were settled there are unknown, but they probably came from Elephantine to which they were brought before the Hellenistic conquest, as indicated by another papyrus from that place[174]. Admittedly the numerous Greek names among those Jews suggests that they may have been in the military, for the laws of the Ptolemaic kingdom forbade people to adopt Greek names without special permission of, and registration by, the authorities. Research has discovered that illegal change of name or ethnic designation ($\pi\alpha\tau\rho\grave{\iota}\varsigma$ $\kappa\alpha\grave{\iota}$ $\check{o}\nu o\mu\alpha$) was considered a serious crime punishable by death. It was viewed as a serious matter in Roman times as well, but then the penalty was only the confiscation of a quarter of the offender's property[175]. Thus the Jews must have changed their names while serving in the army, but the question is when they did so. The answer is perhaps provided by the testimony of Josephus (*Antiquitates*, XI 345) on Alexander the Great, who took along to Egypt the soldiers of Sanbalat who had helped him in the siege of Tyre, and there allotted them "land estates" ($\kappa\lambda\acute{\eta}\rho o\upsilon\varsigma$ $\gamma\tilde{\eta}\varsigma$) "in the Thebes area" ($\grave{\epsilon}\nu$ $\tau\tilde{\eta}$ $\Theta\eta\beta\alpha\acute{\iota}\delta\iota$) "and assigned them to guard that country" ($\varphi\rho o\upsilon\rho\epsilon\tilde{\iota}\nu$ $\tau\grave{\eta}\nu$ $\chi\acute{\omega}\rho\alpha\nu$ $\alpha\grave{\upsilon}\tau o\tilde{\iota}\varsigma$ $\pi\rho o\sigma\tau\acute{\alpha}\xi\alpha\varsigma$)[176]. It is very possible that under those very circumstances (and perhaps later) the local Jews were conscripted

---

173 See Cowley, Nos. 81-82.

174 The reference is to Cowley, No. 38, which contains a defective paragraph from a letter of a man named Uziah from *Abut* (Thebes) to the head of the community in Elephantine; and see commentaries on the document.

175 See Taubenschlag, pp. 475-476.

176 It is important to note that Arrian, (III 5) said specifically that Alexander's army reached Upper Egypt and the vicinity of Elephantine, and he meant the armies under the command of Apollonides of Chios. The accuracy of the testimony in Josephus has in general been suspected. The main argument was that there was no corroboration from other sources, and that upon it could not be based the establishment of the village of Samareia in the Fayûm, which was founded only in the time of Ptolemy II Philadelphus (see, e.g., Niese, *GGMS*, vol. 2, p. 112, n.2; Tcherikover, *Hellenistic Civilization and The Jews*, p. 272 and n.11). However, in evaluating the report they did not take into consideration the papyri mentioned here. In general, there was a tendency to accuse Josephus of apologetics and falsification wherever he wrote about Jews in military service with Alexander, but at least this report (on the Samaritans) does not deserve the same attitude.

to reinforce the Samaritan settlement[177]. A similar co-existence of Jewish and Samaritan settlement seems to have taken place also in Samareia in the Fayûm[178].

The Cowley papyri are important also because they demonstrate the existence of organized Jewish community life already in that early period. Its existence is particularly clear from Papyrus 82 (line 5) which notes that *rashei ād[eta]* (= the community heads) received a certain sum of money from an individual. Thus the local community was well organized and institutionalized, and authorized to hold public funds and collect money from its members. Also Papyrus 81 (line 39) mentions a man designated as *kahana* (= priest) who evidently carried out religious functions in the community.

More information on the Jews of the place has survived from the second century B.C.E., most of it on ostraca[179]. The occupational and social cross section emerging from them does not permit a definitive determination of the legal status of the Jews, for it is hard to decide, for instance, who of them were royal tenants and who military settlers. In any case, the mention of a Jew named Iasibis ('Ιασίβις) in one of the papyri (*CPJ*, I 27, of 158 B.C.E., and see p. 48 above) as holder of the prominent military post of "*epistates* of a hipparchy" supports the impression that in the middle of the second century B.C.E. there were Jewish military settlers in the city and its environs. They may even have been organized in a Jewish unit, commanded by Jews, as Iasibis' position suggests. No explicit direct information on the type of Jewish community organization in the place is available, but it probably persisted in the same form as those in other Jewish military settlements in Egypt. Perhaps the presence of a Theban synagogue in Arsinoe in the Fayum is indirect evidence of that[180].

---

177 There were no special problems or conflicts raised by their joint service, of course, since the friendly relations between the Jews of Elephantine and the Samaritans was well known (Cowley, No. 30).

178 See on Samareia above. In contrast, as noted by Josephus (*Antiquitates*, XII 10; XIII 74-79) good relations between Jews and Samaritans in Alexandria were not the rule.

179 *CPJ*, I 48-68, 73-74, 76-92, 94, 108. Some were receipts of tax-farmers, and some of taxpayers.

180 See pp. 140-141 above. It is interesting that in Cowley papyrus No. 81 (line 4) Arsinoe is mentioned as *Arsin*. The context is not clear but it is instructive, since it may provide an explanation for the affinity of the two communities and for the establishment of the Theban synagogue in Arsinoë.

Edfu — Apollinopolis Magna

As in Diospolis Magna, remains of Aramaic papyri from the early
Ptolemaic period were found in Apollinopolis Magna[181]. They too
mention Jews with Greek names[182], which can be explained in the
same way as those from Diospolis Magna. One of the papyri refers to
a man called *Honiah Saphra* (= Onias the scribe)[183]. The remnants of
the papyrus do not say whether he was a government employee,
such as "the village scribe" or "the district scribe", or the scribe of
the Jewish community, but the latter seems more likely as the entire
papyrus, including the man's title, are in Aramaic. If so, we have
additional, very early evidence of community organization among
the Jews of Upper Egypt.

From the end of the second century B.C.E. on, a bit more information is available on the Jews of the town. Three ostraca are receipts
issued by the local bank to Apollonios son of Dositheos, the tax
farmer, for the *apomoira* (*CPJ*, I 71, 72, 110)[184]. It is impossible to
tell whether the people he collected tax from were Jews. But a comparison of the receipts given to him with other receipts from Diospolis Magna and other places in Upper Egypt suggests that there were
a good many Jews there, as the totals on them are 270, 4500 and
300 drachmas. There is no way of knowing whether the Jews were
royal tenants or military settlers. Dositheos himself was a plantation
owner (*CPJ*, I 111) which status fits in with his government post and
Greek name.

Another ostracon (*CPJ*, I 139) from the first century B.C.E.
lists the names and titles of contributors to joint holiday meals.
Although the holiday is not specified[185], the fact that there were
communal feasts indicates active community life. As donations were

---

181 See Lidzbarski,*Ephereris*, vol. 2, pp. 243-248; and cf. with documents *BIFAO*, 38 (1939),
   pp. 38 (No. 113), 57 (No. 120).
182 Lidzbarski even proved that the monetary terminology in these documents, even though
   it was aramaic, denoted Greek coin denominations; thus "revia'(a)" meant δίχαλκον and
   the letter N ὀβολός.
183 See *BIFAO*, 38 (1939), p. 57 (No. 120, line 3).
184 Levied on owners of orchards and vineyeards, this tax could be paid directly to a bank or
   through a tax-farmer (see Préaux, p. 171f.). Tcherikover thought that in view of the
   amounts, Appolonius was a tax-farmer (*CPJ*, I p. 196).
185 A. Fuks thought that the Passover holiday was meant, since the two Passover feasts in

involved, the meals were perhaps arranged for the indigent, but in any case point to the existence of community funds.

The titles of the donors too cast some light on the organization and institutions of the community. The title of the first on the list is missing, but the second was apparently called a "sage" (σο[φός]). that is, the Torah teacher in the synagogue[186]. The title of the third contributor is not clear. The original editor, Manteuffel, reconstructed it as ἐνα(γώγος)[187], while Fuks suggested the possibility of ἐπα-(γωγός)[188]. However, ἀνα(γνώστης) (= translator) seems more likely, as it fits in more logically with "sage", as in other communities of the Diaspora[189]. That would be a reaonable proposal if we assume that the local Jews were not fluent in Hebrew and required a translator to read and interpret the Torah. The fourth on the list is described as "priest" (ἱερεύς); he was probably among the local bigwigs, and may consequently have carried out religious functions as well. Two other ostraca of the second (or first) century B.C.E., likewise from Upper Egypt (perhaps actually from Apollinopolis Magna) mention Jewish priests[190]. The presence of Jewish priests there as in other cities provides support for Josephus' assertion that genealogical charts of priestly families were kept in the archives of Jewish communities (*C. Apionem*, I 31-36; *Vita*, 6), and that means that the Apollinopolis Magna community had its archives as well. Manteuffel

---

the Diaspora occur on the 15th and 16th of Nissan, which fits the dates in the document, especially since the name of the month is not mentioned there; and see *CPJ*, I p. 255.

186 Cf. a similar name in Josephus, *Bellum*, I 648, II 433, 445 et al. See Krauss, *Syn. Alt.*, pp. 167, 176, 181. Cf. similar titles in Rome also — *CIJ*, I 508; and in Sardis — *BASOR*, 187 (1967), p. 29; cf. L. Robert, *REG*, 80 (1968), p. 517, n.478.

187 *OE.*, 368, line 4.

188 *CPJ*, I 139 — notes to line 4.

189 See, e.g., an inscription from Nicomedia (*CIJ*, II 798) and see also Krauss, *Syn. Alt.*, pp. 134, 138, 167, 176, 177, 229; Juster, vol. 1, p. 455, n.1.

190 See *CPJ*, I 120, 121. and following a list of most of the mentions of priests in the cities of the Hellenistic-Roman Diaspora: Ephesus — *Acts* 19:14; L. Robert, *Hellenica*, 11-12 (1960), p. 381; Sardis — *BASOR*, 187 (1967), p. 29; Corycos — *CIJ*, II 785; Termesos — *TAM*, III No. 807; Rome — *CIJ*, I 346-347, 355, 375; cf. 315 (see Leon, *The Jews of Ancient Rome*, pp. 192-193); Berenice — *SEG*, XVII 823; Leontopolis — *CIJ*, II 1514. On the use of the title "priest" on gravestones of Jews from outside Israel who were buried in Beth She'arim, see Schwabe-Lifshitz, *Beth She'arim*, vol. 2, Nos. 49, 66, 68, 148, 180, 181, and also Avigad, *Beth She'arim*, vol. 2, pp. 23, 53.

further opined that the traces of a synagogue were discernible from the letters EYXH in a damaged parchment of a local inscription which he reconstructed to [ΠΡΟΣ]ΕΥΧΗ[191].

Archaeological finds from the Roman period are more illuminating in regard to the Jewish community and its members. The Polish-French expedition led by Manteuffel found clear evidence of a Jewish quarter known as "the fourth(=*delta*) quarter"(δ ἄμφοδον)[192], a name Josephus applied to one of the Jewish quarters of Alexandria. Within the quarter were brick houses of more than one storey, with very strong outer walls which apparently constituted the outer wall of the quarter (and the town). The rooms in the houses, which had domed ceilings, were contiguous, without corridors or patios, suggesting crowded conditions and a dense population. The many ostraca found there refer mainly to the reigns of Vespasian, Titus, Domitian and Trajan, that is from 79 C.E. to 116. Only a few date from the reigns of Nero, Galba, Otto and Vitellius[193], and twenty-nine from 151-165 C.E.[194] The archaeological hiatus between 116 and 151 is doubtless due to the great disturbances of the Jewish uprising in Trajan's time[195]. The last two ostraca before the gap, indicating the regular collection of taxes from the Jews of the town, bear the dates of 28 April 116 (*CPJ*, II 369) and 18 May 116 (*ibid.*, 229), after which payments evidently ceased when the rebellion spread to the area[196].

In the opinion of Fuks and Lewis, the quarter became Jewish only at the start of the Roman period, in the reign of Claudius or Nero. They believe that the absence of findings from the Jewish quarter in the Ptolemaic period seems to prove that it did not exist, and that the Jews were scattered throughout the city[197]. However,

---

191 Manteuffel, *Fouilles*, p. 363; as to the date of the inscription, cf. Fraser, *JEA*, 40 (1954), 125. Tcherikover, (*CPJ*, I p. 109, n.1) expressed doubts about this reconstruction, but did not offer an alternative.
192 See *OE*, Nos. 70, 78, 82-84, 86-87, 104-105, 110-111, 115-117, 151-152, 279, 282, and see other reports on this quarter: *CPJ*, II 194, 209, 212, 213, 329, 350.
193 See *CPJ*, 230-236.
194 *CPJ*, II 375-403.
195 Cf. the opinion of Fuks and Lewis in the introduction to *CPJ*, II Section IX (p. 109); cf. Applebaum, *Jews and Greeks in Ancient Cyrene*, pp. 268, 294-296.
196 These dates are likely to reinforce the chronlogical reconstruction of the course of the rebellion which Tcherikover proposed, *Jews in Egypt*, p. 171f.; Fuks, *CPJ*, II, Section IX; Applebaum, *ibid.*, p. 294ff.
197 See *CPJ*, II p. 109; and see *CPJ*, I 139 (first century C.E.).

scholars agree that there was organized community life earlier, which would require a residential concentration. The absence of archaeological evidence from the Pharaonic period of a separate Jewish residential area is hardly decisive, in view of the general paucity of material on that time. Furthermore, the city was densely populated for millennia, from early pharaonic times to the Arab period, and that itself is enough to account for the non-survival of early archaeological evidence. In the Ptolemaic period the Jewish population may well have been small and concentrated in a small neighborhood or even a single street; later in the Roman period Jews began to stream in from the rural periphery to the *metropolis*, and the large Jewish quarter was constructed. The increased Jewish population can be explained by the attractive economic conditions in the *metropolis* and the reduced rural income resulting from the Roman tax policy and oppressive administration. If so, the growth of the Jewish community and its expansion from a street or neighborhood to a whole quarter occurred in the reigns of the Julio-Claudian emperors. At any rate, a Jewish quarter is clear evidence of properly organized community life, separate from that of the city. There may have been some connection between Apollinopolis Magna and Alexandria, evidenced by the identical names and signs of the Jewish quarters in the two places, but in the absence of additional information it is difficult to verify the nature of that connection. It should be noted that residing in a quarter of their own did not prevent the Jews from owning land in the city territory, and in this respect they resembled the Alexandrian Jews who were members of the Jewish *politeuma* and owned land in the city *chora*[198].

No information has survived on the way the community was organized, for most of the finds are the receipts individuals received for various tax payments. Yet they indicate, albeit indirectly, the existence of a recognized community organization. For example, the testimony on the bath tax, one of the levies the Jews of the town were subject to[199], suggests that there was a community bath house, for it is hard to imagine a bath house (ritual or not) shared by Jews and non-Jews. The reference to a Jewish collector of bath tax (*CPJ*, II 240) probably means that he was appointed for the purpose of

198 See *CPJ*, II 241, 294; and cf. *CPJ*, II 142, 143.
199 *CPJ*, II, Index 4, s.v. βαλανευτικόν.

collecting the tax from the members of the Jewish community. Various other taxes[200], also testify to an organized community, for they were ordinarily exacted from organized bodies and groups who were responsible for the payment and imposed it among their members[201].

Even ostraca reporting the "Jewish tax" ('Ιουδαίων τέλεσμα) or "the price of two denars of the Jews" (τιμὴ δηναρίων δύο 'Ιουδαίων)[202] do not reveal the organizational pattern of the local community. What can be deduced is that the list was apparently compiled by the *amphodarches*, as in the case of Arsinoe in the Fayûm[203], and its collection was assigned to a special staff. Evidently the authorities took care to collect the tax separately and issued special receipts, refraining from adding receipts for other tax payments[204]. One ostracon (*CPJ*, II 181) mentions an official described as "the collector of the Jewish tax", who was probably a member of the special staff. Another ostracon (*CPJ*, II 166) includes a signature at the bottom, evidently of a tax collector. Unfortunately the names of the two officials provide no clue to whether they were Jewish or not. If they were, that would perhaps indicate that the collection was assigned to the Jewish communities themselves. Ironically, as noted in the case of Arsinoe (p. 143 above), the fact of the collection of that tax after the destruction of the Temple in Jerusalem should be interpreted as official recognition of the right of the Jewish people to continue practicing its religion, and thus also to organize in communities defined and recognized by law.

Another damaged papyrus from the second century C.E. (*CPJ*, III 452a) contains some muffled data that may cast light on the life of the community. It is a listing of employees of an estate who made payments for various purposes, such as for sheep (or lambs), for a beam (or girder), and for "the night celebration of the Feast of the Tabernacle" (ἡ παννυχὶς τῆς σκηνοπηγίας; lines 15-16). It is not

---

200 *Ibid.*, s.v. μερισμός; see: *CPJ*, II p. 111.
201 See Tcherikover, *Jews in Egypt*, pp. 75-76.
202 On the names of the tax, which changed at various times, see Tcherikover's explanation, *ibid.*, p. 88f. His explanations there are more comprehensive and instructive than in *CPJ*, II pp. 112-113.
203 Cf. *CPJ*, II 421, and if it was indeed the *amphodarch* who compiled the lists, this indirectly provides further support for the reports of Jews residing in their own quarter.
204 See Tcherikover, *Jews in Egypt*, p. 93.

clear who compiled the list and who collected the money, but according to the names, half the people listed were Jews[205]. In his interpretation of the document Stern suggested that the "night celebration" was the water-drawing festival (the second night of *Sukkoth*)[206]. The Feast of the Tabernacle was one of the most important holidays for Diaspora Jews during that period. An inscription from Berenice in Cyrene testifies to the organization at that season of community congresses which made communal decisions[207]. Pseudo-Chrysostomus indicates that the *archontes* of the Jewish community of Antioch on the Orontes were chosen in September[208], and the reference may be to a community convention with many participants on the occasion of the Jewish New Year or Feast of the Tabernacle. The great importance of *Sukkoth* for the Jewish community of Alexandria was noted by Philo, who mentioned also the custom of holding a large popular celebration (*In Flaccum*, 116ff.). It may not have been at all accidental that in Flaccus' incumbency, riots took place throughout September, coming to a head during *Sukkoth*. In other words, the trouble-makers may have deliberately focused on the time of the High Holidays when a Jewish community is engaged in particularly intensive activity. In describing the calamity, incidentally, Philo stressed that his coreligionists were

---

205 There are twenty-two names mentioned in the document, Ishmaelos occurring seven times and Pasias three times, in other words, fourteen different individuals are mentioned. Of these, six are undoubtedly Jews: Ishmaelos, the three brothers, sons of Annaios ('Αvvαῖος is probably חנן), who were called Bokis, Pasias and Pesouris, and also Simon and Iesous. It appears that at least three of the remaining six were also Jews, as is shown by their participation in the payment for "the *pannychis* of the Feast of Tabernacles". For the same reason it appears that another twenty-three unnamed people were also Jews, and they are mentioned as a group of hired laborers who participated in the payment for the same festival (lines 14-15).

206 In support of his opinion and reasoning (which are based mainly on Philo), a long list of Talmudic traditions can be presented which prove that the holiday celebrations were held at night, to the light of torches, etc. — *Sukkah*, V:3; *Tosefta Sukkah*, iv:2; iv:4 (Zuckermandel, p. 98); *T.J. Suk.*, V 55b-c; *T.B. Suk.*, 53a. It is possible that the mention of payments for the water-conduit and the sheep (or lambs) in the papyrus under consideration is somehow connected with the *Sukkoth* holiday and the water-drawing festival. Since this is only hypothetical, based upon the association of water with the water-drawing festival and of sheep with the *Sukkoth* sacrifice, I refrain from further elaboration, especially since I have no suggestion as to how to connect the girder (or beam) to these holidays.

207 *CIG*, III 5361; *REG*, 62, 283f.

208 See Schürer, vol. 3, p. 86.

obliged to remain in their homes after nightfall (*ibid.*, 119), suggesting that evening celebrations were held in Alexandria as well[209]. These similarities indicate that in Apollinopolis Magna too there was considerable activity at *Sukkoth* time in the Jewish community, a sign of vital vibrant Jewish life. Finally it should be noted that if all the people listed in *CPJ*, III 452a were indeed Jews, the different amounts collected from them were presumably community *liturgiai* aimed at financing various activities and needs of the local Jewish population[210]. That possibility is another element in the evidence pointing to the separate and independent organization of the Jewish community (in relation to the Greek *metropolis*) and its defined and recognized legal status.

---

209 All-night holy assemblies were also held by the therapeutai, according to Philo, *De Vita Contemplativa*, 83. Cf. also *De Cherubim*, 92, and Stern, who took these references into account.

210 On this subject, the inscription from Berenice — *CIG*, 5362 (*REG*, 52, p. 90) should be mentioned. It noted the decision of the Jewish *politeuma* to exempt one of its members from the *liturgia* because of his contribution to the community. This does not refer to the city *liturgia* (i.e. of the *polis*), for it is hard to imagine that this would be within the authority of the Jewish community.

Chapter IV

Comments on the Organization of Alexandria as a Polis

A. The Truncated Sovereignty of the Polis of Alexandria

It is important to clarify the political status of Alexandria in order to shed light on the rights of the Jews within it, and also to clarify the extent if any to which those rights were dependent on the *polis* authorities. It appears that for the Hellenistic period it is often very difficult to distinguish between *polis* and other forms of settlement, and even the writers of antiquity cannot help very much. However, the main political feature differentiating the *polis* include: a) a distinct group of citizens, including a general assembly (ἐκκλησία); b) the division of citizens into tribes (φυλαί) and demes (δῆμοι) which were the political and municipal units for the purposes of registration of citizens; c) a city council (βουλή) elected by the tribes; d) a well-defined constitution and a judicial and police system; e) its own elected magistracy; f) city territory; g) municipal coinage and the right to manage its own economy (taxation and budgeting); h) municipal deities and religion; i) autonomy (αὐτονομία), that is, the possibility of conducting municipal affairs according to its own laws through its own officials; j) freedom (ἐλευφερία), that is, non-subordination to any outside political authority.

An examination of Alexandria (and many other Hellenistic cities) according to these criteria shows that it conforms only at first glance. In fact, the reasons for its deficiencies are inherent in its establishment. For while the Classical *polis* evolved with the development of the ancient tribal society, the Hellenistic city was established as a small unit in the large political framework of the Hellenistic monarchy, on the initiative of the king and the basis of a fortuitous group of citizens. Its establishment was dictated by imperial needs, which were its only justification. In view of this fundamental difference, and the fact that the Hellenistic kingdom was based by nature on centralized authoritarian rule, it was clearly impossible to maintain the governmental methods of the Classical *polis*. The sovereignty of the *polis* was thus overshadowed by the royal authority, and in this respect there was no difference between the new cities and the old ones (that is, the former city-states) in the Hellenistic empires. Legal formalities described them as the "allies" of the kings as though alliances between equals were involved, but this was just a political and judicial fiction. In practice each king was the absolute master of his realm, and it was he who determined the terms of the alliance and thus the political status and rights of any city[1]. It is no wonder that there was a conflict of principle between the monarchical and *polis* systems, that is, between the authoritarian government and autonomous liberatian conceptions, and this was particularly true of Egypt with its long tradition of extreme monarchical regimes[2].

The most ancient of the Egyptian *poleis* was Naucratis, which was a *polis* many years before the Hellenistic conquest. However, it lost its sovereignty in the Ptolemaic period as indicated by a number of facts[3]:

a) Except for the short time between the death of Alexander the Great and the accession of Ptolemy I son of Lagos, it did not have its own coinage.

b) From the time of Ptolemy II Philadelphus, the cultivation of its land was directed by royal decree.

c) Administratively it was subordinate to the Saïte nome, and only during the Roman empire did it attain its own nome (Pliny, *Natural History*, V 49).

d) A royal garrison was stationed within the city.

e) During the reign of Ptolemy IV Philopator, financial and economic supervision was exercised by government officials.

Thus the central government in effect limited the autonomy of the *polis* to the narrowest municipal affairs.

The same situation obtained in Ptolemaïs. Although it was ostensibly the Ptolemaic king's "ally" to which he sent envoys (*OGIS*, 49),

---

1 See Bickermann, *Rev. de Philol.*, 65 (1939), p. 346f. On this subject Bickermann disagreed completely with Heuss, *Stadt und Herscher*, pp. 213, 248-299.

2 See Ehrenberg, *The Greek State*, p. 195f.; A.H.M. Jones, *The Greek City*, p. 95; Jouguet, p. 1f.; Bevan, p. 82.

3 See full details in Bevan, pp. 90-91; Jouguet, p. 42; Bouché-Leclerq, vol. 3, p. 145; vol. 4, p. 11; A.H.M. Jones, *CERP*, p. 303.

and in the third century B.C.E. had its own council, magistracy and judicial system (as evidenced by inscriptions)[4], in fact it was totally subject to the supervision of the Ptolemaic monarchy as the following facts show:

a) The participation of imperial officials in the municipal magistracy[5].

b) The lack of authority to issue coinage without any connection with the imperial monetary system.

c) Placement within the city of the main royal military camp for Upper Egypt[6].

d) The intervention of the king in its religious life[7].

The situation in Alexandria was not very different. Actually, its sovereignty was even more restricted, and the nature of its status as a *polis* quite obscure, given the following circumstances:

a) Alexandria was the seat of the Ptolemaic kings (and later of the Roman praefects) and thus subject to their direct jurisdiction[8]. Although in the Roman period its citizens were exempt from the *laographia*, it cannot be considered *civitas libera et immunis*. Exemption from the *laographia* was the outcome of the political realism of the Romans who, wishing to avoid unnecessary disturbances, adopted Ptolemaic governmental traditions.

b) The presence of a royal garrison within the city was also a proof of subordination to the central government[9], and the same

---

4 See full details in A.H.M. Jones, *CERP*, p. 306f.; Plaumann, *Ptolemais*, p. 35f.

5 For example, we hear, from the second century B.C.E., of the Theban *epistrategos* who were a chief πρύτανις and gynmasiarch in the city (Schubart, *Klio*, 10 (1910), p. 54) and of another man who was commander of a hipparchy in the Ptolemaic army and at the same time was a life *pritanis* and also a scribe of the municipal *boulé* committee (*OGIS*, 51, 728), and it appears that this reflects the Egyptian custom.

6 Plaumann, *Ptolemais*, pp. 31-32; and cf. Bouché-Leclerq, vol. 3, p. 145; vol. 4, p. 11.

7 A case from the time of Ptolemy XII Auletes (75 B.C.E.) is very instructive — a royal edict to the city authorities about granting the right of asylum to the shrine of Isis established by the Theban *epistrategos* (within the city limits). Bevan correctly deduced from this (p. 106) that the city was not authorized to decide about this right, even though the shrine was within its boundaries.

8 See Bevan, pp. 101-103; Jouguet, p. 30; Ehrenberg, *The Greek Stage*, pp. 195, 203-204, Taubenschlag, p. 575. For an exhaustive survey of the whole system of relations between the king and the city, see Fraser, vol. 1, pp. 93-131.

9 See pp. 173-174 below and n.23. The same was true in other cities outside of Egypt which were under Ptolemaic rule, such as Soli (Welles, *Roy. Corres.*, No. 30); Samos (*SEG*, I 364), Thera (*OGIS*, 102), etc. In regard to cities in the Seleucid kingdom, see Bicker-

applied during the Roman period.

c) There were local officials such as "city governor" (ὁ ἐπὶ τῆς πόλεως) and "city commander" (στρατηγὸς τῆς πόλεως) appointed by the central government[10].

d) The central government was in complete charge of civic registration. During the Ptolemaic period the kings could grant or withhold Alexandrian citizenship . at their exclusive discretion[11]. The Romans were even stricter, especially in regard to the lists of ephebes and the granting of citizenship[12], and even the operation of private gymnasia without central government supervision was forbidden. Throughout the whole principate period Alexandrian petitions to the emperors requesting the establishment of a *boulé* (= city council) were rejected.

e) Alexandria did not have its own coins. The coins minted there were related to the royal monetary system, and bore the portrait of the reigning king or emperor and a designation of the date according to his regnal year[13].

f) All documents written in Alexandria bore the official Ptolemaic or Roman dates.

g) Despite the city's special status as *Alexandria ad Aegyptum*, it was subject to government edicts[14].

h) The city's constitution was formulated and arranged by the

---

mann, *Inst. Sél.*, p. 32f.; Rostovtzeff, *SEHHW*, p. 524f. As to Atalid Pergamon, see Rostovtzeff, p. 557f.

10 On this subject in general see Schubart, *Klio*, 10 (1910), pp. 68-69; Bengston, *Die Strategie*, vol. 3, pp. 128-133; and on Alexandria in particular see Bevan, p. 103; Ehrenberg, ibid., p. 201f.; Taubenschlag, p. 575. It should be noted that Alexandria was not the only Hellenistic city in which there were such positions (see A.H.M. Jones, *The Greek City*, pp. 105, 317, n.19). Recently Fraser clarified the difference between them, one being civilian and the other of a military nature. For full details, see Fraser, vol. 1, pp. 106-107; vol. 2, pp. 193-195, (nn.94, 99, 101, 104).

11 For example, we know that Ptolemy IV Philopator established a new civic tribe in Alexandria, and even made its members preeminent (see Satyrus' report: *FGrH*, IIIc, no. 631, p. 180f.). It is also known that Ptolemy VIII Euergates II revoked the Alexandrian citizenship of many people and granted it to others (see Justinus, XXXVIII, 8, 7). On the poor relations of this king with the Alexandrians, see full details in Fraser, vol. 1, p. 121f.

12 See, e.g. *P. Lond.*, 1912 (= *CPJ*, II 153), line 52f. Note also Trajan's reply to Pliny the Younger, stressing the principle accepted by the emperors of not granting Alexandrian citizenship lightly (Pliny, *Epist.*, X 7).

13 Poole, *Catalogue of the Coins, passim*.

14 See Fraser, vol. 1, pp. 107-109.

central government[15].

i) While Alexandria had a municipal magistracy, it is not clear whether it was appointed by the central government (as in Cyrene) or elected and appointed jointly (as in Ptolemaïs). In any case it was closely supervised by the government, as was the citizens' assembly[16].

j) There was no *boulé* in Alexandria at least from the middle of the second century B.C.E. to the time of Septimius Severus (200 C.E.)[17].

k) While a *gerousia* existed in Alexandria from the second (or first) century B.C.E.[18] it was probably appointed by the government, judging by Ptolemy I's practice in Cyrene (*SEG*, IX, lines 20-25).

It should be noted that the existence of a *gerousia* does not necessarily imply the absence of a *boulé*, but the mention of the former only points to the less than total sovereignty of the Alexandrian *polis*. Modern scholars do not agree on the nature and functions of the *gerousia*. Some believed that it was a public institution operating mainly in matters of religion which sometimes took part in the administration of the city, that is, an institution of significance in the life of the *polis*. Others believed that the *gerousia* was a body repre-

---

15 See, e.g., Fraser, vol. 1, pp. 110-115, about the Ptolemaic period.

16 See full details of this in Fraser, vol. 1, pp. 95-100.

17 Opinions on this subject in scholarly literature differ widely. The clearest sources are: Spartianus, *Scr. Hist. Aug., Vita Severi*, 17, 2; *P. Lond.*, 1912 (lines 66-72); Cassius Dio, LI 17; *PSI*, 1160 (the *"Boulé* Papyrus"). However, all of them are from the Roman period and they cannot serve as definitive sources for certain conclusions about the existence of *boulé* in the Ptolemaic period. While it is true that Spartianus's report definitely states that Alexandria did not have a *boulé* at that period, this was questioned because the report was from a later time. For a survey of the research and the problems on this subject, see Fraser, vol. 1, pp. 93f., 797-798; vol. 2, pp. 173-176 (nn.3-11). Apparently most scholars accepted the principle that Alexandria did have a *boulé* in the Ptolemaic period, but that it no longer existed at the time Augustus captured the city. On exactly when it was abolished there are various opinions, among which the most current are: a) Schubart's view that it occurred in the time of Ptolemy VIII Eurgetes II, i.e. between 145 and 116 B.C.E. (Schubart, *BIFAO*, 30 (1931), pp. 407-415); b) Bell's view that it might also have taken place in the reign of Ptolemy IV Philopator, in connection with the reforms he instituted in the organization of the municipal demes and tribes (Bell, *Aegyptus*, 12 (1932), pp. 173-184); c) Fraser's view reinforcing the opinion of the first publishers of the papyrus that the *boulé* was abolished only in the time of Augustus, but in fact not putting forward any new decisive arguments (Fraser, *loc.cit.*).

18 Selected bibliography on this subject: Momigliano, *JRS*, 34 (1934), pp. 114-115; El-Abbadi, *JEA*, 50 (1964), pp. 164-169; Musurillo, pp. 108-110; Fraser, vol. 1, p. 95; vol. 2, pp. 176-177, nn.14-16 (where extensive, exhaustive bibliographical details are to be found).

senting a social organization, such as "older citizens" or "younger citizens", which at most had some political influence in the life of the city. Its social nature is indicated by its close connection with the gymnasium[19]. In Oliver's view, the various *gerousiai* in the ancient world should be classified on the basis of ethnic and geographic groups, and varied accordingly[20]. One way or the other, it is impossible to ignore the fact that the *gerousia* was less powerful than the *boulé*. In Alexandria, at any rate, they were not equal, and that is demonstrated by the frequent efforts of the Alexandrians to establish a *boulé*. That alone shows how small was the political value of the *gerousia* as an institution representing the sovereignty of the *polis*, and what a poor substitute it was for a *boulé*[21]. The important point here is that the Greek community organization in Alexandria had a *gerousia*, just as the Jewish *politeuma* had, and in that respect had no advantage. This fact is evidence of the *isopoliteia* that the Jews enjoyed according to Josephus (see Chapter VIII below).

In regard to points (c) and (i) above, the failure of the sources to differentiate between government (or imperial) magistracy and municipal magistracy in Alexandria is most illuminating[22], as it indicates how overshadowed the latter was by the former. This is shown in an excerpt from Strabo depicting the situation at the end of the Ptolemaic and start of the Roman periods:

"Egypt is now a Province; and it not only pays considerable tribute, but also is governed by prudent men — the praefects who are sent there from time to time. He who is sent has the rank of king; and subordinate to him is the administrator of justice (δικαιοδότος), who has supreme authority over most of the law suits; and another is the official called *Idiologus*, who inquires into all properties that are without owners and that ought to fall to Caesar; and these are attended by freedmen of Caesar, as also by stewards (οἰκονόμοι), who are entrusted with affairs of more or less importance. There are also three legions of soldiers, one of which is stationed in the city and the others in the coun-

---

19 The basic studies of the *gerousia* and its spread in the Greek and Roman world include Poland, *Vereinswesens*, pp. 98-102, 577-587, Oliver, *The Sacred Gerousia*. In support of the first opinion, see, e.g., Poland, *op.cit.*, p. 98f.; Ziebarth, *Vereinswesens*, p. 3, and other scholars concurred. For the second opinion, see e.g., A.H.M. Jones, *The Greek City*, pp. 255f., 353, n.31; idem, *JRS*, 34 (1944) pp. 145-146; and cf. Fraser's middle-of-the-road opinion, vol. 1, p. 95.

20 Oliver, *The Sacred Gerousia*, p. 7f.

21 Cf. Ehrenberg, *The Greek State*, p. 201.

22 Cf. Fraser, vol. 1, p. 96f. The subject is exemplified by inscription *SB*, 2100, which mentions a man (named Likarion) who is described as honorary *archigeron, dioiketes, exegetes*, commander of the city (ὁ ἐπὶ τῆς πόλεως) and *gymnasiarches*, all at once.

try; and apart from these there are nine Roman cohorts, three in the city, three on the borders of Aethiopia in Syene, as a guard for that region, and three in the rest of the country. And there are also three bodies of cavalry, which likewise are assigned to the various critical points. Of the native officials in the city, one is the Interpreter (ἐξηγητής), who is clad in purple, has hereditary prerogatives, and has charge of the interests of the city; and another the Recorder (ὑπομνηματογράφος); and another the Chief Judge (ἀρχιδικαστής); and the fourth the Night Commander (νυκτερινὸς στρατηγός). Now these officers existed also in the time of the kings, but since the kings were carrying on a bad government, the prosperity of the city was also vanishing on account of the prevailing lawlessness (Strabo XVII, 1, 12, c797 trans. H. L. Jones, LCL, ed.)[23].

An exmination of the nature of the municipal posts reported by Strabo reveals the following picture: The "Recorder" (or memorandum-writer) was a high official in the service of the Ptolemaic king[24]. The "Chief Judge" was not a municipal official either, but had judicial authority in Egypt as a whole, and only resided in Alexandria like most of the high officials[25]. The "Night Commander" was apparently an official equivalent to the *praefectus vigilum* in Rome. Bevan proposed identifying him with the "Commander of the city" (στρατηγὸς τῆς πόλεως) in the belief that the post was patterned after that of the *praefectus urbi* in Rome[26]. In either case he was clearly not a municipal official, but appointed by the central government. As to the *exegetes*, Bevan claimed that on the basis of Strabo's description he should be identified with the annual eponymous priest of Alexander, who according to Pseudo-Callisthenes (III 33) was "overseer of the city" and stemmed from among the king's favorites or the royal family. Since these priests were not actually municipal magistrates, Bevan spectulated that the *exegetes* was the honorary head of the civic body, and not an official with any real authority[27]. It seems strange that Strabo made no mention of the

---

23　Cf. Josephus, *Bellum*, II 387; Tacitus, *Historiae*, I 11 (and also V 1).

24　Fraser, vol. 1, p. 96; vol. 2, p. 179, n.29.

25　In the opinion of Wilcken-Mitteis (vol. 2, p. 27), in the Ptolemaic period the *archidikastos* was a municipal functionary, but Schubart (*Archiv*, 5 (1909-13), pp. 61-70) took violent issue with this, and Fraser (vol. 1, p. 96) agreed with him.

26　See Bevan, p. 103, but Box, in his commentary on *In Flaccum*, 120 disagreed, and his argument is fairly convincing. Cf. also Fraser, vol. 1, p. 98. The fact that Philo mentioned "the night guard" is in itself instructive, and according to his description they were indeed entrusted with guarding the city at night. On the νυκτερινὸς στρατηγός in Egyptian cities see Fraser, vol. 2, p. 100, n.34, where there is also an extensive bibliography. There were such guards in Asia Minor, too, e.g. in Ephesus (*SEG*, IV 519) and in Tralles (*CIG*, 2930).

27　Bevan, p. 103; cf. Fraser, vol. 1, p. 97; vol. 2, p. 180, n.33.

post of gymnasiarch which was so well known in the Roman period, and whose incumbents were the most enthusiastic spokesmen of Alexandrian interest. Perhaps in his day the gymnasiarchs were not yet imported in Alexandrian public life and only after the consistent refusal of the emperors to repair the deficiencies of Alexandria as a *polis* did they become the standard bearers of opposition to Rome. This alone testifies to the defective nature of the Alexandrian *polis*.

As a matter of fact, the relations between Alexandria and the Ptolemaic kings were probematic from the reign of Ptolemy IV Philopator on, and especially beginning in the second century B.C.E., as modern research has shown[28]. The testimony of Polybius (in *Strabo*, XVII 1, 12, c797) reflects clearly the imcomplete sovereignty of Alexandria, as a result of the deterioration of these relations:

> "At any rate, Polybius who had visited the city is disgusted with the state of things then existing; and he says that three classes (γένη) inhabited the city: first, the Aegyptian or native stock of people, who were quick-tempered and not inclined to civic life (ὀξύ καὶ ἀπολιτικόν); and secondly the mercenary class, who were severe and numerous and intractable (for by an ancient custom they would maintain foreign men-at-arms, who had been trained to rule rather than to be ruled, on account of the worthlessness of the kings); and third, the tribe (γένος) of the Alexandrians, who also were not distinctly inclined to civil life (οὐδ᾽ αὐτὸ εὐκρινῶς πολιτικὸν), and for the same reasons, but still they were better than those others, for even though they were a mixed people (μιγάδες) still they were Greeks by origin and mindful of the customs common to the Greeks. But after this mass of people had also been blotted out, chiefly by Euergetes Physcon, in whose time Polybius went to Alexandria (for, being opposed by factions, Physcon more often sent the masses against the soldiers and thus caused their destruction) — such being the state of affairs in the city, Polybius says, in very truth there remained for one, in the words of the poet, merely "to go Egypt, a long and painful journey" (*Odyssea*, 4, 483).

That testimony certainly speaks for itself[30].

During the Roman period, relations became even worse and except for short periods there was constant friction between the Alexandrians and the Roman emperors[31]. Augustus initiated the policy of reservation and suspicion to Egypt in general and Alexandria in

---

28 See a broad, exhaustive survey in Fraser, vol. 1, pp. 81-82, and especially p. 115f.

29 See Jones's translation and his comment on the exact textual meaning, *Strabo, ad. loc.*; and see also Fraser, vol. 1, p. 61; vol. 2, pp. 144-145, n.184.

30 For full details of the relations of Ptolemy VIII Euergetes II with Alexandria see Fraser, vol. 1, p. 121f.

31 See Mommsen, *Röm. Geschichte*, vol. 5, p. 582f. On the stormy character of Alexandria and the frequency of bloody riots there, see Ammianus Marcellinus, XXII 11, 4. As a matter of fact, the Alexandrians hated the Romans even before the latter captured the city; see Fraser, vol. 1, pp. 90, 125-128, 488, 545, 550, 794-795.

particular, and bequeathed it to succeeding generations[32]. Although he did not assume a lofty tone with the Alexandrians in the conquest of their city, he did not hide his disparagement of it. Riots broke out in the city already in his own reign, actually between 25 and 21 B.C.E.[33] From then on there was a continual series of anti-Roman outbreaks[34], with sporadic intervals of calm due to fright or to hope for prospective improvement in the situation. Except for Caligula and Nero, all the emperors of the principate period viewed Alexandria with dismay and distrust, chiefly because the character of its citizens and its rebellious inclinations contradicted their policy of *Pax Romana*. The negative evaluation of the city in Roman literature was by no means gratuitous[35]. Philo too reports that the prefects were always suspicious of the Alexandrians and established the practice of conducting arms searches every three years (*In Flaccum*, 93). The embers of Alexandrian enmity to Rome were fanned in particular by the gymnasiarchs, and its main means of expression was the

---

32 The reason was that Egypt was a convenient geo-strategic base for seceding from the empire. In the words of Tacitus: "For Augustus among the other secrets of absolutism, by prohibiting all senators or Roman knights of the higher rank from entering the country without permission, kept Egypt isolated" (trans. Moore and Jackson, *LCL*) (*Annales*, II 59; and cf. Cassius Dio, LI 17). According to Tacitus, Tiberius also "rebuked him (Germanicus) with extreme sharpness for overstepping the proscription of Augustus by entering Alexandria without imperial consent" (*ibid.*). In line with his policy, Augustus appointed a special governor for Egypt, *praefectus Aegypti*, from the equestrian class, and not a *legatus pro praetore* from the senate, as was customary in other provinces. He also forbade Egyptians who acquired Roman citizenship to serve as senators in Rome (Cassius Dio, LI 17, 1-2).

33 Cassius Dio, LI 16, 5; Strabo, XVII 1, 54 (819c).

34 This situation was especially serious from the Claudian period onward; but at that time the main thrust was against the Jews, while the Roman emperors and prefects were only showered with scorn and abuse (cf. Seneca, *Dial.*, XII 19, 6). Later genuine riots erupted against Roman rule, e.g. the tension during the time of Vespasian (Cassius Dio, LXVI 8, 2-6; and cf. *Epit.*, 65, 8-9; Suetonius, *Vespasian*, 19); the Alexandrian rebellion in the time of Hadrian (See Spartianus, *Scr. Hist. Aug.*, *Vita Hadriani*, 12, 1; and cf. Cassius Dio, LXIX 8, 1; Wilcken, *Antisemetismus*, p. 816); the riots during the time of Antoninus Pius, in which the Roman governor was killed (see P. Meyer, *Klio*, 7 (1907), p. 123); the slaughter of Alexandria's citizens by Caracalla (Cassius Dio, LXXVII 22-23; and cf. Spartianus, *ibid.*, *Vita Caracalla*, 6). An instructive expression of the hatred of the Alexandrians for the Roman rulers is given in Dio Chrysostomus's report (*Orationes*, XXXII 69-72) noting the readiness of the rabble there to riot despite the intervention of the Roman legions. See also Smallwood, p. 214.

35 E.g. Seneca, *Dial.*, XII 19, 6; Diodorus Siculus, I 83, 8; Pliny the Younger, *Panegyricus*, 31; Tacitus, *Annales*, I 11; Dio Chrysostomus, *Orationes*, XXXII 1, 29-32, 69-72, 86, 95-96, 99; Cassius Dio, LI 17, 1-2, cf. also Josephus, *Bellum*, II 385.

mime literature[36] and farces, as well as venomous propaganda[37]. The death sentences that various emperors pronounced on the gymnasiarchs did not reduce the animosity of the Alexandrians. On the contrary, they aroused the next gymnasiarchs to wield even more assiduously the pens of incitement, vilification and indictment. The protracted hatred had a long history rooted first and foremost in the truncation of the sovereignty of the Alexandrian *polis*, and indicating that the city did not enjoy the Roman emperors and was much hampered under their rule.

B. The Political Organization of Alexandria (according to Tarn)

The deficiencies in the political sovereignty of Alexandria and its sister cities which were established throughout the empire by Alexander the Great were well known to Tarn. According to him the Alexandrian cities were founded not as ordinary *poleis* but as political bodies that were multi-ethnic in character, organized as a collection of *politeumata*, of which the most important was that of the Greeks[38]. As to Alexandria, it too was "a collection of *Politeumata*, based on nationalities, the Greek *politeuma* being much the most important; outside these stood a few privileged Macedonians at one end and the mass of Egyptians at the other"[39].

As Alexander's stay in Egypt was short, it is difficult to ascertain his activities there. According to the meager information in the sources, he did not stay to direct the establishment of the city of Alexandria, but entrusted the task to the first governor, Cleomenes[40]. The details of Alexander's instructions in regard to the citizens there are not known; in any case, it is understood that they were all

---

36 From both literary and papyrological sources we know that the Mime literature and the plays and farces connected with it, were very popular in Alexandria. See, e.g. Cicero, *Pro Rabirio*, 12, 35. And cf. also Dio Chrysostomus, *Orationes*, XXXII 86, 99. For papyrological sources see Musurillo, p. 49f.; Wilcken, *Antisemitismus*, p. 807f.; and also Page, *Greek Literary Papyri*, nn. 73-79. Literary sources include Wüst, *RE(PW)*, vol. 15, p. 1730 (s.v. Mimos); Reich, *Der Mimus*; Box, *Phil. Alex.*, p. 88f. and see n.37 below.

37 This literature was titled "Acta Alexandrinorum". Musurillo included all the items from the papyri in his book.

38 Tarn, p. 148; see also Tarn, *The Greeks in Bactria*, p. 18; in his opinion the Alexandrian cities became *poleis* only in Seleucid times, as indicated in, e.g., *OGIS*, 233, line 114.

39 See Tarn, p. 185. It was in fact Engers who first expressed this idea. See Engers, *Mnemosyne*, N.S. 54 (1926), p. 161.

40 See complete details on the founding of the city in Fraser, vol. 1, p. 3f.

"Hellenes", at least when Polybius visited the city in the second century B.C.E. (in *Strabo*, XVII 1, 12, c797). Still, a residential quarter was allotted in the new city to some native Egyptians from the fishing village of Rhacotis and other villages[41]. Thus there were autochthonic Egyptians among the original inhabitants of the city, so that perhaps there is a historical basis for the testimony of Peusdo-Callisthenes (who reeks of legend) that the city was founded through synoecism (living together, union) of populations from extensive areas in its vicinity[42]. It is not clear, however, to what extent these were included in the civic body[43].

It is odd that all the testimony on the founding of Alexandria fails to mention soldiers, for this does not accord with what is known about the establishment of other cities in the east by Alexander, which in all cases revolved around a settlement core of soldiers, either regular or retired[44]. However, Alexandria was not an exception in this respect; an important papyrus from mid-third century B.C.E. specifically mentions military personnel (οἱ στρατιῶται) from Alexandria, of whom at least some were classified as citizens[45].

The status of the "Macedonians" is related to this problem which has produced various scholarly solutions. Schürer, Juster, Bevan and others considered the "Macedonians" to be the citizens par excellence

---

41 See full details in Fraser, vil. 1, pp. 5-6; vol. 2, pp. 7-8, nn.17-19.

42 *Ps. Callist.*, I 31, 8; and it can be assumed that the description found there applies to the Alexandrian *chora* as well. As will be shown below, this was a common and accepted phenomenon in the Hellenistic world, that new cities were established by synoecism, that is, a sort of federative union, or an integrated merger of various political groups, military units, different communities, villages, etc.

43 Fraser tends to view these communities as intended for physical but not constitutional synoecism, that is, the villagers achieved the right of residence in Alexandria in this way, but did not become part of its citizenry (see Fraser, vol. 1, p. 41).

44 A number of these cities, particularly where the two military elements — Greek mercenaries and retired "Macedonians" — figured prominently in the population alongside the local residents, were: 1) Caucasian Alexandria (Arrian, VI 22, 4; Diodorus Siculus, XVII 83, 2; Curtius Rufus, VII 3, 23); 2) Alexandria on the Tanais (Arrian, IV 4.1); 3) Alexandria on the Acesines (*ibid.*, V 29, 8); Alexandria Kharkis (Pliny, V 27, 138); Arigaeum in India (Arrian, IV 24, 7), etc. For more details see Tcherikover's books, *Städtegründungen*, and *Jews and Greeks in the Hellenistic Period*, (1931), p. 85.

45 *P. Hamb.*, 168a, lines 5-10; and cf. *P. Hal.*, lines 156-165. Fraser even made a considerable list of soldiers who resided in the Fayûm and were citizens of Alexandria but had not yet completed all the formalities needed for full citizenship (Fraser, vol. 2, pp. 133-134, n.1040. This problem is discussed also in chap. 5 below.

of Alexandria[46], while Schubart and others claimed the opposite[47]. Among these was Tcherikover, who carried the investigation further, and was able to distinguish four types of "Macedonians" in the various cities of the Hellenistic East[48]: a) Macedonian garrisons of the regular army, stationed near (or in) ancient Greek cities and assigned to defend them (sometimes hired by the city itself); except in some extraordinary cases, these soldiers were not considered citizens of the *polis*. b) Macedonian garrisons in the service of the Hellenistic kings, charged with maintaining public order in the newly founded cities; these were not citizens either, but directly subordinate to the king. c) Military settlements of Macedonians which developed into real Hellenistic cities in the course of time. d) Macedonian veterans in Alexander's service, who were among the founders of his new cities and citizens of them.

In Tcherikover's opinion, Alexander did not have any Macedonian veterans at his disposal when Alexandria was founded, as he was just beginning his military exploits. Consequently the Macedonians settled in Alexandria at the time were a regular garrison and not part of the citizenry. The situation was perpetuated by the Ptolemies who kept the soldiers outside the civic body and subject to direct royal discipline[49]. This view is supported by the fact that they lived apart, close to the royal court, in a genuine residential quarter rather than a military barracks[50]. As there were in Ptolemaic Egypt military units organized as *politeumata*[51] the "Macedonians" in

---

46 Schürer, vol. 3, p. 122; Juster, vol. 2, p. 7; Bevan, p. 98.
47 Schubart, *Archiv*, 5 (1909-1913), pp. 111-112; Engers, *Klio*, 18 (1922-23), p. 89; Bell, *JEA*, 13 (1927), p. 173; Wilcken-Mitteis, p. 63; Fuchs, p. 88; Heichelheim, pp. 38-43; Launey, vol. 1, p. 308f.; Fraser, vol. 1, p. 52f.
48 Tcherikover, *Jews and the Greeks* etc., (1931), Hebrew, pp. 328-329. Fraser (*ibid.*) distinguished between two kinds of "Macedonians" for purposes of the discussion on Alexandria: soldiers (the royal bodyguard) and civilians. He did not think the former were citiznes of the *polis*, but admitted their superiority and special position (p. 80). On the other hand, contrary to Schubart, he considered the "Macedonians" of the latter class less important, and did not think they enjoyed any preferential civil status (see also *ibid.*, pp. 69, 80, 88).
49 *Ibid.*, p. 330. Cf. also Fraser, vol. 1, p. 52f. On "Macedonian" military colonies separately organized in other *poleis*, see Oertel, *RE(PW)*, 11 (1921), p. 3. A similar situation existed in the cities of the Seleucid kingdom as well, see Bar-Kochva, p. 22f.; Rostovtzeff, *SEHHW*, pp. 500-502.
50 Cf. Schubart, *Archiv*, 5 (1909-1913), p. 112.
51 See, e.g., Launey, vol. 2, p. 1064. Examples are the Cretan *politeuma* in the second century B.C.E. (*W. Chr.*, 448 = *P. Tebt.*, I 32); the Boetian *politeuma* from 165 B.C.E.

Alexandria may have been the first of these, especially in view of the existence of equivalent organizations there, such as the ·Phrygian *politeuma*[52] and the Lycian *politeuma*[53]. There is also testimony on the organization of a *"politeuma* of soldiers serving in Alexandria" (τὸ πολίτευμα τῶν ἐν Ἀλεξανδρείαι φερομένων στρατιωτῶν) from the end of the second century B.C.E. or the beginning of the first, which had its own magistracy[54]. It may have been composed of several ethnic elements, as Fraser suggests[55], in which case it was perhaps established as a federation of small *politeumata* of the ethnic type noted. To these should be added the Jewish *politeuma* which was likewise apparently established on the basis of a military settlement[56]. It is not clear whether there were other ethnic or religious associations in Ptolemaic Alexandria[57].

(*SEG*, II 871); the Idumaean *politeuma* of 112 B.C.E. (*OGIS*, 737); and the Cilician *politeuma* (*SEG*, VIII 573). Some scholars believe that there were also Achaean and Thracian *politeumata* (Perdrizet and Lefebvre, *Graffites d'Abydos*, p. XI; Henne, *BIFAO*, 25 (1924), p. 179) and Mysians and Persians (Lesquier, pp. 143f., 151). See also Fraser, vol. 1, pp. 59, 89, 194, 280-281.

52 *OGIS*, 658 — Although the inscription (from 3 B.C.E.) was found in Pompeii in Italy. Dittenberger definitely proved its connection with Alexandria, mainly because of the phrasing of the date, which was based on the Egyptian calendar. Ruppel (p. 443) suggested two reasonable explanations for the inscription being found in Pompeii, which it is unnecessary to give here. It should also be mentioned in this context that the rites of the Phrygian Cybele (the goddess of fertility, nature and life) were very popular in Alexandria; about this see Fraser, vol. 1, p. 277f. It is true that Fraser did not think that cult was necessarily connected with any special ethnic elements among the city population, but it appears that he was wrong.

53 *SEG*, II 848, from 120 B.C.E.; and see Heichelheim, p. 115. Ruppel (pp. 448-449) was doubtful about its Alexandrian origin, even though it was found in Alexandria, but his reasons are not very convincing.

54 See *SEG*, II 499.

55 Fraser, vol. 1, p. 89.

56 The *Letter of Aristeas*, 310; Strabo (in Josephus), *Antiquitates*, XIV 117; on the subject of the connection with military colonization, see *Bellum*, II 487-488; *C. Apionem*, II 35, 42; *Antiquitates*, XII 8. A spècific discussion of these reports appears below in chap. 8.

57 From the report of Polybius (V 36, 4-5) it appears that in 220 B.C.E. there were in the Alexandria garrison 3,000 Peloponesian mercenaries, 1,000 Cretan mercena⁻ies, and some from Syria and Caria as well. It is not clear as to whether they were organized in civil bodies, but this is not impossible in view of the organization of a Cretan *politeuma* in the Arsinöite nome (*P. Tebt.*, I 32 from 145 B.C.E.). In support of this assumption it should be noted that document *P. Tebt.*, III 700 (Col. II, lines 37f.) tells of the existence in Alexandria of various *gymnasia, politeumata* and *synodoi* against which Ptolemy III Eurgetes II took harsh measures, but it is not clear whether this refers exclusively to Alexandria.

Still the picture that emerges appears to confirm Tarn's assumption that "Alexandria was a collection of *politeumata*"[58], particularly since Hellenistic cities like it in being less than completely autonomous tended to contain a number of *politeumata*[59]. In this respect there was no difference between the Hellenistic period and the Roman; only the terminology changed.

Magnesia, for instance, in 244 B.C.E. had a *politeuma* of Smyrnans (the town garrison) federated with the local *polis* (*OGIS*, 222) but retaining a separate organization even though the members became local citizens[60]. Two first-century B.C.E. inscriptions from Berenice in Cyrene mention a Jewish *politeuma*. The editors correctly noted that *"singulae urbes Cyrenaicae diversas constituebant civitates"*[61], and this is illuminating in view of the fact that the arrangements in Cyrene resembled those in Egypt, as both places shared the Ptolemaic heritage. Later (in 56 C.E.) the community was called a συναγωγή (*SEG*, XVII 823) which was the synonymous term[62].

In Sidon there were tombstones dating from the end of the third century B.C.E. or the start of the second, of soldiers from four different *politeumata*, originating in Asia Minor; this too is probably due to the Ptolemaic heritage[63]. After the rebellion of slaves in Delos in 130 B.C.E., a federation of several *politeumata* was established on the ruins of the city, the *politeumata* having been organized by foreign merchants subject to an Athenian government[64]. According to Strabo, Emporium in Spain was originally a double city (δίπολις) divided by a wall. One part was inhabited by Emporitans and the other by natives, Indiketans. The latter had their own government (ἰδίᾳ πολιτευόμενοι) but eventually the two merged into one *politeuma* combining "barbarian" with "Hellenic" laws (*Strabo*, III

---

58 Indirectly, Fraser held this opinion (vol. 1, pp. 280-281).
59 On this subject cf. Tarn (*Alexander*, p. 135), who argued that there were both Greek and non-Greek organizations in the Asiatic Alexandrias. It should be added that Alexander even allowed the establishment of a *politeuma* among the citizens of an older city — e.g. in Chios a *politeuma* of exiles was organized with his permission, see *Syll.*, 283; Ruppel, p. 57f.
60 See Ruppel, p. 295; and for more details see Bar-Kochva, p. 57f.
61 Franz and Boeckh, *CIG*, 5361-2; and see also *REG*, 62 (1949), p. 290f.
62 See Applebaum, *Jews and Greeks*, pp. 162, 192.
63 See Ruppel, p. 310 and bibliography. See also L. Robert, *BCH*, 59 (1935), p. 428f.; Rostovtzeff, *SEHHW*, pp. 341, 1401 (n.137).
64 Ferguson, *Hellenistic Athens*, p. 380; Tarn, pp. 264-265.

4, 8). Livy (34, 9) notes that Julius Caesar was said to have attached
Roman settlers to the united city. That means that Emporium was
organized as a federation of three ethnic groups — Greeks, Spaniards
and Romans.

Strabo reported that Megalopolis in Cappadocia Pontica was
founded by Pompey as a *polis* of two communities, Camisene and
Colupene. Eventually the Roman prefects split the two communities
into a number of units, putting an end to Pompey's achievement in
the place (*Strabo*, XII 3, 37). A third-century B.C.E. inscription from
Cos mentions three people, two of whom were *archontes* of a local
politeuma (*OGIS*, 192). In view of the date noted on it, the inscription is probably from Egypt, especially since Cos had connections
with the Ptolemaic kingdom[65]. It has even been suggested that the
politeuma was Jewish, founded by emigrants from Egypt[66], and thus
to be added to the list of Jewish *politeumata* in the Classical world.

In regard to Seleucia on the Tigris, Josephus noted that the
population consisted of three elements — Macedonians, Hellenes and
Syrians. In regard to the latter he worte: "not a few Syrians holding
civic rights" (ἔστι δέ καὶ Σύρων οὐκ ὀλίγον τὸ ἐμπολιτευόμενον)[67].
Tarn seems to have been right to maintain that the word τὸ ἐμπολιτευόμενον is derived from *politeuma* rather than *polis*, which means
that there was a Syrian *politeuma* in Seleucia[68]. In his view when a
non-Greek group was attached to a Greek city, this was done in the
framework of a *politeuma*, or *katoikia* in Seleucid terminology[69].
On these grounds it can logically be assumed that the Jews too were
so organized in some cities. At any rate, that appears to have been
the case in regard to the Jewish *katoikia* of Hierapolis in Phrygia
(*CIJ*, II 775), and perhaps also to the Jews of Sardis[70].

---

65 For details see Fraser, vol. 1, pp. 69, 124, 307, 344, 660, 784;vol. 2, p. 462, n.11. See
   also Josephus, *Antiquitates*, XIII 349; XIV 112; Appian, *Bell. Civ.*, I 102, and also *OGIS*,
   42.
66 See Ruppel, pp. 437-438. Cf. S.M. Sherwin-White, *Zeitschrift für Papyrologie und Epigraphic*, 21 (1976), p. 186.
67 *Antiquitates*, XVIII 372; and cf. also *ibid.*, 378.
68 See Tarn, p. 157 (and n.3); cf. Tarn, *The Greeks in Bactria*, p. 18.
69 Tarn, pp. 157-158; and also pp. 147-148. He thought the same was true of Antioch on
   the Orontes and Antioch-Edessa, as well as Pisidian Antioch.
70 If we judge by what appears in *Antiquitates*, XIV 259: ὅι κατοικοῦντες ἡμῶν ἐν
   τῇ πόλει Ἰουδαῖοι πολῖται; and according to *IGRR*, iv 1387: ἡ Ἰουδδῆνων κατοικία.
   On this inscription see Radet, *De Coloniis a Macedonibus, s.v. Judeni*, p. 282 (cf. p. 22);

Inscriptions of the second or first century B.C.E. from Heraclea in Thrace mention a *politeuma* of Romans permanently settled there[71]. In considering Roman settlements, a distinction must be made between colonies of veterans which were designed to carry out military functions and were set up near the Hellenistic cities as separate bodies[72], and other groups of Romans, particularly in the cities of Asia Minor, whose settlements were often called *epoikisis*[73]. The cities they lived in considered these groups "Romans resident [with us]" ('Ρωμαίων οἱ [παρ' ἡμῖν] κατοικοῦντες) which means they were not citizens[74]. There is evidence of a few groups which had federative connections with the towns through a *sympoliteia*[75], and this shows that the groups were organized and well defined, for a *sympoliteia* could only be formed by agreement of the two parties. It should be kept in mind that the *sympoliteia* indicated only the federative citizenship, along with which the previous citizenship could be retained[76]. Presumably the Romans would have been interested in retaining their own organization, by reason of their Roman citizenship. In brief, in the Roman period too it was common for the Hellenistic cities to contain two (or more) organized associations, either totally separate, or federated.

It should be noted that a frequent occurrence in Hellenistic times

L. Robert, *Villes*, p. 282; Launey, vol. 1, p. 551, n.4; Bar-Kochva, p. 228, n.114.

71 See *IG*, IX 2, 1; and Ruppel, pp. 435-436.

72 See, e.g., A.H.M. Jones, *CERP*, pp. 41, n.3, 141.

73 See Bowersock, *Augustus*, p. 64; Broughton, *TAPA*, 66 (1935), pp. 2f., esp. 21f. For example, Appian applied the term "colony" to the Roman settlement Lampsacus dating from the time of Julius Caesar (*Bell. Civ.*,V 137). Strabo (XII 3, 6, 11) reported similarly about Bethynian Heracleia and Sinope, each of which contained a "colony" of Romans which had occupied a part of the city and its *chora*. By the way, according to the same report there was a colony of Miletian people in Sinope, too, and also in Amisus, Tralles, Cyzicus and other places.

74 See Ruppel, p. 435. Roman organizations of this kind, defined in Latin as *conventus civium Romanorum* were not subject to the *polis* and even maintained their own courts, and their own religion and way of life. On their legal status, see Mitteis, *Reichsrecht*, pp. 143-150; e.g., from the time of Augustus on, a group of Roman citizens is known to have resided in Chios and engaged in a legal battle with the local citizens, and both parties (ἑκάτερον μέρος) were clearly distinguished as two separate sections; see Ehrenberg and Jones, *Documents*, No. 317.

75 That is, a treaty for reciprocal interchangeable citizenship, see, e.g., Bowersock, *Augustus*, p. 64, n.3.

76 Ehrenberg, *The Greek State*, p. 126. On dual *politeumata* see also Levick, *Roman Colonies*, p. 70f.

was the establishment (usually by kings) of cities on the basis of a merger of various communities. Antioch on the Orontes was a union of an Athenian community (from Antigoneia on the Orontes) with a Macedonian community, and the same was true of Antigoneia in Bithynia (later Nicaea)[77]. One of Alexander's successors, Lysimachius, arranged a synoecism of small towns in order to found his city, Lysimachia in the Chersonese, and he had similar plans for Teos and Lebedus in Lydia. His wife Amastris also founded a city named after her on the Paphlagonian shore of the Black Sea, based on a merger of four Greek settlements. The same policy was applied by Seleucus I in regard to three cities of his realm, Seleucia on the Calycadnus, Alexandria near Issus, and Seleucia in Pieria[78]. It appears that both Antioch and Apollonia in Pisidia arose from the union of several military settlements; and Nysa in Caria, Antioch on the Maeander and adjacent Tripolis were produced by the merger of Hellenized Carian communities[79]. Attaleia in Lydia, later Apollonis, was founded as the merger of a number of Macedonian settlements, and Pharnaceia in Pontus of two Greek ones. Bithynian Nicomedia in Pontus and other cities of the vicinity were mergers of small towns. Mylasa in Caria developed through a *sympoliteia* of various communities[80]. As early as 408 B.C.E. a number of Carian communities established as demes united in a *sympoliteia* in the city of Rhodes[81]. The Seleucid authorities encouraged the union of small communities into a large political unit, as a surviving royal edict indicates. Sometimes the unification was desired by the parties and sometimes it was imposed, but in either case the parties continued to maintain their pre-merger organization[82]. An interesting instance was that of Demetrias, which united with neighboring Pegasae, in which a wall separating the two created two clearly defined quarters in a single city[83].

All these examples support Tarn's thesis, and there was a similar evolution as well in Memphis, the most important Egyptian city before the Macedonian conquest. Herodotus (II 154) reported mili-

---

77 A.H.M. Jones, *The Greek City*, p. 7.
78 *Ibid.*, p. 11.
79 *Ibid.*, p. 15.
80 *Ibid.*, p. 17.
81 *Ibid.*, p. 28.
82 *Ibid.*, pp. 43-44.
83 Tarn, p. 68.

tary settlement there of Greeks and Carians in the reign of Psammeti-chus I (664-610 B.C.E.) in "camps" on opposite banks of the Nile; later, on orders of King Amasis, the Carians were moved to the same bank as the Greeks in order to better defend the city. They were settled in separate districts in the city, a fact known also to Stephanus Byzantius[84]. These groups were thus *landsmanschaft*-type associations, and the available information indicates that they were not the only ones of that kind in Memphis. The Zenon papyri too refer to "Egyp-tian Phoenicians" as a distinct group (*PSI*, 531) and to urban quarters with ethnic designations, such as the "Syrian-Persian quarter", the "Carian quarter", and the "Hellenic quarter" (*PSI*, 488). Further-more, in 112 B.C.E. Memphis contained a *"politeuma* of Idumaeans" founded by a local police unit, which had a definite "congregation" and its own magistracy and priests[85]. The deduction must be that Memphis was a collection of *politeumata*, following a pattern that undoubtedly preceded the Hellenistic conquest[86]. That it was an analogue of Alexandria is noted by Strabo: "The city [Memphis] is both large and populous, ranks second after Alexandria, and consists of mixed races of people (μιγάδων ἀνδρῶν) like those who have settled together (συνῳκισμένων) at Alexandria"[87].

All in all, the partial autonomy granted to Hellenistic cities, com-bined with government supervision of their constitutions and organi-zation, created the conditions for the establishment within them of political bodies like the *politeumata*. The various units may have had equal status from the political and legal standpoints, or one of them may have been more privileged.

---

84 Steph. Byz., s.v. Ἑλληνικὸν καὶ Καρικόν (*FGrH*, II, p. 98). See also Porten, *Archives*, p. 8f.
85 *OGIS*, 737; and see also Ruppel, p. 306f. See pp. 49 (n.50), 61 above.
86 This was the opinion of quite a few scholars, see Schubart, *Klio*, 10 (1910), p. 63; Wilcken-Mitteis, p. 18; Ruppel, pp. 306-309; cf. also Bevan, p. 108; Jouguet, *Macedonian Imperialism*, p. 332.
87 Strabo, XVII 1, 32. The term μιγάδες characterized the residents of Alexandria in Polybius as well (Strabo, XVII 1,12). As to the second term, συνῳκισμένων it should be noted that the Jews were also described in the Claudian Edict (*Antiquitates*, XIX 281) συγκατοικισθέντας Ἀλεξανδρεῦσιν. On this Tarn correctly noted that the refer-ence was to the Jewish *politeuma*, which was organized alongside the Greek *politeuma* (see Tarn, p. 222, n.3), and it appears that this interpretation is correct regarding Strabo's report on Memphis also.

C. Jewish Settlement in Alexandria[88]

Information on the earliest Jewish settlement in Alexandria is derived from Josephus. *Bellum*, II 487f. notes that as a reward for their military aid, Alexander gave the Jews the right to settle in Alexandria, "on terms of equality with the Greeks". This right was confirmed in the period of the Diadochi who even assigned them their own residential section and allowed them the title of "Macedonians". *Contra Apionem*, II 37 also mentions royal letters of Alexander and Ptolemy I, documents of subsequent kings[(x)], and a stele of Julius Caesar's defining the rights of the Jews (τὰ δικαιώματα). *C. Apionem*, II 42 places the Jews among the founders of Alexandria, but *Antiquitates*, XII 8 states that it was Ptolmey I son of Lagos who made the Jews "citizens of equal rights (ἰσοπολίτας) with the Macedonians".

Reservations regarding Josephus' reliability here were expressed by many scholars and summed up by Tcherikover. In his view the reservations stem from the contradictory statements whereby Josephus attributes the granting of Jewish rights to Alexander (in *C. Apionem*), to Ptomemy I (in *Antiquitates.* XII 8) and to the Diadochs (in *Bellum*, II 488), and therefore "we are not obliged to follow Josephus in these matters, especially since he himself expresses three different opinions on the same matter"[89]. This is, however, a somewhat distorted representation, taken out of context. Paragraph II 487 of *Bellum*, for example, says explicitly that it was Alexander who gave the Jews the right to live in Alexandria and made them equal to the "Macedonians" in this respect, and paragraph 488 says only that this right was confirmed by the Diadochs. Moreover, further on in that paragraph Josephus says that the Romans did not permit any "diminution of the honours conferred on the Jews since the time of Alexander". Thus one of the contradictions is eliminated, leaving the one in *Antiquitates*, XII 8 to be dealt with. In judging it, the context cannot be ignored, and it must be borne in mind that the statement was part of Josephus' reply to the vilification of Agatharcides of Cnidus. As the latter had attacked the

---

88 The question of privileges is dealt with below in chap. VIII.
(x) Josephus subsequently repeated this exactly in *C. Apionem*, II 72, so that it was clearly not a slip of the pen.
89 Tcherikover, *The Jews in Egypt*, p. 43.

"superstition" of the Jews by means of the story of Ptolemy I's conquest of Jerusalem, it is no wonder that Josephus sought to rebut him on his own grounds. He therefore claimed that despite having fought the Jews and taken them to Egypt as captives, Ptolemy I respected them, precisely because of their faith, and in this matter acted as Alexander had:

> "And as he recognized that the people of Jeruusalem were most constant in keeping their oaths and pledges, as shown by the reply which they gave to Alexander when he sent an embassy to them after defeating Darius in battle, he assigned many of them to his garrisons, and at Alexandria gave them equal civic rights with the Macedonians and exacted oaths of them that they would keep faith with the descendants of him who had placed them in a position of trust." (trans. Marcus, *LCL* ed.).

The statement must be understood as an analogy to Alexander's action[90], so that there is no contradiction here. At most an apologetic tinge can be imputed to Josephus' testimony in regard to the identification of the person who granted the Jews the rights. But as there are many literary traditions, in fact non-Jewish ones, ascribing the accomplishment of many deeds unhistorically to Alexander, Josephus' testimony cannot be considered an unusual exception. It is not contradictory, therefore, to maintain that the first Jewish settlers of Alexandria arrived at the time of Alexander the Great, and that later in the reign of the first two Ptolemies they were followed by large groups of immigrants then granted privileges defining their political status.

The second point on which Josephus was suspected of apologetics is in the matter of Jews serving in Alexander's army, since that service was connected with their civic status[91]. Other testimony on Jews in the Hellenistic armies — such as that in *Antiquitates*, XII 147-153 on the Jewish military settlement in Phrygia and Lydia founded by Antiochus III — was treated with similar skepticism, but has proven reliable[92]. The participation of conquered peoples in the armies of the Hellenistic kingdoms is a well known fact. Alexander's father, Philip conscripted "barbarians" into his army, and Alexander not only granted equality with Greeks to his Asiatic recruits but even

---

90 Josephus wrote in similar vein in *C. Apionem*, II 44.

91 See, e.g., Tcherikover, *Hellenistic Civilization and the Jews*, pp. 272, 320.

92 See Marcus's survey (*Josephus*, VII, App. D, p. 743f.) which cites scholars rejecting the report, such as Schubart, Laquerer, Willrich, Wellhaüsen, Niese. As opposed to this opinion, see Schalit, *JQR*, 50 (1959-60), p. 289f.; Bickermann, *REJ*, 100 (1935), pp. 4-35.

sometimes preferred them to Greek mercenaries[93]. It was his custom
to take auxiliary troops from the conquered peoples, both as conscripts and volunteers. His demanding that the Jews should send him
military help for the siege of Tyre (*Antiquitates*, XI 317) fits in with
that policy, as does the Samaritan compliance with his appeal (*ibid.*,
321). In accordance with the same policy, he ordered the Samaritan
troops serving him to settle in Thebes, and on the basis of their
settlement set up a "cleruchy" for the defense of the region (*ibid.*,
345). In regard to Jews in Alexander's army, Josephus citing Hecataeus of Abdera supplies two stories. One (*C. Apionem*, I 201-205)
concerns the mounted archer Mosollamos, and the other the refusal
of the Jews to take part in the task of reconstructing the temple of
Bel in Babylonia which Alexander had assigned to his troops (*ibid.*,
192ff.). While the authenticity of these two stories is still a matter
of dispute[94], and there is no denying that they were written in order
to idealize Judaism and inveigh against superstition, they may very
well contain a genuine historical core[95]. Arrian (III 5) reported the
great caution Alexander exercized in the administrative arrangements
he made for Egypt. He deliberately split civil authority and the military command into many units headed by people of varied ethnic
origin, even appointing two governors of Egyptian stock, so that
power would not be concentrated in just a few hands. Such a practice would undoubtedly allow for the involvement of Jews and
Samaritans in certain military services, so that Josephus' testimony in
this matter stands the test of logic, and too much of it would have to
be refuted before it could be rejected.

The only external testimony (aside from Josephus) on Jewish
settlement in Alexandria in Alexander's time is a Jewish interpolation

---

93 See Lesquier, p. 137. As already noted (p. 148 and n.176) Niese's and Tcherikover's
doubts about this should be reconsidered. It should be borne in mind that Tcherikover's
negative evaluation of Josephus's report on Alexander's relations with the Jews and
Samaritans (*Antiquitates*, XI 297-347) is based on the opinions of Büchler (*REJ*, 36
(1898), pp. 1-26) and Schalit (*Levy Memorial Volume*, p. 252f.) which are obsolete
because of the discoveries and archaeological finds from the Samaritan cave in Wadi
Dalieh (Cross, *BA*, 26 (1963), pp. 110-121; *HTR*, 59 (1966), pp. 201-211). See also
Kasher, *Beth Mikra*, 20 (1975), pp. 187-208.
94 Of recent studies on this subject, see, e.g., Schaller, *ZNW*, 54 (1963), pp. 15-31; Gager,
ZNW, 60 (1969), pp. 130-139. See also Fraser, vol. 2, pp. 698-699, n.115.
95 See Levy, *Studies in Jewish Hellenism*, pp. 56ff.; Gutman, *The Beginnings of Jewish
Hellenistic Literature*, vol. 1, pp. 60ff.

in Version C of Pseudo-Callisthenes' novel about Alexander[96], reporting that on the occasion of the foundation of the city, Alexander
proclaimed the worship of God in the Jewish quarter. Although
admittedly legendary, it may well contain a grain of historical truth.
The fact that it was written in the first century C.E. does not invalidate this testimony, for most of the reports on Alexander are even
later. Furthermore, the bits of information it supplies accord with
those of Josephus, in particular as regards the allocation of a Jewish
residential quarter, designed to allow ancestral ceremonials to be
carried on without hindrance (*Bellum*, II 487f.).

Early Jewish settlement in Alexandria from the first half of the
third century B.C.E. is demonstrated by epigraphical finds such as
for instance Jewish tombstones from the nearby El-Ibrahimïya cemetery[97]. Some are in Aramaic, indicating that Greek was not yet
current among the Jews. Archaeological evidence of very early
Jewish settlements were found in Cyrene as well, at latest from the
start of the third century B.C.E., and Applebaum assumed they were
nuclei of military settlement[98]. The *Letter of Aristeas* (12-14, 35)
also described very early military settlement by Jews, in the reign of
Ptolemy I. Inscription *CIJ*, 1440 from Schedia near Alexandria also
supports the conclusion on the antiquity of Jewish settlement there.
Thus military settlement of Jews in Egypt, including Alexandria,
started at the latest in the reigns of the first two Ptolemies. The
pioneers of Jewish military settlement may certainly have arrived and
settled in Egypt in Alexander's time, as noted above, but larger scale
settlement began during the reign of Ptolemy I. Josephus indicated
this in two places, relying on Hecataeus of Abdera. In one place
(*C. Apionem*, I 186-189) he reports the immigration of the priest
Ḥezekias and his coterie after the battle of Gaza in 312 B.C.E.,
and in another he notes that Ptolemy I, like Alexander, placed Jews
in the fortresses ($\varphi\rho o\upsilon\rho\iota a$) of Egypt, and when he conquered Cyrene
he dispatched them to its various cities to settle ($\kappa a\tau o\iota\kappa\eta\sigma o\upsilon$) there[99].

---

96 See Pfister, *Heidelberger Akademie*, V, Abt. XI, pp. 22ff. See the quotation of the above
    addition: Marcus, *Josephus*, VI, App. C, pp. 514-515. For a complete survey of Alexander-
    Romance see Fraser, vol. 1, p. 676f.
97 The earliest of these inscriptions are *CIJ*, II 1424, 1425, 1426, 1431.
98 Applebaum, *Jews and Greeks*, pp. 58, 130f.
99 *C. Apionem*, II 44. These two reports have already passed the test of historical criticism;
    and see pp. 40-41 above.

The third point considered justification for rejecting Josephus' testimony relates to the "Macedonians". According to Tcherikover, since they were not among the founders of Alexandria, the report of Jewish settlement there when it was found is a figment of the imagination of Jewish apologists, Josephus having failed to distinguish between "Macedonians" and "Hellenes" and attributed a racial significance to the former, as indicated by the fact that he mentioned the equal rights of the Jews once in relation to "Macedonians" and another time in relation to "Hellenes"[100]. It was Tcherikover's contention that Josephus placed the start of Jewish settlement in the city in Alexander's time for apologetic motives aimed at supporting his claims regarding civic status, and for the same reason Tcherikover had doubts about the service of Jews in Alexander's army.

The matter of the army service having been cleared up above, the question of the "Macedonians" remains. Josephus does not seem to have attributed a racial connotation to the term, for he reported (*C. Apionem*, II 36) the existence of a tribe (φυλή) of "Macedonian" Jews in his own time. Furthermore, he stated (in *Bellum*, II 488) explicitly that the Diadochs allowed the Jews "to take the title of Macedonians" (χρηματίζειν ἐπέτρεψαν Μακεδόνας) clearly indicating a distinction. Thus he obviously used the title to refer to a legal status deriving from its functional military denotation in early Ptolemaic times, just as it is used in papyri of Augustus' time which also mention Jewish "Macedonians" (*CPJ*, II 142-143). It is interesting to note that while Tcherikover himself pointed out that the combination of the verb χρηματίζειν with "Macedonians" duplicated the usage in official papyri, he did not admit that Josephus might have used the term in the same meaning[101]. It is worth taking note of a passage in *Bellum* (V 460) where "Macedonians" has a clearly military denota-

---

100 Tcherikover, *Hellenistic Civilization and the Jews*, pp. 322-323; and see also *CPJ*, I (Prolegomena), p. 14.

101 Tcherikover, *Jews in Egypt*, p. 42. In regard to the use of the verb χρηματίζειν see Preisigke, *Wörterbuch*, s.v., 4; Bickermann, *HTR*, 42 (1949), p. 111f. On the functional significance of the term "Macedonians" in the Hellenistic period, see Launey, vol. 1, pp. 321, 330, 353, 360f. In this connection, Tarn's view (p. 218) that the Macedonian Jews mentioned in the papyri from the time of Augustus were converts should be treated with reserve. His opinion shows that he could not bring himself to believe in the possibility of Jews being Macedonians, influenced, no doubt, by the attitude belittling the military aptitude of the Jews in ancient times that developed through a mistaken projection from the situation in Europe in modern times.

tion. In describing one episode in the Jewish war against the Romans, Josephus says:

> "Meanwhile there appeared on the scene Antiochus Epiphanes (son of Antiochus IV, king of Commagene), bringing with him besides numerous other forces a bodyguard calling themselves "Macedonians", all of the same age, tall, just emerged from adolescence, and armed and trained in the Macedonian fashion, from which circumstances indeed they took their title, most of them lacking any claim to belong to that race". (trans. Thackeray, *LCL* ed.).

That statement is very clear, and leaves no room for doubts as to what the term "Macedonians" meant for Josepnus[102]. In fact his use of the term in describing events of his own time explains its use in the statements in *C. Apionem*, II 36 and *Bellum*, II 488 and other places. Evidently then the first Jewish settlers in Alexandria were military settlers who belonged to a unit of "Macedonians", and this fits in with the conclusions above on the participation of military personnel in the founding of the city.

Conclusion

It is hard to determine definitely whether there was organized Jewish military settlement in Alexandria in Alexander's time, for Josephus' testimony could be interpreted as a typical attempt to attribute the start to that great leader, as other traditions have done in other connections. Probably the organized settlement of Jews in Alexandria took place first in the reigns of Ptolemy I and Ptolemy II, but it is also possible that the very earliest settlers dated from the time of Alexander himself.

---

102 Arrian (VII 6) relates that Alexander the Great himself recruited 30,000 "youths just grown into manhood" whom he called "epigoni" (i.e. afterborn, or simply offspring). They were "all of the same age" and "they had been accoutred with Macedonian weapons and exercised in military discipline after the Macedonian system". According to Arrian, "the arrival of these is said to have vexed the Macedonians, who thought that Alexander was contriving every means in his power from future need of their services" etc. Further he continues to describe this dissatisfaction in detail and among the reasons for it, he states that some "Persians were picked out and enrolled among the foot-guard in addition to the Macedonian officers" and "Macedonian spears were given to them instead of the barbarian javelins", etc. In view of this it can be deduced that as early as the time of Alexander the term "Macedonians" had a functional and pseudo-ethnic significance.

Chapter V

The Meaning of "Alexandrians" in the Papyri

A. The Ptolemaic Period

The political connotation of the term Ἀλεξανδρεῖς was a matter of serious dispute until Schubart proffered the solution, which has been virtually uncontested. He suggested that Alexandrian citizenship was not monolithic[1]. In his view, the terms "citizen" (πολίτης), "Alexandrian" (Ἀλεξανδρεύς) and "Alexandrian (of the *Epigone*) among those unregistered in a certain deme" (Ἀλεξανδρεὺς [τῆς ἐπιγονῆς] τῶν οὔπω ἐπηγμένων εἰς δῆμον τὸν δεῖνα) denoted different statuses, for they figured simultaneously in one group of documents and sometimes even in a single document[2]. Schubart assumed that people with full civc rights were only those registered in a deme, while "Alexandrians" were of lower status, and the "Alexandrians of the *Epigone*, etc." were in the middle[3].

Although Jouguet first suggested that the term "Alexandrians" was applied to citizens of Alexandria when outside it, even in the Egyptian *chora* which was considered by law to be foreign parts in relation to Alexandria, he eventually eliminated that possibility since even documents from the *chora* clearly distinguish between ordinary "Alexandrians" and those registered in demes[4]. He then suggested on the basis of Schubart's hypothesis, that "Alexandrians" like "Ptolemaeans" (citizens of Ptolemaïs) who were not registered in demes were considered to have individual civic rights but lacked community political rights[5]. Jones agreed, and reinforced the argument

---

1 Schubart, *Archiv*, 5 (1909-1913), esp. pp. 81f., 104f. For a bibliographicai iist ot those agreeing with his opinion, see El-Abbadi, *JEA*, 48 (1962), p. 106, n.1.

2 Schubart, *ibid.*, pp. 104-111. Particular attention should be paid to n.1 on p. 105 (in regard to *P. Reinach*, 9 from the end of the second century B.C.E.).

3 Schubart, *ibid.*, pp. 106-108.

4 Jouguet, pp. 9-10; and cf. Schubart, *ibid.*, p. 104, n.1 (where sources are indicated).

5 Jouguet, p. 11. Cf. also pp. 17, 121-122. In his opinion the private rights were the right

for various levels of rights, claiming that it evolved from the timocratic constitution of Alexandria, judging from the Cyrenean constitution in the Ptolemaic period. However he cautiously noted that the distinction may not have been so clearcut in practice, and in his view it did not exist at all until the reign of Ptolemy III, since an official document of that time (*P. Halensis*, lines 245-248) stated that every citizen had a *demos*. Consequently he concluded that the various ranks developed after that king's reign[6].

El-Abbadi disagreed sharply and denied any difference in rank among citizens of Alexandria[7]. Although he did not admit it, he may have been influenced by Plaumann who contended that in Ptolemais there was no difference between the citizens registered in demes and those described as "Ptolmaeans"[8]. He maintained that if the "Alexandrians" were really of lower status, they should logically have been more numerous, but in fact that term is rather rare in official documents[9]. As to the claim regarding intermediate status, he noted that it was an oddity, especially as it seems to have existed only from the middle of the third century B.C.E. to the middle of the second[10]. On the basis of two important documents — *P. Hamb.*, 168 and *P. Halensis* — he claimed that the terms Ἀλεξανδρεύς and πολίτης as well as registration in a deme were synonymous, and there was no ranking within Alexandiran citizenship. For as *P. Hamb.*, 168 has πολῖται in the demes lists (lines 7-8), πολῖται must have been equivalent to registration in the deme in his view, and the same held true for Ἀλεξανδρεύς and πολίτης mentioned together in *P. Halensis* (lines 219-221). In brief, El-Abbadi maintained that an Alexandrian citizen

---

to purchase land (γῆ ἔγκτησις) and the right to marry citizens (ἐπιγαμία).

6 A.H.M. Jones, *CERP*, p. 304. Schubart also had similar difficulties, even attempting to attribute the creation of the intermediate class (the Alexandrians who were not yet registered in one of the demes) to the time of Ptolemy IV Philopator, on the basis of Satirus's problematic report; see Schubart, *ibid.*, pp. 89-90.

7 El-Abbadi, *ibid.* p. 106f.

8 Plaumann, *Ptolemais*, p. 21. On the differences of opinion between him and Jouguet, see Jouguet, p. 17, n.2.

9 El-Abbadi, *ibid*, p. 107. This term is mentioned only twice, he claims, in official documents (*P. Eleph.*, 3, and *P. Reinach*, 9), all the other references being in inscriptions of dedication, etc., which in his opinion are not phrased as legal documents should be. But this argument is not valid, see Fraser, vol. 1, pp. 47-48; and especially vol. 2, pp. 130-131, n.100.

10 In attacking Jones's opinion, which attributed the distinction discussed to developments after the time of Eurgetes I, El-Abbadi indicates *P. Eleph.*, 3 from 285/4 (*ibid.*, p. 110).

could describe himself in three equal ways: a) by "citizen" (πολίτης);
b) by "Alexandrian"; c) by his name and the deme in which he was
registered.

A careful examination of El-Abbadi's thesis, however, shows that
the ostensible synonymity operates in only one direction. It can
be claimed that all the people registered in the demes were also
"Alexandrians", but not that all the "Alexandrians" were registered
in the demes. Similarly, it can be agreed upon that all those registered in the demes were "citizens" but not that all "citizens" were
registered in the demes. The same situation exists in regard to "Alexandrians" and "citizens". For it cannot be argued that all "citizens"
in Egypt were "Alexandrians" since there were "citizens" in other
poleis as well, and furthermore the term *politai* could also be
applied to members of *politeumata*.

Despite his efforts to disprove Schubart's theory, El-Abbadi
could not deny that the citizenship of Alexandrians who were not
registered in any deme was defective in comparison with the citizenship of those who were [11]. Nor is there any question that as long
as the ceremonial and legal procedures for registration in a deme
were not completed, the persons concerned were not full citizens.
Most of the latter were soldiers or descendants of soldiers settled in
the *chora*, especially in the Fayûm, cultivating their κλῆροι or other
categories of leased land[12]. It is not known whether their registration
was delayed for technical or circumstantial reasons, or deferred for
some other reasons. In any case it is clear that the individuals here
concerned were not young people who had just finished their education in the *ephebeion* and were awaiting the completion of formal
arrangements for full citizenship; most were grown men connected
one way or another with military service[13]. Moreover, Al-Abbadi's

---

11 El-Abbadi, *ibid.*, pp. 111, 114.

12 Lesquier, pp. 157-158; Jouguet, pp. 12-17; A.H.M. Jones, *CERP*, p. 304; Fraser, vol. 1,
p. 49f. Schubart (*Archiv*, 5 [1909-1913], p. 104f.) believed that the term "Alexandrians
of the Epigone" did not have military significance at all, but simply indicated the descendants of citizens who were to receive full citizenship. Other scholars who delved
deeply into the problems of "the Epigone" in general accepted this; see n.22 in chap. 1
above. This problem has not yet been finally solved. In any case, no one now denies that
these Alexandrians were soldiers (see n.43 below).

13 For a full list of the documents, see Fraser, vol. 1, pp. 113, 134 (n.104); on their connection with the military, see Uebel, p. 3. It should be pointed out that one of the men
was fifty years old in 237 B.C.E. (*P. Petr.*, III 6a, line 43f.), so not all of them were
young.

claim of equivalence between "Alexandrian" and a person registered in a deme was based mainly on two documents. One of them (*P. Tebt.*, III 815, Fr. 1, col. II 2) mentioned the name of a man described as an Alexandrian of the unregistered with no designation of any deme ('Ελεξανδρεύς τῆς ἐπιγονῆς τῶν οὔπω ἐπηγμένων). The other (*P. Hibeh.*, I 32, lines 2-3) mentions a name of a man termed Καστόρειος τῶν οὔπω ἐπηγμένων. Thus in this case the deme, Kastoreios, is mentioned, but the term "Alexandrian" is not used. In El-Abbadi's opinion the two designations are abbreviations, and are equivalent in their juridical and political implications.

This conclusion is based on the same misinterpretation as the previous one, for it cannot be proven that all "Alexandrians" figured in the deme rolls. Although the listing in *P. Hibeh*, I 32 might certainly be considered shortened[14], there is no assurance that the person mentioned belonged to Alexandria at all[15]. The other document (*P. Tebt.*, III 815 I, col. 2) however, seems flawed or rather incomplete, because the legal requirement of the designation of the deme was not complied with. The reasons could be simply a slip of the pen, or chance omission[16]. Be that as it may, a doubtful and isolated case of this kind cannot support a conclusion as important as El-Abbadi's. Similar conclusions emerge from *P. Reinach*, 9 as well, which refers to two people, one termed 'Αλεξανδρεύς and the other Χαριστήριος (the name of a deme). Their different designations suggest that they were not synonymous, and in this instance there is even doubt about whether that deme belonged to Alexandria[17].

The testimony of Satyrus on the reform that Ptolemy IV Philopator instituted in the tribal structure of Alexandria may indicate that membership in a deme of the Dionysian tribe granted a higher status than membership in those of other tribes[18]. If so, it provides

---

14 See Uebel (p. 337, n.5), who thought the full text should be "an Alexandrian from among those unregistered in the Castorius deme" (if "Alexandrian" is meant and not "Ptolemaean"; see n.15 below). At any rate, we have at least one other example like this, in *BGU*, 1962; and see Uebel, p. 321, n.3.

15 Wilcken (*Griechisch Ostraka*, vol. 1, p. 433, n.3) and Bouché-Leclerq (vol. 3, p. 146) thought that there was a deme called "Castorius" in the city of Ptolemaïs, also. And indeed, the same papyrus mentions a man who belongs to a deme called "Philoterius", which all agree did belong to the city of Ptolemaïs.

16 Cf. Uebel's opinion, p. 149-150, n.8 (to No. 476).

17 Jouguet, e.g., was inclined to think that particular deme belonged to Naucratis (p. 127).

18 See *FGrH*, III, No. 631 (p. 180f.).

support for Schubart's thesis on differential Alexandrian citizenship.
Schubart's view is preferable to El-Abbadi's also in line with Jones'
logical argument on the timocratic nature of the original Alexandrian
constitution (the model for the Cyrenean constitution as well).
Fraser further confirmed it in his excellent monograph on Alexandria, proving that the same was true in Rhodes as well as in Ptolemaic
Cyrene[19]. It is important to note his firm conviction that the term
politai covered extensive groups with varying rights.

In general there seems to be a solid basis for positing that Alexandrian citizenship was "graduated", in the Ptolemaic period and in
particular when the expression Ἀλεξανδρεὺς (τῆς ἐπιγονῆς) τῶν
οὔπω ἐπηγμένων εἰς δῆμον τὸν δεῖνα was current. However, since
those so designated were connected with military service, the epithet
Ἀλεξανδρεὺς may perhaps have been equivalent to an ordinary
ethnic designation (πατρίς) that was commonly used for soldiers,
and the rest of the description simply defined the precise political
and legal status[20]. That situation may explain the frequency of
Ἀλεξανδρεῖς in the epigraphy of the Ptolemaic period[21]. From
there to its signifying an ordinary *origo* is not a great distance[22]. It
may have been popularly employed, mainly at the end of the Ptolemaic period, to denote residents of Alexandria, of some *politeia* or

---

19 See Fraser, vol. 1, pp. 47-49; vol. 2, pp. 130-133, nn.100-102.
20 An examination of *P. Hamb.*, 168, esp. lines 5-10, appears to call for this conclusion.
     The document distinguishes between soldiers with πατρίδες who were not "citizens"
     and those who were "citizens". From the phraseology it appears that it was not necess-
     ary to list the πατρίς (homeland) for the latter, and the reason is clear: indication of
     citizenship (including listing of the deme) fulfilled this function. The term"Alexandrian",
     then, should be thought of as an ordinary ethnic designation, and this view is strongly
     supported by *SB*, 4313, where it is noted explicitly in connection with a woman: πατρίς
     Ἀλεξάνδρεια Μακεδονίς. Cf. also *P. Ent.*, 88, and see Heichelheim, p. 7, and n.21
     below.
21 I shall cite two inscriptions as examples. In one (*SB*, 6252) we read Ἀγαθόδωρος
     Ἀγαθοδώρου Ἀλεξανδρεὺς τῆς β ἱπ(πα)ρχ(ίας), and in the other (*ibid.*, 6253), in
     connection with the same person): Ἀλεξανδρεὶς ἱππάρχης ἐπ᾽ ἀνδρῶν κατοίκων
     ἱππέων κτλ... Cf. also with inscriptions from Ptolemaic Egypt, *SB*, Nos. 17, 38, 593,
     3479, 3733, 3772, 4261, 5863.
22 In inscriptions outside of Egypt the term "Alexandrian" is fairly common, and can be
     clearly interpreted as referring to origin. Rostovtzeff should be noted here, for he
     thought that possibly the title indicated the *metoikoi* (permanent residents), who for
     some reason are not mentioned in documents from Alexandria, see Rostovtzeff, *SEHHW*,
     vol. 2, p. 1064. Unfortunately, this idea was not developed and has not yet received the
     scholarly attention it deserves.

other (within the city). Polybius, for instance, distinguished between "Alexandrians" and Egyptians and mercenaries, but in regard to the former failed to divide them into groups, and contented himself with merely noting that they were "a mixed people" and "not distinctly inclined to civil life". That statement. suggests the presence of more than one *politeia* in the city and justifies Tarn's thesis. Moreover, if by "Alexandrians" Polybius meant the citizens of the *polis*, it would be strange to imagine that he did not discern the *metoikoi* who were certainly among the inhabitants of the city. The absence of any reference to them suggests that he used "Alexandrians" rather loosely to some *politeia* or other, and therefore did not mention the Jewish *politeuma* in the city explicitly. He could not of course failed to realize that it existed.

B. The Roman Period

The scholarly difference of opinion on the quality of Alexandrian citizenship is even sharper in regard to the Roman period. The frequent occurrence of the term ἀστοί in the Roman period aroused heated arguments about its relation to the term "Alexandrians". Jouguet tended to assume that they were citizens resident in the *chora* who were inferior in status to those registered in tribes and demes, but had difficulty in classifying them[23]. Plaumann and Schubart however maintained that the *astoi* were superior in status to the "Alexandrians". The discovery of the papyrus of the *Gnomon of the Idios-Logos*[24] further exacerbated the controversy and evoked new theories as well[25]. Among the latter was that of Carcopino, suggesting that the term was confined to "Hellenes" from the Egyptian *metropoleis* who had no *politeia*, while Taubenschlag claimed

---

23 See Jouguet, p. 121f. His opinion may be based on classical Greek sources, which reserved the term ἀστοί for those having only "civic rights" to distinguish them from πολῖται, who also had "political rights". On this matter, see Liddell & Scott, s.v. ἀστός.

24 This papyrus contains a selection of the regulations which affected the office of *idiologus*. This high official, like the prefect, was of the equestrian class, and was charged with making up the "special report" (*idios-logos*) which listed revenues for the imperial treasury which came not from ordinary taxation, but from fines, expropriations, and heirless property.

25 Plaumann, *Ptolemaïs*, pp. 20-21; Schubart. *Archiv*, 5 (1909-1913), p. 104; see detailed bibliographical lists in Taubenschlag, p. 18, n.49; El-Abbadi, *JEA*, 48 (1962), p. 115. It is possible to consider here only a few theories.

that it applied to both *polis* citizens and members of various *politeumata*[26]. Segré's original and interesting suggestion was that the Roman administration had enlarged the citizenry of Alexandria by adding all the "Alexandrians" to it, so that there was no longer any difference[27]. El-Abbadi accepted his idea, and especially Bickermann's, which stressed the *astoi*'s connection with Alexandria, but continued to maintain that just as in the Ptolemaic period, in the Roman period too there was just one type of Alexandrian citizenship[28]. He held that in the first two centuries C.E. by law (as reflected by the *Gnomon of the Idios-Logos*) the terms *astoi, politai* and "Alexandrians" were completely synonymous, and all people designated by any of them were registered in tribes and demes.

An examination of El-Abbadi's thesis reveals that it is based on dubious assumptions: For one, the term *astoi* was not confined to Alexandria, for it figures even in an official document from Ptolemaïs, of the second century B.C.E.[29] Secondly, according to the *Gnomon of the Idios-Logos* a clear distinction was made between *astoi* and "Alexandrians", and the terms are not used interchangeably. El-Abbadi based his opinion as well on the fact that the *astoi* did not have a *politeia* (according to §47 of the *Gnomon*) and, on the assumption that *astoi* was the Roman substitute for the Ptolemaic *politai*, deduced that the citizens of Alexandria were meant. He seems however to have forgotten that there were other *poleis* in Egypt as well as the various *politeumata*, and that the members of all of these were called *politai*. If so it could be maintained that *astoi* denoted the latter as well, as Taubenschlag believed[31]. El-Abbadi

---

26 Carcopino, *Rev. des Èt. Anc.*, 24 (1922), p. 114 (cf. Uxkull-Gyllenband, *BGU*, 5 (1900), pp. 23-26; Arangio-Ruiz, *Rev. Int. des Droits de l'Antiq.*, 4 (1940), pp. 7-20; Taubenschlag, p. 18, n.49.

27 A Segré, *Atti della Pontificia Accad. Romana di Arch., Rendiconti*, 16 (1940), p. 183f. Earlier he expressed a completely different opinion (in line with the views of Plaumann and Schubart), see idem., *BSAA*, 28 (1933), p. 149f.

28 Bickermann, *Rev. de Philol.*, 53 (1927), pp. 362-368. El-Abbadi, *JEA*, 48 (1962), p.166f.

29 See, e.g., *P. Merton*, 5, and see Rostovtzeff, *SEHHW*, p. 1381; Taubenschlag, p. 18, n.49.

30 Cf. the opinion of Uxkull-Gyllenband (*BGU*, V p. 25), who concluded from this distinction that the "Alexandrians" were a small and exclusive group within the ἀστοί. I cannot agree since it seems to me (following Schubart and Plaumann) that the opposite is the case, as will be explained below.

31 See Taubenschlag, p. 18, n.49, and cf. Rostovtzeff, pp. 304, 1069; and also F. Zucker, *Beiträge*, p. 52f. As a matter of fact El-Abbadi himself took this possibility into account; see his article in: *JEA*, 48 (1962), p. 120.

for some reason also disregarded the important fact that the term *politai* figured in official document of the Roman period too, and in explicit connection with Alexandria[32]. Furthermore, since the ἀστικοὶ νόμοι were first mentioned as a juridical term only in the second century C.E.[33], there are grounds for arguing that the πολιτικοὶ νόμοι still applied at least during the first century of Roman rule in Egypt, so that the *astoi* cannot be identified with the *politai* so definitely (despite El-Abbadi). The scholarly confusion still prevailing on the matter only goes to show that in the absence of adequate criteria, it is meanwhile impossible to determine the precise political import of the term *astoi*, and certainly impossible to indicate its relation to other terms[34]. El-Abbadi was right on one point concerning Alexandria, that the *astoi* were among those registered in tribes and demes[35].

As to "Alexandrians", faithful to his method El-Abbadi claimed that in the Roman period too the term was assigned to citizens registered in tribes and demes, on the basis of *P. Flor.*, III 382, which is a petition for exemption from the liturgies (= payment for public services required of the rich of the city). The petitioner, Heron, was registered in the Ἀλθαιεύς deme, and had acquired citizenship in the normal way after passing the ephebic test[36]. He described himself in two ways by noting the name of this tribe and deme (line 28) and by the term "Alexandrian" (line 35). El-Abbadi found nothing wrong in the latter designation and concluded that the two forms of registration were synonymous. However, only the first was couched in the manner prescribed by law, giving the name, the father's name, the tribe and the deme, and no arguments, however sophisticated, can persuade us that the term "Alexandrians" embraced all that

---

32 See, e.g., in a papyrus from the second century C.E.: Ἀλεξανδρέων πολῖται (Wilcken-Mitteis, No. 372, line 25f.) and the same term recurs a number of times in the same document. Cf. *PSI*, 1160; *P. Lond.*, II 260, p. 51, line 120, and there are other references.

33 See *P. Oxy.*, IV 706, line 9 (from 115 C.E.); and cf. Rostovtzeff, *SEHHW*, p. 1069; Taubenschlag, pp. 17-19.

34 Tcherikover admitted this, and see *CPJ*, I (Prolegomena), p. 41, n.102.

35 This is Schubart's opinion; cf. El-Abbadi's method of validation on the basis of a document from the beginning of the third century C.E. (*BGU*, IV 1034), in which a citizen (with his deme indicated) together with his sister are mentioned as ἀστοί (the particular reference is to line 4 and 10). According to Philo (*De Vita Mosis*, I 35) the *astoi* were at the top of the political ladder in Alexandria (see detailed discussion of this in chap. VIII).

36 This is indicated in line 73; and it appears that his father was also an *ephebos* (line 82).

information. Obviously there was no sense in repeating the legal form so soon, and only in line 78 does the full form recur. Furthermore, the context implies that the term "Alexandrian" is meant only to indicate Heron's origin as proprietor of land in the Hermoupolis region. In other words, the term denotes only *origo*, and does not embody any real juridical meaning. El-Abbadi made a similar mistake in regard to *PSI*, XII 1232 from Antinoupolis (Antinoe), concluding from it that a citizen of that *polis* could be designated by his tribe and deme or by the term 'Αντινοεύς[37], but in fact the designations in that document show that the two are not synonymous and that 'Αντινοεύς refers only to the man's origin[38]. El-Abbadi also disregarded many other examples from Antinoe which show a clear distinction between 'Αντινοεῖς and those registered in tribes and demes[39], and also ignored the expression πολιτεία 'Αλεξανδρέων ἰθαγενής (in one of the inscriptions) which Smallwood believed indicates graduated Alexandrian citizenship[40].

One of the cases that El-Abbadi entirely neglected is the petition that the Jew Hellenos son of Tryphon submitted to the Roman prefect, in regard to payment of the *laographia*[41]. It is actually the only official document in which "Alexandrian" is applied to a Jew, and is consequently of great importance. Examination of the papyrus, which is very badly preserved, suggested that it was written by a scribe or clerk rather than by the petitioner himself, as the same handwriting was found on another document totally unrelated to this petition[42]. The petition begins: "To Gaius Turrianus from

---

37 El-Abbadi, *ibid.*, p. 119, n.1.

38 The text reads as follows: 'Αυρ. Βερενικεὺς ὁ καὶ 'Ωρίων Νερουάνειος ὁ καὶ Προπατόρεως καὶ ὡς χρηματέιξει 'Αντινοεύς. If the indication of tribe and deme was interchangeable with 'Αντινοεύς, why are they mentioned together? 'Αντινοεύς was evidently meant to indicate only the individual's origin. At first glance it would seem to have been more difficult to deal with *P. Lond.*, III 1164F, p. 161, and it is odd that El-Abbadi did not refer to it. It mentions three brothers only one of whom (the eldest) inherited the father's full citizenship and was listed in the tribe and deme lists, while the other two were called 'Αντινοεῖς. Schubart proved conclusively, on the basis of the mother's being Egyptian, that the three brothers were not of equal status and that the status of the eldest was higher (Schubart, *Archiv*, 5 (1909-1913), p. 10). El-Abbadi ignored this document, perhaps because Schubart's proof did not fit in with his argument.

39 Schubart, *ibid.*, pp. 109-110.

40 *IGRR*, IV 1519 — an inscription from Sardis, see Smallwood, p. 8, n.6; and cf. Taubenschlag, p. 592, n.40.

41 The request was published by Schubart in *BGU*, 1140 (= *CPJ*, II 151).

42 See *BGU*, 1130; Schubart, *Archiv*, 5 (1909-1913), pp. 38 (n.2), 109, 119.

Helenos son of Tryphon an Alexandrian ('Aλεξανδρέως)", but the last word is crossed out and replaced by "a Jew from Alexandria" ('Iουδαίου τῶν ἀπὸ 'Aλεξανδρίας). Some scholars have claimed that the correction was designed to describe the identity of the petitioner more accurately, because the term "Alexandrian" was too general for that purpose[43]. Others have argued that the erasure meant that Helenos was not an Alexandrian citizen, and the correction described his precise legal identity as merely a resident of Alexandria[44]. The latter interpretation was based on the assumption that the erasure and correction were made by the competent official. Consequently Tcherikover asserted that since Helenos was unable to prove his civic status (as citizen of Alexandria) he was forced to designate himself by the humble and civically insignificant title of "Jew from Alexandria"[45]. According to him, if Helenos had been a citizen of the *polis* he would have replaced "Alexandrian" with a designtion of his deme. Since he did not do so, and because the form ὁ δεῖνα τῶν ἀπὸ 'Aλξανδρέίας cannot possibly apply to a citizen of the *polis*, the designation must reflect the official usage in regard to the native-born[46]. An examination of the various forms of official registration reveals that native Egyptians were indeed registered by that formula, with their names filling the slot of ὁ δεῖνα[47], but for precisely that reason the correction in the petition cannot be classified as such, for ὁ δεῖνα is replaced not by the name alone, but by the ethnic designation of "Jew" as well, and papyrological research has demonstrated that ethnic designations in Egypt had definitely political significance[48]. The word ἀπὸ does of course mean "from" and thus the phrase τῶν

---

43 See Schürer, vol. 3, p. 718; Juster, vol. 2, pp. 9-10; and cf. De Sanctis, *Rev. di Filol.*, 51 (1924), p. 499. On general and unclear use of the term "Alexandrian" in various sources, see Fraser, vol. 2, pp. 4 (n.19), 149 (n.203), 167 (n.323), 501 (n.35), 580 (n.188), 662f. (n.445), 634 (n.512), 656 (n.53), 737 (n.140), 741 (n.172).

44 Schubart, *ibid.* See also Wilcken, *Antisemitismus*, pp. 787-788; Tcherikover, *CPJ*, II 151, p. 30; and many other thought so, too.

45 Tcherikover, *The Jews and Greeks*, p. 247.

46 *CPJ*, II 151, p. 31.

47 See Bickermann, *Archiv*, 8 (1924), pp. 220, 234f.

48 See Heichelheim, p. 5. A broad specification of the problems of registration is to be found in Bickermann's excellent study (*ibid.*, p. 217f.), which indicates important distinctions between the two typical methods of registration, one, for aliens, for whom the characteristic way was listing the ethnic designation, and the second, for Egyptian natives, where the usual practice was merely by local origin (in his words, "*Herkunftszeichen*"), that is, the cities and villages of the *chora* where they settled (*ibid.*, p. 220f.).

ἀπὸ Ἀλεξανδρείας meant a person who lived in Alexandria, but the prefixing of the ethnic designation clearly indicates membership in an independent ethnic organization, and the formula ὁ δεῖνα τῶν ἀπὸ (ἐκ) itself also points to a connection with some community body[49]. Similar designations were applied to members of all Jewish communities throughout Egypt[50], which fact Tcherikover was aware of. Thus Helenos son of Tryphon belonged to the Jewish *politeuma* of Alexandria, and the correction was merely aimed at precision in this respect.

Papyrological evidence shows that sometimes permanent residents who were non-citizens, and even slaves, were described as "Alexandrians" in official documents[51], and a similar situation obtained in other cities including those of the *metropoleis*. The controversy regarding the status of Helenos son of Tryphon is therefore superfluous, since "Alexandrian" can also denote the *origo,* and is not just a technical term defining a citizen of Alexandria. The large number of erasures and corrections in the petition (at least seventeen) suggest that it was a draft, for it is difficult to imagine that a document on such an important matter could be submitted to the authorities in such a bureaucratic regime in such a badly mutilated state[52]. And since it was a draft, the corrections were stylistic changes rather than

49 See Bickermann, *ibid.*, p. 234f.; and cf. also Ruppel, p. 448, n.289; and also Cl. Préeaux, *Recueil Soc. Jean Bodin*, p. 161.

50 E.g. οἱ ἀπὸ Ξενεφύρεος Ἰουδαῖοι (*CIJ*, II 1442); τῶν ἀπο Σύρων κώμης Ἰουδαῖοι (*CPJ*, I 46); τῶν ἀπὸ Ὀξ(υρύγχων) πόλ(εως) Ἰουδαῖοι (*CPJ*, II 423); οἱ ἐν Ἀθρίβει Ἰουδαῖοι (*CIJ*, II 1443); οἱ ἐν Κροκοδίλων πόλει Ἰουδαῖοι (*CPJ*, III 1532A). It was the same outside of Egypt, and cf. τῶι πολιτεύματι τῶν ἐν Βερενίκῃ Ἰουδαίων (*CIG*, 5361-2) and also ἡ συναγωγή τῶν ἐν Βερνεικίδι Ἰουδαίων (*SEG*, XVII 823). The forms οἱ ἐν and οἱ ἐκ were typical of the Ptolemaic period, while οἱ ἀπὸ was more characteristic of the Roman period, particularly after the first century B.C.E. (see Bickermann, *ibid.*, p. 234; Jouguet, p. 55, n.3). This manner of registration appears in Josephus in exactly the same form (in connection with Jewish communities in the Diaspora), see, e.g. *Antiquitates*, XIV 213: XVI 160, 169, 172, 213; *Bellum*, VII 41, 110, 361-363; *Vita*, 55, 61; and there are many other places.

51 Thus, e.g., Tiberius Julius Alexander's famous edict mentioned "Alexandrian natives" (ἐγγενεῖς Ἀλεξανδρεῖς) who were subject to the heavy *liturgiai* usual for residents of the *chora* (χωρικαὶ λειτουργίαι), and because of the heavy burden, he came to their aid; from which it can be concluded that they were discriminated against and of inferior civil status. On this subject see also Taubenschlag, p. 616. On other "Alexandrians" of low status, see also *ibid.*, pp. 587-588; Jouguet, p. 106.

52 Cf. Turner, *Greek Papyri*, p. 128: "This document, unreadable because of its alterations, could never have been submitted to the prefect; we do not know whether the final form incorporated these alterations or the reason they were made."

the result of a legal investigation of Helenos' status. The erasure of the term "Alexandrian" does not indicate that the man did not deserve the designation, for why was he different from his father who was so described (*BGU*, 1140, 1.3)? And if his father was an Alexandrian citizen, why was he not lawfully registered in a tribe and a deme? It is no wonder that the problem produced some highly speculative solutions. Wilcken, for instance, thought that the father must have acquired citizenship in the *polis* after the birth of his son, so that the latter did not acquire it. Although Tcheikover agreed, he also suggested that Helenos might have been illegitimate or had a non-citizen mother. These solutions seem contrived and artificial and must be rejected[53]. Actually, the answer is simple: The father's designation was not corrected because he was not the subject of the petition, but as the petitioner, his son was obliged to comply with legal requirements and employ full precise legal form[54]. For that reason the scribe found it necessary to replace the general term "Alexandrian" with a more accurate term and indicate clearly the group Helenos legally belonged to. The term "Alexandrian" did not meet legal requirements, not even in regard to a citizen of the *polis*. Its infrequent appearance in official documents indicates that it was not acceptable to the authorities, at least not in that early period. It was probably a popular term designating provenance[55], and in epigraphical documents is quite common in reference to Jews[56].

---

53 See *CPJ*, II 151 (p. 32); cf. Fraser, vol. 2, p. 139, n.144. If, e.g., Helenos had been an illegitimate son, he would not have been called after his father, and would probably not have mentioned him very much. On the other hand, if the father were married to someone from among the "natives", he then must have broken the law of Alexandria which specifically forbade this. In fact, the document does not enable us to determine in what way the son's status differed from that of his father. Moreover, the definite title applied to the father ("Alexandrian") was applied first to the son. This in itself, and the natural way it is written, shows that they were of equal status. The erasure, then, must be accounted for in some other way. It is worthwhile noting here that the idea denouncing intermarriage with aliens is well known in Athens too (see, e.g. Plato, *Menexenus*, 245c ff.; Demosthenes, LVII 16-17 ;LIX 30ff.; Aeschines, III 168, 172; Plutarch, *Pericles*, 37). No wonder therefore that Pericles passed a law according to which only people whose parents were both citizens could claim Athenian citizenship as well (Plutarch, *ibid.*).

54 See *P. Hamb.*, 168, lines 5-10.

55 Cf. El-Abbadi, *JEA*, 48 (1962), p. 122.

56 See, e.g., the inscription on the gravestone of Nicanor the "Alexandrian" which was fund on Mount Scopus (*PEF*, 1903, p. 93; Schwabe, *Sefer Yerushalayim*, vol. 1 (1956), p. 367) and the inscription from Jaffa in the *Sefer Ha-Yishuv*, p. 83. It is reasonable to

Looking at the problem from another angle, Tcherikover ascribed
a juridical meaning to the term "Alexandrian" for an additional
reason. He thought that Helenos son of Tryphon feared that being
obliged to pay the *laographia* might deprive him of Alexandrian
citizenship, for as the document states, he risked the loss of his
"homeland" ($\pi\alpha\tau\rho\iota\varsigma$, lines 6-7). To Tcherikover the word *patris*
suggested an association with testimony in Philo (*In Flaccum*, 46)
that the Jews of the Diaspora considered the Greek cities they lived
in as $\pi\alpha\tau\rho\iota\delta\varepsilon\varsigma$. Thus Tcherikover sought to have it both ways, for
if Philo called the Jews of his city "Alexandrians" with no political
or legal implications[57], how could Alexandria be their *patris*? By his
own logic, Tcherikover should have argued that in Philo *patris* too
was used metaphorically and had no political or legal import, and it
is odd that he cited that testimony in support of the contrary. What
did Helenos actually mean when he said he feared the loss of his
patris? Clearly he referred exclusively to Alexandria[58]. If we accept
Tarn's thesis that Alexandria was a collection of *politeumata*, it is
understandable that for Helenos, as a "Jew of Alexandria" (that is,
a member of the Jewish *politeuma* there), the city was really his
patris.

Helenos' education (which most scholars mistakenly deemed to
have been acquired in the gymnasium)[59] might seem to have been

---

assume that there was a Jewish community of Alexandrian Jews in Jaffa, an impression
also gained from another inscription (*CIJ*, II 918) which mentions a *frontistes* of the
Alexandrian Jews ($\varphi\rho o\nu\tau\iota\sigma\tau\eta\varsigma$ Ἀλεξανδρέων). It is interesting that one of the Jaffa
inscriptions contains the form ἀπὸ Ἀλξανδρείας, which shows us that it can be synony-
mous with Ἀλεξανδρεύς; see Klein, *Sefer Ha-Yishuv*, pp. 80 (No. 4), 83 (No. 25), and
cf. an inscription from Tiberias — Schwabe, *Memorial Book to Y.h. Levi* (Hebrew),
p. 210. A recently discovered as yet unpublished Jewish tomb inscription in the Jaffa
Museum of Antiquities also contains the form ἀπὸ Ἀλεξανδρείας.

57 See Tcherikover, *The Jews and Greeks*, p. 250. Smallwood (p. 255) held the same
opinion.

58 On the adoption of a new *patris* see Taubenschlag, p. 584.

59 See *CPJ*, II 151, line 5f. and cf. *ibid.*, line 13f. In fact, there isn't an ounce of proof in
the entire document. Lines 5-6 mention "his compatible (or "appropriate", see n.60
below) education", which in the opinion of Tcherikover and other scholars refers to
gymnasium education. This assumption was supported by a doubtful reconstruction of
lines 13-14. There υμνασιον was read as [γ]υμνάσιον, based on an illegible word where all
the letters were damaged. In another place they read τὴν ἀπὸ τῆς ἐφηβεί(ας), words
whose reconstruction is doubtful to a like degree. Prof. Momigliano drew my attention
to the fact that the article τὸν which appears in the text cannot be combined with
γυμνάσιον, which is a common noun, so in any case the proposed reconstruction is
impossible.

mentioned in order to prove his Alexandrian citizenship, but that is impossible because it does not accord with the correction to "Jew of Alexandria". In other words, since the official clerk (the writer of the document) knew that Helenos was not an Alexandrian citizen, it is not reasonable to suppose that Helenos would have tripped himself (and his father) up by stressing the way he deceitfully became part of the citizen group. Nor would he have requested Alexandrian citizenship on such unconvincing and dubious grounds as "although my father was an Alexandrian and I have always lived there, receiving the compatible education, as far as my father's means allowed" (lines 3-6). If his education had fulfilled legal requirements (for obtaining Alexandrian citizenship) why did he describe it in such apologetic terms as "compatible"[60] and "as far as my father's means allowed".

It might be claimed that he wished to be counted in the privileged group of gymnasium graduates (οἱ ἀπὸ γυμνασίου) and thus gain exemption from the *laographia*. However, the date of the petition is 4 or 5 B.C.E., and papyrological findings indicate that Augustus' thirty-fourth regnal year (4/5 C.E.) was the first for the registration of genealogy and its examination for the above-mentioned purpose by the authorities[61]. Thus it must be concluded that Helenos son of Tryphon could not have requested an exemption or reduction on the basis of his being one of the οἱ ἀπὸ γυμνασίου, since that was not yet officially recognized as grounds at the time. Furthermore, considering that Helenos was more than sixty years old when his petition was written[62], his education had been acquired long before the Roman conquest of Egypt, during the time when anarchy prevailed in that area, and individual initiative could be exercised[63].

---

60 *Ibid.*, line 6 — ἀρεσκούσης, and this adjective embodies a tinge of sanctimoniousness, and see Liddell and Scott, s.v. ἄρεσκος. Therefore, "compatible" seems preferable to "appropriate" (as Tcherikover maintains).

61 Wilcken-Mitteis, No. 147; *P. Oxy.*, 257, 1266, 1452, 2186; *PSI*, 457.

62 Lines 22-23 of the document clearly suggest that he had recently reached the age of sixty.

63 It appears that even Egyptians could take part in the activities of the gymnasium; see Launey, vol. 2, pp. 865-869; see also Delorme, *Gymnasium*, pp. 421-480; Fraser, vol. 1, p. 77. The last reference to a private gymnasium (almost certainly a vestige of the Ptolemaic period) is from 2 C.E. (*BGU*, IV 1201); and cf. others like it at the end of the first century B.C.E. in *BGU*, IV 1188, 1189. On the social and cultural character of the gymnasia in the Egyptian *chora* see Rostovtzeff, *SEHHW*, pp. 1058-1060, 1395 (n.121), 1588 (n.29).

Could Helenos have been educated in a private gymnasium? Actually his apologetic and sanctimonious explanation suggests that such may have been the case. The gymnasium may in fact have a Jewish one, as perhaps indicated by one of the fragmented and corrected sentences of the petition[64]. Why did he mention his education? His petition, it should be kept in mind, involved a complaint about an injustice he felt had been done him in connection with the *laographia*, and the mention of his education should be considered in connection with that rather than with Alexandrian citizenship. Obviously Helenos thought his education would constitute a recommendation likely to help earn him an exemption or reduction. The sanctimonious tone is a sign that it could not have been formal grounds. No wonder he also presented the argument that the "first governors" had never bothered him nor had the prefect Turranius, to whom the petition was addressed. That fact was not formal grounds either, for the situation could have been caused by a persistent error; thus that too was only an auxiliary argument. Only at the end of his complaint did Helenos pull his strong card out of the pack, his age. That actually constituted real grounds. Taking that into account as well as the auxiliary reasons submitted, the authorities, he hoped, would admit he was the victim of a purely bureaucratic mistake.

To sum up, then, the terms "Alexandrian" and "Jew from Alexandria" can be said to be equivalent, with the latter being more accurate from the legal viewpoint as it noted membership in the Jewish *politeuma* of Alexandria. Despite scholarly doubts, it is a fact that the term "Alexandrian" at times denoted simple provenance. To the extent it acquired special political significance, it can be deemed to have applied to residents of Alexandria classified as *politai* because of a connection with any of the separate political bodies there, and not exclusively to citizens of the *polis*. It cannot be imagined that Jews were part of the tribal system of the Alexandrian *polis*, for all the constituent demes were somehow or other connected with pagan

---

64 The reference is to lines 12-13 and the correction over line 13; and cf. also Tcherikover's translation "... my father to his ancestral gymnasium" (*CPJ*, II p. 31). Philo's positive or neutral attitude towards gymnasium education (see *De Spec. Leg.*, II 229f., 246) perhaps reveals the situation in his youth (Philo was born ca. 20 B.C.E.), when Jews could still participate in gymnasium education, or maintain gymnasia of their own. In any case, the parallel with Philo's report is quite illuminating.

cults, as their very names show[65]. If Helenos son of Tryphon had wished to pretend he was a citizen of the *polis*, he would probably have done so through some religious overtures, but there are no traces of such attempts in his petition.

---

65 See Fraser, vol. 1, p. 44f.

Chapter VI

The Alexandrian Jews in Apocryphal Literature

The information on the Jews of Alexandria that appears in *the Letter of Aristeas* and in *III Maccabees*, although quite scanty, is of great importance because those sources are so early[1].

A. The Jewish Community and Its Organization According to the Letter of Aristeas

The most important piece of information on the Jewish community of Alexandria is given at the end of the *Letter*, in §§ 308-310:

"When the work was completed, Demetrius assembled the congregation of the Jews (τὸ πλῆθος τῶν Ἰουδαίων) in the place where the translation had been made and read it over to all in the presence of the translators who met with a great reception also from the congregation (παρὰ τοῦ πλήθους), because of the great benefits which they had conferred upon them. They bestowed warm praise upon Demetrius, too, and urged him to have the whole law transcribed and present a copy to their leaders (τοῖς ἡγουμένοις αὐτῶν). After the books had been read, the priests and the elders (οἱ πρεσβύτεροι) from among the translators and from among the people of the *politeuma* (τῶν ἀπὸ τοῦ πολιτεύματος) and the leaders of the congregation (οἱ τε ἡγούμενοι τοῦ πλήθους) stood up and said that since so excellent and sacred and accurate a translation had been made, it was only right that it should remain as it was and no alteration should be made in it."[2]

---

1 There is a serious controversy over the date of the *Letter of Aristeas*. The most popular opinion attributes it to the middle of the second century B.C.E.: see, e.g., Wendland (in Kautsch), *Die Apokriphen*, vol. 12, p. 3; Bickermann, *ZNW*, 29 (1930), pp. 280-298; Tcherikover, *Jews in the Greek and Roman World*, pp. 316-338; Fraser, vol. 1, p. 689ff., especially pp. 696-699. On the other hand, there are some who date it earlier, at the end of the third century B.C.E., such as: Schürer, vol. 3, p. 608f.; Vincent, *RB*, 5 (1908), pp. 520ff.; 6 (1909), pp. 555ff. See also Tramontano, *La Lettera di Aristea*; Pelletier, *La Lettre d'Aristée*. For a recent opinion supporting the earlier date, see Rappaport, *Studies in the History of the Jewish People and the Land of Israel*, vol. 1 (1970), pp. 38-50. As to *III Maccabees*, some tend to place it as late as the Roman period, and on this subject Tcherikover's opinion is generally accepted (*ibid.*, pp. 339-365). In contrast, J. Gutman (*Eshkoloth*, 3 [1959], pp. 49-72) thought the book was written in the Ptolemaic period, apparently in the second century B.C.E. In my opinion this date is to be preferred, for reasons which will be explained later.

2 The differences of opinion and approach regarding this translation are discussed below.

Without a doubt the most important bit of information cullable from this testimony relates to the way the community was organized. It must be stressed first of all that it was defined as a *politeuma*. The term accords perfectly with the official terminology that was used in Ptolemaic Egypt in relation to foreign ethnic groups who lived in it and its cities, and were organized and recognized as legal political bodies with certain privileges. It should be noted that the same term was used to describe the Berenice Jewish community in two inscriptions of the first century B.C.E. (*REG*, LXII pp. 283, 290 = *CIG*, 5361-2), and was 'certainly a legacy from the Ptolemies. Probably the Alexandria Jewish community was not the only one so organized, and various documents contain confirmation of this. Clearly the basis for the separate organization and autonomy of the Alexandria community was the right to "live according to ancestral laws", a basic right cited in a good many documents, not exclusively in connection with Jewish *politeumata*[3]. The *Letter of Aristeas* says so too, and one of its passages indicates that it applied the term *politeuma* to people who arranged their lives according to the laws of their forefathers[4].

An interesting controversy regarding the structure and leadership of the community developed as a result of divergent interpretations of the passage cited above. Some scholars maintained that "the congregation of the Jews" (τὸ πλῆθος τῶν Ἰουδαίων) was identical in meaning to "the people of the *politeuma*" (οἱ ἀπὸ τοῦ· πολιτεύματος)[5]. Others contended that the *politeuma* was a limited group of privileged people within the broad Jewish "congregation"[6], suggesting that the Jewish *politeuma* (like the *polis*) was composed of two circles, the inner one made up of full members and the outer one of the peri-

---

3 On the use of this formula in the Greek and Roman world see, e.g., *OGIS*, 442, 449; Abbott and Johnson, *Municipal Administration*, Nos. 15c, 19, 40, 52, 67. See also *Antiquitates*, XII 142; XIV 195, 199, 213-215, 223, 227, 235, 242, 246, 258, 260-261, 263; XVI 163, 171, 172; XIX 283-285, 290.

4 See *Letter of Aristeas*, 81 —τῶν κατ' αὐτὰ πεπολιτευμενῶν καὶ πολιτευομένον ἀνδρῶν — cf. the parallel in *Antiquitates*, XII 38; and also I 10 — "I found then that the second of the Ptolemies, that king who was so deeply interested in learning and such a collector of books, was particularly anxious to have our Law and the political constitution (διάταξιν τῆς πολιτείας) based thereon translated into Greek."

5 Schürer, vol. 3, p. 72; and also Tcherikover, *CPJ*, I p. 9, n.24. Cf. also Fraser, vol. 2, p. 139, n.145.

6 Fuchs thought so (p. 89f.); and also Ruppel, p. 281; Box, Introd., pp. xxii (n.2), xxv; Tramontano, *La Lettera di Aristea*, p. 243.

phery. The latter view seems correct, and is supported by a comparison of the text of the *Letter* with Josephus' paraphrase (*Antiquitates*, XII 107f.), for "the congregation of the Jews" seems synonymous with "all (πάντες) The Jews" in Josephus. In any case, from the context in both sources it is evident that "congregation" (πλῆθος) and "community" (πολίτευμα) are not synonymous[7]. That conclusion accords with historical logic, for it is not reasonable to suppose that all the Jews of Alexandria were members of the *politeuma*. Probably the *politeuma* was established on the base of a military settlement, as were other *politeumata* in Egypt. In that case the "congregation of Jews" was most likely the general Jewish public, including those under the protection of the *politeuma* but not actually members of it.

The scholarly controversy also concerns the nature of the community leadership. As § 310 of the *Letter* is couched in rather vague terms, some scholars have considered "elders" as applying not only to "translators" but also to "the people of the *politeuma*" whom they therefore sought to identify with members of the *gerousia*[8]. Tcherikover, in Tramontano's wake, attempted to demonstrate the weakness of that interpretation, arguing that to admit it would mean that οἱ πρεσβύτεροι was to be understood literally as "aged" with the word "translators" and as having political-institutional import with the phrase "people of the *politeuma*". Taking note of the Josephus version (*Antiquitates*, XII 108) where the word "elders" applies only to "translators", Tcherikover favoured Williamovitz's solution interpreting "people of the *politeuma*" to mean "leaders of the people". He therefore offered the following translation — "and the men (i.e. representatives) of the community, those who were the leaders of the people" — and attempted to solve the problem by pointing to the use of τε in the text[9]:

This tempting proposal must however be rejected, for a number of reasons: a) It does not diminish the distinction between πλῆθος and πολίτευμα, but actually strengthens it, contrary to Tcherikover; b) The term πρεσβύτεροι is used with "translators" in two other

---

7 In clause 108 (in Josephus) the distinction between the two terms is very clear.
8 See, e.g., Schürer, vol. 3, p. 72; Fuchs, p. 89f.; Ruppel, p. 281, and many others thought the same. In contrast, Smallwood (p. 5, n.4) could not decide and wavered between the two possibilities.
9 Tcherikover, *CPJ*, I p. 9, n.24; Cf. Fraser, vol. 2, p. 139, n.145.

instances in the *Letter of Aristeas* (§§ 39, 42) and the description of their nature there leaves no doubt that the author meant men that were distinguished and steeped in the Torah. Thus there is no basis for claiming that the term has two meanings in one context. c) The word τε clearly separates τῶν ἀπὸ τοῦ πολιτεύματος (= the people of the community) from οἱ ἡγούμενοι τοῦ πλήθους (= the leaders of the congregation) as it does repeatedly in all other versions of the *Letter*. Moreover, the linguistic points made by Wendland and Ruppel justifying the presence of τε seem convincing[10]. While Josephus' paraphrase can help clarify some matters, it is too free to allow for the correction of the text of the *Letter*. All in all, πλῆθος and πολίτευμα can be distinguished, and the term πρεοβύτεροι understood to have a political-institutional connotation.

As to the structure and organization of the community, the *Letter* provides considerable information. Probably the *politeuma*-type organization complied with the usual standards in the Ptolemaic kingdom for military and administrative people[11], and evidently the Macedonian tribe (φυλή) that Josephus noted (*C. Apionem*, II 36) was a remnant of the internal organization that seems to have reproduced the tribal division within the *polis* itself[12]. It appears to have been headed by a collegium of elders (certainly members of the *gerousia*) among them the "leaders of the people" or *archontes*[13]. Doubtless all of them also acted as the leadership of the "congregation of Jews" under the protection of the *politeuma*. The language of the *Letter* does not make it clear whether the "priests" were part of the community leadership or of the "translators", but the first alternative seems more likely[14].

B. Jewish Rights and Status According to III Maccabees

III Maccabees is certainly one of the important sources for the clarification of the legal status and rights of the Alexandrian Jews.

---

10 Wendland in: Kautsch, *Die Apokriphen*, vol. 2, p. 30, n.3.
11 On Jews in the military and administrative service of the Ptolemaic kingdom in its early period see the *Letter of Aristeas*, 12-13, 35-37.
12 There is no question about the "Macedonian" Jews having belonged to the Jewish *politeuma* in view of *CPJ*, II 142/3, for these documents indicate that they deposited their wills in the "Jewish archives."
13 Cf. Schürer, vol. 3, p. 72.
14 See chap. III above, p. 162 and n.190; cf. R.B. Schwartz, *JBL*, 97 (1978), pp. 567-571.

The book is divided into two parts, I 1–II 24 dealing with the Battle of Raphiah and Ptolemy IV Philopator's visit to Jerusalem, and the rest reporting the king's persecution of the Jews of Egypt and Alexandria. There is no doubt of the historical reliability of the first part[15], and Tcherikover's reservations regarding the report of Philopator's Jerusalem visit must be rejected[16]. The historical reliability

---

15 On this matter I accept the argument and reasoning of Gutman, *Eshkoloth*, 3 (1959), pp. 51-59.
16 Tcherikover admitted that the description of the Battle of Raphiah was based on accurate historical information (*Jews in the Greek and Roman World*, pp. 340-341) but he nevertheless questioned the accuracy of the story about Philopator's breaking into the Jerusalem Temple. In his opinion, the author of *III Macc.* was influenced from a literary point of view by the story in *II Macc.* about Heliodorus (*ibid.*, pp. 343-344). The reasoning against Tcherikover's dating, most of which I learned from Prof. Efron, is given below. In fact, Emmet (in Charles), *Apocrypha*, vol. 1, p. 156f. already perceived the fact that *III Macc.* was independent of *II Macc.*, but he did not go into the details of the problem.

It appears that the similarity between the two stories is only external, vague, and can be summed up in three points: the desire to break into the Holy of Holies, the ferment in Jerusalem, and the prevention of the desecration by divine intervention. On the other hand, the differences are many and extremely significant: a) In *II Macc.* Heliodorus (a minister and not a king) comes to fulfill a political mission, designed to extract money from the Temple as a result of the information of Simon the Hellenizer against Onias III, but in *III Macc.*, Philopator, the Ptolemaic monarch himself, comes to Jerusalem as part of the state visits he made to Syrian cities after the victory of Raphiah. Ptolemy IV Philopator was not motivated by greed for money, but by curiosity, which was later transformed into pride, spite, and scorn for the Jewish religion. b) Even though both stories describe ferment in Jerusalem, *III Macc.* tells of an attempt at resistance by force, while in *II Macc.* there is no such incident. c) In *III Macc.* the king's ministers tried to stop him, while *II. Macc.* has nothing to this effect. d) *III Macc.* cites a long prayer made by the High Priest, in which biblical quotations, mainly from *Psalms*, are embroidered, while *II Macc.*, although describing a public prayer, does not give its contents or mention the participation of the High Priest. e) In *III Macc.* the description of Ptolemy IV Pilopator's invasion of the Temple is very short and contains no exaggerated descriptions. The king is smitten by God himself and falls down in a faint, in all, a simple, purposeful, and reasonable explanation. In *II Macc.*, however, the description is full of unreal exaggerations about a "mighty apparition", in which "a rider of terrible aspect" and "two young men of surpassing strength and glorious beauty" are placed, a veritable epiphany, containing most of the artistic elements of Hellenistic literature including strong dramatic emphasis. f) *II Macc.* has it that Heliodorus's companions pleaded with the High Priest to ask the Lord to restore Heliodorus to consciousness, which was done; and moreover, the heroes of the heavenly "apparition" appeared again and urged Heliodorus, who recovered, to thank Onias for his recovery. In *III Macc.*, on the other hand, the king's companions and bodyguards dragged him away and after a time he recovered consciousness. Here, too, the description in *III Macc.* is simpler and more credible. g) According to *II Macc.*, Heliodorus thanked Onias for his recovery, made a sacrifice, swore oaths, and even admitted the existence of the power of God in the Temple. In *III Macc.* the king is

of the second part has however been seriously questioned. One of the main reasons is Josephus' story (in *C. Apionem*, II 53-56) about Ptolemy VIII Physcon (Euergetes II) ordering the Jews of Alexandria to be chained and thrown naked in front of intoxicated elephants when he fought Onias, Cleopatra II's military commander. The attempt was unsuccessful because the elephants attacked the king's men rather than the Jews. Eventually the king rescinded the order, after a terrible vision and his mistress's urging. In commemoration of the event the Alexandrian Jews initiated an annual holiday. Tcherikover claimed, for instance, that Josephus' story is more credible, and that *III Maccabees* is simply an additional edited version of the persecutions in the reign of Ptolemy VIII Physcon[17]. Although that proposal seems to fit the historical background of the king's early days, there is not reason enough to reject the *III Maccabees* version, because the time of Philopator seems an even more suitable historical background. It should be borne in mind that Ptolemy VIII Physcon (Euergetes II) battled Cleopatra II, whom the Jews were allied with, for only a very short time (in 145 B.C.E.), and in fact there is epigraphical evidence of synagogues being dedicated to him (*CIJ*, II 1441-2). On the other hand Philopator's hostility to the Jews

---

said not to have changed his mind, but to have become even angrier. *II Macc.* (III, 12f.) emphasizes the right of asylum (protection against desecration of holy places) which was granted to the Jerusalem Temple (first by Antiochus III the Great; see *Antiquitates*, XII 145-146; Bickermann, *Syria*, 25 [1946-8], pp. 67-85), by means of which Onias II the High Priest tried to keep Heliodorus from desecrating it. In *III Macc.* there is not a trace of this matter, which indicates the antiquity of the event.

These comparisons suffice to show that the two stories were not based on a common tradition. The simplicity of the story in *III Macc.* points to its antiquity; while the embroideries and Hellenistic artistic features of *II Macc.* attest to its later date. The first part of *III Macc.* in its Hassidic spirit is closer to *I Macc.* (written in Judaea), mainly in its emphasis on the gulf between Judaism and the gentiles. It should also be noted that evidence of unrest in Judaea and its neighborhood even after the victory of Raphiah can be found in various sources. Among these see, e.g., the demotic inscription Gauthier and Sotas, *Un décret*, p. 32f.; see also Gutman, *Eshkoloth*, 3 (1959), pp. 58-59. Tcherikover, at the beginning of his study of *III Macc.* claimed that "the inflated style, and many contradictions and exaggerations" of the author attest to his being "a writer without taste and an irresponsible historian" (*Jews in the Greek and Roman World*, p. 339). Nevertheless, this did not prevent Tcherikover from developing far-reaching theories based on *II Macc.* (such as dating the Hasmonaean revolt before the persecutions of Antiochus IV Epiphanes), even though the author of *II Macc.* himself said of his work that it suffered from those very faults (*II Macc.*, II 23-32; XV 38-39).

17 *Hellenistic Civilization and the Jews*, pp. 274-5, 282; *Jews in the Greek and Roman World*, pp. 344-348.

is easily explainable against the background of the stance of the Palestinian Jewish community, his friendship with the Egyptian priests, and the negative attitude of the Jews to the new state religion, the cult of Dionysus. The fact that the Josephus version diverges only shows he was not familiar with the book, and drew his information from another tradition, and the dilution of the Josephus version strengthens the impression that *III Maccabees* is the reliable source[18].

III Maccabees was one of the bases for Tcherikover's thesis on the legal status of the Jews. His main evidence for the lateness of its composition was Philopator's order (*III Maccabees*, II 28-30), especially the section in which the *laographia* is associated with the "condition of servitude" according to the terminology prevalent at the start of the Roman period[19], and this seems unacceptable. Philopator's order reads as follows:

> "That none who did not sacrifice (i.e. worship the king) should be allowed to enter their sacred rites (τὰ ἱερὰ αὐτῶν) and that all Jews should be degraded to the rank of natives and the condition of servitude, and that those who spoke against it should be taken by force and put to death; and that those who were registered should even be branded on their bodies with an ivy-leaf, the emblem of Dionysus, and be reduced to their former limited status. But that he might not appear an enemy to all, he added: But if a few of them prefer to join those who are initiated into the mysteries, they shall have equal rights with the citizens of Alexandria"[20] (a revised translation of Emmet, in Charles' *Apocrypha*).

The Jews and the Dionysian Cult

According to Tcherikover, in a strange manner the author of *III Maccabees* combined the "Jewish question" with the Dionysian cult

---

18 For more details of the inferiority of the Josephus version see Gutman, *Eshkoloth*, 3 (1959), p. 61f. It appears that Tcherikover was also carried along after those scholars who tried to find various literary models for what is stated in *III Macc.*, relying on dim historical associations of a kind which he himself viewed with reservation; see, e.g., *Jews in the Greek and Roman World*, p. 348f.; see also Schürer, vol. 3, p. 489f.; Emmet in: Charles, *Apocrypha*, vol. 1, p. 156f.

19 Tcherikover, *ibid.*, pp. 349-353. Cf. Fraser, vol. 1, p. 703; vol. 2, p. 982f. (n.176). In this context it should be noted that there are some scholars who believed that the terminology in *III Macc.* was more suited to the Ptolemaic period; see Emmet, *loc. cit.* and also Bickermann, *RE(PW)*, XIV 1, p. 797f.

20 *III Macc.*, II 28-30: μηδένα τῶν μὴ θυόντων εἰς τὰ ἱερὰ αὐτῶν εἰσιέναι, πάντας δὲ τοὺς Ἰουδαίους εἰς λαογραφίαν καὶ οἰκετικὴν διάθεσιν ἀχθῆναι, τοὺς δὲ ἀντιλέγοντας βίᾳ φερομένους τοῦ ζῆν μεταστῆσαι, τοὺς τε ἀπογραφομένους χαράσσεσθαι καὶ διὰ πυρὸς εἰς τὸ σῶμα παρασήμῳ Διονύσου κισσοφύλλῳ, οὓς καὶ καταχωρίσαι

and Alexandrian citizenship, and in order to do so modified a royal order he found in some unknown writer or collection of Ptolemaic decrees. In support Tcherikover pointed to a number of documents with similar phraseology[21], but for some reason refrained from making a precise comparison in regard to one of them, in which the Dionysian cult occupies a prominent place as it does in the decree quoted in *III Maccabees*. That decree is *BGU*, 1211, which reads as follows:

> "By decree of the king. Persons who perform the rites of Dionysus in the interior shall sail down to Alexandria, those between here and Naucratis within ten days from the day on which the decree is published and those beyond Naucratis within twenty days, and shall register themselves before Aristobulus at the registration office within three days from the day on which they arrive, and shall declare forthwith from what persons they have received the transmission of the sacred rites for three generations back and shall hand in the sacred book sealed up, inscribing thereon each his own name"[22] (translated by Hunt & Edgar, *Select Papyri*, II No. 208, *LCL* ed.).

In his analysis of *III Maccabees* Tcherikover remarked that it is inconceivable that Jews should have taken part in the Dionysian cult of their own free will, as it was not open to all, so that the author's view of this matter was "naive", because according to the order quoted, the participation in the ceremonies was at the exclusive discretion of the Jews[23]. However, though the secrets of the cult were indeed closed, the "naive view" did have a basis, and in this connection two problems need to be considered: a) the "free" desire of the Jews to join in the Dionysian cult, and b) their actual participation in it. As to the first aspect, at first glance it might seem that there is a difference between the two orders, for *BGU*, 1211 is addressed to such as already took part in the Dionysian cult, while

---

εἰς τὴν προσυνεσταλμένην αὐθεντίαν. ἵνα δὲ μὴ τοῖς πᾶσιν ἀπεχθόμενος φαίνηται, ὑπέγραψεν 'Εὰν δέ τινες ἐξ αὐτῶν προαιρῶνται ἐν τοῖς κατὰ τὰς τελετὰς μεμυημένοις ἀναστρέφεσθαι, τούτους ἰσοπολίτας 'Αλεξανδεῦσιν εἶναι.

21 Tcherikover, *ibid.*, pp. 341-343 and n.8.

22 Βασ[ιλ]έως προστάξαντο[ς]. τοὺς κατὰ χώραν τελοῦντα[ς]τῶι Διονύσωι καταπλεῖν εἰς 'Αλε[ξ]άνδρειαν, τοὺς μὲν ἕως Ναυκράτε[ως] ἀφ' ἧς ἡμέρας τὸ πρόσταγμα ἔκκειται ἐν ἡμέραις ι, τοὺς δὲ ἐπάνω Ναυκράτεως ἐν ἡμέραι<ς> κ, καὶ ἀπογράφεσθ[αι] πρὸς 'Αριστόβουλον εἰς τὸ καταλογεῖον [ἀ]φ' ἧ[ς] ἂν ἡμέρας παραγένωνται ἐν ἡμέρ]αις τρ[ι]σίν, δισαφεῶ δὲ εὐθέως καὶ π[αρὰ τ]ίνων παρειλήφασι τὰ ἱερὰ ἕως γενε[ῶν τρι] ῶν καὶ διδόναι τὸν ἱερὸν λόγον ἔ[σφ]ραγισ[μένον] ἐπιγράψαντα [το ὄνομα] ἕκαστ[ον] τὸ αὖ [το]ῦ ὄνομα. For general information and bibliography on this papyrus see Tondriau, *Aegyptus*, 26-27 (1946-7), p. 84f.; id., *Chr. d'Égypte*, 25 (1950), pp. 299f.

23 Tcherikover, *ibid.*, p. 342.

the order in *III Maccabees* notes the possibility of joining in it, ostensibly according to the "choice and free will" of the Jews (II 30). Also the bait — Alexandrian citizenship — included in the latter order seems to strengthen that impression. In fact, however, such a pre- sentation is contradictory to the true meaning of the testimony in *III Maccabees*. Verse 30 should not be separated from its prede- cessors (28-29) which leave no doubt that the point is a royal edict, aimed at imposing the Dionysian cult through threats of drastic punishments, including death[24]. Consequently, the alternative being slavery or death, the "choice and free will" cannot be taken seriously[25].

Faithful to his method, Tcherikover argued that the branding of the Jews with the sign of Dionysus was not a punishment but rather an honor, as Philopator himself was so branded[26]. However, from the Jewish standpoint it was persecution, for it was contrary to an explicit biblical command (*Leviticus*, 19:28), and the ivy leaf was definitely a pagan symbol. The intention was a royal sign of recogni- tion ($\chi\alpha\rho\alpha\kappa\tau\dot{\eta}\rho$)[27] of the kind that was impressed on the bodies of slaves and war captives, and it should be borne in mind that the order said that "all the Jews would be degraded ... to the condition of servitude". Kahana correctly pointed out that the reference was to a brand ($\sigma\tau\dot{\iota}\gamma\mu\alpha$) burned on to the bodies of slaves so that they could be identified and their escape prevented[28]. Hunt and Grenfell pub- lished a papyrus dating from the start of the Ptolemaic period dealing with sailors marked with the royal brand and with ways of recovering them if they fled. That the men were slaves or war captives employed

---

24 Cf. *III Macc.*, III 1, 25f.; IV 14; VI 34, 37-38; VII 3f.; and cf. also IV 2f.; 21, 38f.

25 It is interesting in connection with this to recall the anti-Jewish decrees of Antiochus IV Epiphanes, which also contained many enticements (see, e.g., *I Macc.*, II 18; *II Macc.*, VII 27; *IV Macc.*, VIII 7; XII 5). From the fact that "many in Israel accepted the foreign worship sacrificing to idols", etc. (*I Macc.*, I 43) it might be deduced that in this case, too, there was a choice, but in fact, matters were such that "the penalty for disobed- ience was death" (*I Macc.*, I 50). A comparison with the persecutions in *III Macc.* on this point is instructive.

26 See Tcherikover, *ibid.*, p. 342 and n.11; as to Ptolemy IV Philopator himself, Tcheri- kover was probably referring to the report of Stephanus, and see *Etymologicum Magnum* (p. 220) s.v. Γάλλος ῾Ο Φιλοπάτωρ Πτολεμαῖος διὰ τὸ φύλλα κισσοῦ κατεστίχϑαι ὡς οἱ Γάλλοι.

27 Cf. *III Macc.*, II 29: οὕς τε ἀπογραφομένους χαράσσεσϑαι καὶ διὰ πυρὸς εἰς τὸ σῶμα.

28 Kahana, *Ha-Safarim Ha-Ḥizoniim*, vol. 2, p. 244 (commentary on *III Macc.*, II 29).

as royal sailors and consequently branded with the king's brand[29], was proven by those scholars, who also recalled the tesimony in *III Maccabees* (II 20). The branding was usually done with a hot iron, to criminals as well as slaves and war captives. It was a common practice in Ptolemaic Egypt and in Hunt and Grenfell's view inherited from the Pharaohs[30]. The marking was customary in the entire Greek world as well, by tatooing if not by branding with a hot iron[31]. That explanation of *III Maccabees*, II 29, throws new light on the nature of the decree and removes the grounds for Tcherikover's contention that no punishment was involved.

As to the participation in the Dionysian cult, a distinction must be made between a general public ceremony and that of initiates. Gutman claimed that Philopator introduced various ceremonies and practices in honor of Dionysus that were not restricted to initiates. It was his view that the celebrations reported by Ptolemy of Megalopolis (Philopator's contemporary) that were conducted in the presence of guests from all the cities were of the public variety[32]. That might explain the "naive" statements in *III Maccabees*, as the uninitiated would then be able to participate[33], except that *III Maccabees* clearly notes that Jews were invited to take part in the mysteries, and not merely in the public celebrations. How does this accord with Tcherikover's just claim that the Dionysian mysteries were not open to all?

A careful examination of II 30 reveals that in fact not all the Jews were invited but merely "a few of them" ($\tau\iota\nu\epsilon\varsigma\ \dot{\epsilon}\xi\ \alpha\dot{\upsilon}\tau\tilde{\omega}\nu$). As presumably the king had already had inscribed on a slab in his court the decree that compelled all the Jews to be classified with the "natives" and "slaves" (II 28) it is clear that the beginning of II 30 applies to a minority of Jews only. That is obvious from the text itself: "But

---

29 See *P. Hibeh*, II 198, line 86f.; about this type of slave see Lesquier, pp. 256-258.

30 See Grenfell and Hunt, *The Hiebeh Papyri*, vol. 2, pp. 98-99.

31 The tatooing was done (as it still is) by means of heated needles which scratched designs on the skin which were inked in various colors. On the tatooing of salves in Greece, see, e.g., Aristophanes, *Aves*, 760; of captives, Herodotus, VII 233; Plutarch, *Pericles*, 26, and others. On the tatooing of slaves in Ptolemaic Egypt see *M. Chr.*, 369; *P. Lille*, I 29. On the tatooing of temple slaves see *UPZ*, 121.

32 See Gutman, *The Beginnings of Jewish Hellenistic Literature*, vol. 1, p. 144.

33 Gutman (*ibid.*) argued likewise, on the basis, among others, of Poland, *Vereinswesens*, p. 288f.

that he might not appear an enemy to all, he added: But if a few of them prefer to join those who are initiated into the mysteries (τὰς τελετὰς μεμυημένοις), etc." It is most illuminating that the last part quoted has the same meaning as *BGU*, 1211 regarding "persons who perform the rites of Dionysus" (τοὺς τελοῦντας τῶι Διωνύσωι). There is no doubt that the reference is to special ceremonial and ritual practices, such as initiation or religious purification[34]. Who then were the "few of them" that *III Maccabees* reports as having been invited to take part? The answer is provided by verse III 21 which refers to those the king sought to make "partners with the priests forever" (μετόχους τῶν ἀεὶ ἱερεῶν)[35]. Verse II 31 even defined them as people who, "hating the price paid for the religion of [their] city" (i.e. Jerusalem), easily joined in the praise that was expected of the king's adherents. A good example was certainly Dositheos son of Drimylus, mentioned in *III Maccabees* (I 3) as a Jewish apostate who rose to serve as an eponymous priest at Philopator's court as early as 222 B.C.E. (*CPJ*, I 127d-e). There is general agreement that the first part of verse 31 of chapter II is hard to fathom, mainly because of the word ἐπιπολαίως. It appears in only two minuscule MSS of version V, and even there as a correction, while three other minuscules have ἐπιπολέως. It seems preferable to accept what most MSS of version A have — ἐπὶ πόλεως — especially since fragments of the Codex Sinaiticus, which is the earliest of the manuscripts, confirm it[36]. To whom then did ἔνιοι... ἐπὶ πόλεως refer? Grimm considered logically that it meant those who headed a quarter or community in Alexandria[37]. If so, it might be a reference to the several Jewish

---

34 Zuntz proved that the expression τελεῖν τῷ Διονύσῳ has to be interpreted in this manner, distinguishing it from the ordinary rites which were defined by means of the verbs θύεω, εὔχεσθαι. He corroborated his conclusions by means of an interesting comparative study, as well. See Zuntz, *Hermes* 91 (1963), p. 230; and cf. Bevan, p. 234. It should be added that in ordinary language the word τελεσταί indicated participants in the mysteries, and it is no accident that the site of the mysteries in Elusis was called the τελεστήριον (my thanks to Applebaum who drew my attention to this).

35 The word ἱερῶν (holy objects, or holy customs — in short, holy things) is found in only one version of *III Macc.*, and also in Grotius's correction. On the other hand, all the other versions have ἱερεῶν. See, for details, the critical apparatus of Rahlfs, *Septuaginta, III Macc., ad loc.*; Hanhart, *Septuaginta, III Macc., ad loc.* Gutman was the first to see this, *Eshkoloth*, 3 (1959), p. 65.

36 See Hanhart, *ibid., ad loc.* In regard to the Sinaiticus version, see Baars, *Vetus Testamentum*, 13 (1963), p. 85.

37 Grimm, *Handbuch, ad loc.*

leaders whom the king tempted with eminent positions (such as was granted to Dositheos son of Drimylus), who may actually have been priests. As is well-known, Ptolemy IV Philopator instituted a religious reform in his kingdom, grafting the royal cult onto Dionysian rites[38]. As various theological traditions show, Dionysus was identified with many oriental gods, including Israel's, and the king may very well have believed that the Jewish ritual could combine with his[40], and that some Jewish priests would be initiated into his cult. The fact that only a few (ἔνιοι) were tempted to worship the king, and the majority (οἱ πλεῖστοι) abhorred "those who parted from them" (τοὺς ἀποχωροῦντας ἐξ αὐτῶν) and compared them to "enemies (πολεμίους) of their nation"[41], indicates the unfavourable reaction of the Jews to Philopator's proposal. From the Jewish standpoint, the "mysteries" current in the pagan world were identified with lechery and promiscuity (that is, abominations)[42], and the Dionysian mysteries were no exception. It is no wonder then that *III Maccabees* presents the king's decree and the "bait" he offered as religious persecution par excellence. The "naive" outlook on the matter expressed there is consequently not surprising, and the descriptions there provide no grounds for the impression that "admission to the mysteries

---

38 Perdrizet, *Rev. Ét. Anc.*, 12 (1910), pp. 217-247. Cf. Rostovtzeff, *CAH*, 7 (1964), p. 151; Tarn, p. 212. Tondriau (*Aegyptus*, 33 [1953], pp. 125ff.) showed that the dynastic rite of Ptolemy IV Philopator was introduced around the time of the battle of Raphia! (*ibid.*, p. 129), and this fits in with the historical reality described in *III Macc*.

39 Of the Eastern gods, Osiris, e.g., should be mentioned, as his image was identified with Dionysus to a great extent, see, e.g., Herodotus, II 42, 48, 123, 144, 156. As to the God of Israel, who was also identified by some classical authors with Dionysus, see the testimony of Valerius Maximus (*Epitome de Julius Paris*, I 33), Plutarch (*Quaestiones Conviviales*, IV 6) and Tacitus (*Historiae*, V 4). About this see Levy, *Studies in Jewish Hellenism* p. 129 and n.62. The blood libel of Damocritus was also described as part of the rites of Dionysus, as shown by Flusser, *Levy Memorial Volume*, p. 104ff.; Stern, *Greek and Latin Authors*, vol. 1, p. 531.

40 See Perdrizet, *op.cit.* in n.38; Tarn, p. 212; Jouguet, p. 140.

41 *III Macc.*, II 32-33. It seems to me that "Niketas son of Jason the Jerusalemite" should also be considered a renegade, as he made á contribution to the Dionysian rite in the Asia Minor city of Iasos (see *CIJ*, II 749). Tcherikover himself suggested that he was a Hellenizer, especially in view of the fact that the inscription is from the middle of the second century B.C.E., that is, from the Hellenizing period. He even compared his contribution to that of the Hellenizing delegation from Jerusalem to the Heraclean rite in Tyre (*II Macc.*, IV 18-19); see *Hellenistic Civilization and the Jews*, p. 352, but cf. p. 350.

42 See, e.g., Gutman, *The Beginnings of Jewish Hellenistic Literature*, vol. 1, p. 144f.; and to this may be added some places in Philo, such as *De Spec. Legibus*, I 56, 319-320.

was dependent only on the will of the Jews, as if they were open to every person"[43].

Nature of the Census

Tcherikover attempted to point out contradictions in the *III Maccabees* descriptions in order to prove that the census and the conversion order were two different things which the author mistakenly put together. In his view "every consus in Egypt had but one aim, levying taxes, and taxes are not levied on people sentenced to death"[44]. Of course this categorical assertion was based on the belief that the aim of the census was the *laographia*, and accordingly Tcherikover dated the composition to the Roman period, but the error is based on a mistaken interpretation of the purpose of the census.

The language of the decree in *II Maccabees* leaves no doubt that the purpose was to ascertain who would adopt the royal cult and who would not. The imposition of the *laographia* and slavery on the Jews[45] was not the purpose, but a punishment, countered by the reward of Alexandrian citizenship offered to those who agreed to be initiated into the mysteries. Even if it is assumed that the census was conducted for the purpose of taxation, there was some sense in it even though all the Jews were sentenced to death, as *III Maccabees* says. For verse VII 22 stresses that after the king repented his iniquity, he ordered the Jews to be given back their property as recorded by the census[46]. The inference thus is that the census was aimed at registering the property of condemned Jews prior to its confiscation. If account is taken of the situation of the Jews who complied with the decree and gained equal rights with the Alexandrians, there are grounds for concluding that the census might have had a fiscal purpose (although that is hard to believe). *BGU*, 1211, however, reports a census conducted by Ptolemy IV Philopator that was of a completely different character, relating entirely to the registration of those initiated into the Dionysian mysteries[47]. Evidently then

---

43 See Tcherikover, *Jews in the Greek and Roman World*, p. 342f.
44 *Ibid.*, p. 344f.
45 The meanings of these terms in *III Macc.* are discussed below.
46 Cf. III 28, where confiscation of Jewish property is also hinted at.
47 See, e.g., lines 7f.: ἀπογράφεσθαι πρὸς Ἀριστόβουλον εἰς τὸ καταλογεῖον κτλ ...

censuses were taken in Egypt not only for fiscal purposes but sometimes for clearly religious ones, and the census described in *III
Maccabees* was of the latter type.

The purpose of the census and the annihilation decree had a deep
religious logic connected with the persecution of those who rejected
the divinity of Dionysus, and *III Maccabees* indicates this (in IV
14-15). Büchler already discerned that the preparations for the
execution of the Jews as described have the character of a religious
ceremony[48]. Indeed, the sentence was to be carried out at dawn[49], the
time set for the punishment of those denying Dionysus[50]. Gutman's
suggestion that the trampling by elephants was a kind of spectacular
ceremonial punishment culminating the maltreatment of anti-Diony-
sians, is very apt[51]. It was probably for that reason that Philopator's
decree was displayed on the tower in the courtyard of his palace
(*III Maccabees*, II 27) and that the elephant trample was supposed
to take place in public at the hippodrome of Schedia[52].

The king's behavior too was quite ceremonial, for he arranged his
wine feast in the temples of his gods (IV 16). The elephants too were
prepared ritually, since they were given frankincense and wine (V 2,
45). The drink does not seem to have been aimed merely at making
them wild, for as war elephants they were in any case trained to kill
by trampling. From the military point of view, it was senseless,
because intoxicated elephants might easily lose all control and turn
against their handlers, as indeed they did in this case (VI 21). The use
of frankincense — common in ceremonials including the Dionysian
ones — reinforces the impression of the ceremonial-ritual nature of
the preparations for killing the Jews. Moreover, madness and frenzy
were typical of the punitive operations undertaken against the
"unbelievers" in Dionysus[53]. Gutman also discovered the connection

---

48 See Büchler, *Tobiaden und Oniaden*, p. 180, n.9.

49 *III Macc.*, V, 23-24 and cf. V, 1-, 26, 27, 46.

50 See Gutman, *Eshkoloth*, 3 (1959), p. 70.

51 Gutman, *ibid.*, pp. 68-70.

52 *III Macc.*, IV, 11; V, 46. This spectacle may be the reason that the census of the Jews
    was held in Alexandria and not in their places of residence, and thus explains another
    point that Tcherikover wondered about. In any case, the royal decree of *BGU*, 1211 also
    ordered the census to take place in Alexandria and even specified the times that mem-
    bers of the *chora* were to arrive there.

53 Cf. Euripides, *Bacchae*, 144, 1222, 1228, 1230 (cf. also 300-305) and also Herodotus
    (IV, 79).

between elephants and the Dionysian ritual, particularly in relation
to the persecution of "heretics"[54]. The Jews certainly provided
Ptolemy IV Philopator with sufficient pretext for conducting an
anti-heretic spectacle. They not only refused to worship Dionysus,
but were in some cases even dissenters (ἀντιλέγοντες) who dared to
publicly voice their scorn of the few who had heeded the king's
call[55]. There was consequently sufficient reason for a census and a
ceremonial execution, and that explains the apparent contradictions
which Tcherikover sought to solve.

Another ceremonial element in the story is the reward for those
denouncing the Jews (III 28). Aside from money and property, they
were to receive also καὶ τῇ ἐλευθερίᾳ στεφανωθήσεται. The Syriac
translation has ve-ḥaruta ve-kalila nekabel, and that rendering has
some support in one of the Lucian versions[57]. At first glance it
seems to refer to people of lowly origin that would receive "freedom"
in return for their denunciations, and Emmet thus proposed to identify them with Egyptian natives[58]. That proposal does not however
accord with the Ptolemaic objections to such civic promotions, and
in any case the term "freedom" is meaningful in relation to slaves
rather than Egyptian natives. For the same reason the people concerned could not be Jews, and the "freedom" could not mean their
being granted equal rights with the Alexandrians. The solution must
be sought on a different plane, not in the wording of the Syriac or

---

54 This appears from the reports of Diodorus Siculus, III, 65, 7; and Athenaeus, 31 (20cd);
   and see Gutman, *Eshkoloth*, 3 (1959), p. 69. His evidence is supported by other reports of
   Ptolemy IV Philopator's deep religious feeling about elephants. It appears that he believed
   that they prayed to God because of an inner drive and purified themselves by bathing in
   the sea. Ptolemy IV Philopator is cited as saying that they worshipped the rising sun by
   raising their trunks (as though in a prayer of supplication), and were consequently beloved
   by the gods. After the victory of Rapiaḥ, he is said to have sacrificed four elephants, but
   when he had nightmares in which the gods expressed anger at his peculiar deed, he performed many rites of appeasement and even built a bronze monument in memory of
   his sacrifice. On all this see Plutarch, *Bruto Animalia*, 972c; Aelian, *De Nat. Anim.*,
   VII 2, 44; Pliny, *Nat. Hist.*, VII 1f.; Cassius Dio, XXXIX 38, 5. The story in *III Macc.*
   fits in with this picture very well.
55 *III Macc.*, II 28; cf. II 33; III 23.
56 It seems that the genetive-case versions of A and V manuscripts are to be preferred to
   that quoted here, which appeared in only one miniscule (55).
57 The reference is to L'-58-311, where a few words are even added to finish the sentence.
   Kahana's Hebrew translation was apparently based on this version or the Syriac one.
58 Emmet in: Charles, *Apocrypha, III Macc., ad. loc.* (p. 167).

Lucian texts[59]. For Dionysus was described as the "liberator" (ἐλευθερεύς) and the "free" (ἐλεύθερος) and the term ἐλευθερία was sometimes applied to a holiday in honor of that god[61]. The expression should be interpreted to mean crowning with the diadem worn on the Dionysian holiday, which fits in very well with the ritualistic character of the projected punishment. Thus Tcherikover's contention that the persecutions of Jews described in *III Maccabees* had no religious tinge is quite odd[62]. One of his arguments, by the way, based on verse 28 — "that none who did not sacrifice (i.e. worship the king) should be allowed to enter their sacred rites (τὰ ἱερὰ αὐτῶν)" — claimed that τὰ ἱερά could not possibly refer to synagogues because they were not temples. However, that term should not be translated as "temples" but rather as "sacred things" or

---

59 Lucian was very free with the style and grammar of the Septuagint. The Syriac translation is at times also free, and sometimes parallels the Lucian version; see Emmet in his introduction to *III Macc.* (*ibid.*, p. 155).

60 See Kern, *RE(PW)*, V 1 (1903), p. 1028; Jessen, *RE(PW)*, V 2 (1905), p. 2345; cf. Roscher, *Lexicon*, vol. 1, p. 1070

61 *Thesaurus Graecae Linguae* s.v. ἐλευθερία. The same is true of the corresponding Latin term *liberalia*. See Schur, *RE(PW)*, XII 1, pp. 81-82; and also about the term *liber* (op.cit., p. 68). The "freedom" motif is very closely tied up with the figure of Dionysus, the "liberator", as may be seen in Euripides, (*Bacchae*, 55-57, 440-450, 497-498, 512, 545-549, 609-610, 614, 616, 634, 643, 648, 651, 653-654, 793, etc.).

62 *Jews in the Greek and Roman World*, p. 354.

63 See *ibid.*, pp. 341-342. Even so, a series of sources contradict his opinion and indicate that Jewish holy places were given this name: a) Jos., *Antiquitates*, XIII 66, and see Gutman's comment in *The Beginning of Jewish Hellenistic Literature* (Hebrew), vol. 1, p. 146, n.8. b) Apparently the synagogue in Syrian Antioch was also so named, see *Bellum*, VII 45, and also J. Chrysostomus, *Adv. Jud. Or.*, I 6. c) Agatharchides of Cnidus, quoted by Josephus, attested to the Jews' refraining from work on the Sabbath, and indicated that they are accustomed only to "pray with outstretched hands in their temples (ἐν τοῖς ἱεροῖς) until evening" (*C. Apionem*, I 209). Krauss pointed out correctly that the plural used here was not a scribal error indicating many temples in Palestine, and that the reference was to synagogues (see Krauss, *Syn. Alt.*, p. 58). d) In two inscriptions from *Beth She'an*, a local synagogue was called τὸ ἱερόν (Krauss, *ibid.*, p. 210). e) Tacitus (*Historiae*, V 5) noted that the Jews "set up no statues in their cities, still less in their temples (*templa*)", and see Levy, *Studies in Jewish Hellenism*, p. 125 and n.61, and also Krauss, *ibid.*, p. 28, n.6. f) The inscription from the Jewish synagogue in Hadara (near Alexandria) has the word τὸν ἱερόν and it is not clear to which word it is associated. Most editors of the inscription connected it with περίβολον (see *CIJ*, II 1433) but it can also go with τοπός. In any case, the reference is to a sacred precinct around a synagogue, and therefore the word is part of the terminology relating to Jewish synagogues. g) Another inscription, also from a synagogue in Egypt, (found in the vicinity of Cairo) indicated specifically that it was granted the right of asylum by the king (see *CIJ*, II 1449) just as temples were.

"sacred rites", just as in *BGU*, 1211 (lines 11-12)[64]. In any case, the term cannot be the authority for Tcherikover's view that the persecutions as described in *III Maccabees* were not religious in character.

The Dionysian Cult and Alexandrian Citizenship

Dionysus was the god that Philopator claimed descent from[65], and this was a departure from the traditional dynastic generalogy of the Ptolemaic kings before him who, like Alexander the Great, traced their descent from the god Heracles[66]. Philopator's divergence may well have had reverberations among the Alexandrians, and even evoked discontent and criticism. In any case his ceremonial innovations and exaggerated devotion to the new Dionysus (Νέος Διόνυσος) aroused vigorous opposition[67]. Interestingly enough, like *III Macca-bees* Plutarch connected the wild cruelty of Dionysus with the wickedness of Phalaris, and stressed that the result was catastrophic for Egypt[68]. According to Athenaeus, Queen Arsinoe herself expressed disgust and contempt for the Dionysian practices Philopator had adopted[69].

The king's devotion to that cult had political ramifications as well, for he established in Alexandria a new tribe called Dionysia (composed of demes whose names were borrowed from the mythological attributives of Dionysus) which enjoyed great prominence[70]. It is easy to understand that the establishment of such a privileged tribe produced a class differentiation among Alexandrian citizens and consequent feelings of discrimination. They may have been one of the reasons for the dissatisfaction with Philopator's devotion to the new Dionysian cult, and the unfavourable attitude to this king in Greek historiography[71] probably reflected the position of the Alexandrians[72]. Thus the Jews were not alone in their opposition

---

64 J. Gutman, *The Beginnings of Jewish Hellenistic Literature*, vol. 1, p. 146 and n. 8.
65 On his innovations in the dynastic rites, see Fraser, vol. 1, p. 219f.
66 See, e.g., Theocritus, XVII 20ff. (esp. 26-27); and cf. *OGIS*, 54.
67 Fraser, vol. 1, p. 204f.
68 *Quomodo Adul.*, 12 (56) E; *III Macc.*, V 20, 42. Phalaris (tyrant of Acragas) symbolized a cruel tyrant in the Greek world.
69 Athenaeus, 276A-C (*FGrH*, 241, Fr. 16).
70 See Perdrizet, *Rev. Ét. Anc.*, 12 (1910), pp. 218f.
71 See, e.g., Polybius, V 107, 2-4; Strabo, V 34, 3-5, 9-11; XVII 1, 11.
72 See Gutman, *Eshkoloth*, 3 (1959), p. 66. And cf. Preaux, *Chr. d'Égypte*, 40 (1965),

to Philopator, and this is clearly indicated in a number of passages in *III Maccabees*. One of them (III 8-10) notes that the "Greeks" in Alexandria were friendly to the Jews, sympathized with them and were prepared to vouch for them and try to save them. Another (IV 11) states that one of the reasons for confining the Jews in the hippodrome outside the city was "so that they might neither communicate with his army or in any way claim protection of the walls". That attitude of the Greeks was diametrically opposed to that of the "gentiles" (ἀλλόφυλοι) who should certainly be identified as Egyptians[73]. Such a situation does not fit the Roman period, when there was already a deep rift between the "Greeks" and the Jews, but harmonizes very well with the background of Ptolemy IV Philopator's time[74]. Probably the new Dionysian tribe was open to people particularly hostile to the Jews, and yet not accepted by the Hellenes. They may have included members of the Egyptian priesthood which had become prominent after the battle of Raphiah[75]. The king's submission to Egyptian priestly interests could have been the reason for his deteriorating relations with both the Jews and the Alexan-

---

pp. 364-375; Fraser, vol. 2, p. 144, n.180. Should not the change of name of the Dionysian tribe to "Berenike" after Philopator's period (on this see Fraser, vol. 1, p. 44) be seen as rejection of his reforms?

73 Tcherikover did not think so. In his opinion the conflict between the "Greeks" and the "gentiles" was purely imaginary. In order to prove this he tried to relocate various passages. In his view, the transposition of the sections *III Macc.*, III 1-7 and 8-10 would eliminate the problem (see *Jews in the Greek and Roman World*, pp. 363-364, n.54). His proposal appears very artificial, its only goal to fit the writings to his purposes, and should therefore be rejected; cf. *III Macc.*, IV 1f. Even Willrich did not fail to identify Jew-haters with the native Egyptian population in this context (see Willrich, *Judaica*, p. 129); cf. also Bell, *Juden und Griechen*, p. 7. On the other hand, Heinemann's reservations about their views should be completely rejected — Heinemann, *RE(PW)*, Suppl. V, pp. 7-8.

74 That does not mean that the writing should be attributed to the period of Ptolemy IV Philopator. The mention of Daniel and his comrades (*III Macc.*, VI 6-7) makes this impossible (on the literary and ideational unity of the Book of Daniel see Efron, *Beth Mikra*, 29 (1974), pp. 466-504). Therefore, the emphasis on these figures in the prayer of Eleazar the Priest, and also the tense atmosphere of martyrdom in the entire piece, makes it probably that it was written around the time of the Hasmonaean revolt. It seems to me that the reflection of the Ptolemaic period in the book (as explained above) strengthens the impression that it was indeed written in the second half of the second century B.C.E. or at the latest at the beginning of the first century B.C.E., as Emmet and Bickermann thought (see n.19 above).

75 As can be seen from the Canopic edict (*OGIS*, 56) and also from the dedicatory inscription of the Egyptian priests to Ptolemy IV Philopator after the victory of Raphiah. See Gauthier and Sottas, *Un décret*, p. 32f.; Bevan, p. 338.

drians. The priests were already armed with anti-Jewish propaganda, and very likely set it to work on Philopator. There is quite a patent hint in *III Maccabees* that the king was influenced by the malicious advisors surrounding him[76], and verses III 8-10 and IV 1 suggest that they may be identifiable with the priests, since the Greeks were sympathetic to the Jews. It is reasonable to assume that it was on the advice of these new friends of his that out of all those opposed to him the king chose the Jews as objects of the Dionysian punishment. The Jews were chosen probably for other reasons as well: a) Their objection to the cult was undoubtedly uncompromising, and based on solid religious principle; b) Their heresy was considered a sign of treason and insurrection[77]; c) Their coreligionists in Palestine were enemies; d) They were a convenient scapegoat.

As according to III *Maccabees* it is clear that Alexandrian citizenship was a prize (both political and material) for those agreeing to Dionysian initiation[78], the refusal of the Jews to accept the prize must be explained as stemming from their religious beliefs. *III Maccabees* contains no echo of any controversy among the Jews for or against Alexandrian citizenship[79]. They refused it not only because it was not offered to all of them, but mainly because of the religious obstacle, for accepting it would have meant definite heresy. In any case, there is no need to attribute "Zionist" notions to *III Maccabees* in regard to the rejection of Alexandrian citizenship[80] when the reason for that rejection was obviously the apostasy involved.

The Debasement of the Jews — Laographia and Slavery

One of the problems preoccupying scholars is connection with Philopator's order that "all the Jews should be degraded to the rank of natives and condition of servitude" (πάντας δὲ τοὺς Ἰουδαίους εἰς λαογραφίαν καὶ οἰκητικὴν διάθεσιν ἀχϑῆναι; *III Maccabees*, II 28). There is a difference of opinion as to whether *laographia* here means "census" as in the Ptolemaic terminology, or "poll-tax" as in the Roman, and the solution is important in particular in dating the

76 *III Macc.*, II 25; V 3, 39, 44; VII 3.
77 *Ibid.*, III 7, 19, 24-25; VII 3-5, etc.
78 *Ibid.*, II 30; III 21.
79 Cf. the opinion of Tcherikover, *The Jews in the Greek and Roman World*, p. 362.
80 See Tcherikover, *ibid.*, p. 365.

composition of *III Maccabees*. Tcherikover insisted on the second
meaning: "The author of *III Maccabees* speaks in one breath of the
'laographia' and 'condition of slavery'; he thus identifies the two
concepts or considers the first a preparatory phase for the second".
Accordingly, "the combination of the two concepts — payment of
the laographia and enslavement — is a notion typical of the Roman
period: payers of the poll-tax are *dediticii*, subjects"[81]. In support
of his view Tcherikover cited IV 14 which ostensibly "the author
more precisely indicates the condition of servitude as τῶν ἔργων
λατρεία, that is, hard forced labor"[82].

Tcherikover's proof is quite weak, and does not take into account
the complete phrase τῶν ἔργων κατὰ πόνον λατρείαν (in the best
examples of version V, and cf. IV 14 below), which does not mean
"hard forced labor" at all. For the expression πόνον λατρεύω has the
idiomatic meaning of "render due service to the gods"[83], so that the
phrase as a whole should be translated "the act(s) in the service of
the gods". That meaning for the noun λατρεία (or verb λατρεύω)
was quite common in Jewish Hellenistic literature, including the
Septuagint[84], and even appears in *III Maccabees* itself (VI 6). Plutarch
used the expression as well in reference to the worship of Philopator[85].

Finally, verse IV 14 clearly hints at a previously mentioned
census, probably the one referred to in II 29, which has been shown
above to have had mainly religious import. If so, *III Maccabees*
provides no textual authority for identifying the *laographia* with
a condition of "hard forced labor", and in any case a denotation
rooted in the period of Roman rule should not be ascribed to it. The
terms "*laographia*" and "condition of servitude" describe two conditions, both lowly, but different[86], and the distinction was character-

---

81 *Ibid.*, pp. 351-352; and cf. *ibid.*, p. 264; *Hellenistic Civilization and the Jews*, pp. 317-
    318.
82 *The Jews in the Greek and Roman World*, p. 351.
83 See Liddell and Scott, s.v. λατρεύω (3). From a linguistic standpoint the combination
    πόνον λατρεύω shows that it is the *accusativus cognatus* which gives them the meaning
    as stated.
84 Hatch and Redpath, *Concordance to the Septuagint*, s.v. Cf. also *I Macc.*, I 43; II 19, 22.
85 Plutarch, *Quomodo Adul.*, 12, E (56).
86 The fact that the word καὶ divides them may also reinforce the conclusion that they are
    not the same.

istic of the Ptolemaic period, as indicated, for instance, by the Rainer papyrus[87].

The historical connection of the Philopator decree cited in *III Maccabees* to the Ptolemaic period is revealed also by a comparison of II 28 and 29. Obviously the words of the first verse ("All the Jews will be degraded to the rank of natives and condition of servitude") are paraphrased by those of the second ("and be reduced to their former limited status"). At first glance there might seem to be a contradiction between the two since from the first verse it might be thought that the Jews were never before in that situation, while the second indicates that their original status was limited. In fact, however, the contradiction is more apparent than real, as Gutman already pointed out. The "former limited status" according to him was the status of the Jews before the liberation decree of Ptolemy II Philadelphus (*Letter of Aristeas*, 22ff.), while their "degradation to the rank of natives and condition of servitude" in Philopator's time was aimed at abolishing the reductions and privileges granted in the reign of Philadelphus[89]. Indeed the *Letter of Aristeas* more than once defined the status of Jewish war captives of Ptolemy I's time with the term "servitude" (οἰκετεία)[89]. They were actual war captives (τὰ αἰχμάλωτα) handed over to soldiers as booty[90].

The *III Maccabees* descriptions of the detention of the Jews fit the usual treatment of war prisoners that were enslaved. They were rightly described as "enslaved captives" (ἀνδράποδα)[91], and it is not surprising that they were branded with the royal brand, as customary in such cases. In other words, it was Philopator's intention to have the Jews revert to the status they had several generations earlier.

Alexandrian Citizenship and the Status of the Jews Prior to Philopator's Decree

As noted above, II 28 leaves no doubt that according to *III Maccabees* the imposition of the *laographia* and condition of servitude on

87 See Liebesny, *Aegyptus*, 14 (1936), pp. 257f.; Westermann, *AJPH*, 59 (1938), pp. 1-30; idem, *Upon Slavery*, passim; Rostovtzeff, *SEHHW*, pp. 341-344.
88 Gutman, *Eshkoloth*, 3 (1959), pp. 67-68.
89 See *Letter of Aristeas*, 14, 15, 16, 24.
90 *Ibid.*, 12, 23, 33, 35. The *Letter of Aristeas*, 22, stressed that the soldiers became masters of the Jewish slaves (σωμάτων). In regard to the use of the term "slave" (σῶμα) cf. *Letter of Aristeas*, 20, 24.
91 III 25; IV 7, 9; V 6; VI 27.

the Jews indicates that they were not in that situation before the decree. In other words, *III Maccabees* did not consider them "natives" and "slaves" in the intermediate period between the liberation decree of Ptolemy II Philadelphus and the edict of Ptolemy IV Philopator. On the other hand, they were not Alexandrian citizens, for if they had been, the king would not have had to tempt at least some of them with the right to that status.

What then was the status of the Jews as described in *III Maccabees*? Verse III 4 says "Yet worshiping God, and living according to his Law (καὶ τῷ τούτου νόμῳ πολιτευόμενα) they held themselves apart in the matter of food, and for this reason they were disliked by some". The use of the verb πολιτεύω is most illuminating and is solid grounds for the conclusion that what was meant was the existence of a Jewish *politeuma*, whose organizational basis was the laws of the Torah, and which was thus different from other organizations. Verses III 9 and VII 3 reinforce that conclusion since they refer to the Alexandrian Jewish community and its other counterparts in Egypt as *systema*[93], and Josephus too employed the same term to denote Jewish communities in the Diaspora (*C. Apionem*, I 32). The usual meaning of the term was "an organized body" but it quite commonly had a military meaning (like συντάγμα)[94], and F. Poland showed that it could also denote a religious association like σύνοδος or συναγωγή[95]. Thus it meant something very like *politeuma* and indeed there is confirmation of this in Classical literature[96]. It is

---

92 *Ibid.*, VII 5. ἀνδράποδα is a common term in the papyri from the Ptolemaic period, and appeared for the first time in a royal decree from the time of Ptolemy II Philadelphus — *P. Hibeh*, I 27, lines 1, 4, 6, 8. For more details of its frequency in papyri literature, see Taubenschlag, p. 67, n.2.

93 The first to reveal this was Ostersetzer, *Braude Jubilee Volume*, p. 14. Version A of verse VII 3 has τὰ συστήματα, that is, the plural rather than the singular.

94 See examples in Liddell and Scott, s.v. Polybius, e.g., used this term for the "Macedonians" as well as other military units (XV 26, 9). The same use of the term can be found in papyri, see Uebel, p. 378. It is more illuminating, of course, to find this use in *II Macc.* (VIII 5; XV 12). On the military significance of συντάγμα, see Lesquier, p. 95f.

95 See Poland, *Vereinswesens*, p. 248. It is interesting to note that in the Patristic literature as well (in a later period, of course), this term was also used to denote organized communities (see Lampe, *A Patristic Greek Lexicon*, p. 1351).

96 See, e.g., Polybius, VI 10, 14 (κάλλιστον δέ σύστημα τῶν καθ' ἡμᾶς πολιτειῶν); II 36, 6. See also Diodorus Siculus, XII 11, 3 (συστησάμενοι δε πολίτευμα δημοκράτικον); Strabo, XVII 1, 42, 813c (σύστημα πολιτικὸν ἐν τῷ Ἑλληνικῷ τρόπῳ) in his remarks on the Egyptian city of Ptolemaïs; V 2, 10 (πολιτικὸν σύστημα); XII 3, 37, (560c).

therefore reasonable to suppose that the two words had similar if not identical meanings in regard to Jewish communities as well[97]. As in Ptolemaic Egypt the various *politeumata* were established on the basis of military units; and as *III Maccabees* itself supplies clear data on the connection of Jews with the army[98], it may be concluded that the term σύστημα as applied to Jewish communities referred to an association of the *politeuma* type[99]. Thus Philopator's edict was designed to withdraw from the Jews their right to their own organization, a right which granted them intermediate status higher than that of "natives" but lower than that of Alexandrian citizens. That is the status that is congruous with membership in a *politeuma*.

It is not wonder then that as members of a body organized on ethnic lines they were termed a "people" or "national community" (τὸ ἔθνος)[100] in contrast to "other peoples" (ἀλλοεθνέσιν) in Egypt[101]. For the author of *III Maccabees*, the Jews of Egypt were "a strange people in a foreign land" (λαὸν ἐν ξένῃ γῇ ξένον; VI 3) and their settlement was a "colony (of immigrants)" (ἀποικία; VI 10), "sojourning (in a foreign land)" (παροικία; VI 36; VII 19), all terms that denoted their "exile"[102]. The separateness of the Jews from the world around is stressed in the book and deeply impressed in the author's outlook, as something self-evident[103]. The fact that they rejected Alexandrian citizenship with all its material benefits shows that their true aim was a separate independent life. That was always the essence of the Jewish struggle, and it is therefore surprising that Tcherikover claimed that "there were not many among the leaders and supporters of the community who could agree to such a principal stand, since the renunciation of 'the fight for emancipation' seemed to them political suicide"[104]. In order to adapt the text to his

---

97 Cf. Scramuzza, *Emperor Claudius*, p. 73.
98 *III Macc.*, II 11, VI 25, and cf. IV 11; III 7.
99 A similar phenomenon is known in regard to the Jewish communities in Cyrene, which were called πολιτεύματα (*CIG*, 5361-2) or συντάγματα (*Antiquitates*, XIV 116) at the same time. See Applebaum, *Jews and Greeks in Ancient Cyrene*, p. 131.
100 *III Macc.*, II 27, 33; or ὁμοεθνεῖς – ibid., IV 12; cf. also τὸ γέους τῶν Ἰουδαίων – III 2, 6; VII 10; VI 4, 9, 13; cf. also τὸ φῦλον – IV 14; V 5; or οἱ ὁμόφυλοι αὐτῶν – IV 12; VII 14.
101 *III Macc.*, IV 1, 6; cf. III 20; V 6, 13; VI 9, 13, 15, 26. Cf. also ἀλλόφυλοι – ibid., III 6.
102 See Tcherikover, *The Jews in the Greek and Roman World*, p. 364.
103 See *III Macc.*, III 4, 7. And cf. also II 33.
104 Tcherikover, *ibid.*, p. 362. In this context it should be emphasized that historical retro-

opinion, Tcherikover stated that the social circle to which the author of *III Maccabees* belonged was not that of the prestigious rich, but of "the broad mass of Jewish populations in Alexandria"[105]. The book does stress that few of the Jews were tempted by the king's offer[106], and notes explicitly that Eleazar, one of the leading Jewish priests in Egypt, and with him the elders (πρεσβύτεροι) were among the persecuted majority that spurned Alexandrian citizenship (VI 1). Moreover, prominent among those who punished the few renegades were a group from the aristocratic echelon in the Jewish community, the priests (VII 13).

Unfortunately only obscure echoes have survived on the Jewish leadership. Only "priests" and "elders" are mentioned, but it is not clear whether the reference is to the Jewish community of Alexandria or to other Jewish communites of Egypt as well. In any case, the mention of "elders" fits in with the information in the *Letter of Aristeas*, and it appears that the communities were headed by a leadership collegium of the *gerousia* type. Probably it was aristocratic in nature, as was the case in most Jewish communities, and encompassed the priests in one way or another, probably in functions of a religious character. The extent of the authority wielded by the Alexandria Jewish leadership, and of its acceptance by the public can be indirectely deduced from the castigation and complete ostracization of the few backsliders who adopted the king's cult (II 33). Such measures are inconceivable in the absence of a strong, well-developed leadership in full control of the Jewish populace[107]. The inauguration of a salvation holiday in both Alexandria and Ptolemaïs[108] also supports that conclusion. Furthermore, the holiday

---

jection of modern concepts (such as "a war of emancipation") to the reality of ancient times is unacceptable.

105 *Ibid.*, p. 363. However, it does not appear reasonable to classify as part of the masses a person who was a well-educated author.

106 *III Macc.*, II 30-33. Verse VII 15 even gives their number — "above three hundred men" — and this is a very small minority of the large Jewish population of Alexandria.

107 The same is true of the right given by the king to put the Jewish traitors to death (*III Macc.*, VII 12). Even if this is patently an exaggeration, the king's recognition of the Jewish leadership and the right of the communities to define independent existence and to control of their members is discernible.

108 Most commentators believe the reference is not to the famous Ptolemais in Upper Egypt but to another small city of this name located south of the Delta, to be more exact, in the Fayûm. A hint of this can be seen in the fact that it was a place where roses were grown (cf. Ptolem. IV 5, 75) as stated in *III Macc.*, VII 17.

was proclaimed in Ptolemaïs by a community decision engraved on a stele and marked by the establishment of a "place of prayer" (τόπον προσευχῆς; VII 20). These facts clearly demonstrate that Jewish community life was ordered and organized, and that the leadership was both acknowledged and powerful.

Chapter VII

The Rights of the Alexandrian Jews
according to Philo

The sharp scholarly debate on the civic status of the Jews of Alexandria has centered mainly around the testimony in Josephus and papyrological findings, while Philo's writings have been accorded relatively little attention, even by Tcherikover whose coverage of the subject is most comprehensive. Most scholars, especially those who reject Josephus, have done their best when referring to Philo, to solve the contradictions between his testimony and papyrological evidence, and thereby reinforce their suspicions regarding apologetic inaccuracies in Josephus. As modern scholars so often employed Philo's writings to support theoretical generalization on Jewish rights, they did not pay attention to the concrete details he provided or systematically examine the political and legal terminology he used in connection with Jewish rights.

In several places Philo called the Jews in Alexandria "Alexandrians"[1], which was confusing to scholars, especially those who attacked Josephus for the same usage, and most of them were inclined to interpret the term as lacking any political or legal significance[2]. A careful scrutiny shows that Philo applied the term both to the citizens of the Greek *polis* and the Egyptian rabble in the city[3]. That itself is enough to eliminate the argument that he was apologetic in applying the term to Jews, for his hostility to the Egyptian rabble is well known. It is thus hard to avoid recognizing that for him "Alexandrians" meant Greeks, Jews and Egyptians. Willrich was right in claiming that Philo's differentiation of Greek from Egyptian (or

---

1 *In Flaccum*, 80, and cf. *ibid.*, 123, *Legatio*, 194, 350.
2 See, e.g., Bell, *Jews and Christians*, p. 14; Tcherikover, *Hellenistic Civilization and the Jews*, p. 315.
3 The citizens of the *polis* — *In Flaccum*, 78-79; *Legatio*, 183; and cf. *In Flaccum*, 41, 141; *Legatio*, 152. The Egyptian rabble — *Legatio*, 120, 162-4, 166-170, and cf. *In Flaccum*, 41, 108.

moderate from extremist) Alexandrians derived from his desire to
point out the Jew-haters and condemn them[4], but that does not
mean that he tried to play down the difference between Greek and
Jewish Alexandrians. In fact, although he called his coreligionists
"Alexandrian Jews" (*Legatio*, 350; *In Flaccum*, 80), he separated
them from "the group of the other Alexandrians" (ἡ τῶν ἄλλων
Ἀλεξανδρέων μερίς)[5]. By failing adequately to study that distinction, scholars overlooked an important criterion for understanding
the entire matter of Jewish rights and legal status in Alexandria.
Philo did not consider the Jews of Alexandria citizens of the Alexandrian *polis*, nor did he ascribe to them any desire to be such. He
described their assiduity in safeguarding their rights as a separate
body politic independent of the *polis*. If the Jews fought for equal
rights it was for equal status of two parallel organizations, a status
which endowed them with equal political and legal rights as individuals as well. That, for Philo, was the essence of the Jewish *politeia*.

In a number of instances Philo used the words πολῖται and πολιτεία,
or cognate terms, to denote the status and rights of the Jews in the
cities of the Roman empire, including his own[6]. Not even once did he
say, however, that the Jews of his city had "Alexandrian *politeia*", so
that clearly he did not consider them citizens of the Alexandrian
polis[7]. What did he mean in applying these terms to the Jews? Jones
very logically explained that to Philo *politeia* meant the rights of the
Jewish *politeuma* in the city, and *politai* meant its members[8]. Engers

---

4 Willrich, *Judaica*, pp. 128-130. Cf. also the views of Box, p. 79, Smallwood, pp. 225,
   245.

5 This distinction is discussed below, pp. 246ff.

6 See *In Flaccum*, 47, 53, 80, 123; *Legatio*, 193, 194, 211, 265, 349, 363, 371.

7 Box (Introduction, pp. xxi-xxii) and Smallwood (*Jews Under Roman Rule*, p. 227)
   tried to argue that one of Philo's books (*Quod Omnis Probus Liber sit*, 6) hints that
   numerous Jews were citizens of the Alexandrian *polis*. On the conrary, it must be emphasized that what Philo wrote was entirely a theoretical generalization. Aside from not
   mentioning any particular city, he did not identify any Jew among its residents (who
   participated in its assembly, courts, council, and in the management of the market and
   the gymnasium). In fact, the reference cannot possibly be to Alexandria, for how could
   he have then cited participation in the city council (βουλεύοντας) when there was no
   boule there at the time. Smallwood's statement, therefore, the "βουλεύοντας must bee used
   loosely" (idem, n.34) is not convincing.

8 H. St. Jones, *JRS*, XVI (1926), pp. 27-28; cf. the opinions of Fuchs, p. 96; Smallwood,
   pp. 8-9; and also Colson, *Philo*, vol. 10, p. xxvii. To this must be added Ruppel's opinion
   that from a linguistic standpoint the word *politeuma* can indicate an association of
   politai just as τεχνίτευμα indicates an association of τεχνῖται (see Ruppel, p. 238).

was also of that opinion, and went so far as to say that "in territorio urbis Alexandreae utique duas civitates liberas fuissue, quae idem valerent et aequo iure fruentur"[9], so that his analysis accords with Tarn's on the political organizational structure of Alexandria as a collection of *politeumata*. Furthermore, as Philo has a large number of synonyms for *politeuma* and *politeia* as do other Greek writers[10], it is possible to argue that what he called ἡμετέρα πολιτεία[11] (*In Flaccum*, 53) was in essence the totality of rights of the Jewish *politeuma* in Alexandria. Is there confirmation of this in his text, or is it a matter of speculative interpretation? Unfortunately neither Jones nor Engers related sufficiently to the actual writings of Philo, and based their ideas mostly on the *Letter of Aristeas* (§310) testimony on the existence of a Jewish *politeuma*, and on the testimony of Strabo which presented the Jewish ethnarch in the city "as if he were the head of a sovereign state" (ὡς ἂν πολιτείας ἄρχων αὐτοτελοῦς; cited by Josephus, *Antiquitates*, XIV 117)[12]. There is however evidence in Philo indicating the existence in Alexandria of a Jewish *politeuma* from which the Jews derived their rights.

In Flaccum, 53, describes exactly the political-legal situation of the Jews of the city:

> When then his attack against our laws by seizing the meeting-houses without even leaving them their name appeared to be successful, he proceeded to another scheme namely the destruction of our *politeia* (ἡμετέρα πολιτεία) so that when our ancestral customs (τὰ πάτρια) and our participation in political rights (ἡ μετουσία πολιτικῶν δικαίων), the sole mooring on which our life was secured, had been cut away, we might undergo the worst misfortunes with no cable to cling to for safety. (trans. F.H. Colson, *LCL* ed.).

Some support for this view can be found in inscription *OGIS*, 592, the first line of which mentions the Caunian *politeuma* (Καυνίων τὸ πολίτευμα) and the fifth line its members (τοὺς αὐτῶν πολίτας). See also Smallwood, *Jews Under Roman Rule*, pp. 229-230.

9 Engers, *Mnemosyne*, N.S., 54 (1926), p. 159. He expressed a similar opinion as early as 1923 in a paper witten even before the publication of the Claudian Letter to the Alexandrians, see idem, *Klio*, 19 (1925-26), p. 84 ; and cf. Bludau, *Juden und Judenverfolgungen*, p. 17; Davis, *Race Relations*, p. 102; Cary, *History of the Greek World*, p. 274. For a recent treatment, see Smallwood, *ibid.*, pp. 228-230, 359-360.

10 See Wolfson, *JBL*, 63 (1941), p. 165f.; whose opinion is discussed below. About the synonymity of the terms emerging from Philo's writings, see below, Appendix, pp. 359-361.

11 Along with the emphasis on "ours" (ἡμετέρα), the Jews in their relations to each other are described as τῶν ἰδίων πολιτῶν (*Legatio*, 211).

12 Cf. Bell, *Jews and Christians*, p. 16.

That wording reveals quite a clear legal formula: The basis of the
Jewish *politeia* was a combination of "ancestral customs" and "participation in political rights". *Legatio*, 371, puts the matter even more
clearly:

> What political right (πολιτικὸν δίκαιον) those who order their lives according to Jewish
> traditions (τὰ πάτρια τῶν Ἰουδαίων) would not be overthrown? Both the specifically
> Jewish Laws (τὰ ἐξαίρετα νόμιμα) and their general rights vis-à-vis each individual city
> (τὰ κοινὰ πρὸς ἐκάστας τῶν πόλεων αὐτοῖς δίκαια) would be overthrown, shipwrecked
> and sent to the bottom of the sea (trans. E.M. Smallwood)[13].

The two excerpts show that the rights of the Jews derived from
their own *politeia*, and not from that of the "group of the other
Alexandrians". Tcherikover was of course aware of this, but did not
consider all the implications[14]. Actually, the same conclusion can be
drawn from other passages in Philo's historical writings[15]. In his
bitter words at the beginning of the third book of *De Specialibus
Legibus* he refers to the Jewish *politeia* and bewails the necessity of
leaving the world of philosophy and being plunged "in the ocean of
civil cares" (εἰς μέγα πέλαγος τῶν ἐν πολιτείᾳ φροντίδων)[16].

As the Jews had their own *politeia*, how can the expressions
ἡμετέρα πολιτεία (*In Flacum*, 53) and ἡμετέρα Ἀλεξανδρεία
(*Legatio*, 150) be reconciled? If they were not contradictory, why
didn't the Jews have "Alexandrian *politeia*"? And if they were, as
appears likely, how can the second expression be explained? The
difficulty can be resolved by Bell's suggestion about the *origo* denotation of the term "Alexandrians" (see note 2 above). In other
words, it can be claimed that Philo considered Alexandria his city,
because his conationals had lived there for generations. However, the
careful reader will discern a deeper meaning. *In Flaccum*, 46, notes
that Alexandria like other cities was "homeland" (πατρίς) for its
Jewish inhabitants. In Philo's view, Jews settled in the cities of the
Diaspora as "immigrants" (στειλάμενοι), and their settlements were
"colonies" (ἀποικίαι) of the *metropolis* of Jerusalem[17]. Significantly,

---

13 Attention should be paid to the total correspondence of the terms and phrases in the
two reports, and especially to the fact that the same formula is used twice in Philo's
historical works, revealing his well-formed legal perception of Jewish rights.
14 Tcherikover, *Hellenistic Civilization and the Jews*, p. 315.
15 *Legatio*, 349; and on this see Bell, *Jews and Christians*, p. 13. See also *Legatio*, 363;
and cf. *ibid.*, 193-194. These clauses will be discussed in detail later.
16 See *De Spec. Leg.*, III 3, 5.
17 Cf. also *Legatio*, 281-282.

in the same context (*ibid.*, 47) Philo calls the settlers *politai*. The terms ἀποικία and εἰς ἀποικίαν στέλλειν or εἰς ἀποικίαν ἐκπέμπειν in Classical literature are applied to the establishment outside the metropolitan area of colonies of immigrants which generally had an independent political character[18]. Evidently Philo attempted to describe the status of the Jews in terms the Greek reader was familiar with. Consequently he presented them as ordinary immigrants who laid the foundation for a "colony" which according to its organization and rights was an independent body (such as a *politeuma*). Henceforth therefore the Jews of Alexandria will be termed "Jewish" *politai* (οἱ πολῖται Ἰουδαῖοι) as Philo himself called them (*In Flaccum*, 47) and not simply *politai*.

That Philo was using terms that the Greek reader would more easily understand is demonstrated also in other writings of his, including his biblical commentaries where he often chose to apply contemporary terms (a practice quite frequent in all exegetical literature). Thus in *De Vita Mosis*, II 232, he compares the Israelites who went to Egypt to "settlers abroad or inhabitants of other regions" (οἱ ξενιτεύοντες ἤ ἑτέρωθι οἰκοῦντες) and even to "a nation" (ἔθνος) whose country is too small to contain it and which therefore sent "colonies" (ἀποίκιαι) all over. He also asserted that such people were not "deprived of rights" or "wrongdoers" (ἀδικοῦσιν) deserving to "be deprived of equal privileges" (ὡς στέρεσθαι τῆς ἴσης τιμῆς). The analogy to the situation in his own time is striking, and furthermore the wording itself closely resembles that figuring in *In Flaccum*, 46-47, and *Legatio*, 281-282. Thus from his point of view the Jewish "colony" deserved "equal status" (ἰσοτιμία)[19] with other "colonies". A similar judgement is discernible in *De Conf. Ling.*, 77-78 in his comments on biblical passages dealing with "stranger and sojourner". There Philo rose to philosophical heights in noting that the Heavens were not a "colony" for the souls of sages which ascended to there. On the contrary, for them

---

18 An instructive definition of ἀποικία: "Die griechische Colonie ... ist ein Niderlassung von Griechen in fremden Lande, die ein selbstttädiges Staatswesen, eine Politie (= πολιτεία) bildet, unhabhängig von der Mutterstadt und eine neues Bürgrecht begründet" etc., (*RE(PW)*, I, p. 2852). See also Busolt, *Griechische Staatkunde*, vol. 1, p. 229.

19 That is, an equal position as an independent body, and not equality within that same organized body. It should be noted that Philo used the same terminology as Josephus.

"the heavenly region where they live as citizens (ἐν ᾧ πολιτεύονται)[20] is their homeland (πατρίς); the earthly region in which they became sojourners is a foreign country. For surely a colony (ἀποικία) for immigrants is a host homeland (ἡ ὑποδεξαμένη πατρίς) substituting for the *metropolis*, but to the travellers abroad the *metropolis* is a place they yearn to return to."

Probably that description too was based on political concepts Philo had formulated, and the expressions, wording and import are remarkably like those in his historical works. Thus the true meaning of "homeland" in *In Flaccum*, 46 is undoubtedly "host homeland" or "second homeland" (δεύτερα πατρίς)[21], in contrast to the genuine original one, which was and always will be Jerusalem. That conception was rooted in the Roman outlook as well, as expressed by Cicero[22], to which Philo's view was amazingly similar. Alexandria, then, was not a Greek *polis* that Philo construed as a "homeland". He did not claim citizenship in it, and on one occasion in dealing with a contemporary matter stated explicitly that the Jews and "the rest of the population" in the city did not have a common "homeland" (*De Somniis*, II 124). In other words, Alexandria could be considered a "homeland" only in the political sense, for it was a place in which a Jewish "colony" — organized as a separate ethnic union with a recognized political and legal status (*politeuma*) — had been established.

Another Philo passage — *De Vita Mosis*, I 34-36 — is even more illuminating (it was Wolfson who first pointed out the relationship between the terminology there and that applicable to the civic status of the Alexandria Jews)[23]. Here too Philo projected the legal and political terms of his day on to the earlier situation. In analyzing the circumstances of the Jews who went to Egypt before Moses, he wrote:

---

20 To be more exact, "carry on political life in it."

21 Cf. *De Vita Mosis*, I 34; this report is discussed further below. It is interesting that in the remains of a Jewish inscription from Phrygia the term *patris* refers to the city of Acmonia, see Ramsay, *Cities and Bishoprics*, vol. 2, No. 561 (pp. 651-652). In regard to Leontopolis and Alexandria, see pp. 127f., 204 above.

22 "unmquid duas habetis patrias? an est una illa patria communis? nisi forte sapienti illi Catoni fuit patria non Roma, sed Tusculum. Marcus: Ego me hercule et illi et omnibus municipiis duas esse censeo patrias, unam naturae alteram civitatis, ut ille Cato, quom esset Tusculi natus, in populi Romani civitatem susceptis est, ita quom orto Tusculanus esset, civitate Romanus, habuit alteram loci patriam, alteram iuris" (Cicero, *De Legibus*, III 2, 15). From the foregoing, a distinction between a "natural homeland" and a "judicial homeland" or "civic homeland" can be discerned.

23 Wolfson, *JBL*, 63 (1949), pp. 165-168, and cf. also idem, *Philo*, vol. 2, pp. 399ff.

"The Jews, as I have said before, were strangers (ξένοι)... They were, in a sense, suppliants, who had found a sanctuary in the pledged faith of the king and the pity felt for them by the inhabitants. For strangers, in my judgement, must be regarded as suppliants of those who receive them, and not only suppliants, but settlers (μάτοικοι) and friends who are anxious to obtain equal rights with the burgesses (σπεύδοντες εἰς ἀστῶν ἰσοτιμίαν) and are near to being citizens (γειτνιῶντες ἤδη πολίταις) because they differ little from the original inhabitants (οἱ αὐτόχθονες). So then these strangers, who had left their own country and come to Egypt hoping to live there in safety as in a second fatherland (δευτέρᾳ πατρίδι) were made slaves by the ruler of the country and reduced to the condition of captives taken by the custom of war, or persons purchased from the masters in whose household they had been bred. And in thus making serfs of men who were not only free (οἱ ἐλεύθεροι) but guests, suppliants and settlers, he showed no shame or fear of the God of liberty and hospitality and of justice to guests and suppliants Who watches over such as these." (trans. F.H. Colson, *LCL* ed.)

Wolfson believed that the passage above faithfully reflected the political status of the Jews of Alexandria in Philo's day. They were represented as deserving to be *politai*, that is, to have an intermediate status between *astoi* and *laoi*. And since the *astoi* were citizens of the *polis*, the *politai* in this context were members of the Jewish *politeia* (= *politeuma*).

Although correct in his approach, by mistakenly identifying the "original inhabitants" (αὐτόχθονες) with the Egyptian "natives" (λαοί) Wolfson failed accurately to discern the civic status of the Jews as indicated in the passage, and consequently placed the Jews in an intermediate position between the *laoi* and the *astoi*[24]. While this view is ostensibly tenable, an examination of the use of the word αὐτόχθονες in various other Philo passages reveals that it was applied to the more high-born people, namely aristocrats (εὐπατρίδες)[25], in other words, it referred to the *astoi*. It would therefore be more exact to say that according to the passage, the *politai* were an intermediate class between *astoi* and *metoikoi*. Keeping in mind Applebaum's thesis regarding the legal problem that arose in connection with requiring the Jews of Cyrene to pay the *metoikion* tax[26], it

---

24 Cf. also Smallwood's opinion, p. 9. Actually, it qas Bludau (*Juden und Judenverfolgungen*, p. 19) who first proposed this idea, but not in connection with the report of Philo under consideration here, cf. also H. St. Jones, *JRS*, XVI, p. 29; Ostersetzer, *Broda Jubilee Volume*, pp. 21, 26, 35.

25 See, e.g., *De Spec. Leg.*, I 52. Philo discusses the problem of "in-comers" (ἐπηλύται) that is in essence similar to the problem under consideration here, especially since he bases himself on the verse "you were strangers in the land of Egypt," in reference to which the report discussed here was written. And cf. *De Cherubim*, 120. It is interesting that Wolfson himself identified the "autochthons" with the original "citizens" who are referred to elsewhere (*Philo*, II p. 355).

26 Applebaum, *Jews and Greeks*, pp. 184-185, and see p. 288 and n.86 below.

seems clear that the Philo passage reflects a similar situation. In both places there was a question of whether the Jews should be defined as *metoikoi* or *politai*. If they were the former, they would have to pay tax to the *polis*, which they were extremely dependent on. If however they were *politai*, they were organized in a recognized body with specific privileges (a *politeuma*) directly subordinate to the central government rather than to the *polis*. It is only natural that the lack of clarity on this matter should have resulted in a fundamental conflict that produced literary polemics, judicial disputes, street confrontations and bloodshed.

Philo's historical testimony (*In Flaccum*, 53; *Legatio*, 371) cast light on the term "our *politeia*" from another angle. The first and most important component of the *politeia* related to "ancestral customs" (τὰ πάτρια) or "special laws". (τὰ ἐξαίρετα νόμιμα). These terms and others like them are frequent in Philo's writings[27]. As the right to keep ancestral laws was a basic element in the legitimate ethnic-religious associations like the *politeuma*, that right is of help in identifying those associations. In any case, Philo's repeated explicit statements on the point show that in his view it was the juridical basis for the existence of the Jewish community in Alexandria and, as will be seen below, his chief concern as the community's official spokesman.

The second element of the formula relates to the "civic rights" (or the "political rights" — τὰ πολιτικὰ δίκαια) of the Jews. At first glance this seems like quite an obscure theoretical generalization, but an examination of Philo's writings reveals that it is possible to define its actual content, rooted in the juridical conditions of Egypt.

One of the most celebrated rights concerned the matter of flogging. In Egypt of that time, the type of punishment for crime depended on the civic stratification of the offender, and one of the chief authorities for that conclusion is Philo's testimony on the different

---

27 a) τὰ πάτρια – *In Flaccum*, 47; *Legatio*, 117, 153, 208, 215, 232, 240, 249, 306, 313, 327.
  b) ἔθη πάτρια – *In Flaccum*, 52-53; *Legatio*, 300.
  c) τὰ ('Ιουδαϊκὰ) ἔθη – *In Flaccum*, 48, 50; *Legatio*, 115, 134, 161, 170, 360.
  d) οἱ νόμοι (τῶν 'Ιουδαίων) – *In Flaccum*, 52-53, 97, 117; *Legatio*, 115, 134, 195, 210, 240, 279, 332.
  e) τα ('Ιουδαϊκὰ) νόμιμα – *In Flaccum*, 50; *Legatio*, 152-153, 159, 161, 240, 256, 322, 369, 371.

way Egyptian natives and "Alexandrians" were flogged[28]. While he says (*In Flaccum*, 80) that Jewish criminals were flogged "more suggestive of free men and citizens" (ταῖς ἐλευθεριωτέραις καὶ πολιτικωτέραις), that does not mean he considered the Jews citizens of the *polis* of Alexandria. In fact the expression "in relation to us too" (καὶ ἐπὶ τῶν ἡμετέρων) in that connection (*ibid.*, 79) suggests that they were not included in that category[29]. According to the passage, there were two types of flogging "by the social standing (τὰ ἀξιώματα) of the persons to be beaten" (*ibid.*; 78) and the type inflicted on the Jews was a sign of their honorable status. The use of the comparative form of adjectives (ἐλευθεριωτέραις, πολιτικωτέραις) reinforces that impression, as it concerned the way they were flogged and not the definition of their status as citizens of the *polis*. It was in this way that Philo presented Flaccus as a person who flouted accepted customs and laws[30]. Not without reason did he castigate

---

28 *In Flaccum*, 78-80: "There are differences between the scourges used in the city, and these differences are regulated by the social standing (τὰ ἀξιώματα) of the persons to be beaten. The Egyptians actually are scourged with a different kind of lash and by a different set of people, the Alexandrians with a flat blade, and the persons who wield them also are Alexandrians. This custom was observed in the case of our people (ἐπὶ τῶν ἡμετέρων) by the predecessors of Flaccus and by Flaccus himself in the first years of office. For it is surely possible when inflicting degradation (ἀτιμία) on others to find some little thing to sustain their dignity (ἐπιτιμία), or when wantonly mistreating them, to find some accompaniment to counteract the wantonness... Surely then it was the height of harshness that when commoners among the Alexandrian Jews (τῶν ἰδιωτῶν Ἀλεξανδρέων Ἰουδαίων) if they appeared to have done a thing worthy of stripes, were beaten with whips more suggestive of freemen and citizens (ταῖς ἐλευθεριωτέραις καὶ πολιτικωτέραις), the magistrates (τοὺς ἄρχοντας), the Senate (τὴν γερουσίαν), whose very name implies age and honour, in this respect fared worse than their inferiors and were treated like Egyptians of the meanest rank and guilty of the greatest iniquities" (trans. F.H. Colson, *LCL*, ed.) See Box, pp. 103-104; Westermann, *RE(PW)*, Suppl. VI, p. 1052. It appears that Philo's distinction between the two kinds of flogging is based on the Roman practice of differentiating between punishment by the *virga* (rod for beating) or *fustis* (stock, staff, cudgel), and punishment by means of the *flagellum* (whip, scourge). See Th. Momsen, *Röm. Strafricht*, p. 983. It should be noted in this context that the Jerusalem Talmud also distinguished between בעל הזמורה, בעל האגמון and בעל הרצועה (*J.T. Sotah*, IX 24b), and apparently the reference is to the Roman practice and the terms noted above.

29 This reasoning appears to invalidate Momigliano's opinion (*Emperor Claudius*, p. 96, n.25) that the Jews were citizens of the *polis* according to Philo's report — *In Flaccum*, 80; see also Engers, *Klio*, 18 (1922/3), p. 85; Weber, *Hermes*, 50 (1915), p. 62; Premerstein, *Hermes*, 57 (1922), p. 300; Fuchs, p. 94; Tcherikover, *Hellenistic Civilization and the Jews*, pp. 316-317.

30 He accused him, e.g., of not putting off the punishment of the Jews, as custom dictated

him for inflicting "degradation" (ἀτιμία)[31] on the thirty-eight Jewish
gerontes and three Jewish archontes, which was contrary to the custom (τὸ ἔθος) followed in the past and by himself as well. In other
words, Flaccus was accused of ignoring the rank of the victims, the
fact that they were politai with their own politeia, and in this case
even gerontes and archontes whose eminence was unquestionable.
The relationship of the Jews to the "civic law" system, clearly shown
in papyrological literature, verifies what was said here, and confirms
beyond all doubt the existence of Jewish politai. That system of laws
defined what Philo called "their political rights" (τὰ πολιτικὰ δίκαια)
and their "social standing" (τὰ ἀξιώματα). On that basis they enjoyed "participation in political rights" (In Flaccum, 54) or "general
rights vis-à-vis each individual city" (Legatio, 371), that is, rights
common to Jews and members of other associations who were like
them in being politai. Examination of the Philo testimony from this
angle eliminates the question of whether or not the Jews of Alexandria were citizens of the polis.

The same sort of test should be applied to Flaccus' proclamation
(πρόγραμμα) which defined the Jews as "foreigners and aliens"
(ξένοι καὶ ἐπήλυδες; In Flaccum, 54). Engers admitted that the terms
might at first glance be understood to mean the opposite of politai,
but in In Flaccum, 172, felt that they would better be considered to
mean katoikoi[32]. Indeed the remorseful statement attributed to
Flaccus — "I cast on them the slur that they were foreigners without civic rights, though they were inhabitants with full franchise"
(ὠνείδισά ποτε ἀτιμίαν καὶ ξενιτείαν αὐτοῖς ἐπιτίμοις οὖσι κατοίκοις
— trans. by F.H. Colson, LCL ed.) — implies that just as "disgrace"
(ἀτιμία), namely, being deprived of civic rights, is contrary to their
status of possessing "full franchise" (ἐπιτίμια), their "foreignness"
(ξενιτεία) is contrary to their status as "inhabitants" (κάτοικοι).
However, Engers' original impression hit on the truth, for "possessors
of civic rights" (ἐπίτιμοι) is equivalent to politai, while ἄτιμοι is the

---

in view of the celebration of the emperor's birthday. See In Flaccum, 74, 81-84. For
details of this custom see Box, p. 105; Blumenthal, Archiv, 5 (1909-1913), p. 336f.;
Bell, Jews and Christians, p. 32.

31 It is accepted that ἀτιμία means the loss of all civil rights, and that ἄτιμος is like an
enemy (see Liddell and Scott, s.v.). The antonyms of these terms are ἐπιτίμια and
ἐπίτιμος, and their use by Philo is discussed below.

32 Engers, Klio, 18 (1922/3), p. 83f.

opposite. Thus Flaccus expresses regret for having deprived the Jews of their status as both *politai* and *katoikoi*. The statement may contain an indication of the lack of legal clarity in the status of the Jews (that is, between *metoikoi* and *politai*) as in the case of the Jews of Cyrene. The same situation applied to the Jews of Sardis who according to Josephus (*Antiquitates*, XIV 259) were described in a resolution passed by the local citizens as οἱ κατοικοῦντες ἡμῶν ἐν τῇ πόλει Ἰουδαῖοι πολῖται[33]. Here too there is an apparent contradiction between κατοικοῦντες and πολῖται, but it is only apparent, because the *politai* here are not citizens of the *polis* but are Jewish *politai*, namely, members of the Jewish *politeuma* who were "permanent residents" of the city, separately organized from the *polis*. And indeed, the resolution of the Sardis citizens used the word πολιτεύωνται to describe the right of the Jews to conduct their own political (civic) life[34]. The same is true of the Hierapolis Jewish community which in one inscription is designated as "the *katoikia* of the Jewish residents of Hierapolis" (ἡ κατοικία τῶν ἐν Ἰεραπόλει κατακούντων Ἰουδαίων; *CIJ*, II 775). There is no redundancy in the use of the terms κατοικία and κατοικοῦντες, for the first describes the way the community was organized — retaining the trace of its origin as a military settlement — while the second describes the simple fact that the Jews were permanent residents of the city.

Flaccus' declaration that the Jews of Alexandria were "foreigners and aliens" must be interpreted as persecution in the full sense of the word, for until its publication they were not so counted[35]. Its pur-

---

33 Cf. similar terminology in connection with organizations of Roman citizens in Hellenistic cities of Asia Minor (above, p. 183).

34 See *Antiquitates*, XIV 260; and Marcus's comment (Marcus, *Josephus*, vol. 8, p. 589, n.b.) should be cited: "The reference is to the organization of the Jewish community (*politeuma*) in Sardis."

35 Cf. Philo, *Legatio*, 350, which notes that the Jewish question was not discussed for four hundred years, only raised for the first time in a legal forum in his time. Contrary to the opinion of Heinemann (*RE(PW)*, Suppl. V, p. 9f.), the plots against the Jews had a definitely religious character and recall to a great extent the religious persecutions of Antiochus Epiphanes. The following examples show this: a) Forcing women to eat pork (*In Flaccum*, 95-96) as a means of identifying Jewish women (the means of identifying Jewish men may be easily guessed by reference to Suetonius, *Domitianus*, 12); b) Cancellation of the Feast of Tabernacles (*In Flaccum*, 116f.); c) Deliberate restriction of Sabbath-keeping (*De Somniis*, II 123f.); d) Desecration of synagogue, their seizure, and the placing of icons of the emperor in them (*In Flaccum*, 41-43, 45, 47-53; *Legatio*, 132-139, 165, 191, 335, 346); e) Encouragement of Jew-hatred on grounds of the Jews' opposi-

pose was to negate the basis of the existing Jewish *politeia*, that is, to cancel the right of the Jews to live permanently in the city and form their own political organizational union. Furthermore, the declaration actually outlawed them by making it possible to treat them and their property as if they were enemies, allowing them no defense[36]. The logical progression of the persecution in two stages is readily discernible. First the Jewish *politeia* was abolished, and a few days later (*In Flaccum*, 54), the Jews were accorded a new status. The object of the exercise was to turn the Jews over to the Alexandrian *polis*, as it had specifically requested (*ibid.*, 23, 172). The fact that the order was given by the prefect is a definite indication that the rights of the Jews derived not from the authority of the *polis*, but from the central government. The abolition of the Jewish *politeia* meant the intentional recognition of the Alexandrian *politeia* as having the exclusive right to authority in the city. Consequently the Jews were no longer recognized as an organized group with political privileges, and being "foreigners and aliens" they were handed over to the *polis* (as individuals) for good or for evil.

One of the most interesting applications of the term *politeia*, figuring in *Legatio*, 194, may clarify the problem of Jewish rights from another angle. There Philo proffered an argument that was axiomatic for him. He and his delegation, he claimed, could not be expected to fight for the rights of the Jews in Alexandria while the existence of "the more general *politeia* of the Jews" (ἡ καθολικωτέρα πολιτεία τῶν Ἰουδαίων) was imperiled. Little attention has been paid to this phrase, though Smallwood entertained the notion that it might be a reference to the various political rights enjoyed by many Jewish communities in the Diaspora, while she admitted that it was a "compressed expression" or a "puzzling phrase, since there was no single and universal πολιτεία embracing all the Jews in the empire"[37]. Philo's own words clarify the matter, for he explicitly stated that "the more general *politeia* of the Jews" was jeopardized by Caligula's idolatry edict. Philo's original mission was to submit two claims

tion to the emperor cult (*Legatio*, 115-120, 133, 169-177, 268, 335, 346, 353, 355, 361-362).

36 *In Flaccum*, 54, 56; and cf. *ibid.*, 62f., 94f.

37 Smallwood, p. 258. See the reasoned objections of Pelletier, *Legatio ad Caium*, p. 204, n.3.

(ὑποθέσεις) to the emperor, which were outlined in a short general
memorandum (γραμματεῖον) and a more detailed petition. They
touched on two matters, the suffering of the Jews of Alexandria,
and their demands of the authorities[38]. Both of the claims can be
said to aim at what Philo described as "our *politeia*" which was
essentially based on two components, "ancestral customs" and
"participation in political rights". As in Philo's view Caligula's edict
eliminated the possibility of keeping "ancestral customs" (see
Legatio, 191ff.) the campaign could deal only with the second component, "participation in political rights". Philo rejected that possibility, however, for under those conditions the campaign would be
tantamount to heresy (*ibid.*, 193). That is not surprising, since for
him "ancestral customs" were the main element of the Jewish *politeia*
in Alexandria. Consequently when that was invalidated, the second
lost its validity as well (*ibid.*, 195). Because of Caligula's idolatry
edict, Philo considered his mission a "private matter" (ἰδίου τινος)
secondary to "the general interests" (τῶν ὅλλων) that were being
threatened. As he said, "It is essential that we subordinate minor
matters to important ones, and the interests of the few to those of
the whole nation, since the loss of the latter means the overthrow
of our *politeia*" (*ibid.*, 193; trans. E.M. Smallwood). In his view the
relation between private and public matters exactly paralleled the
relation between "one part of the Jewish people (μέρει τοῦ Ἰουδαϊκοῦ)
and "the whole nation collectively" (συλλήβδην ἅπαντι τῷ ἔθνει;
Legatio, 184; cf. *In Flaccum*, 1). In other words, the Jewish community in Alexandria was only "one part of the Jewish people",
representing a local *politeia*. On the other hand the people in Palestine together with the Jewish communities in the Diaspora constituted
"the whole nation collectively" representing a "more general *politeia*"
to which the "name common to the whole nation" (τὸ κοινὸν τοῦ
ἔθνον ὄνομα) is applied[39]. Its validity was symbolized by the Temple

---

38 *Legatio*, 178-179, 195. Although unfortunately Philo did not quote the contents of the
   memorandum, it can be inferred from various hints in his *Legatio ad Gaium*. Understandably the first subject dealt mainly with religious persecution and the suffering it caused,
   and the second subject presented the demands of the Jews to maintain political rights.
   For a fairly exhaustive discussion, see Colson, *Philo*, vol. 10, Intr., p. XXVIf.
39 *Legatio*, 194. See Wolfson, *Philo*, vol. 2, pp. 397ff. By association, this may have an indirect
   implication in regard to the term "Alexandrian Jews" frequent in Philo's writings. It
   appears that its first element, "Jews," refers to "the name common to the whole nation,"

in Jerusalem and was conditional on the existence of the latter
(*Legatio*, 194). The reference was not to a uniform imperial *politeia*
that was formulated by law, but rather to the basic element of all
Jewish *politeias*, the right to worship as their forefathers had, and
maintain ancestral customs (through the connection with Jerusalem).
That does not mean, of course, that all Jewish communities enjoyed
the same specific rights, for these certainly varied according to local
legal and practical traditions[40].

Various other passages in Philo indicate that the Jewish community
as an organized body was separate from the *polis*. In *In Flaccum*,
43, he clearly distinguished between two different sectors in Alexandria, noting that "the city had two kinds of inhabitants, us and them"
(ἡ πόλις οἰκήτορας ἔχει διττούς, ἡμᾶς καὶ τούτους). He also used the
expression "the rest of the city" (οἱ πρὸς τὴν ἄλλη πόλιν) to describe the non-Jewish of Alexandria[41]. Accordingly the Jews were
designated as "their own countrymen" or more precisely, "their own
politai" (τῶν ἰδίων πολῖτων) while the others were termed "those

---

while the second element, "Alexandrians," indicated only the name of the community,
which represented only "one section of the Jewish people" (ἐνὶ μέρει τοῦ Ἰουδαϊκοῦ,
ibid., 184). A similar approach is found in the symbolic description of the High Priest
(*De Spec. Leg.*, III 131): "The whole nation has a kinsman and close relative common to
all in the high priest, who as a ruler dispenses justice to litigants according to the law,
who day by day offers prayers and sacrifices and asks for blessings, as for his brothers
and parents and children, that every age and every part of the nation as a single body
(πάντα μέρη τοῦ ἔθνους ὡς ἑνὸς σώματος εἰς μίαν) may be united in one and the
same fellowship, making peace and good order their aim." This idea of partnership and
unity of communities of one religion is also expressed in Christian thought, see I *Corinthians*, 12:12f.; and see Baer, *Zion*, 15 (1950), p. 13f.; Juster, (vol. 2, p. 166f.) collected many examples from ancient literature showing the existence of a feeling of frater-
nity and common destiny among Jews of the Diaspora. Cf. also Willrich, *Haus des
Herodes*, p. 66f.; Heinemann, *RE(PW)*, Suppl. V., p. 12f.

40 This is clearly indicated, e.g., from the inscription on a tombstone from the city of Tlos
in Lycia (placed on the lintel of the entrance to the gravesite) which states that the tomb
"shall be the property of the Jews and if anyone will bury there, he will have to pay a
fine to the people of Tlos of −? − drachmas" (*CIJ*, II 758 − the first century C.E.). In
contrast, on two gravestones from Hierapolis in Phrygia the fine is to be paid to "the
katoikia of the Jews residing in Hierapolis" or to "the Jewish community" (λαός) (see
CIJ, II 755-6 − from the second and third centuries C.E.). In Nicomedia in Bithynia, on
the other hand, payment was to the synagogue of the Jews and to the Roman treasury
(*CIJ*, II 799). This shows that although in each place the details of the rights were different, yet they were all based on one basic privilege.
41 *In Flaccum*, 76; cf. 139, and also "the other public" − ἡ ἄλλη πληθύς − *De Somn.*, II
124.

of another tribe" (ἀλλόφυλοι)[42]. The distinction made between the citizens of the *polis* and the Jews is clear in the passage on flogging (*In Flaccum*, 78-80) particularly in the phrase "and also in relation to us" (καὶ ἐπὶ τῶν ἡμετέρων) as already indicated above[43].

The concentration of the majority of Jews in particular neighborhoods of their own reinforces the conclusion that they had a separate organization, very like a *landsmannschaft*. Quite a few Jews were of course scattered throughout the city, but two of the five sections of the city were known as Jewish quarters, because of their Jewish population[44]. Josephus (*Bellum*, II 495; *C. Apionem*, II 33-36) has made it possible to identify and locate one of these, known as "Delta". Strabo too (cited in Josephus, *Antiquitates*, XIV 117) noted that "In Alexandria a large part of the city was allocated to this nation" (trans. R. Marcus, *LCL* ed.), but does not specify whether that "part" was one quarter or more, and his "large part" (μέγα μέρος) may not be identical with Philo's "two quarters" (δύο μοῖραι). In any case, Tcherikover's attempt to apply Strabo's testimony to the Delta quarter alone does not accord with the information in Philo and required rather a tortuous interpretation[45]. The division of the city into separate residential sections is indicated by Philo in several places[46]. Papyrological evidence too shows that the metro-

---

42 *Legatio*, 211. Wolfson proposed understanding the term "tribe" (ψυλή) here as one of the tribes of citizens in Alexandria (*Philo*, vol. 2, p. 398, n.13) but his proposal is based purely on association.

43 Pp. 240-241 and nn.28-29. And cf. *In Flaccum* 96 where there is a similar usage (ἡμέτεραι) in regard to Jewish women who were attacked during the riots of 38 C.E.

44 *In Flaccum*, 55 (cf. 62). The designation of the city quarters with letters of the Greek alphabet was reported by Pseudo-Calisthenes (I 32, 9), and see more details in Fraser, vol. 1, p. 34f. According to Diodorus Siculus (XVII 52, 6) the "free" population of Alexandria in the first century B.C.E. was more than 300.000. As *In Flaccum*, 55 supplies quite a firm basis for assessing the Jewish share in Alexandrian "free" population, the relative proportion probably exceeded the number of 120,000 (i.e. ⅖ of 300.000) Jews. If Diodorus referred to males only, the real figures must have been approximately one million for the total population and 400,000 for the Jews. It is difficult to accept or reject these numbers because the data at our disposal is quite poor. The same is to be said about the figures of one million Jews resident in Egypt given by Philo (*ibid.*, 43) and 7½ millions of the total Egyptian population (excluding Alexandria) given by Josephus (*Bellum*, II 385). Indeed, these are clearly imprecise figures, but there are no better ones as yet. See: Box, p. 94; Juster, I, p. 209, Baron, *Social and Religious History*, I, p. 170; Stern, 'The Jewish Diaspora', pp. 119, 122-3; idem, *Enc. Judaica*, VI (1971), p. 9; Fraser, I, pp. 90-92; II, pp. 164 (n.315), 171-2 (n.358).

45 See *CPJ*, II, p. 2, n.2.

46 See *In Flaccum*, 62, 73, 144; *Legatio*, 124, 127-128, 132. See also Smallwood, p. 215f.

politan cities in the Egyptian *chora* were divided into administrative-
topographical units, or "quarters" (ἄμφοδα), and here and there these
had clearly ethnic characters, such as in Arsinoe, Oxyrhynchus and
Memphis[47]. The Jews formed part of that picture like other ethnic
groups. The Delta quarter in Apollinopolis Magna, for instance, was
Jewish, and Oxyrhynchus had a section known as "the Jewish quarter"[48]. There is evidence as well of Jewish lanes (or streets —λαῦραι)
withi:. non-Jewish quarters[49]. A similar situation may have obtained
in Alexandria (not only in regard to Jews), and if so, that is confirmation from a different angle of Tarn's thesis on the city as a collection of *politeumata*. Furthermore, Philo's testimony on Jews spread
throughout the city and not confined to Jewish neighborhoods
accords with what is known of the situation in the metropolitan
cities. However, the Jewish "streets" in the non-Jewish parts of the
city must also have been organized in the *landsmannschaft* fashion,
for it would be hard otherwise to explain the spread of synagogues all
over the city (*Legatio*, 132), which must have served the Jewish
population in their vicinity[50]. Thus the Jewish quarter of Alexandria
cannot by any means be considered a *ghetto*. Residence in a separate
ethnic quarter was a privilege granted by the Ptolemaic kings, and the
Jews were no different from other ethnic groups in this respect[51].

On the basis of an associative analogy involving the number 5,
some scholars have posited identity between the five quarters of
Alexandria and the five tribes mentioned in *P. Hibeh.*, I 28 (205
B.C.E.)[52]. It is by no means certain, however, that the document

47 See chap. 3 above, pp. 139, 145, 150-151.
48 On Appolinopolis Magna see *CPJ*, II, Section IX, p. 108f.; on Oxyrhynchus, see *CPJ*,
    II 423; and see p. 150 above.
49 See *CPJ*, III 468, 485, and cf. No. 454.
50 The discovery of an inscription from a synagogue in the western part of the city, in
    today's Gabbari area, seems to corroborate this (*CIJ*, II 1432 = *OGIS*, 742). It is reason-
    able to assume that this synagogue was established close to Jewish places of employment
    in the neighborhood of Eunostos Bay and the port of Kibotos. Cf. Fraser, vol. 1, p. 56;
    vol. 2, p. 140, n.152.
51 On the view that the Jewish quarter was a "ghetto", see Willrich, *Klio*, 3 (1903), p. 406;
    Balsdon, *Emperor Gaius*, pp. 132-133; Bludau, *Juden und Judenverfolgungen*, p. 12;
    Wilcken, *Antisemitismus*, p. 788, n. 8; Wilcken-Mitteis, vol. 1, p. 24; Jouguet, p. 19.
    For contrary opinions, see Juster, vol. 2, p. 177f., Fuchs, p. 104f. ;Bell, *JRS*, 31 (1941),
    p. 1; Stern, *Greek an Latin Authors*, p. 399.
52 See, e.g., Jouguet, p. 11; cf. Schubart, *Archiv*, 5 (1909-13), pp. 92, 140; Fraser, vol. 1,
    p. 39f.

refers to Alexandria[53]. Secondly, if the reference is in fact to Alexandria, we would have to agree, taking Philo's testimony into account, that two of the five urban tribes were Jewish. That would make it impossible to avoid the conclusion that the Jews were involved in the tribal system of the *polis*, and were citizens of it, a conclusion that even the same scholars were reluctant to draw[54]. The difficulty can be circumvented only if it is argued that the five tribes were not identifiable with the five urban quarters, or that such an equivalence did not apply in the period from 265 B.C.E. to Philo's time, due to government intervention[55]. The testimony of both Philo and Josephus seem to be grounds enough for concluding that the two Jewish neighborhoods were separate and well-defined units, with no relation to the tribal divisions of the *polis*.

Although it is hard to locate all the Jewish residential areas precisely, quite a lot of information is available on the location of the quarter that Josephus termed Delta (*Bellum*, II 495). It has generally been agreed that his topographical descriptions (*C. Apionem*, II 33-36) fit the northeastern part of Alexandria, near the sea shore, east of the royal palace in Lochias[56], on the basis of Strabo's data (XVII 1, 9)[57]. The discovery of Jewish gravestones (from the early Hellenistic period) in the El-Ibrahimiya cemetery three kilometers northeast of the city[58] supports locating the Jewish quarter in that vicinity. Philo's descriptions too fit that area. In *In Flaccum*, 55-56, he noted that the Jews were forced by their enemies into "a most

53 See *The Hibeh Papyri*, vol. 1, pp. 157-158. Jouguet (p. 10) and Fraser (*ibid.*) agreed with this explanation.
54 See, e.g., Jouguet, p. 19; Fraser, vol. 1, p. 55.
55 Fraser (*ibid.*) thought that the residential areas of the Jews were recognized as Jewish quarters only in the time of Ptolemy VI Philometor, their patron, and he may be right.
56 From Apion's provocative words it appears that the Jews "settled by a sea without a harbour, close beside the spot where the waves break on the beach" (trans. Thackeray, *LCL*, ed.). Later, in his response, Josephus emphasizes that "the seaboard forms part of the city and is, by universal consent, its finest residential quarter." He also complains about Apion: "I do not know what Apion would have said if the Jews had been quartered in the neighbourhood not of the palace, but of the necropolis!" The necropolis was at the end of the city, while the royal palace lay near the eastern part of the port.
57 See, e.g., Breccia, *Alexandria ad Aegyptum*, p. 57; and cf. Zogheb, *Études*, pp. 9-10; H.L. Jones, *Strabo*, vol. 8, p. 32, n.3; Thackeray, *Josephus*, vol. 1, p. 304; Puchstein, *RE(PW)*, I, p. 1388. Full topographical details of Alexandria can be found in Fraser, vol. 1, p. 7f.
58 Breccia, *op.cit.*, pp. 82-83; Fraser, vol. 1, p. 57; vol. 2, p. 141, n.165.

narrow quarter" (ἑνὸς μοῖραν βρχυτάτην) and because of their great
numbers "they poured out over beaches, dunghills and tombs". In
another place (*Legatio*, 127-128)) he stated that they were pushed
"into a very small part" of the city (*ibid.*, 124), "into a confined
space on the edge of the city" (*ibid.*, 128) where they felt "terribly
choked" (*ibid.*, 125) and then "overflowed on to the desert, the
shores and the cemetery" (*ibid.*, 127, trans. E.M. Smallwood). The
mention of the cemetery tends to be misleading because it might be
misconstrued to refer to the western part of the city. But Philo used
the term μνήματα rather than νεκρόπολις, and they should not be
interpreted as indicating the same place. For east of the city was a
whole valley of graves from the Ptolemaic period, and Philo was
undoubtedly referring to that area. The impression from *In Flaccum*,
74, is that the procession of the Jewish leaders to the theatre located
near the Jewish quarter wended its way through the main streets of
Alexandria so that their humiliation could be seen. Probably they
proceeded southwards to the splendid Canopic street that went the
length of Alexandria from east to west, marched westwards to the
museum area, there turned north to the Emporium, and then east to
the theatre[59]. That route traversed the most important sites in the
city, and was suitable for such a procession. Another indication that
the Jewish quarter was in the eastern part of the city was the fact
that the Jews were near the "camp" (τὸ στρατόπεδον) of the "night
watch" (νυκτοφυλάκες) so close to the royal palace that they clearly
heard the soldiers and cavalry bustling about when Flaccus was
arrested (*In Flaccum*, 120). The proximity of the quarter to the
gymnasium (reported in *Legatio*, 134-135) likewise confirms its
location in the eastern part of the city[60]. It should be noted also
that some of the Alexandrian papyri from the Augustan period
found at Abusir el-Meleq (published in *BGU*, IV) refer to Jews and
mention two city quarters designated as Beta and Delta[61], which may

---

59 Cf. *In Flaccum*, 84-85, 95; *Legatio*, 131.

60 The gymnasium lay south of the hippodrome in the eastern part of the city center.
   The pulling of Cleopatra's chariot to the Great Synagogue is described as a hasty and
   spontaneous action, so it must be concluded that the synagogue was near the gymnasium.
   This fact may very well explain the Jewish-Greek tension and the Jewish harassment of
   the gymnasium, as is indicated in the analysis of Glaudius' Letter to the Alexandrians
   below. It is interesting that archaeological excavations in Sardis revealed the proximity
   of the gymnasium and the synagogue in that city as well.

61 *CPJ*, II 142-149.

mean that Jews were connected with those quarters. However, one of these documents (*BGU*, IV 1151, verso II, line 40) contians topographical data indicating that the Delta quarter was in the western part of the city, contrary to both Josephus and Philo. Fraser suggested that the only possible explanation was that a change had been made in the numeration of the quarters between the time of Augustus and that of Philo and Josephus[62]. As to the second, unnmamed, Jewish quarter mentioned by Philo, if it was the Beta quarter it was in the center of the city[63].

The separate character of the Jewish communities in Egypt, including that of Alexandria, is shown also in regard to tax collection. In his commentary on Deuteronomy 24:16 — "The fathers shall not be put to death for the children, neither shall the children be put to death for the fathers; every man shall be put to death for his own sin" — Philo cited a story of his own time beginning "Recently a tax collector was appointed with us" (*De Spec. Leg.*, III 159f.). The story was designed to condemn the reprehensible practice long prevalent in Egypt of imposing collective responsibility in tax collection[64]. The term "with us" ($\pi\alpha\rho'$ $\dot{\eta}\mu\hat{\iota}\nu$) and to some extent the objection to collective responsibility perhaps point to the separate organization of the Jews. Unfortunately the nature of those taxes, which would certainly cast light on the legal status and organizational arrangements of the Jews, is unknown.

In *In Flaccum*, 24, the "Jews" are differentiated as a separate group from the other Alexandrians, here as legal and political rivals meriting representation. This is clear from Philo's castigation of Flaccus for refusing to hear their complaints[65], and for ignoring their equal right to speak ($\iota\sigma\eta\gamma o\rho\iota\alpha$). The fact that he summoned representatives of the two sides ostensibly to achieve a compromise between them (*In Flaccum*, 76) shows that they were both recognized and representative parties for negotiations. This is shown too by the dispatch of the Jewish delegation to Rome, as the legal opponent of the Alexandrian delegation[66].

---

62 See Fraser, vol. 2, p. 109, n.270; and cf. *ibid.*, p. 79, n.182.

63 See Fraser, vol. 1, p. 109, nn.267-268.

64 About this system, which is a heritage from the Pharaonic and Ptolemaic traditions, see, e.g., Preaux, pp. 200, 500f., (esp. p. 509). Cf. also Tarn, p. 220.

65 Cf. a similar claim about Gaius Caligula's habit in regard to the Jews, *Legatio*, 183.

66 On the Jewish delegation see the following: *Legatio*, 180f., 192, 195, 349-350, 369-371.

The right of decision ($\psi\acute{\eta}\varphi\iota\sigma\mu\alpha$) enjoyed by the Jews of Alexandria is likewise proof of separate organization[67]. That right was one of the basic ones granted to organized communities, including those forming a *politeuma*-type union[68]. At first glance it might seem from Philo's report that the decisions of the Alexandrian Jews were purely honorary in nature, but since they were restricted by limitations connected with the Jewish religion, in certain circumstances they might have had some political implications[69]. In other words, a simple honorary "decision" could acquire important political significance if it was conditional on certain principles, and the same was true of failure to make one. The fact that the Jews avoided decisions connected with the worship of Caligula disadvantaged them politically and aroused suspicions that they were politically disloyal and prone to rebellion. Their abstention could be interpreted as a decision not to decide, and thus have political motives imputed to it. On the other hand, an honorary decision of the Alexandrian *polis* could also lead to political difficulties, because of an excess of reverence, as in the deification of the emperor[70]. Indeed there are clear indications in Philo that the decisions of the Jews had a distinctly political character. This is especially evident in the "memo" sent to Caligula which specified the demands for justice (*Legatio*, 178). As the dispatch of the Jewish delegation to Rome had great political significance, it was no doubt preceded by a carefully weighed decision

---

Since the dispatch of the delegation was so important a matter, the whole work is called by that name. See full details about this in Smallwood, mainly pp. 36ff. Josephus also reported the dispatch of the delegation (*Antiquitates*, XVIII 257-260) as did Eusebius (*Historia Eccl.*, II 5f.) and others (for reports in patristic literature see Schürer, vol. 3, p. 677f.; Smallwood, ibid.). On the Alexandrian delegation see *Legatio*, 172, 349-350, 353, 355, 361-362; and cf. *Antiquitates*, XVIII 256f.; *Claudius' Letter to the Alexandrians* (*P. Lond.*, 1912, lines 75, 88) — see Tcherikover's commentary (*CPJ*, II 153, pp. 49-50; and also *CPJ*, II 155-159).

67 See *In Flaccum*, 97-101. One of the first to see this was Engers, *Klio*, 18 (1922/3), pp. 84-85.

68 See, e.g., Wilcken-Mitteis, vol. 1, p. 332, n.23.

69 That should be the approach to *In Flaccum*, 97: "We had decreed and ratified with our actions all the tributes to Gaius which were possible and were allowed by the laws and had submitted the decree to Flaccus" etc. (trans. F.H. Colson, *LCL*, ed.). Cf. also *ibid.*, 50; *Legatio,* 116-118, 154, 236, etc.

70 This can be learned from *Claudius' Letter to the Alexandrians* — *P. Lond.*, 1912 (line 20f.) — from which it appears that the emperor refused the exaggerated honors for clear political reasons.

taken in the competent, authoritative forum. The wording of the "memo" and contents of the "argument"[71] were no doubt meticulously worked out in the community institutions, for they were designed to formulate an authorized stand-point and determine courses of action and legal tactics. Such a project could be carried out only by a body with an active, functioning establishment, and decision-making authority. Moreover, the Jewish "memo" was essentially an ordinary legal petition for justice, and research has shown that in Egypt the right of group petition was granted only to organized bodies like a *polis*, a gymnasium or a *politeuma*[72]. Thus the petition and the judicial activity of a properly representative delegation constitute proof that the Jews of Alexandria were organized into a separate political body that was officially recognized.

The fact that the Jewish community of Alexandria had an establishment separate from that of the *polis* is indicated by a number of points reported by Philo:

a. The existence of the post of genarch (*In Flaccum*, 74) which was no doubt identical with that of ethnarch noted by Strabo (cited in *Antiquitates*, XIV 117)[73]. The fact that the Jews had an ethnarch of their own is illuminating in view of the existence in Egypt of non-Jewish ethnarchs[74] who evidently headed other ethnic unions.

b. The existence of a Jewish *gerousia* (*In Flaccum*, 74, 80) which Philo termed "our *gerousia*". The first-person possessive adjective is clear evidence that there was more than one *gerousia* in Alexandria, and this is confirmed by some epigraphical and papyrological material[75]. According to Philo, it was Augustus who appointed a *gerousia* for the Jews, ın his order to the prefect Magius Maximus in 11/12 C.E. In Momigliano's view, the Jewish *gerousia* had been dissolved at

---

71 See *Legatio*, 181, 195, 350, 352. It is important to note that emphases such as "the statement of your case" (τῆς ὑμετέρας ὑποθέσεως — *ibid.*, 181) or "the statement of our case" (ἡμῖν τῆς ὑποθέσεως — *ibid.*, 186) show that the other side also had its argumentations and that the formulation of the Jewish ὑπόθεσις was to a certain extent a polemical one.

72 Taubenschlag, p. 605.

73 Box's argument (p. 102) about the terms' being synonymous is fairly convincing, mainly because in a number of instances Philo uses the term γενάρχης in reference to γένος and ἔθνος at the same time. See *De Somn.*, I 167; *Q. Rev. d. Heres*, 278-9; *De Vita Mosis*, I 189; Solomon, *JQR*, 61 (1970), pp. 119-131.

74 See Strabo, XVII 1, 13 (c798). See also Schürer, vol. 3, p. 76f.; Fuchs, p. 90f.

75 See above, chap. 4, n.18.

the end of the Ptolemaic period (following deteriorating relations
with the government) and reconstituted by order of Augustus; and if
it had not been favored by the Jews, Philo would not have extolled
the measure[76]. Tcherikover, however, viewed the matter very differently. He connected the Philo testimony with the information in
Claudius' edict (*Antiquitates*, XIX 283) and argued that the latter
implied that during Aquila's prefecture the last ethnarch in the
dynasty of Jewish ethnarchs died, and thereafter Augustus prohibited the appointment of a new one, which prohibition was officially
announced during the term of the succeeding prefect, Magius
Maximus. The stress put in the edict on the fact that Augustus did
not prevent the appointment of additional ethnarchs appeared to
him to be pure apologetics aimed at refuting claims to the contrary,
and thus attributable to the "Jewish counterfeiter" of the edict[77].
As Augustus' declarations were considered decisive and binding in
regard to Jewish autonomy, Tcherikover felt that the abolition of
such an important post was contrary to the emperor's pro-Jewish
policy, and a good reason for the alteration by the "Jewish counterfeiter"[78]. However, this view is groundless, for nowhere is it stated
that the post of ethnarch was abolished or replaced by the *gerousia*.
Box's explanation is much more satisfactory. In his view, the post
remained but was included in the new *gerousia*, the ethnarch being
among the "heads of the *gerousia*" noted by Josephus (*Bellum*, VII
412), and perhaps even its president[79]. Quite possibly the down-
grading of the post was rooted in the reform whereby the authority
of the ethnarch, which had been monarchic in nature (according to
Strabo cited in *Antiquitates*, XIV 117), was considerably reduced. In
Box's view the reform was designed to appoint a collegial leadership
from among the Jewish aristocracy, and this accorded with Augustus'
general policy favoring that type of leadership rather than a monar-

---

76 See Momigliano, *JRS*, 34 (1944), p. 114; Cf. Schürer, vol. 3, p. 78; Box, pp. 102-3.

77 Tcherikover, *Hellenistic Civilization and the Jews*, pp. 412-413. Possibly he was influenced
    by Motzo, who thought a change for the worse in the status of Jews took place after the
    abolishment of the office of ethnarch, and see Motzo, *Attid. r. Accad. di Scienze di
    Torino*, 48 (1912-13), pp. 577-598.

78 *CPJ*, I (Prolegomena), p. 57, esp. n.22.

79 Box, p. 403. And cf. the introduction to the book, p. xxvif. See also Schürer, vol. 3,
    pp. 76-79, Fuchs, pp. 90-93. See also Stern, *Greek and Latin Authors*, vol. 1, pp. 280-
    281.

chistic one. And this, as Momigliano too believed, was congenial to the Jews. The exclusive rule of the ethnarch may have disturbed the members of other prestigious families in the community, who also wished to share in the leadership. The fact that some time elapsed between the death of the ethnarch (10/11 C.E. — *Antiquitates*, XIX 283) and the appointment of the *gerousia* (12 C.E. — *In Flaccum*, 74) may mean that after his death a rivalry for his post ensued, and was solved by the compromise of a collegial leadership, which was perhaps the outcome of a Jewish appeal to Augustus. If so, that would point up even more the institutional separation of the Jewish community, as its form of leadership was in such dispute that the problem was submitted to the emperor. The exact limits of the authority of the Jewish *gerousia* are not specified by Philo, who says only that it was established "to supervise the affairs of the Jews"[80], which definition alone indicates the separate organization of the Jewish community.

c. The existence of Jewish *archontes* (*In Flaccum*, 76, 80, 117) *Legatio*, 5) whom Philo referred to as "our *archontes*" (*In Flaccum*, 76). Here again his use of the first-person possessive adjective shows that the Jewish leadership was separate from the city magistracy, especially since there is also some indication of the latter in his writings[81].

d. The existence of Jewish educational institutions independent of the *polis*. The Alexandria authorities never maintained general educational institutions for the whole population. In the Ptolemaic period, all educational institutions including the gymnasia were privately owned[82]. In the Roman period, the gymnasia became public institutions under government supervision[83], but the other facilities, in particular the schools (διδασκαλεῖα), continued to be private[84]. Thus probably the Jews also maintained their own educational institutions.

---

80 *In Flaccum*, 74. Strabo (in *Antiquitates*, XIV 117) described the function of the ethnarch in the past in exactly the same way. See also Fraser, vol. 1, p. 56f.; Stern, *loc.cit.*

81 The reference is to οἱ ἐν τέλει which are mentioned in *In Flaccum*, 141. Philo used this expression to denote both the Jerusalem functionaries (*Legatio*, 222, 300) and those of Rome (*Legatio*, 26, 108, 110, 144). On the city magistracy in Alexandria see details in Jouguet, p. 39f., and esp. pp. 166-181; Fraser, vol. 1, pp. 96-110, 112-113, 299.

82 Full details are in Taubenschlag, p. 636f.; and see also chap. V above, n.63.

83 See Taubenschlag, *loc.cit.*; A.H.M. Jones, *CERP*, p. 319.

84 See, e.g., *P. Oxy.*, 471 (line 113) from the second century C.E.

Since the various ecctors of the population of Egypt (such as the
Greeks and the Egyptians) imparted a definitely religious tinge to
their schools[85], the Jews were not likely to attend them unless they
converted. As Jewish education too certainly had religious content,
the logical conclusion is that Jews had their own independent institutions.

As the references to schools in Philo, Wolfson was of the opinion
that there are such, to higher education or adult education[86]. *De Vita
Mosis*, II 216 reports that on the Sabbath the Jews "occupy themselves with the philosophy of their fathers" and devote their time to
acquiring knowledge and contemplating nature, that in every town
the synagogues served also as study houses (termed also διδασκαλεῖα)
for learning "prudence and courage and temperance and justice and
also of piety, holiness and every virtue by which duties to God and
man are discerned and rightly performed" trans. Colson, *LCL* ed.).
De Spec. Leg., II 61-63 notes in passing that Jews gathered on the
Sabbath in their "schools", of which there are "thousands in every
city", to educate the Jewish masses in the subjects noted above. At
each gathering one of the teachers "of special experience" would
guide his audience in recognizing the good and the useful in order to
direct their lives into desirable channels. The passage describes a
great assembly of Jews on the Sabbath[87] where one of the priests or
"elders" read the Torah and explained it to the assembled. Although
the context is not that of Philo's time, Wolfson made the reasonable
assumption that the assembly described was analogous to those of
Philo's own period, particularly as it has a parallel in the description
of the Therapeutic customs which Philo was familiar with[88]. However,
despite Wolfson, these descriptions do not appear to refer to institutions of higher learning, but rather an ordinary event in his congregation, the reading and explanation of the Torah on the Sabbath to
all Jews, not just a limited group of students[89]. Philo's attribution of

---

85 See Wilcken-Mitteis, vol. 1, p. 137f.
86 Wolfson, *Philo*, vol. 1, p. 79f.
87 On studying on the Sabbath, as a precept from the Torah in Philo's view, see also *De
    Opf. Mundi*, 128; Eusebius, *Praep. Evangelica*, VIII 7, 359d-360a; *Hypothetica*, 7, 13.
88 *De Vita Contemplativa*, 30-32.
89 Cf. the opinion of Schürer, vol. 3, p. 499. The same is true of the school of the *Therapeutai*
    which was called the "common sanctuary" and in which they used to meet on the
    Sabbath in order to hear the sermon of "the senior among them who also had the fullest

an academic character to these occasions probably derived from his well-known interest in idealizing Judaism. In any case, the possibility should not be rejected that this description of the synagogues indicates the additional function they fulfilled in the daily life of the Alexandrian community as schools or academies, and perhaps as centers of other cultural activity. Philo's direct historical testimony too confirms this. *Legatio*, 156-157, for instance, tells of the Jews' custom of gathering in their synagogues, especially on the Sabbath, to publicly recite the wisdom of their forefathers and explain the laws of the Torah. In *Legatio*, 115, Philo took pride in the presence of teachers and tutors in Jewish communities throughout the ages, and in the teaching of the oral and written Law. Moreover, in *Legatio*, 312, he called the synagogues "schools of sobriety and justice" and it is not clear whether he meant only their educational role, or also a judicial role in the life of the community. Furthermore, evidently the synagogues were also places for general festival gatherings such as the one described in *In Flaccum*, 116-118, on the *Sukkoth* holiday[90], which was probably the occasion for the public reading of the Torah, etc. as well.

e. The existence of synagogues protected from defilement by order of the central government. In several places Philo mentions the situation in Augustus' reign which was a model in the principate period insofar as the laws and synagogues of the Jews were concerned[91]. He also extols the good relations with the first emperors, as shown by the prayers for their health in the synagogues, the dedication of gilded shields, and crowns, and monument inscriptions in their honor[92]. That fact should be interpreted as official recogni-

knowledge of the doctrines" (*De Vita Contemplativa*, 31-32). About study of the Torah of this kind Josephus also commented — *C. Apionem*, II 175; *Antiquitates*, XV 43. In the New Testament there are many indications that one of the main activities in the synagogue was that described by the verb διδάσκειν (e.g., *Matthew*, 4:23; *Mark*, 1:21-22; *Luke*, 4:15, 31; 6:6; 13:10; *John*, 6:59; 18:20, and more).

90 In regard to the assemblies on the Feast of Tabernacles, cf. the inscription from Berenice (*CIG*, 5361); and also in the Water-drawing Festival in Appolinopolis Magna, see chap. III (end).

91 Cf., e.g., *In Flaccum*, 50; *Legatio*, 152-158, 291, 311, 315-316, 322.

92 See *Legatio*, 133, and Smallwood's excellent commentary in this connection (p. 22f). However, she did not pay attention to the fact that in *In Flaccum*, 53, Philo wrote that Flaccus seized the synagogues and even destroyed their names (τοὔνομα). The reference may be to the dedicatory inscriptions in honor of the kings and rulers placed over their gates, like those noted in a large number of synagogues in Egypt and also in Alexandria

tion of the sanctity of the synagogues, and indeed Philo noted that they were recognized as "sacred precincts" and so no different from other holy places in the city[93]. He also stressed that Jews were permitted to convene in their synagogues (to study and interpret the Torah, and collect donations of half a *sheqel* to hold holiday assemblies) and were not subject to the prohibition against gatherings that obtained from the reigns of Julius Caesar and Augustus on[94]. It is therefore not surprising that Philo censures the desecration of the synagogues as a departure and a breach of the law without precedent (*In Flaccum*, 41). The fact that this was a new development is shown in several passages, as is its practical meaning; the desecration of Jewish holy places was equated with conspiracy against Jewish law in general[95]. Thus Philo very logically stressed the danger that the

---

itself (see, e.g., *CIJ*, II 1432 — Alexandria; *ibid.*, 1440 — Schedia; *ibid.*, 1441 — Xenephyris; *ibid.*, 1442 — Nitriai; *ibid.*, 1443 — Athribes, and more). But the same extent the reference may be to signs of inscriptions outside the synagogue which gave notice of the nature and sacredness of the building (see *CIJ*, II 878 — bronze tablets from Phoenician Ornithopolis ; and cf. an inscription from Corinth — *CIJ*, I 718).

It should be noted that the dedicatory plaques honoring kings and rulers in synagogues did not include the title θεός in their lists of titles. In Walter's opinion (*Der Thoraausleger*, pp. 24-25), this was a result of the prohibitions of the Jewish religion; cf. also Fraser, vol. 1, p. 283. It appears that the wording of the Jewish dedications, beginning with "in honor of" (ὑπέρ) was chosen for the same reason, so as not to give the impression that they were meant for the actual rites of the kings (like the pagan dedications which were phrased in direct language, using the dative case). On this subject, cf. Philo, *Legatio*, 137-138, 141-142, 148, 356-357; and Josephus, *Antiquitates*, XIII 67. See also Fraser, vol. 1, pp. 226-227, 282f.

93 See, e.g., *In Flaccum*, 48. Similar uses of the term ὁ ἱερὸς περίβολος can be found in epigraphical material and even in an inscription from Alexandria itself (*CIJ*, II 1433). Philo used another term also — τέμενος — by which he defined the sacred precinct of the synagogues (*Legatio*, 137), and by which he refers to other holy places in the city as well (cf. *Legatio*, 150, 151; *In Flaccum*, 51). Sacred precincts like this existed in the other Jewish communities in Egypt, as can be learned from inscriptions and papyri.

94 On the prohibition of organizations (*collegia*) see Seutonius, *Julius*, 42, 3; and also *Augustus*, 32, 1. Philo also mentioned this prohibition (*In Flaccum*, 4-5), but stated definitely that the assemblies of the Jews were not considered prohibited meetings (*Legatio*, 312, 316); see Smallwood's commentary on *Legatio*, 156 (p. 236), which gives important details of this ban in general, and also a research survey on the subject. Furthermore, the letters of Pliny the Younger to the Emperor Trajan contain information on the suppression of various clubs in Bithynia in Asia Minor (*Ep. Plin. ad Traj.*, 96, 7; and cf. also Sherwin-White, *The Letters of Pliny*, p. 608. See the brilliant and comprehensive analysis on the *lex Julia de collegiis* offered by Yavetz, *Julius Caesar and his Public Image*, pp. 85-96.

95 *In Flaccum*, 47; *Legatio*, 157, 165; and in regard to the Temple cf. also *Legatio*, 208, 292, 300, 333. The "innovation" is emphasized by the use of the verb νεωτερίζω.

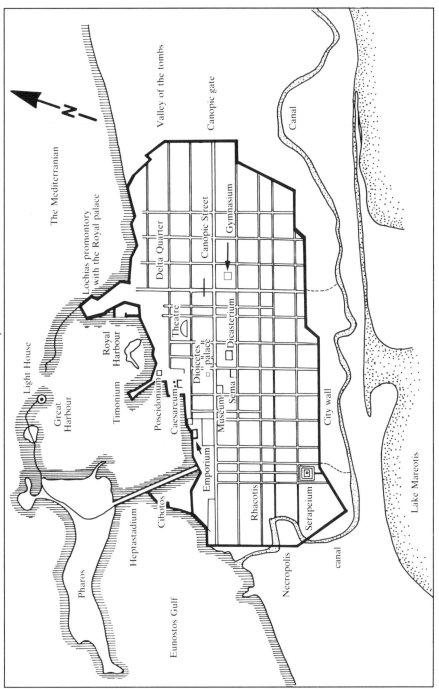

Alexandria in the days of Philo

Alexandria precedent constituted for all Jewish communities in the Roman Empire[96].

It should be noted in conclusion that in applying the term "nation" (or "people") to the Jewish community in his city or in others[97] Philo meant the organized groups of the Jewish people as bodies responsible to themselves[98].

The main inferences from Philo's writings can be summed up as follows:

1. The Jews were termed "Alexandrian" without any implication of political significance indicating citizenship in the *polis*, for a distinction is made between "Alexandrians" and "Jewish Alexandrians"

2. The Jews were considered *politai* because they had their own independent *politeia*, that is, they constituted a *politeuma*.

3. The *politeia* of the Jews was grounded on the right to maintain ancestral laws and customs, and on their participation in general civic rights shared by all those classified as *politai*.

4. The formal validity and actual existence of the Jewish *politeia* was dependent exclusively on the central government, and not on the *polis*.

5. Flaccus' edict for the first time abolished the Jewish *politeia*; thereafter, by proclaiming the Jews "foreigners and aliens" he made them subject to the *polis* at the latter's request, because it wanted only one *politeia*, its own, in the city.

6. Philo considered Alexandria a "colony" (ἀποικία) and "homeland" (πατρίς) for the Jews living there, with no implication in regard to citizenship in the *polis*.

7. The Jews by law enjoyed the right to live in Jewish neighborhoods. Separate residential areas on an ethnic basis were also common

---

96 *In Flaccum*, 45-47, 152; and cf. *Legatio*, 346.

97 τὸ Ἰουδαίων ἔθνος — *In Flaccum*, 191; *Legatio*, 210, 373 (cf. 217); ἔθνος alone — *In Flaccum*, 1; *Legatio*, 119, 133, 137, 160, 171, 178, 184 (ἅπαντι τῷ ἔθνει against ἑνὶ μέρει τοῦ Ἰουδαϊκοῦ), 194, 196, 214, 215, 279, 301, 351 (like in 184). The term was used in regard to other nations also: see *Legatio*, 10, 19, 116, 147, 183 (ἀλλοεθνεῖ), 256. Sometimes Philo used the term τὸ Ἰουδαίων γένος (*Legatio*, 178, 346; and cf. *ibid.*, 3-4, 201, and in reference to other nations he also used the term γένος, and cf. *Legatio*, 265). The instances of the term οἱ Ἰουδαῖοι are too numerous to list here. Cf. also ὁμοφύλοι (*Legatio*, 193, 327, 332) as opposed to ἀλλοφύλοι (*ibid.*, 200, 211).

98 Otherwise we could not be able to understand the terms ἡμετέρα πολιτεία (*In Flaccum*, 53), τοῖς πολίταις αὐτῶν Ἰουδαίους (ibid., 47), πολιτεία Ἰουδαϊκή (*Legatio*, 157), etc.

in the Egyptian *metropoleis* and are evidence of separate independent organization.

8. The Alexandrian Jews described as *politai* were ranked between the *metoikoi* and the *astoi*, and as such were treated like "free people" and "citizens" insofar as punishments were concerned.

9. As an organized body the Jews had the right to make "decisions", to submit group petitions, to appoint representative delegations, and have communal legal representation, all just as the *polis* had.

10. The Jewish community had its own leadership institutions unconnected with those of the *polis*.

11. The Jews had synagogues whose sanctity was recognized by law and protected by order of the central authorities, and also independent educational institutions.

12. The Jews were recongnized as a definite ethnic group separate from others in Alexandria and elsewhere.

13. The just demands of the Jews, their "claims" and the dispatch to Rome of their delegation to confront their Alexandrian rivals in court were all aimed at safeguarding their *politeia*, that is, their right to comply with ancestral laws, with all it juridical implications. It is inconceivable, even ridiculous, to think that Philo and his delegation aspired to attain citizenship in the Greek *polis*, which was led by confirmed anti-Semites like Apion, Lysimachus, Isidoros and Lampon[99], who strove diligently to have a single *politeia* in the city, a Hellenic one, necessarily associated with the municipal cult.

Thus there are no grounds for Tcherikover's claim that "Philo's picture is far from complete" because it was "affected by the desire to avoid disrupting relations with the Greeks, for the Jews wished to get into the citizen list, that is, to be people of the city, not its enemies"[100].

---

99 This subject is discussed at greater length below. Ostensibly one may offer a reason in line with Tcherikover's opinion: Did not the Jews of Western Europe strive for emancipation (in the modern period) even though the countries they lived in were governed by antisemites? This sort of anaology is questionable, since it is based on an alien and remote historical projection. For example, the Jewish fighters for emancipation in Western Europe played down the national character of their Judaism, which for them was a hindrance on their way to civic naturalization; in contrast, the Jews of Egypt bore their Jewish nationality painfully aloft, and declared specifically that Jerusalem was their *metropolis,* and even suspended their local struggle in times of trouble in Jerusalem.

100 Tcherikover, *The Jews in the Greek and Roman World,* p. 292.

Chapter VIII

The Status and Rights of the Alexandrian Jews according to Josephus

The works of Josephus supply most of the available information on the civic status of the Jews in the Hellenistic and Roman Diaspora. A few scholars took his testimony literally and decided that it meant that the Jews enjoyed civic equality in the Greek *poleis*. Most however suspected it of falsification or apologetics and at times even rejected it with insufficient justification[1]. Neither of these approaches is entirely tenable. The claim of the former was totally refuted by the celebrated papyrological discovery containing the letter of Emperor Claudius to the Alexandrians (*P. Lond.*, 1912) which clearly indicates that the Jews were not citizens of the Greek *polis* and thus did not enjoy full civic equality. On the other hand the fact that Josephus dealt extensively with the subject out of a sense of justice and great pride and on the basis of many documents (e.g. *C. Apionem*, II 36-37; *Antiquitates*, XII 119-126, 187-189, 213-267; XVI 27-65, 160-178; XIX 280-291) indicates that he was not fabricating. Furthermore, there is confirmation of some of the documents in Philo (e.g., *Legatio*, 311-320). Admitting that many people doubt the genuineness of the documents preceding Roman rule which were not deposited in any public archives, Josephus stresses that the reliability of the documents of the Roman imperial period is unquestionable (*Antiquitates*, XIV 187-188). That may mean that in the conflict between the Jews and the citizens of the Greek *poleis*, the latter denied the official validity of any Jewish document from the Hellenistic period; no such claim can however be made in regard to the Roman period, when anti-Semites could not resort to propaganda (cf. *Antiquitates*, XII 126; *C. Apionem*, II 65; and see below).

---

1 On the rights of the Alexandria Jews, see n.3 below. In regard to the Jews of Asia Minor, see Marcus, *Josephus* (*LCL*), vol. 7, Appendixes C, D, p. 737ff.; Roth-Gerson, *Jews in Asia Minor*, p. 53ff.

Josephus certainly had recourse not only to the archives of the Jewish community, but also to the document files of the Roman emperors which were open to him by kind permission of his benefactors, the Flavian emperors. That is sufficient reason to refrain from a hasty rejection of his testimony. It is hard to imagine that Josephus would indulge in falsifications on such a sensitive matter as they could easily inspire hostile propaganda. The most that can be said is that his reports on the Hellenistic period are not accurate enough, due to the paucity of detailed data and the lapse of time, but he should not be suspected of deliberate prevarication. Presumably he tended to view the rights of Jews in the Hellenistic period through the prism of his own, and this retrospection led to errors here and there, but could not have totally distorted the picture. For ultimately the status of the Jews in the Roman period was determined by criteria inherited from the Hellenistic period, as admittedly the Romans introduced few innovations in this area.

In considering the testimony of Josephus it is important to keep in mind that the main question that preoccupied scholars was whether or not the Jews of Alexandria and of other cities in the Graeco-Roman world were citizens of the *poleis*. Almost nobody questions the assumption that the conflicts between the Jews and the citizens of the *poleis* revolved around that question. Most scholars have claimed that the Jews fought for recognition of their rights as citizens of the *poleis*, while their opponents objected. For them it was the real "Jewish question", and it is not surprising that Tcherikover called it a "war of emancipation"[2]. However, this is obviously a projection from the remote situation of eighteenth and nineteenth century Europe, and a basic fault. A careful reading of Josephus will make it possible to ascertain the actual rights of the Jews and the real significance of their struggle, and the point of departure is necessarily the edict of Claudius (*Antiquitates*, XIX 280f.).

A. Was there an edict and when was it written?

Whether the edict is authentic is the main key question in all

---

2 See, e.g., *Hellenistic Civilization and the Jews*, p. 311ff.; *Jews in Egypt*, pp. 152, 155; *Jews in the Greek and Roman World*, pp. 291, 364; etc. See also *CPJ*, I, p. 60ff. (esp. p. 74).

relevant research, and if it is, the second question is whether its contents is reliable from the legal and historical point of view. As a rule
the two questions have been so interwined that they have been
practically inseparable, and scholarly opinions have divided into
three main groups: 1) Those who viewed the document as genuine
and authority for the civic equality of the Alexandria Jews, and at
most proffered a few reservations; 2) Those who rejected it totally
on the grounds that it was an apologetic forgery; 3) Those who
claimed that it contains grains of true facts which were however
embellished by some Jewish counterfeiter, perhaps Josephus himself[3].

Most scholars have treated the problem on the basis of quite a
completely formed subjective evaluation of Josephus' writings. Their
considerations naturally focused on the contents of the edict in
particular, in order to ascertain whether it showed signs of Jewish
apologetics. Their answers determined their stand on whether there
was an edict at all. Unfortunately almost no scholar examined that
question by itself, unrelated to the problem of its contents. That
situation itself led to the neglect of objective historical criteria in
seeking a solution. The only attempt to judge and examine the edict
of Claudius unfettered by that subjective assessment of Josephus
seems to have been made by Amusin[4], and there is historical justification for his thesis verifying the existence of the edict and determining its dating.

According to Amusin, the dispute in the city of Dora is likely to
supply rather solid proof of the authenticity of the edict. In *Antiquitates*, XIX 300-310 Josephus reports a quarrel between the city
of Dora and the local Jews after Agrippa I's return from Rome.
Several young townsmen desecrated the local synagogue by placing
the emperor's statue in it. Agrippa immediately complained to the

---

3 Group A: Schürer, vol. 3, p. 121ff.; Juster, vol. 2, p. 1ff.; Alon, *History of the Jews*,
   vol. 1, p. 206ff.; Momigliano, *Emperor Claudius*, p. 96, n.25; De Sanctis, *Riv. di Fil.*,
   52 (1924), p. 473ff.; cf. Dessau, *Gesch. der römischen Kaiserzeit*, vol. 2, p. 668ff.
   Group B: Jouguet, p. 19, n.7; Dobschütz, *AJTh*, 8 (1904), p. 737, n.20; Zielinsky,
   Rev. de l'Univ. de Bruxelles, 32 (1926/7), p. 128ff.
   Group C: Most scholars belong to this group, but Tcherikover's research is the most
   comprehensive and exhaustive, and contains most of the bibliography. See *Hellenistic
   Civilization and the Jews*, pp. 309ff., 409ff.; *Jews in Egypt*, p. 116ff.; *CPJ*, I, pp. 39-41,
   56f., 62, 69-74; II, pp. 25-107.
4 "The Letter and Edict of Claudius Caesar" appeared in Russian (Amusin, *VDI*, 2 (1949),
   pp. 221-228.

Syrian governor Petronius about the desecration of ancestral laws. The latter was furious and in an order to the leaders of Dora vigorously denounced the perpetrators of the crime and demanded that they be put on trial. His order referred four times to the edict (or edicts) of Claudius. First the governor stressed that some people of Dora had behaved with "such mad audacity" that they disobeyed the emperor and flouted his order (διάταγμα) permitting the Jews to keep their ancestral laws (ibid., 304). Second he noted sarcastically that "it is ridiculous for me to refer to my own decree after making the mention of the edict of the emperor" (ibid., 306, trans. Feldman, LCL ed.). Third, he wrote that he ordered the centurion Proclus Vitellius to send him the people who dared these "in defiance of the edict of Augustus" (ibid., 307). And foruth, he stressed that so that the city of Dora could learn to understand his policy he was attaching to his letter "the edicts (διατάγματα) which were published in Alexandria" (ibid., 310). On the basis of these passages Amusin correctly claimed that it was hard to imagine that Josephus had fabricated the emperor's edict, the more so because the passages contain quite a number of details that accord with Roman practice in the provinces[5]. In his opinion, the Claudian edict referred to in the Petronius letter was actually the edict and not the emperor's Letter to the Alexandrians (P. Lond., 1912). That opinion is supported by a number of convincing facts:

a) Claudius' Letter to the Alexandrians cannot be considered an edict because of both its form and its opening, and because the term itself does not appear even once in the text. Furthermore, Aemilius Rectus, the Roman prefect of Egypt who made it public specifically called it a "letter" (ἐπιστολή; lines 4, 7). At most it might belong to a certain category of "official replies" (ἀποκρίματα) delivered to the people concerned through a legatus[6]. On the other hand, Claudius' edict was meant not solely for Alexandria, but for Syria as well (Antiquitates, XIX 279) and the term διάταγμα does figure in it (ibid., 285)[7]. The letter could not have been sent to Petronius, as it was intended for a different recipient, and as it was worded like an "official reply" was probably issued by the office of

---

5 See Amusin, ibid., p. 221.
6 See H. St. Jones, JRS, 16 (1926), p. 19.
7 The variant διάγραμμα (or dicta in Latin) likewise confirms that it is an edict.

the *ad responsa Graeca* to the people concerned, in this case   citizens of the Alexandrian *polis*. The letter in its entirety dealt with purely Alexandrian matters, and the quarrel with the Jews was just one of its items. The edict on the other hand concerned basic Jewish problems, and therefore mentioned both Alexandria and Syria.

b) In his letter to the city of Dora, Petronius noted that Agrippa read out the emperor's orders (διατάματα) and the use of the plural eliminates the possibility that the letter was meant. The plural may mean that King Agrippa read out to Petronius two Claudian edicts, possibly the Alexandrian Syrian one (*ibid.*, 280-285) and the World one (*ibid.*, 287-291).

c) The Syrian governor referred to the edict as a document already long known, and thus wrote "it is ridiculous for me to refer to my own decree after making mention of the edict of the emperor" (*ibid.*, 306). The final paragraph of the World edict can likewise explain its publication, as it specifies instructions on the matter, such as: "it is my will that the ruling bodies of the cities and colonies and *municipia* in Italy and outside Italy and the kings and other authorities through their own ambassadors shall cause this edict of mine to be inscribed, and keep it posted for not less than thirty days, in a place where it can plainly be read from the ground" (*ibid.*, 291)[8].

d) Petronius wrote to the city of Dora that the statue of Claudius should rather have been placed in a temple dedicated to him, and not elsewhere (*ibid.*, 305), that is, not in a synagogue. Would Petronius have written that, asks Amusin, if he had read Claudius' letter to the Alexandrians in which he totally rejected the idea of erecting a temple to him? Petronius' suggestion must therefore be considered his own judgment, independent of Claudius' policy on the matter which he only learned of later[9].

---

8 Feldman pointed out that the final words fit the Latin version, *ut de plano recte legi possi(n)t*, known also by the initials *u.d.p.r.l.p.* See Feldman, *Josephus*, vol. 9, p. 352.

9 *P. Lond.*, 1912, and see Amusin, *VDI*, 2 (1949), p. 222. It might be claimed that Claudius' policy on the emperor cult (in his lifetime) was eventually more flexible, for there was a temple to him in Britain from 44 C.E. on (Seneca, *Apoc.*, 3; cf. also Tacitus, *Annales*, XIV 31). Furthermore, it appears that Claudius by no means disliked to be addressed by his divine title (see Charlesworth, *Class. Rev.*, 39 (1925), p. 114ff.). At the same time there is no evidence that this was done at his behest or that he approved it, so that in this respect there was no difference between him and Augustus. On the other hand it should be kept in mind that the Dora affair and the conflict in Alexandria occurred in 41 C.E., a short time after he was crowned, when Caligula's deification

e) The reconstruction of the chronological order of the events connected with Dora suggests that they occurred shortly after King Agrippa's return to Palestine, that is, in the spring or early summer of 41 C.E. If that date is accepted, Petronius cannot possibly be thought to have relied on the Claudius' Letter, which was issued in Egypt only in the fall of that year, on 10 November 41 (*P. Lond.*, 1912, lines 11-12).

The dating does seem to be correct. Josephus' report of the Dora case (*Antiquitates*, XIX 300) begins with "A very short time after this" referring to the initial arrangements Agrippa made in his realm after returning there (*ibid.*, 294ff.). Those arrangements evinced his great concern to win his people's hearts, a course typical of anyone interested in rapidly acquiring a favorable image[10]. Agrippa naturally made initial arrangements soon after his return, and when can that have been? According to Josephus, Claudius dispatched him immediately (αὐτίκα) to receive his kingdom (*ibid.*, 292) and indeed "since he was to go back with improved fortunes he turned quickly (μετὰ τάχους) homewards" (*ibid.*, 293). Agrippa was crowned in Rome in mid-winter, "a few days later when the sacrifices to the dead were offered" (*ibid.*, 272), that is, the *Paternalia*, which came between the 13th and 21st of February[11]. Despite his haste,

---

madness was fresh in people's minds, so that there is good reason to believe that then Claudius wished to dissociate himself from the deification cult. At most it can be assumed that in the course of time his stance changed, as he was known to be erratic and easily influenced by his advisors. However, some scholars consider the British temple a deviation (so far as Claudius is concerned) designed to provide the pagan island with a replacement for the Druidic cult that was abolished. There being no evidence in the sources that the erection of the temple in Britain was initiated or supported by the emperor, it is more likely to have been a private local project, analogous to those in Asia Minor reported in two inscriptions (*IGRR*, III 328; *BCH*, XI, p. 307). For further details on this problem see Bell, *Jews and Christians*, p. 7; Scramuzza, *Emperor Claudius*, pp. 145, 249, n.18.

10 This is shown by the thanksgiving sacrifices he made omitting nothing stipulated by Law, the release from Nazirite vows of many people (apparently the poor) as in the days of the Hasmonaeans, and the presentation of a gold chain to the Temple. These things were probably done at the outset of his stay in Jerusalem, as they seem to indicate a desire to be approved by his people from the beginning of his reign. The dismissal from the High Priesthood of Theophilus son of Hanan (who was Vitellius' appointee) and the nomination of Simeon son of Boethus called Cantheras were similarly motivated. The appointment of Silas as commander was also made quickly, as a new king could reasonably be expected to choose his own general early in his reign. See notes in Feldman, *Josephus*, vol. 9, p. 353ff.

11 See Feldman, *ibid.*, p. 340, note a.

he was unlikely to have sailed during that season of Mediterranean storms, so that his stay in Rome probably lasted until spring. He seems to have departed shortly after 30 April, when he was still in Rome in connection with the trial of Isidorus and Lampon[12]. There is no data available making it possible to follow his later activites precisely. On the basis of *Antiquitates*, XIX 310, Tcherikover assumed that on his way to Palestine Agrippa stopped in Alexandria and there read in public the Claudian edict that was composed at his request[13]. There is not the slightest hint anywhere, however, that he visited Alexandria at the time. What reason could there be for concealing such a visit, especially if it had the character of a political mission and was not played down like Agrippa's previous visit in 38 C.E.? And what reason did King Agrippa have for returning to Alexandria? He already knew that the problem of the Jews of that city had been solved by the edict issued at his behest and under his influence. And the Alexandrian leaders had been defeated on the legal confrontation with him, and executed. A careful reading of the text makes it impossible to accept Tcherikover's interpretation of Agrippa's visit to Alexandria. The fact that he was in a hurry to return to Judaea is self-evident. Furthermore, the report of the Dora case notes most clearly that Agrippa came to Publius Petronius "without delay" (*Antiquitates*, XIX 301), meaning that he personally appeared before the Syrian governor. Consequently the statement in *Antiquitates*, XIX 310 must mean that Agrippa read the Claudian edicts when he was arguing or contending (δικαιολογησάμενος) at the legal tribunal of Petronius[14]. Despite the absence of evidence from 30 April, 41 C.E. on, it is probably the case that Agrippa sailed for Palestine shortly thereafter, at latest at the end of May, and that his initial activities as well as the Dora episode took place in June and July.

The Mishnah (*Sotah*, VII 8) also appears to confirm that chrono-

---

12 See Tcherikover, *Jews in Egypt*, p. 142, *CPJ*, II, pp. 68, 73.

13 Tcherikover, *Jews in Egypt*, pp. 141, 143, 147.

14 That was the way Feldman rightly edited his translation (see *Josephus*, ad. loc.). The expression δικαιολέγομαι περὶ τινος means "to defend someone in court" so that the βῆμα on which he pleaded was no doubt that of the tribunal. There is no reason to think that Petronius first learned of the edicts at the trial concerning the Dora affair. He himself noted that they were already known to all (*Antiquitates*, XIX 310). King Agrippa read them aloud because, acting as he did on the legal plane, it was natural for him to cite the imperial edicts which were designed to serve as grounds for the complaints he was making against the Dora people (see *Antiquitates*, XIX 301 — καταλέγει).

logy, though indirectly. It reports that on the eighth day of *Sukkoth*, that is, at latest in mid-October, Agrippa read the Book of Deuteronomy to an enraptured audience. Schürer correctly stated that this occurred in 41 C.E. which was also a fallow year[15]. According to the mishnaic description, Agrippa was praised for reading while standing, but evidently not only for that. It is reasonable to suppose that the audience was enthusiastic because he had previously proven himself praiseworthy for important accomplishments. The latter were apparently those specified in *Antiquitates*, XIX 294ff., and his efforts for the Jews of Dora was one of them. Even if this hypothetical structure is too speculative and imaginative, the mishnaic testimony is important because it provides an additional date when Agrippa was in Jerusalem, a full month before the publication of the letter to the Alexandrians on 10 November 41.

Thus, the reconstruction of the events connected with the Dora episode shows that it occurred about the time when Agrippa returned to Judaea, that is, in the spring or early summer of 41 C.E. Acceptance of that date automatically eliminates the possibility that in his communication Petronius referred to Claudius' Letter to the Alexandrians, published on 10 November, and makes it necessary to concur in Amusin's assumption that Petronius was referring to the edicts or edicts mentioned by Josephus.

f) That the edict did in fact exist is supported also by the letter to the Alexandrians, which contains a number of phrases suggesting that it was preceded by some other document dealing with the relations between the Alexandrians and the Jews. A number of scholars have justifiably agreed that the words "having heard both sides" and "as I have confirmed (Jewish customs)" (line 88) refer to the edict[16]. Also the following sentences — "Even now therefore

---

15 Schürer, vol. 1, p. 555; idem (Vermes & Millar ed.), vol. 1, p. 447. Although some scholars — Büchler, *Die Priester*, p. 12ff.; Epstein, *Introduction to the Mishna* (Hebrew), p. 40ff.; Safrai, *Pilgrimage*, p. 197ff. — sought to ascribe the episode to the reign of Agrippa II, Schürer's view seems preferable. Cf. Stern, *Joseph Amorai Memorial Volume*, p. 127f., n.30.

16 See, e.g., Tcherikover, *Jews in Egypt*, p. 144; *CPJ*, II, p. 49; Ostersetzer, *Braude Jubilee Volume*, p. 31; Amusin *VDI*, 2 (1949), p. 222. Amusin supported that conclusion linguistically as well, claiming that the use of the *aorist* meant that Claudius had previously heard the two sides and confirmed Jewish rights (see line 88; διακούσας, ἐβεβαίωσα). For Claudius' other instructions are given in the present and future tenses; see lines 30, 32, 36, 37, 46, 49, 53, 54, 57, 61, 67, 79, 82, 89, 98, 99, 105.

I conjure the Alexandrians to behave gently and kindly towards the Jews" etc. (line 82ff.) and "and on the other hand I order the Jews", etc. (line 87ff.) — indicate clearly that the letter was preceded by another document which also called the two parties to order[17], as the edict itself says "and I enjoin upon both parties the greatest precaution to prevent any disturbance arising after the posting of my edict" (*Antiquitates*, XIX 285). Another hint in the letter appears in the sentence "but I harbour within me a store of immutable indignation against those who *renewed* the conflict" (Tcherikover's translation)[18], which implies that the dispute between the Alexandrians and the Jews had already been reported to the emperor who had made his decision on it before sending the letter.

At first glance it seems logical to assume that the edict was formulated in the initial days after Claudius was crowned emperor. Taking into account the absence of *consul* among Claudius' titles in the edict (*Antiquitates*, XIX 281) and its presence in the World edict (*ibid.*, 287) and the Letter to the Alexandrians (line 15), Amusin concluded that there was a lapse of time between the two edicts, since Claudius became *consul designatus* for the second time on 28 February 41. Thus according to Amusin the Alexandrian edict could have been issued at the latest in the second half of February, and the World edict on the 28th at the earliest, and he suggested that the Alexandrian edict was composed at the beginning of the month[19].

That proposal seems somewhat contrived, considering that the epitome of paragraph 280 (in *Antiquitates*) of the Alexandrian edict does have the title of *consul*, like the other two documents. Thus the title must have been inadvertently omitted in the original version of the edict, as was the title of "high priest" which appears in the other two. The date Amusin proposed is not tenable because the report of Caligula's death (on 24 January) could not have reached Egypt before the middle of February. Tcherikover correctly pointed out that the voyage from Rome to Alexandria normally took two weeks, but in the winter storms in the Mediterranean probably took longer[20]. While Josephus says that the Jews immediately (εὐθέως)

---

17 This is intimated in particular by the stressed words, "Even now, therefore" (διόπε ἔτι καὶ νῦν).
18 Lines 77-78. The emphasis πάλιν speaks for itself.
19 Amusin, *VDI*, 2 (1949), p. 225.
20 Tcherikover, *Jews in Egypt*, p. 143, n.45. For the same reason he rejected the suggestion

took up arms (*Antiquitates*, XIX 278), reports of the disturbances in Alexandria could not have arrived in Rome before the end of March. For despite Josephus' report of immediate Jewish action, the violent confrontations no doubt developed gradually, as they usually do in such cases. Probably small clashes turned into street fighting and became general only as irritation grew, and the process would have taken a few days. In view of the likelihood that the Roman rulers in Alexandria at first sought to persuade the rioters to compromise, the report to Rome may have been delayed for another few days. It is impossible to say whether the report of the riots was carried to Rome by the second Alexandrian delegation headed by Barbillus, or earlier. That the delegation brought the report along seems reasonable since the disturbances were the motive for its departure for Rome. If so, the report reached Rome in April, for Barbillus was present at the trial of Isidorus on 30 April. If however the disturbances were reported directly by the prefect, likewise a reasonable possibility, the report could have arrived by the end of March. No doubt upon learning of the situation Claudius immediately dispatched urgent instructions to the Egyptian prefect calling on him to restore order as soon as possible, as dictated by the *Pax Romana* policy, but that does not mean that the edict was appended to those orders. Josephus says that the instructions and the edicts were two separate documents, the former reaching Egypt in the form of a letter, and the edict in the form of an order or command[21]. Tcherikover properly noted that it was hard to believe that Claudius hastened to issue the edict before hearing the two sides[22]. If it is admitted that the words of line 88 ("having heard both sides", etc.) really refer to the edict, it must be concluded that it was necessarily preceded by a judicial debate that took some time. Tcherikover suggested that the parties to the debate were the same two delegations which confronted each other during Caligula's reign, that is, the Jewish one led by Philo, and the Alexandrian one headed by Apion. If so, the edict was composed at the earliest in mid-April. The trial

---

regarding the immediacy of the events made by Premerstein (*Hermes*, 67 (1932), pp. 174-196, esp. 182f.

21 See *Antiquitates*, XIX 279, and the distinction between καὶ Κλαύδιος ἐπιστέλει and πέμπει δὲ καὶ διάγραμμα. The words δὲ καὶ indicate the difference between the two documents. Cf. also *ibid.*, 285.

22 Tcherikover, *Jews in Egypt*, p. 144ff.

of Isidorus and Lampon, whose outcome indicates the anti-Alexan-
drian policy of the emperor, took place at the end of April. Accordingly, it is reasonable to assume that the date of issuance of the edict
was near that of the trial, and the fact that Agrippa was connected
with both supports that assumption[23].

Although Tcherikover's proposal on the chronology of events is
impeccably logical, his evaluation of the circumstances is not. A
central claim of his was that there was a change for the worse in the
emperor's attitude to the Jews, suggested by the fact that he learned
that the riots had been resumed on their initiative and by the fact
that neither Philo's delegation nor Agrippa's were in Rome, and
demonstrated by the letter which was definitely not supportive of
the Jews[24].

That evaluation seems erroneous, for three reasons: a) The Jews'
responsibility for the resumption of disturbances is actually referred
to in the edict (*Antiquitates*, XIX 278). b) Claudius stated clearly
in his letter that he was not at all interested in ascertaining who were
guilty of precipitating the riots, even though the Alexandrians had
made the most serious charges (line 75ff.). c) Tcherikover felt that
the sentence "but I harbour within me a store of immutable indignation against those who renewed the conflict" was evidence that
Claudius' anger was directed against the Jews, especially since it was
contiguous to warnings to the Jews[25], and claimed that Claudius'
description of the hostilities as "the disturbances and rioting, or
rather to speak the truth, the war against the Jews" (lines 73-4),
which might be construed to the contrary, was simply "a grammatical
turn of phrase and nothing more"[26]. Rather than being a slip of the
pen, however, the phrase seems to represent an effort to select the
right wording, carefully thought out. A comparison of these statements with Josephus' assessment of events preceding the publication
of the edict reveals two contrasting formulations. For according to
Josephus (*Antiquitates*, XIX 276), the disturbances erupted among
the Jews "against the Greeks" (πρὸς Ἕλληνας), while the *Letter* has
it that they erupted among the Greeks "against the Jews" (πρὸς

---

23 On the trial see *CPJ*, II 156a, lines 16-19; *CPJ*, II 156b, line 11. For the edict, see *Antiquitates*, XIX 279; cf. also *ibid.*, 288 in regard to the World edict.
24 Tcherikover, *Jews in Egypt*, p. 149.
25 See line 98ff., and see Tcherikover's interpretation, *CPJ*, II, p. 48.
26 See his explanation of line 73 (*CPJ*, II, p. 47).

'Ιουδαίους). It seems reasonable to suppose then that the emperor's anger against those who "renewed the conflict" was directed at the Alexandrians rather than the Jews.

Tcherikover's contention (in the same context) that the emperor concurred in the Alexandrian view of the conflict, is untenable, not only because there is no authority for it in the source, but because the emperor deliberately refrained, as he himself said, from clarifying the affair. According to Tcherikover, the evidence that the Jews were blamed appears, as noted above, in *Antiquitates*, XIX 278. But strangely enough that passage is followed by the edict, which all agree is favourable to the Jews. Moreover, since the hostilities on the part of the Jews began in February (as Tcherikover pointed out) and came to the attention of the emperor in April[27], why would he wait till the end of October to reprimand the Jews[28]? Also, at the trial of Isidorus and Lampon attended by Agrippa which took place at the end of April, the emperor was obviously sympathetic to the Jewish cause, although news of the distubances had already reached him[29]. The only possible explanation is that the letter was motivated by a new wave of riots that erupted around October. The phrase "those who renewed the conflict" (line 78) seems to support this view, as it seems designed to censure the perpetrators of riots that broke out for the second time in Claudius' own reign. For it is not reasonable to assume that the word πάλιν should be interpreted to mean a second time after the first time in Caligula's reign (in 38 C.E.). The first disturbances, about which there is no doubt, erupted in February as a new emperor took over in Rome. Claudius ordered his governor in Egypt to suppress them, and after investigating the matter, issued the edict whose basic prupose was to eliminate the travesties of the Caligulan period and relegitimize the situation prevalent in Augustan times (*Antiquitates*, XIX 282-285). From that standpoint the edict can be viewed as the expression of a policy aimed at locating the causes of the riots in Alexandria and restoring order. Inevitably, both the edict and the trial of Isidorus and Lampon

---

27 Tcherikover, *Jews in Egypt*, p. 146.
28 The letter was certainly written then, for on 10 November 41 the Roman prefect promulgated it in Egypt.
29 In that trial, Isidorus was explicit: "My Lord Caesar, I beseech you to listen to my account of my native city's suffering" (*CPJ*, II 156a, col. 2, line 10f.). The emperor agreed and gave him permission to speak (*ibid.*, line 12f.).

provided the Alexandrians with a powerful motive for reviving the clashes. They must have found it hard to swallow the edict which restored Jewish rights and nullified their own considerable achievements in Caligula's time. Furthermore, the execution of their leading spokesmen, Isidorus and Lampon, certainly offended and infuriated them. Presumably the joy of their adversaries (the Jews) also exasperated them and incited them to riot. To sum up, then, the edict was composed in about April, 41 C.E., following riots initiated by the Jews in about February, and the letter was composed in October, following a new outbreak initiated by the Alexandrians in mid-September, the period of the Jewish High Holidays[30].

B. The Reliability and Legal Terminology of the Edict.
The term "Alexandrians" as used by Josephus.

The edict begins "Having from the first known that the Jews in Alexandria called Alexandrians" (*Antiquitates*, XIX 281), and the question is what the term "Alexandrians" meant in that context. Most scholars, among both those accepting and those rejecting the authenticity of the edict, have claimed that it meant the citizens of Alexandria[31]. Feldman even argued that the term "Alexandrians" could not refer to place of residence (*origo*) because in that case the wording "would be redundant, in speaking of the Jewish inhabitants of Alexandria, who are called inhabitants of Alexandria". He therefore considered it a technical term with juridical significance denoting the citizens of the *polis*[32].

Josephus applies the term to the Alexandria Jews only three times (*Antiquitates*, XIX 281; XIV 188; *C. Apionem*, II 38) but in all three cases it is preceded by "the Jews in Alexandria" (οἱ ἐν Ἀλεξανδρείᾳ Ἰουδαῖοι) or just "the Jews" (οἱ Ἰουδαῖοι) and that itself shows that they were not actually citizens of the *polis*. If so, what did he mean

---

30 The riots during Flaccus' prefecture also occurred during that season (*In Flaccum*, 116).

31 Scholars accepting the edict include Schürer, vol. 3, p. 121ff.; Juster, vol. 2, p. 1ff.; Momigliano, *Claudius*, p. 96, n.25; De Sanctis, *Riv. di Fil.*, 52 (1924), p. 473ff.; Alon, *History of the Jews*, vol. 1, p. 220ff.; Among those denying its authenticity see e.g. Willirch, *Klio*, 3 (1903), p. 403ff.; Fuchs, p. 79ff., esp. p. 89f.; Wilcken, *Antisemitism*, p. 787; Tcherikover, *Jews and Greeks*, pp. 245, 323ff.; idem, *CPJ*, I, p. 70, n.45; and many more.

32 Feldman, *Josephus*, vol. 9, p. 344, note d.

by the term "Alexandrians"? The fact that the citizens were termed "Alexandrians" in the edict might suggest that he meant to ascribe citizenship in the *polis* to the Jews, particularly since in *Antiquitates*, XIV 188 he stated clearly that the Jews were "Alexandrian *politai*" (Ἀλεξανδρέων πολῖται). However, that was not his intention, although he did not use the term to indicate only origin. At first glance this might seem like grasping both ends of the stick, but the applications show that the use of the phrase "Alexandrian *politai*" for Jews was meant to stress their equal status with the citizens of the *polis*. It does not mean that the Jews had the same *politeia* as the Greeks, but that they were *politai* of their own political organization, and because the existence of that organization in Alexandria was legally recognized, they could be called "Alexandrians". In other words, that designation, as a technical term with a juridical meaning, defined the residents of the city who were classified as *politai*, but not necessarily of the *polis*[33]. Admittedly, calling the Jews "Alexandrian *politai*" may be misleading, but probably unintentionally so. It does not seem likely that Josephus would have wanted to misinform his readers on a patently legal matter that could easily be verified. And as noted above, in the three instances cited the Jews were also described as "the Jews in Alexandria" or "the Jews" which terms do not fit in with citizenship in the *polis*. In other instances Josephus used still other definitions such as "the Jews residing in Alexandria" (οἱ ἐν Ἀλεξανδρείᾳ κατοικοῦντες Ἰουδαῖοι)[34], "the Jewish people" (τὸ Ἰουδαίων ἔθνος)[35], which undoubtedly refer to the Jews as a national group organized as a separate political body. A similar situation also obtained in regard to the Jews of Antioch who were called "Antiochans" and "the (Jewish) inhabitants of Antioch" in one passage (*C. Apionem*, II 39) and elsewhere "the Jews in Antioch" (*Bellum*, II 41) or "the Jews from Antioch" (*ibid.*,

---

33 Another possibility was suggested by Motzo (*Atti d. r. Accad. di Scienze di Torino*, 48 [1912-1913], p. 583ff.) who claimed that the term "Alexandrians" denotes merely a particular degree of citizenship in the *polis*, such as that of people not registered in demes or tribes, that is, *politai* (contrast to *astoi*). A similar opinion was expressed by Tarn (p. 222) who maintained that the Jews had "potential" citizenship in Alexandria. Both these views must be rejected, however, for reasons discussed in on pp. 278ff. below.

34 *C. Apionem*, II 7, 33, 44; *Antiquitates*, XIV 113, 117; cf. also *C. Apionem*, II 55, 63.

35 *Antiquitates*, XIX 278, 285, Cf. *Antiquitates*, XIV 117-118; *C. Apionem*, II 43; *Bellum*, II 487, 495.

VII 44, 47, 54, 111). Jews settled in other cities of the Hellenistic world in a recognized framework on the basis of their separate *politeia* were also called after their city of residence by Josephus (*C. Apionem*, II 39). But at the same time they were defined in a way that indicates their separate organization, such as "the Jews in Delos" (*Antiquitates*, XIV 213), "The Jews who lived in the (Greek) cities" (*ibid.*, XVI 27), "The Jewish *politai*[36] living in our city (= Sardis)" (*ibid.*, XIV 259), "the Jews in Cyrene"(*ibid.*, XVI 160, 169). It should be kept in mind that Josephus cited the authority of Strabo, who defined the Jewish community in Alexandria as "an independent *politeia*" (*ibid.*, XIV 117) and called the Jews of the land of Onias *politai* (*ibid.*, XIII 287).

For Josephus in *C. Apionem*, II 38 the term "Alexandrians" and the like had a rich significance. Alexandria and other such cities were founded as "colonies" (ἀποικίαι) and consequently their inhabitants regardless of ethnic origin were known by the name of the founders. This presentation accords perfectly with Philo's explanation (pp. 236 ff. above) and like Philo Josephus obviously sought to define the settlement of Jews in the cities of the Diaspora in terms familiar to the Greek reader. From his point of view the Jews were considered ordinary immigrants who took part in the establishment of the "colonies". And since they were by nature and according to their organization and rights separate independent bodies, they were known by the name of colonies. Furthermore, in citing the example of the Antiochean Jews, Josephus noted that "our residents in Antioch are called Antiocheans, having been granted *politeia* by its founder Seleucus" (*C. Apionem*, II 39). At first glance it might be thought that *politeia* is citizenship in the *polis*, and for that reason the Jews were called "Antiocheans", but in fact Josephus did not specify which *politeia*, did not clearly define it as the *politeia* of the citizens of Antioch, and meant, as will be seen below, the Jewish

---

36 The term *politai* here refers to Jews as members of an independent *politeuma*. This is definitely proved by the wording of the Sardis resolution regarding the Jews living in their city: "... they may, in accordance with their accepted customs, come together and have a communal life (πολιτεύωνται) and adjudicate suits among themselves," etc. (*Antiquitates*, XIV 260). Cf. a similar use of the verb πολιτεύεσθαι (πολιτεύω) in Antiochus III's bill of rights to the Jewish people, as quoted by Josephus: "And all the members of the nation shall have a form of government (πολιτευέσθωσαν) in accordance with the laws of their forefathers" (*Antiquitates*, XII 142).

politeia[37]. The fact that the name of the city figuring in the designation of the Jews does not indicate their citizenship in the *polis* is explicitly indicated further in the passage: "Similarly those at Ephesus and throughout the rest of Ionia bear the same name as the indigenous (αὐθιγενέσι) citizens". The distinction Josephus makes between the Jews and the local citizens is thus quite clear and cannot be obliterated. The ostensibly irrefutable argument that Claudius' Letter to the Alexandrians contains a clear distinction between "Alexandrians" and "Jews" does not affect Josephus' terminology one way or the other, for the edict he cites also makes the distinction twice (*Antiquitates*, XIX 281, 284). However, in the Letter to the Alexandrians Claudius also addresses the Jews directly (lines 80, 86ff.) a most illuminating point[38].

One of the main reasons for rejecting the words "called Alexandrians" in the edict is derived from document *BGU*,1140 (= *CPJ*, II 151) in which the designation "Alexandrian" has been crossed out from the petition of the Jew Helenos son of Tryphon and replaced by "a Jew from Alexandria", but that document is in fact a two-edged sword; the change was made merely to comply with the official requirement of precision in the designation form, for in practice there was no substantive difference between the two terms, and indeed throughout the document the petitioner's father continues to be called an "Alexandrian"[39]. The designation of Jews by that term is clearly shown in epigraphical examples more than once[40], indicating that there was nothing wrong with it and Jews could in fact be so referred to. Furthermore, a certain papyrus shows that Jews owned land in the Alexandrian *chora*; can it not therefore be assumed that they were entitled to be called "Alexandrians?" It might even be deduced that they were citizens of the *polis*, on the basis of the commonly held opinion that due to the contraction of the municipal

---

37 See a fuller treatment of the problem, pp. 297ff. below. But even the quotations cited here suggest that the *politeia* is not that of the *polis* but an independent one.
38 Schubart and Tcherikover admitted this, but made unconvincing attempts to explain it away. See Schubart, *Gnomon*, p. 33; Tcherikover, *CPJ*, II, p. 49.
39 See a fuller treatment of the petition, pp. 200ff. above.
40 See *CIJ*, I 644, 699; *OGIS*, 599; *Sefer ha-Yishuv, Yaffa*, Nos. 4, 25, 26, 27 and cf. Klein, *JPCI*, Nos. 135, 137, 141, 154.
41 See *CPJ*, II 142, lines 9-11.

chora ownership of its land was restricted exclusively to citizens[42]. Such a deduction is however, invalid, for those Jews were designated as "Macedonians" and their connection with the Jewish *politeuma* in Alexandria is unquestionable[43]. Obviously, then, just as the term *politai* was used in an ambiguous and rather imprecise way for citizens of both the *polis* and the Jewish *politeuma*, so was the term "Alexandrians", which also acquired the meaning of "provenance" in the common popular sense. Most probably the leaders of the citizens of the *polis* sought to eliminate the double and arbitary application of these terms so that they would be confined entirely to *polis* members. That would seem to be the reason for Apion's complaint: "Why then, if they are citizens (*cives*) do they not worship the same gods as the Alexandrians?" (*C. Apionem*, II 65).

Of course by this statement he disputed the right of the Jews to be called *politai* and "Alexandrians", for in his view the terms applied exclusively to citizens of the *polis*. In other words, he denied the existence of any other *politeia* in the city besides that represented by the *polis* based on unequivocal Alexandrianism, whose hallmark was the municipal cult. It is reasonable to suppose that the stipulation in the edict regarding the Jews' right to be called "Alexandrians" indicates that the clash with the Alexandrians involved that matter as well. For the struggle of the Jews concerned in the main not the desire for citizenship in the *polis*, but the right to organize as a separate political body, independent of the *polis*. Apparently the adversaries of the Jews even disputed their right to be called *politai* or "Alexandrians", so that a conflict in the area of terminology constituted still another aspect of the Jewish fight for *isopoliteia*.

Isopoliteia

In the solution of the complex problems related to the rights and status of the Jews, many scholars have considered the key to be the concept of *isopoliteia*[44]. There is no doubt that the more important

---

42 On that opinion see A.H.M. Jones, *CERP*, p. 305f.; Mitteis, *Reichsrecht u. Volksrecht*, p. 75.

43 This was definitely proven by *CPJ*, II 143 which notes the connection of one of the Jewish "Macedonians" with the "Jewish archives" in regard to this will. See especially line 7f. and the commentary of Fuks. Note that there were also "city archives" (*BGU*, 1131, lines 14, 32).

44 The fact that this is the key to the solution of these problems was stressed by Tarn,

segment of the word is *politeia*. The political philosophers of the Greek world attributed a number of simultaneous meanings to it, such as "regime", "constitution", "government", "civic status" or "citizenship" and "civic body". A careful analysis of the use of the term by Josephus reveals that he too understood the term to have all those meanings[45]. However, the instances in which he used it in the sense of "civic status" (or "citizenship") are the least frequent, and those in which it designated "constitution" are the most numerous. It is most instructive that in the vast majority of the latter, the "constitution" referred to was the laws of the Torah, and indeed that was the common usage in Hellenistic Jewish literature too[46]. It is therefore not surprising that he used the verb πολιτεύειν (or πολιτεύσθαι) to mean the establishment of community life according to the laws of the Torah[47]. It is important to note also that for Josephus the terms *politeuma* and *politeia* were synonymous and interchangeable[48]. That must be borne in mind while considering the meaning of *isopoliteia* in his works.

As a rule, *isopoliteia* in scholarly literature is defined as the reciprocity of civic rights between two cities as stipulated in a treaty between them[49]. But is that what Josephus meant? Did he really mean the citizenship of the Jews in the *polis*[50] by virtue of reciprocity of civic rights rather than the quality of the Jewish *politeuma* with the Greek *polis*? At first glance it appears that the second question should have an affirmative answer, ostensibly supported by Josephus' indirect testimony on the Claudian edict which is cited in connection with the conflict that erupted in Dora early in the rule of

---

p. 221f.; De Sanctis, *Riv. di Fil.*, 52 (1924), p. 473ff.; Scramuzza, *Emperor Claudius*, p. 75; Davis, *Race Relations*, p. 102; and others.

45 See the Appendix, p. 361ff.
46 E.g., *Antiquitates*, III 84, 213, 322; IV 45, 184, 191, 193-196, 198, 230, 302, 310, 312; V 98, 132, 179, 186; VI 35; X 275; XI 140; XII 240, 280; XIII 2, 245; XV 281; etc. Cf. *II Maccabees*, IV 11; VIII 17; XIII 14; *IV Maccabees*, III 20; VIII 7; XVII 9.
47 *Antiquitates*, XII 38, 142; XIV 260; and cf. *ibid.*, XI 112, 279. A similar usage figures in *II Maccabees*, V 2; XI 25; *III Maccabees*, III 4; *IV Maccabees*, II 7; IV 23; cf. also IV 1, 19. For similar uses of the verb, although not in connection with the laws of the Torah, see *Antiquitates*, II 330; XV 264; XVII 16, 60; XVIII 372, 378; XX 234.
48 See the Appendix, p. 363ff.
49 See, e.g., Tarn, pp. 72-85; Oehler, *RE(PW)*, 10 (1921), p. 2227f.; Glotz, *Greek City*, pp. 356-360; Hirzel, *Themis Dike u. Verwandtes*, p. 267; Ehrenberg, *Greek State*, p. 106ff.; Larsen, *Greek Federal States*, p. 203.
50 See e.g., Tcherikover, *Hellenistic Civilization and the Jews*, p. 411.

Agrippa I (*Antiquitates*, XIX 306). In a description attributed to
Petronius, governor of Syria, "the edict of the emperor permits Jews
to follow their own customs, yet also, be it noted, bids them to live
as fellow citizens with the Greeks" (συμπολιτεύσθαι τοῖς Ἕλλησιν).
This statement does not refer to the Jews' citizenship in the *polis*,
but is meant to stress that their rights are composed of two elements:
their right to keep their own particular laws (that is, their ancestral
laws), and their participation in general civic rights by virtue of their
connection as *politai* to the "civic laws". Philo too — in *In Flaccum*,
53 and *Legatio*, 371 (see pp. 235 ff. above) — proffered a similar
formulation, and he is considered particularly reliable on this subject.

As to *isopoliteia* in connection with the Claudian edict, a treaty on
reciprocal civic rights between the Jewish *politeuma* in Alexandria
and the *polis* seems doubtful, for several reasons: a) No such arrangement is known between Greeks and non-Greeks[51]. b) No precedent
for reciprocity of civic rights is known between a *politeuma* and a
polis. c) In the case of Alexandria, there was profound enmity between
the two that went so far as war. d) One party to the conflict denied
the validity of the other party's separate organization and thus also
of the civic status of the latter's members. e) Since citizenship in the
polis involved, or at least might involve, participation in the municipal
cult, it is hard to imagine that the Jewish community and its leaders
would be party to an agreement that would authorize heresy. Tarn
sought to circumvent that pitfall by arguing that *isopoliteia* means
the Jews' potential citizenship in the *polis*[52], but in fact even citizenship of that ilk could not be acceptable to God-fearing Jews. His
solution might have been tenable if he had claimed, for instance,
that the *isopoliteia* did not derive from a treaty, but was ordained by
the central government, so that the possibility of citizenship in the
polis was available, or subject to the individual decision of every Jew,
on condition that he would participate in the municipal cult. How-

---

51 That was the opinion of Tcherikover (*CPJ*, I, p. 40, n.104), and cf. Applebaum, *Gedalyahu Alon Memorial Volume*, p. 198.

52 See Tran, p. 222, who believed that "citizenship" could be fully implemented only
if the Jews agreed to participate in the municipal cult; and sought thus to justify the
application of the term *politai* to the Jews. In his view "potential citizens" were the
contrary of *astoi*, who were full citizens. However, serious doubts regarding the distinction between full and potential citizens in that period were raised by Hammond, *Harvard
Studies in Classical Philology*, 60 (1951), p. 169, n.40.

ever, that solution too seems contrived and artificial and obviously intended to solve the dilemma arising from a desire to interpret the term to mean "equal citizenship" and thus verify the edict and settle the contradictions between it and the letter to the Alexandrians.

Bell made the most significant stride towards the solution of the problem[53]. Out of a desire to settle those contradictions, he proposed a new interpretation for *isopoliteia* as Josephus used the term, an equal civic regime. In other words, Claudius meant not "equal citizenship" for the Jews (as individuals) but rather equality of rights of the community and its status as a political body. In his opinion, the scope of its separate rights was so broad that a condition of equality can be said to have existed between it and the *polis*. He further stressed that Josephus said nothing explicit regarding the granting of civic rights to the Jews, so that *isopoliteia* is not to be so interpreted in the edict, and the problem should be related to Srabo's testimony (in *Antiquitates*, XIV 117) regarding the organization of the Jewish community as an "independent *politeia*"[54]. Consequently that community can be considered a city within a city, with its own quite similar authority and separate organization[55]. Engers, Scramuzza, Smallwood, Davis, Ostersetzer and Feldman followed Bell's lead[56]. All of them, however, Bell included, continued to believe in the Jews' desire to attain Alexandrian citizenship, and thus forfeited the advantage of their method.

The addition of Version E to paragraph 284 of the edict — "And the Alexandrians rose up against the Jews among them who attained *isopoliteia* with the other Alexandrians"[57], etc. — can cast light on the problem. The distinction made between two groups of "Alexan-

---

53 Bell, *Jews and Christians*, p. 10ff. That study is important first of all because it was the first to deal with the connection between the edict and the Letter to the Alexandrians.

54 In support of Bell's impression it should be noted that the contiguity of the edict to Strabo's testimony is indicated also by the mention of the ethnarchs.

55 See Bell, *Jews and Christians*, p. 16f. Strictly speaking, this idea was first proposed, in a restrained and somewhat hesitant manner, by Jouguet, in 1911 (p. 20), before he could have compared the edict to *Claudius' Letter*, which was published only in 1924.

56 See Engers, *Mnemosyne*, n.s. 54 (1926), p. 159, whose chief conclusion merits repetition: "In territorio urbis Alexandreae utique duas civitates liberas fuisse, quae idem valerent et aequo iure fruentur." See also Scramuzza, *Emperor Claudius*, p. 76; Davis, *Race Relations*, p. 93ff.; Smallwood, *Jews Under Roman Rule*, p. 225ff. Smallwood, p. 10. Cf. Ostersetzer, *Broda Jubilee Volume*, p. 31ff.; Feldman, *Studies in Judaism*, p. 44 b; idem, *Josephus (LCL)*, vol. 9, p. 348.

57 See Niese, *Flavii Josephi Opera Omnia*, ad. loc.

drians" is quite clear, and provides no grounds for thinking that the Jews identified with the citizens of the *polis*[58]. Furthermore, the expression "other Alexandrians" accords with Philo[59], and also supports the conclusion that "Alexandrians" applied to the Jews as well. The distinction between the two groups is also quite apparent in paragraph 285 of the edict which refers to "the people of the Jews (τὸ Ἰουδαίων ἔθνος) and their own customs" (τοῖς ἰδίοις ἔθεσιν)[60], and what is more important, makes an explicit distinction between "both parties" (ἀμφοτέροις... τοῖς μέρεσι)[61]. The "Jewish Alexandrians" and the "other Alexandrians" were thus two separate and different groups, but the status of the first in relation to the second was defined by the term *isopoliteia*.

The edict and other passages indicate that in Josephus' writings the term *isopoliteia* defined an equal (or similar) organizational-political status of two parallel and separate bodies, and thus are evidence of the existence in Alexandria of a Jewish *politeuma* separate from the *polis*. For if the edict meant to present the Jews of Alexandria as citizens of the *polis*, why did it not state their rights as such? In fact nothing of the sort is specified; as in all Josephus' passages about the rights of the Jews in Alexandria and other cities, only Jewish rights are mentioned, that is, the right to keep ancestral laws, maintain their own organization and a well-defined Jewish way of life. That alone shows that the edict and like it other documents reflected the efforts of Jewish communities in the Diaspora to exist as separate organizations (such as *politeumata*) while the Hellenistic *poleis* sought to destroy them and impose their laws and rule on the Jews.

The data in Josephus demonstrates that from the outset Jewish settlement in Alexandria had a definitely territorial character. *Bellum*, II 488 states that the Ptolemaic kings "assigned them a quarter of their own" and that accords perfectly with the Strabo statement (in *Antiquitates*, XIV 117) that "in the city of Alexandria a great part of

---

58 Cf. also *C. Apionem*, II 64 which has *aliis Alexandrinis* while II 63 describes the Jews as *Iudaeis in Alexandria commorantibus*.
59 *Legatio*, 183; *In Flaccum*, 76, 139; and see p. 234f. and 246f. above.
60 Or, the "customs of the Jews," according to some versions (M, W, E) where the word Ἰουδαίων was replaced by ἰδίοις.
61 This distinction is supported by Philo (*Legatio*, 355) and *Claudius' Letter to the Alexandrians* (*P. Lond.*, 1912); see especially line 88 and cf. lines 75, 80, 102.

the city has been allocated to this nation". The use of the verb
ἀφορίζω here stresses the separation of the Jewish dwellings[62], indicated in *C. Apionem*, II 33-36 by the words "part (μέρος) of the city"
and "place (τόπος) of residence" as well as by the topographical
description of the Jewish quarter[63]. In *Bellum*, II 495 Josephus
supplied the name of that quarter — Delta — and noted that "there
the Jews settled together (or concentrated)". On the basis of that
description, the Jewish quarter can be termed a συνοικία, that is, a
settlement of a group of people (a community) living together as an
organized body. Josephus said the very same thing in *C. Apionem*, II
32: "the Jews in Alexandria living together alongside them." Tarn
and Davis are certainly right in assuming that the almost identical
wording of the edict describing the Jews as "fellow colonists...
jointly with the Alexandrians" (*Antiquitates*, XIX 281) proves the
existence of a Jewish *politeuma* alongside the *polis*[64]. *Bellum*, II
488 also provides a logical explanation for the allocation of a separate
residential section: "in order that through mixing less with aliens,
they might be free to observe their rules more strictly". Thus "living
together alongside them" was designed to safeguard "the ancestral
law" (πάτριος πολιτεία) of the Jews[65]. It is therefore not surprising
that the edict treated the "living together" and the *isopoliteia* in
one venue.

The edict states explicitly that the documents and orders the Jews
had served as official authority for the defense of their rights (τῶν
δικαίων αὐτοῖς) connected with their own organization, the religion of their forefathers (τὴν πάτριον θρησκείαν) and their own
customs (τοῖς ἰδίοις ἔθεσιν). All these are summed up in the term τὰ
δικαιώματα[66], which places the Jewish community (i.e. the *politeuma*)
in a status equal or similar to (that is, in *isopoliteia* with) the Greek
communal organisation. The fact that the rights of the community
were defined in a separate *politeia* is shown also in *Antiquitates*, XII
121 which states that the Antiocheans and the Alexandrians asked
Vespasian and Titus "that the Jews should no longer continue to

---

62 See Liddell & Scott, s.v.
63 For particulars on its location, see p. 247f. above.
64 Tarn, p. 222, n.3; Davis, *Race Relations*, p. 102, n.4.
65 On Josephus' use of the phrase, see the Appendix, p. 362.
66 See *Antiquitates*, XIX 281, 283, 285, and cf. *C. Apionem*, II 37; *Bellum*, VII 110.

have the rights of their *politeia*"[67], but "they still did not deprive
them of their existing rights of the *politeia*, mentioned above" (*ibid.*,
123ff.). This meaning of *isopoliteia* is even more evident in the World
edict of Claudius (*Antiquitates*, XIX 286-291). There the Roman
emperor clearly noted that the defense of Jewish rights throughout
the Roman empire was not merely a favor granted at the request of
his royal friends (King Agrippa and King Herod of Chalkis, but was
dictated by his overall policy of equality for all, Jews and non-Jews.
He explicitly asserted that "in particular I did so because I hold it
right that not even Greek cities should be deprived of these privileges,
seeing that they were in fact guaranteed for them in the time of the
divine Augustus. It is right therefore that the Jews throughout the
whole world under our sway should also observe the customs of their
fathers without let or hindrance" (*ibid.*, 298f.). Obviously the contrast between "Jews" and "Greek cities" corresponds to the contrast
of the rights (τὰ δίκαια) of the two sides. It is therefore not surprising
that the emperor required the Jews too "not to set at nought the
beliefs about the gods held by other peoples but to keep their own
laws" (*ibid.*, 290)[68]. The clear differentiation between "the people of
the Jews" (τὸ Ἰουδαίων ἔθνος; *ibid.*, 284) and the "other peoples"
(τῶν ἄλλων ἐθνῶν; *ibid.*, 290) is very significant; and it should be
noted that in Jewish inscriptions from the Roman Diaspora some
communities are called "the people of the Jews" and contain also
synonyms of "people" (ἔθνος) and *politeuma*[69]. It is important to
remember that the same applies to the Jewish community of Alexandria which Strabo, for instance, referred to as both *ethnos* and
politeia in a single context (in *Antiquitates*, XIV 117).

Isopoliteia was not the only term Josephus used to define the
rights of the Jews. In *C. Apionem*, II 35, for example, he wrote: "In
fact, however, it (that is, the Jewish quarter in Alexandria) was
presented to them as their residence by Alexander and they obtained
privileges on a par with those of the Macedonians" (ἴσης παρὰ τοῖς

---

67 The syntactic form τὰ δίκαια τὰ τῆς πολιτείας justifies the translation "the rights of
their *politeia*."

68 It appears that the Jews too were pugnacious in regard to the holy places of their adversaries; a similar case figures in *Claudius' Letter to the Alexandrians* (chap. 9, a below).

69 See Schürer, vol. 3, p. 74. The synonymity is especially obvious in inscription *CPJ*,
III 1530A from Leontopolis about Abramos the *politarches*, i.e. the man who "wore
the wreath of magistracy for the whole people" (see pp. 125-127 above.)

μακεδόσι τιμῆς ἐπέτυχον). On the other hand *Bellum*, II 487 says that "at Alexandria there had been incessant strife between the native inhabitants and the Jewish settlers since the time when Alexander, having received from the Jews very active support against the Egyptians, granted them, as a reward for their assistance, permission to reside in the city on terms of equality (ἐξ ἰσομοιρίας) with the Greeks". The Liddell & Scott dictionary defines ἰσοτιμία as "equality of rights" and thus a ἰσότιμος was a person enjoying such equality. The latter term under the Ptolemies was applied to prominent persons whose status equalled that of various ranks of courtiers such as "the king's kinsmen", "the first friends", etc[70]. The term ἰσομοιρία has a similar meaning: "equal part" or "equal share" in some asset[71].

The passage in *C. Apionem*, II 35f. shows that Josephus merely wished to present the Jews of Alexandria as having equal status, from the standpoint of their privileges, with the Macedonians, and to prove that he stressed that even in his time there was still a "tribe" of Jews known as "Macedonians" (*ibid.*, 36). That this statement is accurate is definite, for such Jews are mentioned in Alexandrian papyri dating from the reign of Augustus (*CPJ*, II 142-143). However, Josephus' statement is somewhat exaggerated and may give the impression that all Alexandrian Jews were of that class[72], which of course was not the case, but he did retain the Ptolemaic sense of the term *isotimoi*[73], for only thus did those Jews obtain their privileges and the right to be called "Macedonians".

Tcherikover believed that Josephus applied the term "Macedonians" to the citizens of Alexandria as well, in simple error rather than in an attempt to mislead[74]. He argued that Josephus just did not distinguish between "Greeks" (or "Hellenes") and "Macedonians", considering both citizens of the *polis*, and attributing an ethnic denotation to both terms. His main authority for this view was *Bellum*, II 487-490 which refers to "Greeks" (*ibid.*, 487, 490), "Macedonians" (*ibid.*, 488) and "Alexandrians" (*ibid.*, 490) in the

---

70 See Rostovtzeff, *CAH*, 7 (1964), p. 166; and see also Fraser, vol. 2, p. 187, n.73.

71 See Liddell & Scott, s.v.

72 That impression might be gotten from the beginning of the passage in *C. Apionem*, II 33.

73 There are three other instances of such a usage in his works: *Antiquitates*, VII 284, XVI 98, XIX 317.

74 *Jews and Greeks* (1931), p. 330; *Hellenistic Civilization and the Jews*, p. 323f.

same context. A careful scrutiny however reveals that Josephus did
not confuse the terms. In *Bellum*, II 487 he said merely that the
Jews were given the right "to reside in the city on terms of equality
(ἰσομοιρία) with the Greeks". As he did not refer to any civic political
right, but only to the right of residence, there are no grounds for the
notion that he identified the Jews with citizens of the *polis*. The
isomoiria here means only that they were allotted "a quarter of their
own" like the Greeks.

According to Tcherikover, as shown in several passages, Josephus
considered the "Greeks" citizens of the *polis*[75], as did other Greek
writers like Polybius, for instance[76]. But that was not Josephus' view
of "Macedonians". In *Antiquitates*, XII 119, reporting that Seleucus
I Nicator declared the Jews in Antioch and other cities "to have
equal privileges (ἰσοτίμους) with the Macedonians and Greeks who
were settled in these cities", the use of the two terms (i.e. "Macedonians" and "Greeks") indicates that for Josephus they were not
synonymous, or else he could have simply written "citizens of the
polis". As described below, Antioch and its sister cities (Seleucia
Pireia, Apamea on the Orontes, and Laodicia) were founded within
the framework of Seleucus I's military colonization program, and
their original population was mixed, like that of Alexandria. The
outstanding element consisted of "Macedonians", and the rest were a
mixture of people of extremely varied ethnic origin whom the general
inclusive term "Greeks" (or "Hellenes") aptly described[77]. Tcherikover himself claimed that the "Macedonians" differed from the
urban communities beside which they were settled, and there is no
reason to believe that Josephus' description did not reflect that
situation, particularly since he used the two terms, "Macedonians"
and "Greeks" together. Furthermore, any doubt about Josephus'
construction of "Macedonians" is eliminated by *Bellum*, V 460,
where the term clearly has a purely functional, military meaning, and
no ethnic content at all[78].

---

75 *Antiquitates*, XII 119, XV 160f., XIX 306; and cf. *ibid.*, XX 173 in regard to the designation of the citizens of Caesaraea as "Syrians".
76 Polybius, in Strabo, XVII 1, 12 (797c). It is important to bear in mind that he does not
   mention "Macedonians" among the Alexandrian citizenry.
77 For details see below, p. 299.
78 That passage deals with Antiochus' bodyguard from Commagene "calling themselves
   Macedonians" whose members were "armed and trained in the Macedonians fashion,

Thus the Jews' equality of rights with the "Macedonians" is no more than literal. In other words, Tcherikover's only conclusion should have been that the privileges of the "Macedonian" Jews were the outcome of their military service, as were those of other "Macedonians", and as such they were placed "outside the community of citizens" (that is, the *polis*), as he himself said[79].

The question then is, what is the point of the Jews' equality of rights with the "Greeks"? And the answer is that since as a definite political body the "Macedonians" resembled the community of citizens (that is, the "Greeks") in their privileges and organization, there was reason to compare the status of the Jews to that of both other groups. Even if Tcherikover's contention that for Josephus "Greeks" and "Macedonians" were synonymous terms defining the citizens of the Alexandria *polis* is accepted, that still does not mean that what Josephus said about Jewish equality of rights refers to citizenship in the *polis*. Although, as Tcherikover suggested, in the course of time (after Alexander the Great) "Macedonians" probably intermigled with the citizenry, it is not unreasonable to suppose that they did not do so as an organized body (*politeuma*). Furthermore, the existence of a "Macedonian" tribe within the Jewish community could mean a parallel "Macedonian" group within the citizen community. If that was the case, the comparison of the Jews' status as an organized group with that of the other two was logical. Such a conclusion of course accords with the notion of Alexandria as a collection of *politeumata* proffered by Tarn, and with the view that the similar status of them all was defined by the term *isopoliteia*.

Light can perhaps be cast on the problem from another angle as well. The term *isopoliteia* may very well derive from the lexicon of concepts prevailing in Greek philosophy on democracy, as an abstract political ideal, and Josephus may have based his use of it on the fact that the constitution of the Alexandrian *polis* followed the Athenian model[80]. The Athenian philosophers deemed equality to be the

---

from which circumstance indeed they took their title, most of them lacking any claim to belong to that race." See also the end of chap. 4.

79 See *Jews and Greeks* (1931), p. 330, and his discussion on p. 327ff. See also Fraser on the special status of "Macedonians" unrelated to Josephus (Fraser, vol. 1, pp. 53, 80).

80 On the Athenian pattern of the Alexandrian constitution, see *P. Hal.*, lines 35, 50, 57, 62, 66, 79, 82, 115, 128, 173; cf. *P. Oxy.*, 2177; see also Fraser, vol. 1, p. 110ff.

cornerstone of a democratic regime[81], and to be the enjoyment "of
equal and similar things"[82]. Therefore every citizen in such a society
was an "equal and similar citizen"[83], and democracy was termed an
"equal and similar *politeia*" ($\pi o\lambda\iota\tau\epsilon\iota a$ ἴση καὶ ὁμοία)[84]. The term
isopoliteia as Josephus used it may thus have derived from those
abstract notions of equality of Greeks democracy, especially since
the Hellenistic kings used to set democratic constitutions as the norm
in the cities of their kingdoms. But that is not the case with the terms
isotimia and *isomoiria* which seem to be genuine technical terms
defining a very specific situation, and as such Josephus used them
according to their original meaning.

The same conclusions can be drawn from reports on the rights of
Jews in Cyrene and Asia Minor. *Antiquitates*, XVI 160f. notes that
the kings granted the Jews "equal rights" ($i\sigma o\nu o\mu ia$) and that Augustus "granted them the same equality of taxation ($i\sigma o\tau\epsilon\lambda\epsilon ia$) as
before". The first term appears likewise to come from the notions
of Greek democracy[85], and should not be construed to denote any
particular political arrangement. Indeed in Philo's historical works it
is used to describe the ideal situation that obtained at the start of
Gaius Caligula's reign (*Legatio*, 13). The term *isotoleia*, however, is a
genuinely technical term for the equality in taxation granted the
metoikoi in relation to the citizens of the Greek *polis*. In other words,
people having *isotoleia* were exempt from the *metoikion* tax, and in
that respect equal to the citizens of the *polis*, while otherwise their
status was between those of citizens and *metoikoi*. The testimony of
Strabo (in *Antiquitates*, XIV 115) shows that the Jews had that intermediate status, since they were not counted as either Cyrenean
citizens or *metoikoi*[86]. The description in Philo (*De Vita Mosis*, I
34-36) of the Jews as intermediate in rank between *astoi* and *metoi-*
koi accords nicely with that of Josephus. It is worthwhile mention-

---

81 See Aristotle, *Politics*, IV 4, 129lb (31-35). The Greek democrats took pride in a *politeia*
   based on the equality of citizens and their resemblance to each other (*Politics*, III 6,
   1279a, 9).
82 Demosthenes Or., 21, 112, A19.
83 *Syll.*, 333. line 25: 421, line 13; 742, line 45.
84 *Ibid.*, 254, line 6; 312, line 25; and cf. Aeschines Or., 1,5.
85 See Hirzel, *Themis, Dike und Verwandtes*, pp. 228-320, and esp. pp. 240ff., 263ff.
   See also Glotz, *Greek City*, p. 129; Ehrenberg, *Polis und Imperum*, p. 279ff.
86 It was Rostovtzeff, *SEHHW*, (p. 333) who first compared the fourfold division of the

ing here Marcus' opinion that the status of *isopoliteia* was "quasi-citizenship"[86a].

C. A Comparative Study of the Rights of the Jews of Caesarea Maritima

Like Alexandria, this city appears to have quite a similar conflict about *isopoliteia* between the Jews and Greeks. While examining and reconstructing the episodes leading to the great Jewish revolt against the Romans, Levine referred several times to the political status of the Jews in the city, indicated in *Antiquitates* (XX 173, 183) by the term *isopoliteia*. Following the accepted view of the meaning of the term, he maintains that when using it Josephus referred to a legal situation wherein, in a number of *poleis* throughout the Diaspora, Jews possessed civic rights equal to those of their neighbors (i.e. the citizens)[87]. While discussing the difference between the accounts in *Bellum* and in *Antiquitates*, Levine suggests that Josephus might have introduced some changes and corrections in the latter work for apologetic reasons rather than in order to describe an historical reality[87a]. Although Levine has drawn some quite persuasive conclusions about the uniqueness of the Caesarean struggle, it seems that the *isopoliteia* question in Caesarea deserves further study.

In fact, Josephus presented two versions of the Jewish-Greek quarrel in Caesarea (*Bellum*, II 266-270, 284-292; *Antiquitates*, XX 173-178, 182-184). According to both accounts, the city population was divided into two distinct groups, "the Jews" on one hand and "the Syrians" (or "the Greeks") on the other[88], each organized as a

---

Cyrenean population (reported by Strabo) with the division of the Egyptian population, and reached the conclusions noted above. See also Applebaum, *Jews and Greeks in Ancient Cyrene*, p. 190.

86a See Marcus, "The Hellenistic Age", in *Great Ages and Ideas of the Jewish People* (ed. L.W. Schwarz), 1956, p. 115: "Instead of citizenship, the Jewish residents of Alexandria, Antioch, Ephesus, and other Hellenistic cities had the status of *isopoliteia* or 'quasi-citizenship'. Accordingly, organized in separate corporation or *politeuma* within the *polis*, they enjoyed religious and cultural autonomy, and exemption from those civic obligations that conflicted with the Jewish religion". Significant evaluation, indeed!

87 *JJS*, 25 (1975), pp. 381-397, especially p. 385ff.

87a *Ibid.*, pp. 386-387. Most of the scholars who have dealt with Josephus' evidence about the civic status of the Jews in Alexandria have adopted the same attitude.

88 On th tendentious systematic uses of these terms by Josephus, see Levine. *op.cit.*, pp.

self-contained body with its own magistrates. The leadership of the Jewish community was in the hands of "the Elders"[88a], also known as "the Heads of the Jewish inhabitants of Caesarea"[88b], or "the Jewish Notables"[88c]. The other group in the city was led by "the Heads of the Syrians in Caesarea"[88d]. Ranking above the Jewish and the Syrian leaders were the Roman authorities[88e]. In this respect, the situation in Caesarea was very similar to that in Alexandria and Antioch, cities which were main centers of administration in their provinces, and to which delegates from Rome were posted. The Roman method of rule as adopted to the management of Palestine city life was based on a combination of government control and partial autonomy[89]. Such a method could create suitable conditions for establishment of several political organization within the cities[90]. It is not surprising, therefore, that the Jewish community in Caesarea was a political ethnic body recognized by the authorities as one representing a legal personality (i.e. *politeuma*). The separation

---

381 (n.3), 387 (n.35). The distinction between the two sections of the city is evident mainly in *Bellum*, II 266, where Josephus deals with the "Jewish portion of the population" (τῶν ἀναμεμιγμένων Ἰουδαίων) as distinguished from the Syrian. The two sides are referred to several times as two parties (οἱ δε ἕτεροι, ἑκάτεροι, ἀμφοῖν, ἑκατέρωθεν; *Bellum*, II 266-7, 270) who sent deputies (πρέσβεις ibid. 270) to Rome. In *Antiquitates* (XX 174, 178) also a clear distinction is made between the two different sides (ἀμφοτέρωθεν, ἀμφότερα).

88a *Bellum*, II 267: οἱ γεραιοί.

88b *Antiquitates*, XX 182: οἱ πρωτεύοντες τῶν τὴν καισάρειαν κατοικούντων Ἰουδαίων.

88c *Bellum*, II 287: οἱ δυνατοὶ τῶν Ἰουδαίων. They were twelve in number (*ibid.* 292) and were described in *Antiquitates*, XX 178 as "those who were of eminent rank" (προύχοντας κατὰ τὴν ἀξίωσιν).

88d *Antiquitates*, XX 183: τῶν ἐν καισαρείᾳ οἱ πρῶτοι Σύρων, cf. Niese, apparatus criticus, *ad loc*. It seems that they are those referred to in *Acta Apostolorum* 25:23 as "the principal men of the city" (ἀνδράσιν τοῖς κατ' ἐξοχὴν τῆς πόλεως); cf. Schürer, vol, p. 137, n.173.

88e In *Bellum*, II 269 there is a reference to "the magistrates" (οἱ ἔπαρχοι) as those who were at pains to repress the disorders in the city. It seems that this term applies not only to the procurator and his military staff but also to the governor of the city (either ὁ ἔπαρχος τῆς πόλεως or ὁ τῆς πόλεως ὕπαρχος or perhaps some sort of ὁ ἐπὶ τῆς πόλεως or στρατηγός τῆς πόλεως). This impression may find support in the version of *Antiquitates*, XX 174, where οἱ τῆς χώρας ἔπαρχοι (in the plural) are mentioned again. For other contemporary instances of such an office in Palestine, see *ibid.*, 333; *Vitae*, 74, 89; *Bellum*, II 615; Avi-Yonah, *Historical Geography of Palestine*, p. 64.

89 A.H.M. Jones, *Cities*, p. 258ff.; idem, *The Greek city*, pp. 170ff.; 270ff.

90 Apparently this phenomenon originated in the Hellenistic period. For details, see Applebaum, "The legal status" etc., pp. 452ff.; and see also pp. 181ff. above.

between "the Jews" and "the Syrians" was such that each group was allowed to send official delegates to Rome[90a]. In fact the Roman procurator would not have negotiated with Caesarean Jewish leaders unless they had indeed been authorized to represent their community[90b].

Until the days of Felix, when relations between the two parties reached the point of explosion, there prevailed to a certain degree a state of coexistence in the city which was termed *isopoliteia* (*Antiquitates*, XX 173, 183). In other words, Caesarea saw an equality between two political bodies, the Greek *polis* and the Jewish *politeuma*, each of which had the privilege of living by its ancestral laws and of maintaining its own leadership, and was equally dependent on the central government. Yet such a description is too simple, since Caesarea was after all a Greek *polis*, a fact which implies that the Greek community (or the Syrian *politeuma*) was legally identified with the *polis*[91]. Another logical inference from this situation is that the political standing of "the Greeks" (or "the Syrians") was superior to that of "the Jews". In other words, the status of the former in comparison with the latter was, in a sense, that of *primi inter pares*. No wonder, therefore, that only "the Greeks" were designated as "Caesareans" (see above note 91), whereas "the Jews" were called "the Jews in Caesarea", or "the Jews living in Caesarea", or "the Jewish inhabitants of Caesarea"[92]. Although there is epigraphic proof that the title "Caesareans" was applied to Jews as well[93], and although the phrase "the Greek Caesareans"[93a] might suggest a corresponding title like "the Jewish Caesareans", it appears that the latter was not a formal but merely a popular turn of phrase

---

90a *Bellum*, II 270; *Antiquitates*, XX 182-3.
90b *Bellum*, II 287-8, 292.
91 See, for instance, *Antiquitates*, XIX 356, 361, 364, 365; *Bellum*, II 284, 285, 289, 290, 291, references in which the Greeks are called either Καισαρεῖς or οἱ Καισαρέων Ἕλληνες.
92 *Bellum*, II 285: οἱ ἐν Καισαρείᾳ Ἰουδαῖοι; VII 361: οἱ Καισάρειαν Ἰουδαῖοι κατοικοῦντες. *Antiquitates*, XX 184: οἱ κατὰ τὴν Καισάρειαν Ἰουδαῖοι; cf. *ibid.*, 175; see also *Beluum*, II 457: τοὺς παρ' ἑαυτοῖς Ἰουδαίους; cf. VII 363. It is worth noting that a similar situation existed in Hellenistic Jaffa, the citizens of which were called "the *politeuma* of the *Joppitai*", or simply "the *Joppitai*", whereas the Jewish residents were regarded as "the Jews who dwelt among them (i.e. the *Joppitai*)"; see *II Maccabees*, 12:3, 7.
93 See *CIJ*, I, nos. 25, 370. Cf. *CIJ*, I 716 (probably from Athens).
93a *Bellum*, II 284: οἱ Καισαρέων Ἕλληνες; cf. *ibid.*, 285, 289-291.

which, at the most, could designate their *origo*[94].

Let us now examine the roots of the strife between the Caesarean rivals in order to clarify the Jews' political status in the city. According to the narrative in *Bellum* (II 266), the Jews rose against the Syrians claiming that the city was theirs: they refused to admit that Caesarea was really a Greek *polis*. The picture is presented differently in *Antiquitates* (XX 173), where Josephus states that the quarrel between the two parties involved the subject of *isopoliteia*, and that the Jews insisted on being as superior in status[95]. The analogy of the two versions suggests that "to be superior in status (or "to have the precedence")[95a] in a situation of *isopoliteia*, meant either the identification of one group with the *polis*, or simply the recognition of the members of one group as the masters of the city. In this there is a great difference between the Jewish strife in Caesarea and that in Alexandria, because the Caesarean Jews did not content themselves with political coexistence with their neighbors, but firmly denied the exclusive right of the Greek community to be identified with the *polis*, a right which they demanded for themselves. By contrast, the Jewish struggle in Alexandria, conducted and controlled for the most part by quite moderate leadership, was concentrated upon the very existence of the Jewish community as a legal organization. Consequently, a peaceful coexistence with the Alexandrian *polis* was the main goal in the eyes of the local Jewry.

The controversies between the two sides in Caesarea can prove the hypothesis presented above. The Jewish townsmen supported their claim for superiority (or precedence) by emphasizing the Jewish origin of King Herod, the founder of the renewed city[95b]. Although the Syrians did not deny this fact, they refused to accept the Jewish argument as relevant to the dispute. They supported their claim to rule the city with two arguments: a) Herod's intention was to build a Greek city, otherwise he would not have erected so many statues or pagan temples there (*Bellum*, II 266); b) no Jews were living in the

---

94 The same was evident in Alexandria, where Jews were also described as 'Αλεξανδρεῖς; see Philo, *In Flaccum*, 80, 123; *Legatio*, 194, 350; cf. Bell, *Jews and Christians*, p. 14; Smallwood, pp. 10, 255. For a detailed discussion of this subject, see above pp. 233ff.

95 When writing οἱ μὲν γὰρ Ἰουδαῖοι πρωτεύειν ἠξίουν Josephus must have had in mind a conception of political rank and dignity.

95a See the translation of Feldman, *Josephus*, (*LCL* ed.), vol. 9, p. 483.

95b *Bellum*, II 266; *Antiquitates*, XX 173.

city before Herod's time, when it still bore the name of Strato's Tower (*Antiquitates*, XX 173). It cannot share Levine's opinion that the second argument is much weaker than the first[96]. On the con-- trary, it might be better evaluated as the Syrian trump card when arguing with Jewish envoys at the Emperor's tribunal in Rome. One can easily imagine that the Syrian deputies pressed their complaint against the Jews by blaming them for the illegal occupation of the city by Alexander Jannaeus. Such an argument might gain the sym- pathy of wide circles in Rome itself as well as the support of Greek public opinion, which viewed Pompey as a real liberator of Hellenistic city life in Palestine, who restored conquered *poleis* to their "legi- timate citizens"[97]. On the other hand, what political profit could the Jews gain by arguing for the right to rule the city on the unstable basis of Jannaeus' conquest? At most, it might have served the Jews' internal needs[98]. In any case the striking fact is that Caesarea was excluded by Talmuduc tradition from the boundaries of Eretz-Israel and was assigned to the so-called *Eretz ha-Ammim*[99]. But the most significant fact in this context is that the city is referred to by the old name of Strato's Tower[100]. For generations it was regarded by the Jews as the "*Metropolis* of Kings" and was offensively symbolized as the "Daughter of Edom (= Rome)", a title which emphasized its deep enmity to Jerusalem[101].

It stands to reason that the Caesarean conflict did not break out overnight during the administration of Felix; such quarrels developed gradually and reached fever pitch slowly, as a rule. Alexander Jan-

---

96 Levine, *op.cit.*, p. 382, n.8.

97 Ἃς πάσας τοῖς γνησίοις ἀποδοὺς πολίαις; (*Bellum*, I 156-7), cf. *Antiquitates*, XIV 75-6; Strabo, XVI 2, 40, 76; A.H.M. Jones, pp. 256-258. For further details about the negative attitude of the Greco-Roman historiography toward Alexander Jannaeus, see Efron, *Gedalyahu Alon Memorial Volume*, pp. 78ff.; Stern, *Jacob Liver Memorial Volume*, p. 375ff.; idem, *Gedalyahu Alon Memorial Volume*, p. 169ff.

98 In this sense I understand the Talmudic traditions of the *Scholion* to *Megillath Ta'anith* (ed. Lichtenstein), p. 327; *B.T. Megillah*, 6a; *Tos. Oholoth*, xviii 16 (ed. Zuckermandel, p. 617); Levine, *op.cit.*, p. 392, n.79.

99 On this subject see the studies of Heldesheimer and Klein, in *Studies in the Geography of Eretz-Israel* (Hebrew Trans.), pp. 24ff., 123, 150ff., 162.

100 Nevertheless, it is difficult to decide whether or not the *halakhic* exclusion of Caesarea from the boundaries of *Eretz-Israel* was the result of Nero's decision in favor of Hellenic control of the city, cf. Liberman, *Tarbiz*, 2 (1930), p. 107; Alon, *Studies in Jewish History etc.* vol. 2, p. 14; Klein, *op.cit.*, p. 150ff., 158.

101 See for example, *B.T. Megillah*, 6a.

naeus' occupation, as well as the settlement of Jews in the city[102], had sown the seeds of calamity which sprouted and put forth thorns after Herod's death. Of course Herod had turned a new page in the history of the city, but most probably he would not have dared to alter the political order imposed by Pompey and Gabinius according to which the Greek townsmen were entrusted with the management of the city. To whatever extent the foundation of Caesarea had conformed with Herod's cosmopolitan conception of Hellenism[103], it does not follow that he totally ignored local Jewish interests. On the contrary, when he gave a new constitution to the city[104], he must have made some juridical provision for the Jewish community. It is difficult to believe that as a distinguished fighter for Jewish rights in Greek cities of the Mediterranian basin[104a], he would not have taken notice of such rights in his own realm. It is very likely that he introduced to Caesarea some relevant regulations derived from juridical standards of the Hellenistic heritage. It stands to reason that the Jews of Caesarea, like the Jews of other *poleis* throughout the Greco-Roman world, constituted a community (*politeuma*) which enjoyed the basic privilege of living by its ancestral laws as well as the right to have independent institutions of leadership. As in Alexandria, the Jews must have been granted a *politeia* of their own, based on specifically Jewish laws, in addition to general civic rights[105]. Such a system of royal supervision and partial autonomy (granted to more than one group in the same city) might be relied upon to cause severe conflicts in times of cirsis and political suspense.

The first eruption of emotions in Caesarea known to us followed upon the death of King Agrippa I (44 C.E.), when the Greek townsmen, together with those who were then in military service, demonstrated their hatred by disgraceful behaviour towards the late Jewish

---

102 Cf. *Megillath Ta'anith* (ed. Lichtenstein), p. 327.
103 Cf. *Antiquitates*, XV 293; Stern, *Tarbiz*, 35 (1966), p. 235ff.; idem, *The Jewish People*, vol. 1, p. 270ff.
104 I fully agree with Otto and Schalit that Herod imposed on each of the new cities he founded a new polity or constitution (i.e. πολιτεία), possibly including a certain code of civic laws (πολιτικοὶ νόμοι); see: Otto, *Herodes*, p. 120ff.; Schalit, King Herod (Hebrew), p. 159.
104a *Antiquitates*, XII 125-127; XVI 27-65.
105 Cf. *In Flaccum*, 53; *Legatio*, 371, and see pp. 235ff. above. The "general civic rights" were those applied to *politai*, viz. citizens of the *polis* and members of the Jewish *politeuma*.

king and his family. The rigorous policy of the Emperor Claudius restored order in the city, but it could not suppress the conflict completely[105a]. It is not surprising, therefore, that the procuratorship of Felix 52-60-?- C.E.), which was the turning point in Jewish-Roman relations in Judea[106], had aroused factious adults and passionate youths alike among the Jews to strive for dominance in Caesarea[106a]. Thenceforth, Jews openly demanded political superiority in the city and used force to back their claims. It is not easy to decide whether or not the hottempered among the Jews were in fact connected with the Zealot movement. The famous speach of Eleazar son of Yair on Massada indicates that the Jews of Caesarea "had not even contemplated revolt from Rome" (*Bellum*, VII 362), but his words should not necessarily be taken to imply the lack of such connection[107]. In the beginning Felix acted alone and in maintaining his authority as procurator tried to bring the situation under control by force — force directed mainly against the Jews. When he realized that emotions had become even more inflamed, he decided to send delegations from both sides to Rome, so that they could put their claims directly before Nero himself (*Bellum*, II 270).

At this point the two versions of Josephus differ once again. According to *Antiquitates* (XX 182) the Jewish envoys "went up to Rome to accuse Felix"; their journey coincided with the termination of his service in office (60 C.E.?). As regards the nature of the mission and its date, the two accounts complement each other at this stage. But further on their differences become much more explicit. According to *Antiquitates* (XX 182-184), the Syrian leaders were assisted

---

105a *Antiquitates*, XIX 356-366.

106 Cf. Schürer, vol. 1, pp. 571ff.; idem (eds. Vermes & Millar), vol. 1, p. 460ff.

106a *Bellum*, II 267ff., 286, 290; cf. *Antiquitates*, XX 178, 182.

107 It is not easy to decide whether or not their advantage in physical strength (σωμάτων ἀλκῇ, *Bellum*, II 268) might imply the numerical superiority of Caesarean Jewry (so Levine, *op.cit.*, pp. 382-3). The general view is that Caesarea might have been inhabited at the time 50,000 persons, among whom there were approximately 20,000 Jews; cf. *Bellum*, II 457; Schürer (eds. Vermes & Millar), vol. 1, p. 465, n.41. If the Jewish population was really in the minority, it would appear that in order to be victorious in the street clashes (*Antiquitates*, XX 176; *Bellum*, II 270), the Jews must have found some support from their coreligionists in the surrounding area (cf. *Bellum*, II 291). It is not unlikely that the *Knishta maradeta de-Kisrin* which is mentioned in some Talmudic traditions (such as *J.T. Bikkurim*, iii, 65d; *J.T. Berakhoth*, iii, 6a; *J.T. Nazir*, vii, 56a; *Ekhah Rabbati* (ed. Buber) p. 32), can lend support to the tentative indications of the relations of the Caesarean Jews to the Zealots.

by Felix's brother Pallas, who was able to exert some influence upon
the Emperor, and by a certain Beryllus, whom they bribed successfully to use his position as *ab epistulis Graecis* to induce the Emperor
to decide in their favor. Taking their advice, Nero promulgated an
imperial rescript annulling the *isopoliteia* of the Jews. Without going
into the chronological problem here[107a], it may be said that the
similarity of the two versions in regard to Nero's verdict (*Bellum*, II
284; *Antiquitates*, XX 183) indicates that the handing over of power
in Caesarea to the Greeks (or the Syrians) and the abolition of the
Jewish *isopoliteia* were two sides of the same coin. The inference
from the first version is that there was no place for any *politeia* in
Caesarea other than the Greek one, once the city government was
transferred wholly to the Greeks. The second version might suggest
that when the *isopoliteia* was abolished, the Jews' right to maintain
a self-contained body independent of the *polis* could no longer exist.
The desecration of the Jewish synagogue by Greek rioters (*Bellum*,
II 289ff.) should be interpreted in this light, as an act which was
intended to impose by force the Greek exclusive *politeia* in the city.

Thus, it appears that the political order in Caesarea, like that in
other large cities of the Greco-Roman world, was based on the existence of different communities, whose rights and legal positions in
the city were defined by the term *isopoliteia*. The term applied to
an equal organizational status of independent bodies deriving their
rights, including that of internal self-government, from authoriza-
tion by the central government. A further scrutiny of Josephus'
evidence on the conflict in Caesarea shows that despite the theoretical
equality between the two communities there, in practice the Greek
one enjoyed precedence. To this fact it owed a number of political
advantages, the most outstanding of which was expressed significantly
in its identification with the *polis*. However, because of their superior
wealth and physical strength[108], and their feeling of greater confi-
dence in their native land, the Jews of Caesarea were more impor-
tunate in their political demands than those of any other city in the
Diaspora. Their political ambitions and efforts were designed to

---

107a On this matter, see Schürer, vol. 1, pp. 577-579; idem (eds. Vermes & Millr), vol. 1, pp.
      465-6, n.42; cf. Stern, *The Jewish People* etc., vol. 1, p. 74ff.
  108 See note 107 above. It is worth noting that the Jews were deeply involved in the eco-
      nomic life of Caesarea, and it is likely that they held the chief customs office in the
      city-port; see *Bellum*, II 287; Schalit, *op.cit.*, pp. 152-3.

shatter the basis of the existing *isopoliteia*, according to which they were inferior in status; they wished to win the precedence in Caesarea and to gain control over the city. But the result of their efforts was, ironically, the opposite of what they had intended.

This conclusion is undoubtedly highly instructive when applied to the problem of *isopoliteia* in Alexandria. The Alexandrian Jews, on their part, struggled for the very right of self-organization, so that they were content in political coexistence (i.e. *isopoliteia*) with the Greeks. The difference derived probably from the different historical circumstances in Alexandria and Caesarea.

D) *A Comparative Study of the Rights of the Jews of Antioch on the Orontes*

According to Josephus' description, just as the Jews of Alexandria were known as "Alexandrians", their co-religionists in Antioch were called "Antiocheans" ('Αντιοχεῖς), for "Seleucus the founder (of the Seleucid kingdom) granted them their *politeia*" (τὴν γὰρ πολιτείαν αὐτᾶς ἔδωκεν ὁ κτίστης Σέλευκος; *C. Apionem*, II 39). He says, furthermore, that "they also received honour (τιμή) from the kings of Asia when they served with them in war. For example, Seleucus Nicator granted them a *politeia* in the cities which he founded in Asia and Lower Syria and in his capital, Antioch, itself, and declared them to have equal privileges (ἰσοτίμους) with the Macedonians and Greeks who were settled in these cities, so that this *politeia* of their remains to the very day" (*Antiquitates*, XII 119)[(*)]. On another occasion Josephus noted that "the Jewish race" was scattered all over the inhabited world, mainly in Syria. "But it was at Antioch that they specially congregated, partly owing the greatness of the city, but mainly because the successors of King Antiochus (i.e. Epiphanes) had enabled them to live there in security... they even allowed them to participate in the city equally with the Greeks" (*Bellum*, VII 43-44)[109]. We shall content ourselves for the time being

---

(*) The English translation cited here is that of Marcus, *Josephus* (*LCL* ed.), vol. 7, *ad loc.* The only reservation I have to this translation concerns the words "equal rights" (in their context), which I would rather translate as follows: "declared them of equal honour" etc.

109 The English translation offered here is of Thackeray, *Josephus* (*LCL* ed.), vol. 3, *ad loc.*, except for the last sentence. Its meaning and legal implications are further dealt with below.

with these testimonies and attempt to elucidate the problems deriving from them, in the process of which we shall also investigate other evidences. Like the conflict in Caesarea Maritima, the conflict in Antioch too was one of long standing and Josephus was intimately acquainted with the juridical and political terminology connected with it.

The statement of Josephus about the Jews of Alexandria and Antioch, namely, that they were among the early founders of these cities, have been questioned. One of the most important scholars who expressed his doubts about it was Tcherikover[110]. On the basis of the testimony in *Bellum*, VII 43-44, he concluded that when Josephus wrote *Bellum Juadaicum* he had not yet heard of the granting of rights by Seleucus I Nicator and thought that these rights originated with the successors of Antiochus IV Epiphanes, that is, 150 years after Seleucus I[111]. However, such a construction completely ignores the purpose of the testimony in *Bellum Judaicum* and artifically pulls out isolated sentences of their context. Such a method is fundamentally faulty as it opens the door to reliance on half truths. It must be kept in mind that what Josephus wrote in *Bellum Judaicum* was an account of the danger of destruction which threatened the Jews of Antioch, when the Great Jewish Revolt erupted in Palestine (66 C.E.). He specifically stated that he wished to introduce the subject by some notes on the tragedy of the Antioch Jews, in order to report more comprehensively about the developments and latest events there (*Bellum*, VII 41-42). His digression takes up clauses 43 to 53, most of which is devoted to the evil deeds of the apostate Antiochus, whose libels about a Jewish conspiracy against the citizens of Antioch were minor when compared with his malicious incitement of the aroused populace to force the Jews to make sacrifices in the Greek manner. The Antioch mob responded enthusiastically to the challenge, and after the apostate set a "personal example", the Jews were put to the test. Only a few submitted,

---

110 Tcherikover, *Hellenistic Civilization and the Jews*, pp. 289, 328-331.

111 Some scholars tried to identify the Antiochus in clause 43 with Antiochus I Soter; see, e.g., Thackeray, *ibid.*, p. 517, n.c; C.H. Kraeling, *JBL*, 51 (1932), p. 137, n.47. On the other hand, some believed him to be Antiochus III the Great; see e.g., Marcus, *ibid.*, appendix c, p. 739. Both proposals must be rejected, primarily because clause 44 clearly specifies that Antiochus IV Epiphanes is meant. In this matter Schürer's view should be accepted (see vol. 3, p. 122); to Tcherikover's credit, he had not the slightest doubt of this.

and the objectors were slaughtered. Antiochus, however, was not satisfied with that, but persecuted his former brothers cruelly, and in particular he opposed keeping of the Sabbath. He was so zealous about it that the abolition of that holy institution soon became a policy to be imitated by other cities as well. The entire description of Josephus follows the pattern of an ancient tragedy — the persecu-, tions of Antiochus IV Epiphanes. Even the name of the Jewish apostate was likely to awaken such an association in Josephus' heart. It is no wonder therefore that Josephus prefaced this story with the important and relevant background remark regarding the kings who followed Antiochus IV Epiphanes. In other words, he' wished to stress, in connection with his story, that since the time of Antiochus IV Epiphanes there had been no legal basis for treating the Jews in that fashion. Consequently, the reference to Antiochus IV Epiphanes should not be construed as aiming to establish earliest date for the rights that have been accorded to the Jews of Antioch.

As contradictions between the report in *Bellum Judaicum* (VII 44) and those in *Contra Apionem* (II 39) and *Antiquitates* (XII 119) are removed, the latter two sources can be credited with greater relia-bility. The antiquity of the Jewish community in Antioch (noted above) seems to be indirectly confirmed by Talmudic sources, which seek to identify the city limits with places known to the Jews from old traditions (such as *Hamath* and *Rivlah*). Although the historical value of such identifications is dubious, they nevertheless may con-tain some grains of truth, thus lending indirect support to the testi-mony of Josephus about the antiquity of the Jewish community in the Seleucid period. The same may be true of the Talmudic tradition describing Nebuchadnezzar's meeting with the great Sanhedrin at Daphne (a suburb of Antioch)[112].

Let us now look at other evidence: modern research has proven that the four "sister cities" (Antioch, Seleucia Pierea, Laodiceia and Apamea on the Orontes) were founded by Selucus I Nicator within the framework of his military program. For that reason the original population of Antioch was a considerably mixed one consisting of Macedonians, Athenians, retired soldiers, Parthians, Cypriots, Argives,

---

112 For details, see Krauss, *REJ*, 45 (1902), p. 29ff.; C.H. Kraeling, *op.cit.*, p. 131ff.
113 Downey, *A History of Antioch*, p. 79ff.; idem, *Ancient Antioch*, p. 28ff.; Bar-Kochva, p. 29ff.

Heraclides and Syrians[113]. Strabo reports that the city was organized after the pattern of "*tetrapolis*, since it consisted of four parts" (XVI, 2, 4, 750c). Each section of this quartet was surrounded by a wall of its own which joined the general wall that encircled the whole city. Two of the four quarters were established by Seleucus I Nicator. The population of the first consisted of Greek elements, the most prominent among which were those from Antigoneia (the capital of Antigonus Monophthalmus, one of the Diadochs) who were transferred to the new city; the population of the second quarter consisted of a "multitude ($\pi\lambda\acute{\eta}\vartheta o\upsilon\varsigma$) of settlers" (*loc.cit.*). All scholars are in agreement that the first quarter was the nucleus for the body of the citizens of the new city, while the inhabitants of the second quarter are particularly identified with Syrian natives[114]. It appears that, as far as the population of Antioch is concerned, it resembles Polybius' description (cited by Strabo, XVII 1, 12, 797c) of Alexandria, whose population was made up of three elements: military men, Alexandrians, and natives (i.e. Egyptians). It is interesting that it was the Alexandrian group that Polybius described as "mongrels", or "mixed people" ($\mu\iota\gamma\acute{\alpha}\delta\epsilon\varsigma$) and "masses" ($\pi\lambda\acute{\eta}\vartheta o\upsilon\varsigma$). A comparison of the terminology suggests that the second quarter of Antioch may have been settled by elements other than the natives, possibly also by Jews.

The political organization of Antioch in the early days is not sufficiently clear. In any case, Downey's research has refuted to a considerable extent the common views (held by Bickermann, A.H.M. Jones and Holleaux) regarding Antioch's organization as an ordinary Greek *polis* from the start[115]. As in other Seleucid cities, and especially in Egyptian Alexandria, there was an *epistates* governing Antioch, a royal governor with both civil and military powers. Like Alexandria, Antioch too was a royal capital, and its relations with the kings were rather sensitive, beset with mutual suspicion and sometimes with even enmity. In the opinion of Tarn and Downey, the non-Greek population of Antioch, including the Jews, was organized in *politeumata*, as was organized, for instance, Seleucia on the Tigris[116].

---

114 Downey, *A History of Antioch*, p. 80.
115 Bickermann, *Les institutions des Séleucides*, p. 57; A.H.M. Jones, *The Greek City*, p. 7; Holleaux, *Études d'épigraphie et d'histoire greques*, p. 127ff.; Downey, *ibid.*, p. 112ff.
116 Downey, *ibid.*, p. 115; Tarn, p. 158. In their studies they based themselves among others

C.H. Kraeling accepted this hypothesis and even believed that the nucleus for the Jewish community of Antioch was a military settlement[117.] Josephus' statement in *Antiquitates*, XII 119 ("they also obtained honours from the kings of Asia when they went to war with them") may perhaps imply that. Scholars like Willrich and Tcherikover, who doubted the authenticity of the information regarding the beginning of the Jewish settlement in Antioch, claimed that if the Jewish community achieved any importance, it was not before 200 B.C.E., at the time of Antiochus III the Great. Their error seems to have arisen from their preliminary assumption that the Jewish settlers in Antioch must have been connected, one way or the other, with Palestine. For some reason, these scholars ignored the existence of a populous Jewish diaspora in Babylonia which was subject to the first Seleucids. Furthermore, that Jewry had a glorious military tradition that was closely connected at times with the fate of Seleucid kingdom. Babylonian Jews played an important military role, for instance, in the war against the Galatians during the reign of one of the early Seleucid kings (*II Maccabees*, 8:20)[118]. In the reign of Antiochus III the Great we know of the establishment in Phrygia and Lydia of military settlements founded by Babylonian Jews[119]. In Herod's days, Zamaris and the unit under his command emigrated from Babylonia, settled first near Antioch, and then were moved by Herod to the *Batanea* (in northern Trans-Jordan on the *Trachonitis'* border) to serve him militarily (*Antiquitates*, XVII 23-27). Consequently, Herzfeld's view, that the Jewish soldiers who took part in the establishment of Antioch came from the Babylonian Jewish community appears rather reasonable[120]. Taking into account the information credited to Hecataeus of Abdera on the

---

on *Antiquitates*, XVIII 372, 378 and argued that the Greek verb ἐμπολιτευόμενον applied to the Syrians in Seleucia, is derived from πολίτευμα.

117 Downey, *ibid.*, p. 79ff.; C.H. Kraeling, *JBL*, 51 (1932), p. 131ff.

118 There was a tendency to ascribe this episode to the period of Antiochus I Soter, but Bar-Kochva recently proposed setting it in the so called "The Brothers' War" of Seleucus II Callinicus and Antiochus Hierax. See full details in: *Proceedings of the Cambridge Philological Society*, 119, N.S. 19 (1973), pp. 1-8.

119 *Antiquitates*, XII 147-153; and see: Schalit, *JQR*, 50 (1959/60), pp. 289-318.

120 Hertzfeld, *Handelsgeschichte der Juden des Altertums*, p. 224. Applebaum has confirmed this impression, in view of the "Babylonian village" on the coast of southern Syria between Tyre and Sidon, which may well have been a military settlement of Jews who came from Babylonia; cf. Applebaum, *Studies in the History of the Jewish People and the Land of Israel*, vol. 1, pp. 79-88; cf. also Luria, *The Jews in Syria*, p. 94.

Jews serving in the army of Alexander the Great, and the papyrological information on such service for the early Ptolemies, it is not
farfetched to assume a similar situation for the early Seleucids.

In *Bellum*, VII 100ff., Josephus reports that the *boulé* (i.e. the
city-council) and the *demos* (i.e. the citizens' body) of the Antiocheans received Titus in their city with honor and splendor and at
that time asked him to banish the Jews. As he declined this request
in a rather diplomatic fashion, they pressed with an additional
request, that he should remove the bronze plates on which the rights
of the Jews (τὰ δικαιώματα τῶν Ἰουδαίων) were inscribed (*op.cit.*,
110). It may be recalled that both Philo and Josephus used the exact
same words to describe the rights of the Jews of Alexandria.

A careful examination of the first request, to banish the Jews from
the city, shows that in effect it sought to elicit from the Roman
rulers an admission that the Jews were "aliens" and "enemies".
The Antiocheans probably believed that under the circumstances
(i.e. the Great Jewish Revolt against the Romans), they could easily
obtain it, especially since they knew that Vespasian and Titus were
much troubled in their war with the Jews (*Antiquitates*, XII 122)[121].
It is reasonable to assume that unlike their counterparts in Alexandria
(in 38 C.E.) who sought first to abolish the Jewish *politeia* and only
subsequently to declare the Jews "aliens and foreigners" (*In Flaccum*,
53) the Antiocheans in requesting to banish the Jews, chose a short
cut[122]. By cancelling the right of the Jews to live in Antioch, they
hoped to eliminate the necessity of combatting Jewish rights. It was
only after their first request was denied that they presented themselves with their second request. Titus, however, did not comply
with the request either, and, on the contrary, allowed the Jews of
Antioch everything in accordance with the situation that had prevailed earlier[122].

From this evidence it can be concluded with complete certainty
that the Jewish rights did not derive from the Greek *polis* (Antioch)
but exclusively from the central authorities. It was the Hellenistic

---

121 The statement was made in connection with the Antiocheans' request to rescind the
Jewish rights in the wake of the Jewish revolt itself.
122 *Bellum*, VII 111; cf. also *Antiquitates*, XII 122 stating that Vespasian and Titus, despite
their annoyance because of the revolt in Judea, "they still did not deprive them of their
existing *politeia*". The last term is translated of course by Marcus as "rights of citizenship".

kings and Roman rulers who had granted and confirmed those rights, and only they could either maintain or abolish them. The appeal of the *polis* to the emperor to abolish the rights indicates that the citizens were well aware of it. In other words, the Jews as a community were excluded from the dominion of the *polis*, as their rights derived from the authority of the central government.

That this was indeed the status of the Jews is clearly shown by the "affair of the oil". According to Josephus, it was Seleucus I Nicator who decided that those Jews who were unwilling to use foreign oil should receive from the gymnasiarchs a sum equal to the value of the oil (*Antiquitates*, XII 120). At first glance, this statement could be construed in either way, as indicating that the Jews were directly dependent on the king's order, or that they were dependent on the Greek *polis*. Let us, however, examine the matter carefully. Rostovtzeff has shown that like the Ptolemies in Egypt, the Seleucids made the production and supply of oil an imperial monopoly. An inscription from one of the cities of the Hellespont, from the time of Antiochus III the Great (*SEG*, II 663), indicates that olive oil was, among other things, an important ritual commodity, and supplying it to the cities was, to a large extent, the result of a royal commitment to provide the cities with their religious needs[123]. As the oil monopoly operated on all levels, it is not surprising that the central government issued regulations regarding the distribution of the oil, in order to facilitiate supervision. It appears that the gymnasiarchs were appointed to be the foremost supply agents, for the institution they managed were the largest consumers of oil in any city[124]. The Jews' application to the gymnasiarchs in this matter should therefore be interpreted as an application to the imperial civil servants, and not to the *polis* administration, for the role of the gymnasiarchs was limited to carrying out imperial instructions. They had no authority to make decisions. If they had had any, and did not need the permission of the provincial governor, they certainly would not have given the hateful Jews the monetary equivalent of the oil which they (i.e. the Jews) did not use. As we know, several cities allocated part of their revenue

---

123 See: Rostovtzeff, *CAH*, vol. 7, pp. 178-9.
124 See: *Syll.*, 691; *IG*, V ii, 46-48; 50; XII ix, 236; Pliny, *Epist.*, X 23. Probably this was the situation in Egypt too, judging by the permission given by the "Gnomon of the Idios Logos" (clause 102, lines 229-231) to the gymnasiarchs of Alexandria to import oil duty-free in time of scarcity.

for the purchase of additional oil[125], and even set up special funds for that purpose, with money donated by philanthropists (mainly the gymnasiarchs themselves). We can therefore assume that the gymnasiarchs must have been reluctant to pay the Jews the cost of oil, which ultimately come from their own pockets.

Obviously, Seleucus' order was primarily designed to enable the Jews to practice their religion, and, indeed, Josephus' statement implies that religious motives impelled the Jews to avoid using the oil of the Gentiles. The religious motive may seem surprising, for the *Mishnah* says: "The following articles of the heathens are prohibited but prohibition does not extend to all use of them: Milk which an heathen milked without an Israelite watching him, their bread and oil — Rabbi and his court permitted the oil"[126]. However, it appears that the law regarding the prohibition of Gentile oil developed in three stages. During the first stage, from the early days of the Second Temple[127] to the time of Josephus[128], there was in force an absolute prohibition of eating and benefiting because of possible contamination by unknown non-Jews. The second stage begins after the destruction of the Second Temple, or, more specifically, during the Usha's period[129], when there was a relaxation, allowing the use of Gentile oil for benefit, but not for eating[130]. Stage three set in a result of the regulation by Rabbi (i.e. Rabbi Judah the Patriarch, the editor of the *Mishnah*) who allowed Gentile oil for both eating and benefit. It thus appears that the testimony of Josephus related to the stage when the strict prohibition was still in force, this confirming its own authenticity[131].

---

125 A.H.M. Jones, *The Greek City*, pp. 221, 351 (n.23).

126 *Mishnah, Abodah Zarah,* ii: 6; cf. *B.T. Abodah Zarah*, 36a: "R. Samuel b. Abba said in the name of R. Johanan: our masters sat and made investigation concerning [the use of heathens'] oil [and found] that its prohibition had not spread among the large majority of Israelites; they accordingly relied upon the dictum of Rabban Simeon b. Gamliel and R. Eliezer b. Zadok who declared: We make no decree upon the community unless the majority are able to abide by it."

127 See: *Judith*, x:5; xxii:1-4; *Tobit*, i:11, *Daniel*, i:8-15; cf. alon, *Studies in the History of the Jewish People*, vol. 1, pp. 127-8; cf. *B.T. Shabbath*, 17b, see the detailed study of Ben-Shalom, *The Shammai School*, pp. 562ff., esp. 578-579.

128 Indeed there are two other references in his writings to the importation of oil from the Land of Israel for the Jews of Syria, despite its high cost: *Bellum*, II 591ff.; *Vita*, 74.

129 According to the list of sages in chapter two of the *Mishnah* (*op.cit.*)

130 The main reason was the possibility of forbiden cockery, as indicated in the Babylonian Talmud.

131 I am grateful to my friend A. Oppenheimer who helped elucidate the halakhic development of the matter.

To sum it all up, it is thus reasonable to assume that just as Philo cited the episode of the lashes inflicted upon the *archontes* of his community to show the equality of rights enjoyed by the Jews of Alexandria (*In Flaccum*, 78-80), Josephus dwelt on the oil episode to demonstrate the equality of rights enjoyed by the Jews of Antioch.

In *Antiquitates*, XII 119, Josephus, following again the example of Philo, used the term *politeia* to define the bill of rights and the legal status of the Jews of Antioch. Most scholars have construed this as referring to citizenship in the Greek *polis*, suspecting Josephus of apologetics and falsification — charges they did not dare to make against Philo. However, a careful examination of Josephus' uses of the term *politeia* shows that these uses allow also for another interpretation, namely, the right to organize as a *politeuma*[132]. Josephus does not state that Selecus granted the Jews a *politeia* of the cities of his kingdom, so that the meaning is not necessarily citizenship in them[133]. Furthermore, the distinction he makes between "the Jews from Antioch" (*Bellum*, VII 44, 47, 54, 111 etc.) and "the *demos* of the Antiocheans" (*ibid.*, 47, 100, 107; *Antiquitates*, XII 120, 123) is glaring, and may very well indicate that in his view these were two separate bodies. It is in this spirit, that the application of the term *politai* with regard to the Jews of the city should be interpreted. Thus, the reference would not be to the citizens of the *polis* but to the members of the Jewish *politeuma*. This is evident from the report on the deeds of the apostate Antiochus. It notes that he "domineered with severity over his (Jewish) fellow-citizens" (χαλεπὸς ἐφειστήκει τοῖς αὐτοῦ πολίταις, *Bellum*, VII 52), that is, the members of his *politeuma*. Moreover, in relation to the Jews of his city he was described as "one of them" (εἷς ἐξ αὐτῶν, *Bellum*, VII 47). And he and "his fellow-citizens" (τοῖς αὐτοῦ πολίταις) are clearly differentiated from those "alien Jews" (ξένους Ἰουδαίους) whom he accused of taking part in the plot to burn down the city, and who certainly did not belong to the Jews of his city[134]. Josephus' asser-

---

132 See the Appendix below.
133 In fact, *Antiquitates*, XII 119 contains no genetive case construct connected with the *politeia*, but only a dative. It should therefore be imterpreted as "Seleucus Nicator awarded them a *politeia* in the cities he founded" etc. Thus the reference is not to the *politeia* of those cities.
134 These appear to have been Jews from Palestine suspected of belonging to the Zealots' movement.

tion that the Jewish *politeia* survived to his own day are not just
words, for the same term is applied to the Jewish community of
Antioch by Bishop Johanes Chrysostomus (end of the fourth century C.E.)[135]. The analogy with Alexandria is illustrative, for Strabo
(*apud* Josephus, *Antiquitates*, XIV 117) used this term to describe
the Jewish community there, and Philo too employed it in defining
that community' bill of rights and legal status (cf. *In Flaccum*, 53;
Legatio, 371).

The separation of the Antioch Jewish community from the *polis*
(as an organized and recognized body) is clearly indicated by the fact
that the community had its own magistrature. Josephus mentions
the post of *archon* (*Bellum*, VII 47) which persisted at least up to the
time of Johanes Chrysostomus, who also noted the post of *prostates*[136]. Elsewhere, in a source likewise attributed to that bishop, we
learn of the custom of the Antioch Jews to choose their magistrates,
called *archontes*, once a year[137]. Libanius' letter to Priscianus (364
C.E.) notes as well the existence of a leadership of its own in the
local Jewish community. In his analysis of that document, Schwabe
pointed out that the local administration in Syria did not intervene
in the appointment of the Jewish community leadership, and that
the Jews enjoyed the autonomy of a recognized, sovereign body, a
sort of state within a state[138]. It is important to note that Josephus

---

135 *Adv. Jud. Orat.*, I 3(*PG*, XLVIII, p. 847). Krauss (*REJ*, 45 (1902), p. 36, nn.3-4) maintained that the term *blateia* (found in some *Midrashim*) is but the Hebrew transcription
of πολιτεία.

136 *Ibid.*, V 3 (*PG*, XLVIII, p. 887).

137 Juster, vol. 1, p. 445, n.1; Schürer, vol. 3, p. 86. See more M. Stern, *The Diaspora in
the Hellenistic-Roman World*, pp. 167, 335 (n.41) (Hebrew).

138 See: Schwabe, *Tarbiẕ* , 1 (1930), pp. 107-121 (esp. p. 118). The main subject of Libanius'
letter was the objection of the Antioch Jews to the appointment of "an old sinner"
(πονηροῦ τινος γέροντος) over them. Schwabe assumed that the γέρων was supposed
to serve as a *gerousiarches* or *prostates*. His proposal can be supported by the inscription
from Beth-She'arim — "Apsis of Idasios the Antiochean *gerousiarches*". See: Schwabe
& Lifshitz, *Beth-She'arim*, vol. 2 (The Greek inscriptions), No. 207. The epithet
"Antiochean" fits in with the statement in *Contra Apionem* (II 35) that the Jews were
so described. Cf. also the application of the term to Jews in two inscriptions from
Apamea on the Orontes (*CIJ*, II 803-4) and from Tiberias (Schwabe, *Levy Memorial
Volume*, p. 220). The Apamea inscriptions indicate that in 391 C.E. the local Jewish
community and the Antiochean group within it had a well organized leadership among
whom were the *archisynagogoi, presbyteroi* and the *gerousiarches*. Most likely the
subsidiary Antiochean community in Apamea was organized along the lines of the main
community; if so, we have additional confirmation of its well developed internal organization.

distinguished between the Jewish and the *polis* magistratures[139], in
order to explain that they were completely separate from each other.
The evidence of the Talmudic tradition with regard to the existence
of "courts (*Erka'oth*) in Syria" and "two people who had a trial
in Antioch"[140] reinforces the contention that the Jewish community was organizationally distinct from the *polis* and had autonomous status. Th existence of a Jewish court is also attested to by
Johanes Chrysostomus who bitterly complains that many Christians
preferred to submit their cases to the Jewish court in Antioch
because of impartiality, and because the Jewish oath seemed to them
stricter and more committing[141].

The status of the Jewish community as an organized legal entity
is also indicated in the Justinian Code which preserves a ruling by
Emperor Caracalla of 213 C.E., stating: "The Emperor Antoninus
to Aulus Claudius Tryphoninus: what Cornelia Salvia bequeathed in
her will to the Jewish community (= *universitas*) established in the
city of Antioch it is impossible to claim" (*Cod. Just.*, I 9, 1). Although
the ruling denied the community the right to execute the will, this
should not be construed as proof that the community did not have
the status of a legal entity, since we know that other communities
in the empire did have that right[142]. In fact, the very recognition
implied of the community (*universitas*) as a separate body in the
ruling is proof that it was a legal entity. Furthermore, Cornelia
Salvia would not have bequeathed her property to the community
if she had not honestly believed that such a step was lawful. Allon's
solution to this problem seems rather convincing. In his opinion,
Cornelia Salvia was a "God fearing" Roman gentile lady; and Emperor
Caracalla's ruling was designed to "break the connection of Gentiles

---

139 In *Bellum*, VII 47 he comments on the convening of the Greek people's assembly; in VII
55 he refers to the square market of the city, the government building and the city
archives; in VII 107 he also mentions the city council (*boulé*).

140 *J.T. Sanhedrin*, III 21a; and cf. *B'T. Sanhedrin*, 23a — the subject seems to be rules of
finance. The *T.B. Arakhin*, 22b (cf. also *B.T. Ketubboth*, 88a) tells of Rabbi Yitzḥak
Nafḥa, an *amora* of the second and third generation, who issued a ruling in Antioch on
matrimonial matter (i.e. a *Ketubbah*).

141 See: *Adv. Jud. Orat.*, I 3 (*PG*, XLVIII, p. 847). At the same time Johanes Chrysostomus
was furious that many Christians used to go to the synagogue of Daphne and to sleep
there (*ibid.*, I 6). He was angry also because many Christians used to fast on Jewish fast
days (*ibid.*, I 4) and celebrate Easter as Passover (*ibid.*, III 4); cf. also *Homilies on Titus*,
III 2.

142 See: Juster, vol. 1, pp. 432-434.

to Judaism, in accordance with Septimius Severus' order forbidding conversion[143]. In other words, the emperor did not deprive the Jewish community of its rights as a legal entity (empowered to receive donations and bequests), but subjected it to the laws governing contracts and relations with non-Jews.

Thus, the Jewish community of Antioch had its own *politeia*, was recognized as a political body with its own magistrature; and its right derived from the central government and not the *polis*. Having independent status, it can be considered as an organization paralleling and resembling the *polis* itself, with which, however, it did not necessarily have to have reciprocal relations[144].

The equal rights of the Antioch Jews are mentioned twice by Josephus, in *Bellum*, VII 44 and in *Antiquitates*, XII 119. The first reference notes that the kings after Antiochus IV Epiphanes "allowed them (i.e. the Jews of Antioch) to participate in the city equally with the Greeks" (συνεχώρησαν αὐτοῖς ἐξ ἴσου τῆς πολέως τοῖς Ἕλλησι μετέχειν).This sentence has generally been translated "granted them citizen rights on an equality with the Greeks"[145]. C.H. Kraeling was aware of some incongruity in the sentence, but contented himself with noting only that there was an unclear use of the term *isopoliteia*[146]. The translation proposed above is preferable, first of all because it is linguistically more accurate. The verb μετέχειν takes a genetive and dative (μετέχω τινός τινι) and according to Liddell & Scott's Lexicon means "to partake of something in common with another; enjoy a share of". The words ἐξ ἴσου are intended only to emphasize the relationship between the Jews and the Greeks. How then is the "equal share" of the Jews in the city to be explained? It must be explained in the context of the other details and facts mentioned (*Bellum*, VII 43-53). There is no doubt that first and foremost it refers to the right of "residence (κατοίκησιν) without fear" (*ibid.*, 43). No less important must have been their fight to live according to their ancestral laws, and to conduct their religious rites and ceremonies unhindered. The testimony also indicates the existence of an independent organization (separate from the *polis*)

---

143 Alon, *History of the Jews* etc. vol. 2, p. 110.
144 See the important concluding remarks of Smallwood, *The Jews under Roman Rule*, p. 358ff.
145 See e.g. Thackeray, *Josephus (LCL*, ed.), vol. 3, *ad Loc.*
146 C.H. Kraeling, *JBL*, 51 (1932), p. 138.

with an independent leadership of the community. Moreover, since members of the Jewish community are referred to there as *politai*, obviously their equal share (with the Greeks) in the city cannot be participation in the same *politeia*, but an equivalent status of *politai*, and the difference is significant.

Supportive of this interpretation is also the second excerpt (from *Antiquitates*, XII 119) which states that Selucus I Nicator granted the Jews of Antioch a *politeia* and "declared them of equal honour (ἰσοτίμους) with the Macedonians and the Greeks" etc. The use of the term *isotimoi* and *isotimia* in various contexts shows that he meant a degree of honour equal to that of people of high ranks and titles[147]. In this case it was their *politeia* that placed them at an equal rank with the Macedonians and other Greeks; and that was the result of the "honour" (τιμή) they had earned through their military service. Josephus does not give the slightest hint of Jews having rights as citizens of the *polis*. In fact, he was always careful to stress that the struggle of the Jews resulted from their eagerness to survive as Jews, and their desire to protect their rights to an independent organization. The fact that the citizens of Antioch sought to force their religion on the Jews indicates that they wished to abolish the Jewish *politeia* and to maintain only one *politeia* in the city, based on one religion. They could not tolerate a situation in which the political status of the Jewish community was equal to that of their own organization (i.e. the *polis*). Apparently, they wished to abolish the *isopoliteia* in favor of *sympoliteia* which would lead to an integrated union of the two political organizations and in effect result in the abolition of the Jewish *politeia*. However, in reality not only did they fail to abolish it, but it stood the test of the most severe political storms. Even the Jewish war against the Romans did not have a detrimental effect on it. In fact, the Jews made great strides, for they regularly attracted masses of Greeks to their religious ceremonies, to the point that the latter almost became assimilated (*Bellum*, VII 45). This makes clear how unbearable the situation must have become from the point of view of the Antioch citizens, for the Jewish community not only succeeded in surviving, but even grew stronger.

---

147 Cf. *Antiquitates*, VII 284; XVI 98; XIX 317.

Chapter IX

Various Problems Connected with Claudius'
Letter to the Alexandrians

Since its publication by Bell in 1924 (*P. Lond.*, 1912), *Claudius'
Letter to the Alexandrians* has been the subject of dozens of studies,
the most comprehensive of which are by Tcherikover[1]. A number of
solutions proposed for various problems are however unsatisfactory,
and the most important of these concerns the attitude of the Jews to
gymnasium education and consequent citizenship in the *polis* of
Alexandria.

A. Jewish Harassment of Competitions Arranged by Gymnasiarchs and Cosmetes

According to Tcherikover, two passages of the *Letter* indicate
that the Jews sought to gain Alexandrian citizenship by infiltrating
into the local gymnasium, one being an indirect reference (line 32f.)
and the other a direct one (line 38f.). The first cites the emperor's
decision: "To all those who have been registered as ephebes up to the
time of my principate I guarantee and confirm the *politeia* of the
Alexandrians (τὴν Ἀλεξανδρέων πολιτείαν) with all the privileges
of benefits enjoyed by the city, with the exception of any who
though born of slave-parents have made their way into your ephebate." That passage is very reminiscent of the *Boulé Papyrus* (*PSI*,
1160, lines 1-6) stating "I submit then that the Council (= *boulé*)
will see to it that none of those who are liable to enrolment for the
poll-tax diminish the revenue by being listed in the public records
along with the *epheboi* for each year, and it will take care the pure
(?) citizen body of Alexandria (τὸ π⟨ο⟩λίτευμα τῶν Ἀλεξανδρείων
ἀ[κ]έραιον) is not corrupted by men who are uncultured and uneducated". In Tcherikover's view that document reflected the situa-

---

1 Bell, *Jews and Chritians*; see the comprehensive bibliography – *CPJ*, II, p. 36f.

tion in Augustus' time, and aimed its arrow chiefly at the Jews who had then embarked upon their "war for emancipation"[2]. However, the *Boulé Papyrus* makes no explicit or substantive reference to Jews[3]. Secondly, there are no grounds for dating it to the Augustan era, and the two objections are closely connected, making it necessary to consider the document in relation to the "indirect" passage in *Claudius' Letter to the Alexandrians* (line 52f.).

The scholars who published the *Boulé Papyrus* were of the opinion that it was composed a short time after the conquest of Egypt, that is, in about 30 B.C.E. Tcherikover modified this a bit, to 19-20 B.C.E. because the term *laographia* which appears in the papyrus is first mentioned in ostraca of 22 B.C.E.[4] He dated the document to the Augustan period for the additional reason that it contains the word "caesar" which he believed could refer only to Augustus[5]. Bell's first reaction was to question the dating and for paleographic reasons place it later, not before the reign of Tiberius. Following further study, he suggested that despite the uncertainty of the paleographic evidence, the document must have been written after Augustus' reign, perhaps in that of Claudius[6]. He thus came to agree with Schubart who was the first to propose the reign of that emperor. Musurillo concurred, and after an additional paleographic comparison concluded that it dated from the end of the first century B.C.E.[7]

There were differences of opinion in regard to the nature of the document as well. Some scholars considered it an official document[8], and others part of a cheap literary work like the *Acts of the Alexandrian Martyrs*[9]. Bell's philological grounds seem to favor the second

---

2 *Hellenistic Civilization and the Jews*, pp. 312-314; *Jews in Egypt*, p. 137; *CPJ*, II, p. 27.

3 While not unaware of the fact, Tcherikover tried to overcome it with a not very convincing argument designed to have the document as a whole serve his thesis; see *CPJ*, II, p. 27 in particular.

4 See *CPJ*, II, p. 26f.; *Jews in Egypt*, p. 119. On the year — 22 B.C.E. — see *O. Strassb.*, 38; see also Johnson, p. 534. The idea for this correction was undoubtedly based on a similar idea of Oliver's (*Aegyptus*, II [1930/1], p.165f.).

5 *CPJ*, II, p. 29 (explanations of line 21).

6 See *Aegyptus*, 12 (1932), p. 173ff. (esp. p. 176); *JJP*, 4 (1940), p. 26.

7 Schubart, *BIFAO*, 30 (1931), p. 407ff. (esp. 411ff.); Musurillo, p. 83f.; cf. also Amusin, *VDI*, 4 (1951), p. 213ff.

8 Schubart, ibid., p. 407ff.; cf. also Tcherikover, *CPJ*, II, p. 26; Wilcken, *Archiv*, 9 (1930), pp. 254-256.

9 That was the opinion of Oliver, *Aegyptus*, II (1930/1), p. 167f.; Bell, *Aegyptus*, 12 (1932), pp. 175f., 184. Cf. Also Musurillo, pp. 85-87; Amusin, *VDI*, 4 (1951), pp. 213,

view, and those of Oliver, regarding the literary character of the document which is in the form of a dialogue full of rhetoric, tip the scales. Oliver also rightly argued that the words *caesar* and *epitropos* are typical of that literary genre and appear also in the *Acts of the Alexandrian Martyrs*. That seems to solve the difficulty that Tcherikover noted in this regard, and indicates that the preferable interpretation is the one that rejects the official nature of the document and dates it to the reign of Claudius.

At the same time, just as in regard to the *Acts of the Alexandrian Martyrs*, the historic value and authentic sources of the document should not be denied[10]. The attribution of the document to Claudius' reign around the time of his *Letter to the Alexandrians* is most illuminating. Amusin showed that all the reasons and proposals of the Alexandrians regarding the establishment of a *boulé* (as listed in the *Boulé Papyrus*) elicited substantive responses in *Claudius' Letter*, to the point of exact correspondence between the two documents[11]. Despite considerable effort, Tcherikover was not able to refute those conclusions. The main problem in both the *Boulé Papyrus* and the "indirect" passage in *Claudius' Letter to the Alexandrians* (line 52f.) concerns the matter of the establishment of the *boulé*. The point of uneducated, uncultured people infiltrating into the list of the *epheboi* was merely the justification given for setting up the *boulé*, and as such was associated with another justification, the loss of imperial revenue. Only Tcherikover focused on the fiscal reason and presented it as the crucial point. In any case, there is no specific mention of Jews in the document, and no grounds for suggesting that they were concerned. Furthermore the Jews (as an organized political body) not only refrained from seeking entry into the Alexandria gymnasium, but actually opposed and attacked it. In addition, the conjunction of the *Boulé Papyrus* and *Claudius' Letter to the Alexandrians* actually shows that any communal Jewish desire to join the gymnasium is imaginary. While some individual Jews may have been interested in the gymnasium in order to gain Alexandrian citizenship, they were most probably apostates, and their small number could.

---

216. The latter strongly supports Bell. Oliver, by the way, pointed out the cursive writing as being more suitable for literary texts than for official documents.

10 Cf. Bell, *ibid.*, p. 184.

11 See the detailed consideration on this by Amusin, *VDI*, 4 (1951), pp. 214-216.

not have created a problem great enough to bring to the attention of the emperor. Nor is it reasonable to suppose that such Jews would have "infiltrated"; they would rather have joined openly, and been welcomed by the Alexandrians.

To whom then was Claudius referring in his *Letter to the Alexandrians* (line 56ff.) as people "born of slave parents" (ἐγ δούλων γεγονότες) who appeared as Alexandrian citizens by fraudulent registration as *epheboi*? Beyond a doubt he meant the offspring of Alexandrian fathers and slave women, people "born of servile mothers"[12], in Bell's apt translation. Already in the Ptolemaic period (at least from Ptolemy VI Philometor on) such people were required on all official documents to append only their mother's name to theirs, to show their illegitimate birth, for according to law (though perhaps not in practice) the fathers were considered to be unknown[13]. It was natural for such men to deceive the authorities either by concealing the names of their mothers or by failing to register in the specified manner, so that they could attain the status of citizens. Since during the Roman period the criterion for citizenship of "a citizen son of citizens" no longer had legal validity, having been replaced by gymnasium education, the wall of exclusivity of Alexandrian citizenship developed cracks, at least at the outset, and many people were able to enter the ranks of the *epheboi* in explicit violation of the law[14]. The practice may have been related to the fact that at the time of Julius Caesar's Alexandrian War, the citizens were obliged to arm numerous slaves (*Bell. Alex.*, 2, 2) and many of them were of the dubious category described above. Claudius' sensitivity to people of "slave origin" posing as Alexandrian citizens is understandable against the background of his legislative intervention on the same matter in Rome itself[15]. Thus it is clear that the problem

---

12 Bell, *Jews and Christians*, p. 28.

13 See Westermann, *Slave System*, p. 53; Fraser, vol. 1, p. 85.

14 See details in Westermann, *ibid.*, p. 103 and n.24; Bell, *Jews and Christains*, p. 34; cf. *BGU*, V, line 113ff.

15 Connected with Claudius' name was an explicit senate decision (*senatus consultum Claudianum*) heavily penalizing Roman female citizens who copulated with slaves, to the extent of depriving them of their freedom. See Gaius, *Institutiones*, I 84; Tacitus, *Annales*, XII 53. It will be recalled that a Jewish law invalidates the legitimacy of children born to a female slave or bondmaid (*Mishnah Kiddushin*, III 5b) so that the people of slave descent (that is, "born of servile mothers") which *Claudius' Letter to the Alexandrians* referred to could not have been Jews.

was not related to Jews, and it is therefore not surprising that neither the "indirect" passage in *Claudius' Letter to the Alexandrians* nor the *Boulé Papyrus* makes any subśtantive reference to Jews.

That the Jews as a body opposed the gymnasium is deducible from the second passage in *Claudius' Letter* (line 73ff.) which explicitly mentions the conflict between the Jews and the Alexandrians. According to Tcherikover, the Jews were warned "not to intrude themselves (ἐπισπαίεω) into the games presided over by the gymnasiarchs and cosmetes, since they enjoy what is their own, and in a city which is ṇot their own possess an abundance of all good things"[16]. In Tcherikover's view, that passage proves that the Jews sought to gain Alexandrian citizenship through infiltration into the gymnasium. That proof, however, is based on a single word, ἐπισπαιεω. The first editor of the papyrus read the word as ἐπισπαίρειν[17], but was unable to fathom its meaning, for until the discovery of the papyrus concerned, only one instance of the verb was known, in Plutarch[18]. It was generally translated as "to palpitate, to be alarmed" or "to pant" and the like, a meaning which did not satisfy Bell in the context in the *Letter*. He therefore proposed rendering the problematic word as equivalent to μετέχειν (= participate), and argued accordingly that Claudius' warning was to be understood as directed against the participation of Jews in the contests presided over by the cosmetes and gymnasiarchs[19]. His interpretation appealed to numerous scholars, and Schwartz was the first to propose reading the word ἐπισπαιεω (that is, dropping the *rho*) to provide Bell's interpretation with a textual basis[20]. That correction was enthusiastically accepted by many scholars, mainly because it supported their notion that the Jews sought to "intrude" into gymnastic games[21].

---

16 Lines 83-85; see Tcherikover, *Jews in Egypt*, p. 137f., and Smallwood, *Jews Under Roman Rule*, p. 249.

17 He noted explicitly that the letter *rho*, though damaged, could be distinguished. See also Bell, *Jews and Chritians*, p. 37.

18 Plutarch, *De fort. Alex.*, I 3 (*Mor.*, 327c).

19 Bell, *Jews and Christians*, p. 37.

20 E. Schwartz, *DLKIW*, n.s. 1 (1924), p. 2094.

21 Bell too accepted that version. See Bell, *JEA*, 11 (1925), p. 95, n.2; id., *Juden und Griechen*, p. 6; *Cults and Creeds*, p. 43. For the view of other scholars, see especially Th. Reinach, *REJ*, 79 (1924), p. 128; H. St. Jones, *JRS*, 16 (1926), p. 29; Hunt & Edgar, *Selected Papyri*, II No. 112 (*ad. loc.*); Lösch, *Epistula Claudiana*, p. 11; Scramuzza, *Claudius*, p. 66; Charlesworth, *Documents*, p. 5; Box, *Introduction*, pp. xx, xxix-xxx, Turner, *JRS*, 44 (1954), p. 58; Tcherikover, *CPJ*, II 153 (ad. loc.).

The first dissenter was Radin, who preferred the original reading
(ἐπισπαίρειν) which he claimed meant to "jeer" or "scoff"[22]. He
did not however support his interpretation with philological parallels,
so could not prove it. Lagrange too objected to Bell's emendation,
claiming that ἐπισπαίειν would require a further correction, the
insertion of the letter *eta* to form ἐπεισπαίειν, for which there is no
basis in the text. He objected to Schwartz's correction from a historical
standpoint as well, because normally the Jewish leadership disliked
the gymnasium and were therefore not likely to wish to infiltrate it.
In his view, the original letter was in Latin, and the problematic
word was merely a mistranslation of the Latin *trepidare*, meaning "to
be agitated" or "to attack"[23], but unfortunately his interesting and
original proposal was presented with great brevity and unsupported
by philological and historical evidence.

One of the few scholars who rejected that reading and all it implies
was Amusin[24]. First of all, he claimed that the emendation leads to
a syntactical error since the verb ἐπεισπαίειν requires the preposition
εἰς with the accusative case, and there are no instances of its use
with the dative, as suggested for *Claudius' Letter*. Furthermore, he
proved that the word ἐπισπαίρειν means "to oppose something or
someone", or "to cause obstructions" or "to resist"[25]. In support,
he examined the verb's philological cognates in other Indo-European
languages and showed that the verb σπαίρειν figures in Herodotus
(VII 5) in the meaning of "oppose"[26]. He noted as well that the verb
ἀσπαίρειν had a similar meaning in Greek, "to fight", "to struggle"[26].

How does this interpretation of Amusin's fit the text? As noted,
various scholars considered that reading to be textual evidence of
Jewish surreptitious penetration into the gymnasium. However,
Claudius also used more specific phrases such as "all those who have
been registered as *epheboi* (ἅπασι τοῖς ἐφηβευκ ώσει; line 53) and
those who "have made their way into your ephebate" (ἐφηβεῦσαι

---

22 See the review of Bell's book, Radin, *Class. Phil.*, 20 (1925), p. 370.
23 Lagrange, *RB*, 40 (1931), p. 272f.
24 Amusin, *JJP*, 9-10 (1955/6), p. 176.
25 *Ibid.*, p. 183f.
26 See Liddell & Scott, *Lexicon*; cf. other verbs derived from the same root, such as
ὑποσπαίρω, περισπαίρω, σπαρίξω, ἀσπαρίξω. See also *Thesaurus Linguae Graecae*
(ed. H. Stephano), vol. 5, p. 8552b. Amusin notes that the Latin equivalent of σπαρίξω i
is *sperno*, and there is quite a lot of support for that view; see Frisk, *Griechisches etymo-
logische Wörterbuch*, vol. 2, p. 775f.

line 56f.). These phrases suggest that the penetration into the ephebe lists was an act of trickery, as indicated by the verb ὑπέρχομαι. Such trickery is characteristic of, and possible for, individuals but not for a mass of people, let alone a highly organized body like the Alexandria Jews. Furthermore, according to the information available, the central authorities exercised strict supervision of the ephebe lists, for under the Romans[27] the gymnasia and the ephebia ceased to be private institutions. It is therefore difficult to imagine that Jews could at that time really penetrate the gymnasia or that the Alexandrians would not have called attention to that penetration and objected vociferously. Such a development is especially inconceivable at that time, for there are no grounds for believing that such infiltration was possible just prior to *Claudius' Letter*, that is, in Caligula's reign. Actually it would be logical to expect there to be a total deterioration in the situation of the Jews at that time, as indeed there was. Dessau evidently discerned this difficulty and advanced the hypothesis that Claudius' warning to the Jews forbade their "becoming involved" (his rendering of the word in question) in the struggle for "the elections of the gymnasiarchs and cosmetes"[28]. His proposal has been rejected by many scholars; De Sanctis above all contradicted it as far back as 1924, when the *Letter* was first published[29]. However, there has been general acceptance of the hypotheses of Bell and Schwartz that the Jews were prohibited from "participating", "penetrating", or "infiltrating" the games arranged by cosmetes and gymnasiarchs which were reserved exclusively for citizens of the *polis*[30].

Against this explanation it must be noted that Claudius' warning was part of a passage dealing with the disturbances and quarrel with the Jews of the city, or rather with the "war" against them, as the *Letter* puts it (line 73f.). Consequently it seems logical to assume that the "games" or "competition" (ἀγῶνες) referred to were held in the presence of great crowds of spectators[31], for a "war" could break out where large numbers of people were involved, and not

27 See Wilcken-Mitteis, vol. 1, p. 142; Bell, *JEA*, 12 (1926), pp. 245-247; Boak, *JEA*, 13 (1927), p. 152ff.; Taubenschlag, p. 699ff.
28 Dessau, *Geschichte*, vol. 2, p. 675.
29 De Sanctis, *Riv. di Fil.*, 52 (1924), p. 507.
30 Cf. *CPJ*, II, p. 53 (explanations of line 92f.).
31 For this meaning see Liddell & Scott, *Lexicon*, s.v.

at games limited to an exclusive circle such as the competitions of
the ephebes. De Sanctis in fact was at first inclined to such a view,
and suggested that Claudius' warning was directed at the clashes
of rival factions at circus performances. While subsequently retract-
ing in order to avoid contradicting Schwartz's emendation, he continued to interpret ἐπισπαίρειν as meaning *subsulto*, that is, "to be
in an unbalanced condition"[32]. The mention of the cosmetes supports
the conclusion that well-attended public performances were concerned, as those functionaries were known to have participated in
the financing and organization of popular spectacles of that kind[33].

Radin and Amusin fully concurred in De Sanctis' views. While
Radin accepted the basic point that the competitions were games
held before a large and emotional crowd which even produced some
bloodshed[34], he properly rejected the identification of the games
with circus performances. Amusin however accepted De Sanctis'
view in toto, even expanding it[35]. Actually the three scholars held
quite similar views, and of them, although the least elaborated, the
most credible seems to be that of Radin, namely, that the games or
competitions were great public events involving masses of people
who might easily be incited to bloodshed. The games may have taken
place either in the city hippodrome or the city theatre, both of
which were adjacent to the main Jewish quarter (Delta).

The theatre was the venue for the Alexandrian popular assemblies,
and there was a case of a clash between Jews and Greeks on such an
occasion in 66 C.E. (*Bellum*, II 490f.). Philo too, in describing the
riots of 38 C.E., castigated the Alexandrian mob that flocked into
the theatre to ridicule King Aprippa and plan the desecration of the
synagogues (*In Flaccum*, 41f.). The insults were composed at the
gymnasium by "authors of farces (= mimes) and jests" (*ibid*. 33f.).
As mime literature was very popular in Alexandria[36], the theatrical

---

32 See De Sanctis, *Riv. di Fil.*, 53 (1925), pp. 240-245.

33 See Oertel, *Die Liturgie*, p. 329f.

34 Radin, *Class. Philol.*, 20 (1925), p. 370. For support he cited Philostratus, *Vita. Ap. Ty.*,
V 26.

35 Amusin, *JJP*, 9-10 (1955/6), p. 184f.

36 See Cicero, *Pro Rabirio*, 12, 35; see also Musurillo, p. 49f.; for papyrological fragments
on the mime plays see Page, *Greek Literary Papyri*, Nos. 73-79. General literature on the
subject includes Reich, *Der Mimus*; Wust, *RE(PW)*, 15 (1932), p. 1730; Musurillo,
p. 247f.; Smallwood, p. 321; see also the interpretations of Box to the above citations
from Philo.

performance of Carabas and his friends in a typical mime about King
Agrippa (*ibid.*, 36f.) is not surprising[37]. Philo's detailed descriptions
of the "play" presented in 38 C.E. suggest that some Jews may have
attended the performance. Another "happening" in the theatre in
38 C.E. was not a play but an actual event. The Jewish *gerontes*
were dragged into the theatre and flogged in full view of the audience,
like native Egyptian criminals (*ibid.*, 74f.). This incident took place
at the time of the popular celebrations of Caligula's birthday[38].
According to Philo, the "performance" was organized in detail;
the first act lasted from dawn until the third or fourth hour, that is,
until sunset. Jews were flogged, hanged, chained to the rack, and led
across the orchestra to their deaths. Following that exhibition,
the audience was treated to interludes of dancing, mime and music,
as well as "stage games" (σκηνικῶν ἀγώνων – *ibid.*, 85). Philo's
use of the term ἀγῶνες in that context is most illuminating, especially
in view of its employment in *Claudius' Letter to the Alexandrians*
(line 93). These facts suffice to show that the city theatre was the
center of anti-Jewish activity[39], and that the public torture and
execution of Jews were conducted there as an organized spectacle.
The theatre was a center of anti-Jewish activities in other cities as
well. During the great Jewish revolt against the Romans, a shameful
scene involving the burning of several Jews was enacted in the
Antioch theatre (*Bellum*, VII 47f.). And Malalas reported that in
40 C.E. after a clash in that theatre, a great "war" broke out between
Jews and Greeks in the course of which synagogues were burned
down and many local Jews killed[40]. A similar situation obtained in ·
the Palestinian city of Caesaraea, where Graeco-Jewish clashes
occurred. A talmudic tradition concerning Rabbi Abbahu (a third-
century *amora*) relates that the Caesareans cursed him and ridiculed
Jewish customs while sitting in theatres and circuses[41]. Another
tradition, cited by Reish Lakish, assessed the mime plays as follows:

---

37 Note in particular the expression ὡς· ἐν θεατρικοῖς μίμοις; cf. also *In Flaccum*, 72
and *Legatio*, 359.

38 *In Flaccum*, 81, 84; cf. 74 end. See Box's excellent explanation of 81 (his book, p. 105).

39 That it was a magnet for the rabble is shown indirectly in Dio Chrysostomos (Or., XXXII
51), for a Roman guard unit was stationed near it.

40 See Malalas, *Chron.*, X (p. 244f. in Bonn ed.). However, it is hard to know the source of
his information, and he may have invented the episode on the basis of what happened
in Alexandria.

41 *Ekhah Rabbati*, XVII (Buber ed., p. 14).

"We should be grateful to the pagans for introducing mimes to their theatres and circuses to play with, so that they would not hold to disputations with one another and thus be incited to useless quarrels."[42] This assessment of the mime plays reveals the rabble's predilection for crowding the theatres and circuses where boisterous spirits sometimes led to bloodshed. From early times on Judaism's attitude to the gymnasia and ephebia was obviously unfavorable, due to the fear of their harmful effect on Jews and the dislike of idolatry[43]. In later periods the sages also condemned theatres and circuses, not only for idolatry but also for "bloodshed" and being the "seat of the scorners" (or "frivolous company")[44], undoubtedly a reference to the mime plays.

Despite such censure, it should not be concluded categorically that the Jews everywhere kept away from the gymnasia and theatres. In fact in some Diaspora communities they may have established such institutions of their own[45]. Furthermore, Jews participated actively in certain gymnasia and ephebia such as those in Cyrene[46]. Excavations in Sardis showed that the synagogue and the municipal gymnasium were adjacent[47], so that evidently peaceful co-existence marked the activities of the two institutions there. Thus the attitude of the Jews to Greek educational and cultural institutions largely reflected the relationship between the local Jews and the Greeks in the various cities. Where relations were good, probably Jews of a certain type had no qualms about taking an active part in the life of

---

42 *Bereshith Rabbah*, LXXX 1.
43 *I Maccabees*, I 14-15; *II Maccabees*, IV 9-17. Josephus too (*Antiquitates*, XV 267f.) noted Jewish opposition in Herod's time to the erection of a theatre in Jerusalem, the introduction of gymnastic games and contests. He notes that these innovation were contrary to ancestral laws and led to neglect in everything connected with the fear of God (*ibid.*, 267); blood spectacles were also condemned (*ibid.*, 274-276). Jeiwish objections to all these were described by Herod as "superstition" (*ibid.*, 277) and that may well indicate its religious and uncompromising nature.
44 See *Mishnah Abodah Zarah*, I 7; *J.T. Abodah Zarah*, I 40a; *B.T. Abodah Zarah*, 18b.
45 See Applebaum, in *Fourth World Congress for Jewish Studies*, vol. 1, p. 107f.; *Jews and Greeks*, pp. 167, 178, 185. Cf. J. Gutman, *The Beginning of Jewish Hellenistic Literature*, vol. 2, p. 68f. The Ἰουδαῖοι νεώτεροι mentioned in an inscription from Hypaipa in Lydia may have been members of the Jewish gymnasium (cf. Schürer, vol. 3, p. 91); Frey, *CIJ*, II 755, S. Reinach, *REJ*, 10 (1885), p. 74f.; but cf. Krauss, *Syn. Alt.*, pp. 231, 395f.
46 See *QAL*, 4 (1981), pp. 19-20 (Nos. 6-7).
47 See *BASOR*, 170 (1963), p. 38f.; 174 (1964), p. 30f.; 177 (1965), p. 17f.; 182 (1966), p. 34f.; 186 (1967), p. 17f.; 187 (1967), p. 9f.

those institutions. Where relations were bad, however, as in Antioch, Alexandria and Caearaea, the institutions were hotbeds of anti-Jewish activity and consequently also the prime target for Jewish opposition and retaliation.

According to the interpretation here proposed, Claudius did not warn the Jews against penetrating the ranks of the ephebes, but rather sought to dissuade them from "harassing" (ἐπισπαίρειν) the public performances organized by the gymnasiarchs and cosmetes since such action could readily inflame tempers and so cause another "war". It should be borne in mind that the section in *Claudius' Letter* referring to the Jews was aimed entirely at restoring order and preventing the recurrence of the "war against the Jews". All the passages of that part of the *Letter* reflect the emperor's concern to reestablish the *status quo ante* in the spirit of the Augustan policy of *Pax Romana*. Consequently, just as he enjoined the Alexandrians not to violate Jewish customs and religion, he enjoined the Jews not to attack the Alexandrian Greeks' popular spectacles. It should be noted too that Claudius' warning to the Jews in the world edict as cited by Josephus is remarkably similar to his warning to the Alexandrians in the *Letter*: "It is right therefore that the Jews throughout the whole world under our sway should also observe the customs of their fathers without let or hindrance. I enjoin upon them also by these presents to avail themselves of this kindness in a more reasonable spirit, and not to set at nought the beliefs about the gods held by other people but to keep their own laws" (*Antiquitates*, XIX 290)[48]. According to Claudius' policy, each of the rival groups was supposed to display tolerance for the other. Both were ordered to refrain from offending each other, since experience had shown that hostile acts and bloody clashes were likely to ensue.

To sum up, *Claudius' Letter to the Alexandrians* does not deal with any surreptitious infiltration by Jews into the Alexandrian gymnasium in order to gain citizenship in the *polis*. It simply warns the Jews "not to harass" (μηδὲ ἐπισπαίρειν)[49] the "games" arranged by the gymnasiarchs and cosmetes, a warning that may be taken as

---

48 Cf. a similar policy in the Dora affair (*Antiquitates*, XIX 305).

49 Or "oppose," "run riot," "attack," and the like, as per Amusin. Consequently, the Latin original of the letter may very well have had the term *asperno*, which the Greek translator changed to ἐπισπαίρω; see also above, p. 315f. and nn.25, 26.

showing that the Jews were hostile to the Alexandrian gymnasium which had humiliated them not long before (e.g. Philo, *In Flaccum*, 34). The emperor's warning to the Jews paralleled the one directed at the Alexandrians and was aimed at preventing the recurrence of violent disturbances. The fact that the Jews were the initiators in 41 C.E. (*Antiquitates*, XIX 278) suggests that they chose the popular Alexandrian spectacles to focus their retaliation on for the events of 38 C.E. The proximity of the gymnasium and theatre to the dwellings of the Jews may also help to explain both their choice of a traget and their success in attacking it.

The *Letter to the Alexandrians* does not name the gymnasiarchs of the time, but their predecessors or collaborators are known. Prominent among them was Isidorus, who is known from the *Acts of Alexandrian Martyrs*[50], and Lampon, who was assigned the office as a *liturgia* by the prefect Flaccus[51]. Both of them became martyrs following their trial before Claudius in 41 C.E. That fact that such confirmed Jew-haters were then gymnasiarchs makes it all the more unlikely that Jews could have "infiltrated" into the gymnasium they presided over[52]. On the contrary, their leadership spurred the Jews on to combat that institution that had so embittered them just a few years earlier. Such an interpretation casts new light on the struggle of the Jews in Alexandria. It totally refutes the grounds for the well-known thesis that the Jews of Alexandria yearned for citizenship in the *polis* and sought "emancipation" through the gymnasium. *Claudius' Letter to the Alexandrians* provides the true facts: it shows the Jews as an organized body independent of the *polis* and fighting for self-determination. While the Alexandrians opposed that aim, either by interfering with the practice of the Jewish religion or attempting to deprive the Jews of their autonomy, the Jews did not sit by idly, but fought for their rights to the point even of initiating acts of revenge.

---

50 See *CPJ*, II 156d, col. 3, lines 8-10; *CPJ*, II 156a, col. 2, line 2f.; *CPJ*, II 156b, lines 42f., 46. Its connection with the gymnasium is clear also from Philo who reports that he made groundless accusations against Flaccus before the rabble in the gymnasium (*In Flaccum*, 139).

51 *In Flaccum*, 130, and see Box's explanation.

52 That is so even if "penetrate" (ἐπισπαίεω) is accepted.

B. Additional Demands of the Jews

Claudius' clear assertion in his *Letter* that the Jews were entitled
to live in Alexandria in safety and peace and keep their customs as in
Augustus' day demonstrates that he confirmed their *politeia*. This
was unsatisfactory for the Alexandrians, and they did all they could
to oppose the Jewish *politeia* and abolish it. On that point the
emperor's decision was unequivocal: the Augustan policy was firm
and abiding in his reign as well. However, one passage in his letter
suggests that the Jews sought to obtain "more than they had previously" (line 89f.).

Tcherikover considered it self-evident that the something "more"
was citizenship in the *polis*[53], which fit in very well with his notion
of a "struggle for emancipation" by the Alexandria Jews. But the
Letter contains not the slightest hint to support that view, particularly since it has been demonstrated that there was no "penetration" or "infiltration" by the Jews into the games presided over by
gymnasiarchs and cosmetes. Unfortunately, *Claudius' Letter* does not
specify the additional benefits requested by the Jews. It is clear,
however, that those demands were formulated to counterbalance the
desires of the Alexandrian delegates, especially those of Dionysus
son of Theon[54]. Assuming that the adversaries of the Jews wished to
abolish the legal validity of the Jewish (separate) *politeia*, the Jews
would have insisted at least that it be maintained, but that would
not constitute an additional demand. It should be borne in mind that
Philo's delegation left for Rome while Caligula was still emperor,
armed with "just demands" which were composed in the form of a
"memoradum" handed to King Agrippa (*Legatio*, 178f.). As noted
above, Philo's mission as well as the "memorandum" were designed
to submit two points to the emperor (*ibid.*, 195), one describing the
suffering of the Alexandria Jews and the other demanding the protection of what Philo termed "our *politeia*". Thus no demands for
new rights were made[55]. The additional demands mentioned in
Claudius' Letter must then have come from a group that did not
include Philo and his delegation, namely, from the second of the two
Jewish delegations referred to in *Claudius' Letter* (line 90f.). Tcherikover indicated the differences in the composition and methods of

---

53 See *CPJ*, II , p. 50.
54 See *CPJ*, II 153, line 75f.
55 This conclusion can be drawn from Philo as well. Cf., e.g., *Legatio*, 183, 350.

the two delegations[56]. Philo's delegation most probably represented the Jewish *politeuma's* traditional aristocratic leadership which favored moderate diplomatic means in the fight to safeguard Jewish rights. The other delegation apparently represented more popular groups who favored the methods employed by the Zealots of Judaea[57]. They may have demanded that Alexandria be opened to more Jews[58], and perhaps also that Jewish rights be expanded and extended to Jews outside the restricted membership of the *politeuma*. All these would have been reason enough for a rift between two Jewish delegations as well as for Claudius' anger[59]. The grounds for any definite assertions on this score are unfortunately extremely shaky; it cannot however, be claimed that the additional demands were related to citizenship in the *polis*.

C. When did the Two Delegations Report to Claudius[60] ?.

Tcherikover estimated that the second Jewish delegation arrived in Rome a short time after the second Alexandrian delegation headed by Barbillus, that is, in April 41 C.E., for the purpose of defending the violence the Jews had employed since February and thwart

---

56 See his explanation of lines 90-91 (*CPJ*, II, pp. 50-53). Tcherikover's comprehensive analysis is excellent, except that it is not reasonable to suppose that Philo's circle were interested in citizenship in the *polis* (p. 52), or that the conflict was a "war of emancipation."

57 Amusin was the first to discern the influence on the Jews of Alexandria at the time of the Palestinian zealots who immigrated to Egypt (suggested in the Letter, lines 96-100); see Amusin, *JJP*, 9-10 (1955/6), p. 196f. The fanaticism of the extremist groups among the Alexandria Jews could actually be attributed to the local situation rather than Palestinian influence. The easily aroused Alexandrian rabble might well have provoked a similar Jewish reaction. In any case, the short tempers and impatience of the Alexandria Jews was well known, and reflected in talmudic tradition; see *Tosefta, Yoma*, IV 13 (Zuckermandel, p. 188); cf. *B.T. Yoma*, 10a, *Menahoth*, 100a.

58 See line 96ff. – Nor are they to bring in or invite Jews coming from Syria or Egypt," etc. – (cf. Amusin, *ibid.*, p. 198f.). Probably the arrival of those Jews displeased both the citizens of the *polis* and the Roman authorities.

59 The stance of the extremist popular groups could have jeopardized the achievements of Philo and his delegation. And on the other hand, Claudius did not wish to disturb the status quo, so that he would have disliked the violence of the extremists. It is not surprising that he hinted that he might "be forced to conceive graver suspicions" against them and "proceed against them in every way as fomemting a common plague for the whole world." On the meaning of "plague" (νόσος) which has political connotations, see *CPJ*, II, pp. 53-54.

60 Tcherikover, *Jews in Egypt*, pp. 146, 148f.

possible Alexandrian machinations. He even suggested that the news of renewed disturbances initiated by the Jews led to less favorable imperial policy toward them.

That interpretation is untenable for a number of reasons[61] :
a) The emperor was not concerned with who caused the disturbances, as he actually said in the *Letter*. b) As Tcherikover himself admitted, the edict which was favorable to the Jews was issued in April after the emperor had already learned of the renewal of disturbances. c) The death sentence was passed on Isidorus and Lampon on 1 May, indicating that the emperor's hostility to the Alexandrians had not abated, even in the face of the recommendations of his personal friend Barbillus who headed the second Alexandrian delegation. d) Claudius explicitly stressed in his *Letter* that there was no precedent for dispatching two Jewish delegations, and he wrote that in October! It is not reasonable therefore to suppose that he became angry in October about something that happened in April. Furthermore he said that they should not send two "embassies" in the future, which "has never been done before", and his words should be understood literally to mean that such a thing had not ever been done before October.

The background for the two Jewish delegations must have been different, and there appear to be two possibilities:

a) If it is assumed that the Alexandrian delegates remained in Rome even after the trial of the gymnasiarchs[62], then it is reasonable to suppose that Philo's delegation remained as well to look out for Jewish interests[63], so that the second Jewish delegation appeared only after a new wave of riots in September (see pp. 272-274 above). Its arrival in Rome at that time fits in with our conclusions that the Greeks were responsible for that second outbreak. This delegation was evidently not content with complaining about the resumption of hostilities, but made demands of the emperor as well.

b) Philo's delegation may have returned to Alexandria in May, having been satisfied by the issuance of the edict and the sentences of Isidorus and Lampon. However, as a result of the renewed distur-

---

61 Cf. pp. 272ff. above.
62 As per Tcherikover, *ibid.*, p. 143.
63 Contrary to Tcherikover's view that Philo's delegation already returned in the spring (*ibid.*, p. 149). See below for another possibility.

bances in September, the Jews sent out two delegations, one of them to operate on the basis of the line Philo had taken, and the other to submit demands to the emperor using different tactics. They were opposed of course by a united Alexandrian delegation which made no change in its arguments or positions. The emperor was no doubt surprised by the development, and confused and perplexed by the presence of two Jewish delegations speaking two different languages. He was therefore annoyed with the Jews and scolded them. It is hard to decide which of the two possibilities is correct, but in either case the month was October, as the data in *Claudius' Letter* shows.

D. ἀλλοτρία πόλις

Claudius' Letter to the Alexnadrians contains a passage (line 94f.) saying that the Jews "enjoy what is their own (τὰ οἰκία) and in a city which is not their own (ἐν ἀλλοτρίᾳ πόλις) they possess an abundance of all good things". Generally ἡ ἀλλοτρία is construed to mean "alien country" so that ἡ ἀλλοτρία πόλις is applied to people who are temporary residents[64]. Tcherikover admitted that Claudius could not have meant the term in that sense because, as the emperor himself wrote, the Jews had lived in Alexandria for ages (line 84). However, Tcherikover believed that although they were considered permanent residents of the city, Alexandria was "alien" to them in the civic-juridical sense, and was the homeland (*patris*) only for the citizens of the *polis*. In his view that was decisive proof that the Jews were not citizens of the *polis*, and in using that term the emperor wished to counter their arguments on citizenship[65].

The Alexandria Jews were not of course citizens of the *polis*, but Tcherikover's contention that the emperor's words were meant to define their "foreignness" from the civic standpoint is untenable. One cannot grasp the stick at both end. If the term ἡ ἀλλοτρία πόλις did not have a precise legal significance that defined the Jews as out and out "foreigners", it cannot be proof of their civic status. Accordingly, the argument that Claudius ostensibly wished to point out that Alexandria was not a homeland for the Jews has no basis, aside from the fact that it contradicts what Philo had to say on the subject[66].

---

64 See Tcherikover's interpretations of the passage, *CPJ*, II, p. 53, line 95.
65 See his interpretations of line 95 (*ibid.*) and also *Jews in Egypt*, p. 151.
66 See *In Flaccum*, 46, and the discussion of the matter, pp. 236-238 above.

The term ἡ ἀλλοτρία πόλις must obviously be explained differently in line with Churgin's construction[67], and should be understood literally, without the slightest relation to the civic status of the Jews. It should be kept in mind that Claudius refrained from investigating the causes of the conflict, and his sole aim was to restore quiet and prevent hostilities. His statement that the Jews should "enjoy what is their own" (τὰ οἰκῖα) is contrasted with "a city which is not their own" simply to stress that Alexandria, like all of Egypt, was the private possession of the emperor[68], and they therefore could not do as they liked in it. This is made clear by Claudius' ending to his *Letter* (lines 100-104): "If you both give up your present ways and are willing to live in gentleness and kindness with one another, I for my part will care for the city as much as I can, as one which has long belonged to my house (ἐκ προγόων οἰκίας ἡμῖν ὑπαρχούσης...). In short, the expression ἐν ἀλλοτρίᾳ πόλις has nothing to do with civic status.

E. The Tone of the Warning to the Jews.

In Tcherikover's view, Claudius' tone was sharper in regard to the Jews than to their adversaries, as evidenced by "I conjure (διαμαρτύρομαι) the Alexandrians" (line 82) and "I order (κελεύω) the Jews" (line 89). According to him the first expression is softer and more polite, suitable for addressing an ally, while the second is tougher and fits the formal, severe attitude to the native born (see *Jews in Egypt*, p. 149.; *CPJ*, II p. 49). However, the difference in the terms should not be viewed as expressing different political attitudes to the two parties, for the emperor deliberately avoided taking sides, and was known to choose his words carefully. The explanation seems to be much simpler: Claudius "ordered" the Jews because he knew very well that he could not get them to swear. An emperor as intelligent and thoughtful as he was could be expected to know that after having twice encountered the Jews in his courts, and noted their reactions when called upon to testify. For as Philo noted (*De Decalogue*, 86, cf. 82-95), "For an oath is an appeal to God as a witness on matters in disupte, and ... the height of profanity."

---

67 Churgin, *Studies in the Times of Second Temple*, p. 269f., n.9. I am grateful to Prof. Efron for calling my attention to the point.
68 Cf. Tacitus, *Annales*: II 59; *Historiae*, I 11.

Chapter X

Jewish Civic Status and Rights according to Anti-Jewish Literature

Anti-Semitism in the ancient world has been dealt with comprehensively by modern scholarly research. The various causes and manifestations have been considered, and some studies were devoted to Alexandria in particular[1]. The focus here is on anti-Jewish literature in Alexandria, in order to ascertain its objectives and the interests it served, and to explore the political significance of the accusations made against the Jews. These included their base origin, misanthropy, superstition, impiety and sacrilege, and rebellious conspiratory nature, and the slanders sought to prove that their character had been cast at the dawn of their existence, thus providing "lawful justification" for persecuting them, abolishing their civic status, and out-lawing them. As most of the available information on the Alexandrian anti-Jewish writers comes from Josephus, and since the basic arguments of most were similar[2], the discussion will be limited to Manetho and Apion, they having the largest bodies of work and being dealt with most extensively in Josephus.

A. Manetho

The most ancient examples of anti-Jewish propaganda were composed by Manetho and cited by Josephus in *Contra Apionem*[3]. He was an Egyptian priest with a Greek education, who lived at the time of the first two Ptolemaic kings, and was well-steeped in the anti-

---

1 Such as Musurillo; Wilcken, *Zum Alexandrinischen Antisemitismus; Heinemann RE(PW)*, Suppl. V, pp. 3-43; Bell, *JRS*, 31 (1941), pp. 1-18; Dobschütz, *AJTL*, 8 (1904), pp. 728-755.

2 The difference lay in the way the anti-Jewish libels were developed.

3 *C. Apionem*, I 73-90, 94-102, 229-251. See the comprehensive survey of his literary work in Fraser, vol. 1, p. 505ff. See also Kasher, *Studies in the History of the Jewish People and the Land of Israel*, vol. 3, p. 69ff.

Jewish tradition prevalent in Egypt since antiquity[4]. No wonder
Josephus considered that his being Egyptian was the root of his
hatred of Jews, and indeed in several places noted that the Egyptians
were confirmed enemies of the Jewish people[5].

In Manetho's day, the prestige of Judaism and the Jews had been
enhanced following the translation of the Pentateuch into Greek[6],
as demonstrated by the intellectual interest in it of members of the
Ptolemaic court, foremost among them Hecataeus of Abdera. On the
other hand an Egyptian priest and writer like Manetho, for whom
Egypt was the cradle of civilization, could very well have felt that the
translation would dim the splendor of his motherland, particularly
since the salvation of Israel in the Bible involved the defeat and
humiliation of his people. Probably the disappointment in the attitude of the king (Ptolemy II Philadlphus) to the Egyptian intelligentsia[7], in contrast to the admiring royal interest in Jews and Judaism, aroused Egyptian hatred of the Jews and zeal for the honor of
Egypt. All these factors impelled Manetho to collect the ancient
traditions defaming the Jews, and record them.

As might be expected, his work followed the pattern of polemic
and apolgetic literature in which the controversial motif is predominant[8], though not exclusive. He does not appear to have wished to
take a purely defensive position, but to launch a mighty propaganda

---

4 *C. Apionem*, I 105, 228, 287. Some scholars tried to refute that claim and question
  whether Manetho was a Jew-hater at all, but such views are groundless. See details in
  Kasher, *ibid.*, p. 72ff.; Stern, *Greek and Latin Authors*, vol. 1, p. 62ff. On the development of Jew-hatred among the Egyptian priesthood, see Yoyotte, *RHR*, 163 (1963),
  p. 133f.

5 *C. Apionem*, I 70, 223-226, 251. Fraser (vol. 1, p. 509) tried to mitigate the matter by
  attributing general xenophobia to the Egyptian priesthood, but was mistaken, as he
  failed to take into account contradiction in ritual and faith that already aroused hatred
  in earlier times (e.g. in the Persian period).

6 It was Fraser's opinion (vol. 1, p. 589f.) that there is a real historic basis at least in regard
  to the start of the translation at that time. The fact that the Jews of Alexandria annually
  celebrated the event on the isle of Pharos (see *De Vita Mosis*, II 47) likewise verifies the
  details (cf. *Letter of Aristeas*, 301ff.).

7 Tarn rightly pointed out that even if Ptolemy I considered involving Egyptians in intellectual activity in Alexandria, that possibility vanished almost completely in the reign of
  Philadelphus. See Tran, *JEA*, 14 (1928), p. 254. On the lack of any influence of Egyptian literature, see also Fraser, vol. 1, p. 685ff. Its influence grew only many years later
  (from the reign of Philopator on, especially in the first century B.C.E.).

8 Josephus himself sensed this (*C. Apionem*, I 223-225). Cf. Tcherikover, *Hellenistic
  Civilization and the Jews*, p. 363ff., and see below.

campaign against Jewry and the Jewish faith, hoping thus to redress the effects of the Septuagint. For that purpose he adopted a proven literary method — ethnographic investigation — whose purpose was to prove that the Jewish people still embodied the evil heritage of their forefathers. From this point of view Manetho did not differ from other ethnographic writers of antiquity, as for them too the investigation of the pasts of various peoples served as a means of revealing their natures in the present. It was then generally accepted that the character of a people was determined by the circumstances of its birth, the manner of its development, and the settlement pattern of its founders. The ethnographic writers delved assiduously into these matters for the purpose of exploring the roots of the favorable or unfavorable traits in the peoples under discussion, depending on their attitude to any particular people. There are even tactical instructions provided by rhetoricians on the subject, which were evidently quite effective propaganda tools[9]. Indeed, Josephus in his introudction to the leper libel noted that defamation was employed by numerous writers, and not only against the Jews (*C. Apionem*, I 220). Manetho too was faithful to the typological method of ethnographic literature as he sought thereby to prove the principle that the character pattern of the Jewish people was formed with its inception, and only in that way was it possible to expose its true face in the present as well. His testimony combined ethnographic motifs with polemics to form an integrated whole which constituted the basis of his propaganda attack against Judaism.

In opposition to the notion of "chosen people" Manetho presented the Jewish people as a contemptible rabble of aliens (Hyksos) who joined with the leprous, diseased and maimed among the Egyptians, in other words, a foul bunch that the country must disgorge as it is purified from the religious standpoint[10]. In contrast to the scriptural description of the exodus from Egypt symbolizing true salvation through divine might, Manetho stressed that the Jews were forcibly expelled and persecuted as despicable people. While the Bible described Joseph as having saved Egypt and ruled it wisely, Manetho presented Osarseph[11] as a destructive figure who ruined the country.

---

9 Levy, *Studies in Jewish Hellenism*, pp. 94ff., 138.
10 *C. Apionem*, I 229, 241, and cf. 234, 256, 257, 260, 273, 278. Cf. also the Chaeremon version (*ibid.*, 289, 295) and the Lysimachus version (*ibid.*, 306).
11 On the linguistic problem I am inclined to accept the view proffered by Reinach (*Textes*

330 Chapter X

Manetho's revision of the exodus from Egypt was designed to
emphasize several features of the Jewish people that marked it from
its birth and ever after. One of these was that they were war captives
and slaves, showing that such had been their original condition[12].
According to their name the Hyksos were "captives"[13], and the
lepers were people banished to slavery in the quarries east of the
Nile[14]. The fact that in Manetho's time (the reigns of Ptolemy I and
Ptolemy II) a considerable proportion of the Jews in Egypt were
actually captives and slaves[15] shows that he sought to provide "legal
justification" for that situation through his ethnographic description
of the origins of the Jewish people[16].

Another possible interpretation of his point is that it was a polemical attack against Ptolemy II's growing inclination to change the
lowly status of the Jews which Manetho deemed justified. His testimony may even have involved an apologetic note here, for how could
the Egyptians remain on the lowest rung of the civic ladder while the
descendents of "nameless people" and unclean Egyptians and disease-
ridden individuals oppressed into slavery were favored? Probably his
accusation that the Jews were misanthropic[17] was also designed to
serve the same end. That epithet signified an absence of humane
feelings, and was considered an attribute of barbaric peoples[18]. According to ancient anti-Semites, the misanthropy of the Jews were
demonstrated by their aloofness, segregation from others, and laws

d'auteurs grecs, p. 33, n.1) that the last part of the name contains the name "Joseph"
and the first part is based on the replacement of Jo (= יהך) by "Osiris" (with the suffix
Seph (= סף). Sayce, Alte Denkmaeler im Lichte Forschungen, p. 59, made the interesting suggestion that "Osarseph" combined the figures of Moses and Joseph (cf. Tcherikover, op.cit. in n.8, p. 363, n.80). However, an ethnographic writer cannot be expected
to have attended to historical niceties when his aim was primarily propagandistic. Furthermore, ancient anti-Jewish literature quite often brought the figures of Joseph and Moses
together in disregard of historical truth. Trogus Pompey, e.g. (in Justinus, 36, 2, 7ff.;
see Reinach, ibid., p. 252) made Moses the son of Joseph from whom he learned magic,
and Chaeremon had Joseph and Moses as contemporary leaders of the expelled Jews
(C. Apionem, I 290). Thus Manetho's juxtapositioning of the two is not surprising.
12 Cf. III Maccabees, II 29.
13 C. Apionem, I 83, and cf. 91f.
14 Ibid., 235, 237, 267.
15 Letter of Aristeas, 2-16, 20-25, 36-37.
16 A similar case of "justification" figures in Tacitus. See also Levy, op.cit. in n.9, p. 150ff.
17 C. Apionem, I 75f., 239f., 248f., 269f.
18 See e.g. Cicero, Tusc., IV 25-27; Pliny, Nat. Hist., VII 80; Diodorus Siculus, I 67, 10;
etc. See Levy, op.cit. in n.9, p. 147ff. and nn.145, 146.

and a way of life different from those of all other peoples. These traits were emphasized in Manetho by primitive drawings easily understood by anyone even superficially familiar with Jewish customs. In brief, as an ethnographic writer he endeavored to prove that the Jews and their Torah were deviant in human civilization, and that they still harbored the evil legacy of their past. The obvious conclusion was that they should be treated as they deserved. In the same way Manetho proved his accusation of rebelliousness, which he considered the outcome of their misanthropy. From his standpoint the Jews were enemies, traitors and rebels, for their birth as a nation was marked by rebellion[19], and by sworn conspiracy[20], and besides their divinity was the mutinous Seth-Typhon[21]. Such ethnographic accusations are probably part of a deliberate campaign against the assignment of Jews to the military and administrative services of Ptolemy II Philadelphus.

As an ethnographic writer, Manetho sought to demonstrate that from the dawn of its history the Jewish people had been characterized by impiety[22], and that implied both violation of law and disloyalty to the throne. In the ancient world, laws were deemed to be god-given, so that Jewish non-acceptance of the gods meant non-acceptance of law, with the result that the Jews were accused also of lawlessness (ἀνομία). As the laws reflected human morality, the Jews were immoral and blamed for adhering to a new Law whose provisions contradicted those of the Egyptians[23]. Moreover, as failure to acknowledge the gods was equated with disregard of the royal cult, the Jews could be represented as faithless, treacherous, hostile and insurgent, and deserving to be dealt with accordingly. At the very

---

19 *C. Apionem*, I 238, 240, 245, 272, 275f., etc.
20 *Ibid.*, 238f., 261. In classical literature the term συνωμοσία meant a sworn conspiracy. See e.g. Thucydides, VI 27, 60; VIII 49; Plutarch, *Antony* 2, 13; *Cato the Younger*, 29; *Sertorius*, 22; and so on.
21 Seth is known in Egyptian mythology as the murderer of Osiris, his brother and usurper. Typhon was also considered a rebel and identified with one of the Titans in the depths of the earth (the son of Tartarus and Gea) who was sent to the netherworld after being hit by Zeus' thunderbolt because he wanted to revolt and destroy the heaven of the gods. Seth and Typhon were identified in Egyptian mythology and by Manetho (according to Plutarch, *De Iside et Osiride*, 62) as representing the forces of darkness and evil, night and desolation, plagues and diseases, and other natural disasters (Plutarch, *ibid.*, 49).
22 *C. Apionem*, I 76, 239, 244, 248f., 261, 264, etc.
23 *Ibid.*, 239.

least, according to Manetho, these "facts" ought to suggest certain
conclusions about the political and juridical status of the Jews.

B. Apion[24]

Josephus states that Apion's libel concerning the base origin of the
Jews was the debt the latter felt he owed the Alexandrians in return
for the citizenship they granted him, since he was aware of their
hatred for the Jews[25]. The fact that Josephus mocked Apion's Egyptian lineage might suggest that the Jews were not above ethnic slander
either, in the Alexandrian-Jewish controversy[26]. However, the revela-
tion of Apion's Egyptian ancestry should probably be understood as
an attempt on Josephus' part to destroy the bases of Apion's argument against the right of the Jews to be considered *politai*. Fighting
Apion with his own weapons, Josephus derided Apion for denying
his true background and falsely representing himself as an "Alexandrian"[27]. He thus showed that Apion had contradicted himself, for
if the Egyptian origin of the Jews made them unfit to be *politai*,
that would apply to Apion himself. Leaving aside that dialectical
argument, Josephus vigorously denied the accepted "fact" that the
Jews were originally Egyptian[28]. In settling the accounts, he proffered an explanation of Apion's motivation in claiming that the
Jews were of base origin: It was natural for people to take pride in
their homeland and denounce those who do not (*C. Apionem*, II 30).
According to Josephus the imputation of base origin to the Jews
served two purposes. It was designed on the one hand to enhance the
reputation of the Egyptians (by connecting them with the Jews)
and on the other to mar that of the Jews by association with the
Egyptians (*ibid.*, 31). At first glance such a double purpose seems
based on a contradiction, for what was the advantage to the Egyp-

---

24 See for full details, Stern, *Greek and Latin Authors*, vol. 1, p. 389ff.
25 *C. Apionem*, II, 32 (and cf. also 6f.) suggests a connection between his version of the
exodus from Egypt and his defamations of the Alexandria Jews.
26 That was Josephus' complaint against Manetho (*C. Apionem*, I 73). See Waddel,
Manetho, Introduction (*LCL*); Fraser, vol. 1, p. 506ff. Chaeremon too was of Egyptian
descent (see Porphyry, *De Abstinentia*, IV 608; Schürer, vol. 3, p. 538ff.; Stern, *op.cit.*
in n.24, p. 41f.). There are many references in Philo censuring the Jew-haters among the
Egyptian population of Alexandria.
27 *C. Apionem*, II 29, 41.
28 *Ibid.*, 28, and cf. 8 and others as well.

tians of kinship with the dregs of humanity? Yet there was some sense in it, for if the worst and lowest Egyptians had obtained considerable political advantage from the country's rulers, why should the real respectable Egyptians not achieve it as well? On the other hand, if Egyptian descent did not provide political privileges, why did the basest of Egyptians obtain them? While there is no documentation for such an argument, it can be inferred from Josephus' report.

Josephus attributed the argument to Egyptians in general rather than to Apion, who was an Alexandrian citizen and seems to have voiced purely Alexandrian arguments. Yet Josephus juxtaposed his analysis of that Egyptian argument to his treatment of Apion, because of his assessment of Apion and all the Jew-haters of Alexandria. In his view Apion was, and remained, fundamentally an Egyptian. Apion's libels and diatribes against the Jews originated in Egyptian sources, as he himself says[29]. Thus for Josephus Apion's arguments were a synthesis of Egyptian and Alexandrian ones just as the man himself represented such a synthesis as an individual and an author[30].

In other words, his hatred of the Jews was the ancient Egyptian animosity in a new Alexandrian wrapping. According to Josephus, when Alexandrian citizenship was restircted to Greeks, no conflicts developed between them and the Jews. It was only when masses of Egyptians acquired Alexandrian citizenship that the trouble began, instigated by citizens like Apion (*C. Apionem*, II 69). For the Alexandrians were no longer purely Greeks, but a base admixture. In noting that Apion thanked the Alexandrians through his anti-Jewish writings, Josephus meant that he served the interests of the Egyptian rabble[31], who had attained citizenship in the *polis* during the period of confusion and disturbances. Not surprisingly, Josephus therefore asserted axiomatically that all the anti-Jewish slander originated with people of Egyptian descent, noting that it was motivated by a mixture of hatred and envy because a) the ancestors of the

---

29 He said he got them from Egyptian ancestors (*C. Apionem*, II 8, and cf. also 13ff.). Josephus also stressed the resemblance between Apion's traditions and those of his predecessors, chiefly Manetho and Chaeremon (*C. Apionem*, II 2-3).

30 In fact he wrote his *Aegyptiaca* (see *C. Apionem*, II 10) as an Egyptian. On the other hand, he is famous as a commentator on Homer (*C. Apionem*, II 14) and as a teacher of rhetoric at Rome during the reigns of Tiberius, Caligula and Claudius.

31 Philo too, it will be recalled, blamed the anti-Jewish disturbances on the Alexandrian rabble, identified with the Egyptians.

Jews (the Hyksos) had ruled Egypt, b) the Jews had returned to
Egypt and were again successful there, and finally c) there were
basic differences in ritual and religion between them (*C. Apionem*,
I 223-225).

In accusing the Jews of misanthropy, rebelliousness and conspiracy,
Apion said nothing new. However, his libels were vastly improved
from the literary viewpoint, reaching an apogee with the so-called
blood libel (*ibid.*, II 89f.). Flusser provided an excellent analysis of
the way that libel evolved as well as of the tactics of its propagadistic
utilization, and also showed how it served Apion's interests in his
political struggle with the Jews[32]. For Apion's contention was that
the Jews' hateful, rebellious and conspiratorial propensities were
directed at the Greeks, rather than at the Egyptians or other people.
The political implications were quite clear: The Jews represented
pure "barbarism" and could not therefore be accorded social, legal
or political equality.

Apion's accusation of the Jews as "impious" served his political
interests best of all. Fortunately Josephus provided a quotation of
one of the basic arguments: "Why then if they are citizens do they
not worship the same gods as the Alexandrians?" (*ibid.*, 65).
Numerous scholars have pointed to that argument as incisive proof
that the religious obstacle was what prevented the Jews from fully
participating in the public political life of the Greek *polis*[33]. Even
scholars claiming that the Jews were citizens of Alexandria (and of
other Hellenistic cities) accepted the validity of that interpretation,
although they advocated some explanations that evaded the point[34].

Fustel de Coulages pointed out that the definition of the term
"citizen" (πολίτης) must first and foremost pass the test of religion,
for to be a "citizen" meant to participate in the city ritual[35]. At the
same time, he noted that this applied to the period before the great
democratic revolutions, and although the ancient posts and public

---

32 Flusser, *Levy Memorial Volume*, pp. 104-125.
33 See, e.g., Bell, *Jews and Christians*, p. 11; Tarn, p. 221; Segre, *Jew. Soc. St.*, vol. 6
    (1944), p. 277; Fuchs, p. 79; Tcherikover, *Jews in Egypt*, p. 130; idem, *Hellenistic
    Civilization and the Jews*, pp. 310ff., 374-376; Willrich, *Hermes*, 39 (1904), p. 258;
    Ostersetzer, *Braude Jubilee Volume*, pp. 10ff.
34 See e.g., Schürer, vol. 3, p. 126; Askowith, *The Toleration*, p. 194.
35 Fustel de Coulanges, *The Ancient City* (Engl. trans.), p. 193f. Cf., e.g., Aristotle, *Athen-
    ian Constitution*, 42, 1; Xenophon, *Memorabilia*, IV 4, 16; see also Glotz, *The Greek
    City*, p. 133.

religious ceremonies still persisted thereafter, religion no longer had a crucial influence, in particular in government and political life[36]. That reservation does not however seem adequate to solve the problem of Jewish citizenship in the Greek *polis*. It is true that the Hellenistic period saw the end of the Classical *polis*, since the religious and political standards imposed on many Greek cities altered their constitutions, rituals, sovereignty, and the criteria for citizenship in them. The granting or withholding of citizenship, for instance, was no longer the exclusive prerogative of the *polis*, for the government now intervened. During the Roman period, the supervision of the cities became even stricter, and indeed Alexandria conducted a protracted campaign against the Roman Empire urging the removal of the restrictions to municipal sovereignty. Under the circumstances of central government supervision of the cities, it was at least theoretically possibly for the Jews to be citizens of the *poleis*. There is no doubt that there were religious obstacles for Jews who aspired to public posts which generally involved explicit religious obligations. On the other hand, Jews as individuals could apparently be citizens of *poleis* whose constitutions did not contain strict religious requirements for ordinary citizens. The city of Rome itself placed no impediment of a religious nature to the acquisition of Roman citizenship by Jews.

In reality, however, the main road to citizenship in most Greek *poleis* in both the Hellenistic and Roman periods was gymnasium education, which was closely involved with Greek religious practices. Thus observant God-fearing Jews could not participate in the life of that institution, and consequently could not become citizens of the *polis*. And yet there seem to have been cases of Jews becoming citizens in just that way, in Ptolemaîs of Cyrene and in Cyrene itself, as indicated by the names of Jewish ephebes on stelas bearing dedications to Greek gods[37]. These inscriptions raise a difficult problem: Did those ephebes belong to the city *ephebeion* or to a private one? If they belonged to the former, those Jewish ephebes who took an active part in the life of the city gymnasium must have converted, but the retention of Jewish names seems to contradict that possiblity

36 Fustel de Coulanges, *ibid.*, p. 318ff.
37 See Applebaum, *Jews and Greeks*, pp. 167f., 177f., and ch. IX, n.46.

which would have involved the adoption of Greek names[38]. Perhaps the explanation is that they participated only partially in gymnasium life, or had special permission to absent themselves from the Greek rites. Even so, they could not have been orthodox Jews in the Palestinian sense. They must have made certain allowances for themselves so as to find a way to integrate Judaism and Hellenism. Applebaum sought to explain the existence of Jewish ephebes in the two Cyrenean cities on the basis of the local laws which made it possible[39]. The fact that there is an illuminating temporal proximity between the two ephebic lists (one was written in 2 C.E. and the other in 24 C.E.) indicates that the Jews still acquired a gymnasium education in those cities at the end of the first century B.C.E. That certainly represented a change in the situation described by Strabo when the Jews (as a body) were not citizens of Cyrene, and the same was true of Berenice, where the Jews were separate from the municipal citizenry (see *CIG*, 5361-5362 = *REG*, LXII 1949, pp. 283, 290). Quite a different possible explanation for the difficulty mentioned above is that the Jewish ephebes got their education in private rather than city gymnasia. In any case, however, the dedications to the Greek gods in those stelas generates doubt as to the sincere Jewish faith of the ephebes listed there.

Another inscription from Cyrene show that later (in the sixties C.E.) there was a Jewish *nomophylax* in the city, and indicates that conditions then made it possible for Jews to hold public office there[40]. Applebaum demonstrated that the *nomophylakes* were *inter alia* in charge of recording the laws of the city and safeguarding the archives of official documents. He found that the holders of that office had to have administrative ability, knowledge of the law, an inclination for official duties, and the courage to impose the laws on

---

38 See Applebaum, *loc. cit.* Similarly, an inscription from Iasos in Asia Minor, containing a list of ephebes from the early Roman period, has a number of clearly Jewish names: Judah, Dositheos, Theophilos, etc. See L. Robert, *REJ*, 101 (1937), p. 73f.; *Hellenica*, vol. 3, p. 100f. On the other hand, an inscription from Iasos (*CIJ*, II 749) from the Hellenistic period mentions "Niketas the Jerusalemite," undoubtedly Hellenized as he made a contribution for the Dionysian celebrations.

39 See the explanations of Applebaum, *Jews and Greeks*, p. 183ff.; idem, "The Legal Status of the Jewish Communities", pp. 447f., but unfortunately Applebaum did not deal with the religious difficulties raised by these inscriptions. Cf. M. Stern, *The Diaspora in the Hellenistic-Roman World*, pp. 186-187 (Hebrew).

40 Applebaum, *Jews and Greeks*, p. 178.

other city officials who flouted them[41]. No evidence is available on any religious qualification for that post in Cyrene. Although the inscription mentioning the Jewish *nomophylax* included a dedication to one of the gods, there is no doubt that the man was Jewish, for his name was Eleazar son of Jason, and he too, like the ephebes noted above, would have adopted a Greek name if he had converted. Nevertheless, the dedication to a Greek god generated doubt as to his sincere Jewish faith, like in the case of the ephebes mentioned above.

The situation in Alexandria was not however analogous to that in Cyrene. It must be borne in mind that all cities did not have identical laws (cf. *Antiquitates*, XVI 176). Cyrene had a timocratic constitution and under those historical circumstances of no stringent religious restrictions in regard to citizenship, certain Jews could become citizens there. That does not indicate the absence of an organized separate Jewish *politeuma* in the city. In fact the Jews there might well have had dual "citizenship", in the *polis* and in the Jewish *politeuma*[42]. Such was not the case in Alexandria, Apion's rhetorical question (*C. Apionem*, II 65) suggests that citizenship in the Alexandrian *polis* was conditional on participation in the municipal cult, so that Jews could not become citizens unless they converted[43].

In order to better understand Apion's rhetoric and provocative question (*loc. cit.*), it is necessary to keep in mind that the granting of citizenship was closely supervised by the central authorities, who were especially strict in regard to Alexandria (see p. 171 above and nn. 11, 12). Alexandria conducted a persistent campaign against the Hellenistic kings and Roman emperors in regard to its sovereignty, and the question of citizenship was no doubt crucial, control of it being a clear indication of municipal sovereignty. In that campaign the Alexandrians certainly employed sophisticated tactics, and may well have attempted another ploy, opposition to Jewish rights. An

---

41 *Ibid.*, p. 188.
42 Dual citizenship was quite common in the Hellenistic and Roman period, and the emperors sought unsuccessfully to abolish it.
43 It should be borne in mind that in Alexandria the registration of citizens was effected through the tribes and demes, both of which were pagan by nature (Fraser, vol. 1, p. 39f.) and that itself was a serious obstacle for a Jew desiring to be a citizen of the *polis*. On the pagan rites regularly conducted in Alexandria in general, see Fraser, vol. 1, p. 189ff.

examination of Apion's position shows that its point of departure
was that there was only one *politeia* in the city, that is, the Greek
one, and that was in fact what his Alexandrian logic sought to
achieve. In his fight against Jewish rights he strove to eliminate the
complexities and vagueness that prevailed in regard to the ambiguity
of the terms *politai* and "Alexandrians" since they were applied to
the members of both the Jewish *politeuma* and the "pure *politeuma*
of the Alexandrians"[44].

Support for this interpretation can be found in a similar case that
took place in Ionia and was tried before Marcus Agrippa. It appears
that the citizens of Ionian cities "petitioned Agrippa that they alone
might enjoy the *politeia* given them by Antiochus, Seleucus' grandson, called Theos by the Greeks, and claimed that if the Jews were to
be their kinsfolk, they should worship their gods" (*Antiquitates*, XII
125-126). The phrase "that they alone might enjoy" indicates that
politeia was not given exclusively to the Greeks[45]. What the Greeks
seem to have wanted was that in each of their cities only one *politeia*
should be recognized, and that the Jews should lose the right to their
own. The chief argument was that "if the Jews were to be their
kinsfolk, they should worship their gods". The term "kinsfolk"
(συγγενεῖς) seems equivalent to *politai*, a term more correct in the
context, and yet the choice must have been deliberate. For the
Greeks evidently wanted a single *politeia* based on συγγένεια (kinship, brotherhood). Since at the time the term no longer had an
ethnic denotation, they wished to establish it according to a religious
criterion. It should be noted, at any rate, that not a single report on
the disputes in the Ionian cities contained any argument explicitly
denying the Jews' right to be *politai*. In the Roman period, it will be
recalled, the term *politai* applied to members of three different
groups: citizens of the Greek *poleis*, Roman citizens, and members
of *politeumata*. That alone refutes the claim that the Jews as such
were not entitled to be so called.

The verdict in the Ionian conflict reveals another aspect of the
struggle: Josephus notes that when "the matter was brought to trial,
the Jews won the right to use their own customs" (*Antiquitates*,

---

44 That was the wording in the *Boulé* Papyrus (*PSI*, 1160, line 5).

45 Other versions of the text, in which the word μετέχωσιν is replaced by μετέλθωσιν
(*possiderent* in the Latin translation), likewise confirm that impression.

XII 126). The verdict definitely suggests that the Greeks wanted to prevent the Jews from following their own customs. In other words, they wished to abolish the Jewish *politeia* and impose their own laws on the Jews. That is made even clearer in *Antiquitates*, XVI 27ff., where Josephus reports that the Jews of Ionia complained to Marcus Agrippa about the pressure being put upon them in the cities where they were living:

"... the mistreatment which they had suffered in not being allowed to observe their own laws and in being forced to appear in court on their holy days because of the inconsiderateness of the examining judges. And they told how they had been deprived of the monies sent as offerings to Jerusalem and of being forced to participate in military service and civic duties and to spend their sacred monies for these things, although they have been exempted from these duties because the Romans had always permitted them to live in accordance with their own laws." (trans. Marcus, *LCL* ed.)

Nicolaus of Damascus, the Jews' defender in that dispute, proffered and incisive argument: the source of the rights of the Ionian Jews being the Roman government, which alone had the authority to grant them (*ibid.*, 32), it was inconceivable that they could be infringed by such as had not granted them (*ibid.*, 57). By illtreating the Jews, he stressed, the Greeks were offending the Romans themselves as they were seeking to abolish favors that were a Roman gift (*ibid.*, 34), and whether those favors were large or small, "it is shameful for the granters not to confirm them" (*ibid.*, 33). "Even a madman" would not wish to abolish the favors of Rome, he said (*ibid.*, 38), and the implication is clear. Concluding his address he requested one thing of Marcus Agrippa, that the Romans should not allow others to deny rights which the Romans themselves had dispensed (*ibid.*, 57).

Evidently the Jews' right to preserve their ancestral religion without interference provoked envy or resentment (τὸ ἐπίφϑονον) in the Greeks (*ibid.*, 41), the reason being that the legal and religious autonomy enjoyed by the Jews seemed exaggerated, and emphasized the restricted autonomy of the Greeks. While the Ionian arguments are not cited, they can be surmised from what Nicolaus of Damascus as defender of the Jews had to say.

The Ionian complaints seem to have been following the conventions of anti-Jewish propaganda. Thus the Jews were accused of disloyalty to Rome[46], apparently due to their "misanthropy" (*ibid.*,

---

46 See, e.g., *Antiquitates*, XVI 50ff.; 41 perhaps also vaguely suggests this.

42) and "impiety"[47]. This was clever tactics attempting to direct Roman attention to sensitive points, and thereby gain advantages for the city. In his rebuttal Nicolaus proved not only that there were no grounds for accusing the Jews of disloyalty and impiety, but that it was the Greeks who were actually guilty of these. A number of scholars have considered the astute statements of Nicolaus to be an ordinary apologia (edited by Josephus) especially the part referring to the glory of Roman rule[48], and indeed the speech might be deemed smooth talk full of flattery. However, the speech can be demonstrated to accord precisely with the principate's political stand, which was a subject of considerable philosophical thinking by Romans in the first century C.E.[49] At most Nicolaus can be accused of being a great advocate who was skilled at finding point common to his defense of the Jews and basic Roman policy. No wonder he stressed that the Jews owed their felicity to Roman rule, and only wished to follow their ancestral religion without interference (*ibid.*, 41). In that connection he noted that "this itself would not seem to be a cause for resentment, and is even to the advantage of those who grant this right". He further stressed that disrespect for the laws of the Jews was "not because this is called for by legal agreements" (*ibid.*, 45). Although the "legal agreements" were not specified, the inference is that they were between the Roman authorities and the cities of Ionia. It should be noted that the term συνάλλαγμα (= agreements) comes from the verb συναλλάσσω, one of whose meanings is "to be reconciled". It may thus well be that the "agreements" were signed, probably at the insistence of higher authority, after local clashes.

The separate independent existence of Jewish communities within their boundaries was a thorn in the flesh of the Ionian cities. The Jews' right to maintain a parallel organization to the *polis*, send money to Jerusalem, be exempt from the *liturgia* and enjoy full consideration of their laws all highlighted the *poleis'* own limited sovereignty and total dependence on Rome. It is therefore no wonder

---

47 The last accusation is inferrable from the pugnacious rebuttal of Nicolaus, who tried to direct it at the Greeks themselves.

48 The reference is to *Antiquitates*, XVI 38ff. See, e.g., Laqueur, *Der jüdische Historiker*, pp. 221-230.

49 Cf. the opinion of Schalit, *King Herod* (Hebrew), pp. 217-222.

that those cities missed no opportunity to seek a change in the situation. One method undoubtedly consisted of accusing the Jews of "impiety", which if confirmed would lead to the abolition of the Jewish *politeia*. That would leave just one *politeia*, the Greek one, based on a single *syngeneia* of a clearly religious nature.

The Ionian situation makes it easy to understand the argument of Apion (*C. Apionem*, II 65) who represented similar interests when in the name of the Alexandrians he fought against the existence of the Jewish claims that they had equal right, he recalled that they had not benefited from the distribution of free grain during the famine in Cleopatra VII's reign (*C. Apionem*, II 60), and that they had not figured among the recipients of cheap corn in 19 C.E. during Germanicus' visit (*ibid.*, 63). Obviously Apion sought to refute the Jews' insistence on equal rights with facts known to all (which Josephus did not deny). His point was that the basic right to allocations of grain was limited to citizens of Alexandria. As an Alexandrian citizen he could not swallow the idea that the Jews could enjoy equal rights without being citizens of the *polis*. And since the fact that they were not allocated grain meant that they were not citizens, there was no legitimate basis for their claim that they enjoyed equal rights. Josephus disregarded Apion's dialectical exercise but dealt with facts that were controversial, and without touching on the matter of citizenship, examined the question of whether or not the Jews were entitled to allotments of corn.

Josephus is not at all clear on that point. On the one hand his apologetic style implies that the Jews were not entitled to allotments as Alexandrian citizens were, although that did not mean they did not have equal rights in other area. On the other hand, the impression gleaned is that the two cases Apion mentioned were exceptional, and no conclusions about the right to allocations of corn equal to those of the Alexandrians can be drawn from them. That seems to be the impression that Josephus intended. Cleopatra' animosity to the Jews, in his view, was easily the reason for discrimination in the first case, and he took advantage of the point to defame that queen, censure her policies and at the same time vaunt the Jews' collaboration with the Romans against her (*ibid.*, 57-61). In fact he achieved a propaganda triumph, noting that the Jews could only be proud of not having bread provided by her on their tables (*ibid.*, 60).

In regard to the second case, Josephus was in some difficulty, and could only apologetically state that "if Germanicus was unable to

distribute corn to all residents of Alexandria that merely proves a
barren year and a dearth of corn and cannot be made an accusation
against the Jews" (*ibid.*, 63). In this case, as Germanicus was fond of
the citizens of Alexandria[50], Josephus could not point to Jewish-
Roman collaboration, and proffered a weak excuse that ignored
Germanicus' policy. It is not clear why Josephus refrained from
attacking the Germanicus visit to Egypt which was definitely contrary to the regulation of Augustus and annoyed the emperor Tiberius. He could have argued that everything Germanicus did was illegal,
including discriminating against the Jews in the allocation of grain.
He must have known of the Germanicus affair which so irked Roman
public opinion; his apologetic stand therefore suggests that in fact
the Jews were not entitled to allocations of grain like the citizens of
Alexandria. Nevertheless that does not mean that they did not enjoy
equality in other rights for their equal rights were not conditional
on membership in the *polis*. Moreover, in the present case Josephus'
wording was more exact for he specifically included the Jews among
the "residents of Alexandria" and differentiated them from "the
rest of the Alexandrians" (*ibid.*, 63-64), thus not tying his argument
on their equality of rights to the claim of citizenship in the *polis*.

C. The Status of the Jews in the Acts of the Alexandrian Martyrs

The *Acts of the Alexandrian Martyrs* (henceforth *AAM*) is actually
propaganda directed mainly against the Roman rulers[51], but it contains certain information relating to the present subject. *P. Giss.*, 46
(= *CPJ*, II 155) for instance mentions someone as a prosecutor who
disputed before the emperor Gaius Caligula with the Alexandrian
gymnasiarch Isidorus by whom he was described as "a foreigner,
receiving unregistered *politeia*" (ξενι[κὸς] γὰρ μᾶ[λον κατα]λαβὼν
πο[λ]ιτείαν ἀ[να]πόγραφο[...) While the text does not specify the
politeia, probably Isidorus was referring to Alexandrian citizenship.
The assertion that it was "unregistered" means that the man avoided
the census (ἀπογραφή κατ᾽ οἰκίαν) which determined the taxes he

---

50 On Germanicus in Alexandria see Tacitus, *Annales*, II 59; Suetonius, *Tiberius*, 52. See
also Hunt & Edgar, *Select Papyri*, No. 211 (pp. 76-78); Willrich, *Klio*, 3 (1903), p. 95ff.;
Wilcken, *Hermes*, 63 (1928), p. 48ff.; Hennig, *Chiron*, 2 (1912), p. 349ff.; Weingartner,
Die Aegyptenreise des Germanicus, esp. pp. 91-99.
51 Musurillo's study still seems to be the best treatment of the subject.

was subject to including the *laographia*. While such a Tcherikoverish interpretation is possible and logical, it says nothing about any inferior Jewish status. The prosecutor is not identified and there are no grounds for deciding that he was a Jew. And even if he was, that does not indicate an inferior status. For the document describes the situation in Caligula's time, when the Jews were defined as "foreigners" ($\xi\acute{e}\nu o\iota$), but that was not the case in earlier periods. The document perhaps confirms that the Alexandrians succeeded in canceling the validity of the Jewish *politeia* in Caligula's time, yet seems to reveal that the Jews endeavored, and to an extent managed, to disregard that and to avoid the fiscal census. Isidorus' assertion that his accuser received a *politeia* may be interpreted otherwise as well, to mean that the accuser was unwilling to give up the *politeia* he had before Caligula, and continued to claim possession of it.

Other fragments of *AAM* literature make explicit reference to Jews. While they embody no innovations from the propaganda point of view, they are important because they refer to particular people and events. This in 41 C.E. Isidorus defamed King Agrippa by describing him as "a Jew worth three obols," in other words, the son of a whore[52], thus deriding his royal lineage and his people. That was the old tried and true method of using lowly origin as propaganda ammunition. Another time Isidorus accused the Jews of stirring up contention the world over[53], seeking thus to censure them as rebels disloyal to the emperor and consequently not entitled to his favors[54].

Further on he ranted that "they are not of the same nature as the Alexandrians but live rather after the fashion of the Egyptians. Are they not on a level with those who pay the tax?"[55] This assertion relates directly to the status of the Jews, but surprisingly it has heretofore not been noted that it reflects a controversy over the principle of *isoteleia*. Isidorus' stand shows that he did not recognize that Jews had equality in matters of taxation, and compared them with Egyptian natives. The tax ($\varphi\acute{o}\rho o\varsigma$) referred to is probably the poll-tax (or *laographia*)[56], and that means that he wished to represent

---

52 *CPJ*, II 156b, col. 1, line 18; cf. the similar accusations Isidorus and Emperor Claudius flung at each other: *CPJ*, II 156d, col. 3, lines 7-12.

53 *CPJ*, II 156c, col. 2, lines 20-24.

54 Cf. a similar argument by Isidorus cited in Philo, *Legatio*, 355.

55 *CPJ*, II 156c, col. 2, lines 25-27.

56 Cf. Tcherikover's interpretation of the document: *CPJ*, II, p. 79, and Smallwood, *The Jews under Roman Rule*, p. 252.

344 Chapter X

the Jews as having the lowest status on the civic scale. Agrippa's very interesting retort was that the governors levied taxes ($\varphi \acute{o} \rho o\iota$) on the Egyptians but not on the Jews. Tcherikover deemed that to be an evasive and propagandistic reply aimed at concealing the fact that the payment of the *laographia* established an inferior status for the Jews of Alexandria. However, Agrippa's reply is based on a fundamental historical argument, that the taxes were levied on the Egyptians, not on the Jews, so that it does not appear to be an attempt to deny the truth. The deduction might then be that if Jews did pay the *laographia*, it was not because of their Judaism[57]. A reexamination of the Isidorus statement shows that he was speaking generally of the whole mass ($\tau \grave{o} \nu\ \acute{o} \chi \lambda o \nu$) of Jews and not specifically of those in Alexandria. Such a generalization was certainly incorrect, for there were at least some Jews who held Roman citizenship and were undoubtedly exempt from the poll-tax. Thus Isidorus' statement was based on a half-truth. It is true that many Jews (especially in the *chora*) were considered natives and paid the *laographia*, but that is still far from being equitable with members of the native class. Aside from Jews with Roman citizenship there were the descendents of *katokoi* of whom thousands were scattered throughout Egypt, and they cannot possibly be considered on a par with lowly Egyptians. It is therefore quite astonishing that Tcherikover did not discern Isidorus' propaganda motive here, as he did in relation to Agrippa's reply. Apparently it was the undefined status of Jews that provoked a controversy. Jew-haters sought to ignore the fact that there were Jews at all levels of civic stratification, and disputed the right of some of them to *isolteleia* with the Alexandrians. By analogy with the Cyrene situation (*Antiquitates*, XVI 161)[58], it can at least be presumed that there were Jews in Alexandria who attained equality in taxation, and they were probably from among the descendents of the *katokoi* or the Jewish "Macedonians" who were in the highest social class of the Jewish *politeuma* in the city.

The ";base origin" of the Jews was for the Alexandrians an axiom which did not require any proof, as is especially evident in the *Acta Hermaisci*. By sneering at Trajan that his council was full of Jews[59],

57 Cf. Musurillo, p. 139.

58 See Applebaum, *Gedalyahu Alon Memorial Volume*, p. 195ff.

59 *CPJ*, II 157, col. 3, line 50f., and see also the explanation of Musurillo, p. 168f.

the author meant to disparage the entire imperial company, as clearly demonstrated by the subsequent exchange between him and Trajan. When the emperor denounced that audacity, Hermaiscus replied ironically: "So then the word Jew is offensive to you?"

That same source also used the charge of impiety as a conventional and self-evident propaganda tool[60]. The purpose was clear and the *AAM* literature contains nothing new on that score. The term "impious Jews" (οἱ ἀνόσιοι Ἰουδαῖοι) however, also figures in documents which are not part of that literature but refer specifically to the Jewish revolt during Trajan's reign[61]. Musurillo determined that the historical background described in *Acta Hermaisci* dates to Trajan's early regnal years, before 113 C.E.[62] The surviving fragments refer to some trial conducted following disturbances around that time in Alexandria, between Greeks and Jews[63]. The trial involved a Jewish delegation confronting a Greek one. The wording clearly demonstrates that the Jews had the right to send their own delegation[64] which was even permitted to engage a lawyer "an Antiochian in origin")[65], exactly the same rights accorded to the Alexandrian delegation[66]. The "two parties" faced each other before the emperor in order to voice their complaints[67], so that obviously each of them represented a separate legal entity. That fact, figuring as it does in a hostile source, is most illuminating, and provides additional support for the conclusion that the Jewish community of Alexandria had its own organization separate from the *polis*, of which it was legally and politically independent.

---

60 See *CPJ*, II 157, col. 3, lines 43, 49f.; cf. *CPJ*, II 158, col. 2, line 13; col. 4, line 14. See also Musurillo, p. 177 (explaining line 49).

61 See Tcherikover, *Jews in Egypt*, p. 176ff.

62 Musurillo, pp. 164-168; cf. Weber, *Hermes*, 50 (1915), p. 76ff.

63 A hint of this appears in *CPJ*, II 157, col. 2, line 36f.

64 *CPJ*, II 157, col. 1, lines 11-13, has "When the Jews learned this they too elected envoys from their own people."

65 *Ibid.*, line 15f. It is not clear whether or not he was Jewish. His name, Sopatros, provides no clue, but as the Jews could be expected to hire a lawyer sympathetic to them, he may well have been Jewish. The words "Antiochean in origin" (Ἀντιοχεὺς τῷ γένει) prove that the adjective "Antiochean" denoted *origo*, and that has implications for the problem dealt with above (pp. 177ff., 212f., 241, 249-253).

66 *Ibid.*, line 19f.

67 *Ibid.*, line 25f.: "And he [the emperor] appointed the day on which he would hear both parties," etc.

Chapter XI

The Alexandrian Jewish Community in Talmudic Traditions

Numerous talmudic sources indicate that the Jews of Egypt, including those of Alexandria, had quite close connections with Jerusalem. These ties took several forms: pilgrimages, dispatch of the half *sheqel*, priestly gifts, tithes, first fruits and the like[1], and indirectly provide information on the internal organization in the communities of the Diaspora. For instance, the fact that the pilgrims were organized in caravans[2] preceded by careful preparation[3] indicates that the communities from which they set out were well organized. The preparations and arrangements connected with the pilgrimages were not confined to the pilgrims' places of residence, but closely coordinated with the life in Jerusalem. Various communities maintained their own synagogues in Jerusalem to serve the pilgrims and provide for their needs[4]. Among the synagogues was "the synagogue of the Alexandrians"[5] which no doubt served the Alexandrians permanently settled in Jerusalem who were in charge of preparations for the festivals.

An indication of the close relationship of the Alexandria Jewish community to the Temple in Jerusalem is the fact that some High Priests came from Alexandria. The *Mishnah* has Hananel the Egyptian in a list of preists who prepared a "red heifer" (*Parah*, III 5)[6].

---

1 See Safrai, *Pilgrimages*, p. 59ff.

2 See *ibid.*, p. 106ff.

3 Cf., e.g., Philo, *Legatio*, 156.

4 Which can be learned from the famous Theodotus inscription found on Mount Ofel. See Klein, *JPCI*, (1920), pp. 10-104; Clermont-Ganneau, *Syria*, 1 (1920), pp. 190-197; Schwabe, *Sefer Yerushalayim*, vol. 1, pp. 362-365.

5 *Acts*, 6:9, *J.T. Megillah*, III 3d; *Tosefta, ibid.*, III 6 (Zuckermandel ed., p. 224) and see S. Liberman, *Tosefta Kifshutah, Megillah*, p. 1162.

6 He is generally identified with Hananel the Babylonian of Herod's period (see, e.g., Schürer, vol. 2, p. 269 and n.5), but Safrai proposed indentifying him with the priest

Josephus too notes an instance, reporting that Herod appointed the Alexandrian Simeon son of Boethus to the High Pristhood[7], and says that he was "a priest of the prestigious" (*Antiquitates*, XV 320). No doubt his lineage became known in Jerusalem from the genealogical records kept in the archives of the Alexandria Jewish community[8]. These facts indicate how well organized the community was, and how reliable its archives were deemed by Jerusalemites.

The close ties between the Jerusalem Temple and the Jews of Alexandria are reflected also by the commissioning of craftsmen from Alexandria to repair damaged Temple accessories[9], and by gifts of splendid ornaments such as the gold plating of the nine gates of the Temple court, donated by the *Alabarach* Julius Alexander (Philo's brother)[10], and the famous copper doors for the Nicanor gate, donated by Nicanor the Alexandrian[11]. The involvement of the Alexandria Jews in the life of the Jerusalem Temple is shown also by their inviting priests who were specialists in "how to prepare the shew-bread" and "how to prepare the incense" to overcome the difficulties caused by the priests of the House of Garmu and the House of Abtinas[12]. Actually, those Alexandrian priests may have been from the temple of Onias, since "Alexandria" in the Talmud represented Egypt as a whole, as can be seen in the talmudic legends about the founding of the temple of Onias.

The relations between the Alexandria Jewish community and the sages of Palestine are demonstrated also by the story of Judah son of

---

Ḥanan whom Josephus mentions in *Antiquitates*, XX 197-198 (Safrai, *op.cit.* in n.1, p. 60).

7 *Antiquitates*, XV 320. His sons later held that prominent post (*Antiquitates*, XIX 297-298).

8 Cf. *C. Apionem*, I 31. *Antiquitates*, XII 187 likewise suggests that the Jews of Alexandria scrupulously took lineage into account in regard to matrimony.

9 See *B.T. Arakhin*, 10b; and cf. *Tosefta Arakhin*, II 2c-d (Zuckermandel ed., p. 544).

10 *Bellum*, V 201-206; and cf. *Mishnah Yoma*, III 5; *J.T. Yoma*, III 41a, and the parallel *B.T. Yoma*, 38a. See also *Mishnah Middoth*, I 4; II 3.

11 The man is known from an inscription (dating from the first century) found on Mount Scopus in Jerusalem which says, "The bones of Nicanor the Alexandrian, who made the doors" (See Schwabe, *Sefer Yerushalayim*, vol. 1, p. 367). He is also known from talmudic tradition: *J.T. Yoma*, III 41a; *Tosefta Yoma*, II 4 (Zuckermandel ed., p. 183); *B.T. Yoma*, 38a, and seems to have been suggested in the *Mishnah* itself (*Yoma*, III 6); cf. Safrai's view, *Pilgrimage*, p. 61.

12 *J.T. Yoma*, III 41a; *B.T. Yoma*, 38a; *B.T. Shekalim*, 14a; *Tosefta Yoma*, II 6 (Zuckermandel ed., p. 184); cf. *B.T. Arakhin*, 10b.

Tabbai's refusal to assume the heavy burden of President of the Court (= *Nasi*), and his flight to Alexandria[13]. Only after the urging of the Jerusalem people and the letter from Simeon son of Shetaḥ did the nominee become reconciled and return to Palestine to accept the post[14]. The interesting point is that he chose to depart for Alexandria; no doubt he had personal ties there that developed from contacts on the halakhic plane. Joshua son of Peraḥiah, a colleague of Judah son of Tabbai, is celebrated for having rejected "wheat that comes from Alexandria" as unacceptable "because of their baling machine", after which the sages disputed his ruling and declared the wheat pure[14a]. This episode shows the close relations between Palestine and Egypt in *halakhic* matters as well.

The affair of the "kidnaped women from Alexandria"[14b] which the aged Hillel adjudicated likewise indicates the close ties between the two Jewish communities, and at the same time reflects the considerable influence on the Alexandria Jews exerted by the Hellenistic-Roman laws prevailing in Egypt[14c].

---

13 *J.T. Ḥaggigah*, II 77d; *J.T. Sanhedrin*, VI 23c.

14 Efron proved that the *B.T.* tradition substituted Joshua son of Peraḥiah for Judah son of Tabbai and had the latter leave for Egypt ostensibly because of the Jannaeus persecutions. Contrary to scholars who accepted that, Ephron discovered its inferiority compared to the *J.T.* tradition. See *Gedaliahu Alon Memorial Volume* (Hebrew), p. 75ff.

14a See *Tosefta Makhshirin*, III 4 (Zuckermandel ed., p. 675). *antalia* comes from ἀνταλια, that is, "baling out bilge-water", "pumping" (with wheels and buckets), see Jastrow, *Dictionary*, p. 84. The possibility of contamination was suspected in case water had been sprinkled on the wheat.

14b *Tosefta, Shabbath*, II 3 (Zuckermandel ed., p. 111f.); Lieberman, *Tosefta Kifshutah*, p. 68. Cf. also *J.T. Yebamoth*, XV 14d; *Ketubboth*, IV 28d; *B.T. Baba Metziá* 104a.

14c The passages above suggest that according to the betrothal customs of the Jews of Alexandria (and evidently of Egypt as a whole) the betrothal document was in the form of an agreement (*omologia*) which served as both a "betrothal contract" and "marriage writ." However, it contained an explicit condition ("when you come to my house you will be my wife according to the religion of Moses and Israel") which would invalidate the marriage in advance if for some reason the bethrothed did not marry the man. She would thus not need a bill of divorcement, and her children from a subsequent marriage (in the terms of the passage "her kidnapper") would not be *mamzerim* (i.e. bastards, illegitimate children). Scholars have remarked traces of that custom in Philo (in *De Spec. Leg.*, III 72, e.g.) and claimed that they derived from Hellenistic-Roman juridical norms applying in Egypt. See A. Büchler, in *Festschrift zu Israel Lewy's Siebzigsten Geburtstag*, pp. 111-144, esp. 122ff.; I. Heinemann, *Philons griechische und jüdische Bildung*, p. 300; Gulak, *Tarbiz* 3 (1932), p. 361ff.; *Tarbiz* 5 (1934), p. 127, n.7; Albeck, *Moshe Shur Memorial Volume*, pp. 12-24; B. Cohen, *PAAJR*, 18 (1949), pp. 67-136,

An examination of Philo's writings shows that he too was well versed in the *halakha* of Palestine[15], no doubt thanks to the close relations between the Jews of his city and the sages of Palestine. In later generations too, the Alexandrian Jews relied on Palestine in *halakhic* matters, as is demonstrated by the "twelve things" they asked Rabbi Joshua son of Hananiah regarding purification rules[16] and festival rules[17]. The questions were put to the Palestinian sage who happened to be in Alexandria (the occasion and purpose are unknown), and the Alexandrian Jews took advantage of his visit to clarify various problems in *halakha* that they were unable to solve on their own. They may actually have directed the questions at Rabbi Joshua who was celebrated for his knowledge of Greek philosophy as well as the *halakha*[17a]. That the Jews of Egypt were dependent on Palestine in connection with *halakhic* matters is demonstrated also by the problem that Rabbi Johanan Ben-Nuri (of the Yavneh generation) submitted to Rabbi Tarfon in connection with the lighting of the Sabbath candles. Since Rabbi Tarfon stipulated that "one lights only with olive oil", Rabbi Johanan Ben-Nuri asked him what Diaspora Jews should do if they have no such oil, and counted among them the Jews of Alexandria who customarily used "turnip oil", it being cheaper[17b]. Quite possibly the tradition in the *Tosefta* about the existence of a rabbinical court in Alexandria[18] which appeared to have survived until the uprisings in Trajan's reign, is evidence of the *halakhic* connection between Alexandria and Jerusalem.

The organization of the community life is elucidated by an important tradition relating to the great synagogue, which is preserved in three different versions, one in the *Jerusalem Talmud*, one

---

esp. 92ff.; Lieberman, *Tosefta Kifshutah, Ketubboth*, p. 246f.; M. Alon, *Hebrew Law*, p. 351f.

15 On this see Ritter, *Philo und die Halacha*; Belkin, *Philo and the Oral Law*.

16 B.T. *Niddah*, 69b; cf. also *Mishnah Nega'im*, XIV 13; *Tosefta Nega'im*, IX 9 (Zuckermandel ed., p. 630).

17 See, e.g., *J.T. Erubin*, III 21c.

17a On the astuteness of the questions submitted to Rabbi Joshua son of Ḥananiah, and on the Alexandrian school in Judaism, see Lieberman, *Proceedings of the Rabbinic Assembly of America*, 12 (1948), pp. 273-281 ; Lieberman, *Sifrei Zuta*, pp. 29-31.

17b See *Tosefta Shabbath*, II 3 (Zuckermandel ed., p. 111f.); cf. *B.T. Shabbath*, 21a ; Lieberman, *Tosefta Kifshutah, Shabbath*, p. 26.

18 *Tosefta, Pe'ah*, IV 6 (Zuckermandel ed., p. 23); *Ketubboth*, III 1 (Zuckermandel ed., p. 263); *B.T. Ketubboth*, 22a. See also Lieberman, *Tosefta Kifshutah, Mo'ed (Sukkah)*, p. 889f.; *Pe'ah*, p. 182; *B.T. Ketubboth*, 25a.

in the *Tosefta* and one in the *Babylonian Talmud*[19]. The Jerusalem version is as follows:

It has been taught, R. Judah stated, He who has not seen the double colonnade[20] of Alexandria in Egypt has never seen the glory of Israel. It was like a huge basilica, one colonnade[21] within the other, and it sometimes held twice the number of people that went forth from Egypt. There were in it seventy[22] cathedras of gold adorned with precious stones and pearls[23], corresponding to Seventy Elders[24] ... and a wooden platform in the middle upon which the minister (*Ḥazzan ha-Knesseth*) stood[25]. When someone stood up for reading, the officer in charge (*ha-Memuneh*)[26] waved the scarf and they[27] responded Amen ... However they did not sit mingled, but sat each craft by itself[28], so that in case a guest (*akhsenai*)[29] comes in he would join his fellow-craftsmen's [place] where his livelihood is provided. And who destroyed it? The wicked Trogionus[30].

A comparison of the various versions shows the Jerusalem Talmud one to be preferable, for a number of reasons: a) The description of the construction of the synagogue is more detailed, covering, for

---

19 *J.T. Sukkah*, V 55s; *Tosefta Sukkah*, IV 6 (Zuckermandel, ed., p. 198); *B.T. Sukkah*, 51b. See also Lieberman, *Tosefta Kifshutah, Mo'ed (Sukkah)*, p. 273.

20 The reference is to διπλῆ στοά; and in *B.T.* and *Tosefta diplestion, diplestton, (διπλόστωον)*. The *J.T.* version seems more accurate; see also Lieberman, *ibid.*, p. 889f.

21 *Stav*, that is, στοά or στοία; see also Lieberman, *ibid.*, p. 890.

22 In the *B.T.* and *Tosefta*: Seventy-one, or 71; see n.24 below. Cf. with other talmudic sources in Lieberman, *ibid.*, p. 890.

23 The words "set with precious stones and pearls" do not appear in the *Tosefta* and *B.T.*

24 The *Tosefta* has "corresponding to seventy-one elders" and *B.T.* has "corresponding to seventy-one of the Great Sanhedrin." Thus some scholars deduced that a Sanhedrin was established in Alexandria modeled after the Great Sanhedrin of Jerusalem. These included Schürer, vol. 2, p. 249f.; idem (ed. Vermes & Millar), vol. 2, p. 210f.; Honig, *The Great Sanhedrin*, p. 87f., but this view is untenable, as discussed below.

25 The *Tosefta* has quite a different version here; see also Lieberman, *Tosefta Kifshutah*, p. 891.

26 The *memuneh* is not mentioned in the *B.T.* and *Tosefta* versions. Lieberman, *ibid.*, p. 892, n.13, contends that *memuneh* is synonymous with *ḥazzan* (cf. Lieberman, *ibid.*, p. 529, n.64), but in the present context there is a discernible distinction between the former and the functionary described as *ḥazzan ha-Knesseth*, and see p. 354 below.

27 The *B.T.* and *Tosefta* have "all the people."

28 The *B.T.* and *Tosefta* have "but goldsmiths by themselves and silversmiths by themselves, and blacksmiths by themselves and wool weavers (*Gardyim*) and flax-spinners (*Tarsyim*) by themselves." See also Lieberman, *ibid.*, p. 892 and note 34 below. J. Brand (*Glass Vesseles in Talmudic Literature*, pp. 91-94) has recently suggested that *Tarsyim* (טרסיים) were glass craftsmen. Quite different explanations were offered long ago by Herschberg (*Culture Life in Israel* etc., pp. 161-162) and Nathane filio Jechielis (ed. A. Kohat, *Aruch Completum*, vol. 4, p. 87).

29 The *B.T.* has "a pauper" (*ani.*)

30 The words, "And who destroyed it? The wicked *Trogionos* (Trajan) do not figure in the *B.T.* and *Tosefta*, but the *B.T.* has an additional sentence: Abbaye stated: Alexander of Macedon slew them all".

instance, the cathedras (set with pearls and precious stones). b) It is more likely that there was a special "officer" (*Memuneh*) to "wave the scarf" for the prayers than that the minister (*Ḥazzan ha-Knesseth*) was expected to do so. c) The replacement of אכסנאי (in the *J.T.*) by עני (in the *B.T.*) is senseless. d) The ascription of the destruction of the synagogue to Trajan's reign is historically reasonable, while its ascription to Alexander the Great's time (as in the *B.T.*) is not, and is obviously a product of later *amoraic* editing. This anachronism was indeed recognized by the later exegetes of the Talmud[31].

This tradition implies a number of things about the organization of the community: The splendid large synagogue was undoubtedly built with donations from the members of the Alexandria community. Its decorations were certainly fashioned by Jewish craftsmen such as embellished the Temple in Jerusalem. The architecutral design may also have been Jewish. The execution of such a large project and the ongoing maintenance of the building undoubtedly imply an institutionalized community organization, and the existence of community funds authorized to collect money for the needs of the Jewish public, and suggest that the community was a legal entity recognized by the central authorities.

Presumably the synagogue was located in the heart of one of the Jewish residential districts[32], on land owned by the community. As noted by an epigraphical find (*CIJ*, II 1443) in regard to another synagogue in Alexandria, this one too no doubt surrounded by a "sacred precinct"[33] and similarly enjoying the right of *asylia*. According to Philo, it was the largest and most splendid synagogue and one of the chief targets of the Alexandrian rabble during Caligula's reign (*Legatio*, 134-135). Its proximity to the municipal gymnasium implied by Philo suggests that it was located in the Delta quarter.

The efficient organization of Alexandria Jewish community life is discernible in talmudic tradition in the description of synagogue practices. It appears that prayer services were conducted in an orderly manner with someone reading the weekly portion in the *Torah* (or

---

31 Cf. the marginal notes to the *B.T.* version made by the Gaon Rabbi Eliyahu and by Rabbi Beẓalel of Regensburg.

32 The reference is to the Delta quarter, in particular on the basis of Philo's information (see below).

33 Cf. Philo, *In Flaccum*, 49; and see also above ch. III, n.108.

the blessing) aloud, and a special officer (*Memuneh*) supervising
the participation of the congregation. It appears also that the regular
synagogue-goers "did not sit mingled, but sat each craft by itself".
The crafts, unnamed in the *J.T.*, are listed in the *B.T.* and *Tosefta*,
but it is not clear whether the list is genuine or simply an illustration
of the synagogue seating arrangement[34]. As other talmudic passages
report that Alexandrian craftsmen decorated the Temple in Jerusalem, they no doubt included goldsmiths, silversmith, and other metal
workers. Philo also provided a vocational cross section of Alexandrian Jewry (*In Flaccum*, 57) noting that it included farmers, landowners[35], ship-owners who carried mainly grain[36], merchants,
money-lenders[37], and artisans[38]. It is quite possible that the community had craft guilds that were quite well developed and recognized as an integral part of Jewish organization, as that was the case
in other communities. In Phrygian Hieropolis, for instance, there was
a "presidency of the purple-dyers", and a "*synedrion* of carpet-
weavers" (*CIJ*, II 777) and in Corycus a guildmaster of goldsmiths
(*CIJ*, II 793) and two perfume dealers who were involved in the
community leadership as *presbyteroi,* namely, members of the council of elders (*ibid.*, 790, 792). The proximity of the Sardis synagogue
to Jewish businesses and stores[39] supports this view of the community organization, especially since according to the Talmud there
was a close connection in Alexandria between the great synagogue

---

34 Cf. Alon, *History of the Jews of Eretz Israel in the Period of the Mishnah and the Talmud*, vol. 1, p. 104; cf. also Applebaum, *Tarbiz*, 28 (1959), p. 419; idem, "The Social and Economic Status of the Jews in the Diaspora," in: *The Jewish People in the First Century*, vol. 2, p. 717. For further details on crafts and commerce see Alon, *op.cit.*, p. 102f. Lieberman too (*ibid.*, p. 892, and in a personal communication) confirmed the conclusion that this source is full of τόποι, and there are insufficient grounds for analyz-ing the examples in order to arrive at definite conclusions.

35 Jewish landowners in the Alexandrian *chora* are mentioned also in *CPJ*, II 142-143.

36 See information on them in Box's commentary on *In Flaccum*, 57; and see also *CPJ*, II 404. Cf. *Mishnah Kelim*, XVI 1, and Albeck's commentary (*Tohoroth*, p. 68).

37 The source has τῶν πορωτῶν, that is, "suppliers," but the term can also mean "usurer" as M. Stein has it in his Hebrew translation. *CPJ*, II 152 also refers to Jewish money-lenders.

38 Unfortunately Philo used this general term and did not specify. *In Flaccum* implies Jewish "workshops," which seems to refer to the workshops and stores of the various craftsmen. For additional information on Jewish crafts in later periods see Applebaum, "The Social and Economic Status of the Jews in the Diaspora," p. 702ff.

39 See *BASOR*, 170 (1963), pp. 49-51. Applebaum even thought of the possibility that Sardis had a Jewish quarter; see Applebaum, "The Organization of the Jewish Communi-ties in the Diaspora," p. 479.

and the craft guilds of its members[40]. Epigraphical findings from Sardis indicate that Jewish goldsmiths were involved in the *Boulé* council of the city[41], and it seems logical therefore to assume hat they were also involved in the leadership of the Jewish community[42]. Such craft guilds are also reported in the Palestinian cities — Lod, Tiberias, etc. — in the mishnaic and talmudic periods[43]. That form of organization was most probably modeled to a large extent on the organization in the Greek cities. Data from Asia Minor in the Roman period shows that organization by craft was quite common[44], and the members of each guild may even have lived in their own residential area[45]. The talmudic reports on the Alexandria synagogue indicate that it was customary for hospitality to be extended to Jewish craftsmen from out of town by members of the appropriate guild. That practice itself seems to point to well developed craft organization and probably also craft leadership. The apostle Paul also benefited from the custom: In Corinth he was the guest of Aquila since both men were tent-makers[46].

---

40 On this point see Krauss, *Syn. Alt.*, pp. 261-263; Goodenough, *Jewish Symbols,* vol. 2, p. 85f., who claimed that the Great Synagogue in Alexandria was a *basilica,* and only a commercial center at first, before being turned into a synagogue. This view seems contrived, in the light of the finds at Sardis. In any case, *basilica* is explainable as a technical term describing only the form of the building (i.e., an oblong hall with double colonnade and apse).

41 Robert, *Nouvelles Inscriptions,* pp. 44-55 (Nos. 6, 13, 14). This is not surprising as the period is a late one, the fourth century.

42 Applebaum made the interesting suggestion that the "tribe" Leontios mentioned in an epigraphical find from Sardis might be the goldsmiths' guild. See Applebaum, *op.cit.,* in n.39, p. 479f.

43 See Alon, *History of the Jews,* etc., vol. 1, p. 103ff.

44 See, e.g., Ramsay, *The Cities and Bishoprics,* vol. 1, p. 105ff.; vol. 2, pp. 371, 440f., 462 ; Ziebarth, *Das Griechische Vereinwesen,* p. 120ff. See also Rostovtzeff, *SEHHW,* p. 178f.; vol. 2, p. 619f.; Applebaum, *op.cit.,* in n.39, pp. 480-482.

45 That was the situation in Apamea in Asia Minor, and in Theatera; see A.H.M. Jones, *CERP,* pp. 70, 83f.

46 *Acts,* 18:3: "And because he was of the same craft, he abode with them and wrought; for by their occupation they were tentmakers." Cf. also *Acts,* 20:34; *I Corinthians,* 4:12. I am grateful to Prof. Applebaum for calling my attention to these passages, and to the fact that in Theatera too Paul was in touch with craftsmen, such as the "seller of purple" (*Acts,* 16:14) and in Ephesus with a coppersmith (*II Timothy,* 4:14). On Synagogues as hostels for Jewish visitors and wayfarers see C.H. Kraeling, "The Synagogue," *Excavations at Dura Europos, Final Report,* vol. 7 (1956), p. 328; Ben-Zvi, *JPOS,* 13 (1933), pp. 94-96; Sukenik, *JPOS,* 15 (1935), p. 167; Cook, *PEFQS,* (1921), p. 22f.; Marmorstein, *PEFQS,* (1921), pp. 23-28; Schwabe, *Sefer Yerushalayim,* vol. 1, pp. 362-365; Mazar (= Maisler), *Yediot,* 9 (1942), p. 15f. Cf. *B.T. Pesaḥim*, 101a.

Two functionaries in the Great Synagogue are mentioned in the
Talmud, *Ḥazzan ha-Knesseth* and *ha-Memuneh*. The adjacency of
Ḥazzan and *Knesseth* shows that the second word denotes the worship-
ers, that is, the congregation (= synagogue)[47]. The term *Ḥazzan ha-
Knesseth* is well known from the *Mishnah*[48], and the duties of that
functionary were numerous: He was the beadle of the synagogue
who had to prepare the Torah scroll for reading, the teacher of the
youngest children, and the agent of the rabbinical court charged with
implementing sentences of flogging[49]. According to the *Tosefta*
(*Sukkah*, IV 11-12; Zuckermandel, p. 199) he was also in charge of
blowing the trumpet to signal the start of the Sabbath. The Greek
terms equivalent to *Ḥazzan* were ὑπηρέτης and νεώκορος, and these
have been mentioned in connection with other Jewish communities
in the Diaspora[52]. Evidently in later periods (e.g., the fourth century),
the *Ḥazzan* was called διάκονος[53], and the title was especially common in Christian congregations that were organized largely on the
Jewish model.

The officer in charge (*ha-Memuneh*) according to the Jerusalem
Talmud was supposed to wave the scarf to ensure the proper order
and uniformity in the prayer service. He does not seem to have been
equivalent to the φροντιστής, which post figured in several Diaspora
communities, including that of Alexandria. An inscription by an
incumbent of this post was found in Jaffa; he apparently served the
Alexandrians who settled there, and it appears that the post was
named after one so designated in the mother community[54]. Holders

---

47 Cf. Schürer, vol. 2, p. 504ff.; vol. 3, pp. 74f., 81-85, 106, 717; idem (ed. Vermes &
   Millar), vol. 2, p. 429ff. On the use of the term συναγωγή see p. 156 above.
48 *Mishnah Sotah*, VII 7-8; *Yoma*, VII 1; *Makkoth*, III 12; *Shabbath*, I 3.
49 See Krauss, *Syn. Alt.*, p. 126ff.
50 *Antiquitates*, IV 214; *Luke*, 4:20.
51 Cf., e.g., Philo, *De Praem.*, 74.
52 See, e.g., *CPJ*, I 129, line 7 from Alexandru-Nesus in the Fayûm; *CIJ*, II 805 from
   Syrian Apamea; *CIJ*, I 172 from Rome. For further details on the duties, see Juster,
   vol. 1, p. 454; Schürer, *Gemeindeverfassung*, p. 28; Frey, *CIJ*, I, p. xcix; Baron, *Jewish
   Community*, vol. 1, pp. 102, 104; Leon, *Jews of Ancient Rome*, p. 190. Frey (loc. cit.)
   does not accept Krauss' view (*Syn. Alt.*, p. 128) that the post of ὑπηρέτης was the model
   for the διάκονος of early Christian communities, but Krauss seems to be right. Cf. also
   Schürer (Vermes & Millar ed.), vol. 2, p. 438.
53 Thus, e.g., an inscription from Syrian Apamea (of 391 C.E.) calls one of the donors of
   the mosaic for the local synagogue both 'Aṣṣáva and διάκονος' See *IGLS*, 4 (1955),
   No. 1321. Cf. *CIJ*, I 805.
54 Quite a substantial collection of gravestones (with Greek inscriptions) of Jews from

of such a post are known in other communities as well — two in Rome (*CIJ*, I 337, 494), one in Aegina in Greece (*ibid.*, 722) and one in Side in Pamphylia (*ibid.*, 781). Since in non-Jewish sources frontistes was the equivalent of procurator, he can be considered a general manager in administrative and financial matters[55]. That makes it unlikely that the *ha-Memuneh* was identical with the *frontistes*. The most that can be assumed is that the former was in some way or other subordinate to the latter, but even that assumption is rather dubious.

Alexandria of the third to fourth centuries C.E. were found in Jaffa (see, e.g., *Sefer ha-Yeshuv* (Hebrew), Jaffa, Nos. 4, 25, 26, 27). This type of "Landsmannschaft" association was quite common in Palestinian cities at the time, so that an "Alexandrian" association in Jaffa is not surprising.

55 Frey described the post as "administrateur des biens" and suggested that the official was in charge of community property including the synagogue building, the cemetery, etc. *CIJ*, I p. xcif. See also Baron, *Jewish Community*, vol. 1, p. 102; Leon, p. 191.

Conclusion

In regard to various aspects of the civic and political status and bill of rights of the Jews of Egypt as individuals and organized communities, the sources examined lead to the following conclusions:

a) The civic status of the Jews of Egypt was not uniform. Their stratification was quite diversified, and determined a large extent as early as the Ptolemaic period by functional criteria.

b) The Jewish communities throughout Egypt were generally organized as separate independent bodies, sometimes even within well-defined territorial limits. The larger ones were recognized legal entities operating on the basis of fundamental rights such as the right to maintain ancestral laws, the right to have their own leadership institutions, the right to make community decisions, the right to own community property, the right to have public funds, the right of asylum for community sacred places.

c) The basic organizational form of the larger communities was the *politeuma*, which resembled that of other ethnic groups, and generally derived from military service in the Ptolemaic period.

d) As members of *politeumata* Jews were classified civically as *politai*, and as such enjoyed the protection of the "civic laws" (πολιτικοὶ νόμοι).

e) The Jews of Alexandria were not citizens of the Greek *polis* there.

f) The Jewish community of Alexandria was organized as a *politeuma*, independent of the Greek *polis*, its rights and political status having been accorded by the central government.

g) The existence of the Jewish *politeuma* within the city limits of Alexandria was a thorn in the flesh of the *polis*, as it demonstrated the flawed sovereignty of the latter.

h) The Greek *polis* in Alexandria aspired to establish within the city a single *politeia*, based on one kinship (*syngeneia*) linked to the municipal cult. It consequently hoped to abolish the Jewish *politeia* and sought to designate the Jews as "foreigners" or at most "permanent residents" (*metoikoi*).

i) The Jews of Alexandria could legitimately be called both *politai* and "Alexandrians", the former term denoting their membership in the Jewish *politeuma*, and the latter their permanent residence in the city.

j) The status of the *politai* of the Jewish *politeuma* was intermediate between *astoi* and *metoikoi*.

k) The bill of rights of the Jews of Alexandria is defined accurately in Philo's statement that "the Jewish *politeia* is a combination of ancestral customs (or laws) and participation in general civic rights".

l. The Jews in Alexandria fought to maintain their own *politeia*, and not to attain citizenship in the *polis*.

m) The Jews put their trust in the central government, and consequently their Alexandrian adversaries associated their hatred for the Jews with their fight against the country's rulers (that is, the Ptolemaic kings and Roman emperors).

n) There is no source documenting any desire on the part of Jews as an organized group to fraudulently infiltrate the Alexandrian gymnasium (so as to gain citizenship in the *polis*). On the contrary, there is evidence of their resentment of the gymnasium and attempts to harass it.

o) The Jewish striving for *isopoliteia* meant the desire for equality between two political bodies in Alexandria, the Jewish *politeuma* and the Greek *polis*.

The Term *Politeia* in Philo and Josephus

The term *politeia* had important political and philosophical content and was thus the subject of considerations by the best minds of
the Classical world, Plato and Aristotle among them. The Greek
philosophers deemed the *polis* to be the apogee of human creation[2],
and its organizational form was consequently a crucial matter both
lofty and invaluable. The truth is that they could not imagine a *polis*
without a definite political organization, what is now termed a "government" or "regime", which in ancient Greece was called *politeia*.

At the beginning of the third book of *Politics* (1274b) Aristotle
notes that "for the student of government and of the nature and
characteristics of the various forms of constitution (πολιτεία), almost
the first question to consider is in regard to the state (πόλις)"[3]. As the
"*polis* is a collection (πλῆθος) of citizens" (πολῖται)[4] and as a citizen is someone who has the opportunity of participating in governing functions[5], and "for inasmuch as the *polis* is a kind of partnership
of citizens and is in fact a partnership of a *politeia* ... and when the
form of the *politeia* has been altered and is different it would appear
that the *polis* is no longer the same *polis*"[6], it thus appears that *polis*
and *politeia* are two that are one. Furthermore, since the regimes
determined the shape and nature of the laws[7], the *polis* also identified with a special set of laws; that is, what is today called constitution, which in Classical Greece was again defined by the term

---

1 The analysis relates to the use of the term in Philo and Josephus in general, and not
specifically in relation to the Jews of Egypt, as those instances have been treated in the
body of the book. For references, see G. Mayer, *Index Philoneus*, p. 238; Rengstorf, *A
Complete Concordance to Flavius Josephus*, III, pp. 474-5.

2 See, e.g., Aristotle, *Politica*, I 1251a (1,1).

3 The translator is H. Rackham, in the *LCL* edition.

4 *Politica*, III 1274b 45 (1,2).

5 *Ibid.*, III 1275b 17-20 (1,12).

6 *Ibid.*, III 1276b 1ff. (3,7).

7 *Ibid.*, IV 1289a 10-15 (9-10).

politeia. Moreover, as "a constitution (πολιτεία) is the ordering of the *polis* in respect of its various magistracies and especially the magistracy (ἀρχή) that is supreme over all matters. For the government (πολίτευμα) is everywhere supreme over the *polis* and constitution (*politeia*) is the government (*politeuma*)"[8]. However, no mistake should be made regarding the meaning of the last term, for it does not have only the conventional meaning of "authority" or "magistracy" (i.e. ἀρχή); Aristotle himself stressed explicitly "I mean that in democratic states, for example, the people are supreme, but in oligarchies on the contrary the few are"[9]. The "government" (*politeuma*) was a term that denoted the body of citizens who undertook the duties of authority[10]. And the circle closes where it began, with the assertion that as regimes differ from each other in type, the inevitable conclusion is that the definition differs for the citizen (πολίτης) of each *politeia*[11], and thus also for each *polis*[12]. Aristotle's exposition makes it clear why the Greeks applied the word *politeia* to the concept of "citizenship" too. The lack of discrimination between the concepts of regime, constitution, government and citizenship led to the fusion of all of them in the consciousness of the Greek philosophers and resulted in the use of a single vague term — *politeia* — which encompassed all the meanings noted.

Philo, as a philospher, was familiar with the political concepts of the Greek world, and it is no wonder that his use of the term *politeia* followed their pattern. Josephus, however, was not likely to have had a knowledge of the Greek philosophers gained directly from the sources. His acquaintance with Greek political and philosophical notions may have been made through secondary sources such as literary anthologies, or the works of Jewish Hellenistic authors (such as Philo), and yet his conceptual world was the same.

A. Philo
1. Politeia meaning Government, Management of the State, Statesmanship

---

8 *Ibid.*, III 1278b 10ff. (6,1) and cf. *ibid.*, 1279a 25 (7,2).   9 *Ibid.*
10 It should not be thought that the reference is to a leadership like the *archontes*. In a democratic regime, the *archontes* merely carry out the decisions of the sovereign body, the *ecclesia*.
11 *Ibid.*, 1275b 1-5 (1,9).
12 Cf. *ibid.*, 1276b 1ff. (3,7).

A clear case of this meaning occurs in *De Josepho*, 38. Here Philo compares the statesman to the manager of a household, and state (*polis*) management to the management of a household (οἰκονομία). His opinion is well rooted in the political concepts of the Greek philosophers[13]. In *De Josepho*, 54, he lists three fundamental traits of a statesman — that of a shepherd, that of the manager of a household, and that of a person with self-control, noting in particular that the last was actually related to "statesmanship" (*politeia*). Other similar usages appear in *Quod. Omn., Prob. Lib. sit*, 83; *De Fuga et Inventione*, 35-36; *De Ebrietate*, 88, 91-92; *De Somniis*, I 220; *De Josepho*, 32, 78, 150, 218; *De Praem. et Poen.*, 11; *De Spec. Leg.*, I 33; *De Decalogo*, 14; *Quod Det. Pot. sol.*, 7, 28; *De Plantatione*, 56; *De Mutatione*, 150; *In Flacc.*, 141.

2. Politeia meaning Community, Body of Citizens (politeuma)

Philo sometimes employed the term to mean *politeuma*, as did some Greek authors as well[14]. In some cases the word *politeia* is used with the verb ἐγγράφω to denote those "registered in the body of citizens": *De Spec. Leg.*, I 63; *De Gigantibus*, 61; *De Vita Mosis*, II 211. In others Philo uses the word *politeuma* with that verb: *De Josepho*, 69; *De Spec. Leg.*, II 45; *De Conf. Ling.*, 109; *De Agricultura*, 81; *De Opif. Mundi*, 143, a most instructive parallelism. Aside from this phrase, there are numerous instances in which *politeia* is synonymous or analogous to *politeuma*: *De Spec. Leg.*, I 51, 105; II 123; III 170, 181; IV 10, 100, 120; *De Vita Mosis*, I 241; II 51; *De Virtutibus*, 87, 127, 219; *De Conf. Ling.*, 196; *De Gigantibus*, 89; *De Ebrietate*, 36, 109.

3. Politeia Meaning Regime, State.

Philo as well as the Greek philosophers sometimes used *politeia* to name "regime". It is often difficult to distinguish between the denotations of "regime" and "constitution", and the list below includes only instances that are clearly "regime" or "state". Philo was concerned with the philosophical investigation of the ideal state or regime, and even asserted categorically that the political regime

---

13 Cf. Plato, at the beginning of *Statesman*, I 259c; Aristotle, *Politica*, I 1252a.
14 E.G., Polybius, XXX 6,8; 7,9; 13, 12; 32, 8, etc.

described in the Pentateuch merited that description. See *De Spec. Leg.*, I 51, III 24, 167; IV 55; *De Somniis*, I 219. Like Plato, Aristotle and the Stoics, Philo distinguished "good" and "bad" regimes, "right" and "unright" ones (ὀρθή; οὐκ ὀρθή). He noted, for instance, that oligarchy, ochlocracy and tyranny were bad[15], while democracy, monarchy and aristocracy were good[16]. Thus Philo sought to show that the regime specified in the Torah was the best of the good regimes as it embodied the finest features of them all[17].

4. Politeia Meaning Constitution.

As noted above, it is difficult to distinguish the sense of "regime" from that of "constitution". Philo did, however, use the term in the phrase ἡ πάτριος πολιτεία which is known from Classic Greek literature as signifying "ancestral constitution"[18]: *De Migrat. Abr.*, 38; *De Vita Mosis*, I 241; II 49; *De Abr.*, 61; *De Josepho*, 29-31; *De Conf. Ling.*, 2; *De Spec. Leg.*, IV 55; *De Virtutibus*, 219.

B. Josephus

1. Politeia meaning government, state management.

There is a very fine distinction between this sense of *politeia* and that meaning "regime", which is not always easy to discern, as for instance in *C. Apionem*, I 220. However, in two instances *politeia* is associated with προστασία τοῦ ἔθνους (leadership of the nation)[19], so that it clearly means political leadership. In several cases *politeia* is used with the verb καθίστημι[20], to mean to establish or install a government (or constitution), a combination familiar from classical Greek writings[21], as is the combination of *politeia* with the verb πολιτεύω, which Josephus employed as well[22].

---

15 *De Fuga*, 10; *De Agricultura*, 46; *De Decalogo*, 155; *De virtutibus*, 180; *De Abrahamo*, 242; *De Conf. Ling.*, 108.
16 *De Abrahamo*, 242; *De Spec. Leg.*, IV 237; *De Conf. Ling.*, 108; *Quod Deus sit Immut.*, 176; *De Virtutibus*, 180.
17 *De Spec. Leg.*, IV 161f.
18 See, e.g., Polybius, II 70, 4; *BCH*, 44 (1920, p. 73 (no. 4); *SIG*, 390 (lines 14f.).
19 *Bellum*, I 169; *Antiquitates*, XX 251.
20 *Bellum*, I 169; *Antiquitates*, III 322; VI 35.
21 Cf., e.g., Plato, *Laws*, VII 536b 3; 555b 5.
22 See, e.g., *Antiquitates*, XIV 91.

2. Politeia Meaning Regime.

A substantial number of passages show that for Josephus *politeia* involved the establishment of some political regime or other — monarchy, aristocracy, oligarchy, and the like. See for instance *Antiquitates*, VI 36, 44, 83-85, 223, 268; XI 11-112; XIV 91; XX 229, 251; *Bellum*, I 169. Other passages contain *politeia* in a similar sense, but perhaps closer to "state" (*C. Apionem*, II 188; *Antiquitates*, XIV 117; XVIII 9; XIX 172-173.

3. Politeia Meaning Constitution.

Josephus seems to use *politeia* most often in the sense of "constitution" as demonstrated by its frequent occurrence together with "laws". See, for instance *C. Apionem*, I 250; II 222, 227, 264, 273, 287; *Antiquitates*, I 10; III 213; IV 193-198, 228-230, 292, 310, 312; V 98, 132, 179; X 275; XI 140; XII 240-241, 280; XV 254, 281; XIX 183.

In this sense the word frequently figures in characteristic phrases:

a. the ancestral constitution (ἡ πάτριος πολιτεία); in the table of contents of *Antiquitates*, XII (x); *Antiquitates*, XIII 2, 245; *C. Apionem*, II 264. Cf. *Antiquitates*, XII 240, XV 281.

b. the constitutional disposition (ἡ διάταξις τῆς πολιτείας): *Antiquitates*, I 10; IV 45, 194, 198, 292; V 98. This phrase is common also in Classical Greek literature.

c. the order of the constitution (ὁ τῆς πολιτείας κόσμος): *Antiquitates*, III 84; IV 184, 312; V 132, 179, 186; XIX 173.

4. Politeia Meaning Civic Status.

Politeia in the meaning of "civic status" is infrequent in Josephus and almost always appears with a verb denoting "giving" or "granting":

a. with δίδωμι: *C. Apionem*, II 32, 41 (Alexandrian citizenship granted to Apion); *Antiquitates*, XIV 137 (Roman citizenship granted to Antipater, Herod's father);

b. with δωρέω: *Bellum*, I 194 (Roman citizenship granted to Antipater);

c. with μεταδίδωμι: *C. Apionem*, II 260 (granting of Spartan citizenship);

d. with τιμάω: *Vitae*, 423 (granting of Roman citizenship to Josephus himself);

e. with λαμβάνω: *Antiquitates*, XVI 53 (Roman citizenship granted to Antipater);

f. with μεταλαμβάνω: *C. Apionem* II 41 (Roman prohibition against the granting of Roman citizenship to Egyptians).

C. Josephus' Use of the Term Politeuma

Josephus used the word *politeumà* ten times, and in every case its denotation fits all the senses of *politeia* except "citizenship".

In *C. Apionem*, II 145, in refuting the degamations of Jew-haters, he says, "I desire to give to the best of my ability a brief account of our constitution as a whole and of its details" (περὶ τῆς ὅλης ἡμῶν καταστάσεως τοῦ πολιτεύματος). In *C. Apionem*, III 184 Josephus lauds the Law of Israel, which he says was originally formulated in accordance with God's will, and praises it extravagantly. In one of his pointed rhetorical questions he expresses doubt about the possibility of changing what he calls "the overall system of the constitution" (τὴν ὅλην κατάστασιν τοῦ πολιτεύματος). The connection with the verb καθίστημι is noted above. Ruppel understood the expression a bit differently, as "management of the state" (*Einrichtung des Staatswesens*)[23]. Even if he is right, the sense of *politeia* parallels one of the meanings of *politeuma*.

In *C. Apionem*, II 164-165, Josephus notes the diversity of the laws and customs adopted by people the world over:

"Some people have entrusted the government of their states (τὴν ἐξουσίαν τῶν πολιτευευμάτων) to monarchies, and some entrusted it to oligarchies, and others to the masses. But our Lawgiver, however, was attracted by none of these forms (of polity) but gave to his constitution (ἀπέδειξε τὸ πολίτευμα) the form of what — if a forced expression is permitted — may be termed "theocracy", placing all sovereignty (τὴν ἀρχήν) and authority (τὸ κράτος) in the hands of God," (trans. Thackeray, *LCL*, ed.).

The term *politeuma* figures twice in this passage, in what appear to be two different senses. Ruppel preferred to translate it in its first sense as *allegemine Staatsbegriff*[24], for quite convincing reasons. One way or another, however, the excerpt demonstrates how flexible the term was for Josephus even in a single passage.

In *C. Apionem*, II 250 Josephus censures the distorted conception Greek legislators had of divinity. As they did not really understand it, they were not able to "attain and to make the rest of their consti-

---

23 Ruppel, p. 287.
24 *Ibid.*

tution conform to it" (τὴν ἄλλη τάξιν τοῦ πολιτεύματος). The final phrase recurs in *Antiquitates*, I 5 where it has the same meaning as ἡ διάταξις τῆς πολιτείας noted above, and this in a single context (cf. *Antiquitates*, I 10). In *Antiquitates*, XI 157 Josephus completes his survey of the regulations of Ezra the scribe, and the latter's description of the moving occasion of the reading of the Torah on the *Sukkoth* festival. After the eight days of the festival, he relates, all the people returned to their places "expressing their thanks to Ezra for rectifying the offences against the laws of the state (τὸ πολίτευμα)". There is no doubt that this meaning fits the sense of the passage better than any other. It is interesting to recall that in another passage discussing the breaking of ancestral laws in Ezra's time, Josephus uses the term *politeia* in the same sense (*Antiquitates*, XI 140).

While in Josephus *politeuma* is most frequently used to mean "constitution", it is employed to denote other concepts as well. In *Antiquitates*, I 13, Josephus wrote "The things narrated in the sacred Scriptures are, however, innumberable, seeing that they embrace the history of five thousand years and recount all sorts of surprising reverses, many fortunes of war, heroic exploits of generals, and political revolutions (πολιτευμάτων μεταβολαί)". In *C. Apionem*, II 257, in rebutting Apollonius Molon on Jewish misanthropy, Josephus notes proudly:

> "... in particular, Plato followed the example of our legislator. He prescribed as the primary duty of citizens a study of their laws, which they must all learn word for word by heart. And in order to prevent strangers from mingling with them, took precautionary measures to maintain a pure body of citizens (τὸ πολίτευμα) of law-abiding people." (trans. Thackeray, *LCL*, ed.).

While *politeuma* could here be interpreted to mean "state" as well, and would then be synonymous with *politeia* which figures in the same context (*ibid.*, 256), there is an occurrence of *politeuma* with that meaning in *Antiquitates*, XII 108, that is, "body of citizens" or "community"; and that passage parallels the *Letter of Aristeas*, 310, discussed earlier in the book.

Bibliography

Abbott F.F., A.C. Johnson, *Municipal Administration in the Roman Empire*, Princeton 1926.

Abel E.L., 'The Myth of Jewish Slavery in Ptolemaic Egypt', *REJ*, CXXVII (1968), pp. 253-258.

Abrahams, 'The Third Book of the Maccabees', *JQR*, IX (1897), pp. 39-58.

Adriani M., 'Note sull' Antisemitismo antico', *Studi e Materiali di Storia delle Religioni*, XXXVI (1965), pp. 63-98.

Aimé-Giron, N., *Textes araméens d'Égypte*, Cairo 1931.

Albeck H.'Betrothal and Marriag Writs', *Moshe Shur Memorial Volume*, New York 1945, pp. 12-24.

Alberro C.A., *The Alexandrian Jews during the Ptolemaic Period* (Dissertation), Michigan State University, 1976.

Alon G., *Studies in Jewish History in the Times of the Second Temple, the Mishnah and the Talmud*, I-II, Tel-Aviv, 1957 (Hebrew).

–– *History of the Jews in Eretz-Israel in the Period of the Mishnah and Talmud*, I-II, Tel-Aviv, 1958 (Hebrew).

Alon M., *The Hebrew Law*, Jerusalem 1978 (Hebrew).

Amusin I.D., 'К эдикту Тиберия юлия Александра (*OGIS*, II 669)', *VDI*, I (1949), pp. 73-76.

–– 'Письмо и эдикт императора Клавдия,' *VDI*, II (1949), pp. 221-228.

–– 'К вопросу о датировке Флорентийского папируса *PSI*, X, 1160', *VDI*, IV (1951), pp. 208-219.

–– 'Ad *P. Lond.* 1912', *JJP*, IX-X (1955/6), pp. 169-209.

Andrieu J., *César – Guerre d'Alexandrie*, Paris 1954.

Applebaum S. 'The Rebellion of the Jews of Cyrenaica in the Times of Trajan', *Zion*, XIX (1954), pp. 81-95 (Hebrew).

–– 'A Hypothesis Concerning a Jewish Military Settlement in Cyrenaica', *Yediot*, XIX (1956), pp. 188-197.

–– 'Three Additional Remarks on the Jewish Rebellion in Cyrene under Trajan', *Zion*, XXII (1957), pp. 81-85 (Hebrew).

–– 'Three Inscriptions on Tombstones in the Cemetery of Teuchera in Cyrene', *Yediot*, XXII (1958), pp. 74-77 (Hebrew).

–– 'Corpus Papyrorum Judaicarum, I' (book review), *Tarbiz*, XXVIII (1959), pp. 418-427 (Hebrew).

–– 'New Jewish Inscription from Berenice in Cyrenaica', *Yediot*, XXV (1961), pp. 167-174 (Hebrew).

–– 'The Jewish Community of Hellenistic and Roman Teucheira in Cyrenaica', *Scripta Hierosolymitana*, VII (1961), pp. 27-52.

–– 'Cyrenensia Judaica – Some Notes on Recent Research Relating to the Jews of Cyrenaica in the Hellenistic and Roman Periods', *JJS*, XIII (1963), pp. 31-43.

–– 'Jewish Status at Cyrene in the Roman Period', *Parola del Passato*, XIX (1964), pp. 291-303.

–– 'The Jewish Amphitheatre in Berenice at Cyrene', *Fourth World Congress of Jewish Studies*, I (1967), pp. 107-108 (Hebrew).

–– 'Jewish Diaspora of the Mediterranean Basin in the Hellenistic and Roman Period',

in: *The Mediterranean, its place in the history and culture of the Jews and other nations,*
The Historical Society of Israel, 1970, pp. 49à56 (Hebrew).

—— 'The Civic Status of the Jews at Cyrene', *Gedalyahu Alon Memorial Volume*, Tel-Aviv,
1970. pp. 192-202 (Hebrew).

—— 'the Zealots: The Case for Revaluation, *JRS*, LXI (1971), pp. 155-170.

—— 'The Legal Status of the Jewish Communities in the Diaspora', *The Jewish People*
in the First Century (Safrai & Stern, eds.), I (1974), pp. 420-463.

—— 'The Organization of the Jewish Communities in the Diaspora', *The Jewish People in*
the First Century (Safrai & Stern, eds), I (1974), pp. 464-503.

—— 'The Social and Economic Status of the Jews in the Diaspora', *The Jewish People in the*
First Century (Safrai & Stern, eds.), II (1976), pp. 701-727.

Arangio Ruiz V., 'Intorno agli astoi dell' Egitto Greco-Romano', *Rev. Inter. der Droits de*
L'Antiquité, IV (1940), pp. 7-20.

Askowith D., *The Toleration of the Jews Under Julius Caesar and Augustus*, New-York
1915.

Atkinson K.M.T., 'The Third Cyrene Edict of Augustus', *Ancient Society and Institutions*
(Studies presented to Victor Ehrenberg on his 75th birthday), Oxford 1966, pp. 25f.

Avi-Yonah M., *Historical Geography of Palestine*[3], Jerusalem 1962 (Hebrew).

—— 'The Epitaph of T. Mucius Clemens', *IEJ*, XVI (1966), pp. 258-264.

Avigad N., *Beth She'arim* (III: The Archeological Excavations), Jerusalem 1971 (Hebrew).

Avogadro S., 'Alcune Ossenratio sulle tasse del bestiame nell' Egitto Greco-Romano',
Aegyptus, XIV (1934), pp. 293-297.

Baars W., 'Eine neue griechische Handschrift des 3. Makkabaerbuches', *Vetus Testamentum*,
XIII (1963), pp. 82-87.

Baer I.F., 'The Origins of the Organization of the Jewish Community in the Middle Ages',
Zion, XV (1950), pp. 1-41 (Hebrew).

Balsdon J.P.V.D., *The Emperor Gaius*, Oxford 1934.

—— 'Notes Concerning the Principate of Gaius', *JRS*, XXIV (1934), pp. 13-24.

Bar-Kochva B., 'On the Sources and Chronology of Antiochus I's Battle against the Galatians, *Proceedings of the Cambridge Philological Society*, CXIX, N.S. XIX (1973), pp.
1-8.

—— 'The Battle of Ela'sa', *Beth Mikra*, 58 (1974), pp. 419-434 (Hebrew).

—— *The Seleucid Army, Organization & Tacties in the Great Campaigns*, Cambridge 1976.

—— *The Battles of the Hasmonaens: The Times of Judas Maccabaeus*, Jerusalem 1980
(Hebrew).

Barnard L.W., 'Judaism in Egypt, A.D. 70-135', *Church Quarterly Review*, XLX (1959),
pp. 320-334.

Baron, S.W., The Jewish Community — *Its History and Structure to the American Revolu-*
tion, I-II, Philadelphia 1948.

—— *Social and Religious History of the Jews*, Philadelphia 1953.

Barrow R.H., *Slavery in the Roman Empire*, London 1923.

Baynes N.H., '(Review) Bell. H.I., Jews and Christians in Egypt', *JRS*, (1974), pp. 17-23.

Beek M.A., 'Relations entre Jérusalem et la Diaspora égyptienne au 2 siècle avant J-C',
OT ᴴᴵᴵ (1943), pp. 119-143.

Belkin S., *Philo and the Oral Law*, Cambridge (Mass.) 1940.

—— 'The Alexandrian Source of Cont. Apionem II', *JQR*, XXVII (1936/7), pp. 1-32.

Bell H.I., *Jews and Christians in Egypt*, London-Oxford 1924.

—— *Juden und Griechen im römischen Alexandreia — Eine historische Skizze des alexan-*
drinischen Antisemitismus, (Der alte Orient), Leipzig, Beih. 9, 1926.

—— 'Records of Entry among the Ephebi', *JEA*, XII (1926), pp. 245-247.

—— 'Alexandria', *JEA*, XIII (1927), pp. 171-184.

—— 'The problem of the Alexandrian Senate', *Aegyptus*, XII (1932), pp. 173-184.

—— 'The Economic Crisis in Egypt under Nero', *JRS*, XXVIII (1938), pp. 1-8.
—— 'Roman Egypt from Augustus to Diocletian', *Chronique d' Égypte*, XIII (1938), pp. 347-363.
—— 'The Acts of the Alexandrins', *JJP*, IV (1940), pp. 19-42.
—— 'Antisemitism in Alexandria', *JRS*, XXXI (1941), pp. 1-18.
—— 'Alexandria and Aegyptum', *JRS*, XXXVI (1946), pp. 130-133.
—— 'The Constitutio Antoniniana and the Egyptian Poll-Tax', *JRS*, XXXVII (1947), pp. 17-23.
—— *Cults and Creeds in Greco-Roman Egypt*, Liverpool 1953.
Ben-Shalom I., *The Shammai School and its Place in the Political and Social History of Eretz Israel in the First Century A.D.*, (Diss.), Tel-Aviv University 1980 (Hebrew).
Ben-Haim Z., 'Yeb', *Encyclopaedia Biblica*, III, pp. 425-439 (Hebrew).
Bengston H., *Die Strategie in der hellenistischen Zeit*[2], München 1964.
Bentwitch N., 'The Rightfulness of the Jews in the Roman Empire', *JQR*, VI (1915), pp. 325-336.
Bertholet A., *Die Stellung der Israeliten und Juden zu den Fremden*, Freiburg-Leipzig 1896.
Bevan E.R., *A History of Egypt Under the Ptolemaic Dynasty*, London 1927.
—— 'The Jews of the Dispersion', *CAH*, IX (1932), pp. 428-434.
Bi(c)kerman(n) E., *Das Edikt des Kaisers Carcalla in P. Giss. 40*, Berlin 1926.
—— 'Ritualmord und Eselkult. – ein Beitrag zur Geschichte antiker Publizistik', *MGWJ*, LXXI (1927), pp. 171-178, 255-264.
—— 'A Propos des "Ἄστοι" dans l'Égypte greco-romaine', *Rev. de Philol.*, LIII, N.S.I. (1927), pp. 362-368.
—— 'Beiträge z. antiken Urkundengeschichte', *Archiv*, VIII (1929), pp. 216-239; *Archiv*, IX (1930), pp. 24-46.
—— 'Zur Datierung des Pseudo-Aristeas', *ZNW*, XXIX (1930), pp. 280-298.
—— 'Ein jüdischer Festbrief vom Jahre 124 v. Chr. (II Macc. 1, 1-9)', *ZNW*, XXXIII (1933), pp. 233-254.
—— 'La charte séleucide de Jérusalem', *REJ*, C (1935), pp. 4-35.
—— *Les Institutions des Séleucides*, Paris 1938.
—— 'La cité grecque dans les monarchies Hellénistiques', *Rev. de Philol.*, LXV (1939), pp. 335-349.
—— 'eine proclamation séleucide relative au temple de Jérusalem', *Syria*, 25 (1946-48), pp. 67-85.
—— 'The Names of Christians', *HTR*, XLII (1949), pp. 109-124.
—— 'Une question d'authenticité: Les Privilèges Juifs', *Byzantion*, XXIV (1953), pp. 11-34.
Bilabel F., 'Zur Doppelausfertigung ägyptischer Urkunden', *Aegyptus*, V (1924), pp. 153-173; VI (1925), pp. 93-113.
Bludau A., *Juden und Judenverfolgungen im alten Alexandria*, Münster 1906.
Blumenthal F., 'Der Ägyptisch Kaiserkult', *Archiv*, V (1909-1913), pp. 317-345.
Boak A.E.R., 'The Epikrisis Record of an Ephebe of Antinoopolis found at Karanis', *JEA*, XIII (1927), pp. 151-154.
Bouché-Leclercq A., *Histoire des Lagides*, Paris 1903-1907.
—— *Histoire des Séleucides*, Paris 1913-1914.
Bousset W., H. Gressmann, *Die Religion des Judentums im späthellenistichen Zeitalter*, Tübingen 1926.
Box G.H., *Philonis Alexandrini in Flaccum*, Oxford 1939.
Bowersock, G.W., *Augustus and the Greek World*, Oxford 1965.
Brady T.A., *The Gymnasium in Ptolemaic Egypt*, Univ. Missouri Stud. 1936.
Brand, J., *Glass Vesseles in Talmudic Literature*, Jerusalem 1978 (Hebrew).
Breccia E.V., 'Tribu e demi di Alessandria', *BSAA*, III (1900), pp. 169-186.
—— *Alexandria ad Aegyptum*, Bergamo 1922 (Eng. Trans.).

Broughton T.R.S., 'Some non Colonial Coloni of Augustus', *TAPA*, LXVI (1935), pp. 2f.
— —   *The Magistrates of the Roman Republic*, I, II, New York 1951-2.
Bruce I.A.F., 'Nerva and the Fiscus Judaicus', *PEQ*, 96 (1964), pp. 34-35.
Brücklmeier M., *Beiträge zur rechtlichen Stellung der Juden im römischen Reich*, München 1939.
Büchler A., *Die Priester und der Cultus im letzten Jahrzehnt des jerusalemischen Tempels*, Wien 1895.
— —   'La relation de Josèph concernant Alexandre le Grand', *REJ*, XXXVI (1898), pp. 1-26.
— —   *Tobiaden und Oniaden*, Wien 1899.
— —   'Das jüdisch Verlöbnis Stellung der Verlobten eines Priesters im ersten und zweiten Jaharhundert', *Festschrift zu Israel Lewy's siebzigsten Geburtstag*, Breslau (1911), pp. 111-144.
Bunge J.G., 'Zur Geschichte und Chronologie des Untergangs der Oniaden und der Hasmonäer', *Journal for the Study of Judaism in the Persian, Hellenistic and Roman Period*, 6 (1975), pp. 1-46.
Burr V., *Tiberius Julius Alexander*, Bonn 1955.
Busolt G., *Griechische Staatskunde*, I, II, Göttingen 1920-1926.
Caputo G., 'La sinagoga di Berenice in Cirenaica in una iscrizione greca inedita', *La Parola del Passato*, XII (1957), pp. 132-134.
Carcopino J., 'Le Gnomon de l'Idiologue', *Rev. des Ét. Anc.*, XXIV (1922), pp. 105f.
Cary M., *History of the Greek World from 323 to 146 B.C.*, London 1965.
Casey R.P., 'New Papyri Concerning Incidents at Alexandria', *HTR*, XVIII (1925), pp. 285-287.
Causse A., *Les Dispersés d'Israël*, Paris 1929.
Charles R.E., *The Apocrypha and Pseudepigrapha of the Old Testament in English*, I, II, Oxford 1913.
Charlesworth, M.P., *'Deus* noster Caesar', *Class. Rev.*, XXXIX (1925), pp. 113-115.
— —   *Documents Illustrating the Reigns of Claudius and Nero*, Cambridge 1939.
Churgin P., *Studies in the Times of the Second Temples*, New York, 1949 (Hebrew).
Clermont-Ganneau Ch., 'Découverte à Jérusalem d'une synagogue de l'époque Hérodienne' *Syria*, I (1920), pp. 190-197.
Cohen J., *Judaica et Aegyptiaca*, Groningen 1941.
Cohn L., P. Wendland, S.R. Reiter (eds.), *Phillonis Alexandrini Opera*, I-VI Berlin 1896-1915.
Colorni V., *Leggi ebraici e legge locali*, Milano 1945.
— —   *Gli ebrei nel sistema del diritto comune fino alla prima emancipazione*, Milano 1956.
Colson F.H., G.H. Whitaker, R. Marcus., *Philo* (Loeb ed), vol. 1-X, I-II (Supplements), London 1958.
Cowley A.E., 'Notes on Hebrew Papyrus Fragments from Oxyrhynchus', *JEA*, II 1915), pp. 209-213.
— —   *Aramaic Papyri of the Fifth Century B.C.*, Oxford 1923.
Cross F.M., 'The Discovery of the Samaria Papyri', *BA*, XXVI (1963), pp. 110-121.
— —   'Aspects of Samaritan and Jewish History in the Late Persian and Hellenistic Times', *HTR*, LIX (1966), pp. 201-211.
— —   'Samaria and Jerusalem', *The Restoration — The Persian Period* (ed. H. Tadmor *et al.*), Jerusalem 1983, pp. 81-94 (Hebrew).
Davis S., *Race Relations in Ancient Egypt: Greek, Egyptian, Hebrew, Roman*, London 1951, New York 1952.
Delcor, M., 'Le Temple d'Onias en Égypte', *RB*, LXXV (1965), pp. 188-203.
Delling G., *Bibliographie zur jüdisch-hellenistischen und intertestamentarischen Literatur* (1900-1970) Berlin 1975.
— —   'Biblisch-jüdische Namen in hellenistisch-römischen Ägypten', *BSAC*, 22 (1974/5), pp. 1-42.

Delorme J., *Gymnasium — Étude sur les monuments consacrés à l' éducation en Grèce* (*des origines à l' Empire Romain*), Paris 1960.

Dessau H., *Geschichte der römischen Kaiserzeit*, Berlin, I (1924), II (1930).

Dobschütz von E., 'Jews and Antisemites in Ancient Alexandria', *AJTh*, VIII (1904), pp. 728-755.

Downey G., 'Political Status of Roman Antioch', *Berytus*, VI (1939/40), pp. 1-6.

—— *A History of Antioch in Syria — from Seleucus to the Arab Conquest*, Princeton 1961.

—— *Ancient Antioch — A Condensed Version of a History of Antioch in Syria from Seleucus to the Arab Conquest*, Princeton 1963.

Duff A.M., *Freedmen in the Early Roman Empire*, Oxford 1928.

Edgar C.C., 'Tomb Stones from Tell-el-Yahudieh', *ASAE*, XIX (1920), pp. 216-224.

—— 'More Tomb Stones from Tell-el-Yahudieh', *ASAE*, XXII (1923), pp. 7-16.

Efron J., 'The Sanhedrin as an Ideal and as Reality in the Period of the Second Temple', *Doron sive Commentationes de antiquitate classica docto viro Benzion Katz ... dedicatae* (1967), pp. 167-204 (Hebrew).

—— 'Simeon ben Schetaḥ and King Jannaeus', *Gedalyahu Alon memorial Volume*, Tel-Aviv, 1970, pp. 69-132 (Hebrew).

'The Organic Unity of the Book of Daniel', *Beth Mikra*, 59 (1974), pp. 466-504 (Hebrew).

—— *Studies of the Hasmonean Period*, Tel-Aviv, 1980 (Hebrew).

Ehrenberg V., *Alexander und Ägypten*, Leipzig 1926.

—— *Der Staat der Griechen*, Leipzig 1961, I-II (Zweite Auflage von *Der griechische und der hellenistische Staat*, Leipzig 1932.

—— *The Greek State*,[2] Oxford 1960.

—— *Polis und Imperium — Beiträge zur alten Geschichte*, Zurich 1965.

—— *Society and Civilization in Greece and Rome*, Cambridge (Mass.) 1965.

Ehrenberg V., A.H.M. Jones *Documents Illustrating the Reigns of Augustus and Tiberius*,[2] Oxford 1965.

El-Abbadi M.A.H., 'The Alexandrian Citizenship', *JEA*, XLVIII (1962), pp. 106-123.

—— 'The Gerousia in Roman Egypt', *JEA*, L (1964), pp. 164-169.

Epstein J.N., *Introduction to Tannaitic Literature: Mishna, Tosephta and Halakhic Midrashim*, Jerusalem 1957 (Hebrew).

—— *Introduction to the Text of the Mishna*, I-II, Jerusalem 1948 (Hebrew).

Engers M., 'Die staatsrechtliche Stellung der alexandrinischen Juden', *Klio*, XVIII (1922/3), pp. 79-90.

—— 'Der Brief des Kaisers Claudius an die Alexandriner (p. Lond. 1912)', *Klio*, XXIX (1925/6), pp. 168—178.

—— 'ΠΟΛΙΤΕΥΜΑ', *Mnemosyne — Bibliotheca Philologica Batava*, N.S. LIV (1926), pp. 154-161.

Ewald H., *Geschichte des Volkes Israel*, Göttingen 1852.

Fabre P., *César — La guerre civile*, I, II, Paris 1968.

Fébrier J., *La date, la composition et les sources de la Lettre d'Aristée*, Paris 1925.

Feldman L.H., 'The Orthodoxy of the Jews in Hellenistic Egypt', *JSS*, XXII (1960), pp. 215-237.

—— *Studies in Judaica — Scholarship of Philo and Josephus*, New-York 1962.

Ferguson W.S., *Hellenistic Athens — An Historical Essay*, London 1911, *Greek Imperialism*, London 1913.

Flusser D., 'The Blood Liber against the Jews in the Light of the Views of the Hellenistic Period', *Levy Memorial Volume*, Jerusalem 1949, pp. 104-124 (Hebrew).

Frankel Z., *Vorstudien zu der Septuaginta*, Leipzig 1841.

Fraser P.M., 'Alexandria ad Aegyptum again', *JRS*, XXXIX (1949), p. 56.

—— 'Bibliography in Greco-Roman Egypt', *JEA*, XL (1954), pp. 124-141.

—— 'A Ptolemaic Inscription from Thera', *JEA*, XLIV (1958), pp. 99-100.

—— 'Bibliography, Greco-Roman Egypt, Greek Inscriptions 1959', *JEA*, XLVI (1960), pp. 95-103.

—— *Ptolemaic Alexandria*, I-III, Oxford 1972.

Frey J.B., *Corpus Inscriptionum Judaicarum — Recueil des inscriptions juives qui vont du IIIe siècle avant Jessus-Christ au VIIe siècle de notre ére*, Città del Vaticano, I (1936), II (1952).

Friedlander M., *Das Judentum in der vorchristlichen griechischen Welt*, Wien-Leipzig 1897.

Fuchs L., *Die Juden Ägyptens in ptolemäischer und römischer Zeit*, Wien 1924.

Fuks A., 'Marcus Julius Alexander (Concerning the History of Philo's Family)', Zion, XIII-XIV (1947-1949), pp. 10-17 (Hebrew).

—— 'Notes on the Archive of Nicanor', *JJP*, V (1951), pp. 207-216.

—— 'The Jewish Revolt in Egypt (A.D. 115-117) in the Light of the Papyri', *Aegyptus*, XXXIII (1953), pp. 131-158.

—— 'Dositheos son of Drimylos: A Prosopographical Note', *JJP*, VII-VIII (1953/4), pp. 205-209.

—— 'Aspects of the Jewish Revolt in A.D. 115-117', *JRS*, LI (1961), pp. 98-104.

Fuller J.F.C., *Julius Caesar — Man, Soldier and Tyrant*, London 1965.

Fustel de Coulanges N.D., *The Ancient City* (Eng. Trans.) New York 1956.

Gager Jr. J.G., 'Pseudo-Hecataeus Again', *ZNW*, LX (1969), pp. 130-139.

Gabba E., *Iscrizioni greche e latine per lo studio della Bibbia*, Turino 1958.

Gauthiér H., H. Sottas, *Un décret trilingue en l'honneur de Ptolémée IV*, (Service des antiq. de l'Égypte), Cairo 1925.

Gelzer M., 'Iulius (Caligula)', *RE(PW)*, X (1921), pp. 381-423.

Gilboa A., 'The Grant of Roman Citizenship to Antipatros', *Studies in the History of the Jewish People and the Land of Israel*, I, Haifa, 1970, pp. 71-77 (Hebrew).

Ginsburg M.S., 'Fiscus Judaicus', *JQR*, N.S. XXI (1931), pp. 281-291.

Glotz G., *The Greek City and its Institutions*, London 1929.

Goodenough E.R., 'Philo and Public Life', *JEA*, XII (1926), pp. 77-79.

—— *The Jurisprudence of the Jewish Courts in Egypt*, New Haven-London 1929.

—— *'By Light Light' — The Mystic Gospel of Hellenistic Judaism*, New Haven 1935.

—— *The Politics of Philo Judaeus — Practice and Theory*, Yale 1938.

—— *Jewish Symbols in the Greco-Roman Period*, I-XII, New-York 1953-1965.

Gordon Milton D., 'The Excavations in Sardes' *BASOR*, 1963 (No. 170), pp. 51f.; 1964 (No. 174), pp. 30f.; 1965 (No. 177), pp. 17f.; 1966 (No. 182), pp. 34f.

Grätz H., 'Präcisirung der zeit für die, die Judäer betteffenden Vorgänge unter den Kaiser Caligula', *MGWJ*, XXVI (1877), pp. 97-107, 145-156.

—— 'Die Stellung der Kleinasiatischen Juden unter der Römerherschaft', *MGWJ*, XXXV (1886), pp. 329-346.

—— *Geschichte der Juden von den ältesten Zeiten bis auf die Gegenwart* , I-XI, Leipzig 1897-1911.

Gregoire, H., 'H.I. Bell: *Jews and Christians in Egypt*' (Recension), *Byzantion*, I (1924), pp. 638-647.

Griffith G.T., *The Mercenaries of the Hellenistic World*, London 1935.

Grimm C.L.W., *Kurzgefasstes exegetisches Handbuch z. den Apocryphen des A.T. — Dritte Lieferung, Das zweite, dritte, vierte Buch der Maccabaer*, Leipzig 1856.

Grintz Y.M., *Sefer Yehudith (The Book of Judith)*, Jerusalem 1957 (Hebrew).

Guignebert Ch., 'Remarques sur l'explication de la "Lettre de Claude" et l'hypothèse de M.S. Reinach', *RHR*, XC (1924), pp. 123-132.

Gulak A., 'Betrothal contract and things bought in saying according to the Talmudic law', *Tarbiẓ*, III (1932), pp. 361-367 (Hebrew).

Gutman J., 'The Origin and main purpose of the Letter of Aristeas', *Ha-Goren*, X (1928), pp. 42-59 (Hebrew).
— — 'Hana and her seven sons in Legend and in the Books of Maccabees', *Levy Memorial Volume*, Jerusalem 1949, pp. 25-37 (Hebrew).
— — 'The Historical Importance of III Maccabees' *Eshkoloth*, III (1959), pp. 49-72 (Hebrew).
— — *The Beginnings of Jewish Hellenistic Literature*, I-II, Jerusalem 1958, 1963 (Hebrew).
Gutmann M., 'Enslavement for Debt in Jewish Teaching', *Dinaburg Anniversary Book*, Jerusalem, 1949, pp. 68-82 (Hebrew).
Hadas M., 'Aristeas and III Maccabees', *HTR*, XLII (1949), pp. 175-184.
— — 'III Maccabees and the Tradition of Patriotic Romance', *Chronique d'Égypte*, XXIV (1949), pp' 97-104'
— — *Aristeas to Philocrates; Jewish Apocryphal Literature*, New-York 1951.
— — *The Third and Fourth Book of Maccabees; Jewish Apocryphal Literature*, New-York 1953.
Haddad G., *Aspects of Social Life in Antioch in the Hellenistic-Roman Period* (Diss), Chicago 1949.
Hammond M., 'Germana Patria', *Harvard Studies in Classical Philology*, LX (1951), pp. 147-174.
Hanfmann G.M.A., 'The Ninth Campaign at Sardis', *BASOR*, CLXXXVI (1967), pp. 17-52; CLXXVI (1967), pp. 9-62.
Hanhart R., *Septuaginta, Vetus Testamentum Graecum auctoritate Societatis Litterarum Göttingensis editum*, Götingen 1936.
Harper G.M., 'Tax Contractors and their Relation to Tax-Collection in Ptolemaic Egypt', *Aegyptus*, XIV (1934), pp. 49-65.
Hassoun J(ed.), *Juifs du Nil*, Paris 1981.
Hatch E., H.A. Redpath, *A Concordance to the Septuagint*, Oxford 1897.
Hauber, H., 'A Jewish Shipowner in Third Century Ptolemaic Egypt', *Ancient Society*, X (1979), pp. 167-170.
Heichelheim F.M., 'The Text of the Constitutio Antoniniana and Three other Decrees of the Emperor Caracalla Contained in *P. Giss. 40*', *JEA*, XXVI (1940), pp. 10-22.
— — 'Die auswärtige Bevölkerung im Ptolemäerreich', *Klio*, Beiheft 18, 1925.
Heinemann I., 'Antisemitismus', RE(PW), Suppl., V (1931), pp. 3-43.
— — *Philons griechische und jüdische Bildung*, Breslau 1932.
— — 'The Attitude of the Ancients Towards Judaism', *Zion*, IV (1939), pp. 269-293 (Hebrew).
Hemer C.J., 'The Edfu Ostraka and the Jewish Tax', *PEQ*, CV (1973), pp. 6-12.
Hengel M., *Judaism and Hellenism*, I-II, London 1974.
— — *Juden Griechen und Barbaren*, Stuttgart 1976.
— — 'Proseuche und Synagoge. Jüdische Gemeinde, Gotteshaus und Gottesdienst in der Diaspora und in Palästina', in: *Tradition und Glaube*. Fest. für K.G. Kuhn, Göttingen 1971, pp. 157-184.
Hennig D., 'Zur Ägyptenreise des Germanicus', *Chiron*, II (1972), pp. 349-365.
Herschberg A.S., *Culture-Life in Israel in the Period of the Mishnah and Talmud*, Warszawa 1224 (Hebrew).
Hertzfeld L., *Handelsgeschichte der Juden des Altertums*, Braumschweig 1879.
Heuss A., *Stadt und Herrscher des Hellenismus in ihren Staats-und Völkerrechtlichen Beziehungen*, *Klio*, Beiheft 39, Leipzig 1937.

Hirsch S.A., 'The Temple of Onias', *Jews College Jubilee Volume*, London 1906, pp. 33-80.
Hirschfeld O., *Die keiserlichen Verwaltungsbeamten bis auf Diocletian*,[3] Berlin 1963.
Hirzel R., *Themis, Dike und Verwandtes — ein Beitrag zur Geschichte der Rechtsidee bei den Griechen*, Leipzig 1907.

Holleaux M., *Rome, la Grèce, et les monarchies hellénistiques au IIIe siècle av. J.C.*, Paris 1921.

—— 'Remarques sur une inscription de Thessalonique', *REG*, X (1897), pp. 446-455.

—— *Études d'épigraphie et d'histoire grecques*, I-IV, Paris 1938-1957.

Hopfner T., *Die Juden Frage bei Griechen und Römern*, Prague 1943.

Hopkins, C., 'The Date and Trial of Isidorus and Lampo before Claudius, *BGU, 1, 511* and *P. Cair, 10448*', *YCS*, I (1928), pp. 169-177.

Hunt A.S. and C.C. Edgar, *Select Papyri*, I-II, London 1934.

Isaac J., *Genèse de l' Antisémitisme*, Paris 1956.

Janne H., 'Un passage controversé de la lettre de Claude aux Alexandrins', *Rev. Arch.*, XXXV (1932), pp. 268-281.

Jellicoe S., 'Aristeas, Philo and the Septuagint Vorlage', *JTS*, N.S. XII (1961), pp. 261-271.

—— 'The Occasion and Purpose of the Letter of Aristeas', *NTS*, XII (1966), pp. 144-150.

—— *The Septuagint and Modern Study*, Oxford 1968.

Jessen, 'Eleuthereus', *RE(PW)*, V2 (1905), pp. 2345-2346.

Jessi F., 'Notes sur l'édit dionisiaque de Ptolemée IV Philopator', *JNES*, XV (1950), pp. 236-240.

Johnson A.C., *Roman Egypt to the Reign of Diocletian*, in T. Franks' *Economic Survey of Ancient Rome*, II, Boltimore 1936 (1956).

Jones A.H.M., 'Another Interpretation of the Constitutio Antoniniana', *JRS*, XXVI (1936), pp. 223f.

—— *Cities of the Eastern Roman Provinces*, Oxford 1937 (= *CERP*).

—— 'The Election of the Metropolitan Magistrates in Egypt', *JEA*, XXIV (1938), pp. 65-72.

—— *The Herods of Judea*, Oxford 1938.

—— *The Greek City from Alexander to Justinian*, Oxford 1940.

—— 'J.H. Oliver's *The Sacred Gerusia*' (Review), *JRS*, XXXIV (1944), pp. 145-146.

Jones H.L., *The Geography of Strabo, Book I-XVII*, (Loeb ed.) I-VIII (with an Index and maps in the last volume).

Jones H. ST., 'Claudius and the Jewish Question at Alexandria', *JRS*, XVI (1926), pp. 17-35.

Jouguet P., 'Une lettre de l'empereur Claude aux Alexandrin', *Jour. de Savants*, 1925, pp. 5-19.

—— *La vie Municipale dans l'Égypte Romaine*, Paris 1911.

—— *Macedonian Imperialism and the Hellenization of the East*, London 1928.

Judeich W., *Caesar im Orient; Kritische Übersicht der Ereignisse vom 9 Aug. 48 bis October 47*, Historische Dissertation, Strassburg (Leipzig) 1884.

Jülicher A., 'Zum Brief des Kaisers Claudius', *Die Christliche Welt*, XXXVIII (1924), pp. 1001-1004.

Jullien L., *Les juifs d'Alexandrie dans l'Antiquité*, Alexandria 1944.

Juster J., *Les Juifs dans l'empire Romain — leur condition juridique, économique et sociale*, I-II, Paris 1914.

Kahana A., *Ha-Sefarim Ha-Ḥizonim* (= The Apocrypha), I-II, Tel-Aviv 1959 (Hebrew).

Kasher, A., 'Three Jewish communities of Lower Egypt in the Ptolemaic Period, *Scripta Classica Israelica*, II (1975), pp. 113-123.

—— 'Some Suggestions and Comments Concerning Alexander Macedon's Campaign in Palestine', *Beth Mikra*, 20 (1975), pp. 187-208 (Hebrew).

'The Circumstances of Claudius Caesar's Edict and of his Letter to the Alexandrians', *Zion*, XXXIX (1975), pp. 1-7 (Hebrew).

—— 'Les circonstances de la promulgation de l'édit de l'empereur Claude et de sa Lettre aux Alexandrins (41 ap. J.-C.)', *Semitica*, XXVI (1976), pp. 99-108.

—— 'Some Comments on the Jewish Uprising in Egypt in the Time of Trajan', *Journal of*

Jewish Studies, XXVII (1976), pp. 147-158.

—— 'The *Isopoliteia* Question in Caesarea Maritima', *JQR*, LXVIII (1978), pp. 16-27.

—— 'The Jewish Attitude to the Alexandrian Gymnasium in the First Century', *AJAH*, (1976), pp. 148-161.

—— 'Diaspora Jews in the Period of Antiochus Epiphanes Persecutions and the Hasmonean Revolt', in: Bar-Kochva B. (ed.), *The Seleucid Period in Eretz-Israel*, Tel-Aviv 1980, pp. 205-226 (Hebrew).

Kautsch E., *Die Apokryphen und Pseudepigraphen des AT*, I-II, Tübingen 1900.

Kess H., 'Nitriai', *RE(PW)*, XVII (1936), pp. 774-775.

Kenyon, F.G., 'Phylae and Demes in Greco-Roman Egypt', *Archiv*, II (1903), pp. 70-78.

Kern O., 'Dionysos', *RE(PW)*, V 1 (1903), pp. 1010-1046.

—— *Die Religion der Griechen*, I-III, Berlin 1938.

Kittel G., 'Das kleinasiatische Judentum in der hellenistisch-römischen Zeit', *Theologische Literaturzeitung*, LXIX (1944), pp. 9-20.

Klausner J., *History of the Second Temple*, I-V^5, Jerusalem 1958 (Hebrew).

Klein S., *Jüdische-Palästinisches Corpus Inscriptionum*, Wien-Berlin 1920.

—— *Sefer Ha-Yishuv*, Jerusalem 1939 (Hebrew).

—— 'The Boundaries of Eretz Israel according to the Tannaim', in: *Studies in the Geography of Eretz Israel* (ed. Mossad Harav Kook), Jerusalem 1965, pp. 119-176 (Hebrew).

Klijn A.F.J., 'The Letter of Aristeas and the Greek Translation of the Pentateuch in Egypt', *NTS*, XI (1964), pp. 154-158.

Kornemann E., 'Das Hellenentum der Makedonen in Aegypten', *Aegyptus*, XIII (1933), pp. 644-651.

Korngreen P., *Jewish Military Settlements in Ancient Times*, Tell-Aviv, 1948 (Hebrew).

Kraeling C.H., 'The Jewish Community at Antioch', *JBL*, LI (1932), pp. 130-160.

Kraeling E.G., *The Brooklyn Museum Aramaic Papyri — New Documents of the Fifth Century B.C. from Jewish Colony of Elephantine*, New Haven 1953.

Krauss S., *Griechische und lateinische Lehnwörter im Talmud, Midrasch und Targum*, Berlin 1899.

—— 'Antiochia', *REJ*, XLV (1902), pp. 27-49.

—— *Talmudische Archäologie*, I-III Leipzig 1910-1912.

—— *Synagogle Altertümer*, Berlin-Vienna 1922.

Kromayer J., G. Veith, *Heerwesen und Kriegführung der Griechen und Römer*, München 1928.

Kübler B., 'Peregrinus', *RE(PW)*, XIX (1937), pp. 639-655.

Lagrange M.J., 'Les cultes hellénistiques en Égypte et la judaïsme', *Rev. Thomiste*, XXXV (N.S. XIII) 1930), pp. 309-328.

—— 'La lettre de Claude aux Alexandrins', *RB*, XL (1931), pp. 270-276.

Laqueur R., *Der jüdische Historiker Flavius Josephus*, Giessen 1920.

—— 'Der Brief des Kaisers Claudius an die Alexandriner', *Klio*, XX (1925), pp. 89-106.

—— 'Griechische Urkunden in der jüdisch-hellenistischen Literatur', *Historische Zeitschrift*, CXXXVI (1927), pp. 229f.

Larsen, J.A.O., *Greek Federal States, their Institutions and History*, Oxford 1968.

Last H., 'The Praefectus Aegypti and his Powers', *JEA*, XL (1954), pp. 68-73.

Launey M., *Recherches sur les armées hellénistiques*, I-II, Paris 1949-1950.

Lefebvre, G., 'Inscriptions gréco-juives', *Ann. du serv. des antiq. de l'Égypte*, XXIV (1924), pp. 1-5.

Leipoldt J., *Antisemitismus in der alten Welt*, Leipzig 1933.

Leisegang H., *Index Philonis*, Berlin 1926-1930.

—— 'Philons Schrift über die Gesandschaft der alexandrinischen Juden an den Kaiser Gaius Caligula', *JBL*, LVII (1938), pp. 377-406.

Lenger M.T., *Corpus des ordonances d'Ptolemaées*, Bruxelles 1964.

Lennan H. Mac, *Oxyrhynchus — an Economic and Social Study*, Amsterdam 1968.

Leon H.J., *The Jews of Ancient Rome*, Philadelphia 1960.

Lesquier J., *Les institutions militaires de l'Égypte sous les Lagides*, Paris 1911.

—— 'L'Arabarches d'Égypte', *Revue Archéologique*, VI (1917), pp. 95-103.

Levick B., *Roman Colonies in Southern Asia Minor*, Oxford 1967.

Levine I.L., *Caesarea under Roman Rule*, Leiden 1975.

—— 'The Jewish-Greek Conflict in First Century Caesarea', *JJS*, XXV (1975), pp. 381-397.

Levy J.H., *Studies in Jewish Hellenism*, Jerusalem 1960 (Hebrew).

Lieberman S., *Greek in Jewish Palestine*, New York 1942.

—— *Hellenism in Jewish Palestine*, New York 1950.

—— *Greek and Hellenism in Jewish Palestine*, Jerusalem 1962 (Hebrew).

   Tosefta Kifshutah, a comprehensive commentary on the Tosefta, New York, 1955-1967.

—— 'The Talmud of Caesarea', *Tarbiz*, 2 (1931), pp. 1-108 (Hebrew); English trans. 1968.

—— *Sifre Zutta*, New York 1968.

Lichtenstein H., 'Zur Geschichte der Juden in Alexandrien', *MGWJ*, LXIX (1925), pp. 357-361.

Liddell H.G., Scott, R., *A Greek-English Lexicon,*[9] Oxford 1973.

Lidzbarski, M., *Ephemeris für Semitische Epigraphik*, I-III, Giessen 1902-1915.

Liebesny H., 'Ein Erlass des Königs Ptolemaios II Philadelphos über die Dekleration von Vieh und Sklaven in Syria und Phönikien (EPR Inv. Nr. 24552 gr.)', *Aegyptus*, XIV (1936), pp. 257-288.

Lietzmann H., 'Jüdisch-griechische Inschriften aus Tell-el-Yehudieh' *ZNW*, XXII (1923).

Lifschitz B., 'Fonction et titres honorifiques dans les communautés juives — Notes d'épigraphie palestinienne', *RB*, LXVII (1960), pp. 58-64.

—— *Donateurs et Fondateurs dans les Synagogues Juives*, Paris 1967.

Lösch S., *Epistula Claudiana — Der neuentdeckte Brief des Kaisers Claudius von Jahre 41 n. Chr. und das Urchristentum — Eine exegetisch historische Untersuchung*, Rottenburg 1930.

Magie D., *Roman Rule in Asia Minor*, I-II, Princeton 1950.

Mahaffy J.P., *A History of Egypt under the Ptolemaic Dynasty*, London 1899.

—— 'The Jews in Egypt', *Mélange Jules Nicole*, Genève 1905, pp. 659-662.

Manteuffel J., *Fouilles Franco-Polonaisses, Raports, I-III, Tell Edfou*, Cairo 1937-1939.

—— 'Quelques Textes d'Edfu', (ch. VI, 'le Quartier juif d'Apollinopolis', pp. 110f.), *JJP*, VII (1949).

Marcus R., 'Dositheus, Priest and Levite', *JBL*, LXIV (1945), pp. 269-271.

—— 'Antisemitism in the Hellenistic Roman World, *Essays on Antisemitism*, New-York, 1946, pp. 61-78.

—— 'A Selected Bibliography (1920-1945) of the Jews in the Hellenistic Roman Period', *PAAJR*, XVI (1946-7), pp. 97-181.

—— *Josephus: Jewish Antiquities (books XI-XIV), Loeb Classical Library*, vols. VI-VIII (1931, 1943, 1963).

—— 'The Hellenistic Age', in: *Great Ages and Ideas of the Jewish People* (ed. L.W. Schwarz), 1956.

Marquardt K.J., *Römische Staatsverwaltung*, I-III, Leipzig 1881 (Darmstadt 1957).

Marshall A.J., 'Flaccus and the Jews of Asia (Cicero, Pro Flacco 28, 67-69)', *Phoenix*, 29 (1975), pp. 139-154.

Martin V., *La fiscalité romaine en Égypte aux trois premiers siècles de l'Empire*, Genève 1926.

Mayer G., *Index Philoneus*, Berlin-New York 1974.

Meisner N., *Aristeasbrief* (Jüdische Schriften aus hellenistisch-römischer Zeit, II, 1), Gütersloh, 1973, pp. 35-78.

Mensil Du Buisson Conte du, R., 'Le Temple d'Onias et le Camp Hyksos à Tell el-Yahoudiye', *BIFAO*, XXXV (1935), pp. 59-71.

Meyer Ed., *Ursprung und Anfänge des Christentums*, I-III, Stuttgart-Berlin 1921-1923.

Meyer P.M., 'Papyrusbeiträge zur römischen Kaisergeschichte', *Klio*, VII (1907), pp. 122-137.

Millar F., 'The Date of the Constitutio Antoniniana', *JEA*, XLVIII (1962), pp. 124f.

Milne J.G., *A History of Egypt under the Roman Rule*[3], London 1924.

—— 'The Ruin of Egypt by Roman Mismanagement', *JRS*, XVII (1927), pp. 1f.

—— 'Egyptian Nationalism under Greek and Roman Rule', *JEA*, XIV (1928), pp. 226-234.

Mitteis L., *Reichsrecht und Volksrecht in der östlichen Provinzen des römischen Kaisereiches*, Leipzig 1891.

—— 'Papyri aus Oxyrhynchos', *Hermes*, XXXIV (1899), pp. 88-106.

Momigliano A., 'Il decreto trilingue in onore di Tolmeo Filopatore e la quarta guerra Celesiria', *Aegyptus*, X (1929), pp. 180-189.

—— 'Intorno al Contra Apionem', *Riv. di Fil.*, LIX (1931), pp. 485-503.

—— 'Per la data e la caratteristica della Lettera di Aristea', *Aegyptus*, XII (1932), pp. 161-172.

—— *Claudius — The Emperor and his Achievement*, Oxford 1934.

—— 'The Gerousia of Alexandria', *JRS*, XXXIV (1944), pp. 114f.

—— *Alien Wisdom; the Limits of Hellenization*, Oxford 1975.

Mommsen Th., *Römische Geschichte*, I-V, Berlin 1888-1894.

—— *Römisches Strafrecht*, Leipzig 1899.

Monceaux P., 'Les colonies juives dans l'Afrique', *REJ*, XLIV (1902), pp. 1f.

Modrzejewski J., 'Les Juifs et le droit hellénistique — Divorce et égalité des époux (*CPJud.* 144)', *Jura*, XII (1961), pp. 162-193.

—— 'Servitude pour dettes ou legs de créance? (note sur CPJud. 126)', *Recherches de Papyrologie*, II (1962), pp. 75-98.

—— 'Splendeurs grecques et misères romaines. Les Juifs d'Égypte dans antiquité', in: Hassoun J. (ed.), *Juifs du Nil*, Paris 1981, pp. 17-48; 237-245.

Moreau J., 'le troisième livre des Maccabées', *Chr. d'Égypte*, XVI (1941), pp. 111-122.

Morison W.D., *The Jews under Roman Rule*, New-York 1890.

Motzo B., 'La condizione giuridica dei Giudei di Alessandria sotto i Lagidi e i Romani', *Atti d. r. Accad. di Scienze di Torino*, XLVIII (1912-13), pp. 577-598.

Murray O., 'Aristeas and Ptolemaic Kingship', *JTS*, N.S. XVIII (1967), pp. 337-371.

Musurillo H.A., 'The Pagan acts of the Martyrs', *Theological Studies*, X (1949), pp. 555-564.

—— *The Acts of the Pagan Martyrs — Acta Alexandrinorum, Edited with Commentary*, Oxford 1954.

—— *Acta Alexandrinorum; De mortibus Alexandriae nobilium — Fragmenta Papyracea Graeca*, Leipzig 1961.

Nathane filio Jechielis (ed. A. Kohut), *Aruch Completum*, vols. 1-9, New-York 1892 (Hebrew).

Naveh J., 'Hebrew Texts in Aramaic Script in the Persian Period', *BASOR*, CCIII 1971), pp. 27-32.

Naville Ed., F.L. Griffith, *The Mound of the Jews and the City of Onias*, Egypt Exploration Fund, Seventh Memoire Extra Volume for 1888/9, London 1890.

Neher-Bernheim R., 'The Libel of the Jewish Ass-Worship', *Zion*, XXVIII (1963), pp. 106-116 (Hebrew).

Neppi-Modona A., 'La vita publica e privata degli Ebrei in Egitto nell' età ellenistica e romana', *Aegyptus*, II (1921), pp. 253-275; III (1922), pp. 19-43.

—— 'Antichissimi papiri ebraici rinvenuti recemente a Ossirinco', *Aegyptus*, IV (1923), pp. 31-37, 125-131.

— — 'A proposito del *P. Lond.*, 73-104', *Aegyptus*, VII (1926), pp. 41-48.

— — Πέρσαι τῆς ἐπιγονῆς ἀγώγιμοί, *Aegyptus*, XLII (1937), pp. 472-479.

Niese, B., 'Bemerkungen über die Urkunden bei Josephus Archael., Bd. XII; XIV; XVI', *Hermes*, XI (1876), pp. 466-488.

— — *Flavii Josephi Opera Omnia I-VII*, Berlin 1890-1895.

— — *Geschichte der griechischen und makedonischen Staaten*, I-III, Gotta 1899-1903 (Darmstadt 1963).

Nilsson M.P., *The Dionysiac Mysteries, of the Hellenistic and Roman Age*, Lund 1957 (New York 1975).

Norsa M., G. Vitelli, 'Sul papiro (*PSI*. X. fasc. 1) della ΒΟΥΛΗ d'Alessandria', *BSAA*, VIII (1932), pp. 5-129.

Oates J.F., 'The Status Designation: ΠΕΡΣΗΣ ΤΗΣ ΕΠΙΓΟΝΗΣ', *YCS*, XVIII (1963), pp. 5-129.

Oehler J., "Ἀποικία', *RE(PW)*, 1, 2 (1893), pp. 2823-2925.

— — 'Epigraphische Beiträge zur Geschichte des Judentums', *MGWJ*, LIII (1909), pp. 292-302, 443-452, 525-538.

— — 'Isopoliteia', *RE*(PW), IX (1921), pp. 2227-2231.

Oertel F., *Die Liturgie — Studien zur ptolemäischen und kaiserlichen Verwaltung Ägyptens*, Leipzig 1917.

— — 'Katoikia', *RE(PW)*, XI 1 (1921), pp. 1-26.

Oliver J.H., 'The βουλή Papyrus', *Aegyptus*, XI (1930/1), pp. 161-169.

— — *The Sacred Gerousia, Hesperia*, Supplement VI, 1941.

— — 'Free Men and "Dediticii" ' *Am. Jour. Philol.*, LXLL (1955), pp. 279-297.

Ostersetzer J., 'On the Legal Status of the Jews in Egypt', *Braude Jubilee Volume*, Warszawa, 1931, pp. 77-119 (Hebrew).

Otto W., *preister und Temple im hellenistischen Aegypten*, I, II, Leipzig 1905, 1908.

— — 'Herodes', *RE(PW)*, suppl. II (1913), pp. 1-200.

— — *Zur Gesch. der Zeit der 6 Ptolemaers*, München 1934.

Otto W., H. Bengston, *Zur Geschichte des Niederganges des Ptolemäerreiches (Abh. Bayer, Akad., N.F. 17, 1938)*, München 1938.

Parker H.M.D., *The Roman Legions*, Cambridge 1958. (1971).

Page D.L., *Greek Literaray Papyri* (Loeb ed.) London 1959.

Pelletier A., *La Lettre D'Aristée à Philocrate*, Paris 1962.

— — *Flavius Josèphe adaptateur de la Lettre d'Aristée*, Paris 1962.

— — *In Flaccum, traduction et notes*, Paris 1967.

— — *Legatio ad. Caium, traduction et notes*, Paris 1972.

Perdrizet M.P., 'Voyage dans la Macéedonie premier', *BCH*, XVIII (1894), pp. 416-445.

— — 'Nouvelles et Correspondance (Macédonie, Syrie, Égypte)', *BCH*, XXI (1897), pp. 161-164.

— — 'La fragment de Satyros sur les dèmes d'Alexandrie', *REA*, XII (1910), pp. 217-247.

Perdrizet M.P., G. Lefèbvre, *Graffites d'Abydos*, Paris 1919.

Peremans W., ΕΛΛΗΝΗΣ dans *P. Paris* 66 (*UPZ*, II, 157)', *Chr. d'Égypte*, XI (1936), pp. 517-521.

— — 'Égyptiens et étrangers en Égypte au IIIe siècle avant J.-C.', *Chr. d'Égypte*, XI (1936), pp. 151-162.

— — 'Ptolémée II Philadelphe et les indigènes égyptiens', *Revue Belge de Philologie et d'Histoire*, XII (1933), pp. 1005-1022.

Peremans W., E. Van't Dack, *Prosopographia Ptolemaica*, Louvain 1950-1968.

Petrie W.M.FL., *The Status of the Jews in Egypt*, Fifth 'Arthur Davis Memorial Lecture', London 1922.

— — *Hyksos and Israelite Cities* (ch. IV. — 'The Temple of Onias', pp. 19-27). London 1906.

Pfister P., 'Eine jüdische Gründungsgeschichte Alexandrias mit einem Anhang über Alexanders Besuch in Jerusalem', *Sitzungsberichte der Heidelberger Akademie der Wissenschaften, philoL-hist. Klasse*, V (1914), Abt. XI.

Plauman G., *Ptolemaïs in Oberägypten*, Leipzig 1910.

Poland F., *Geschichte des griechische Vereinswesens*, Leipzig 1909.

Poole R.S., *Catalogue of the Coins of Alexandria and the Nomes* (*A Catologue of the Greek Coins in the British Museum*), Bologna 1964.

Porten B., *Archives from Elephantine. The Life of a Jewish Military Colony*, Berkeley and Los Angeles 1968.

Praechter K., *Die Philosophie des Altertums*, Berlin 1920.

Preaux C., *Les ostraca grecs du Musée de Brooklyn*, Bruxelles 1935.

—— *L'économie royale de Lagides*, Bruxelles 1939 (1947).

—— 'Polybe et Ptolemée Philopator', *Chr. d'Égypte*, XL (1965), pp. 364-375.

—— *Le monde hellénéstique*, vol. I-II, Paris 1978.

Preisigke Fr., *Fachwörterbuch des öffentlichen Verwaltungsdienstes Ägyptens*, Göttingen 1915.

—— *Namenbuch enthalten- alle griechischen, Lateinischen ägyptischen, hebräischen, arabischen Menschennamen soweit sie in griechischen Urkunden Ägyptens sich vorfinden*, Heidelberg 1922.

Preisigke Fr., F. Bilabel, E. Kisselling, *Sammelbuch griechischer Urkunden aus Ägypten*, Strassburg 1915-.

Preisigke, Fr., E. Kisseling *Wörterbuch der griechischen Papyrusurkunden*, Heidelberg-Marburg 1924-.

Premerstein A. von 'Alexandrinisch und jüdische Gestandte vor Kaiser Hadrian', *Hermes*, LVII (1922), pp. 266-316.

—— 'Graf Uxkull Gyllenband — Heidn. Martyrerakten', *Gnomon*, VIII (1932), pp. 201-206.

—— 'Das Datum des Prozesses des Isidors in den sogenannten heidnischen Martyrerakten', *Hermes*, LXVII (1932), pp. 174-196.

—— 'Alexandrinische Geronten vor Kaiser Gaius', *Schriften der Ludwiggs — Universität zu Giessen (1936), Mitteilungen aus der Papyrussammlung der Giessener Universittatsbibliothek*, V, (*P. Giss.*, 46).

Puchstein, 'Alexandria', *RE(PW)*, I (1893), pp. 1376-1388.

Pucci M., *La rivolta ebraica al tempo di Triano*, Pisa 1981.

—— 'The Uprising under Trajan', in: *Judea ana Rome — The Jewish Revolts* (ed. U. Rappaport), Jerusalem 1983, pp. 185-204 (Hebrew).

—— 'The Uprising of the Jews in Egypt under Emperor Trajan', in: *Nation and History — Studies in the History of the Jewish People* (ed. M. Stern), Jerusalem 1983, pp. 125-139 (Hebrew).

—— 'C.P.J., II 158, 435 E La rivolta ebraica al tempo di Traiano', *Zeitschrift für Papyrologie und Epigraphik*, 51 (1983), pp. 95-104.

Rabinowitz J., 'Marriage Contracts in Ancient Egypt in the Light of Jewish Sources', *HTR*, XLVI (1953).

Radet G., *De coloniis a Macedonibus in Asiam cis Taurum deductis*, Paris 1892.

Radin M., *The Jews among the Greeks and Romans*, Philadelphia 1915.

—— H.I. Bell, '*Jews and Christians in Egypt*' (Book review), *Class. PhiloL*, XX (1925), pp. 368-375.

Rahlfs A., *Septuaginta*[9], Sttutgart 1962.

Rahmani L.Y., 'Silver Coins of the Fourth Century B.C. from Tel Gamma', *IEJ*, XXI (1971), pp. 158-160.

Ramsay A.M., 'The Speed of the Roman Imperial Post', *JRS*, XV (1925), pp. 60-74.

Ramsay W., *The Cities and Bishoprics of Phrigia I-II*, London 1897.

— — 'The Jews in the Gracco-Asiatic Cities', *Expositor* VI 5 (1902), pp. 19-33, 92-109.

Rappaport U., 'Les Idumées en Égypte', *Rev. de Philol.*, XLIII (1969), pp. 73-82.

— — 'When was the Letter of Aristeas Written? ' *Studies in the History of the Jewish People and the Land of Israel*, I, Haifa (1970), pp. 37-57 (Hebrew).

Reich H., *Der Mimus — ein literaturentwicklungsgeschichtlicher Versuch*, Berlin 1930.

Reinach S., 'Les Juifs d'Hypaepa', *REJ*, X (1885), pp. 74-78.

— — 'La communauté Juive d'Athribis', *REJ*, XVII (1888), pp. 235-238.

— — 'La première alussion au Christianisme dans l'histoire', *Rev. de l'Hist. des Relig.*, XC (1924), pp. 108-122.

Reinach Th., *Textes d'auteurs grecs et romains relatifs au Judaism — réunies, traduit et annotés*, Paris 1895.

— — 'Quid Ioudaeo cum Verre?', *REJ*, XXVI (1893), pp. 34-36.

— — 'Juifs et Grecs devant un empereur romain', *REJ*, XXVII (1893), pp. 70-82.

— — 'L'Empereur Claude et les Antisémites Alexandrins d'après un nouveau papyrus', *REJ* XXXI (1895), pp. 161-178.

— — 'Encore sur le " Papyrus de Claude",' *REJ*, XXXV (1897), pp. 296-298.

— — 'Nouveaux documents aux Juifs d'Égypte', *REJ*, XXXVII (1898), pp. 218-225.

— — 'Sur la date de la Colonie Juive d'Alexandrie', *REJ*, XLV (1902), pp. 161-164.

— — Les Juifs d'Alexandronèse, *Mélange Jules Nicole,* Genève 1905, pp. 451-459.

— — 'Les Juifs de Xénéphyris', *REJ*, LXV (1913), pp. 135-137.

— — 'Un Code fiscal de l'Égypte romaine: Le Gnomon de l'Idiologue', *Nouvelle Rev. Hist. de Droit Français et Étranger*, LXIII (1919), pp. 583-636; LXIV (1920), pp. 5-134.

— — 'L'Empereur Claude et les Juifs d'après un nouveau document', *REJ*, LXXIX (1924), pp. 113-144.

Reinmuth O.W., 'The Perfects of Egypt from Augustus to Diocletian', *Klio*, N.F. XXI (1935), Beiheft 34.

Remondon R., 'Les Antisémites de Memphis (*CPJud.* 144)', *Chr. d'Égypte*, LXIX-LXX (1960), pp. 244-261.

Rice Holmes T., *The Roman Republic and the Founder of the Empire*, New York 1923.

Rink H., *Strassen und Viertelnamen von Oxyrhynchos*, Giessen 1924.

Ritter B., *Philo und die Halacha*, Leipzig 1879.

Robert J., L. Robert, 'Bulletin épigraphique' *REG*, LXVII (1954), p. 105; LXXII (1959), pp. 275-276; LXXV (1962), pp. 217-218; LXXX (1968), pp. 517-518.

Robert L., 'Notes d'épigraphie hellénistique', *BCH* LIX (1935), pp. 421-437.

— — *Villes d'Asie Mineure*, Paris 1935.

— — 'Un corpus des inscriptions juives (*Rec.*, J.B. Frey, *CIJ*, I-II)', *REJ*, CI (N;S;I) (1937), pp. 73-86.

— — *Hellenica*, I-XII, Paris 1940-1960.

— — *Nouvelles inscriptions de Sardis*, Paris 1964.

Roberts C., T.C. Skeat, A.D. Nock, 'The Gild of Zeus Hypsistos', *HTR*, XXIX (1936), pp. 39-88.

Roos A.G., 'Lesefrucht', *Mnemosyne*, Ser. 3, II (1935), pp. 233-244.

Roscher W.H., *Ausführliches Lexikon der griechischen und römischen Mythologie*, Leipzig 1884-1937.

Rostovtzeff M.I., *A Large Estate in Egypt in the Third Century B.C.*, Madison 1922.

— — 'Pax Augusta Claudiana', *JEA*, XII (1926), pp. 24-29.

— — 'The Exploitation of Egypt in the First Century A.D.', *Jour. of Econom. and Business Hist.*, I (1928/9), pp. 337-364.

— — *Social and Economic History of the Hellenistic World*, I-III, Oxford 1941.

— — *Social and Economic History of the Roman Empire*, I-II, Oxford 1957.

— — 'Ptolemaic Egypt', *CAH*, VII (1964), pp. 109-154.

— — 'Syria and the East', *CAH*, VII (1964), pp. 155-196.

Rostowzew M.I., *Studien zur Geschichte des römischen Kolonatus*, *Archiv*, Beiheft I, Leipzig 1910.

—— 'Frumentum' *RE(PW)*, VII (1910), pp. 126-187.

Roth J.M., *Greek Papyri Lights on Jewish History*, New York 1924.

Rot-Gerson L., *The Civil and the Religious Status of the Jews in Asia Minor from Alexander the Great to Constantine B.C. 336-A.D. 337* (Diss.), The Hebrew University, Jerusalem 1972 (Hebrew).

Roux J., G. Roux, 'Un décret du politeuma des Juifs de Bérénikė en Cyrénaïque au Musée Lapidaire de Carpentras', *REG*, LXII (1949), pp. 281-296.

Rubin Z., 'Further on the Dating of *Constitutio Antoniniana*', *Latomus*, XX (1975), pp. 430.

Ruppel W., 'Politeuma — Bedeutungsgeschichte eines staatsrechtlichen Terminus', *Philologus*, LXXXII, N.F. XXVI (1927), pp. 268-312, 433-454.

Safrai S., 'Eretz-Israel and the Diaspora in the Ancient Period', *Ha-Umah*, III (1963), pp. 221-229 (Hebrew).

—— *Pilgrimage at the Time of the Second Temple*, Tel-Aviv, 1965 (Hebrew).

Safrai S., M. Stern (eds.), *The Jewish People in the First Century*, Compendia Rerum Judaicarum ad Novum Testamentum, Section One, Assen, I (1974), II (1976).

Samuel A.E., *Ptolemaic Chronology*, München 1962.

San-Nicolò, M., *Aegyptisches Vereinwesen zur zeit der Ptolemäer und Römer*, München, ((1913), II (1915).

Sanctis, de-G., 'Claudio e i giudei d'Alessandria', *Riv. di Fil.*, LII (NS, II) 1924), pp. 473-513.

—— 'Giudei e le fazione de Ludi', *Riv. di Fil.*, LIII (NS, III) (1925), pp. 245f.

Sandelin K.G., 'Zwei kurze Studien zum alexandrinischen Judentum', *Studia Theologica*, XXXI (1977), pp. 147-152.

Sayce A.H., *Alte Denkmäler im Lichte neuer Forschungen*, Leipzig 1886.

Schaefer H., 'Προστάτης', RE(PW), Suppl. IX (1962), pp. 1287-1304.

Schalit A., 'The Letter of Antiochus III to Zeuxis regarding the Establishment of Jewish Military Colonies in Phrygia and Lydia', *JQR*, L (1959/60), pp. 289-318.

—— *König Herodes, der Mann and sein Werk*, Berlin 1969; (Hebrew version: Jerusalem 1964).

Schaller B., 'Hekataios von Abdera über die Juden, zur Frage der Echtheit und Datierung', *ZNW*, LIV (1963), pp. 15-31.

Schnebel M., *Die Landwirtschaft im hellenistischen Aegypten*, München 1925.

Schrage W., 'Συναγωγή im Judentum', *Theologisches Wörterbuch*, VII (1964), pp. 806-826.

Schreckenberg H., *Bibliographie zu Flavius Josephus*, Leiden 1969.

Schubart W., 'Alexandrinischen Urkunden aus der Zeit des Augustus', *Archiv*, V (1909-1913), pp. 35-131.

—— 'Spuren politischer Autonomie in Aegypten unter den Ptolemäern', *Klio*, X (1910), pp. 41-71.

—— *Einführung in die Papyruskunde*, Berlin 1918.

—— *Ägypten Von Alexander dem Grossen bis auf Mohammed*, Berlin 1922.

—— 'H.I. Bell, *Jews and Chriastians in Egypt*' (Recension), *Gnomon*, I (1925), pp. 23-37.

—— 'Die Βουλή von Alexandria', *BIFAO*, XXX (1931), pp. 407-415.

Schur W., 'Liber pater', *RE(PW)*, XIII (1926), pp. 68-76.

—— 'Liberalia', *RE(PW)*, XIII (1926), pp. 81-82.

Schürer E., *Die Gemeindeverfassung der Juden in Rom in der Kaiserzeit nach den Inschriften dargestellt*, Leipzig 1879.

—— 'Die Juden im bosphoranischen Reiche und die Genossenschaften der σεβόμενοι θεὸν ὕψιστον ebendaselbst', *Sitzungsberichte der Berliner Akademie*, 1897, pp. 200-225.

—— *Geschichte des jüdischen Volkes im Zeitalter Jesu Christi*[4], I-III, Leipzig 1901-1909.

—— *The History of the Jewish People in the Age of Jesus Christ* (ed. G. Vermes & F. Millar), I-II, Edinburgh, 1973, 1979.

Schwabe M., 'A New Document relating to the History of the Jews in the 4th Century C.E. Libanius ep. 1251(F)', *Tarbiz*, I (3) 1930, pp. 107-121 (Hebrew).

—— 'A New Synagogue from Apamea in Syria', *Yediot*, III (1935), pp. 137-138 (Hebrew).

—— 'Greek-Jewish Inscription from Lyda', *Tarbiz*, XII (1941), pp. 230-233 (Hebrew).

—— 'The Ancient Synagogue of Apamea in Syria', *Qedem*, I (1942), pp. 85-93 (Hebrew).

—— 'Two Inscriptions from the Synagogue in Beth She'arim', *Yediot*, IX (1942), pp. 21-30 (Hebrew).

—— 'On the History of Tiberias; an epigraphical study', *Levy Memorial Volume*, Jerusalem 1949, pp. 200-251 (Hebrew).

—— 'The Greek Inscription of the Second Temple Times', *Sefer Yerushalayim*, I (1956), pp. 358-368 (Hebrew).

Schwabe M., Lifshitz B., *Beth She'arim* (II: The Greek Inscriptions), Jerusalem 1967 (Hebrew).

Schwartz E., 'Zu: H.I. Bell, *Jews and Christians* (1924)' (Rez), *Deutsche Literaturzeitung für Kritik der intenationalen Wissenschaft*, N.F., I (1924), pp. 2093-2101.

Schwartz J., 'Note sur la famille de Philon d'Alexandrie', *AIP*, XIII (1953), pp. 591-602.

Schwartz R.D., 'The Priests in Ep. Arist. 310', *JBL*, XCVII (1978), pp. 567-571.

Scramuzza V.M., *The Emperor Claudius*, Cambridge, Mass. 1940.

Seaver J.E., *Persecution of the Jews in the Roman Empire*, Lawence Kensas 1952.

Segal M.Z., *The Complete Book of Ben-Sira*, Jerusalem 1959 (Hebrew).

Segré A., 'Note sul documento sescutivo greco-egizio', *Aegyptus*, VIII (1927), pp. 293-334.

—— 'Note sullo Status Civiatis degli Ebrei nell' Egitto Tolmaico e Imperiale', *BSAA*, XXVIII (1933), pp. 143-182.

—— 'Note sull' Editto di Caracalla', *Atti della Pontificia Accademia Romana di Archeologia, Rendiconti*, XVI (1940), pp. 183-184.

—— 'Il diritto dei militari peregrini nell' esercito romano', *Atti della pontificia Accademia Romana di Archeologia, Rendiconti*, XVII (1940-1941), pp. 167ff.

—— 'The Status of the Jews in Ptolemaic and Roman Egypt – New light from the Papyri', *Jew. Soc. St.*, VI (1944), pp. 375-400.

—— 'Antisemitism in Hellenistic Alexandria', *Jew. Soc. St.*, VIII (1946), pp. 127-136.

Sevenster J.N., *The Roots of Pagan Anti-Semitism in the Ancient World*, Leiden 1975.

Sherwin-White A.N., *The Roman Citizenship*, Oxford 1939.

—— 'Philo and Avilius Flaccus: a Conundrum', *Latomus*, 31 (1972), pp. 820-828.

Shoucri R.M., 'Égyptologie et Judes-Héllenisme, vers une nouvelle optique', *Mélanges d'études anciennes offerts à M. Lebel*, Quebec 1980, pp. 213-221.

Sijpesteijn P.J., 'Mithradates' March from Pergamum to Alexandria in 48 B.C.' *Latomus*, XXIV (1965), pp. 122-127.

—— 'The Legationes ad Gaium', *JJS*, XV (1964), pp. 87-97.

—— *Liste des Gymnasiarchs des métropoles de l'Égypte romaine*, Amsterdam 1967.

Silberschlag E., 'The earliest Record of the Jews in Asia Minor', *JBL*, LIII (1933), pp. 66-77.

Simon M., 'A Propos de la Lettre de Claude aux Alexandrins', *Bulletin de la Faculté des Lettres de Strabourg*, XXI (1942/3), pp. 175-183.

Skeat T.C., *The Reign of the Ptolemies*, München 1954.

Smallwood E.M., 'The Chronology of Gaius attempt to desecrate the Temple', *Latomus*, XVI (1957), pp. 3-17.

—— *Philonis Alexandrini Legatio ad Gaium* (*Edited with an Introduction, Translation and Commentary*), Leiden 1961.

—— *The Jews under Roman Rule*, Leiden 1977.

Sokolowski F., 'Encore sur le décret dionisiaque de Ptolémée Philopator', *JJP*, III (1949), pp. 137-152.

Solomon D., 'Philon's Use of ΕΘΝΑΡΧΗΣ in *In Flaccum*', *JQR*, LXI (1970), pp. 119-131.

Stähelin F., *Der Antisemitismus des Altertums in seiner Entstehung und Entwicklung*, Basel 1905.

Stählin O., *Geschichte der griechische Literatur*, München 1959.

Stein A., 'Parteikämpfe im hellenistischen Alexandrien', *Preussische Jahrbucher*, CC (1925), pp. 54-73.

— — *Die Prafekten von Aegypten in der römischen Kaiserzeit*, Bern 1950.

Stein M., 'The Author of the Letter of Aristens as an Apologist of Judaism', *Zion*, I (1936), pp. 129-147 (Hebrew).

— — Pseudo-Hcataeus, his Time and the Tendency of his Book on the Jews and their Land', *Meàsseph Zion*, 1934, pp. 1-11 (Hebrew).

— — *Philo of Alexandria: the Writer, his Works, and his Philosophy*, Warszawa 1937 (Hebrew).

— — *Philo the Alexandrian: Historical Writings (In Flaccum, Legatio ad Gaium)*, translated with an Introduction and Commentary, Tel-Aviv 1937 (Hebrew).

— — *The Relationship between Jewish, Greek and Roman Culture* (= a collection of articles), Tel-Aviv 1970 (Hebrew).

Stephano H., *Thesaurus Graecae Linguae*, I-IX, London 1816-1825.

Stern E., *Material Culture of the Land of the Bible in the Persian Period*, Jerusalem 1973 (Hebrew).

Stern M., 'The Death of Onias III, *Zion*', XXV (1960), pp. 1-16 (Hebrew).

— — 'A Fragment of Greco-Egyptian Prophecy and the Tradition of the Jew's Expulsion from Egypt in Chairemon's History', *Zion*, XXVIII (1963), pp. 222-227 (Hebrew).

— — 'Josephus' Way in Writing History', *Historians and Historical Schools, the Historical Society of Israel*, Jerusalem 1962, pp. 25-28 (Hebrew).

— — 'Sympathy for Judaism in Roman, Senatorial Circles in the Period of the Early Empire', *Zion*, XXIX (1964), pp. 155-167 (Hebrew).

— — 'The Political Background of the Wars of Alexander Jannaeus', *Tarbiz*, XXXIII (1964), pp. 325-366 (Hebrew).

— — *The Documents on the History of the Hasmonaean Revolt*, Tel-Aviv 1965 (Hebrew).

— — 'Herodian Policy and the Jewish Society at the End of the Second Temple', *Tarbiz*, XXXV (1966), pp. 235-268 (Hebrew).

— — 'Strabo on the Jews', *Gedalyahu Alon Memorial Volume*, Tel-Aviv 1970, pp. 169-191 (Hebrew).

— — 'Jews in Roman Historiography of the Augustan Period', *Sireni Memorial Volume*, Milano 1970, pp. 79-90 (Hebrew).

— — 'The Kingship of Agrippa I', *Joseph Amorai Memorial Volume*, Tel-Aviv 1973, pp. 117-135 (Hebrew).

— — 'The Jewish Diaspora', *The Jewish People in the First Century*, Assen, I (1974), pp. 117-183.

— — *Greek and Latin Authors on Jews and Judaism*, I-II, Jerusalem, 1974, 1980.

— — (ed.), *The Diaspora in the Hellenistic-Roman Period*, Jerusalem 1983 (Hebrew).

Strack M.L., *Die Dynastie der Ptolemäer*, Berlin 1897.

Sukenik E., *Ancient Synagogues in Palestine and Greece*, London 1934.

Swiderek A., 'La societé grecque en Égypte au III siècle av. n.è. d'après les Archives de Zenon', *JJP*, IX-X (1955/6), pp. 365-400.

Tait J.G., 'Πέρσαι τῆς ἐπιγονῆς', *Archiv*, VI (1924), pp. 396f.

— — *Greek Ostraca in the Bodlian Library of Oxford and various other collections*, 1930.

Taubenschlag R., 'The Ancient Greek City — Law in Ptolemaic Egypt', *Actes du Ve Congrès Intern. de Papyrologie*, Oxford (1938), pp. 471f.

— — *The Law of Greco-Roman Egypt in Light of the Papyri 332 B.C.-640A.D.*, New-York 1944, vol. I-II; idem, 2° Ed., Warszawa 1955.

— — 'The Roman Authorities and the Local Law in Egypt before and after the C.A.', *JJP*,
     V (1951), pp. 121f.

Tarn W.W., *Alexander the Great*, I-II, Cambridge 1951.

— — *Tre Greeks in Bactria and India*, Cambridge 1951.

Tarn W.W., G.T. Griffith, *Hellenistic Civilisation,* [3] London 1952.

Tcherikover V., 'Die hellenistischen Städtegründungen von Alexander dem Grossen bis auf
     die Römerzeit', *Philologus* Suppl. XIX, Heft I. (1927), pp. 1-216.

— — 'Jewish religious influence in Adler Papyri', *HTR*, XXXV (1942), pp. 25-32.

— — 'Syntaxis and Laographia', *JJP*, IV (1950), pp. 179-207.

— — 'The Sambations', *Scripta Hierosolymitana*, I, (1954), pp. 79-98.

— — 'The Ideology of the Letter of Aristeas', *HTR*, LI (1958), pp. 59-85.

— — *Hellenistic Civilization and the Jews*[2], Translated by S. Applebaum, Philadelphia, 1961.

— — 'The Third Book of Maccabees as a Historical Source of Augustus' Time', *Scripta
     Hierosolymitana*, VII (1961), pp. 1-26.

— — 'The Decline of the Jewish Diaspora in Egypt in the Roman Period', *JJS*, XIV (1963),
     pp. 1-32.

— — *Jews and Greeks in the Hellenistic Period*, Tel-Aviv 1931, 2° ed. (revised) 1963 (Hebrew).

— — *The Jews in the Graeco-Roman World*, Tel-Aviv 1961 (Hebrew).

Tcherikover, V.A., A. Fuks M. Stern, *Corpus Papyrorum Judaicurum* I, II, III, Jerusalem,
     1957-1960, 1964.

Tchernowitz Ch., 'The Pairs and the Temple of Omias', *Ginzburg Memorial Volume*, New
     York 1946, pp. 223-247 (Hebrew).

— — *History of the Halakhah*, I-IV, New York, 1934-1950 (Hebrew).

Thackeray H.St.J., *Josephus the Man and the Historian*, New York 1929.

Thackeray H.St.J., R. Marcus, L.H. Feldman, *Josephus with an English Translation* (Loeb
     ed.), I-IX, London 1926-1943, 1963.

Tondriau Jul., 'Les thiases dionysiaques royaux de la cour Ptolémaïque', *Chronique d'Égypte,*
     XXI (1946), pp. 149-171.

— — 'Le décret dionysiaque de Philopator', *Aegyptus*, XXVI-XXVII (1946/7), pp. 84-95.

— — 'Rois Lagides comparés ou identifiés à des divinités', *Chronique d'Égypte*, XXIII
     (1947), pp. 127-146.

— — 'Une thiase dionysiaque à Peluse sous Ptolémée IV Philopalor' *BSAA*, XXXVII (1948),
     pp. 3-11.

— — 'Notes Ptolémaîque', *Aegyptus*, XXVIII (1948), pp. 168f.

— — 'La dynastie Ptolémaïque et le religion Dionysiaque', *Chronique d'Égypte*, XXV (1950),
     pp. 283-316.

— — 'Tatouage, lierre et syncrétismes', *Aegyptus*, XXX (1950), pp. 57-66.

— — 'Quelques problèmes religieux Ptolémaiques, *Aegyptus*, XXXIII (1953), pp. 125f.

Tracy S., 'Aristeas and III Maccabees', *YCS*, I (1928), pp. 239-252.

— — *Philo Judaeus and the Roman Principate*, Williamsport 1933.

Tramontano R., *La Lettera di Aristea a Filocrate*, Napoli 1931.

Turner E.G., 'Tiberius Julius Alexander', *JRS*, XLIV (1954), pp. 54-64.

— — 'An Augustan Document Recovered', *JRS*, XLV (1955), pp. 119-120.

— — *The Hibeh Papyri — Edited with translation and notes*, I-II, London 1955.

— — *Greek Papyri, an Introduction*, Oxford 1968.

Uebel F., *Die Kleruchen Ägyptens unter den ersten sechs Ptolemäern*, Abhand. d. Deutschen
     Akad. d' Wiss' z. Berlin, 1968.

Uxkull-Gyllenband. W. Graf., 'Der Gnomon des Idios Logos', *BGU*, V (1900), pp. 14-28.

Vaggi G., 'Siria e siri nei documenti dell' Egitto greco-romano', *Aegyptus*, XVII (1937),
     pp. 31f.

Van't Dack E., 'La date de la Lettre d'Aristée', Studia Hellenistica, XVI (1968), pp. 263-278.

Varsat, I, Les Juifs dans l'Égypte greque et romain. Aspects sociaux, politiques et institutionnels, Paris 1975.

Viereck P., 'Noch einmal die βουλή von Alexandria', Aegyptus, XII (1932), pp. 210-217.

Vilard U.M. de, 'Sul Castrum romano di Babilonia d'Egitto', Aegyptus, V (1925), pp. 174f.

Vincent H., 'Jérusalem d'après la Lettre d'Aristée', RB, V (1908), pp. 520f. VI (1909), pp. 555f.

Visser C.E., Göter und Kulte im Ptolem. Alexandrien, Amsterdam 1938.

Vlastos S., Isonomia — Studien zur Gleicheitsforstellung in griechischen Denken, 1964.

Vogelstein H., P. Rieger, Geschichte der Juden in Rom, Berlin 1896.

— — History of the Jews in Rome, Philadelphia 1940 (Engl. transl.).

Vogliano A., 'La dedica della sinagoga di Crocodilopolis', Riv di FiloL, XVII (1939), pp. 247-259).

Wachholder B.Z., Nicolaus of Damascus, Berkeley 1962.

— — 'The Letter from Judah Maccabee to Aristobulus. Is II Maccabees 1:10-2:18 Authentic?', HUCA, 49 (1978), pp. 89-133.

Waddel W.G., Manetho with an English Translation (Loeb ed.), London 1956.

Wallace S.L., 'The Ἰουδαίων τέλεσμα in Roman Egypt', TAPA, LXVI (1935), pp. XXXV-XXXVI.

— — Taxation in Egypt from Augustus to Diocletian, Princeton 1938.

— — 'Census and Poll-Tax in Ptolemaic Egypt', AJPh., LXIX (1938), pp. 418-442.

— — 'Receipts for φόρος προβάτων in the Papyrus Collection of the University of Wisconsin', JEA, XXV (1939), pp. 62-69.

Walter N., Der Thoraausleger Aristobulos (Texte u. Untersuchungen z. Gesch. der altchrist Literatur 86), Berlin 1964.

Walton F.R., 'The Messenger of God in Hecataeus of Abdera', HTR, XLVIII (1955), pp. 255-257.

Weber A., 'Eine Gerichtsverhandlung vor Kaiser Traian', Hermes, L (1915), pp. 47-92.

Weingärtner D.G., Die Aegyptenreise des Germanicus, Bonn 1969.

Welles C.B., Royal Correspondence in the Hellenistic Period, New Haven 1934.

— — 'The Ptolemaic Administration in Egypt', JJP, III (1949), pp. 21-47.

Wendland P. (ed.), Aristeae ad Philocratem epistula (Bibliotheca Scriptorum Graecorum et Romanorum Teubeuriana), Tübingen 1900.

Wessely C., Die Stadt Arsinoë im griechischer Zeit (Sitz. K. Akad. d. Wissen., 145), Vienna 1903.

— — 'Topographie des Fajjum', Denkschr. der Wiener Akad. Phil-hist. CL., L (1904).

— — 'Une notice relative à la colonie juive à Arsinoé en Egypte' Actes du XIVe congrès international des Orientalistes, 1905, II (1907), Sect. II, pp. 17-22.

— — 'Das Ghetto von Apolinopolis Magna', Studien zur Paläogr. und Papyruskunde, XIII (1913), pp. 8-10.

Westermann W.L., Upon Slavery in Ptolemaic Egypt, New York 1929 (= P. Col. Inv. 480).

— — 'The Ptolemies and the Welfare of their Subjects', Amer. Historical Review, IV (1937/8), pp. 270-287.

— — 'Enslaved People who are Free (Rainer Papyrus [PER], Inv., 24,552)', AJPh, LIX (1938), pp. 1-30.

— — The Slave System of Greek and Roman Antiquity, Philadelphia 1955.

— — 'Sklaveri', RE(PW), Suppl. VI (1935), pp. 894-1068.

Wilamowitz-Moellendorff U. von, Der Glaube der Helenen, I-II Berlin 1931-2.

Wilcken U., 'Eine Actenstück zum jüdischen Kriege Trajanas', Hermes, XXVII (1892), pp. 464-480.

—— 'Alexandrinische Gesandschaften vor Kaiser Claudius', *Hermes*, XXX (1895), pp. 481-498.

—— *Griechisch Ostraka aus Aegypten und Nubien*, Leipzig-Berlin 1899.

—— *Zum alexandrinischen Antisemitismus*, Leipzig 1909.

—— 'Zum Germanicus-Papyrus', *Hermes*, LXIII (1928), pp. 48-65.

—— 'Der βουλή Papyrus', *Archiv* IX (1930), pp. 253-256.

Wilhelm A., 'Zu den Judenerlassen des Ptolemaios Philadelphos', *Archiv*, XIV (1941), pp. 30-35.

Will Éd., *Histoire politique du monde hellénistique*, I-II, Nancy 1966-1968.

Willrich H., *Juden und Griechen vor der Makkabäischen Erhebung*, Göttingen 1895.

—— *Judaica*, Göttingen 1900.

—— 'Caligula', *Klio*, III (1903), pp. 85-118, 288-317, 397-470.

—— 'Der historische Kern des III Makk.', *Hermes*, XXXIX (1904), pp. 244-258.

—— 'Dositheos', *RE(PW)*, V 2 (1905), pp. 1065-1066.

—— *Urkundenfälschung in der hellenistisch-jüdischen Literatur*, (Forschungen zur Religion u. Literatur des Alten u. Neuen Testaments. NF. XXI), Göttingen 1924.

—— 'Zum Brief des Kaisers Claudius an die Alexandriner', *Hermes*, LX (1925), pp. 482-489.

Wolff H.J., *Das Justizwesen der Ptolemäer*, München 1962.

Wolfson H.A., 'Philo on the Jewish Citizenship in Alexandria', *JBL*, LXIII (1914), pp. 165-168.

—— *Philo — Foundations of Religious Philosophy in Judaism, Christianity and Islam*, I, II, Harvard 1948. Hebrew edition, Jerusalem 1970.

Woess F. von, *Das Asylwesen Ägyptens in der Ptolemäerzeit und die spätere Entwicklung*, München 1923.

Wüst, E., 'Mimos', *RE(PW)*, XV (1932), pp. 1727-1764.

Yaron R., *Introduction to the Law of Aramaic Papyri*, Oxford 1961.

—— 'CPJud 144 et alia', *Iura*, 13 (1962), pp. 170-175.

Yavetz Z., *Julius Caesar and his Public Image*, London 1983.

Yoyotte J., 'L'Égypte ancienne et les origines de l'Antisémitisme', *RHP*, CLXIII (1963), pp. 133-143.

Zeitlin S., 'Did Agrippa write a letter to Gaius Caligula? ', *JQR*, LVI (1965), pp. 22-31.

Ziebarth E., *Das griechische Vereinswesen* (Preisschriften der Fürstlich Jablowski'schen Geselleschaft, XXXIV), Leipzig 1896.

Zielinski T., 'L'Empereur Claude et l'idée de la domination mondiale des Juifs', *Rev. de l'Univ. de Bruxelles*, XXXII (1926/7), pp. 128-148.

Zogheb A.M. de, *Études zur l'ancienne Alexandrie*, Paris 1910.

Zucker F., *Beiträge zur Kentnis d. Gerichtsorganisation im ptolem. und römischen Aegypten*, Leipzig 1911.

—— 'Γυμνασίαρχος κώμης', *Aegyptus*, XI (1931), pp. 485-496.

—— 'Zur Textherstellung und Erklärung von *P. Enteuxis*, fasc. II', *Aegyptus*, XIII (1933), pp. 217-218.

—— 'Dopplelinschrift spätptolemäischer Zeit aus der Garnison von Hermopolis Magna', *Abhandlungen der Königlich Preussischen Akademie der Wissenschaften zu Berlin, Philos-histor. Klasse* 1937, Nr. 6 (1938).

Zucker H., *Studien zur jüdischen Selbstverwaltung im Altertum*, Berlin 1936.

Zuntz G., 'Zum Aristeas Text', *Philologus*, CII (1958), pp. 240-246.

—— 'Aristeas Studies', *Jew. Soc. St.*, IV (1959), pp. 21-36, 109-126.

—— 'Once more: The so-called "Edict of Philopator on the Dionysiac Mysteries" (*BGU*, 1211)', *Hermes*, XCI (1963), pp. 228-239.

Index of Historical Names

Geographical Index

Select Subject Index

Reference Index

A. Literary Sources

Bible

Genesis
14:18−20   117

Exodus
14:2   149

Leviticus
9:28   216

Numeri
24:1   144
33:7   149

Deuteronomium
24:16   251

Jesaias
19:19   133

Jeremias
44:1   1
44:1−15   149
46:14   149

Ezechiel
1:3   144
29:10   149
30:6   149

Psalmi
7:18   117
17:14   117
29:1−2   144
49:14   117
67:35   117

Ecclesiastes
1:7   144

Daniel
1:8−16   304
8:2   144
10:4   144

Ezra
1:8   113

I. Chronicorum
27:31   113
29:6   113

II Chronicorum
8:10   113
24:11   113

Apocrypha

I Esdrae
1:8   113

Tobit
1:11   304

Judith
10:5   304
12:1−4   304

Sirach
45:24   113

Letter of Aristeas
2−16   370
9   59
12−14   3, 59, 189, 211
12−16   108
13   2, 3, 39, 42
14   228
14−27   3
15−16   228
20−25   330
22−25   43, 228

Philo Judaeus

Index of Hebrew and Aramaic Words*

* Words in brackets are transcriptions not included in the text.

Select Index of Greek Words

Select Index of Latin Words